Applause for *The Name Above the Title*

"Invaluable." —*New Statesman*

"Immensely readable." —*New York Daily News*

"Capra's candor is refreshing." —*Washington Post Book World*

"One closes Capra's book with lingering admiration for his gutsy independence and the lifelong battle he fought to make his 'one man, one film' principles prevail." —**Christopher Lehmann-Haupt**, *New York Times Book Review*

"Capra, who could get movies made in peace and war, no matter what, offers enough shop talk from the dream factory to enslave someone who grew up with Capra pictures.... A rare and entertaining [book]." —*Christian Science Monitor*

"Good, gossipy reading.... No other book has given us quite so vivid a picture of the way Hollywood farms out its once infallible filmmakers.... Poignant." —*Time*

"One of the most uncompromisingly honest, spirited, exhaustive, and totally engaging autobiographies by a leading figure in the motion picture world, and certainly one of the best books extant about Hollywood.... Capra's book should enthrall anyone interested in learning what the art and business of moviemaking is about." —*Publishers Weekly*

"A traditional American success story, real and inspirational.... Probably the best autobiography ever written by a Hollywood figure." —*Hollywood Reporter*

"Capra describes with zest and good humor his own adventuresome, often improbable life.... Interesting, candid, and well written." —*Library Journal*

"Warm, forthright, and bubbling over with that spontaneous humanity which was so much a part of his pictures. It is without question the best memoir of a Hollywood personality I have read." —**John Barkham**, *Saturday Review*

"This is the finest, most entertaining book yet written about Hollywood, embracing the whole intricate, complex, and generally stormy fusion of art and commerce. It has many dimensions, both personal and impersonal, with soaring *alleluia* and crushing *de profundis*." —*Daily Variety*

FRANK CAPRA

THE NAME ABOVE THE TITLE

An Autobiography

Foreword by John Ford
New Introduction by Jeanine Basinger

DA CAPO PRESS

Library of Congress Cataloging in Publication Data

Capra, Frank, 1897–
  The name above the title: an autobiography / Frank Capra; foreword by John
Ford; new introduction by Jeanine Basinger.—1st Da Capo Press ed.
      p.   cm.
  Originally published: New York: Macmillan Co., 1971.
  Includes index.
  ISBN 0-306-80771-8 (alk. paper)
  1. Capra, Frank, 1897– . 2. Motion picture producers and directors—United
States—Biography. I. Title.
PN1998.3.C36A3   1997
791.43′0233′092—dc21
[B]   96-47921
                                                                                                              CIP

First Da Capo Press edition 1997

This Da Capo Press paperback edition of *The Name Above the Title* is an unabridged
republication of the edition first published in New York in 1971, here supplemented
with a new introduction by Jeanine Basinger. It is reprinted by arrangement with the
Estate of Frank Capra.

Published by Da Capo Press
A Member of the Perseus Books Group
http://www.dacapopress.com

Manufactured in the United States of America

10 9 8 7 6 5

To the weavers of the Magic Carpet
And to some of my fellow riders
in Memoriam

Aristotle   Robert Riskin
Leonardo da Vinci   Myles Connolly
Athanasius   Jo Swerling

Plateau   Joseph Sistrom
Stampfer   Max Winslow
Daguerre   Art Black

Muybridge   Mack Sennett
Eastman   Harry Cohn
Edison   Sam Briskin

E. S. Porter   Harry Langdon
D. W. Griffith   Jack Holt
                          May Robson

                          Jean Harlow
                          Warner Baxter
                          Gary Cooper

                          Ronald Colman
                          Clark Gable
                          Spencer Tracy

                          Lionel Barrymore
                          Walter Connolly
                          Henry Travers

                          Thomas Mitchell
                          Edward Everett Horton
                          Walter Huston

                          Edward Arnold
                          Claude Rains
                          Hobart Bosworth
                          H. B. Warner
                          James Gleason

Contents

Introduction

On october 12, 1966 Frank Capra sat down to write a letter to his old and trusted friend, the Pulitzer Prize–winning author of A *Distant Trumpet*, Paul Horgan. It had been five years since the release of Capra's last feature film, A *Pocketful of Miracles*, and he had finally faced the knowledge that not only was there nothing on the horizon for him in Hollywood, but there probably never again would be. He was 69 years old, but still vigorous, competitive, restless, eager to achieve more . . . and he had an idea. To Horgan he wrote, "Picture making is over for me because the fun and thrill of personal creation is over. . . . If I wish to continue in personal creation my only other field is writing. . . . I think I've got much to say, many tales to tell. Blatantly presumptuous, I am sending you three samples, varying in mood and content, which I hope you will find time to read."

Having earlier sent a telegram promising a response after the holidays, Horgan replied on January 17, 1967. He was direct with Capra: "I have something to suggest to you. It is something so much more significant, so much more truly commensurate with your great achievement and position than the small pieces you sent me that I hope it will strike you favorably. You should write your autobiography, straightforwardly, as you have felt everything in life, as historically true as your memory will allow and research will assist, full of the amazing energy of your career, without gags, running a straight line of narrative from your early years, into the early years of film, to your great period in the talkies, to your inestimably important (and not understood in contemporary cultural history) invention of the true documentary film, and so on to your final films and their view of society. In all this should be woven your private life—family, your intellectual interests, your basic philosophy, and such—as far as taste and relevance indicate. It will be a long task ... but I know you can do it, and I pray you will do it, for there is not a book I am more eager to have."

Capra respected Horgan and understood what his reliable old friend was telling him: forget these weak stories and write about your own life. He knew at once that Horgan was right, and he plunged in and went to work, taking nearly one year to produce a sample chapter to send out to publishers. The results were rewarding. On September 10, 1968 he signed a standard contract with Macmillan for "an untitled autobiography," 130,000 words in length and for which he would be paid a total of $3000, $1500 upon signing and $1500 upon completion. There was no time limit set, and Capra worked for almost three years before the book finally appeared in print. The time flew by for him, however, because he put all of himself into the project. The research and writing consumed him and filled his life.

Before publication Capra conducted many conversations with his publishers about what the untitled book was to be called. Macmillan wanted something standard, such as *Frank Capra's Hollywood*, or perhaps *Frank Capra, Filmmaker*, or even *The Frank Capra Story*. Capra preferred something more dramatic, and his choice was *One Man, One Film*, the definition of his movie-making philosophy. When the publishers rejected this because "no one would know what it meant," Capra decided on *The Name Above the Title*. Again, the publishers rejected his choice on the basis of its "meaninglessness." It would be *Frank Capra's Hollywood*, they decreed, failing to remember they were dealing with a showman who had outwitted the toughest Hollywood moguls, a man who knew how to get his way. After many more letters and phone conversations, Capra, the wily man of the movie business, placated Macmillan by agreeing to his name going above the title. *Frank Capra: The Name Above the Title (An Autobiography)* was officially published on June 24, 1971 to great fanfare. The Museum of Modern Art declared that date to be "Frank Capra Day" and launched a retrospective of his movies. The *New York Times* ran an in-depth interview, and excerpts from the book were published in the *Los Angeles Times* as well as in *Action* and *Audience* magazines. Almost immediately, the Book-of-the-Month Club announced it as a major selection, and within weeks it appeared on the best seller lists.

The Name Above the Title became a publishing success. It was widely reviewed by major magazines, newspapers, and trade publications. The *New York Daily News* called it "an immensely readable autobiography," and *Daily Variety* said it was "the finest, most entertaining book yet written about Hollywood, embracing the whole intricate, complex, and generally stormy fusion of art and commerce. It has many dimensions, both personal and impersonal, profoundly wise and soul-revealing. It bubbles with humor." The *Wall Street Journal* laid down the word: "This important, entertaining book is valuable to anyone, artist or audience, who loves the dominant art medium of the century."

It wasn't only the big media reviewers who appreciated the book. In the great tradition of Capra's appeal to "the little people," small-town newspapers all over America carried their own reviews, written by someone on their staff. Positive reports came in from Troy, Alabama; Zanesville, Ohio; Wallace, Idaho; Woodward, Oklahoma; Pampa, Texas; Henderson, North Carolina; Traverse City, Michigan; Framingham, Massachusetts. Frank Capra read every one of these local reviews and kept them in his files the rest of his life.

At the same time Capra was receiving an overwhelming number of personal notes from his contemporaries as well as the elite of the current Hollywood scene. His colleagues praised the book, mentioning how they agreed with it, how true it seemed to them, and how grateful they were to him for writing it. Henry King, director of *Twelve O'Clock High* and *The Gunfighter*, said, "It should be required reading in all schools," and William Wyler (*The Heiress, The Little Foxes*) told Capra, "I think you came out on top." Grace Kelly (or "Grace de Monaco" as she signed her letter) thanked him for providing her with a picture of how things were in Hollywood before her time, as did Kirk Douglas. Barbara Stanwyck, who had worked with Capra in several of her best movies, wrote, "When I read your chapter on me, I wept with pride. Your training of me as an actress has never left my heart and soul, and my gratitude and love for you will never leave my heart." Actor-director John Cassavetes call it a "no-crap" book, adding "I don't know how anyone could survive this crazy picture business without knowing that there is someone like you who has been through it all and who would still do it again. The only thing better than reading your book is seeing all your films." Even Capra's son Tom wrote a fan letter: "Dear Daddy, You wouldn't approve of the way I read your book. 'Too fast,' you'd say. I read your book that way because I couldn't put it down. It is fantastic . . . incredible, but true, that we human beings somehow will put more of ourselves on paper than we will into words. As a result, I know you better now than I did before reading the book . . . and I love you more than ever."

Capra's book put him back into the mainstream of both show business and life. Interest in his movies was revived, and his name returned to magazines and newspapers. Capra found his telephone ringing with requests for book signings, appearances, lectures. The book had been published at the right time in the right place. It coincided with the enormous burst of interest in American movies that occurred in the early 1970s, as America rediscovered its film heritage and began to take a national pride in Hollywood filmmaking. The auteur theory had been brought over from France, telling Americans that Hollywood actually *did* make good movies, ones worthy of study and respect. Colleges and universities began offering courses and seminars on directors such as Ford, Hawks, Hitchcock, Walsh . . . and now, Frank Capra. Revival houses and film series programs were mounting detailed retrospectives of all types of American film artists, not just directors, but also producers, stars, writers, and cinematographers. It was a renaissance and Capra's autobiography was like the Rosetta Stone. There was no question but that he was one of the most famous names in film history, and here he was, in print, telling in his own words what it was really like to work in the Hollywood studio system. He was articulate and direct. And he would appear in person to tell even more!

As a result of the book Frank Capra began a second career as a lecturer and teacher, visiting museums, archives, and college campuses to discuss both the book and his movies. He became an ambassador for himself and his work, but also for others of his generation. He was very effective with young people who came to sit at his feet, especially aspiring filmmakers. He found kindred spirits among the young, who didn't mind that he cast himself as the hero of all his tales, because they were Americans and appreciated his lusty immigrant story. The self-congratulatory tone of his work amused them, for they understood the deeper humanity and generosity that lay behind it. Capra had always known how to reach out to ordinary people, and he had always had a youthful spirit. He found he still had the gift to entertain, tell a story, and make people laugh. In making himself available, he gave his book an even longer life, its success continuing past its initial publishing boom.

This edition is being republished on the occasion of Capra's centennial. Usually, such an event kicks off a great reevaluation of the individual's work. Movies have to be hauled up out of the mothballs and explained to a new generation who probably have not heard of them. It provides an opportunity to mount retrospectives, to organize seminars, to write articles. For most centennials, the general audience needs to be educated in the basics. In Capra's case, of course, this is unnecessary: Frank Capra has never gone away. His movies play daily on television, in college classrooms, at revival houses, and in museums and festivals all over the world. Pick up a newspaper during a political campaign and some candidate is sure to quote a Capra movie, claim he is like a Capra hero, or be criticized for being too much like one. At the Frank Capra Archives on the campus of Wesleyan University in Middletown, Connecticut we play host to an international roster of researchers on a steady basis. Some are scholars writing books and articles or doing primary research for classes. Others are journalists, critics, and documentary filmmakers who are studying the work for their own purposes. Many are young filmmakers, some famous, who come to read Capra's handwritten notes on scripts or look at his drawings for camera set-ups. And every holiday season, when *It's a Wonderful Life* is rolled out yet again, we brace ourselves for the flood of requests for interviews, photographs, comments, souvenirs, or just general conversation about the movie. The truth is that Frank Capra's name ranks among the greats, and nothing has unseated him from that position. Although he has (and has always had) many detractors, and although his work is disliked by many (as evidenced by the label "Capracorn" that is so often attached to it), Frank Capra is a name to be dealt with, one that still enjoys household recognition. As a result, his autobiography remains a relevant document.

How does a book published in 1971 hold up and what value does it have for today's readers? There are many rewards to be had from reading *The Name Above the Title*, but the first one is the simplest: it is fun to read. Capra as an author has the basic requirement of all good writers: a personal voice. His prose is frequently slangy and always breezy, conversational in tone. Reading the book is like having Capra sitting in your living room, regaling you with his stories.

Not only does he know how to tell an anecdote, he has the anecdotes to tell. Capra worked with or knew socially everyone in the movie business from Mack Sennett, Charlie Chaplin, and Buster Keaton in the silent era, through the great names of the golden age. He directed Clark Gable, Jimmy Stewart, Cary Grant, Gary Cooper, Bing Crosby, Jean Harlow, Loretta Young, Myrna Loy, Jean Arthur, Claudette Colbert, Barbara Stanwyck, and plenty more. He was an active member of Hollywood's top-level society, and a behind-the-scenes force in the Director's Guild, the Motion Picture Academy, and the Producer's Guild. He knew Churchill, Eisenhower, and George Marshall during World War II, when he supervised America's documentary series, *Why We Fight*. In private life he was a scientist as well as an artist, and he married and raised a family. His is a full and engaging story, and he tells it well. If his style might be called, as one reviewer described it, "sort of a diamond in the rough," I would say it is "the rough" that makes his book so vivid and easy to read.

For those who want to know about Hollywood's history, Capra reveals inside information about a glamorous business, but, unlike many other books, Capra's story is authored by someone who truly was on the inside and in the thick of things. There is also his perspective on larger historical events, both political and artistic. Capra's descriptions of famous people, his memories of significant times and places, are always presented with candor and introspection.

Film students will find Capra's book to be an excellent primer on communication through film, written in simple, direct terms by a man who was unquestionably a master of the medium. Furthermore, they can gain insight into what it is like to enter a tough business, succeed to the highest level, and survive. The trappings—and traps—of success are laid bare. (Too often books by members of the film profession tell film scholars nothing. Often they never discuss the individual's work at all, and many are superficial, providing such insights as "World War II started today, and we had shrimp for lunch.")

Since its original publication Capra's autobiography has been criticized for its tendency to self-aggrandizement. This is not an original insight, because even at the time of publication many reviewers pointed it out. The *Washington Post* complained that "Capra's vanity is bewildering" and the *Boston Herald* bluntly stated, "Capra is not humble enough, and what emerges is his overblown image of himself." The reader needs to accept Capra's strong personality. There is no question that, having lived so much of his life in the limelight, he did not like it when the world temporarily moved past him. He needed to be doing what he did best: telling stories, entertaining people, making them laugh, challenging them. He wrote the book to fulfill these creative needs, but also to call attention to himself. He craved that attention and made no secret of it. Because of this, Capra turns every moment into a scene, and he usually casts himself as the hero of the action. For those who think this might make the book fundamentally dishonest, I would say that, on the contrary, it results in a deeply honest presentation, because Capra reveals his real self. It is also an example of how America allows individuals from humble beginnings to invent themselves, to be who they want to be, and to live by that mythology. Beneath any surface misrepresentations lies a hard truth—the truth in which a strong personality exerts itself and a man endures in a business that is itself one of storytelling and mythmaking. As one reviewer put it, "If Capra appears not so humble in his own estimation of himself, why, why not? Who has a better right? As Al Smith used to say, 'Let us look at the record.' And Capra's record is right up there for all the world to see and admire."

Frank Capra's autobiography is like a Frank Capra movie. What else did anyone expect it to be? Capra himself warns the reader on the very first page: "This is not truly an autobiography—a recording of doings and happenings historically documented. Rather it is mostly random recalls of what went on in my head during my youth and in my forty-odd years of filmmaking." He admits he will telescope conversations that took place over weeks and months into one scene, and promises to describe real people "from the inside of my eyeballs." And he warns everyone: "You may also sense a story: A cheap, egotistical punk grows into a man." All the characteristics of a Capra film—warmth, humor, sentiment, exaggeration, falsification, ups and downs, downs and ups, cruelty and kindness, honesty and dishonesty—will be found in this book. And, of course, there is a happy ending if you want to think of the way it all turned out as a happy ending. If not, the alternative is also available.

And that is a major point—happy or unhappy, what really is this story about? Those who haven't seen any Capra movies lately may have forgotten how contradictory and ambivalent they really are. Many people think of them as only sentimental and happy, but this isn't true. They are complicated and open to interpretation. Arguments among scholars abound: are these films populist or fascist? are they happy or sad? do they celebrate pain or joy? As Terry Curtis Fox once wrote, Capra's movies are "a mass of contradictions riding a yo-yo." There were always two sides to his work, the optimistic and the pessimistic, and that is why people either love him passionately or dislike him intensely. They'll feel the same way about his autobiography . . . but they will never be bored.

In rereading the book, I thought of it as not only about Capra, but also about Hollywood in its greatest years and America at a particular time in its own history. Capra's Hollywood has strange values. It mixes crass commercialism with real art. It is shot through and through with the evils of corruption, nepotism, gross waste, and extravagance. At the same time, it is hard-working, patriotic, high-minded, a place where those who have the least can rise up to become those with the most. It is the stuff our dreams are made of, and also the place many of those dreams originate. Capra's personal tale is the story of one of its most respected and successful participants, a man who experienced the razzle-dazzle of success at the highest level, only to endure rejection and failure later, both personal and professional. Capra could be hard and tough if needed, but he could also be generous and warm. He was a lot of things, most of which he displays in his book, but the main thing he was can never be denied him: one of the most successful film directors in the history of motion pictures, whose movies define an entire American era.

Just as his films endure, his autobiography will endure. Just as his movies can be revived today to laughter and pleasure, this book can be republished to the reader's delight. The flaws in the book that have been pointed out, both in Capra's prose style and in his personality, do exist, but today they only make the book more interesting, more revealing. For anyone who wants to know about Hollywood, who believes in cinema as an art form, and who wants to hear the personal voice of a great raconteur, this book is a very good read—deeply personal and highly original.

Whenever I think of Frank Capra as the person I knew—and I think of him often—I remember his sharp intelligence, his wide-ranging knowledge, his great sense of humor, his love of meeting new people, and his joy in sitting around talking with old friends. Most of all, I remember his wonderful smile and distinctive laugh. Of course Frank laughed when he was happy and something was funny, but he also was able to laugh when things weren't going so well. No matter how unkind or small someone might be to him, Frank could always flash that big smile anyway—wide, warm, and thoroughly disarming. How often I've thought about that smile and of how he must have needed it—and used it—to circumvent his enemies and confound his critics. He just grinned at them and moved on to the next item on his agenda. It was a pleasure to know a man like that and to be in his company. In *The Name Above the Title* anyone can meet him, know him, and enjoy his company. It will be time well spent.

JEANINE BASINGER
Middletown, Connecticut
November 1996

Jeanine Basinger is the Corwin-Fuller Professor of Film Studies and Chairman of Film Studies at Wesleyan University as well as the curator of the Frank Capra Archives. She is the author of The It's a Wonderful Life Book, A Woman's View: How Hollywood Spoke to Women, The World War II Combat Film: Anatomy of a Genre, *and a forthcoming book on silent film stars.*

Foreword

FRANK CAPRA, A WARM AND WONDERFUL MAN, has written a warm and wonderful book, on subjects which he knows as well as any man who ever lived. His genius has been applied not only to the art but to the business of making great motion pictures, and his name on the credits has assured rich satisfactions to bankers, exhibitors, stars, feature players, extras, cameramen, crew, and the theatergoing public for more than half a century. This he has accomplished without compromising his own exacting sense of the good, the beautiful, and the appropriate; without ever losing a friend or having a scene censored.

A great man and a great American, Frank Capra is an inspiration to those who believe in the American Dream. He has called his story *The Name Above the Title*. If he didn't object so strongly to the trite, he might as well have named it *The Land of Opportunity*. For even in early youth he was no stranger to the work, the worry, and the long hours that went with being a poor immigrant boy in a dog-eat-dog society. If all this constituted a deprived childhood, Frank was too busy and too ambitious to notice. Humble beginnings have not deterred his rise to eminence in the arts, letters, and sciences. A great center of learning is proud to honor him as a distinguished alumnus. He has served his country with distinction both in civil and military life. The famous and the notable seek his acquaintance. A series of Frank Capra hits which were to become widely imitated screen classics made Columbia Pictures a major studio. He has earned more awards than he would bother to count. Success has not dulled his wit, his wisdom, or his compassion.

Others have tried to write about Hollywood. Many have failed. Capra brings to his monumental task the sure sense of the professional, and accomplishes the only definitive record I've ever read on the subject. His story is so rich in anecdotes—most of them heart-warming and sympathetic—that there isn't a dull paragraph in the entire book.

For the first time, perhaps, the outsider is given an opportunity to learn how a motion picture is actually prepared, cast, written, and shot, and what it's really like on a motion-picture set, that democratic little monarchy where a hard-nosed director of the "one-picture, one-director" school reigns as king, congress, and court of highest appeal. Frank Capra has every reason to know that it's a good life, quite unlike any other; but only Capra has been also able to depict the agonizing responsibility and the constant struggle between the creator of motion pictures and the concepts of Wall Street, Madison Avenue, and others who would intervene.

Capra has not only achieved a place of distinction in that select company of really fine film directors—men like Bill Wellman, Fred Zinneman, George Stevens, George Seaton, Billy Wilder, Henry Hathaway, the late Leo McCarey, and (abroad) Jean Renoir, Fellini, De Sica, Sir Carol Reed, and David Lean. He heads the list as the greatest motion picture director in the world.

If in his book he administers an occasional gentle slap on the wrist to the proud or the pompous, they can take comfort in the fact that there are picture people by the hundred who would offer their right arms up to the elbow to be mentioned in any frame of reference by a man as great as Capra in a book like his.

I take pride that this American success story should have been written about the industry that both he and I love so dearly, by the only man who could have done it so accurately and so well.

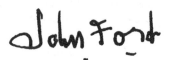

Preface

I HATED BEING POOR. Hated being a peasant. Hated being a scrounging newskid trapped in the sleazy Sicilian ghetto of Los Angeles. My family couldn't read or write. I wanted out. A quick out. I looked for a device, a handle, a pole to catapult myself across the tracks from my scurvy habitat of nobodies to the affluent world of somebodies.

I tried schooling, a technical education. That pole broke in the middle of my vault. I pondered other quick leaps: bootlegging, prize fighting, the ball and bat, con games. When I finally found my vaulting pole, it was not made of bamboo, glass, or metal. In fact, it was not a pole at all. It was a magic carpet—woven with the coils and ringlets of a wondrous peel of limber plastic, whose filaments carried the genetic code of all the arts of man, and from which the abracadabra of science conjured up the hopes, the fears, the dreams of man—the magic carpet of FILM! I vaulted to fame on its witchery.

This is not truly an autobiography—a recording of doings and happenings historically documented. Rather it is mostly random recalls of what went on in my head during my youth and in my forty-odd years of filmmaking. At times I will telescope conversations—which strung out over weeks and months—into one scene. I shall use real names; describe the kings, the queens, and the rogues of Hollywood as I saw them from the inside of my own eyeballs. You may also sense a story: A cheap, egotistical punk grows into a man.

When Eric Gill (one of my heroes), the English illustrator and sculptor —whose iconoclastic ideas about art, sex, money, and mass conformity drop like bombshells from his autobiography—said after his conversion,

"I invented the Roman Catholic Church," I think I understood him. He discovered values already discovered within himself.

When young people discover sex, the experience is so poignantly personal they grant themselves self-issued patents for having invented it.

Similarly, I might say—since some sixty films exist that would not exist had I not created them—that I invented motion pictures. Not true. Motion pictures invented me, and all other filmmakers. The art invented the artists.

The conception of this new, and greatest, art form—comprising and compressing all other art forms into one—was slow and laborious. It took the fertilizing sperm some four thousand years to complete a westward trek of thousands of miles before it found and pierced the ovum of film. That sperm was ejected from the fertile brain of Aristotle in Athens (a square hole in a card projects a round image of the sun on a dark wall); it picked up added genes from the genius of Leonardo da Vinci (camera obscura—a tiny hole projects the image of *any* object on the dark wall).

Leaving Leonardo, the sperm picked up speed and more genes from the intellects of a Jesuit priest, Athanasius (projected paintings on screen); Plateau in Belgium and Stampfer in Vienna (illusion of motion from paintings on a revolving disc); Daguerre in France (discovered photographic emulsions); Muybridge in California (sequential still photos of a running horse); George Eastman (celluloid base for emulsions); the Lumières in France (film projection machine); until finally the sperm found and fertilized the ovum in the brain of the Wizard of Menlo Park—Thomas Edison.

Four thousand years from desire to conception—but once conceived, the new art form sprouted, grew up, and flowered in *one generation*—from Edwin S. Porter's *The Great Train Robbery* (eight minutes), to D. W. Griffith's *Intolerance* (over two hours). All else that has been added—sound, color, techniques—is embellishment.

The overpowering speed of film history has no parallel in human chronology. Like a biblical flood it swept up all the other arts and spread them generously over the earth. Theaters, studios, creative artists, mushroomed from its teeming diluvium. All that we in motion pictures are, have, and do stems from the art itself—from FILM, the magic carpet! I was one of the privileged. I was allowed to grasp the fringes of this flying rug, pull myself up on it, and ride to adventure. Some ride—like riding a meteor!

There are no rules in filmmaking, only sins. And the cardinal sin is Dullness.

PART I
Struggle for Success

It's About Time, You Bum

IT ALL BEGAN WITH A LETTER. A letter from America—when I was a big-eyed child of five. It was the first letter Papa, my forty-seven-year-old peasant father, Salvatore Capra, had received from anywhere. In Papa's old cracked house of stone and mortar, clinging by its toenails to the rocks in the village of Bisaquino, Sicily, the local priest read the letter to a houseful of gaping relatives: Papa, Mama, six ragged children; Papa's four brothers and their families; and all of Mama's kinfolk.

I remember clearly my traumatic shock on learning that not one of my peasant clan could read. I knew people were different—some poor, some rich, some kind, some mean. I knew these things because the children of the poor are born with their eyes and ears open, and know most things before they can walk. And now I knew that peasants were poor and had to work like beasts because they were ignorant. That thought must have burned itself into my child's mind; I never forgot it, never lost my resentment against it. My later mania for education had its genesis in that letter.

It was an astonishing letter, everyone said—unbelievable—from an unheard-of place in California: Los Angeles! Written by an unknown person: Morris Orsatti.

The news spread. Peasants dropped their hoes and ran from the fields. They filled Papa's house, crowded into the doorway: to hear the priest read the letter over and over. It solved Bisaquino's five-year mystery. It was about Ben, Papa's oldest son.

Five years ago, on his sixteenth birthday, Ben had herded Papa's sheep up to the poppy meadows around the hilltop shrine of the Blessed Virgin. The sheep came back. Ben did not. Five years of novenas and lighting of candles

—but not a word from Ben. They mourned him as dead. Now this letter from the other side of the world.

The letter said that Ben ran away from his sheep, ran thirty miles to Palermo, shipped on a Greek trading steamer as a galley helper; that the ship stopped at Gibraltar, Montreal, and Boston. At Boston, young Ben jumped the ship. But two big policemen caught him and brought him back. The ship's captain watched Ben closely at New York and Havana. But in New Orleans the whole crew tried to abandon ship. In the excitement Ben got away. Two days later he lost himself among the workers in sugar cane fields —mostly Negroes and Italians. Ben got a job cutting sugar cane.

The summer was hot and thick with mosquitos, the letter said. People died of the miasma. Ben would have died too, had not a motherly Negro woman nursed him in her shack for weeks.

Ben, Papa's oldest son.

His health restored, the priest read on—or rather paraphrased in short, singsong phrases what he now knew by heart—that Ben lived with his new mother as one of her many children. He brought her his pay. She saved some for him. On his eighteenth birthday Ben asked permission to go to New Orleans, with another young Italian cane cutter, for a celebration. Ben and Mario arrived in New Orleans, met two girls, got very drunk, and were beaten senseless by four rough men with clubs.

When the two young men awoke they found themselves far out to sea again, on a dirty, smelly tramp steamer, with some four hundred other sugar cane workers—Negroes, Italians, Cubans, all moaning and nursing bruised heads. Prisoners they were—slaves!—being taken somewhere by men with guns.

Weeks passed, then months; they lost track of time; from hot weather to cold, then back to hot again.

Finally the ship of sufferings stopped. Loud voices shouted orders. Half dead, the prisoners were dragged up on deck. Ben and Mario saw blue water, white beaches, and palm trees. Short yellow men with slanting eyes marched on board, some had guns. Lifting the prisoners to their feet the new masters led them off the ship.

In a few days Ben discovered they were on a small island owned by Japanese who grew sugar cane. All prisoners were forced to sign statements that they had come to seek work of their own free will. Then they were herded out to the cane fields to join hundreds of Chinese coolies already working at forced labor.

Shortly after Ben's arrival there was a three-day holiday for the prisoners, with parades, firecrackers, masks, and noisy music. Everybody drank foul wine and smoked sweet stuff in pipes. Ben and Mario did not drink or smoke. They watched and planned. They hatched a wild plot to escape come next year's carnival time. During the year Ben and Mario worked so hard the Japanese overseers commended them. In return the boys requested a favor. Would the honorable masters grant the lowly Italians permission to put an Italian entry in the carnival parade—a comical display of Columbus discovering America? Would the noble Nipponese be so kind as to lend the Italians one small rowboat to be the *Santa Maria*?

Carnival time came—with wine, opium, and banging of gongs. At the end of the parade the Italians deposited the *Santa Maria* outside the wharf enclosure and returned to the carousing area. When all was quiet, Ben and Mario stumbled drunkenly down to the rowboat and yelled for the lone guard to open the gate. A swift blow with an oar knocked the guard unconscious. With hearts pounding they slid the boat into the water and silently rowed away into the night. When dawn broke the rowboat was a speck in the middle of the heaving ocean.

But blessed be all the saints, the letter said, a miracle happened! They saw a tiny plume of smoke on the horizon. It was a ship, and it stopped to pick them up—an Australian passenger liner going to San Francisco!

The letter ended by relating how the ship captain had kindly let them off in San Francisco; how they found some Italian friends; how Mario got a job laying Western Pacific tracks going north, while Ben joined a Southern Pacific crew laying track to the south. And how in about a year Ben had worked his way down to Los Angeles where he met Mr. Orsatti, a steamship ticket agent, and how delighted was Mr. Orsatti (father of later famous Frank, Ernie, and Vic) to write a letter for Ben with all the happy news. And, Orsatti added, if the Capra family wished to see Ben again they would all have to come to Los Angeles, because Ben says he is never coming back to Sicily.

And that's the way it was. That's how I came to celebrate my sixth birthday, May 18, 1903, in a howling Atlantic storm; in the *Germania*'s black steerage hold, crammed with retching, praying, terrorized immigrants. Only strong Mama had the courage to brave the wind and spray—hanging on to the deck storm ropes, as she carried trays of food across the heaving deck and down the steep iron stairs to Papa and four seasick children. Josephine was fourteen; Tony, twelve; I was six; little Ann was three. Two older married girls, Luigia and Ignazia, remained in Bisaquino.

Thirteen days of stench and misery in steerage; two more days of panic and pandemonium at Ellis Island; then eight more days of cramped, itchy, hardship in an overcrowded chair car; crying to sleep in each other's laps, eating only bread and fruit Papa bought at train stops.

And finally, finally, after twenty-three days without a bath or change of clothes, our dirty, hollow-eyed immigrant family embraced the waiting Ben at the S.P. station in Los Angeles. Papa and Mama kissed the ground and wept with joy. I cried, too. But not with joy. I cried because we were poor and ignorant and tired and dirty. I didn't know Ben. I just knew he had caused everybody a lot of trouble.

But Ben happily kissed us all, then piled us into a rented one-horse wagon, and drove us to the Plaza Mission, where we all kneeled and thanked God for our safe trip. Then Ben drove us three blocks to a house he had rented on Castelar Street. Castelar Street, Los Angeles—America, America!

The prime challenge an ignorant peasant family faces in a foreign land is to keep alive. Never mind sending kids to school. Get the moola, the hard jingling cash in the pockets, the only *now* defense against the old wolf.

Within a month Papa, Mama, and all the rest of the family found jobs: in brickyards, olive-oil plants, dress shops, candy stores—all except me. I went to school, the Castelar Street school.

To my family I was a maverick. I was jeered at, scorned, and even beaten. But I wouldn't leave school. That meant not only paying for my own education, but putting some change in the family kitty as well. Oh, I loved my family and respected their thrift. But how could they know what I knew, that sure I was born a peasant, but I'd be damned if I was going to die one.

Through the grammar school years I sold papers—mornings, evenings, and Sundays. I gave every penny to Mama. Then came the pow-wow about high school. It was a continuous argument. Papa was on my side but he was out-yelled. "That's enough already," the others argued. "He can read and write now. Time he goes to work like the rest of us. Who's gonna support him?"

Papa finally put his foot down. "If Frankie no ask for money—he go to high school."

At Manual Arts High School, I added three additional moneymaking chores to my paper-selling: two hours of early morning janitor work at school, Sunday night guitar-playing at a Central Avenue bistro, and every Saturday night (this was to be my bread and butter job for years) I "stuffed" papers at the *Los Angeles Times*.

I loved Manual Arts. I lived close to L.A. High, but since I belonged to the riff-raff of Dagos, Shines, Cholos, and Japs, I was sent out to swell the opening of "Siberia" High (an hour-and-a-half car ride for me). There I joined the culls, rejects, and "bad guys" (both students and teachers) two other schools discarded to fill Manual Arts.

The Almighty Himself, always partial to striving underdogs, must have ordained the castoffs would make California and world history. They did. The Unwanted included such names as: opera star Lawrence Tibbett, Generals Jimmy Doolittle, Paul Williams, Harold Harris; Governor Goodwin Knight; District Attorney Buron Fitts; Judges McComb, Kaufman, Brockman, Curtis; major-league ballplayers Irish and Bob Meusel; the beloved athletic Blewetts—George, Bill, Dick and Dotty; actresses Helen Jerome Eddy, Phyllis Haver, Ruth Hammond, Vera Ralston; the world famous Marian Morgan and her dancing girls, including Rose Cowan (Mrs. Covarrubias); writer and historian Rob Wagner; George Arliss's stage director, Maud Howell; and dozens of others who did honor to themselves and their country.

Except for books and lunch money, every penny I made in high school went to Mama. She needed it badly. Papa had bought a small house in the North Broadway district. Mama toiled twelve hours a day in the olive-oil plant. My younger sister Ann worked in a dress shop, while Papa labored as a farmhand on the E.T. Earl Ranch in La Canada. Every nickel that came in was saved and used. Papa's four brothers were helped to come to America, one at a time. My oldest sister and her husband were sent fares to come over. The numerous relatives remaining in Sicily clamored for money from their now rich American kindred. Each month, Mama mailed a half-dozen envelopes with five-dollar bills in them.

My tough family's drive to accumulate money could only be matched by my own stubborn drive to get an education. Naturally I was needled by my brothers and brothers-in-law: "Hey, smart guy. You better turn out to *be* something, with all that schooling. We'll see. We're waiting."

Studies came so easy for me I finished high school in three and a half years, and for a purpose: to work six months to earn some money I could keep. Nobody knew it yet, but I had determined to go to college. So I worked six months at the Western Pipe and Steel plant, "bucking-up" hot rivets, scrunched inside a 36-inch steel pipe, holding a bucking-bar against the butt of a white hot rivet, while a riveter outside, smashed its head down with an air-gun that rattled your teeth. At noontime, when I crawled out of that pipe, I couldn't straighten up and I couldn't hear.

I saved seven hundred dollars in six months. But meantime, Papa was fulfilling a dream of his own. He had bought a fifteen-acre lemon grove in Sierra Madre. It took all the money Papa, Mama, and Ann could scrape together to meet the yearly mortgage payment. Of my savings I contributed four hundred dollars to the ranch, and kept three hundred for my first year's tuition and books. Since I seemed to have a special aptitude for mathematics and science, I entered Caltech, in Pasadena, in February, 1915. (Caltech was then called Throop Polytechnic Institute, but was in the process of being reorganized into the California Institute of Technology.)

At college, I still managed to pay my own way and contribute several hundred dollars a year to my family. Yet, scholastically I was always among the first three in my classes. Books, books, books—I read them all, from science to history to poetry. At Caltech I zeroed in on the Freshman Scholarship Prize. I *had* to win it. In my freshman year, I was fortunate enough to wangle a job as one of the five waiters at the campus dorm which housed sixty-five students. Our pay was room and board.

But only two rooms were allocated to waiters (two to a room). The fifth waiter had to go home nights or rent a room in the neighborhood. I was the fifth waiter. No room at the dorm until next year. My father had moved us to his lemon grove, fifteen miles from school. Mama and my younger sister helped Papa with the ranch. I went back and forth to school. My transportation? A second-hand, single-cylinder, belt-driven Flanders motorcycle, the kind you started up by pushing it on the run.

Okay, I had my board, but no room until next year. But I needed $250.00

for next year's tuition, besides money for books and clothes. I still had my "stuffing" job at the *Los Angeles Times* each Saturday night from nine in the evening till two in the morning. That was good for $5.00 per week. Not enough. (My dormitory laundry agency earned me about $1.00 a day, but that was ticketed for Mama.)

So I got another job at the Pasadena Light and Power plant, doing chores for the night engineer from 3:30 A.M. to 7:30 A.M., seven days a week. The pay: 25¢ per hour. That made another $7.00 per week—all told $12.00. That would get me by the first year.

This was my twenty-four-hour day: up at 3:00 A.M. at ranchhouse, lit small bonfire under motorcycle crankcase to heat up cold oil. Lit acetylene headlight (about as much light as a modern flashlight), then pushed the Flanders down dirt road until single cylinder sputtered into action; leaped on the seat and noisily raced eighteen miles in the dark to the Pasadena Light plant. On rainy nights, the rides were half-drowned ordeals of slips, slides, and muddy spills.

3:30 to 7:30 A.M.: checked boiler fires, polished miles of metal at the Light plant. Then raced three miles to school to help other four waiters wash breakfast dishes for sixty-five dorm students. Ate breakfast while working.

8:00 A.M.: ran to my first class. 11:55: ran with four other waiters to serve lunch at dorm; washed dishes, ate lunch while working. 1:00 P.M.: ran back to class.

5:00 P.M. to 6:00 P.M.: glee-club or football. Then set tables, served dinner, washed dishes, ate dinner.

7:00 P.M.: jumped on motorcycle, raced fifteen miles to Sierra Madre. Last quarter mile of dirt road was so steep had to jump off and push the Flanders. On a rainy night, it was a wrestling match with a wild steer.

7:30 P.M.: backed motorcycle into shed, put paper and sticks under crankcase for bonfire in morning.

7:30 P.M. to 10:00 P.M.: study and homework. 10:00 P.M.: to bed. 3:00 A.M.: up and lit bonfire under crankcase.

What did this schedule do to my studies? Nothing. I won the Freshman Scholarship Prize: $250.00 and a trip around the country, and the sincere congratulations of my proud teachers: Dr. Bates (chemistry), Dr. Van Buskirk (mathematics), Dr. Beckman (German), Professor Sorenson (electrical engineering), Professor Clapp (geology), and proudest of all, Professor Judy (English).

One sun-drenched February morning in 1917, Papa walked through his fifteen-acre lemon grove on the high, frost-free foothills above Sierra Madre, surveying his beautiful trees dripping with large yellowing fruit. A $5,000 crop, Papa estimated, more than enough to make the last mortgage payment due in two weeks. Tomorrow he would gather up pickers in Monrovia to harvest the bountiful yield. God smiled on him.

The first three years he had worked the grove alone, from dawn to sundown: pruning, watering, hauling manure from the Valley, discing behind his old horse—and hoeing until he couldn't straighten up. But two years ago he had ordered Mama and Ann to quit work and live with him at the ranch —a happy day. No more would they ever have to slave, he promised. I'm sure that Papa must have counted his blessings that beautiful early spring morning when all nature gathered its forces for the hallelujah burst of new life, and he probably hummed as he walked through his rose garden, the envy of all nurserymen.

About an hour after breakfast, my seventeen-year-old sister Ann, the youngest and most beloved of the family, heard a strange and fearful whir-ring noise in the grove. She called Papa. No answer. Investigating, she traced the whir to the well-pump house. She looked inside—and froze in horror. Papa was dead, his chest crushed and wedged between the teeth of two large gears. The long, black belt, from the racing motor to the pump, was chewed up and wrapped crazily around his body.

Ann tried to claw Papa out of the gears. She tore off her finger-nails but couldn't budge him. Screaming in terror, she raced the quarter of a mile back to Mama at the house, gasped out what she had seen, and fainted.

Papa's dream of moving his family out of the ghetto and onto his beloved farm was shattered. Stunned Mama and frail Ann forfeited the ranch and returned to Little Sicily, as destitute as the day they had arrived in America fourteen years before.

My educational ambitions were, of course, yanked up short. I would have had to quit had not the good officials of Caltech loaned me the tuition fees for my last three college years, so that—out of my sundry jobs—I could send Mama ninety simoleons a month while finishing school.

By this time I had become somewhat of a hero to my family. My older brothers and sisters, now married, had found out that in America illiterates run so far, then hit a brick wall. Now *I* became the family hope for fame and success. When in June, 1918, I got my degree in chemical engineering, they threw me a wing-ding of a party and drank toasts to the big bank presi-dent in the family. Having been born to worship money, they naturally thought the highest reward for education was to make you the boss of where they kept the money.

Engineering was a vague, disappointing word to them. Sounded too much like the guy in overalls that ran switch engines. When I explained that big industrial corporations were begging engineering graduates to accept draft-exempt jobs at big money, they were re-impressed. But when I told them I wasn't taking *any* job because I was enlisting in the Army, they were sure I'd blown my top. Either that, or I was going to be a bum all my life and *never* go to work, which seemed more likely to them.

Up to that time, in spite of being constantly on the run between classes and jobs, life had been one great big ball for me. Conquering adversities was so simple I began to think of myself as another Horatio Alger, the suc-cess kid, my own rags-to-riches hero.

When I stepped into the Army recruiting station to announce I would enlist if they placed me with an outfit that was going to France immediately, I knew I was doing the "right" thing. All bluebloods enlisted. Noblesse oblige stuff. And if I got a little wound? Fine. That would serve me well later, too. Go! Go! Man.

But as soon as I was sworn in, did they send me to the front to advise the generals? Oh, sure. In two days I found myself teaching ballistic mathematics to artillery officers at Fort Mason up in San Francisco. I never saw a gun, never even drilled. My weapon was a piece of chalk; my front, a blackboard. I slept, not in a foxhole, my face buried in Flanders mud. I slept in a barracks cot not over a hundred yards from the unearthly howling of a foghorn. *It* was my enemy.

Without anyone consulting me the armistice was signed. The world went wild. I went on writing blackboard equations, while the foghorn cheered me on with king-sized Brooklyn raspberries. Returning heroes were given ticker-tape parades. I watched them in the newsreels, then went back to the blackboard and my doodling class. With the gusto of a zombie, I explained parabolic trajectories, wind drifts, and the Coriolus Effect. They yawned. I yawned back. It was exciting.

It was appropriate that my military career was climaxed with the flu epidemic. Men at the base died like flies. Since my discharge papers were due any hour, I prayed hard. But one night, a surge of heat hit me. No mistaking what it was. I didn't report to sick call in the morning. No, I wanted to go home, where my strong mother wouldn't let me die. Scared stiff of passing out on the base, I went AWOL to the city. In an Ellis Street cafeteria, while paying for a bowl of soup, I crashed to the floor, soup and all.

I woke up in a crumbling, water-stained, brick hospital ward (the isolation ward of the French Hospital) the hundred closely-packed beds all squirming with moaning, retching, dying men. In the six days it took the Army to track me down, I never saw a doctor or a nurse. They, too, were dying like flies. Nor did I see any food—not that I wanted any. The almost hourly rhythmic creaking of the wicker basket in which two masked attendants carried out the dead took care of the desire for food.

Back home, I found Mama and my little sister Ann living in the three-room North Broadway house. Both were working. Mama, now aging and gray, was back at the olive plant. Ann, eighteen and bothered with a weak heart, sewed ten hours a day in the dress shop. All my other brothers and sisters were married, well off, and raising families.

But now that *I* was back home, I assured Mama and Ann they would never have to work again. Engineers made big money. I'd buy them fine clothes, *and*—I'd move them out of the ghetto and into a swank neighborhood. Just give me a week or two, Mama.

Confidently, I wrote to all the mining, oil, paper, and paint companies in the phone book. Much to my astonishment the answers were polite but *negative*: "Sorry, retooling for civilian production . . . in a transition period . . . a postwar depression . . . laying off engineers . . . filing your application . . . sorry . . . sorry . . . sorry . . ." Some of these same companies had offered me fat salaries and draft exemption less than a year before.

In a panic I turned to the want-ads. Nothing under "Help Wanted"; but *columns* under "Situations Wanted." My brothers and brothers-in-law came to see me occasionally, jingling cash in their pockets, flipping me quarters for cigarettes—and did they pour on the sarcasm: "When is the Professor going to work, Mama?" "So *this* is what college made outta you—a *bum!* In a broken-down uniform."

They were right—bitterly right. I had no answers. But if Ann was around, she'd break into tears and shout at them: "Oh, leave Frank alone, for God's sake. Isn't he suffering enough?"

But frustration had its lighter faces—the faces of the gimlet-eyed, horny-handed, Sicilian women of the neighborhood. It was a conspiracy with them —indeed, an act of faith—to insist their men were born to work and get married, to work and have children, to work and provide, to work till they died. A grown man, who wouldn't marry and wouldn't work, was both a scandal and a threat to them. Stupid ideas like that could spread to their own men. I had compounded the heresy—a woman worked to support *me!* Santa Maria! They ganged up to scotch this apostate backsliding.

Night after night a gaggle of them just happened to drop in on Mama. Each feigned surprise at the presence of the others. It was a charade, as predictable and formalized as an ancient play. They began the ritual by regaling Mama with the juicy gossip of the day, tittering and gabbling in concert as Mama poured them wine or coffee. They knew I could hear them from the next room—and I knew that they knew.

From gossip they segued into bragging—tall tales of their successful husbands and sons; the matches their daughters had made with good, hard-working young men, and how much money they saved. Money, money— their yardstick of the stature of man. From bragging, they slipped gently into commiserating with Mama. "Donna Saridda, the snow in your hair. How much longer will you work your fingers to the bone? Old age is brutal, every year a bigger rock on your back. You have no husband. A woman alone needs a man for a stick when the hands tremble and the feet take short steps."

But Mama would set her face against them. "I no afraid," was her stock answer. "God made me strong."

The ritual now called for silence and wine sipping—the dramatic pause before the question. Then: "Frankie . . . he find a job today?"

"Frankie's different, like his Papa," Mama would answer, biting her lip. "I pray. But God no answer."

That was the signal to attack—with vinegar-tipped barbs from scandal-ized lips. "Poor Donna Saridda . . . It was the schooling . . . Teach them wrong ideas . . . The Devil hides in books . . . Can't even buy himself a suit

of clothes for his back . . . Who would marry him? Not my daughters . . .
Poor Mama Saridda . . . His shame is our shame . . . But if it is the will of
God . . . He gives us all a cross to bear . . . Courage, Donna Saridda."

I had given my civilian clothes to the Salvation Army a la Beau Geste, so
I still had to wear my—now silly to everybody—uniform with the wide hat
and ridiculous *winding cloth puttees*; with no service stripes, no medals, no
overseas patches. I was a sad-sack ex-soldier. But sad-sack or not, I made the
rounds of the employment offices along with tens of thousands of other
ex-soldiers. No G.I. Bill of Rights then, no jobs back when you returned. It
was brutal. I even tried selling apples on street corners. But when I saw
bitter, uniformed men with chests full of medals, men with missing arms and
legs, begging annoyed people to buy apples, I went home and cried; cried
in Mama's lap, while she stroked my head and said: "Coraggio, figlio,
coraggio." Suddenly her hand went to my brow. "Frankie, you're hot."

"It's nothing, Mama."

"Nothing? Let me see your eyes."

"What eyes? It's nothing."

"I smell something. You vomit today?"

"Yeah, a little."

"You got pain? Like yesterday?"

"Forget it, Ma, will you?"

"Frankie, look at me! You sick again?"

I leaped to my feet, yet remained bent over, both arms locked tight
against my stomach. I screamed at her. "No! I'm not sick again. Nothing
can make me sick again, you hear? Nobody! Not you, not my goddam
brothers, not even God and his stupid goddam angels. Nothing! Nobody!"

My strong, patient mother was tough in the clutch. Seven of her fourteen
children had died in her arms. No, no panic in her when faced with pain or
death. Nor did she run for doctors. With the fatalism of the earthy, she
trusted implicitly in the will of God; you either lived or you died. Besides,
it was the code—if you can't take it you're better off dead.

She put her delirious "wonder boy" to bed, not missing one hour of work,
pasting labels on cans at the olive plant, two blocks away. Four or five
times each day, she ran back to put cold towels and slices of cold potatoes
on my burning head, changed sweat-soaked blankets, hung new herbs round
my neck, lovingly talked me out of my coma till I blinked my eyes in
recognition, prayed, then rushed back to work. Nights, Mama and Ann
spelled each other in a chair beside me. (Twenty years later I was to be
told my appendix had burst at this time.)

Six weeks later I tried standing on my feet. The room spun so fast I
grabbed my mother. We both laughed. We over-laughed, like children
laughing because they're laughing.

"Look at you," she kidded. "Your arms, your legs—like spaghetti. With
sauce and cheese you make one good meal."

"Mama . . . make me some. I'm hungry."

"Thanks, God!" she cried, rushing to the kitchen singing a tarantella.

Embracing her at the door two weeks later, I said, "Good-bye, Mama. Nobody in the world like you."

"I know," she answered. "Gimme your bag."

I handed her my G.I. duffle bag, into which she stuffed loaves of bread, cheese, and salami. I dearly loved strong, fearless Mama, even though I never rated very high on her totem pole—and with good reason. I was the pampered one who went to school while others slaved, the incompetent one who couldn't support his mother and sister, the weak one who absorbed savage insults from family and neighbors without complaint. And so, although our parting was a wrench for both of us, it was also a solution for both of us. We laughed and sniffled and tried to make light of it all.

"Mama!" I said with a big gesture. "When I conquer the world, I'll come back for you. Wait and see. You and Ann will never have to work again. I'll build you a palace, Mama, on top of a hill."

"Bravo! Bravo!" she went along, although tears were rolling down her cheeks. "Never mind the palace. Just get your self-respect back, my son. We pray for you every day. Go. God bless all your footsteps."

She slipped a ten-dollar bill in my Army tunic. I walked away. For a block I passed through a gauntlet of icy stares from gimlet-eyed Sicilian women who stood behind half-opened doors. I bowed and saluted them. They tilted their heads back and smirked—which plainly meant "Ha! It's about time, you bum."

And so I left home; with no real destination in mind—just hop a streetcar to town and let the winds blow—perhaps to the copper mines of Arizona. The North Main streetcar line was only four blocks away. But before I got there, I began to pant and perspire; my knees shook, my head spun. I sat down on the curb, weak as a cold noodle—and laughed out loud. This is ridiculous. If I went back home now, two minutes after my big exit, there'd be a riot in Little Sicily. But I wasn't about to conquer the world unless I could walk. I had to recuperate from that lousy sickness some place. Where? Tony. My brother Tony lived in Van Nuys. That would at least be leaving town. And Tony would understand—maybe.

I rode to town on the yellow car, walked to 4th and Hill, boarded a big red car headed for the San Fernando Valley. It took me through a tunnel, out Sunset Boulevard, past the lemon groves of Hollywood, over the Cahuenga Pass, and down toward Van Nuys. On the way I thought of Tony.

When the fates passed out the sizes they short-changed Tony. He was barely five feet tall. But when they came to moxie they gave him a lion's share. He would fight anything or anybody, on two feet or four—regardless of size. He was twelve when we arrived in Los Angeles; too old for first grade in school, too illiterate for higher classes. They tried him in the third grade, but he was too ornery and feisty to be cooped up in *any* classroom. In an argument with a crosseyed teacher he smashed her right between the eyes. That earned him several weeks in reform school—his total schooling.

In his teens he was alternately a jockey, a horse trainer, a prize fighter, a circus bum, a candymaker. But whatever this midget Midas touched turned into money—lots of it. Besides which, he dressed like a dandy, and loved the girls—all ego-building achievements in a world of bigger men.

Naturally, Tony laughed the loudest when the Brain, his educated brother, couldn't find a job. He bragged he could make more money than any three college jerks—and he did.

But when, by chance, he drove by in his truck and spotted me sitting on a Van Nuys curb, panting like a beached dolphin, he didn't laugh. After all, jerk or not, I was his brother.

"Frank, what're you doin' *here*, sittin' on a curb? My God you're skinny. What's the matter?"

"Nothing, Tony. Did you have to build your house so far from the car line?"

Tony and his lovely wife, Katie, took me in. Having only one bedroom they built a hammock for me between two trees. They fed me, insisted they buy me a suit of clothes to replace my frayed uniform. But by some perverse form of snobbery, I wouldn't give up my uniform. I wore it as my Red Badge of Failure. I wanted the world to know I had worked like hell for an education—and all it got me so far was a scroungy uniform.

The Valley sun, the night air, and the rich eggnogs Katie stuffed into me soon had me pruning apricot trees and singing folksongs with the cheery Mexican crews in my brother's orchards. Songs, Latin jokes, hard work in the open air—the world looked rosy again. I even gave up reading the want ads. But one night, while stuffing myself with Katie's delicious polenta, she showed me a Help Wanted ad she'd saved for me. It read: "Wanted—Tutor; in college math and chemistry." I jumped up, drove to the Van Nuys Western Union office, dashed off a night letter giving my credentials. A reply came—from an attorney—setting up the hour for a personal interview in his Spring Street office.

There were five names on the imposing, paneled office door. I was ushered into the office of the man at the top of the list, a distinguished, gray-haired gentleman who rose to greet me. There was another person sitting in the room to whom I was not introduced—a petite, elegant lady, with a quiet, queenly beauty.

The attorney asked many questions: schooling, background, grades, at the end of which the quiet lady nodded to him. With appropriate apologies the attorney introduced her to me as Mrs. Anita M. Baldwin. The name thrilled me—the daughter of "Lucky" Baldwin, horseman, bon vivant, and discoverer of the fabulously rich Comstock Lode!

In a voice gentle and disarming, she told me that she needed a tutor for her seventeen-year-old son, Baldwin; that he had a brilliant mind, but unfortunately she had probably spoiled him a little and he had not applied himself as he should have, especially to mathematics and science. She feared he would not pass the entrance exams to the University of California. My qualifications were quite satisfactory, but I would have to pass muster with Baldwin himself. He was a headstrong boy, and—since he had already turned down three other applicants—at any rate her home was in Santa Anita, at—

"Mrs. Baldwin," I interrupted, "I know your lovely estate very well. I've rounded the corner of it, at Foothill and Sierra Madre Avenue, hundreds of times on my motorcycle, going back and forth to school."

"Now don't tell me you're the young man who skidded at the turn and flew headlong through our pasture fence?"

"And one of your gardeners, I think, pulled me out of the mud, helped me back on the bike, and pushed me half a block before the darn thing started again. Yes, ma'am."

"Well, I declare—then you will be at the Sierra Madre gate at three in the afternoon tomorrow?" I nodded. "And please, sir, forgive me for prying. Is there some reason for still wearing a uniform?"

"Perhaps you should know this, madam. I haven't worked since I was discharged—months ago."

As the liveried gateman swung open the iron gate I saw Mrs. Baldwin coming toward me down the curving, flower-lined walk. She introduced me to her son; then quickly said "Baldwin, take Mr. Capra to your rooms and have a nice chat with him."

"Oo-ka-a-y," he sighed, taking no pains to hide his boredom. "Follow me, please." He turned and walked toward the house. I followed. From the way he glanced down at me, and wrinkled his nose when we shook hands, I knew he didn't like my looks *or* my smell.

In the rumpus room he slouched on a couch and said "Have a seat." But I couldn't sit down. The room was lined with musical instruments—banjos, guitars, mandolins, horns, saxophones, drums, xylophone, spinet piano. I looked at the slouching beanstalk with a curious interest.

"You play any of these?" I asked.

"I play *all* of them," he said, with that tired insolence of the rich that sandpapers nerve ends.

I walked slowly around the room swallowing a rising resentment—the endemic resentment peasants have for the indolent wealthy. I picked up a beautiful Gibson guitar and strummed an augmented chord. It jolted him out of his slouch.

"Can you play that?" he asked. I looked at him sharply.

"Look, rich boy. You want me around here as a tutor, you better start calling me 'Sir!' Understand?"

"Oh, can that stuff. I asked you if you could play that? Why don't you answer?"

I put the guitar down, turned on my heels, and started for the door.

"Hey! Wait a minute." I kept walking. "Mister! SIR!" I stopped to let him catch up to me. "Gee, but you're touchy. I just asked a simple question."

"Then don't ask it like a fresh punk."

He broke into a mischievous grin. He had charm when he smiled. "Oh, pardon me. Okay. I'll ask you again. Please, sir. Would you mind, sir, if I'm not intruding, sir, do you perchance play a guitar, sir?"

I had to grin back. "That's better. Yes. I can play *all* the instruments in your room."

"Come on, come on back. Let's play something. Everything's tuned up." He was as excited as a kid with his first pair of red boots. Handing me the guitar he picked up a tenor banjo.

I was in. Yesterday, pruning trees as a peon; today, a tutor in mathematics for one of the richest families in the country—because I could play a guitar! Didn't make much sense. But neither did anything else that happened to me for years to come.

Over tea in her famous library the lovely Mrs. Baldwin made me an offer: three hundred per month, and three new suits if I would discard my uniform; I was to live with Baldwin twenty-four hours a day, teach him enough math and chemistry to pass the exams at Berkeley—and keep him out of trouble.

Two months later Baldwin passed the Berkeley exams; I fell in love with Mrs. Baldwin; had a libidinous thought or two about her beautiful daughter, Dextra, and left for the copper mines of Arizona—with two lingering conclusions: the rich have it all, but accomplish little; and, had Baldwin been born a poor boy in New Orleans or Memphis, he might have become one of our great jazz musicians.

Great Week for Screwballs

OVER THREE YEARS—three years on the "bum" all over Arizona, Nevada, California; hopping freights, selling photos house-to-house, hustling poker, playing guitars; running, looking, sinking lower, until here I was in San Francisco again—with only a little change in my pocket, but an offer that would solve *all* my problems.

It was December, 1921. I had just been offered my first job as a "chemical engineer." The head man of a Sicilian syndicate of bootleggers from Los Angeles had tracked me down to my hotel room. Diamonds all over him. He waved ten thousand dollars in my face—if I'd design him some alcohol stills that would work.

I had grown up with this man. He had been one of those push-around tough guys—all fists, mouth, and meanness. Kids hated him, called him "Tuffy." Well, here was Tuffy in my two-bit room. Long black coat, derby, scarf—overdressed, glittering with diamonds, rocks so big they blinded you.

"Chico," Tuffy asked, "what's a brain like you doin' in this fleabag? Alky's big, Cheech. Could be bigger if our cookers didn't stink so much they get knocked off, and the lousy cops hit us for 'grease.' You're smart —engineer—college man. Speak three languages . . ."

"Five," I snapped back at him for some cockeyed reason. "Five and a *half*, if you count Sicilian."

"Okay, okay. You count me the languages, I'll count you the money. Here's ten G's—for pocket dough." He threw the roll of bills on my lap, big rubber band around it.

I said, "No, thanks," and gave him back the roll. Then I walked him through the lobby and out to his block-long limousine.

"Don't be a chump," he said. "Change your mind, Cheech, and I'll make it twenty grand *and*—a cut of the action. I'll be at the Saint Francis for two days."

When I walked back into the lobby, the clerk asked me if any of my friend's diamonds had rubbed off on me. When I told him no, he said, "Too bad. The keyhole to your room's been plugged up."

After a night's sleep in the back seat of a Rolls Royce in the friendly Geary Garage, I got up and walked toward Powell Street. I had never felt so cold or so lonely. I had been arrogant enough to become ashamed of my hardworking peasant family: I knew I deserved my cup of bitterness. I stopped at the corner to look up Powell Street. High up on the hill I saw the Fairmont Hotel bravely holding the fog on its shoulders to keep the gray skies from falling on the city.

Just one block up the street was the St. Francis Hotel, a bootlegger, and twenty thousand dollars waiting for me. It was my moment of truth. My decision would be irrevocable.

Every practical fiber within me urged: "Go on in, fool. Grab that bootlegger's twenty thousand. Sell your knowledge, build his stills. Take care of your own. Get Mama out of that olive plant, and ailing Ann out of that crummy dress shop. Be a success. Be a hero to your family." Yet—everything I had hoped to be screamed against it. "You didn't work your head off getting an education just to make illegal hooch for the Mafia. Gangsters give orders, man. You'd be one of them. Can you take that? Can you sell freedom for bootlegger money?" And yet—the Geary Garage man said no more sleeping in his cars. And I was locked out of my Hotel Eddy room until I raised eighteen bucks—

A Haight District trolley car clickety-clacked across Powell Street's cable tracks. On a sudden impulse I raced after it, catching the handrail just as it was about to pull away. Gracefully, as all ex-newskids hop cars, I swung myself up on the steps and climbed inside. The car was empty except for a turkey-necked conductor who looked up from his morning paper.

"How far do you go?" I gasped.

"To the Park," said the startled conductor.

"Good. Maybe it'll happen there." I pulled out all the change in my pocket.

"What'll happen there?"

"I don't know. But something's gotta happen." I gave him a nickel. Twelve cents were left in my hand. I threw them out the car door. The conductor's Adam's apple yo-yoed up and down his scrawny neck. He handed me his folded paper. "Here. This column is perfect for guys like you. Read it." The column read:

Great Week for Screwballs

Astrologers say the position of the 12 Houses is favorable for dreamers and long-shot players. So, for those who believe in the stars (pun intended), Fireside Productions has announced it is revamping the old Jewish Gymnasium at Golden Gate Park into a Movie Studio. Dreamers, check your horoscopes . . .

Movie studio. What the devil could I do in a movie studio? For that matter, what could I do *any* place, right now? *Has* to be a hunch, though. What can I lose? I'll play it.

In selling wildcat stocks, books, and photos, I had learned the trick of making the buyer feel inferior and deprived; that, yes, he was breathing but not *living* unless he bought what I offered. I'd just smell around at the Jewish Gymnasium, play it by ear until I could make myself superior to somebody —then sell him something.

I stopped against a telephone pole to look around. I was standing in front of an old, yellowing, plaster-cracked building, wide and low. A protruding stone archway, topped with a massive keystone, framed a pair of tall, swinging doors. Must be the entrance, but no number, no sign, no people, and no cars at the curb.

I was about to try the other side of the street when a fluttering bit of ectoplasm, circling through the fog, materialized into a flying pigeon. It flap-landed on the keystone of the old building's archway. Right below him I spotted a barely visible, carved outline of the six-pointed Star of David. I walked in.

Two square unblinking eyes glowed at the far end of the dark, empty hallway. I finally made them out to be small glass peek-panels on wooden double doors. Another streak of light escaped through an open side door, ran across the hall floor, and tried to climb the opposite wall. I looked into the lighted doorway—an empty office; theatrical posters on the wall, bar-bells, bookshelves; a scarred table piled with magazines, coffee cups, cigarette stubs, half-eaten sandwiches; a big iron coffee pot steaming on a small gas stove. The aroma triggered my hunger juices.

"Hello-o?" I called out cautiously. No answer. I continued to the end of the hall, pushing open one of the double doors. A cavernous room—"Gymnasium," I said to myself.

But a naked burning bulb, set on a stake in the middle of the room, fixed the eye. In the lighted area I saw a large, square man in a long, black overcoat, pacing back and forth between the light and a half-circle of empty chairs, as if silently rehearsing a speech. His long, grotesque floor shadow exaggerated his every gesture as it raced alongside and swung around in front of him at the end of his pacing.

"Hello, sir," I called. He slowly and dramatically raised a hand over his eyes, trying to find me in the dark.

"You have the advantage of me, sir," he answered—in a deep, rolling basso, the kind that flutters candle flames. "Are you from the press? It's quiet here today. Jewish holiday."

"Oh, no, sir. I'm from Hollywood." So what's a little lie if you haven't

July 4, 1903. Castelar Street school. After three months in America, I was chosen to lead ghetto kids in pledging allegiance to our flag (in English), by principal Mrs. Isabel Vignolo. Proud Papa bought me a new sailor suit. Brother Tony thinks it's all "a lotta bull."

Baldwin M. Baldwin, sassy, girl-crazy, whoopee-loving "Lucky" Baldwin of Comstock Lode fame. And his tutor who, as yet, only dreamed about girls.

Ten years old, and a ready fist. I hated being poor, hated the ghetto, hated America. "Some day, Annie, some day—"

My halcyon days—wanderer, freight-hopper, door-to-door Hartsook Photo salesman, poker hustler, vendor of Bluesky mining stocks—and now also girl crazy, and making up for lost time.

My first job with a movie company—prop man. "Ain't this house supposed to be on fire?" asks fire chief Dan Mason (of Toonerville Trolley fame) of director Bob Eddy, while the Powerful Katrinka looks on. "Smoke coming right up!" cried the neophyte prop man's voice from inside the house. I was having trouble lighting my first smoke pots.

got to eat? But the effect on him could not have been more startling if I had said, "I'm the Bishop of Canterbury."

"Hol-lywood?" he rolled out. "Well, well, well. I've never met a man from the film Mecca."

I felt like answering, "That makes two of us," but I didn't.

"You may approach me, sir," he beckoned regally, and with him it seemed to come quite naturally.

"I do hope I'm not intruding, sir," I said, with a faint suggestion of a bow. "I read your announcement in this morning's paper, and being up here on a short holiday, I—well, it just came over me to come out and wish you luck on your first venture—I mean, if I'm talking to the right person."

"Oh, you are, you are. And I'm flattered and delighted, sir. I'm Walter Montague. You may have heard of me. In vaudeville. I headline in Shakespeare," offering me his hand.

I took his hand and almost pulled away mine—his fingers were so gnarled and crooked.

"And I'm Frank Capra, sir. And I'm sure you've never heard of me."

"Ah, but I will, I trust. Tell me, what métier are you pursuing in Hollywood?"

"Oh, Mr. Montague—the métier most of us pursue. Learning, sir, just learning. There is so much to learn."

"Charming. Yes. And here I labored under the false impression that all you Hollywood people were braggarts. Refreshing. But you must have some particular segment of the film art you are thinking most about . . ."

"Sir . . . if you'll pardon me, what I'm thinking most about right now is the aroma of that delicious coffee in the other room. It's driving me out of my mind."

"Oh . . . how rude, how rude, how rude of me. Of course, of course. I'll join you in a cup. Time for my aspirin, anyhow." He led me toward the door. "You see, young man, I suffer like Job. But with me, it's my cursed arthritic hands."

In that cold, empty building, trading clichés over coffee and cake with this oddball Shakespearean actor, I got the sickening feeling he had as much money in his frayed pockets as I had in mine. He looked for all the world like a king's page who had been passed up and gone to seed—his get-up so studied for effect I half expected he would be wearing red socks. I looked. He was. Well, better have some more cake. It could be a long day. Anyhow, I thought to myself, slip the expansive gentleman a nudge about money, and get it over with.

"Mr. Montague, I'm dying of curiosity. How much will your—uh—first opus cost, sir?"

"Well, my dear fellow," he answered, awkwardly clawing another aspirin out of a brass pillbox, "though I say it myself, I have few peers in my field of short, dramatic skits; climactic scenes from the classics: Shakespeare,

Chekhov, Poe. But for months now, business friends of mine have urged me to widen my scope. 'Walter,' they say, 'you must transfer your talents from vaudeville to the world screen of the cinema, and we will finance you.' " The word "finance" raised some hopes.

"The daring of this conceit obsessed me like heady wine," he went on, orating. "I pondered it, mulled it, stripped it of its chaff, chiseled the dross of vanity to get to the beauty of truth. 'Walter Montague,' I asked, 'is this a dream of fools? Or can you, at your age, express your artistry in a new *medium*?' 'Yes, Walter,' my inner voice answered, '*emphatically*, yes! The cinema is *not* a new medium. What difference if the performing arts are seen through the many eyes of the audience—or through the single peephole of a camera? It is still THEATER!' Do you agree, Mr. Capra?" his fierce black eyes taking a bead on me over his aiming finger.

"Sir, I'm fascinated. But—uh . . ." (This spear holder is going to talk me to death. I better put my mouth where his money is.) ". . . Forgive my impertinence, Mr. Montague—but in Hollywood the dough-re-me is our number one headache. Are you *fully* financed?"

"Young man," he said, drawing his head back to look down his nose, "in vaudeville it's known as Montague's Law: 'The play's the thing—*if* ducats ring!' Oh, yes, the funds are in the bank, awaiting the stroke of my pen."

"Congratulations!" I exclaimed, beginning to scent pay dirt. "'The play's the thing—*if* ducats ring!' I love that! May I quote you in Hollywood?"

"Freely, freely. Well, then—having resolved that mental hurdle about the cinema, I came to another firm decision: not to adapt *myself* to the film —NO! I would adapt the film to *me*." (He's off again.) "And so, the muses being kind, I chanced upon what may be a new form of film art: From the great treasure-trove of the classic poems, choose the most dramatic. Compress each poem into ten minutes of action—into a one-reeler you call it? Yes. And use the golden verses themselves as titles, superimposed over the action. The priceless words alone will feed the human hunger for beauty. Are you following me, sir?"

"Oh, yes. Thrilling." (Now give him the superiority bit.) "Have you ever made a film, Mr. Montague?"

His coffee cup rattled as he set it down. I'd struck a nerve.

"No-o-o, I haven't. But I mean to innovate, young man, not ape. In Hollywood you move the camera and not the actors. That is wrong! Does the man in the aisle seat," stabbing each word with his finger, "in the second row, of the middle section of the orchestra circle, *move* during a whole performance? NO! And neither should the camera! I will nail my camera down in one spot. My actors will perform the ten-minute poem without a break. And the camera will *photograph* the complete performance, just as the man in the orchestra seat would be *seeing* the whole performance."

He stopped to look at me quizzically and sharply. "Anything wrong with *that*, my young Hollywood friend?"

I thought I detected a clunker in his argument somewhere, but my abysmal ignorance of stage and movies made me cagey. I remembered that at Caltech (odd how many ways an education—any kind of education—comes in handy), while doing research on photographic emulsions, I'd learned a few academic details about film and movie camera, which I had long forgotten. But I gambled on throwing the old gent a high fast ball right at his head. "Mr. Montague, I hate to say it . . . but there's something *very* wrong with your new technique."

"There is?" he exclaimed, visibly sagging.

"It will be impossible for your actors to perform continuously for *ten minutes.*"

"Impossible? I've done it innumerable—"

"Not you, sir, not you. The camera. The camera can't hold enough film to *run* ten minutes."

He sat down heavily, mechanically clawing his pillbox for another aspirin. I sipped coffee casually, knowing I had him on the ropes. Another flurry of technical details should finish him.

"You see, Mr. Montague, if you nail the camera down and replenish it with film every few minutes, the actors must freeze in their positions, as rock steady as wax figures, for the time it takes to refill the camera—a physical impossibility. But let's say you move the camera the Hollywood way. Where, when, and how to move the camera is knowledge that can only be acquired by years of experience."

I swished the dregs in my coffee cup and took a nonchalant sip. The good man's eyes were glassy; his chin sagged low. He was ready for the count.

"Take lighting, for instance," I continued. "The density of light from the actor's face to the camera varies as the square of the distance. That means a mathematical equation for each face, and . . . Oh, I'm wasting your time, Mr. Montague," I said, rising. "Thank you for the coffee, and thanks for a most stimulating conversation. I wish you luck, sir."

He just stared at me. I waved to him and turned to go. This was the moment of truth. If he let me walk out of that door, I'd had it. As a possible excuse for a re-entry, I left my folded newspaper on his desk. I reached the door, faced the wrong way down the hall as a delaying action, then turned and started out.

"Sir!" his voice boomed out. I came back to the doorway.

"Yes, sir? Did I forget something? Oh, my paper. Sorry." Picking up the paper I smiled and turned to go again.

"You said you're here on a vacation?" I thought he'd never ask.

"Just a few days, yes."

"Young man. Would you consider—I mean, just between us—could you find the time to help me plan this first picture?" (Great day in the morning!)

"Oh, Mr. Montague, there are so many more able people—"

"How much would you charge for a few days?"

Wait a minute, I thought to myself. I've been lucky so far but I could be exposed any minute. Taking pay under false pretenses could send me to jail.

"I couldn't accept any salary from you, sir," shrugging it off with a smile. "I'm under contract."

"Perhaps we could call it an honorarium. Help pay for your vacation . . . say, seventy-five dollars?" I nearly collapsed.

"I need your help, son; need it badly, as you know. In the name of the theater itself—say that you will."

"Okay, Mr. Montague. You may count on my help insofar as time and my inabilities will allow."

"Bravo!" he exclaimed, jumping up to shake my hand. "You have the real spirit of the trouper. Here—if I can only find it," rummaging through the mess on his desk and coming up with a small, red vest-pocket book, "it's in here. Our first poem: 'Fultah Fisher's Boarding House' by Rudyard Kipling. You'll like it. Now where's my checkbook?"

I flipped the pages of the small book—when suddenly I remembered I had no carfare.

"Mr. Montague, one small favor. Call it superstition, even nonsense. But every time I get a check for a new picture, I ask for an additional nickel. Brings me luck, I think. Silly, isn't it?"

"Oh, no, my boy. In the theatrical tradition. Of course, of course. Luck pieces. You'll never guess mine." He opened his hand. In it was a crumpled bit of tattered lace.

"A piece of my mother's wedding gown. Gave it to me for my first performance. Held it tight before curtain time ever since. Held it while asking you for help. You see, it worked. Now, here's *your* talisman—"

He took out a nickel, pressed it into my hand, closed my fingers over it, and said: "May you always take the tide at its flood. Now, then, your check—"

"Everything's come up roses," I chortled, stuffing my reclaimed clothes into a duffle bag. And I had enough leftover money to make Reno, and maybe get lucky at poker. Did I leave anything? I felt my pockets . . . hey! Montague's little red book . . . "Ballad of Fultah Fisher's Boarding House" . . . some title . . . should read it . . . owe him that much . . .

It's meller-drama all right. Calcutta barroom . . . hell hole . . . two sailors fight for floozie . . . blue-eyed Dane dies . . . floozie frisks him , . . finds crucifix . . . gets religion, goes straight. Come on! So quick? . . . insult to intelligence. Go *see* a movie.

Golden Gate Theater—Market Street . . . balcony. I see *The Sheik* . . . faraway scenes, closer scenes, big heads filling screen . . . women painted like dolls . . . men like fairies . . . wigs phony, beards phony . . . Hell, *I'd* never do that. Sit through the picture again . . . then again.

I walk the streets. San Francisco—city of dreams. City of hills and the smell of the sea, and battles—with conscience. It's one A.M. I'm hungry. I'd been in that theater nearly twelve hours. Scenes from *The Sheik* race through my brain, colliding with knife fights in a Calcutta barroom.

Next morning I went straight to Montague's office. He was ushering out a young lady.

"That's fine, my dear. Come back tomorrow and you may read for me . . . Well, well, young man. Come in, come in. How did you and the great Kipling hit it off? That young lady wants to play the girl. Said she has played leads for Universal . . ."

"Mr. Montague, please sit down, sir. I have a few words . . ."

"Of course, of course." He sat.

"Well, sir. You paid me some money to help plan your first picture. I stayed up all night. I have a plan for you. I'll give it to you—then I leave. We're even. Agreed?"

"I'm not sure I understand, but go on."

"Fine. Point one. Mr. Montague, wittingly or not, you have dreamed up a novel type of film; *providing*—you preserve that novelty with something new, fresh, daring. With the possible exception of one cameraman, use no technical help that has ever worked professionally on a stage or in a movie studio. Kipling needs the imaginative enthusiasm of the amateur. In your words: *innovators*, sir. Free, young minds, still unfettered by the dull taboos of the tried and true."

My own words astonished me. What was I trying to say? Well, anyway, finish up and run.

"My second point is even more daring," I went on, catching fire with my own enthusiasm, "an artistic concept that defies all the traditional gods of the hackneyed. You will need the guts of a burglar, Mr. Montague—but it could make you the talk of the film world. No make-up, sir . . . no wigs . . . no phony beards . . . and no ACTORS! Go to the waterfront. Pick up real sailors—dirty—smelly—filthy, but real! Put Kipling on the screen, not Montague, not sweet powderpuffs from Universal. You want a whore? The Barbary Coast is lousy with whores. The riffraff in Kipling's bar has got to *reek* of sweat, and grog, and vileness. *Reality*, sir—not fake, painted dolls. The first picturemaker with nerve enough to give the public the Real McCoy— Oh, nuts! What am I blowing *my* top about? Anyhow, you paid me for a plan? We're even. Good-bye."

I flew out of his office, hot, angry, and stewing in my enthusiasm for something I knew nothing about.

"Young man! Young man!" Montague called out, running after me. But I was out the door, half-running down the sidewalk.

"Stop him! Stop him!" Montague yelled to two window washers. They grabbed me roughly and held me. Coming up to me with wide open arms, Montague embraced me warmly.

"Young man, Frank . . . *You* must make Kipling's poem!"

"Me?"

"Yes, yes. You have the concept, the enthusiasm, the technique—brilliant! Brilliant! Daring! I agree with every word. Make the first film for me. Take the tide at the flood. I shall stand with you—to encourage, to learn. Oh, heaven bless this great day . . ."

I was trapped by my own chicanery. Seething with enthusiasm, yet scared stiff of exposure, I stood in a spotlight of my own lighting. Only the surge of adventure and the god-awful gall of the ignorant would lead me to think I could get away with it. Gall, and my ace-in-the-hole—a cameraman, Roy Wiggins, whom I had met while he was on an assignment to photograph the Mount Wilson Observatory. Caltech had appointed me his contact man. We became friends, took out a couple of girls. I knew I could trust Roy. If I could hire him I had it made; he would teach me everything about picturemaking.

Well, I talked him into driving up, and I took him to Marquard's, a fancy night club. Over dinner I told him everything, ending up by exclaiming, "Sounds exciting, huh, Roy?"

"Sounds nuts to me," he said flatly, "but that's your headache. What I'm trying to figure out is why you called me?"

"To show me what to do with the actors—how to direct them, where to put them—"

"Me? I never *saw* anybody direct actors. I ain't ever been inside of a studio."

"Wha-at?"

"I'm a newsreel cameraman. I'm okay in the sunlight, but *studio* lights —that's all Greek to me."

Cripes in a teakettle—Montague's counting on me, who'd never seen a studio—and I'm counting on this bird who'd never been inside one. This was the blind leading the blind, leading the *blind*.

"Okay, Roy, okay, okay—" I was breathing hard and thinking harder. "But can I count on you keeping your trap shut—about me?"

"As long as your money talks, I won't."

"Fine. You'll get your salary—in advance. But you've got to call me *Mister* Capra. I'm the head cheese, see? You ask *me* all the questions, understand? Nobody else. I'll tell you where to put the camera, I'll light the actors, I'll do *everything*. And you just say 'Yes, Mr. Capra,' and *never* contradict me. You got it?"

"Yes, Mr. Capra."

"Oh, you bastard," I laughed, "let's finish this pint. Want to meet some of the chorus dames?"

"Oh, *yes,* Mr. Capra."

The next week was one continuous, hold-your-hat, roller-coaster ride. Nights, I sweated with the "script," on reams of hotel stationery, trying to visualize Kipling's poem in "scenes" with living characters—writing, rewriting; sketching, resketching. "What about photography?" I asked myself. The cameraman had said he was no Rembrandt, the overstatement of the

year. Fine. I'll copy Rembrandt. Light my people from a single realistic
source; paint with light as Rembrandt had with pigment. I might flub it, but
at least talking Rembrandt would make me sound more like a pro.

Daytime, I rushed all over town, renting flats, lights, props. I ran into a
traveling carnival show owner who bragged he and his "crew" could build
me a two-sided saloon set cheap—and "right." My one fear was hiring some
professional who might spot me as a phony.

"Are your men non-professionals?"

"Friend, 'carney' folk don't ask or answer questions. Deal?"

"Deal."

I prowled the waterfront dives for "types": derelicts with peg legs,
chewed ears; the pock-marked, the scarred, the bashed; ruffians of bizarre
ancestry, white, black, yellow; the albino and the piebald. But I laid an egg
with the Barbary Coast whores. Their common answer was "Ten bucks a
day? Take a walk, sport. I make that much in an hour." However, I knew
a Will King chorus girl, overblown, sexy, naive—wouldn't know a Hollywood man from a Piltdown man. She played the lead.

Making a movie in San Francisco was news; the press could kill me. I
asked Montague to protect me from publicity on account of my Hollywood
contracts, and to shield my non-professional actors from embarrassing
visitors.

"Leave the press to Montague, never fear. I will placard the studio with
signs: POSITIVELY NO VISITORS! Brilliant! It will titillate public interest."
Good old Montague.

Came the morning of "shooting." The saloon looked perfect, foggy with
smoke as I ordered, and smelly with beer on the sawdust. The "actors,"
standing around in openmouthed wonderment, were so villainous Kipling
would have loved them. I had every scene in my mind and sketched out in a
pocket notebook; long shots, near shots, face shots—all in chronological
order. A pomaded Montague gripped my hand, wishing me luck.

"Scene One!" I yelled out, giving Roy, the cameraman, my first sketch.

"Yes, sir, Mr. Capra." He set his camera up, while I grouped the
"actors," giving each one of them something to "do" after telling them how
great they looked.

"Gentlemen, you are real skid-row sailors in a real skid-row saloon in
Calcutta. Now, no real saloon in the world would have a director, camera,
electricians, or lights around it, would it? But if you look at the camera or
me during a scene, then you're telling us it's a fake saloon. And if you tell
us it's a fake saloon, I'm going to put fake beer in your beer glasses for
the rest of the day."

"No! No! No fake beer—" shouted the "actors." Montague whispered
"Bravo, Maestro!" in my ear. Roy yelled out, "Ready for camera check,
Mr. Capra."

There are men and there are moments. Lincoln met his moment at Gettysburg; Horatio, at the bridge; Galileo, sitting in church timing the swing of the clock pendulum.

Well, I don't know if I met up with any "moment" when I first looked through the eyepiece of that camera and saw my first movie scene. But I did get the doggonedest attack of goose pimples—and thrills that shook me from head to foot. I couldn't stop looking. Half a century later my eye is still glued to that eyepiece, ever more fascinated by the wonders it reveals.

The *Ballad of Fultah Fisher's Boarding House*, a one-reel film, made by a chemical engineer, with no actors and a newsreel cameraman, at a cost of seventeen hundred dollars opened at the Strand Theater on Broadway, April 2, 1922. The result was astonishing.

Excerpts from Reviews:

> "Ballad of Fisher's Boarding House," Pathe's Kipling Special,
> Booked April 2 for Strand

> . . . justified all claims made for it . . . picture is truly a tribute to Kipling's genius . . . rapt attention . . . all eyes on screen to the finish . . . spontaneous applause . . . Seaport types marvelously well portrayed . . .

> . . . very unusual single reel . . . scenes all intensely dramatic . . . the acting is strong . . . The picture has dignity, beauty, and strength . . . will certainly please the critical audience . . .

Those reviews left me dazed and walking around in a never-never land, where nothing is and everything ain't. "The picture has dignity, beauty, and strength . . ." the critic wrote. The nutty little Montague affair—a smart-aleck scrounging for a quick buck—had backfired into a cockeyed success.

Nothing made sense, especially after a Pathe representative saw the completed one-reeler. He flipped his lid, sent the film to New York, and back came a check for thirty-five hundred dollars (over 100 percent profit) with a contract for twelve more one-reel poems. I was as stunned as if I'd suddenly discovered I could fly. But not Montague—he *was* flying; even sported an elegant new fur collar when he took me to lunch at the Skylight Garden Court of the Palace Hotel and handed me a list of poems from which to select the next production.

I had to make my confession. "Mr. Montague, I lied to you. I know nothing about pictures. I've never—"

"I know. You've never lived in Hollywood. You were locked out of the Hotel Eddy. You slept in garages and worked for a firm that sold worthless mining stock. One of my sponsors, a prudent attorney, had you checked out. Interesting, I said to him, but unimportant. Art is born in the womb; with its own truths. I believed in your initiative, your enthusiasm—the audacity of your creative ideas—and not in a dossier of your misfortunes. You proved me right."

Since he was on cloud nine, he was not about to be ruffled by my refusal to continue to do his films. Blithe spirit that he was, he rhapsodized about "The Village Blacksmith" and departed, leaving me to pay the check.

But my one fleeting glimpse into the wondrous world of films had left me bug-eyed with its magic. I had rubbed Aladdin's lamp; tasted the hashish of creativity—I was hooked. "Is this a dream of fools?" I asked myself, à la Montague. Reason answered, "Yes, it is. Your beat is science, not miracles."

Yet—"The picture has dignity, beauty, and strength," artistic qualities that evoke emotional responses. Fine. Accidents do happen—like chance mutations in biology. Okay, forget Kipling's poem. But one fact did border on the miraculous: Millions of people were seeing a rinky-dink one-reeler, made by a greenhorn, and enjoying it.

Yes, I was hooked. But would I—*could* I—possibly make it as a film director? Man, that would really make my snorting family roll over and bark. That did it. Go, go! man. Learn the tools of filmcraft, the ones you scared hell out of Montague with, for *his* not knowing. Start at the bottom, start with celluloid. Where?

Walter Ball's one-man film laboratory on Howard Street was as clean, precise, and exacting as the man himself. I talked Walt into taking me on as his sorcerer's apprentice, for food and lodging. For the next year and a half I ate, slept, and dreamed celluloid; developing, printing, drying, splicing it.

Ball's business was newsreels, advertising film, and documentaries shot by amateur film buffs. I put these films together in little story forms and began learning one of the most exciting, prime tools—film editing: an art as new as the films.

A dozen scenes can be put together in literally thousands of different combinations—but only one or two will make a "story." Here's an example. A proud father (a Berkeley professor) brought in about twenty hand-held shots of a dog show in which his ten-year-old daughter entered a mongrel. I put his scenes together in chronological order; dogs arriving, being judged, the winners, the losers. The sequence was duller than dishwater. I needed a story, a viewpoint. I re-edited the scenes from the viewpoint of the winning dog—better, but tricky. Then I put the scenes together from the viewpoint of the little girl whose mongrel was given the brush-off. The film exploded into life with laughs and tears.

I was discovering another axiom of entertainment; what interests people most is *people*.

My laboratory apprenticeship had lasted but a short year when Mr. Ball acquired a lucrative processing plum: developing and printing the "dailies" (film shot each day) for Bob Eddy, a Hollywood comedy director, who was making a series of two-reel comedies with Dan Mason of Toonerville Trolley fame. Bob Eddy was shooting his films in Belmont, a small town twenty miles down the Peninsula.

One evening, while Director Eddy was viewing his film in our projection room, he told us his prop man had cut off three fingers on a buzz saw, and did Walt Ball know of any other prop men in town?

"I can fill in, Mr. Eddy," I popped in fast, not knowing exactly what a prop man was.

Bob Eddy looked inquiringly at Walt.

"Frank, here, can do anything, Bob," answered Walt, puffing a cigar stub back to life.

"Well, I gotta have somebody till I get a replacement," said the director. "Bus leaves the Palace Hotel at five thirty. Be there."

A prop man, I learned, must be a magician who grabs things out of the air; things like magazines, furniture, toys, smokes, breakaway vases, flowers, barbed wire, horses, cats, cooked turkeys. His prop chest is a Pandora's box of tools, wire, glue, wigs, safety pins, badges, license plates, first-aid kit, and Kotex. He must produce the impossible *now*, usually by running the hundred in ten flat loaded with tools.

My heaviest cross was playing nursemaid to Eight-ball, an ornery, sway-backed, twenty-year-old white plug of a horse who played a character in the comedies. Eight-ball got his name from being only seven-eighths castrated—enough to take away his can-do, but not his yen-to, and was he sore about it. Many a night the company bus left without me because I was still trying to curry Eight-ball without getting kicked to death. That meant I hitchhiked to town later on or, if too tired, slept in the next stall.

Those were long, tough nights . . . when devil thoughts took over. What in hell was I doing here, rolled up in the stench, shivering under a blanket that reeked of sweat and ammonia? What would my brothers say if they found "wonder boy" in a manure pile?

What would Dr. Millikan, Nobel Prize winner and President of Caltech, think of one of his prize students . . . to whom he had said, "Frank, discipline your imagination and you'll go far." Or, the great Dr. Arthur Noyes, of M.I.T., Chairman of President Wilson's Science Advisory Board, who selected me to research an inflammable liquid that would render enemy gas masks useless—how shocked would he be at his protégé to whom he wrote: "Congratulations for a brilliant piece of research of enormous importance to the war effort. My personal thanks . . ."

Well, what *was* I doing, freezing on wet straw in the hick town of Belmont? Why, learning the tools of the great, new, cinematic art of motion pictures. How? Well, by playing valet to a crow-bait horse; by pulling funny hats off actors' heads with piano wire; by throwing pies in their faces from behind the camera, timing the pie to hit the actor just as he turned his head toward you, so he wouldn't see the pie coming and close his eyes. Tools?

Art? Well . . . "The picture has dignity, beauty, and strength . . ." Ha! You've got your horse, now grab a lance and look for windmills . . .

If you're a prop boy you run when the director says "Get your tail down here!"—even if it is Sunday, and even if that nosy operator did track you down in Lavinia's love nest, where you were making like a sultan as the diaphanous lovely brought you breakfast in bed. I was out of breath as I unlocked the front door of Ball's lab and heard Bob Eddy's voice echo down the stairway: "Goddam this goddam thing!" I'd never even heard him say "darn" before.

I raced up the stairs to the cutting room. There was the director, shirt soggy with sweat, film tangled round his neck and underfoot, cussing and kicking the pedals of the film splicer.

"Frank, come in here!" he yelled, sucking a bloody finger he'd cut with the razorblade film scraper. "Can you work this bloody splicer?"

"Sure, Mr. Eddy. Here, let me patch those scenes for you—don't roll your chair back till I pick up this film. You're in a mess. Where's Peanuts?" ("Peanuts" Yale was his film cutter.)

"He shoulda had the end sequence cut this morning. I bawled him out, so he ups and quits," he said, fighting his way out of tangled film. "Studio wants to see the first cut in Hollywood by tomorrow! Where the hell's Walt Ball? Won't even answer his phone."

"Sunday, Mr. Eddy. Not even the Pope can make Ball work Sundays."

"Sunday! Sunday for everybody! Five times I've tried to raise the studio for another cutter."

He jiggled and pounded the phone. My heart jiggled and pounded my throat. "Mr. Eddy, we can have this print in Hollywood tomorrow. Let me cut the end sequence for you . . ."

He gave me a sour look which said, "Criminy, this is one of those days" . . . "Hello? Try that Hollywood 0301 again for me, will you, operator?"

"Look, Mr. Eddy. I've cut film for a year right in this lab. I know the end sequence by heart, and I know where the film is. I've helped Peanuts here at night . . ."

"Hello! Still don't answer? Aw, to hell with 'em—sorry, Miss."

He banged the phone, let out a string of cuss words, then stopped to glare at me. "You stink as a prop man. What makes you think you can cut *film* —it takes years . . ."

"Right now, you don't smell so good either, Mr. Eddy. I'm just trying to help. You want the print in Hollywood tomorrow? Fine. Come back tonight after dinner and I'll show you a rough cut. You like it, we can put it on the nine o'clock Owl."

At eight forty-five that Sunday night, Bob Eddy and I—and the film shipping can—were speeding in a cab to the Union Station, prodding the driver to make the nine o'clock Owl to L.A. The director had seen my cut sequence but hadn't said a word about it except "Let's go!" when I told him

I had a taxi waiting. At the station I left Mr. Eddy in the cab and ran (with the film) through the depot, out to the loading ramps, past trainmen booming out "All aboar-r-rred!" down the full length of the train to the mail car, heaving the film can up to the clerk just before he closed his doors.

"We made it," I laconically panted to the director as I got back in the taxi. He didn't bat an eye.

"Take us to Leoni's," he ordered the driver.

For the next few minutes neither of us spoke. I sat back with eyes closed, too bushed to even care. Then:

"Eaten anything today?" he asked.

"No, but it's okay. I'll get something at the hotel."

"Frank . . . I don't know how to thank you without sounding sappy. You cut that end sequence beautifully, and you got me out of a big hole with the studio. I'm going to buy you the biggest bottle of champagne, the best dinner in town, and the nicest suit you ever owned. And you can cut all the rest of my films. Okay?"

He said all this without looking at me. I tried swallowing the sudden lump in my throat, but it got bigger. "Jesus, Mr. Eddy," was all I could say.

And so I was initiated into that select circle of "creative minds"—the elite group that has, down through the ages, affected the history of man more than all the kings and generals combined. I sneaked in as the lowest man on the totem pole, a film cutter of slapstick comedies.

Sitting in that cubbyhole of a cutting room in Ball's lab, running film scenes back and forth in the enlarging Movieola, sweating out their right sequential order, I realized I was composing. It was not music, nor was it literature. I was expressing myself in a powerful, new language—FILM—an Esperanto understood throughout the world, one that spoke directly to the heart and mind of man, from Siberia to Patagonia, without words. My lifelong love affair with film had begun, with a honeymoon in that little old cutting room at Ball's lab. And my wildly gyrating compass was settling down to a nervous quiver—pointing at Hollywood.

I edited Bob Eddy's next three comedies for him. I became the blanket to his Linus. In wonderment, I asked him one day why he let me, or anyone else, "compose" his film scenes. His answer was short and curt: "Because I'm a director and *not* a film cutter." But it didn't make sense to me. What if Beethoven had given his original themes to an arranger to orchestrate for him? Would the resulting symphonies have been the arranger's or Beethoven's? And, if the "Shakespeare of Music" had composed with co-creators, would he have left us the *Eroica*, the Kreutzer Sonata, and the monumental Ninth?

Simple thinking? Yes. I had not yet been to Hollywood where most films would be made by committees of producers, writers, directors, actors, and film cutters. I still thought of the medium as a whole. My own zany, single experience with films having been *Fisher's Boarding House*, in which I had done "everything," I naively concluded that one man made a picture, as one man wrote a symphony or a novel.

I was blissfully ignorant then of what I was to learn the hard way later: that the production, distribution, and exhibition of motion pictures was not only an art, but a multibillion-dollar industry, the fifth largest in the country; that a single production might cost millions, at times tens of millions; and that the job expectancy of filmmakers was based on the age-old law of the marketplace—take in more than you spend or you're out.

Because billions were invested in producing and exhibiting this new "art," it became the daffiest of all "Big Businesses." Bankers and industrialists tore their hair trying to standardize; mass-produce winning models; bring order out of chaos. They have never succeeded—and never will. The motion picture is an unresolvable dichotomy of business and art, with art being the safest bet in the long run. Year in, year out, it is the creators who strive for quality, the "one man, one film" artists, who out-succeed the industrially oriented mass producers.

That simple notion of "one man, one film" (a credo for important filmmakers since D. W. Griffith), conceived independently in a tiny cutting room far from Hollywood, became for me a fixation, an article of faith. In my subsequent forty years of film directing, I never forgot it, nor compromised with it—except once. I walked away from the shows I could not control completely from conception to delivery. I approached films with the wonder of a child, but also with the ratiocination of a scientific mind. I knew of no great book or play, no classic painting or sculpture, no lasting monument to art in any form, that was ever created by a committee—with the possible exception of the Gothic cathedrals. In art it is "one man, one painting—one statue—one book—one film."

CHAPTER 3

Comedy and the King

CRANKING UP my second-hand flivver and leaping into the driver's seat before the perverse tin lizzie "crawled" away on me, I shouted to my bride of less than a month, "Wish me luck, honey." She blew me a kiss as I rattled away toward Hollywood Boulevard and to my first interview for a job in a real movie studio.

Hollywood at last! Glamour center of the world. City of the stars: Chaplin, Pickford, Fairbanks, Talmadge, Theda Bara, Valentino. But still an area as off-limits as the Barbary Coast for the Pasadena and Philharmonic bluebloods. I was a defector from the Halls of Ivy; a happy defector—so full of beans I whistled and beat fancy rhythms on the steering wheel.

I had reasons to be cocky. Wonderful things had happened during the last three months in San Francisco. First, Bob Eddy promoted me out of the cutting room and on to the set as his right-hand man—his gag writer. Gags were bits of comedy "business" for the actors to do or to happen to them. To my own great surprise, funny ideas just gurgled out of me, particularly for old Dan Mason and that wonderful sweet giant, Wilma Hervey, who played Powerful Katrinka.

One night Walt Ball asked me to deliver a rush order of film tests to von Stroheim's cameraman. The great von Stroheim was shooting night scenes for *Greed* in a real building on a San Francisco main street. I delivered the tests, then stayed on behind the lights to watch the great man direct a scene. It was a simple scene: a short, nasty argument between two men in an office. But how Stroheim hammed it up! What posturings, torturings, waits, arguments, retakes, retakes—just to get a simple scene.

I stood it so long, then turned away with a loud aside to a group of bit actors: "If that Stroheim's a director, I'm D. W. Griffith."

"Maybe you will be some day," a feminine voice behind me said.

I turned fast at what I assumed was a wisecrack. A very pretty young lady in make-up was smiling impishly; just my type—small, green eyes, auburn hair. Lovely.

"Was that supposed to be funny?" I asked her tartly.

"No—not really."

"Well, let me tell you something. *I* could direct that scene better'n that stiff neck in two minutes."

"Bob Eddy would think so."

"Bob Eddy? You know Bob Eddy?"

"I've played some small parts for him. My name's Helen Howell. You're Frank Capra, aren't you?"

"Why—yeah, but—"

"I've seen you together. He's told me things about you."

"Things you might tell me over dinner?"

She eyed me up and down, then said, "Okay."

That's how it started. It ended five weeks later with the two of us standing with our backs against a fake fireplace in a St. Francis Hotel room—being pronounced man and wife by a Congregationalist minister. I was a Catholic and she was part Jewish. That posed a problem. And since neither she nor I really knew what a Congregationalist was, we decided this gentle old parson would make everything right for us with the merciful powers in heaven.

Then a third wonderful event happened. Having finished his twelve comedies, Bob Eddy suggested that if I would go to Hollywood with him he would introduce me around as a clever young gag writer. He said he had a director friend, Bob McGowan, director of the *Our Gang* kid comedies at Hal Roach Studios, who was always looking for new material. If that failed he had an "in" at the Mack Sennett Studio.

Bob Eddy was a real friend who judged me on face value. What he didn't know was that I was dying to *beg* him to take me to Hollywood; instead, I was playing it cool to the last minute hoping that he would ask *me*. That would make him more responsible for my future. This kind of tortuous thinking, the cunning to use your friends for your own ends, I had picked up in the streets and alleys.

Near the Rancho Golf Course I found the house I was looking for. Taking a deep breath I pushed the bell button. Bob McGowan answered the doorbell himself; a short, square Irishman, wearing a worried look on his slightly pock-marked, Paddy face.

"Frank Capra?"

"Yes, Mr. McGowan? Bob Eddy sent me to—"

"Yeah, yeah. Come in."

I followed him into the den of his modest house. I noticed he dragged one foot and that his hair was limp and flecked with gray. In his rumpled shirt and pants, he resembled a plumber more than a director.

"Ever see any of my kid pictures?" he asked as we sat down in his cluttered little office.

"Who hasn't?"

"They're not easy to make, you know. Last one was a bitch."

Bob Eddy had warned me he'd be shy and uneasy with people, but that I shouldn't worry.

"Are you working on your next one now, Mr. McGowan?"

"Yeah." He crumpled a sheet of paper and threw it at a wastebasket.

"Well, sir," I said, taking off my coat, "I'm an awfully good listener. Why don't we go to work?"

He looked directly at me for the first time. "Bob said I'd like you. I dunno. Salary's forty clams a week, but I got my own way of working, see? Two weeks home, here, preparing; two weeks shooting at Roach. I don't allow nobody on the set . . . not even gag men—kids get nervous. Understand? You think of any gags while I'm shooting, you see me at lunch in the cafeteria. Otherwise stay home and cook up plots for the next one. All I need is simple hookers—to hang gags on—the whole plot in one paragraph, get the idea? I'll try you out for a week. Okay?"

The *Our Gang* comedies were the soap operas of Kiddieland. Now my job was to think up plots and funny gags for bland, small-town children: Mickey, Mary, Farina, Joe—normal youngsters with normal parents. The alley kids I grew up with had really been midget adults—tough, smart, worldly. The fist had been the law, a bloody nose the closing argument. Survival was not predicated on "Wash back of your ears, Mickey," or, "Eat your spinach, Mary." Survival, to us, had meant not being caught alone at night by the Dogtown Dagos or the Ann Street Aztecs. As newskids, it had meant fighting for the possession of better corners—from the outskirts of town to Fifth and Broadway, L.A.'s Metropolitan Opera House for those who sang "Extra! Extra!"

The nine-block area surrounding Fifth and Broadway—with its thirty-six prize corners—had been the big time for the paper hustlers; their own Times Square. Corner by corner you fought your way out of the residential rim toward the business hub, where papers sold fast. When you thought you could "take" the man ahead of you with your fists, you challenged him. If you won, you were one corner closer to the big time. If you lost, you still had a continuous fight on your hands with the kid behind you in this pecking order of bloody noses. At the age of six I started hawking papers around the industrial areas of Main and Alameda. When I quit, ten years later, I had made Third and Broadway, just one block away from the magic square of the big time.

So it was only natural that the first "plots" I submitted to Director McGowan were filled with brawling and chicanery. "No, no!" he objected, throwing my stuff away, "the *Our Gang* kids don't live in slums. They're everyday, small-town children who get sick, get lost, get into trouble trying to grow up. What do normal kids do? They try to imitate their elders and bollix things up because of their innocence. That's the key, that's the humor. Forget this blood-and-thunder junk. Get down to little things that look big to children. You gotta think like a *kid*—not a fight promoter."

Well, innocent kids were not up my alley. I knew the ax was coming. But before it fell I got back into McGowan's good graces by inventing two new *Our Gang* characters: rich, identical-twin boys who had just moved into Ourgangville—good-looking, well-mannered, wealthy twins of Mickey's age, who looked and dressed exactly alike. But one was as tough as scrap iron; the other, a mama's boy who ran if you said "Boo!" Naturally, Mickey's girl, Mary, smiled at the attractive rich twins, and just as naturally Irish Mick had to let the rich brats know who was boss.

But much to Mickey's surprise, one of the twins knocked him flat without mussing a hair; the other cried and ran if Mickey looked at him cross-eyed. And Mickey couldn't tell which was which! That was the kind of gimmick McGowan looked for. A "running" gag, good for long mileage. "Good for half a dozen two-reelers," he enthused. "Audiences will start laughing every time Mickey just sees a twin." McGowan forgot the ax for another month or two.

The Hal Roach Studio, in Culver City, was a swinging lot in late 1924. Contrary to Mack Sennett, Hal Roach was star conscious in his slapstick comedies. When I first walked into his studio, Roach had three "star" series going full blast: *Our Gang*, Will Rogers' Comedies, and the world-renowned Laurel and Hardy laugh getters. In addition, Roach himself was directing a wild, feature action picture. Laurel and Hardy were being directed by Leo McCarey; the cameraman, I believe, was George Stevens.

Since Bob McGowan never really wanted the world to know he used gag writers, I had a dickens of a time getting a pass to enter the studio. "Yes," the suspicious gateman would say, after making several phone calls, "you're on the payroll of *Our Gang*, but what do you do? You're under miscellaneous." And after getting my pass I still felt miscellaneous.

Bob McGowan had no office, which meant I had none. He allowed nobody, but nobody, on his set. The only place I saw the *Our Gang* kids was on a movie house screen. So I wandered around the lot with a pad and pencil, making gag notes; knowing nobody, talking to nobody. At noontime, I waited for McGowan in the cafeteria. When I spotted him in line holding a tray, I'd walk up to hand him a couple of pages of gag suggestions for his current shooting. He would stuff the pages in his pocket without saying a word, in fact, without looking at me.

On paper, a gag suggestion looked like a jerky "shorthand," slapstick hieroglyphics which gag writers and directors translated into visual action. Often the notes were just vague hints to spark the director. The vaguest of all gag suggestions, made by a neophyte writer, became immortalized as a gag line of its own: "Here the kids have five minutes of fun in the grocery store."

I found a faded, yellow pad containing some of my gag suggestions written to Bob McGowan in 1924:

Mary gets into aunt's room—uses cosmetics.

Farina and parrot—grabs Farina's kinks.

Vacuum cleaner—Joe sucks pants off kids.

Skin falls on dog—scares kids.

Mick puts milk bottle in dog's basket—dog up to porch, barks—lady comes out—takes bottle—enters—dog barks more—lady comes out—apologizes—puts nickel in basket.

Indian War Dance—bee stings chief Sonny—jumps around—yells—all stop to applaud his dance—he jumps into rain barrel.

Pony Express mount—goat to donkey.

Kid on piano stool—cat unravels knitted pants—dog after cat.

Kid BB's weather cock off barn—falls into chicken yard—rooster fights it.

Mick milks cow—cow's tail switches cross face—Mick gives tail to dog to hold—dog holds tail tight behind cow.

Kid eating spaghetti—can't come to the end—kid snips spaghetti with scissors.

Some of these gags sound familiar? They are. Gags are just old gags with new twists. A pie in the face is basically the old tomato in the puss. The twists are: what kind of pie, who throws it, who ducks it, who gets it.

You may have noticed that almost every other word in the gag notes is a verb, a visual action verb. The silent comedies were movies that "moved." You may have also noticed there isn't a joke in a carload of gag notes—just a basic, funny, visual situation underlying a string of verbs.

Why these so-called basic situations are funny is a very sticky question which I will try to go into later. But fundamentally, human experience has taught us to know things as they are—or should be—and when they aren't, they strike us as funny or tragic. At any rate, it is still remarkable to see a comedy director take three little words like "cat drinks beer" and conjure up five minutes of laughs from them. Was the cat sure-footed? Now he's got rubber legs. Was he a fraidy-cat? Now he runs dogs up trees. Was he shy? Now he puts a basket on his head, bangs piano keys, and yowls, "It's Three O'Clock in the Morning."

Most writers—and practically all gag writers—have certain pet places to work where ideas seem to come easier: for instance, a chair, a room, a place to walk. Since I had no office I worked outside on the lot—and found my pet place: an old pile of lumber, on which I sat for hours with my yellow pad, away from the noise. Will Rogers walked by me several times a day, to and from his set and dressing room. He began to give me passing glances, but of course I was too scared to say hello to Will Rogers. One day he stopped and said: "Young fella, I know you're not a statue. I can see your pencil move."

I jumped up and muttered something.

"What're you totin' up there? You aimin' to buy this joint or sell it?" he asked, chewing away and smiling. I told him I was a gag writer for Bob McGowan. "Gag writer, huh? Well, come to my dressing room and have a cup of coffee. Tell you what. You try your gags out on me while I take the splinters out of your pants. You like doughnuts?"

In his dressing room he had me in stitches with his stories. What a wit. When he found out I had no office or typewriter he said I could use his dressing room and typewriter and he'd charge me one gag a day—and oh, he'd throw in the coffee and doughnuts. We made a deal. For the next four months his dressing room was my office. I tried to give him one gag a day, but for my one he gave me twenty.

Another fascinating professional I met at Roach's was cartoonist George Herriman, the creator of one of my favorite comic characters, Krazy Kat, that lovable combination of wisdom and innocence who tilted cat whiskers at inhumanities against the ever-changing Arizona backgrounds of Coconino County. Herriman was one of the first intellectual philosophers to comment entertainingly and shrewdly on life's frustrations through the medium of a comic strip.

I don't remember where this talented man lived, but he worked quietly in a studio bungalow in the middle of the Roach lot—"Because," he said, "Krazy Kat feels right at home with all these crazy comics."

I spent many an hour watching this shy humorist draw. Once I asked him if Krazy Kat was a he or a she.

"You know," he answered, lighting his pipe, "I get dozens of letters asking me the same question. I don't know. I fooled around with it once; began to think the Kat is a girl—even drew up some strips with her being pregnant. It wasn't the Kat any longer; too much concerned with her own problems—like a soap opera. Know what I mean? Then I realized Krazy was something like a sprite, an elf. They have no sex. So the Kat can't be a he or a she. The Kat's a spirit—a pixie—free to butt into anything. Don't you think so?"

"I don't know about Krazy Kat, Mr. Herriman, but if there's any pixie around here, he's smoking a pipe."

But the man I watched and admired most was that handsome, black-haired Irish director, Leo McCarey. The ease and speed with which this young genius cooked up laughs on the spot for Laurel and Hardy made my mouth water. He was the first talented director I had seen. And when I found out he was the son of "Pop" McCarey, owner and promoter of the famous Pop McCarey's Fight Pavilion, the best friend us newskids had in town, I just had to introduce myself to Leo.

Leo was the kind of guy you meet and two minutes later you're friends. We talked of all the great champions we had seen at his father's "barn": Benny

Leonard, Al Wolgast, Joe Gans, Joe Rivers, Stanley Ketchell, Harry Wills. And when he asked if I remembered the newskids' battle royals, I lit up.

"Remember them? I was *in* them practically every week."

"So was I," he said. "I used to sneak in to them when Pop wasn't looking. We must have traded haymakers."

Pop McCarey's Fight Pavilion, at Alameda and Main, had been a popular spot for the fight bugs around 1910. Fight nights, I was one of many kids who hustled papers to the straw hat crowds that filled Pop's huge, unpainted, sawdust-floored barn. Pop not only put on good fights, he put on unique shows that rocked the rafters.

One piece of showmanship Pop McCarey served up to the toffs was the Newsboys' Shoe Contest. This was good for ten minutes of continuous laughter. About thirty bona fide newsboys of all sizes and colors stood on the ring's apron outside the ropes. If your voice hadn't changed you were eligible. Each was paid fifty cents before the contest. At the first bell each boy took off his shoes and threw them into the center of the ring. Two attendants mixed the shoes up in a pile. The little old shoes were so beat up and worn they all looked alike. The idea was this: The first boy to find his own shoes, put them on, and tie them would win five dollars.

The second bell rang. Thirty ragged kids scrambled through the ropes, dove into the shoes. The crowd jumped to its feet. Pandemonium broke out. Cheers for the smaller kids, boos for the big ones. It was like throwing thirty strange cats into a cage. The final goal was to find your shoes and put them on. But the immediate goal was to keep anyone else from beating you to it. The moment any kid *looked* like he found his two shoes, others knocked him down, jerked away his shoes, and threw them out into the crowd. The crowd threw them right back. Shoes flew in all directions. If some wise kid tried to sneak out of the ropes to put his shoes on, ringsiders pushed him back into the ring. It was a bedlam of screaming and laughing. Finally, when too many noses got bloody, the bell clanged loudly. Pop McCarey walked into the ring, found a small kid who had drawn cheers, and whether his shoes were tied or not Pop lifted his arm in victory and gave him a five-dollar gold piece. If the crowd cheered long enough for some other kid, Pop would call it a tie and pay off both. Now nickels and dimes showered into the ring. Attendants gathered them up to give to the boys later. When the kids left the ring (to eat all the free hot dogs they could eat), the cheers shook the building. As you can imagine, many a ragged urchin walked off with a gold piece, wearing two left shoes.

In my all-out campaign to become a comedy director I decided that six months at Roach's was long enough to spend on my opening skirmish. At noontime I picked up my closing check and headed straight for the public library to gather ammunition for the siege of my next target—Mack Sennett Comedies. For days I had researched comedy: What makes people laugh? What *is* a laugh?

I found out that animals make grimaces that approximate grins and happy chitterings that denote well-being, but that only humans can laugh— that happy, almost involuntary, explosive, paroxysmic succession of sounds common to all races and tongues. At the moment I was directly interested in Sennett's violent humor, his baggy-pants clowns and fools—especially fools.

The Fool was invented ages ago, to ridicule and poke fun at the "bad guys." Kings, for instance—as a sop to the proletariat, and a prudent thought for their royal necks—appointed court jesters with powers to joke, jeer, and cackle at the courtly machinations of the high and mighty. These jesters were usually dwarfs or grotesque nobodies wearing clown costumes, caps, and bells, and brandishing thin "slapsticks" or inflated bladders as comic symbols of their authority to lampoon. The sarcastic vaporings of the jesters, the kings hoped, would serve as safety valves to prevent the steaming miseries of the unwashed from bursting their boilers.

In the Middle Ages even the sedate and powerful Churchmen saw fit to connive at their own public mockery in their annually sponsored Feast of Fools: A boy, in the role of Bishop, conducted the ceremonies, which degenerated into a travesty of the sacred rites of the Church.

But the mocking Fool idea was too diverting to remain cooped up in courts and chanceries. It spread to the people. The mad charade called burlesque was born. Tattered buffoons (representing the hoi polloi), jeered, jibed, scorned, and swung sticks and inflated bladders at the rich, the greedy, the pompous, the hypocrite—while the plebians howled with laughter.

Mack Sennett's Keystone Comedies—in violent pantomime—were but mad extensions of the jester's japeries, that now—through the magic replication of film—made *millions* laugh all over the world. Nothing was sacred to Mack and his irreverent buffoons. "All is vanity," said Ecclesiastes. "That ain't the half of it," said Sennett. "All is ridiculous!" Virtue, authority, sweet love, wealth—all ridiculous.

In the later words of Richard Griffith and Arthur Mayer, in their handsome volume, *The Movies*: "In Sennett's world all lawyers were shysters, all pious people hypocrites, all sheriffs both stupid and venal, and in that world everybody was caught with his pants down."

But the time-honored weapons for annoying the frauds—the banana peel, the snowball hitting the high hat, the slapstick, the inflated bladder—were too few and too tame for Mack the Momus.

To the banana peel he added such slippery messes as spilled wallpaper paste. He rolled the proverbial snowball—and gathered: flowerpots, bricks, bags of flour, streams from fire hoses. To the token slap of the inflated bladder he added the crunch of maces, bed slats, billy clubs, loose floor boards, stepped-on rakes.

But even with these additions audience interest palled at too much of the same. Insatiable moviegoers demanded bigger and funnier violence. Sennett obliged with higher pratfalls, huge rubber mallets the size of small kegs, vases and statues of thin breakaway plaster to smash on people's heads. Furniture to hurl was built of light yucca or balsa wood that splintered on contact. Windows to dive through were made of transparent candy, and bricks to throw were fashioned of felt.

Ha! But audiences began to sense the new props were phony. Mayhem-in-ersatz lost its punch—and its laughs. A *new* prop was needed: Something that demolished dignity yet looked real—and more important—*was* real to audiences.

They found it! When Ford Sterling, during a scene in a bakery shop, spontaneously picked up a pie—and threw it: Eureka! The PIE! It was safe, utterly devastating—and everyone *knew* it was the Real McCustard. The mallet is dead—Long live the PIE! Burlesque had found its ultimate weapon against pomposity—at Sennett's, by accident.

This humble product of the baker's art has probably made more people laugh than all the other comic props combined. The pie ranks right alongside such major forward leaps as fire, the wheel—and Chaplin's walk. Come to think of it, the Good Book says man came into being as a mud pie: a holy mixture of dust, water, and the Almighty's breath.

Anyhow, there was a gooey finality to a smack in the puss with a lemon meringue pie—as unanswerable as a home run, a scoring forward pass, or Dempsey's left hook—and as crowd pleasing. And, as with these specialties, pie-throwing required uncanny coordination and timing. It developed its own Babe Ruths and Y. A. Tittles—and the greatest of these was—but years later Gene Fowler wrote a great book about Sennett: *Father Goose*. Let Gene delight you with his description of the champ of all pie throwers:

> [The greatest] custard slinger of all time, the mightiest triple-threat man . . . the All-American of All-Americans, the supreme grand lama of the meringue, the Hercules of the winged dessert, the Ajax of the hurtling fritter . . . the unconquerable and valiant flinger of open and closed minced models [was] Roscoe Arbuckle! . . . When Fatty threw a pie it stayed thrown. . . . He could deliver a bake-oven grenade from any angle, sitting, crouching, lying down with a good book, standing on one leg or hanging by his toes from a pergola . . . ambidextrous, he could hurl two pies at once in opposite directions.

Pie throwing was elevated to Olympic Games stature by Leo McCarey with his classic *Battle of the Century*, in which Laurel and Hardy dueled with pies of every crust and fill. At first the duel was slow and ritualistic—a pie for a pie. As the pace picked up, bystanders were drawn into the vortex until it all ended up in an Armageddon of tutti-frutti—and a record-breaking twenty minutes of continuous, side-splitting howls.

These were the kind of thoughts that raced through my mind as I walked hurriedly between houses to our rear cottage. And I had a pang or two about leaving *Our Gang* after six months.

"I know," said McGowan when I talked it over with him, "you want to be a director. *All* gag men want to be directors. That's why I keep them off my set. Okay. I'll call Felix Adler at Sennett's and give you a plug. He's the head writer over there . . ."

The Mack Sennett Studio in Edendale was as unplanned and chaotic as a Keystone chase; twenty-eight acres of hovels, shacks, offices, shops, and open stages, all huddled crazily on the rising flank of a hill. The roofs of the tired wooden shacks had begun to sag and slant at odd angles. Here and there, more imposing new buildings had been added. But, as happens to the invaders of China, the new buildings soon looked slant-roofed, too. Not even stone and mortar could remain sane here.

I parked on Allesandro Street and walked toward a large sign: MACK SENNETT COMEDIES, which arched over a wide, swinging, iron gate—the auto entrance, used only by Sennett. Alongside this big gate was a pedestrian portal, guarded by a studio sentry. This was the entrance to the General Motors of slapstick where laughs were conceived, assembled, and shipped to the world markets in film cans.

Outside the entrance were the usual groups of out-of-work actors four-flushing to each other and hamming it up for gawking visitors—hoping to be seen by directors.

"Mr. Hugunin's office is on the first floor of the tower," said the gateman, handing me a pass and pointing up the raunchy studio street, "that high building up there."

I looked—and gaped for the first time at King Mack's Tower, more famous in comedy circles than the towers of London or Babel. It stuck up as square and forbidding as a Roman fortress. Its first three stories were solid concrete with small windows, its fourth and top floor was all windows —like the control tower at the airport.

Most studios were divided into quiet, lavish, "front offices" and dirty, noisy "back lots." With the exception of the dominating Tower (from which King Mack could scan his empire), Sennettville was *all* back lot. Walking up from the gate I noticed the fronts of the battered buildings had been revamped, repainted, and rephotographed (which often meant demolished) many times. There was a certain amount of sound and fury on all back lots, but here the cacophony seemed to burst from loudspeakers.

The wailing of bandsaws and planers in the mills, the bursts of shouts and guffaws from shooting "companies" on the open stages, the incessant "beat" of dozens of striking hammers, the wind-whipped flapping and drumming of acres of white cloth sun-diffusers over the open stages, all orchestrated fittingly into a silly symphony of slapstick.

Workmen, comics, and pretty girls scurried in all directions. A leather-coated animal trainer came walking toward me hand-in-hand with a chimpanzee. With his free hand the trainer was eating a half-peeled banana. Something was missing in this odd picture, I thought. When the chimp got alongside me it grabbed my pant leg and tugged, with demanding chatters. I got the shivers.

"Well, come on, come on," said the annoyed trainer, "ain't you gonna give it to him?"

"Give him what?"

"Where ya from, Iowa? The cigarette."

With happy noises the chimp grabbed my cigarette palm upward and dragged deep puffs. As they walked away I saw the picture was now complete—the chimp had the cigarette and the trainer the banana.

"Okay," said pleasant Lee Hugunin to me in the ground floor entrance hall of the Tower. He was number three in Sennett's executive pecking order. "Felix Adler interviews gag men. I'll call him down." Stepping over to a narrow stairway he called out, "Felix!" From the second floor another voice took up the call, "Felix!" Then a fainter "Felix!" from the third floor, followed by a still fainter, "Coming!"

"Phones out of order?" I asked innocently.

"Phones? For writers?" retorted Hugunin. "You got to be kidding."

Felix Adler came bouncing down the stairs—a brash extrovert to whom life was just a bowl of gags. I liked him immediately. He shook my hand.

"Hi, Frank. I got an earful of you from Bob Eddy and McGowan. Capra. Means goat, doesn't it? We need a new goat, don't we, Lee? Follow me, Frank. We gotta talk to moneybags."

We went up one floor. Moneybags was John Waldron, number two man; florid, resigned, and pleasantly bewildered. Felix introduced us. "Frank Capra, John Waldron. Only sane man in the asylum. New gag man, John. He's cheap at a thousand a week."

"I know," sighed John, "but he'll take thirty-five."

"Make it forty-five. I got forty from Roach," I argued.

"Who's Roach?" asked John blandly. "Hard rule here, Frank. Beginners start at thirty-five."

"But that'll be going downhill. I want to go up, toward the top."

"When you work at Sennett's you've *reached* the top. Thirty-five, Frank. Take it or leave it."

I swallowed hard; then: "I'll leave it, Mr. Waldron. Thanks, Felix."

"Oka-ay. Let's stop in and see the boss on the way out."

I followed Felix downstairs again. My knees shook. I blew it. My big chance to work at Sennett's—and I blew it. On the ground floor Felix turned to the right, knocked on a door, then opened it. An argument was going on inside.

I had read about Sennett's "office" but it hadn't prepared me for what I saw on entering it. Mack Sennett lay prone and naked on a rubbing table. Abdul the Turk was kneading his buttocks. Two sharp, nattily dressed gentlemen were acting out a scene for Sennett. Otherwise, the room was cell-like and bare except for a big leather chair and a large brass spittoon.

The details of the following scene are hazy, but I recall trying to repeat them word for word to my wife that night. The first words I understood on entering were Sennett's.

"No, no, boys. I don't like it. Where's the theme? You got no theme."

"Mack, we got the greatest theme in the world," argued one of the men in a hoarse whisper. "It's Camille!"

"Camille my foot," shot back Sennett as the Turk handed him a long cigar, "you gotta *man* with T.B."

"But Mack, don't you see? That's our big switch!" argued back the second man.

"Sorry to derail you all at the big switch, gentlemen," apologized Felix, "but Mack, I wanted you to meet Frank Capra before he leaves. And this is Ray Griffith, and Harry Edwards, Frank."

"Well!" I said with open admiration. "Lucky day for me . . . Howdy."

"So you're Frank Capra," said Mr. Sennett, biting off a huge chunk of the cigar and chewing it. "Hal Roach called me up about you."

"Hal Roach?" I asked in astonishment. "Mr. Sennett, in the six months I worked there I never *saw* Hal Roach."

Sennett laughed—a rolling, basso laugh I was to hear many times. "That's what Hal said. But Will Rogers made him call me up to recommend you, because Will said you were the best doughnut dunker in the county. You a friend of Will's?"

"Not really. Just like to hear him talk, that's all. Well, it's been a treat meeting you all." I turned to the door.

"Where you going?" asked Sennett.

"Mack, Frank won't sit still for the beginner's thirty-five," explained Felix. "Wants forty-five."

Harry Edwards became indignant. "Ray," he exploded to Griffith, "did you hear that? Of all the cheek . . ."

Ray Griffith advanced on me shaking an irate finger. He had no voice. He could only whisper. "Forty-five *dollars*! You trying to break the Old Man?"

"Just who do you think you are?" double-teamed Edwards. "Harold Lloyd was only getting thirty when he *left*—"

"Maybe he thinks he's Turpin. Can you look cross-eyed? Look cross-eyed—"

"Can you take a pratfall? Let's see you take a pratfall—"

"How about a double take? Go ahead, do a double take—"

"Quiet, you muzzlers," interposed Felix, "Frank's a *gag* man. Been writing the *Our Gang*'s."

Harry and Ray threw up their hands in amazement. "A writer?"

"Why didn't you tell us?" They pumped my hands and apologized profusely, then turned on Sennett.

"Mack, how dare you offer a writing man a measly forty-five?" berated Ray.

"You're an exploiter of the literati. I'll report you to the Author's League, so help me," threatened Harry.

"Shut up, you clowns," grumbled Sennett, "you're not so funny. Frank, come here. What makes you think you're worth forty-five?"

"Mr. Sennett, what's the difference what you pay me? If you don't think I'm worth it you'll fire me in two minutes anyway."

"He's got a point, Mack!" hoarsely shouted Ray.

"A Clarence Darrow point," added Harry.

"Shut up," growled Sennett. "Whose name is over the front gate?"

Ray and Harry and Felix bowed and salaamed and chanted: "Allah! Allah!"

Sennett nodded and looked for the spittoon. Abdul the Turk ran to get it. Sennett hit it square in the middle. Then he looked up at me. "Frank, I hear you're a college man?"

"Don't admit it," warned Felix. "It's two strikes against you."

"And don't admit that you're Jewish, either," whispered Ray. "That's three strikes and *out*."

Sennett flushed. "Dammit, Ray, don't say things like that. Felix, here, is a Jew. And I let him run the place."

"That's because he told you he was an Arab," chimed in Harry Edwards.

"I didn't say *I* was an Arab," retorted Felix. "I told him my *cousins* were Arabs."

"That's enough!" ordered Sennett. "Felix, he starts at thirty-five or nothing. I'm not breaking one of my own rules."

"Mr. Sennett," I said, "I'm not asking you to break *any* rules. John Waldron starts me on the books at thirty-five. Okay? Tomorrow you raise me to forty-five. Everybody's happy and no rules broken."

"Spoken like a Solomon—an Arab Solomon!" shouted Ray Griffith hoarsely.

Underneath that thick thatch of lank, gray hair there was the faint glimmering of a smile on Sennett's square Irish puss.

"All right—all right—all right," said Harry Edwards with executive brusqueness. "Ray and I approve the deal. Wrap it up, Felix."

Sennett slowly shifted the cud of tobacco from one cheek to the other. It was obvious he enjoyed the clowning.

"Harry, give Frank the commandments," Ray Griffith ordered.

HARRY: Thou shalt punch the time clock at nine, twelve, one, and six.

RAY: Punishment—half a day's pay for a ten minute delay.

HARRY: Thou shalt not speak to directors without permission from the name on the gate.

RAY: Punishment—the gate.

HARRY: Thou shalt not feed Pepper the Cat.

RAY: Punishment—wash Anna May the Elephant.

HARRY: Thou shalt not be seen carrying a book.

RAY: No gags in books, saith the Lord.

HARRY: Thou shalt not gurgle the grape on these holy premises. Nor shalt thou ogle or pinch the Bathing Beauties.

RAY: Punishment for ogling—dinner with Polly Moran. For pinching—in bed with Polly Moran. Understand, Wal-yo?

"Okay. Out. OUT! Everybody," snapped Sennett hopping off the rubbing table. "Ten minutes and not a laugh. Abdul, a steam and a bath."

The Turk ran into the Tub Room, turning on steam and water. The naked Sennett followed him in. There it was: The Tub! The biggest in Hollywood—eight feet long, six wide, and five deep. I was so fascinated by it Adler had to pull me away. As we all were going out the door, Sennett called out: "Ray, Harry. Come back here and tell me how a guy with T.B. can play Camille. I can think better in a bathtub."

On the way up to Waldron's office Adler warned me: "Frank, we kid the Old Man a lot, but don't ever get the idea he's a lunkhead. King Mack is *people*. What makes him laugh makes millions laugh. Hi, John," he greeted Waldron, "you win. Start Frank at thirty-five. Tomorrow raise him to forty-five."

"I what?"

But Felix was bounding up the next stairs two at a time. The third floor was full of files and bookkeepers.

"Accounting department," said Felix. "A writer sneaking out of the Tower has to run the gauntlet of front office stooges. Don't try it without a good excuse. Next floor is purgatory."

We climbed a steep, boxed-in stairway. About halfway up I stumbled noisily. Felix laughed. "Works all the time, our booby trap. Sennett used to sneak up these stairs in stocking feet and catch the gag men sleeping or shooting craps, and there'd be hell to pay. So we conned the head carpenter into raising one riser three-eighths of an inch. Now Mack sneaks up, stumbles, and wakes everybody up. He hasn't caught on yet."

At the top of the stairs was the Gag Room—square and all windows. The "furniture" was a dozen kitchen chairs, two battered tables, two old typewriters, yellow scratch paper everywhere, and two long, high-backed, depot benches—with built-in armrests to fiendishly discourage stretching out for a nap. Felix introduced me to the writers.

"Frank Capra, meet the prisoners of Edendale: Tay Garnett, Brynie Foy, Vernon Smith, Arthur Ripley. Frank's been working on the *Our Gang*'s. It's eight hours a day up here, Frank, and nights, when the Old Man can't sleep. Here's the way we slave: Two men work up a story line, then all the others pitch in on gags. Sennett holds story conferences up here or down in his office. Sometimes he takes us to the projection room to see the rushes. You can scribble out your own ideas, but no scripts for directors. You tell them the story and they shoot from memory. Got it?"

Arthur Ripley, a tall, lugubrious character with the lean and hungry look of Cassius, put in his two-cents worth. "And Frank. You're good for six weeks here if, when Sennett's around, you make like Rodin's "Thinker" and don't open your mouth."

"Oh, yes," added Felix, "the Old Man won't expect much for six weeks. But if you suggest a gag and you don't make him laugh, you're through. If you think of something, tell it to us first, and we'll let you know if it's good enough to tell Mack. Remember that. Okay? So just sit and listen. I'm going back down and watch Ray and Harry try to sell an idea to Mack in his bathtub. They want Turpin to play Camille and Madeline Hurlock the lover."

"Felix, hear what happened yesterday about Turpin?" a writer cracked. "As a gag Johnny Grey calls up Sennett and tells him he heard Turpin was going to a doctor to get his eyes straightened. The Old Man roared like a wounded buffalo and threatened to shoot every doctor in Hollywood."

"Hey, that's an idea," chimed in Brynie Foy. "Let's cook up a story about Turpin going to doctors to straighten his eyes."

"And all the doctors in town end up cross-eyed," pops up another gag man . . .

And that was my introduction to the Gag Room at Sennett's.

A few days later I sat in (making like Rodin's "Thinker") on my first story conference in Sennett's office. Two other writers were sketching out a story line about Chester Conklin, a train engineer who'd lost his marbles because his girl friend had jilted him and taken up with Jimmy Finlayson, the fireman. The story was for Director Del Lord, the highest-paid director on the lot. Although Sennett's stories were now based on "themes"—his pet ones being The False Friend, Cinderella, The Jealous Spouse, and Mistaken Identity—Del Lord still made the wild chase comedies with such preposterous gags as freight trains leaping over each other at crossings; or a freight train and a passenger train hurtling into opposite ends of a single-track tunnel—suspense—then both engines simultaneously emerging with unslackened speed, pulling lines of cars that were half freight and half passenger.

I just listened at my first story conference—and looked. Sennett sat in the big leather chair, suspenders over his undershirt, under which a large paw scratched his hairy chest. Down low over his eyes he wore a straw hat with the top cut out—to ventilate his luxuriant mop of hair—a forerunner of the hatless fad in Hollywood. And with the wad of bitten-off cigar in his cheek —and the handy spittoon alongside—this was his listening attitude. If he laughed it was thunder in the peaks, followed by rolling echoes.

Sennett had seen enough movies about royalty to know that kings always sat on their throne when receiving petitioning subjects. So writers stood, or leaned a hip pocket on the rubbing table which occupied half the narrow room. Behind Sennett's leather chair was a recessed niche—about four by four. In it were the wash bowl and toilet. The toilet was out of sight of writers, but since there was no door, it was not out of hearing—and he insisted writers keep talking to him while he relieved himself.

This was Sennett's office—a far cry from the Taj Mahals in which other Hollywood Maharajas conducted their business. But this earthy, ex-boilermaker, who was awed by the written word, who mistrusted anyone who prated of art and wore flowing ties, who seldom, if ever, uttered a joke—this lowbrow Rabelaisian was the undisputed King of Comedy, or, as Gene Fowler described him: "the Napoleon of the cap and bells [who] created for himself and for millions of the earthbound a voodoo heaven of violent laughter . . ."

I was at Sennett's two weeks before I got up enough nerve to suggest a gag to Sennett—and without consulting with other gag men. It was usual for Sennett to invite the writers to the projection room to view the daily work of the directors. The directors themselves were never allowed to see their rushes. If a sequence seemed slow or unfunny to Sennett, he asked for quick gags from the writers to hop it up.

A scene came on the screen in which Eddie Gribbon, the villain, tried to break through a door. He pulled and rattled the doorknob until it came off in his hand. Then he kicked, pushed, and hurled his shoulder at the door. It wouldn't open. So the villain tore his hair and walked off.

"That's not funny," said Sennett. "We need a topper for the scene. Who's got the topper?"

"I got one, Mr. Sennett," spoke up a writer. "After Gribbon has knocked himself out trying to open the door, let him turn to the audience and say a one-word title: 'Locked!' " Sennett roared, "That's it. We'll use it."

"I got a topper for *that*, Mr. Sennett," I heard myself saying. There was a hush in the room. Felix Adler and the other writers made all sorts of silent gestures for me to keep quiet. Sennett took a shot at his spittoon, then slowly turned his leather rocking chair in my direction.

"You have?" he asked, jingling gold pieces in his pocket. "Let's hear it."

My fellow scriveners raised their eyes to heaven and uttered a few muffled groans.

"Well, Mr. Sennett," my voice had a break in it, "after the heavy says 'Locked!' he looks down and sees a little cat come up to the locked door and push it open with his paw."

Sennett roared—and my co-gag men roared louder, for my benefit.

"Great, Frank. That's a helluva laugh. Then what, Frank?"

"Oh-h-h. Well—uh—then the door closes quietly behind the cat. Gribbon gets an idea. He squats down on hands and knees, crawls up to the door like the cat, and pushes lightly on the door with *his* paw. No soap. Door won't open. Then the heavy throws himself at the door all over again . . ."

"Great!" said Sennett. "We got a routine going. Come on, you guys, keep it rolling. What's next?"

And that's how comedy routines were created by gag men, one idea sparking another, sometimes slowly, often like a string of firecrackers.

It took me six months to lose my beginner's standing—as a kibitzer gag man—and to become a staff writer of original comedies. Sennett himself pinned the accolade on me in his own special lingo.

"Frank, my boy, I think it's time you lost your apprentice bug and rode the stake horses because you've won your wings. See what I mean?"

"Mr. Sennett, you mix in a ten-buck raise with all those metaphors and I'll know exactly what you mean."

"Is that all you writers can think about is money? Okay, go see Dick Jones about it. And Frank. You been a bright boy. Understand?"

"Bright enough to make me a director?"

"A director? And lose a good gag man? You're nuts. Go see Dick Jones."

And who was Dick Jones? Ninety-nine out of a hundred people in Hollywood had never heard of him. I worked for weeks at Sennett's before I knew he existed.

It has been often said that Hollywood had produced only three true geniuses: Chaplin, Disney, and Thalberg. Well, in my estimation Dick Jones was the Irving Thalberg of Sennett Comedies. Each was a supreme creative catalyst, adored and admired by writers, directors, and actors. Each insisted on anonymity—no credits on screen or in publicity. Each functioned as production head of his studio.

Both started in pictures at sixteen, skyrocketed to the top, made a million dollars before they were thirty, and both died in their thirties—killed by the pressure of their jobs.

There was one major difference between them: Thalberg and his superior, Louis B. Mayer, had a passionate hatred for each other—my wife and I saw Mayer dance publicly all night at a cabaret on the Strip the day Thalberg died. Dick Jones admired and praised Sennett's uncanny sense of comedy and graciously gave him all the credit. "Without the Old Man's genius," Jones used to say, "there'd be no Mack Sennett Comedies and no Dick Jones."

However, the writers and directors knew that while Sennett was the heart, the body, and the name of the studio, Dick Jones was the brains. He assigned writers and directors, cast the parts, thought up and listened to story ideas, supervised the editing. Then, without appearing to do so, he had everything tried out on the Old Man. Although Sennett had no great sense of humor—as most of us commonly know it—his reaction to comedy was an infallible audience-barometer. If Sennett laughed, audiences would laugh. If Sennett *didn't* laugh—well, rewrite it or reshoot it, said Dick Jones.

It didn't take me long to sense that Dick Jones knew and understood more about comedy than anyone else on the lot: its construction, the art of timing, the building of a gag, the surprise heaping of "business on business" until you top it all off with the big one—the "topper." Dick Jones was my man. Leech-like I stuck to him night or day, sucking up his know-how. He lived alone at the Hollywood Athletic Club: young (late twenties), handsome, a married bachelor—married to his work. Often I would knock on his door at night.

"Who is it?"

"Frank, Dick. Got an idea for Turpin."

"Go on home. Don't you ever sleep?"

"Sounds like a good gag. Only take a minute."

"All right," as he opened the door, "make it quick. I've got a dame waiting in her car downstairs." (Probably Mabel Normand.)

But once I got started talking he'd catch fire, build on the idea, or invent a new slant that was much funnier. Forgetting the girl, he wouldn't stop till we had a complete "routine," a sequence of funny incidents with a topper— the "blow-off"—a big laugh at the end of the sequence. Toppers were what we knocked our brains out for—the unexpected wow that knocked them in the aisles.

So when Sennett said "Go see Dick Jones about it," I hurried to his office. Conversation with Dick was, for me, intellectual lagniappe.

"A ten-dollar raise," laughed Dick Jones, "the Old Man just phoned me to make it fifteen. You may not know it, but he's had his eye on you since you came up with that cat-opening-door gag. Directors have used a dozen different versions of it, since. Tell me, scientist. I'm curious. Was that a spontaneous flash or did you get it out of Euclid?"

"Well, if you want to know, Dick, I had a marvelous English professor in college by the name of Judy. He once entertained us for an hour with a lecture on what he called "The Intransigence of Inanimate Objects." You know, how a collar button *always* rolls under the bureau; how, if you've got two keys, you always try the wrong one first; and how it always rains when you forget your umbrella, and—well you get the idea. Then he moralized humorously that there was a conspiracy among "non-human" things to frustrate the high and mighty humans, especially the mean and undeserving ones. That's why, he said, untrusting persons are more accident prone than the trusting. That's why mules balk for some and not for others, or why water buffalos charge men on sight yet allow little children to play on their backs, and why Daniel in the lions' den remained unmolested. Well, I've never forgotten that lecture. And when that 'intransigent door' wouldn't open for Gribbon, I thought 'Ha! it will open for a baby—or a cat.' Q.E.D."

"Hm-m-m, what'd you call it? The intransigence of inanimate objects? I can't wait to spring it on some phony highbrows I know. Frank, have dinner with me tonight, Hollywood Athletic Club. Want to talk to you about a small-time vaudevillian the Old Man signed up. A middle-aged, baby-faced guy. I'll show you stills. I haven't got the slightest idea what the hell we can do with him. Name's Harry Langdon."

Little did I dream how much Harry Langdon was to mean to my career. But before relating the almost incredible tragi-comic saga of one of the world's superior comedians, I must tell how an application of my "intransigence of inanimate objects" theory almost finished me off at Sennett's.

Vernon Smith and I were assigned to a Ben Turpin-Madeline Hurlock two-reeler whose plot I've forgotten. But in one sequence, cross-eyed Ben talked the beauteous Madeline into a buggy ride. Object? To smooch in the moonlight. As a Romeo he was lecherous si, Casanova no. Ben panted and pleaded but cold Madeline took out her knitting. He threatened to destroy himself by jumping off a cliff.

The cliff gave me an idea for a running gag that I thought was sure fire—an ornery wheel—the intransigence of an inanimate object. At the start of the buggy ride Ben's jealous rival unscrews the nut that holds the rear wheel on the axle. On the cliff road the rear wheel rolls very close to the edge of the cliff. Intercut the ludicrous love-making in the buggy with the wheel sliding back and forth on the axle, timing it so that with each passionate play Ben makes, the wheel slides off almost to where it falls off. And each time Madeline cools him off, the wheel slides back in place. The topper? When Ben stands up in the buggy and says dramatically "Love me or I leap to my death!" the wheel falls off, the axle drops, throwing Ben over the cliff. Horrified, Madeline rushes down the cliff, embraces the groggy Turpin, and says "My hero. Don't die. I love you . . ."—or some great title only Johnny Grey can write.

My partner, Vernon Smith, liked it; other gag men liked it, so did Dick Jones. I finally told it to Sennett.

"I don't like it, Frank," he said. "Tain't funny." He let the wind out of me. I tried to argue.

"I said it ain't funny," he snapped back, "and don't go telling it to the director—what's his name? Lloyd Bacon. You hear?"

I was so mad I could spit. Secretly I told the routine to a minor comic in the picture. He told it to Lloyd Bacon, as I hoped he would. Bacon loved it—and photographed it.

A few days later Sennett and his gag men were in the projection room seeing the daily rushes. The falling-wheel routine flashed on the screen. Sennett blew a fuse.

"You damn little Dago, didn't I order you not to tell Lloyd Bacon that lousy gag?"

"I haven't been near Lloyd."

"Well, somebody has, and I'm sure as hell gonna fire 'em." He turned to the head film cutter, Bill Hornbeck (later my own film editor for twenty years, and now head of all film editing at Universal). "Bill, don't you dare use that crappy stuff in the final picture. Cut it all out."

My automatic reaction to dictators who demand blind obedience is to say "Nuts!" And persons who consider themselves infallible I consider full of flummery. Job or no job, I wasn't buying any insults.

"Mr. Sennett, I just work here. You're the boss and you can fire me. But you can't insult me. I'm proud of being a Dago, and I'm proud of that wheel gag. And I'm begging you not to cut it out of the picture before an audience sees it."

"You still think that wheel gag is funny?"

"I do."

"Could cost you your job if it isn't."

"If my job means saying yes to you when I don't mean it, it's not much of a job."

"You're nuts. And I'll prove it to you. I'll leave the gag in for the preview. And you, Mr. Know-It-All, I'm taking you to the theater with me— and you're gonna get the lesson of your life."

At the theater the audience laughed all the way through the wheel routine —big laughs! The preview over, I tried to keep from grinning as I walked up to the Old Man outside the theater. He was flushed and scowling. He waggled a finger at me. "Come 'ere, Dago. Whose name is over the front gate?"

"Yours, Mr. Sennett, of course."

"You damn right it is. You're FIRED!"

He walked away, leaving me rooted to the spot. Felix Adler came up to whisper in my ear. "Old Man's sore as hell. It may not work. But walk the gate for three days, see? Be there early, leave late—old clothes, sad look. We've all had to do it, even Chaplin, understand?"

At dawn next morning I showed up at the front gate, unshaven, old clothes, a sandwich in my pocket. On leaving the house my wife had said: "I told you they'd break your heart at Sennett's. Even when you're right they make you eat crow. Don't do it."

"No, Helen, I'm walking the gate. It *was* my fault. Like a dumb cluck I made a fool out of Sennett in public. You just don't step on a general's ego in front of his whole army."

Janitors, and other early working stiffs checking in, guffawed as they saw me pace the gate.

"Hey, fellas, fresh meat at the wailing wall . . ."

"Pound your chest, man, not the sidewalk . . ."

"Repent, you sinner! On your knees . . ."

I laughed and traded banalities with them until the gateman stepped out to warn me that "walking the gate" was a penance, not a picnic, and that the Old Man would not only keep an eagle eye on me from the Tower, but he would also get reports from the gatemen. I got the message.

A half-hour later—two hours before his normal arrival time—Sennett himself rode up in his chauffer-driven Rolls Royce. Humbly, like a penitent seeking mercy, I tried to catch his eye. With imperial indifference he ignored me completely as he drove into the studio. Closing the gate behind the Rolls, the gateman turned to me and nodded approval of my hangdog attitude.

Felix Adler arrived—very early, too. From a distance he looked me over, winked encouragement, and went inside. It was a game, a comic game to onlookers, but deadly earnest to me. My job—my future—was on the line. I had committed the unpardonable sin of challenging the infallibility of the Name over the gate. Now I had to expiate that sin, confess my shame in public, eat humble pie, eat crow—and walk the gate, back and forth, back and forth, underneath the Name I took in vain—openly confessing to King Mack in the Tower that it was mea culpa, mea culpa. Have mercy.

Could my cocky nature take it? I didn't know. But I walked and walked. Time stood still under a broiling sun. I mopped my brow and walked—back and forth—picketing for my job. I've felt sorry for pickets ever since.

After an eternity the noon whistle blew. Instinctively I pulled out my paper-wrapped sandwich, but froze as the gateman rushed to open the gate. Since the big gate opened only for Sennett I threw my sandwich down next to the building and resumed my penitent picketing—it wouldn't do for the King to catch me eating like a contented cow.

Suddenly I heard screaming and yelling. A human stampede came rampaging down the main studio street.

"Look out, Frank!" warned the gateman.

Workmen, actors, stenographers squeezed through the gate like panicky sheep. Before I could get out of their way I got knocked into the gutter. The rabble of employees turned up Edendale Avenue, running like scalded cats toward Sunset Boulevard—uphill and six blocks away. Men hung on to their banging tool belts. Women raised their skirts, revealing all sorts of track-meet underwear. The racing mob spilled out onto the street, snarling traffic. Some fell, rose, and lunged on. None looked back like Lot's wife.

After I picked myself up I asked the gateman, "What in hell's going on?"

"Oh, first time you've seen the bank run, eh?" He went back to his racing form. "Happens now and then. It's payday. Rumor's out—not enough cash in the bank for everybody."

I brushed myself off and looked for my sandwich. The mob had trampled it into a smear.

It was dark before the gate opened for Sennett's car. Again I contritely tried to catch his eye. Again he breezed by me, stone-faced as an Irish Buddha. Tired, humiliated, and ready to bash something, I limped toward my car on my aching dogs.

At home, Helen soaked my feet in hot water, plied me with martinis, called me umpteen different kinds of a fool for letting them do this to me.

"I can't quit now, hon. It's more'n a job, it's a battle. If Chaplin licked it, so can I. Besides, Felix said it never lasts longer than three days."

The second day was pure agony. From dawn till dark nobody noticed me, nobody gave a damn. My picketing had become part of the scenery. I looked so woebegone a kind tourist lady offered me a dime.

The third day I was full of hope—the day of resurrection. Sennett had driven in without looking at me, but that was all right. Felix had tipped me off. The gateman would give me the message when the penance was over. Every hour or so I asked the gateman if he had a message.

"Nope. No message."

Noontime—no message. Two o'clock, four, six—no message. I began to sweat with worry. Was that old bastard going to make it final? He was still in the studio. Seven o'clock, eight, NINE. No message. The gate opened. I saw his car coming. Sure. He'd give me the good word himself. I stood in the headlights—jumped out of the way just in time. The car whizzed by me and roared up the street.

"Go to hell, you lousy son-of-a-bitch!" I shouted at the retreating Rolls.

"Wassa matter?" asked the startled gateman.

"And that goes for you, too, you creep!"

I ran to my car. I clunked it against the curb at my house. Like a wild man I burst through the front door: "Helen! I gotta get drunk!"

"I knew it," she said calmly.

All that night I had wild dreams about destroying Mack Sennett. I set fire to his studio, stage after stage went up in flames, the Tower collapsed in ruins—only that damn name over the gate refused to burn.

In the morning I shaved, put on my best clothes, drove to Sennett's front gate—and waited for him. I was going to stop his car and tell that boilermaker ape just what he could do with his studio, his Tower, and his name over the gate. His car drove up, stopped for the gate to open. The ape was in the back seat. I stepped forward to give him my Patrick Henry speech. He rolled his window down—and beat me to the punch.

"Frank, you little Dago, what the hell you doin' out here? Why ain't you up in the Tower, working?" I gasped. He opened the car door. "Come on, get in. I'll drive you up in style."

I got in; sat limp as a rag. He was smiling.

"Frank," he said as the car started, "your falling-wheel gag's got everybody talking. I'll bet every Poverty Row comic in Gower Gulch'll have it in his picture by next week."

That was life at Sennett's.

CHAPTER 4

Baby Face

HISTORICALLY, man has not progressed at a continuous steady pace, but in surges—great forward leaps called ages, such as the Stone Age, the Bronze Age. Ages begin with epochs, and epochs generally begin with one man. That one man opens a door to hitherto hidden riches of the mind through which others rush to make great new discoveries. Thus Socrates fathered the Golden Age of philosophy—opening the door for Plato, Aristotle, Thomas Aquinas. Copernicus fathered astronomy; Galileo, physics; Mendel, genetics; Einstein, relativity; Goddard, the Space Age.

The Golden Age of Film Comedy was fathered by Mack Sennett. A devout student and disciple of D. W. Griffith (filmdom's first and perhaps greatest artist), ex-boilermaker Sennett launched out on his own to found Keystone's Klown Kollege. Through the daffy doors of this first asylum of violent laughter graduated such greats as Chaplin, Keaton, Lloyd, Sterling, Beery, Dressler—to establish their own new schools of laughter. These luminaries were all scintillating elsewhere when I enrolled at Keystone Kollege in late 1924.

Gone, too, was the all-time great, "Fatty" Arbuckle, who—though proven innocent in court—had been brutally sacrificed on the altar of hate to appease the bigots who howled for his head after the accidental death of Virginia Rappe. Also lost to Sennett was another innocent, all-time great, Mabel Normand, the female Chaplin whom Sennett had hopes of marrying. She, too, had been banned and hounded into oblivion—and early death—by witch hunters who screamed she was connected in some way with the mystery murder of the urbane director William Desmond Taylor.

But despite the flight of stars to brighter skies, and the loss of two irreplaceables to bigots, the Old Man, the founding father and Keeper of Klown

Kollege, was turning out more successful comedies than ever with such lesser lights as Ben Turpin, Chester Conklin, Billy Bevan, Hank Mann; Eddie Gribbon, Fred Mace, Bull Montana; Polly Moran, and Louise Fazenda. The cool, beauteous vamp was Madeline Hurlock; the younger girls: Alice Day, Sally Eilers, Marie Prevost, and a leggy, sexy blonde of sixteen—Carole Lombard.

But Sennett was always scanning the hustings for a new comedy star, and his latest hunch was Harry Langdon—a hunch that wasn't shared by others on the lot.

Harry Langdon and his wife had knocked about for years in the small vaudeville circuits with a comedy act about a new car. All they ever hoped for was to survive and make a fair living. Rumors were that Mrs. Langdon still kept the family savings in a grouch bag around her neck.

Sennett had had Langdon's vaudeville act photographed. He insisted that directors and writers see it. It was my turn. I viewed it with Dick Jones, Arthur Ripley, and two other gag men. The act was billed as "Harry's New Car." It opened with a balky flivver jerking onto the stage, backfiring, steaming, bucking like a wild bronc. Two passengers hung on for dear life. With one last pop, bang, and snort the rearing Lizzie collapsed to a stop as the radiator cap blew off, shooting steam a mile high.

The driver was Harry Langdon, a baby-faced, moon-cheeked little man, wearing a small round hat with turned-up brim, a coat tightly buttoned high but flaring out wide below. His hands and face were pasty white and chubby, like a child's. In fact, his whole appearance was that of an overgrown child, although he was pushing forty. Next to him sat his wife, made up as a dominating, vulture-faced termagant, all feathers and frills. Harry's actions were all in very slow pantomime. Only the wife spoke—in shrieks. Fixing Harry with a killing look, the disheveled, irate wife croaked the equivalent of (Title): "Idiot! Is this what they sold you for a new car?"

Giving her a helpless little smile, Harry got out to survey the steaming, panting new car. Slowly—very slowly—like a child trying to calm a cranky pet, he patted it gently on the radiator. The ornery tin can roared, popped, and lunged at him. Harry turned and ran for his life, holding the brim of his hat in both hands. He was impaled by a shrieking command (Title): "Harry! Come back here!"

Harry came back sheepish and wary. He turned the crank—nothing. He cranked harder—nothing. Impatient, he waggled a finger at the naughty car, like a child scolding a naughty doll. The Lizzie shook. Its motor sputtered into action. Harry jumped into the driver's seat, gave his wife a broad victory smile, and took the wheel. The motor stopped. Befuddled, he got out again. This time the car *door* came off in his hands.

And so the film went for another ten minutes—little Harry, the elf, caught between the devil flivver and the deep blue funk of his shrewish wife.

When the lights went on, Dick Jones said to us: "Well, there he is, fellas.

And we're stuck with him. I don't know what, but the Old Man sees *something* in this Langdon. But so far, in films with other comics he's just another fresh little guy. Any ideas, anybody?"

"Tell you what, Dick," cracked one writer, "this Langdon's no cure for insomnia. Takes him five minutes to blink. I pass; Dick?"

"Now just a minute, you guys," said Dick Jones, "you can't kiss off Sennett's hunches like that. Don't forget, he discovered some big ones. I tried talking the boss out of Langdon, but he says 'No, there's something there. You work on it.' "

"Dick," wryly added another writer, "when you find out what the Old Man sees in this guy that's played in tank towns all his life, you tell me and I'll work on it. Meantime I pass. Okay?"

"Go to hell," said Dick disgustedly, "but while you two bums are passing, stop by and see Del Henderson. He needs an entrance gag for Hurlock when she crashes that social party that snubbed her."

"Oh, we already gave Del a piparoo. Hurlock knocks the dowagers flat on their cans by walking in with a lion sitting on the train of her long dress."

"Hurlock know about the lion?"

"Sure. She said, 'Another stinking lion? Okay. But this time, bring me one that hasn't got halitosis.' See you."

Jones, Ripley, and I were left in the projection room to ruminate about Langdon. Lanky, gloomy Arthur Ripley slouched so low in his seat he sat on his shoulder blades. Between bony fists pressed against bonier cheeks his deep-set eyes still stared at the screen. He came from the New York stage— which gave him status as a theorizer of drama; an analyst, a constructionist. He could spellbind for an hour without anyone discovering what he was talking about. Every picture had to "say" something, he said; had to have a beginning, a middle, an end—and a *theme*. Listening to him ramble on about a theme was like listening to Chopin played backward, or sometimes, Wagner. To lead you to Pasadena, he would circle the globe. But if you could sift through the hyperbole and could stand music played backward—he would eventually get you to Pasadena.

"Arthur," said Jones breaking up the silence, "you're the drayma expert. Got any plots or counterplots kicking around that might help us with Langdon?"

Ripley straightened up and coughed. "Damn chest pains . . . killing me. Well, Dick. I've been analyzing. Now Langdon. What kind of magic could transmogrify that twirp? And since you're stuck with him, and my Aladdin's lamp isn't handy, I suggest prayer. Because at the moment I think only God can help us with Langdon."

I nearly jumped out of my skin. "Wait—a—*minute*," I said, getting up and pacing. "Dick—that could be it! I think Arthur's got something—"

"Sure have—a pain in the chest."

"No, no, Arthur. What you said," I enthused, "that only *God* can help an elf like Langdon. God's his ally, see? Harry conquers all with goodness. Sure! Like the Good Soldier Schweik."

"Who's Soldier Schweik?" asked Dick Jones.

"A little Austrian, a slaphappy soldier. Loved everybody, including the enemy."

"Soldier Schweik," said Ripley coming alive. "*Solid* idea. Like *Pippa Passes*. Leaves a wake of goodness behind. Solid, Dick."

"But where's the comedy?" asked Dick, a little worried about being talked into something.

"Where's the comedy in Chaplin?" I argued. "It's in his character, the Little Tramp. Harry'll be the Little Elf. Look, Dick. Why don't you let Ripley and me kick it around. Give us Harry Edwards as the director."

"Why Harry Edwards?"

"I dunno. He's sensitive—soft—I dunno . . ."

Nearly everybody in the studio went to the preview of Harry Langdon's next two-reel comedy. I have forgotten its title. Next morning the lot buzzed with excitement. "A new star is born!" was the word of mouth.

Sennett called a victory meeting in his office. In Hollywood, happiness is a hit; ecstasy, a *big* hit. While everyone grinned from ear to ear, Sennett praised Ripley, me, and especially Harry Edwards for his fine direction. Then he bit off half a cigar and added: "And I could say something about myself, but I won't."

"I'll say it for you," laughed Dick Jones, "you *told* us so. There's only one Mack Sennett, boss. Right fellas?"

We cheered. Sennett loved it. "Aw, come on, you guys," he huffed like a coy rhinoceros, "one hit does not a swallow make, you know—or somethin'. It's the next one that counts. Right, Dick?"

"Boys have got the next one all blocked out. And, boss, I think we ought to keep this team on Langdon, don't you?"

"You mean they're the *only* guys that can write and direct for Langdon?"

"About the size of it. They invented the character."

"Come on—Langdon was Langdon before they laid eyes on him. But Dick . . . I dunno . . . if you say so. Don't let 'em get a swellhead. You know how they are."

"Mack, I got a favor to ask you," said Harry Edwards. "I know it's against rules, but I'd like permission to have Arthur and Frank on the set when I want them. Harry Langdon's different. And the boys are good at thinking up little goodies on the spot, that Harry can stretch out into big laughs—especially Walyo, here."

"Whoa—hold it. That's busting a rule. What about the other writer guys?" growled Sennett warily.

"Mr. Sennett," I cut in, holding up a hand in defense, "no rule-breaking for me. I don't want to walk that gate again. But this Langdon's something else. He's a gold mine. We'd like to dig into him, study him. We can't do that cooped up in the Tower. We might want to take him to lunch. We can't do that when you order us to have a tuna sandwich and a glass of milk in your restaurant so we won't get logy in the afternoon—"

"You're not kidding anybody, Dago. You wanna be a director. That's why you wanna be on the set."

"Can I put in my two-cents worth, Mr. Sennett?" asked Ripley. "I don't know about Frank wanting to be a director—and he'd make a damn good one if you ask me. But what Frank's trying to say is what he said after the preview—that the theme, the key to Langdon, is innocence. That's a mighty frail reed, Mr. Sennett, not understood by many—not even by Langdon—not even by *us* really, yet. Monkey around with that frail reed and this guy could easily revert back to a small-time comic. That's the reason we'd like to study him—"

"Aw, to hell with you guys," said Sennett giving up. "You're all goddam lawyers. All right. Get out, get out . . ."

Langdon's rise was truly meteoric even for Hollywood—the land of the rising and falling star. In less than a year he became a world-wide "name." Pundits equated him with the Big Three: Chaplin, Keaton, Lloyd. With each two-reeler his fan mail doubled.

It was about that time that Sennett crowned me with his "good conduct" wreath—I became his "pet of the week." The Old Man had grown older, lonelier. The wedding bells that had so often pealed their promise—only to crack into jangled discord before he and Mabel Normand could reach the altar—were now stilled forever by the ugly dampers of scandal. He lived alone in his twenty-one room "Westmoreland Mansion" with its umpteen baths and twice umpteen stiff-liveried butlers. He needed boon companions with whom to let his hair down, to listen to him reminisce; he chose them mostly from those he understood the least but loved the most—his gag writers.

"Frank, how'd you like to bring your soup-and-fish duds tomorrow and come over to the house for some laughs and see some new pictures?" That was the tip-off. I was "pet of the week." I slept, dined, walked, laughed—and listened to the King of Comedy's fabulous anecdotes: apprentice to a boilermaker; singing lessons; New York and a two-year apprenticeship to D. W. Griffith as an "extra"; how he got chummy with the "Unapproachable" by daily walking twenty-three blocks with the Master from his home to studio; how he later became a third leg of the Griffith-Ince-Sennett Triangle Films.

He took me to the Hollywood Hills to walk around a peak he had bought —on which he hoped someday to building a monument, a palace, or something. (His dream had the glimmerings of what Disney was later to realize— Disneyland.)

One morning he took me outside his house to show me something "very cute." Pointing up to his chimney around which some pigeons were cooing, he whispered with boyish excitement: "I was up there yesterday. They were just born. Two of the cutest little squabs you ever saw. I touched them. All fluffy they were, like tiny balls of cotton. Cute."

I looked at Mack Sennett with new eyes. Inside that tough boilermaker I sensed the lilt of the Irish poet. There had to be. He couldn't have been the great Mack Sennett without it.

A few days after my "pet of the week" stint was over, I attended a story conference in Sennett's office.

"Oh, Frank," he said with a gleam in his eye, "remember those two cute little squabs I showed you on my roof, remember? We ate them last night. They were dee-*licious!*"

Although we were completely unlike in nature and manner, Ripley and I enjoyed the affinity of opposites. Ripley was the talker—I, the doer. While he prated ad infinitum about "meanings," I paced and concentrated on scenes. It was like working with the radio on without really hearing it—the drone of his voice cut out all other sensory perceptions, aiding concentration. But subconsciously I must have heard everything he said, because now and then a word or a phrase would flash out of the torrent to spark me into a whole sequence of comedy "business." Similarly, I might come up with an unrelated gag which he would deftly integrate into some other part of the story.

What kind of material did we cook up for Langdon? Why was it *different?* Primarily, because it was based on a unique—but paradoxically, a universal—character. Langdon himself was at heart a child in real life. Now a child can be bratty, whiny, sulky, cruel. We gave the character the "fix" that made him appealing—a grown man with the actions and reactions of a trusting, *innocent* child. Little babe, least of all, among the legs of enemies tall.

Chaplin *thought* his way out of tight situations; Keaton *suffered* through them stoically; Lloyd overcame them with *speed.* But Langdon *trusted* his way through adversities, surviving only with the help of God, or goodness. A few years later I tried explaining this to James Agee (for his *Life* article, "Comedy's Greatest Era") in this fashion: "The key to the proper use of Langdon is the 'principle of the brick.' Langdon might be saved by the brick falling on the cop, but it was *verboten* that he in any way motivate the brick's fall."

Secondly, Langdon's material was non-violent. In a day when comics out-exaggerated each other—longer shoes, baggier pants, higher pratfalls, bigger "take 'ems"—Langdon played scenes delicately, almost in slow motion. You could practically *see* the wheels of his immature mind turning as it registered tiny pleasures or discomforts. Langdon himself was a virtuoso of flitting, hesitant motions. In the middle of extreme danger he could be distracted by a butterfly, or a spot of dirt on his finger.

The "double-take" was a standard item in *every* comic's bag of tricks. The double-take was really two successive looks at an object of intense interest, say a lion in the bedroom, or a passing beauty in a bathing suit. The first look was casual and unseeing, the second, violent and jerky—after the late realizations of what had been seen. The humor lay in the audience waiting for the dumb cluck to become aware of the lion or the girl which they, in their superiority, had seen at a glance.

But Langdon had mastered a *"triple-take"*—two long, beautifully timed, innocent looks at a lion, with plenty of time between looks, before convulsing the audience with his terrified third look—the "take 'em."

Thirdly—the "must nots." Langdon's character must think no evil, see no evil, or do no evil. Thus an innocent, slow-witted, trusting, masterly pantomimist—added up to Baby Face, the star. To deviate from this formula meant reverting to Langdon the vaudevillian.

How did Harry Langdon react to his sky-rocketing fame? One must remember that Mr. and Mrs. Langdon belonged to that peculiar, hardy breed of vaudeville actors—nomads in grease paint playing one-night stands —dressing in rat-infested dressing rooms, eating out of paper bags. Their days were spent riding jerk-water trains, dusty buses, or driving their own rattling trucks if the act carried scenery or props. All hoped to save enough for that chicken farm. Few made it, what with sick relatives, operations, cancellations, or mates that hit the bottle. Their life can be aptly described as "chicken one day, feathers the next." At first, this simple, benighted little man was overwhelmed by what went on at Sennett's. He did what he was told but remained wary, suspicious. He feared it was all temporary. His wife was sure of it. She stuffed his salary in her grouch bag, and kept the suitcases packed.

Then came the reviews and the adulation. The little vaudeville man went Hollywood. He bought a big mansion on Hollywood Boulevard; wore dark glasses, bright scarves, sporty duds; gave parties; acquired secretaries— and discovered girls.

Langdon's lightning success precipitated a shower of offers from other studios. Mack Sennett—never a loose man with a buck—refused to match the offers. After Langdon's last short film at Sennett's, *Saturday Afternoon* —so good it was released in three reels—he signed a million-dollar contract with First National Films for three feature-length comedies and an option for three more. A year before he played the honky-tonks. Now he was marked with the stigmata of stardom—that heady pinnacle of vexations and power. Very few had ever been less prepared to breathe its rarefied atmosphere.

In full command of his own company now, Langdon asked Harry Edwards to join him as his director. Edwards had money enough to ease up and enjoy life. Then, too, he had qualms about accepting the more formidable feature film responsibilities. Edwards and I had become very close. At Sennett's he wanted me constantly at his side during shooting. He consented to go with Langdon providing I went along as his co-director. In turn, I refused to join unless Ripley came with us to head the writing staff. Langdon agreed. And so in November, 1925, we were all reunited with Mr. Harry Langdon in Burbank, to make his first feature-length comedy for First National. It was called: *Tramp, Tramp, Tramp.*

With *Tramp, Tramp, Tramp*, a small, golden stigmata hit me too—in the pocketbook. My salary jumped from seventy-five dollars per week to three hundred dollars. But more important, this was my first opportunity to become involved in all the mysteries of independent filmmaking. I became co-everything: co-producer with Langdon, co-director with Edwards, co-writing head with Ripley—our gag department had been expanded to include Tim Whelan (long a shining light with Lloyd), Gerald Duffy, and J. Frank Holliday. For the first time I worked with a written script (of sorts), a time schedule, and a budget.

I took on all the non-creative chores that others considered drudgery. I wanted to know what the working stiffs were doing, why they were doing it —and the cost. I learned that wasted time was really wasted money that never showed on the screen. In supervising—for the first time—set construction, casting, crews, locations, transportation, film processing, I realized the efficient use of money had to be a *sine qua non* for the successful film producer.

Still another truism dawned upon me: The fragile, intangible film world of creativity—a world of "no rules" where uncertainty is the prevailing mood—is built on and supported by a heavy industry that *has* rules and tangible costs. Labor, materials, equipment, film, time and overtime, are all real and calculable.

Where creativity plans, and heavy industry executes, a hidden rathole of uncertainty may develop down which money can pour: and that rathole is the lack of decision-making by the creators. Making up your mind is the hair-tearing part of film production—the decisions are mostly gut decisions. But those who boldly say "Yes" or "No"—even though proved wrong later —are the respected and admired leaders.

In the shooting of *Tramp, Tramp, Tramp*, a thousand questions were asked of me—for the first time in my career. Pragmatically, I gave a quick "Yes" or "No," fully aware that purely random answers had to be right 50 percent of the time; and, if, in show business you are right 50 percent of the time, you are way ahead of the average.

Yet, with all these added duties, I was almost constantly on the set with Langdon and Edwards. I gained Langdon's confidence and respect with my vetoing of gags that violated the character Ripley and I had created for him. It was amazing to me that neither Langdon nor Edwards really understood, or took seriously, this integrity of characterization—which made Langdon what he was. A funny gag was a funny gag to them, whether in character or not. But they listened to my objections—especially if I managed to twist the gag around to better fit Langdon.

For instance: In a small midwestern town, a black, evil demon—the twisting, terrifying, havoc-wreaking funnel of a tornado—is pursuing Langdon whichever way he runs. Someone suggested that Langdon should pick up a gun and divert the monster by shooting at it. Sounded great. But I said, "No, no!" Langdon would never deliberately fire a gun at anything. Let him pick up rocks—small stones—to throw at the twister. Langdon jubilantly agreed stones were funnier. And out of this came a "topper" we were to use many times in later films: After Langdon's rocks had cowed the tornado's funnel into retreating and turning down a side street, Langdon, in childish cockiness, spits in victory—but the spit goes no farther than his lapel. Then, looking around shamefacedly, he wipes off his lapel with his sleeve.

Tramp, Tramp, Tramp was based on the then popular "cross-country walk-ing races" for prize money. To promote Burton Shoes, millionaire Burton offers twenty-five thousand dollars to the winner of a walking race from New York to California—all contestants to wear Burton shoes. To advertise the race—and the shoes—Burton puts up twenty-four-sheet posters along the route, featuring his beautiful daughter (Joan Crawford), who was to crown the winner. Little Harry needs the money for his father's operation. He enters the walkathon, along with others, including his nemesis—a big, tough Argentinian. The race was the clothesline on which we hung Harry's gags, mishaps, and adventures; including, of course, his falling in love with the beautiful face on the poster, which smiled at him every few hundred yards.

There were three outstanding laugh sequences in the five-reel film: one, his battle with the tornado as described above; two, his escape from a rampaging herd of sheep by leaping over a high board fence—only to get hung up on a fence nail which snags the front of his high-buttoned coat. What he doesn't know—but the audience knows—is that the nail has saved him from a sheer drop of several hundred feet to a busy highway below.

Dangling in mid-air, Harry desperately tries to tear his coat loose from the blasted nail. Here comes the triple-take. Out of breath he stops to take a casual look below. He sees the long drop but it doesn't register. Back he goes to unbuttoning the coat that is choking him. He tears loose the bottom button—drops a foot—the top button still holds. Disgusted he looks down again, sees the busy highway far below. It still doesn't register disaster in his slow innocent brain. He redoubles his efforts to tear off the last button. Suddenly he freezes. What he had seen begins to percolate. Slowly he looks down at the great depths below. In terror he grabs at the nail with both hands. The button rips off. The nail begins to bend, and—well, it was a cliff-hanger.

The third big laugh sequence was a delight for audiences, but a nightmare for Joan Crawford. This was one of Joan's first film roles—and was she a gorgeous girl! Nearing the end of the race, Harry had stopped to moon with love-sick eyes at his dream girl on the poster. A limousine pulls up behind him; out steps the poster girl to cheer him on to the finish.

"Hello, champ!" she says to him.

Harry turns, doesn't recognize her—then does a double-take when he realizes she is the girl! His poster girl—in the flesh—and a thousand times more beautiful! He goes ga-ga; runs back and forth, wide-eyed with joy—then stops. Joan Crawford is shrieking with laughter. Edwards stopped the scene.

"I'm sorry," Joan apologized, "but he's so funny!"

This was her first scene with Langdon, and since she was an inexperienced show girl from New York, everyone on the set thought her break-up was cute and flattering. Let's try the scene again. But when this great star-to-be again exploded into howls when Harry gave her the double-take, it wasn't so cute. And it got less cute when she broke up for the third, fourth, and fifth time.

Now the poor girl got the giggles. She couldn't stop laughing. Embarrassed no end, she began to cry. Her mascara ran. That meant a new make-up. We waited. She came back all fixed up, biting her lip and clutching her hands.

"I'm okay now. I'm so ashamed. I'll do it now. I won't laugh again, dammit!"

Harry Edwards said, "Camera! Action!" Joan steps out of her car, says, "Hello, champ!" Langdon gives her the double-take and Joan collapses in giggles and tears. She runs off sobbing. Edwards runs after her; almost carries her back. Holding the trembling girl in his arms he orders the camera to be set up back of her head, then tells her: "Honey, I've got to get a two-shot with both of you. Close your eyes tight, and don't shake, please! I'll get your close-ups tomorrow without Harry."

And so, one of the greatest of all box-office stars, stood with her back to the camera, eyes and face screwed up tight, mascara tears rolling down her cheeks, and shoulders shaking with fear—as Harry Langdon, one of the great comics, cut his swooning, love-sick didos before her.

Tramp, Tramp, Tramp did not set the world on fire, but it was a box-office hit. And it did cause a slight raising of eyebrows among the Olympian literati of New York. The powerhouse critics (always chary of pulling out all the stops) applauded Langdon daintily as a newcomer to watch, but larded their reviews with many cautious "on the other hands." But exhibitors were more ecstatic, as laughing crowds filled their theaters. All in all, the picture was a hit—and its success did little to disenchant Langdon of his belief that he was the best thing that had happened to films since Mary Pickford's curls. He seldom mentioned Chaplin with whom he was beginning to be compared.

There was one disappointment—Harry Edwards had had it. Having guided Langdon from a frightened little actor to a star owning his own company, Edwards couldn't take Langdon's present approval or disapproval of his every move. He bowed out of the second feature film, suggesting to Langdon that I become his director. Langdon and I had become very close. He agreed to the change—although I sensed the feeling that he would have liked to direct himself, in emulation of Chaplin. But he was still too awed by camera technicalities, and other physical production matters, to take the step.

As for me? I had arrived! Within two years I had leaped from an *Our Gang* gag man to a director of a major feature comedy, guiding a rising star of compelling magnitude. My salary jumped from three hundred dollars a week to six hundred dollars. Now to take care of Mama and little sister Ann. It was about time—I was twenty-nine years old.

The home life of film people can be vexing indeed—unless sensible adjustments and sacrifices are made. During the shooting of *Tramp, Tramp, Tramp* I left home at dawn and returned late at night. Helen hinted I was more married to work than to her. Her two previous marriages had foundered on the rocks of success—both ex-husbands had become top cameramen. Now her third husband was heading hell-bent for the same shoals. She wanted, and needed, a full-time companion husband, not a part-time successful one. Our marriage ship had sprung another, unexpected, leak. Her doctor told her she couldn't have children. Nothing can depress an Italian more than to discover he cannot sire bambinos. But we were adults and fond of each other. We carried on.

I had bought a small lot on Odin Street, near Cahuenga. The plans were all drawn for a two-story house that would also accommodate Mama and Ann. Helen was all for it. She would have company. Although I sent them monthly allotments, Mama and Ann still continued to work. I knew the only way I could get them to quit was to move them in with us. In a few months I would have money enough to start building. The skies never looked brighter as I began preparing for my first directorial assignment, except for one wispy little cloud—Helen was drinking more than usual.

No human being can ever forget the thrill of his "first" accomplishment: a writer—his first novel; a captain—the command of his first ship; a Watusi —his first lion; a director—his first film.

For weeks I had given the writers the Simon Legree treatment—work nights, Sundays; change this, rewrite that. Toppers, toppers! I got to have great toppers. Arthur Ripley laughingly warned, "Hey, Walyo—don't leave your fight in the dressing room."

The day before photography began my wife read me reams from her *Science and Health* to tranquilize the butterflies. But later that evening I copped her bet by kneeling alone in a back pew of the Sacred Heart Cathedral—to remind the Almighty here was another scared sparrow needing His help— even though I was then only a Christmas Catholic.

Next morning, when I stepped on the set to rehearse the first scene, it was no more "Hey, Frank"; or "Shorty"; or "Walyo." It was "Mr. Capra" here, "Mr. Capra" there. The mantle of command had descended on me: I was a film director.

We had cooked up a fine Langdon "story line" with superb routines and gags tailor-made to suit his unique pantomimic talents. Within his limited range—the man-child whose only ally was God—his art approached genius.

As a director I had two sticky problems: one, to keep him on the narrow beam of his range; the other, talking him out of scenes that were not in character—in front of others on the set—without bruising his fast-inflating ego.

Often, he would appeal to the writers to help him overrule me. Surprisingly, Ripley my staunch collaborator, began to agree with him more and more. So, during the shooting, one day Langdon and I would be nuzzling noses in glee at our scenes, the next I might be pulling porcupine quills out of my face for refusing to yield to his whims. But we finished the picture without straying too far from the straight-and-narrow of his character—and, it was a hit at the box office. But more important—and fatal—to Langdon, the big-city critics pulled out all the stops. And, to top it all, the Film Critics Poll selected *The Strong Man* as one of its "Ten Best Pictures" of 1926.

The virus of conceit—alias the "fat head"—hit Langdon hard. His early life had built up no immunity against it. He gave out interviews hinting he was responsible for the story, the comedy, and the directing. Fortunately, we had begun shooting the next feature, *Long Pants*, before the accumulating avalanche of press clippings swamped his dressing room, inflaming conceit into a bad case of Langdonitis.

During the shooting of *Long Pants* our nose-nuzzling days were few and far between. "Pathos," he'd scream at me, "I want to do more pathos."

"Harry, the pathos is in your *comedy*. If you deliberately *try* for pathos, it'll be silly, believe me."

"I believe the New York writers. You know more'n they do?"

They had descended on him from all over the country—and Europe—big-name writers, interviewers, critics, sob sisters, photographers. They paraded through his dressing room, interviewed him at lunch, at dinner—littering the premises with spent flashbulbs, and his mind with flattery.

It was the finale of the picture that spelled "finis" to our long association. I had one more scene to shoot—an "insert": a close-up of Harry's hand slyly reaching for a book titled *Great Lovers* on a library shelf. The crew and I waited and waited. I had sent for him several times. Finally Harry arrived, wearing a gaudy dressing gown and a gaudier scarf, followed by a newly acquired retinue of leeches.

"Why in hell do you keep sending for me? Don't you know I'm through in the picture?" He was as arrogant as Napoleon chewing up a menial officer.

"Sorry, Harry. I need an insert of your hand reaching for this—"

"Insert of my hand? You ain't learned nothing, have you? Directors don't use stars for stupid inserts. They use *doubles*."

"Harry, there isn't another pair of hands like—"

"Oh, shit! You interrupted my interview with two of the biggest critics in New York—for a lousy insert!" He wheeled and strutted out, followed by his comet's tail of hangers-on. Before he was out of earshot he complained loudly to his admiring menage, "See what I have to put up with? Christ! That's what I get for trying to make directors out of two-bit gag men."

I dismissed the crew, shook their hands silently. They understood. It was tantrums like that which made them want to drop lamps on fatheads. The honeymoon was over. But breaking off a relationship with a man you *knew* you'd helped become a star was not easy.

My name was becoming known. One or two more pictures with Harry and other studios would be after me. Should I, or *could* I, lower my tail, become a Langdon "yes man," and bootlick my way into a few more big credits? Or should I quit now—leave with my tail up—take my chances elsewhere? Perhaps it was still possible to "reach" Langdon and not have to take either step. Who was this little Langdon guy?—who could now make me or break me?

Odd, I thought to myself, how in all walks of life there are lives graced by dreams, and lives steeped in dullness. And when greatness strikes, the dreamer is prepared; grace softens the shock. But to the dull, greatness can be traumatic. That was it. Langdon was in a state of shock. Surely, a director should help his actor out of his trauma. I went to Langdon's dressing room. I found him stretched out on a couch looking up at the ceiling, clasped hands under his head.

"Hi, Harry." He did not look at me or answer.

"Harry, I came to tell you what many of us have wanted to say to you for some time, to wit: that you've turned into an impossible, opinionated, conceited, strutting little jerk!"

He gave me a quick, vacant look, then turned away again.

"The happy little guy we once knew and loved has become an ungrateful heel—and you know what kind. But you're still one of the great artists of our times—as great as Chaplin. And you can become greater, if you just stop being a little tin Jesus. And, yes! Stop worrying about copying *Chaplin*. Sure, Chaplin writes his own stuff and directs himself. But he created his own character. He understands it, *better* than anyone else. But you *didn't* create your character. And you don't understand it. And now that you believe your own interviews, you never *will*. But Harry, as a friend, all I'm trying to tell you is that you don't *have* to act, write, and direct to be greater than Chaplin. All you have to do is accept the help of those of us who know you—just as Lloyd accepts all the help he can get, just as Keaton does. One more thing, Harry. Love! Comedians must be loved to get laughs—and right now the only one who loves you around here is you. Think it over, Harry. Why don't you try thanking God for your success—and not yourself? That's all."

I left. He had not uttered a word. But I felt relieved and strangely exhilarated as I drove home. My ego flag was still flying as I drove up to our new house on Odin Street—the house I had built right after *The Strong*

Man, the "palace" I had promised Mama. She and Ann had been living with us for six months, and *not working* for the first time in their lives. And— we had a maid! much to Mama's discomfiture. She could never understand why we should waste money for work *she* should be doing.

I found Mama in the kitchen simmering the meat sauce and rolling out the lasagne dough. As I had done since I first could toddle, I opened my mouth and said "A-a-h." Like a mother bird she glumped a piece of dough into my open mouth.

"God will bless you for all you do for us, Frankie."

"He better hurry up. I think I lost my job."

"Eh-h!" she shrugged. "For every door that shuts another one opens. Don't worry. I got money in the bank."

What an antidote she was for the knots in my stomach. How strong she was, how unafraid, how *real*. I hugged her to absorb some of her earthy strength.

"Ann home, Mama?"

"She out buying Christmas lights like you tell her. Helen be home soon from the shop."

The shop was a dress shop I had bought for Helen on Hollywood Boulevard—with our last twenty-five hundred dollars—in the hope that giving her something to do and worry about would—

"Mama? You like Helen don't you?"

"Like my own daughter."

"Has she—been—"

"No! You crazy? She happy now. She got a shop."

The front door opened. Helen's lovely voice sang out: "Mama! It's me— Oh, Frank, darling. You're home early."

She ran into my arms. I kissed her—and winced. There was liquor on her breath.

Mama was dishing out her mouth-watering lasagne when the front-door chimes rang. "Donga, dinga, danga," Mama sang out in imitation of the chimes. It was Bill Jenner, the business manager for Langdon's company.

"Oh, Bill. Come in, come in."

"I'm *not* coming in Frank. Dammit, I wish I was in Africa, right now."

"I know, Bill. I've been fired."

"Yes, dammit. Here's your closing check, as of tonight."

"Bill, I'd like to finish cutting the picture. No pay."

"Sorry, Frank. Little man was as hard as nails. Said he never wanted to see you again. Good night—and Merry Christmas, dammit!" He practically ran down the walk.

Langdon got his wish to emulate Chaplin: he directed his next three pictures, with Arthur Ripley as his right-hand man. I never ran into Ripley again; Langdon I saw once, years later, under the most pitiful circumstances.

As for *Long Pants*, its box-office returns and critical applause were even greater than for *The Strong Man*. One critic wrote:

> The biggest surprise among the newest of directors of the past year [1926] was Frank Capra . . . responsible for *The Strong Man* and *Long Pants* . . . the year 1927 looks very bright to him.

The year 1927 was to be the un-brightest of my whole life. Out of a job and out of cash in the bank, I looked for an agent to represent me, now that I felt important enough to have an agent. I had heard of Demmy Lampson, an emerging "boy wonder" among the flesh peddlers. In his office, at the Cross Roads of the World, on Sunset Boulevard, he promised the moon if I signed a seven-year contract with him. I did. He said he would go right out to see Henry Henigson, at Universal, and land me a directorial plum in two minutes. Next day he called me. Filled with bright promise I hurried down to his office. "Who needs Harry Langdon?" I chortled to myself.

Before I had time to sit down Lampson curtly handed me back my seven-year contract.

"Get yourself another agent, Frank. I can't do anything for you."

"What?! What happened?"

"When I mentioned your name, Henigson said 'Capra? If he's your client, you keep that lying bastard three miles from my studio or I won't let *you* in here any more.' "

"Demmy, I wouldn't know Henigson if he came up and bit me. He's got to be kidding."

"He wasn't kidding—and neither am I. I don't like clients who don't come clean."

"What the hell's to come clean about?"

"*You*. The story from the First National lot is that you *didn't* direct Langdon. Harry says he directed himself, and that you were a little gag man he brought over from Sennett's for laughs. And when you tried to take directing credit he threw you out on your ass."

"That's a goddam lie."

"Look! Lie or not I can't jeopardize my 'in' at Universal. So get yourself another boy, will you?"

"Demmy," I pleaded, "Langdon's wrong. Help me kill this rumor. Don't tear up my contract. If that comes out, it'll—murder me."

"Baby," he said. "You're in *pictures*. Remember?"

I couldn't remember anything else for the next few weeks. The rumor solidified into fact. I was a four-flusher. Studio executives were too busy to see me or answer phone calls. Other agents gave me the brush-off. All of a sudden I was nobody. Seeking a sympathetic ear I dropped into my wife's dress shop. I was stopped cold by the sight of half a dozen out-of-work actor bums drinking and laughing it up in the back room. I went home, packed a bag, and moved to the Hollywood Athletic Club. A few days later Helen moved out of our house. She rented an apartment in Culver City where she could be near the Rollerdrome, a roller skating rink, in which she had found new friends. Mama and Ann were left alone in our new house.

Ann went back to work designing dresses; Mama dipped into her savings for house money. I walked the streets of Hollywood. "Baby, you're in *pictures.* Remember?"

What was Harry Langdon doing? Well, Harry finished his first self-directed picture (I forget the title) and it flopped.

Langdon's next two features went from bad to worse. His contract was finished and so was Langdon. First National dropped him like a hot potato. The rocket that had flashed into the orbit of world fame lost its rudder and plummeted down faster than it had risen. Later he tried in vain to revive audience interest with some two-reelers he made for Roach. He tried his hand at gag-writing. Then he hit bottom by working in cheap one-reel comedies that served as "fillers" in the lesser theaters. "Baby, you're in *pictures!* Remember?"

It was while he was making one of these "fillers" that I saw him for the first and last time since our break. I peeked into a stage to watch him work. Gone was the elf. He looked like a gargoyle. The camera was running. Harry was going up a set of stairs backward, on his tail, carrying an enormous fat lady on his lap. My heart sank. It was a grotesque replica of the famous scene we did with Mary Astor in *The Strong Man.*

"Faster, Harry, faster!" yelled the irreverent slapstick director. "This is only a one-reeler, you know."

I left—and I could have cried. That great, great artist—whose art was the very essence of slow, slow pantomime—was being hollered at to "go faster!"

In 1944 he died of a cerebral hemorrhage—a long-forgotten man. The tragedy of this supreme talent is that he never knew what made him great, nor why the world forgot him. Quick fame, and the consequent barnacles of conceit that clogged his ego, made him impervious to help from those who *knew* the secret of his magic: the elf whose only ally was God. If, in heaven, he discovers it for himself, he will have the angels falling off their clouds.

The year 1927, which the critic prophesied looked bright to Frank Capra, was four months gone before I even had a smell of another job. Then I met two giant Lilliputians: the Small brothers, Eddie and Morris—small in name and size, but not in craft and imagination. They owned a talent agency, run by Morris, while Eddie was well on his way to making his first of many millions by an uncanny ability to produce big box-office hits at low-budget prices.

"Look, Frank," Eddie said to me, "I don't believe in rumors, not even the ones we start. I believe in my eyes and my nose. My eyes saw your name on the screen, my nose says you've got a big itch. Now there's this producer in New York—you wanna make a picture in New York for Bob Kane?"

"Mr. Small, I'll make a picture in New Guinea for Bob Zilch."

"Morrie, he's got the chutzpah, anyway. What're they offering?" he asked his brother—the two of them would have made one jockey.

"Four hundred plus transportation and hotel," said Morrie.

"You want it, Frank? Sign up with us, we'll try to get it for you."

A week later I checked in at the Manger Hotel, on Times Square, then took a cab for the old Cosmopolitan studio at 125th Street and Second Avenue. We drove through the full length of Central Park. It was April, yet a foot of stubborn snow imprisoned the trees—the bare trunks raising their thin arms to heaven in prayer for spring.

The old Hearst-Cosmopolitan studio, cold and clammy as the Catacombs, was right in the middle of the uptown slums. Joe Boyle, the assistant director, met me at the door. He led me through a labyrinth of Macbethian halls and stairways to the warm office of Leland Hayward, the production manager. Leland was gracious, witty, and full of pleasant blarney (before the picture was finished he would need all the grace, wit, and blarney he had in him).

"Frank," he enthused, "the weather's lousy but I can promise you a helluva press. Only one film being made in New York—ours—and we'll grab all the space. Here's today's papers—whole *columns*. Look at this headline, DIRECTOR OF LONG PANTS PICKS PLUM, and this one, FRANK CAPRA WILL DIRECT HELL'S KITCHEN. Oh, by the way, Frank, we've changed the title from *Hell's Kitchen* to *For the Love of Mike*. Much better. Here, here's the scenario. It's a masterpiece. I should know, I wrote it. And the cast, Frank, you never heard of such a—listen: three of the best comedians in the country—George Sidney, Ford Sterling, Hugh Cameron! Makes your mouth water, huh? No! FOUR great comedians—we've also got Skeets Gallagher. And the leading man? Just the greatest, that's all—Ben Lyon. You know Ben Lyon. But wait. I haven't given you the topper yet. For—the—*girl*? We've come up with a real headline maker, the finest young actress that's hit Broadway in years. Critics rave about her—a sure-fire star, they say— her first film, Frank. Wait'll you see her in *The Barker*—I've got tickets for you already. A star, Frank. She can't miss—CLAUDETTE COLBERT! Huh?"

"Leland," I said, "you must be the greatest promoter in New York."

"Not yet, Frank, but I will be. Now. Tomorrow we're giving a cocktail party to introduce you to the press. Tonight, Bob Kane's giving a dinner party for you at the Twenty-one Club. I'll pick you up at your hotel—seven-thirty . . ."

Bob Kane's dinner party was not exactly all for me. He announced it as a "going away" party. He was leaving immediately for Paris, placing "all responsibility for making *For the Love of Mike* into a great picture in the loyal and capable hands of my right-hand man, Leland Hayward [applause], and in the artistic talents of our director, Frank Capra." A smattering of socialite hands politely tapped each other. But there was much whispering and craning of necks. "Who?" . . . "Didn't get the name . . ." "Could be from Europe . . ."

The story of *For the Love of Mike* was good, but not great, but with that great cast I was certain I could pull off a hit—maybe a home run—and show Langdon and all the other skeptics whether I was a director or not.

The Thinkers.
Co-directors Frank Capra and Harry Edwards (wearing straw hats), Harry Langdon (black hat), and the ingenue and prop man all strain for a funny gag in Langdon's first feature-length film—*Tramp, Tramp, Tramp.*

My first flop came early (1927). Ford Sterling, Hugh Cameron, Claudette Colbert (her first film), Ben Lyon, and George Sidney—in *For the Love of Mike.*

Harry Langdon, rated by some as the world's greatest comic, as he looked in *The Strong Man*, my first feature-length "one man, one film." (Voted by critics one of the ten best, 1926)

But when I came up to bat, that old pitcher Hitch threw me a pitch they called a glich. There was not enough money in Bob Kane's till to make the picture. As I gathered from the scuttlebutt, Bob Kane had not left for Paris on a pleasure jaunt, but on a get-away-from-the-mess trip. He had contracted to deliver ten films to First National. He had delivered nine. Kane counted on financing the tenth film, *For the Love of Mike*, with profits from the first nine. The profits were meager, yet *For the Love of Mike had* to be made; salaries *had* been committed. Photography was begun on the picture in the hopes that profits would pick up and finance the production as it went along.

As a result, Leland Hayward was left holding a skinny bag, but Hayward's charm made what little there was go a long way. For instance, he charmed me into deferring my salary until the end of the picture. On more pressing bills he made token payments to appease collection agencies. But actors all take a dim view of any "Play now, pay later" plan.

In view of the uncertainties of their weekly check, they adopted a plan of their own: "Pay now, play today." Each morning they demanded *that* day's pay in *cash* before putting on their make-up. "People pay at the box office *before* they see us on the screen." Since actors are indispensable, once they get into a film, their argument had the authority of Marshal Dillon's gun.

Where Hayward dug up the cash was a deep mystery. A studio wag said the police had reported a sharp increase in payroll highjackings. Leland didn't think the crack was funny. At any rate, a haggard Hayward showed up early each morning with a handful of envelopes containing each actor's daily salary in cash. This deviation from the norm created some humorous, but vexing, inter-Thespian situations. Actors found out how much *other* actors were being paid—normally a secret. Lesser-paid hams howled in indignation. Egos were bruised; statuses crumbled. Actors called their agents; agents called Hayward; Hayward called Bob Kane in Paris—Kane called for reservations on the Riviera.

There were, of course, days when Hayward couldn't come up with the early morning scratch. The actors sat in their dressing rooms and caught up with their racing forms. That meant we lost a day's work. It also meant Hayward's envelopes had to be twice as fat next morning. These were called the "daily doubles."

Miraculously, despite the bickerings and low morale, we managed to finish seven reels of "presentable" film. But I, who made it, and the wise-acres in Hollywood, knew it was just seven reels of mediocre film. Claudette Colbert, never easily pleased, said that for her it was a disaster, and vowed it would be her first and last film. For me there was an ironic footnote: I never *did* get paid for making the film. Except for transportation and hotel expenses it was all "for the love of Mike." But it was worth it just to meet Colbert, George Sidney, Leland Hayward—and to see the Central Park trees sprout leaves at the incredible rate of about an inch per day.

About August 1, I left for the West Coast, not completely relieved of a growing inner doubt: Could I direct films without Langdon as the star?

No brass bands met me in Hollywood. The Morris office groused about their commissions from the salary I didn't get. They weren't about to break their necks seeking other jobs for such a stupid client. Then, too, divorce papers were served on me by Helen's attorney, demanding a settlement of half the community property and proper alimony. I agreed to the property settlement but balked at alimony, since I had no income. In return for my not contesting the divorce she abandoned alimony. I borrowed eight thousand dollars on the house to pay her off. The court granted her an uncontested divorce on the catch-all grounds of mental cruelty. That ended that.

I returned to my home to live with Mama and Ann—and to knock on studio gates again. I found them closed tighter than ever. By some perverse quirk of guilt-by-association studio executives somehow connected me with Langdon's recent failure.

I was thirty, single again, out of a job, shunned by agents, and tagged as the director of the big flop *For the Love of Mike.* My dreamy love affair with the "new language" of films was on the rocks. Lord, had I made a mistake? Great things were happening in science. My old friend, astronomer Edwin P. Hubble, had just discovered the "red shift" of galaxies—the universe was expanding! Should I, *could* I, go back to Caltech and try for a Ph.D.?

While walking aimlessly down Hollywood Boulevard, brooding over how I could possibly finance myself if I *did* go back to Caltech, somebody slapped my back so hard it almost knocked the wind out of me. It was Mack Sennett.

"Frank, you little Dago," he greeted me, rubbing my head and pushing my chin with a big fist. "Where ya been? What're you doin'? Thought you were a panhandler when I first saw you." His loud laugh caused heads to turn.

"I'll soon be one, Mr. Sennett. I can't get a job."

"Aw, for crying out loud. Why didn't you come and see *me?* You know my studio's always open to old employees. Come on, let's go have lunch at Henry's and hear some stale jokes."

And so, after two years on "the outside," I was back in the Tower as a "prisoner of Edendale"; back as a gag man at seventy-five dollars per week. I took a lot of ribbing: "Couldn't cut it in the big time, hey, Walyo?" . . . "Back for a refresher course, eh?"

"Treat me kindly, boys," I would try cracking back. "I may be hiring you some day."

I was in the Tower for about twelve weeks, and beginning to wonder if it was a life sentence—when I received a "message from Garcia"—a call from Morris Small.

"Frank, Columbia Pictures just called. Want to talk to you about directing a picture."

"Who?"

"Columbia Pictures. They gotta studio—"

"Never heard of them."

"Well, Frank, they probably never heard of you either. But they want to see you."

"Where are they?"

"On Gower Street, near Sunset."

"Oh, come on, Morrie—that's Poverty Row. All fly-by-nighters."

"What the hell do you care? Their money buys groceries, too. Go see the production manager, a guy called Sam Briskin."

The area around Sunset and Gower was known as "Gower Gulch"—infested by shacks and dinky stages where ferret-eyed producers made "fillums" that cost, and sold for, peanuts.

I pulled my cap down over my eyes as I walked through a ragtag herd of extras toward 1438 Gower Street. I opened the door. The place smelled like a rat's nest. A worn-out receptionist behind an enclosure, wearing a uniform that must have come from Mack Sennett's, challenged me.

"What do you want?"

"Frank Capra. I have an appointment with Mr. Sam Briskin."

"Okay. Down the hall, up the stairs, first room on the right."

I walked into a hall so narrow even the skinny had to turn sideways to pass. They would have to grease the walls for a pregnant woman. The office cubicles on both sides of the hall were so tiny the entrance doors overlapped. The smell was more concentrated inside—as gamy as the Green Bay Packers' locker room, without windows. And employees didn't walk, they ran—and bowled you over if you were slow of foot. And nobody talked—they shouted. Some studio.

I found the narrow, closed stairway. It spiraled twice to go up one floor. Before knocking on Sam Briskin's door I had *had* Columbia Pictures. A pleasant secretary said, "Go right in. Mr. Briskin is waiting for you."

"Are you Frank Capra? You're a little guy. I thought you'd be bigger," was Briskin's opening gambit.

All the small men of the world will know how I felt. A psalm discovered in the Dead Sea Scrolls begins with this lament: "I was little among my brethren . . ." Anyhow Sam Briskin was the aggressive, hit-first type; about my age, had a shock of nice-looking hair, and wore thick glasses. Needless to say he was Jewish. To stand the gaff on Poverty Row, you had to be Jewish—even if you were Italian.

"Sit down, sit down. Take the load off," he waved pleasantly. I sat. "Frank Capra. Italiano, huh?" I nodded. "Your last picture wasn't so good, was it?" I burned.

"What *was* my last picture, Mr. Briskin?"

The question threw him off balance. He sputtered something.

"You haven't really seen *any* of my pictures, have you, Mr. Briskin?" With that I got up and started to walk out.

"Hey! Wait a minute—sit down, sit down," motioned Briskin. "My God, you're touchy. What'd I say?"

"Mr. Briskin, why don't you tell me why you sent for me?"

"I didn't send for you, Harry Cohn did. He was looking at a list of unemployed directors, and your name, beginning with *C*, was the first on the list. He said to me, 'Sam, this guy's name's on top. Send for him.' But Harry, I said, read the rest of the list. 'Sam,' he said, 'God picked Abraham because his name came first. Good enough for me. Send for Capra.' So I sent for you."

The first glimmer of interest welled up in me—this madhouse was run by hunch players.

"All right, I'm here. What for?"

"To talk about directing a film. You wanna make a picture here?"

"I'll make a picture anywhere."

"Okay. What's your salary? Or should I talk to Small?"

"No. Talk to me."

"Okay. How much?"

"You name it."

"Oh, you wanna play games. Okay, I'll open the pot. A thousand dollars for directing a film."

"Deal. *If* you let me write it and produce it, too."

"Don't you want a writer?"

"I am a writer."

"And you want to produce, too? What's left for Harry Cohn to do?"

"Harry Cohn can fire me any time—and I can quit any time."

"Wait a minute. Let's get this straight. You want to produce, write, and direct a feature film, for a flat fee of one thousand dollars—no contract?"

"Deal."

"Capra, you're taking all the fun out of this. Let's go see Harry Cohn."

I could see now why everybody ran in this studio—Briskin set the fast pace. We rounded corners on two wheels and skidded to a stop in a reception room, presided over by a secretary I can't recall. It might have been Minna Wallis.

"Tell the boss I'm here with Capra."

"Right away, Mr. Briskin."

The secretary flicked a dictograph switch; announced us. Sam and I waited in front of a huge, paneled door. A loud, angry, door buzzer startled me. Sam pushed open the heavy door, held it open for me. The room was so long I could barely see the other end. In the distant gloom I made out a balding, pugnacious man standing behind a large desk covered with phones and dictographs. Around the edge of a large chair with its back to us I caught a glimpse of two shapely crossed legs. Still holding the door open, Briskin introduced me.

"Harry, this is Frank Capra. He—"

"Okay-okay-okay-*okay*!" interrupted Cohn imperiously. "It's a deal, it's a deal. Scram!"

"But Harry, don't you wanna hear the—"

"For crissake, Sam, will you get your ass outta here. I'm busy. Put 'em to work."

That was my introduction to Harry Cohn, one of the damndest, one of the biggest, and one of the most controversial characters Hollywood has ever known.

As we were leaving, practical-minded Briskin summed up the bizarre goings-on with this comment: "Crazy day today—even for this joint."

CHAPTER 5

Columbia the "Germ" of the Ocean

THE GIMCRACK jumble of Columbia's offices just "grow'd" as breathing space reached the critical staleness that keeled over canaries. I don't know whether Topsy was also turvy but Columbia was. To a dozen or more shacks forming a square around an inner courtyard, succeeding fly-by-nighters had added additions to additions with all the playful abandon of children piling odd-shaped cigar boxes on top of each other—two sides were now three stories high; the third, two stories; the fourth, one and a half.

Narrow halls, rising and falling with the uneven levels, tunneled through the maze; partitions honeycombed it into tiny "offices"; afterthoughts of exposed pipes for water, gas, and heat pierced the flimsy walls; criss-crossing electric wires—inside and out—tied the jerry-built structure together to keep it from blowing away. The last "crazy house" touches were the comical stairways, interior and exterior. Some got you places—others just got you.

I was assigned a 6 by 8 cubicle on the ground floor of the inner court-yard; my "view," a waterless fountain—a catchall for flipped cigarette butts. Those office cribs, facing boardwalks covered by upper boardwalks, reminded me of the crib of a Reno red-light compound—except that Cohn's cribs lacked the Japanese lanterns and the gaudy girls sitting at their windows, and besides which Harry Cohn was hardly the madam type. The sultan of a harem—yes; the procurer—no.

The "back lot" at Columbia was a ramshackle extension of the offices. Within an area not much larger than one big stage at MGM or Warner's, Columbia had squeezed in three cramped stages, a row of shops, an incinerator, a parking place for trucks, and—into a leftover corner—a cubist's nightmare of cutting rooms, film vaults, and projection rooms piled on top of each other, and reachable only by steep, exterior iron stairs.

Yet, within that incredibly small back lot, miracles were created. Harry Cohn was no aficionado of airy architecture and delicate traceries. His forte was men—hot-shot department heads who welcomed the challenge to make do with little or nothing—men like Denver Harmon, head electrician; Ray Howell, props; Joe Walker, camera; George Seid, laboratory; George Yager, lighting; and, ablest of all, Sam Briskin, the production manager. And there was a woman, too: Dorothy Howell, head scenarist—sensitive, intelligent, courageous. Yes, indeed. Decorwise, Columbia was a junkyard; but brainwise, it was a gold mine.

Harry Cohn was the archetype of a breed of moviemakers I had not met before: tough, brassy, untutored buccaneers, second-generation opportunists attracted to a proven bonanza. Spawned in the confining poverty of Jewish ghettos on the East Coast, they broke out like young lions and headed west—to defy the odds and the gods in the carnivorous game of moviemaking. They were not actors, writers, directors, or technicians. They were indigent, hot-eyed entrepreneurs, gamblers who played longshots. Many had been exposed to the fillum fever while working as ushers, ticket takers, messengers delivering cans of film. Some were grub-staked by relatives already in the fillum business—as exhibitors or producers. But most came to Hollywood with little more than guts and gall, knowing they had as good a chance as the next guy to beg, borrow, or steal enough cash to "shoot the dice" and make some cheap, sensational pictures for the thousands of third-rate movie houses.

Harry Cohn, an ex-streetcar conductor and former song plugger for Tin Pan Alley—who snarled out of the side of his mouth with the best of them—was hit by fillum fever. With his wife's money, and his older brother Jack and Joe Brandt as partners, Harry Cohn put together a small film company: C.B.C. (Cohn, Brandt, Cohn) Productions—with its un-unique trademark of a Lady holding up a freedom torch. Arriving in Hollywood, Harry stuck his camel's head under the tattered flaps of a studio on Gower Street. Soon the camel was in, all others out. Unfurling a new sign, COLUMBIA PICTURES STUDIO, he pushed off into the foggy seas of "quickie" production. When I arrived at Columbia Studio, the Lady's torch was still above the waves—the rest of her was anxiously treading water. Lacking foresight, gagsters dubbed Harry Cohn's studios: COLUMBIA THE "GERM" OF THE OCEAN.

I had been there a week or two before I had my first confrontation with Harry Cohn. I had *heard* him every day, storming through the halls, bawling out employees for leaving on lights, smoking, drinking coffee. Dorothy Howell, the scenarist, told me he barked but seldom bit. But in later years I was to see many a sensitive artist walk out of Columbia as if chewed up by a grizzly. Obviously, Columbia was not a place for the weak or the meek. Here they measured you not by what you could do, but by how you did it under Cohn's bullying. I knew our first encounter would be critical. I was determined to get in the first punch.

"Hey, Dago. What've you been doin'? Where the hell's the story?" he barked at me as I walked into his office.

"Mr. Cohn, what are *you* worrying about the story for?"

"COME ON!" he yelled, jumping up and banging his desk with a riding crop. "Are you nuts enough to think I'd fall for that cockamamie idea you cooked up with Briskin? About you producing, writing, directing a whole film? *I* do all the producing around here. *I* run this studio. Me. Alone. HARRY COHN!"

"Then why *don't* you run it—instead of wasting time parading around putting out lights, yelling at people?"

I thought he would burst a blood vessel. "Why you little Dago bastard. I got half a mind to throw you out on your ear right *now!*"

"It's your studio, Mr. Cohn." I was still standing—and ready to go. His voice came down a notch.

"*All right,* come on. Quit screwing around, willya? For chrissake I got more *important* things to do. Come on. I wanna hear the story. What's the story?"

"The story's very simple, Mr. Cohn. Either you stick to the deal—give me control over the whole film—writing, directing, editing—or I walk out. Simple."

He sat down. I got in the first punch. He leaned back, pursed his lips, and tried to stare me down with a fixed look. He broke off. "Hm-m-m. Let me hear the story. I'll decide about the other crap later on."

"Here's the story in a paragraph. A rich socialite owns a big chain of restaurants. He has an only son he wants to groom to take over the restaurants. The son isn't buying. He's more interested in a girl from across the tracks. The old man fumes. The boy insists. The father cuts him off without a dime and throws him out. Boy and girl haven't got a nickel to get married on. But they've got an idea—BOX LUNCHES! They make some. Noontime they take box lunches around in her jalopy to sell to workmen. The lunches are a hit. They grow and grow into a *big business*—and wreck the father's *restaurants.* Old man surrenders. Asks box-lunch owners for merger talks. He is knocked for a loop when owners turn out to be his son and the girl. The two businesses merge, boy and girl merge, boy becomes president."

"Frank, that's a helluva an idea." He jumped up to pace. "Box lunches. Novel. They're bustin' out all over the country. What about the cast?"

"Young man I wrote for at Sennett's, Ralph Graves, would make a good socialite boy. Inexpensive."

"And the girl?"

"I don't know. Depends on your budget."

"Frank, I got just the dame—cute, little—Viola *Dana!* Sexy, too. D'ja ever see her wiggle her ass?"

"Nope."

"Well, she can, take it from me. I'll call New York on it. Wait outside. I wanna show you the back lot."

"Harry, I've been all over your back lot. It's a heap, but your men are great."

"You can bet your Aunt Tilly's tits they're great—the greatest in Hollywood. All right, gwan, beat it! What the hell you waitin' for? Get to work, you damn Dago."

I left his office feeling I had earned at least a draw with the monster. In the general run of humanity, people either give you a lift, or depress you; bore you, or, as with most, leave you indifferent. But not Harry Cohn. Just his presence would make your hackles rise and your adrenals pump furiously. He annoyed and belittled—until he made you hate. Some baseball and football coaches have operated on that principle: John McGraw, Leo Durocher, Vince Lombardi. Add crudeness and sadism to this principle— and you get Cohn.

The title of the box-lunch picture was *That Certain Thing*; a quickie feature film, budgeted at less than twenty thousand dollars, as I remember. Mack Sennett spent twice that for a two-reeler. The shooting of *That Certain Thing* was a postgraduate course in penny-pinching. Not a moment was wasted, not a nickel. We even saved lunch money on location by eating our own props—the box lunches.

There was one minor eyeball-to-eyeball incident in the making of that first film. I had requested fifteen extras for a restaurant scene—the minimum number I could make do with. Only seven appeared on the set. I queried the assistant director. His answer was that "around here the production department automatically puts the shears to every director's request." I told him to stop all work till I got back. I went straight to Harry Cohn's office.

"What the hell you doin' here? Why ain't you on the set?" he growled as I entered.

"Harry, I'll play games with you. All I want to know is what are the ground rules?"

"What the hell are you talkin' about?"

"Harry, I really need a *hundred* extras on that set. I asked for fifteen because I figured that, by juggling, I could make fifteen *look* like a hundred. But I can't make *seven* look like a hundred. Now what are the rules of the game? How-many-people-do-I-have-to-ask-for-to *get fifteen?*"

"Get back on the set, for chrissake!"

"I'll go back and *wait*, Harry."

There were fifteen extras on the set before I got back. All the casting director had to do was lean out the window and whistle. There were always dozens of extras milling around on Sunset and Gower waiting for whistles.

Cohn evidently liked my first picture. He offered me a verbal deal for two more pictures at twenty-five hundred dollars each. "Deal," I said quickly. If I could save up ten thousand dollars working in this dump I might just try for a Ph.D. at Caltech.

In quick succession, six weeks for each picture (two weeks for writing, two for shooting, two for editing), I made two more films: *So This Is Love*, a comedy with Buster Collier, Jr., Johnny Walker, and Shirley Mason, and *Matinee Idol*, a tent-show comedy with Johnny Walker and Bessie Love. In them I tried mixing in another so-called sure-fire ingredient with comedy— a little love story. It seemed to work. Besides which, I "discovered" another directing trick: Don't let the ponderous behind-the-scenes machinery distract from the heroine's fluttering eyelid. People pay to *hear* Heifetz's violin, not to marvel at his fingers. The galaxies and their "red shift" began receding in my mind. In my next scene with Cohn they got lost.

"Dago," he said expansively, "I'm gonna do you a big favor. I'm gonna offer you a contract."

"Wait a minute, Harry. I'm not sure I want to go on with pictures. I've been thinking about going back to school."

"SCHOOL, for chrissake—that's for kids!"

"I know, Harry. But I'm leaving this rat race unless I'm pretty sure I can be successful—very successful. And the only way I can prove that is to have complete control of my pictures. Understand?"

Cohn's faults were legion minus one—he was not stupid. "Dago," he said, "you wouldn't get out of pictures if they stuck a gun at your head. So stop trying to blackmail me for a better deal. This is Cohn. I'll give you a straight one-year contract at five C's a week, with an extra one-year option at seven-fifty. *Wait* a minute—before you open your big mouth. I'll also advance you seventy-five hundred to buy Ben Goetz's house at Malibu, which you rented for a month and went nuts about. How's that, Dago? God-dammit, I'm getting *soft*." He tossed me a legal contract, the first I had ever seen.

"Where's the pen?" I asked.

"Don't you want your agent to read it, you schmuck?"

"No agent. The Small office canceled my contract after I made that first picture deal with you without consulting them."

"Okay, okay. Then *you* read it, smart guy."

"Nope."

"You—you gonna sign a contract without reading it?" he asked in astonishment.

"Harry—you want me to sign this or don't you?"

"Frank, you're either the dumbest bastard in the world, or the smartest. I dunno which. Sign it."

I knew which. I knew Harry Cohn. I was trading money for power I couldn't get at any other studio. In signing my first film contract I was saying good-bye forever to my first love at Caltech. I was marrying the harlot.

I moved into Ben Goetz's house at Malibu—a wonderful two-story house right on the beach, with a tennis court in the rear. I tried taking Mama with me.

"No, Frankie," she said to me at our Odin Street home. "I no move no more. Here I close my eyes. Besides, Ann is getting married." I gulped.

"Ann? Getting *married*?" Of all the sisters in the world, my little sister Ann was the sweetest and the *dearest*. Plagued with a rheumatic heart, working all her life, yet her concern was all for others—never for herself. The thought of her marrying that—

"Mama! Not to Sam?—that bum that hangs around here all day, with his high collar, sitting on the couch reading newspapers—and eating?"

"Frankie, women are like mama birds—wanna make their own nest—in the rocks, in the grass, in the trees—doesn't matter. Don't butt in."

Ann married Sam. I paid for their honeymoon to Seattle. They didn't return. Sam had a job, she wrote. I *knew* who had the job. Then, no word for months. Finally, a letter: she is sick, she owed bills. Would I send some money? I sent a thousand dollars. She returned—without Sam—an empty shell. In Seattle she had developed a tubular pregnancy. At the hospital, because of her heart condition, the doctors cut out her tubes *and* her ovaries. Sam had left for parts unknown while she was in the hospital. She had built her nest for a rat. But she still defended him. That was Ann.

Moving to Malibu I took in a companion; not a wife, but a rollicking *boon* companion—fun-loving, hell-raising Al Roscoe—heaven's gift to the working girls—an actor. No, not *just* an actor. He was the ham what am—with a Hollywood flavor—and loved the part. Al had no equal as a sponger —or as a friend. He would go to hell for you, if you paid the bills. Of late, he had been improving the quality of Wally Beery's life with his sponging-friend bit. But, as with all great con men in love with their art, he had to have a second sucker up his sleeve—just in case. He chose me, and I am eternally grateful that he did.

In my next two pictures for Columbia *Say It with Sables* and *Way of the Strong*, again I experimented—soft-pedaling comedy and pulling out all stops on heavy drama. I knew my experiment with drama was dismal. I was too inexperienced to handle the delicate nuances or the sustained moods of dramatic conflict. But, in the elementary school of trial and error—where I was both student and teacher—I *had* to experiment if I were ever to master this new, universal language of film that was revolutionizing the mores of the world. And mastering film was not just a desire—it had become an obsession! Moreover, I had had no apprenticeship in the theater, no real knowledge of the classic arts. My Hollywood contacts were limited to the bush-leaguers of Gower Gulch. I had yet to step inside the palatial major studios—MGM, Paramount, Warner Brothers, Universal. I had never read a script by an important writer, or watched a top director work—with the exception of that ridiculous (to me) scene I saw Stroheim direct in San Francisco.

One night, from outside the fence at Universal, I did catch a glimpse of an important director shooting a huge exterior mob scene. "He must be a big director," I thought to myself. "All the lights in Hollywood are on his set."

I parked my car close to the fence to watch and learn. I couldn't see the mob of extras (it sounded like thousands), but high up on a platform, silhouetted against the blinding lights, I could see Mr. Director—surrounded by cameras and shouting to the mob through an enormous megaphone. He wore puttees, a long-bibbed cap to shield the lights, a flowing tie, and a coat of many pockets—like a hunter's jacket. I gaped and marveled. Would I ever be up on a platform directing thousands? At Columbia ten extras were a mob scene. I listened intently to catch the words of wisdom from his megaphone.

"Now, children . . . may I have your attention, please!"

Loud shouts of "QUIET! QUIET!" from a dozen assistant directors bounced around the huge set like ping-pong balls. A hush descended. What respect! This was really "big time" moviemaking. His very voice sounded Homeric:

"Children! Tonight we are in danger," came out of the megaphone, "our city is besieged. There is fear in your hearts, but right now—we are only *apprehensive*. Each one of you, turn to your neighbors and say 'Buzz, buzz, buzz!' Nothing *else*, just 'Buzz, buzz, buzz!' All right. Let me hear it."

The buzzing of a million bees filled the air.

"Fine, fine. Now we are *more* fearful. We hear the battle sounds. Turn to your neighbors a little faster and say, out *loud*: 'Chatter, chatter, *chatter*! Chatter, chatter, *chatter*!' Let's hear it."

The chattering of a forest of monkeys swelled the ambient atmosphere.

"Fine. Now I want terror! The enemy has breached the walls! *Run* to your neighbor and *shout*: 'WALLA, WALLA, WALLA! WALLA, WALLA, WALLA!' "

"What kind of crazy directing is this?" I thought to myself. "Buzz, buzz, buzz—chatter, chatter, chatter—walla, walla—it's childish."

"All ready? Camera! Action! Buzz, buzz, buzz—"

The buzzing started, louder than in rehearsal. Extras always give out more when the cameras are running.

"Now! Chatter, chatter, *chatter*!" It sounded like a whole continent of monkeys. "STOP IT, STOP IT." No, no! You're giving me 'WALLA, WALLA, WALLA'—that's for later. I want 'Chatter, chatter, *chatter*'—dammit!—"

I chatter-chattered the hell away from there. If that was directing, I was a monkey's tail.

But on the way home I pondered—and wondered. A director's job is to communicate, evoke responses, and photograph them. He says to a man, "walk"—he walks; to another, "run"—he runs. Simple commands, mechanical responses. But how about emotional or psychological responses—especially unified *mass* responses from two thousand extras? Would I communicate with each *individual*?—leaving the responses up to each extra? Some would faint, others would cower, run, or just stand still. And how would I communicate the "degree" of the response? Come to think of it, that director was not dumb. In fact, he was brilliant! He communicated emotionally with one word: "Fear!" And controlled the degree—from apprehension to terror—with simple *mechanical* commands: "Turn to your

In 1927, His Crudeness (Harry Cohn) comes into my life. Some say the combo made a little film history.

So *This Is Love*, my second Columbia film. These early Columbias cost an average of $20,000. I can't remember why Shirley Mason leaped into the ring to embrace her fallen hero, William "Buster" Collier, Jr.

Early Columbia—*The Matinee Idol*, with Bessie Love and Johnny Walker. Benny Rubin (left) was ostracized from films because he looked too Jewish. So I photographed inserts of his hands and dancing feet.

Say It with Sables, fifth Columbia. Again heavy drama, this time about the bluebloods. Didn't help. The higher the class, the heavier the lead. Plot: son falls for rich father's mistress; stepmother saves the day. Shown here: the mistress (Margaret Livingston), the rich father (Francis X. Bushman), and his wife, the fairy stepmother (Helene Chawick).

Submarine was my first "A" picture. Navy diver Jack Holt has just successfully completed a record 400-foot dive to attach an air hose to a stricken submarine, saving the lives of its whole crew.

neighbors and say, 'buzz, buzz, buzz—chatter, chatter, chatter—WALLA, WALLA, WALLA!'" With two elemental commands, understood by child or professor, he evoked the right mass response from two thousand people, in a jiffy! *That* was directing—and I *was* a monkey's tail. WALLA, WALLA.

I had seen another touch of major studio class hit Poverty Row just before I started *Say It with Sables*. A veteran director, then on the skids, but still suffused with the aura of having worked for years on the fringes of the majors, was hired by Cohn to make a picture; but the veteran insisted on having *music* on the set. It was a time-honored procedure in major studios for small orchestras to "soothe the savage breast" with mood music for the stars. But mood music on Poverty *Row*?! You should live so long!

In a rare moment of aberrant affluence Harry Cohn said "Yes" to the old-time director's request for music. That triggered a chain reaction: *All* the actresses in the studio demanded mood music—including mine in *Say It with Sables*. Cohn raised the roof, but had to agree. The "bad news" spread through Gower Gulch: "Mood music at Columbia! Hoo, hoo, hoo! End of Cohn—thank God!"

I found myself on the set with a three-piece combo—violin, cello, bass—without the slightest idea of how to use them. For a quick "music" lesson I ducked over to the veteran director's set. This is what I saw: An actress playing a passionate scene with an actor. The director, with his *back* to the scene, was conducting the three-piece orchestra with all the soulful fervor of a Toscanini, swiveling his head back and forth from musicians to actors like an ecstatic owl! The scene over, he congratulated the musicians, then rushed into the set to embrace the performers. At least that old director— a paucity of talent wrapped up in a plethora of vanity—was "in the mood." I just made it to the stage door before bursting out laughing.

I tried using my combo for a day or two—to give my actresses equal status—but I couldn't keep a straight face. I let them go. Ironically enough, a year later, when sound hit Hollywood like a tornado, mood musicians were the first casualties. *Sic semper vanitus.*

In my new tux, I had taken a girl to Grauman's Chinese for a gala opening—and to gawk at the stars coming in. "Hey, that's Norma Talmadge . . . and right behind her—Theda Bara . . . No. That's Nita Naldi . . . No, no, it's . . . Oh, my God—look! Look! GARBO! . . ."

During intermission an usher came to me with a message: Mr. Harry Cohn wants you back at the studio. "Right *now*, he said." My girl was impressed. I shrugged it off. I could have told her that Cohn "lived" in his office, and that the muzzler delighted in tracking you down—making you come to the studio at all hours—just to spoil your evening.

Leaving the girl in the car, I went up to Cohn's office and found Harry and Sam Briskin, two obstinate head-butters, nose-to-nose in a purple rhubarb.

"Harry! You're outta your *mind*. Jack and Joe in New York will blow their tops—"

"Screw New York." Then to me, "Two hours I been trying to get you. Get over to the projection room and see two reels of cut stuff. Get going!"

"Harry, I've got a girl in the car."

"To hell with the broad. Go see those reels."

"Why?"

"I'm bleeding and he asks me riddles. GO SEE THOSE TWO REELS!"

The two reels I saw were rough-cut sequences from Columbia's first big splurge into "A" pictures: *Submarine*—budgeted at $150,000—five times the cost of an average Columbia film. I saw Jack Holt and Ralph Graves playing happy-go-lucky Navy men who have a falling-out over a dame, Dorothy Revier. Holt and Graves were so heavily made up they looked like musical comedy sailors. As soon as I was important enough I would get rid of make-up, come actors, come cameramen, come all the Westmores.

But why did Cohn want *me* to see the film? He had to be sweating out some kind of vein-bursting decision.

I went back to Harry's office. He and Sam Briskin were both on the phone with the director, Irving Willat, a respected name. I gathered Willat was pleading to be allowed to finish the underwater photography for which he was noted. I listened—and learned a great lesson. Never plead. Always have your hat on, ready to walk out.

"We'll call you back," said Sam on the phone—respectfully.

"Well, Dago?" asked Harry, anxiety struggling with arrogance.

"Well, what?"

"Come *on*!" he exploded. "What'd you think of the film?"

"Harry," I barked back, "I don't go around criticizing directors."

"Oh, balls! Didn't you think the stuff was lousy?"

"I just work here."

"All I wanted to hear. Sam? Frank's taking over the rest of the picture—"

I nearly jumped out of my skin.

"No, Harry, NO!" pleaded Briskin with the exasperation of a sincere man. "Jack Holt will scream bloody murder. He and Willat are friends. Get an opinion from New York, why don't you—"

"New York couldn't give me the time of day. Frank, get rid of that broad, get in a studio car, go right down to San Pedro where the company's on location, and *finish the picture*. Here's a copy of the script—"

There was a silence. My head spun. The room spun. I gulped big chunks of sweaty air. A small inner voice warned: "Keep cool. Don't let Cohn cut you down or stretch you to fit *his* bed. He'll *own* you." Then I heard my own voice saying: "Not me, Harry. I'm not your repair man. I don't finish *any-body's* show. You want me to take over—it's a new deal. I start from scratch."

"You see, Harry?" argued Briskin, "I *told* you he'd say that. Three weeks shooting'll go down the toilet. We can't afford it."

"We can't afford a *bust*! Sam, I trust this Dago. The other guy worries me—and when I'm worried, I'm scared." Then, turning to me, "You're a fresh punk, you know that?" I started out. "Come back here, you Dago bastard. Don't you *ever* walk out on me, not when I've got fifty G's sunk in a film. Go on. Give me some *reasons* for reshooting everything."

"One's enough—you need a *hit*. The company needs a hit. If you want *me* to tackle it, the chances are better if I do it all *my* way. Harry, you know damn well that if Willat had told you what you could *do* with *Submarine*, you wouldn't take him off the picture. And if I don't tell you the same thing, you'd have no confidence in *me*. So—"

"All right already with the speeches. Get your tail down to San Pedro and take over. I got a hundred people on location eating me up. Gwan, gwan, gwan, BEAT IT!"

That was it. I took the girl home, packed up some work clothes—and was on my way in a studio car, to take over *Submarine*. God help me.

It was one A.M. By the dim light of the limousine I read the script over and over. And I thought about Irving Willat. A gentleman, a distinguished director—with distinguished films behind him—was being taken off a picture because he couldn't face up to Cohn's crassness. Pity. But that was Cohn. He was shrewd enough to know he wasn't fully qualified to judge writers by what they wrote, or directors by their daily photography. So he ran his studio on a more pragmatic, cruder level. He rated writers and directors by their guts, on the raw theory that creators with mettle knew more about what they were doing than the gentle, sensitive kind. *He* might be unsure, but he wouldn't stand for uncertainty in his creative people.

I had often seen Cohn hire a well-known writer, then badger him into turning in fifteen or twenty pages of script. Without reading them, Cohn would call the writer to his office and tear into him. "You call yourself a *writer*?" he would snarl, picking up the man's unread pages and flinging them down. "That's the worst piece of junk I ever read in my life."

If the writer answered, "Look, Mr. Cohn, don't yell at *me*. I think those pages are pretty good," Cohn would back off and bluster, "Oh! That's great! *You* think they're pretty good."

"Yes, I do. If you don't like them, that's just too damn bad."

"Allrightallrightallright, I ain't got time to argue. Get back to work. 'll see you later."

Cohn had tested the writer's mettle. He was in. The pleased bully-boy would smirk to himself, *then* read the man's pages. But if the writer met the attack with servility, he was out, pronto. Many a fine, sensitive artist had been cowed by Cohn's crudeness; Cohn couldn't care less. Call him a gutter executive, a heel, an insensitive boor—yet with his snarling yardstick he was to build up Columbia from a rinky-dink outfit on Poverty Row to one of Hollywood's most successful *major studios*.

And so, because the Crude One had confidence in his Cocky One, I was in a speeding limousine in the early hours of the morning—a lieutenant rushing to replace a general—knowing I was rushing into a hectic war of nerves . . . I leaned back to add things up.

I had directed five cheap films for Columbia in seven months, aptly dubbed quickies; before that, a turkey called *For the Love of Mike*; and two Langdon comedies, which Langdon clouded by telling the world he directed himself. Furthermore, to the entrenched Hollywood Establishment, comedy directors were slapstick freaks—low-down tricksters with piano wire. My goal, as a youth, was to leap across the tracks—to rise above the muck and meanness of peasant poverty. I wanted freedom from established caste systems; and from where I took life's jolts on the chin, freedom could only be won by success.

I attacked films as I did education—with the ardor of a fanatic. I was married to film; the studio was my home. I picked the creative brains of others, stole ideas, made energy count where talent failed. I cashed in on Harry Cohn's weak spots. He trusted most in the sure and cocky. I became his cockiest employee. My measure for all things was simple: Was it good for Frank Capra? And now here I was in a limousine, speeding to replace a "name" director—to take that giant step from quickies to "A" pictures. If this was the "time and tide," I was not only going to take it "at he flood." I was going to use all my cunning and wit to grab it by the scruff of its briny neck!

In the parlance of the fight game, a hungry underdog often beats a 3 to 1 favorite that's eatin' regular. Fight crowds cheer for the hungry one. I was a hungry director—but there were no cheers waiting for me—as I found out from a tired, dispirited Buddy Coleman, the assistant director. Outside the hotel—occupied by the *Submarine* company—he briefed me on the "local" situation:

Jack Holt and Ralph Graves were quitting the picture if I took over . . . Willat was Jack Holt's friend . . . Holt took picture because of Willat . . . Crew and actors all muttering . . . Think it insane for "quickie" Capra to replace "A" picture Willat . . . They would sabotage until I left . . . I was crazy to take the job . . . Everybody loved Willat . . . Should he (Coleman) cancel the call for the morning—the stars and a hundred extras from the Navy? He was sure the actors would not show up . . .

"Good," I said, "situation excellent. I shall attack!"

"What?"

"Nothing. Looks tough, huh? Buddy, I need you—badly. But if you want off the picture, I don't blame you."

"I'm here to assist the director, Frank," he answered quietly. God bless *all* assistant directors.

"Thanks, Bud. Now. Don't cancel any call. We start shooting at eight o'clock. Anyone five minutes late will be fired on the spot. One more thing. Important! No make-up on the actors—*any* actors. That's an order. Where's my room? I'll hit the sack for a couple of hours. Thanks again, Buddy."

I went to my room but not to bed. I sat down to plan the day's work—and the psychological battle. I would attack first, and hard, on the side issue of "no make-up." That would give me the advantage of surprise. I had to win respect and command in the few hours, or take a long step backward. It was one of those many crucial moments you sweat out in show business—moments that make or break you on fragile intangibles that either inspire trust or distrust in others.

In the present pivotal moment the two intangibles that controlled my future were the irreplaceable stars: Jack Holt and Ralph Graves. If they cooperated, I *knew* I could make an important film. If they refused, it would make an idiot out of Cohn; he would probably throw me out on my ear as an incompetent who couldn't handle actors.

Ralph Graves I had written for at Sennett's; he had starred in my first Columbia picture: *That Certain Thing*. Ralph was left-handed—subject to mercurial quirks of temper. He was known to hit first, then tearfully apologize. But he was sensitive; loved pictures, especially comedy; and had aspirations to write and direct. Ralph would be moldable clay.

But Jack Holt was granite—a serious actor, a scion of an old-line family; haughty, ramrod straight, a V.M.I. graduate. He was known to all as a rock-ribbed patriot, a pillar of honor and respectability. Comedy, to him, was for nitwits. Irving Willat was his friend—upper crust, a gentleman of the old school. To replace him with a foreigner, a slapstick director, on a U.S. Navy service picture, was tantamount to degrading the flag. Holt was the cliff I had to scale. I would go-for-broke on one thin rope: *No make-up*. On that "artistic" innovation I could challenge the world *and* Jack Holt.

At 7:30 A.M. I found the working crews (cameramen, electricians, grips, prop men) assembling on the pier, listless and muttering. The one hundred Navy extras were climbing out of shore boats eager for movie excitement. I said a few words to the crews—the Navy boys listened in with avid interest:

"Gentlemen, Mr. Harry Cohn has ordered me, as of this morning, to take over this company as director and producer. I didn't ask for the job. But now I'm here, and I'm asking for your cooperation. For anyone that feels he can't cooperate, there's a studio bus ready to take you to town. But if you decide to stay, and I hope you will, understand this: I'm going to shoot everything over again. That'll put us far behind in time and cost. I want to make it up. When I give an order, don't walk—run. We're going to shoot long hours, and fast—and *good*. The first set-up is on the end of the pier. Two cameras: a thirty-five millimeter lens and a four-inch. Cameras will pan the shore boat, containing Mr. Holt and Mr. Graves, from the battleships to the dock. Watch the focus on the four-inch. Details later. That's all, thank you."

Glumly and slowly, the crews began unlimbering their equipment. As I turned to Buddy Coleman, a loud, juicy, Brooklyn "raspberry" ripped the silence, followed by suppressed tittering. The Navy men looked at each other, surprised at the crude lack of respect. The god of directors was with me. Frank Fay's famous retort—to a heckler's Bronx "cheer" from the balcony—flashed through my mind. Pointing a finger in the direction of the heckler, I said: "Two of those made you, friend." The crews stopped tittering, but the sailors howled. I had won the Navy, and perhaps, the crews. No one left on the bus.

Now for the main event—Holt and Graves. I asked Coleman for Holt's room number, then told him: "Buddy, borrow two well-worn shore-leave uniforms from the Navy boys that will fit Holt and Graves. Oh, and ask George Rhein, the prop man, to get a box of licorice, and—"

"Did you say licorice? What for?"

"Tell you later. And get some BB shot to spit through your teeth—you know. Bring it all to me in Holt's room."

"Check. Frank, you want a laugh? Briskin called to ask if you had any problems."

"Call Briskin back and say: no problems. We start shooting exactly at eight o'clock."

"Not with Holt and Graves, you won't. They've been screaming to Harry Cohn on the phone all morning."

"*With* Holt and Graves."

"But not without make-up. They kicked me out when I mentioned it."

"*Without* make-up."

I went to Holt's door. Graves had the adjacent room. A small army waited outside the doors: hairdressers gingerly combing hairpieces; wardrobe men with meticulously pressed uniforms and mirror-shined shoes; make-up men, each with his devil's box of greasepaints. I gave them a disgusted look. Through Holt's door I could hear an angry voice. I knocked.

"Come in!" I entered.

Jack Holt, as livid as his gray dressing gown, sat scrunched over a phone with his back to me, trying to out-shout the voice on the receiver. Pajama-clad Ralph Graves stood in the doorway between rooms, listening on another phone. I waved to Graves. Seeing me, he quickly turned to Holt. "Jack? Oh, Jack?" But Holt was beyond interrupting his hell-giving on the phone.

"But wait—*wait!* Harry, will you wait just *one-goddam-minute?* I *know* it's your money—but it's *my career.* And I am *not* trusting it to that insolent nincompoop you sent down to replace Willat. Yes, *insolent.* Know the first word he sent us? 'No make-up on the actors—and that's an order.' Why that son-of-a— No, Harry. It's final. I'm walking off the picture."

Down smashed the phone. "YES?" he asked harshly, spotting me in the room.

"Mr. Holt, I beg your pardon for intruding. I'm Frank Capra."

"That's perfect. Now I can say it to your face. I'm leaving this picture."

"Mr. Holt, if you're walking off because of my presence here, please don't. I'll *run* off this show before I see you do that. I see you gentlemen have had breakfast. May I have a cup of your leftover coffee? I've been up all night."

"Sure, Frank," said Graves, pouring me some coffee. Holt listened, stone-faced.

"Last night I was out with a beautiful girl—at Grauman's Chinese, in my first tux—when I get a call from Cohn—and eight hours later, here I am in San Pedro, *annoying* everybody—and having a cup of your nice coffee. Mr. Holt, this isn't the first drink I've had off you. That's right. About ten years ago, a bunch of us seniors from Caltech were in a rathskeller on Spring Street, slopping up beer. When *you* came in, Mr. Holt, in a beautiful white dinner coat—tall, handsome, with a gorgeous girl on your arm. Mr. Holt, we college punks just gaped. You had to be the finest-looking man we ever saw—and without make-up. We were so envious and so full of beer, that we took turns walking back of your chair, muttering adolescent threats. Man that you were, you refused to notice puerile punks. Back at our table we beat our sophomoric chests and bragged that the so-and-so wouldn't fight. Then a waiter walked up to our table. 'Boys,' he said, 'compliments of Mr. Jack Holt. He wishes to buy you college gentlemen a drink.'

"Mr. Holt, you've been a hero of mine ever since—that is, up to midnight last night, I mean: when I saw two reels of this picture, *Submarine*. Mr. Holt, in those scenes you weren't the *man*—the proud, champion Navy diver—able to dive deeper than any other man in the world! No. In that greasepaint, with that hairpiece, wearing that pressed, dandified uniform, you looked to me like a veteran chorus man—masquerading as a Navy diver.

"I took this assignment, Mr. Holt, in the hope that I could make you look like *real* Navy—without greasepaint, no hairpieces, no pressed uniforms—but with a wad of tobacco in that hard cheek, and the love and hates of a champion in that diver's heart. I ask both you gentlemen to accept a challenge: Put yourself completely in my hands for this one day. I will put a rush order on the film we shoot. If you are not satisfied when you see it, just say: 'Sorry, bub'—and I will fold my tent and silently scram. Are you game?"

"Seems fair to me," Graves answered. "I'm willing. Aren't you, Jack?"

"Well . . . I don't know . . ."

There was a knock on the door. "Come in!" I said. "That's Buddy Coleman." Buddy came in with the uniforms and props.

"Gentlemen," I said, "put on these *real* uniforms the Navy boys wear. I'll wait. And come as you are—no make-up. We have ten minutes to make the first shot. And Jack, here's some licorice to simulate the wad of tobacco in your cheek. Ralph, here's some BB shot to spit through your teeth at Jack's neck in the shore boat. I'll explain on the set. Hurry."

All eyes on the end of the pier were as big as saucers as they see Buddy, me, and the two stars—without make-up—hurrying down the pier toward the cameras. Cagey Coleman got an idea. He ran on ahead of us and quietly tipped off the Navy extras to applaud as we approached. The applause and cheers softened old flint-faced Holt. He was the champion Navy diver, as he smiled, chewed a big wad of licorice—and stepped into his seat in the shore boat. We got our first shot at five minutes past the hour of eight.

Around noontime, Sam Briskin arrived expecting chaos. Never was an executive so pleased. I asked him to stay with me, to take all production details—money, sets, locations—off my hands; so I could concentrate on script and shooting—to try to make up the three lost weeks. The Vice President of Columbia became my unit manager.

The rushes arrived early next morning. Holt and Graves saw them together in the theater. Holt found me setting up a camera shot in a shore boat. From the top of the pier he shouted: "Bub! Don't fold your tent."

During the shooting of *Submarine* I played Jack Holt a real dirty trick in the interests of realism. We were on the deck of the aircraft carrier *Saratoga*, commanded by Captain King (later five-star Admiral King, head of the Joint Chiefs of Staff). Holt, the only diver with a chance, was to be flown in one of the *Saratoga*'s aircraft, to the site of the stricken submarine—now lying on the sea bottom—its crew, including Graves, in the last stages of agonizing suffocation. Once there, he would make a desperate, four-hundred-foot dive (never done before) to attach a lifegiving air hose to the sub.

Everything was ready for the take-off—cameras, pilot, plane, crews to guide the plane down the deck. Holt was in the ready room putting on a parachute. He sent for me. He was ashen with fear.

"Frank—in the strictest confidence—I have a terrible phobia about flying. I'm scared to death of planes."

"What?!" I was so mad at this big he-man I wanted to choke him.

"It's in my *contract* with every picture: No flying under *any* circumstances. Now this plane I'm getting into is *not taking off*! Understand?"

I squirmed. I had a long focus lens following him in a close-up, down the runway and through the lift-off to *prove* to audiences it *was* Holt—and not a double. To hell with Holt. The picture came first. He was going to fly *this* time.

"Oh, no, Jack. The pilot will just taxi with you out of camera range—then stop. We'll use a *double* for the actual take-off."

He grabbed a handful of my coat and hoarsely threatened: "No double-crossing. Understand?"

"Come on, Jack. Of course not. Get in the plane."

Shaking like a leaf, Holt climbed into the rear cockpit. Navy men strapped him in. With arm signals I told the pilot to take off, circle, land in the water, and come back alongside—as *planned*. CAMERAS! ACTION!

The amphibian roared, rolled, picked up speed—and took off. There goes Holt on his first flight! The cameraman gave me the "okay" sign. I got myself ready for a stiff punch in the nose. The plane circled and landed in the water. A huge crane would lift it back on the flight deck. As the amphibian taxied alongside the carrier, I gave Holt the "okay" sign. His eyes were like black holes in a white mask. He doubled up a fist and showed me what he was going to do with it. That set me to thinking.

Captain King and all his staff had watched the take-off. I ran over to them.

"Captain King, you might like to know that Jack Holt has an *uncontrollable* fear of planes. But he insisted on flying for this picture. That's his first flight, Captain. I wonder if you'd congratulate him, sir. It would make him feel just great."

"Well, what do you know? His first flight, boys. Congratulate him? Why, we'll do better than—Mac? Bring me a pair of honorary wings . . ."

As Holt stepped off the plane that had been swung aboard, Captain King and his staff surrounded him, slapped his back, shook his hand—and the Captain pinned wings on him—to commemorate his first flight. Holt's white face suffused into a proud pink. When he caught up with me he said, under his breath: "You son-of-a-bitch." But he said it like the Virginian told Trampas to say it—with a smile.

When we ran the rough cut of *Submarine*, there was a hole in the film big enough to ram a destroyer through—no underwater rescue. It cried for scenes of the stricken sub at the bottom of the sea and of the diver's four-hundred-foot dive with the air hose. But Columbia had no experts on miniatures or trick photography, and Cohn would give me no money to hire them. "Use your *verstand*, Dago," he said.

Walking through the prop department for ideas, I stumbled on a large glass case—about 4 feet square by 3 high. The glass was dirty and scratched —obviously an ancient aquarium. Cleaned and filled with water, one could barely see through it.

"What we need is clear plate glass and filtered water," said Joe Walker the cameraman. "This glass is plain, wavy window glass. It distorts; and the tap water is murky."

"I know, Joe. But it's a start," I said, scratching my head.

I haunted the toy shops for a small submarine. Nothing—until I looked over the junk in the corner drugstore. Selah! a toy submarine—about two feet long.

"How much?" I asked the clerk.

"I dunno. Been there for years. Half a buck too much?"

I bought it. We put some sand in the aquarium, filled it with tap water, laid the toy sub on the sand, turned on some lights—and photographed it. On the screen it looked just like what it was—a toy sub in a dirty aquarium. But there was a mysteriousness to the murky water. Perhaps a very small diver would give the illusion of size. No toy divers anywhere. But in the nickel "claw machine" at the corner drugstore, I saw a little metal diver, about two and a half inches high, with helmet and all!

By operating the claw from outside the glass bowl, one tried to "claw up" a visible goodie, such as a comb, a pen, a chocolate bar. But mostly you came up with a gum drop for your nickel. After wasting a pocketful of nickels, I clawed out my little pewter diver. He looked so cute and real, I kissed him. Little Jack Holt.

Now. How do you make bubbles come out of his helmet? I wasn't a chemical engineer for nothing. Pure sodium in contact with water will produce bubbles of gas. I drilled a small hole part way into little Jack's helmet, stuffed the hole full of the soft metal sodium, and held the toy under water. A stream of bubbles floated up out of the helmet!

By attaching air hoses and lifelines to the tiny toy and shooting the lowering of the five-cent diver to the fifty-cent sub in ultra slow motion—the wavy glass, the unfiltered water, the bubbles, and the convection currents generated by the heat of the lights produced an unearthly illusion of eeriness—the lonely, mysterious murky depths of the restless sea. Not all the plate glass and filtered water in the world could have produced such a ghostly, awe-inspiring, dramatic illusion.

Submarine was released about September 1, 1928—ten months after I entered Columbia Studio. It was a solid hit, playing extensive runs in first-run theaters. The proud Torch Lady was almost all out of water. Columbia's earnings rose from $.81 per share in 1927, to $1.75 in 1928—Harry Cohn's personal stock soared into the higher brackets. He took—and deserved—all credit for the success of his hunch to change directors. It consolidated his "one-man rule" over his partners. He could now call moguls like Jack Warner and Louis B. Mayer, and sometimes they would answer—although he *still* had to get on the phone *first*. Harry's finest hour would come later—when *they* had to get on the phone first. Heaven hath no greater glory.

Orally, he thanked me in derailed English: "You little schlemiel—you know what? You coulda made a *bum* outta me, that's what." But, financially, he got back on the track—tearing up my unfinished one-year contract at five hundred dollars per week and offering a straight three-year contract at fifteen hundred dollars per week. Again I signed without reading the contract. When you've got a good thing going, why fool around with it?

CHAPTER 6

The Sound and the Fury

ON THE HISTORIC night of October 23, 1927, Al Jolson's shadow sang from the silver screen. The sound waves of "Mammy" were as devastating as seismic waves. A major earthquake rocked the film world. The silent screen had grown a larynx! Hollywood shook. The inmates took over the asylum.

Volumes could be written about the comedy and the tragedy of sound; the careers it destroyed, those it made. For one thing, it killed pantomime just as it was flowering into great art. For another, the black magic of science began overruling the hunches of showmen. How did Harry Cohn take to sound? With the same fear all Hollywood faced the terrors of the unknown. One dividend for me: my knowledge awed Cohn. He stopped calling me Dago. Not that it mattered. Or maybe it did, some, because I never could call anyone a "Mick," a "Spick," or a "Shine."

"My New York guys say we gotta make all *talkies* now, Frank," he'd moan. "Gimme that science crap about sound again, will ya, Frank?" Sound had no particular terror for me because, paradoxically, what you know well doesn't frighten, and that about which you know nothing at all doesn't either. The least worried are the knowledgeable and the ignorant. Clyde Beatty knew and mastered man-eating "cats"; children play on the backs of man-charging water buffalo. I knew sound, but was blithely ignorant about directing stage actors speaking dialogue.

Not only was I ignorant of all things theatrical, I was also contemptuous of their phoniness. I was raised in my own "school" of naturalness—I had yet to see a top director work. *My* stage was the real world, and the actors had to appear just as real. I considered the camera—and, now, the microphone—as a ubiquitous phantom eavesdropper on the comic or tragic goings-on of people, especially of the outsized characters I had met, loved, and studied in my early wanderings.

I had yet to learn the power of creative art; that Leonardo, seeing with an inner eye, could, with simple brush and canvas, evoke a bewitching smile on Mona Lisa that no all-seeing lens could "see"; that the Psalmist's powerful imagery in nine single-syllable words, "Be still then, and know that I am God," was worth more than ten thousand pictures. Moreover, I was not yet aware that the art of the stage was in its limitations; that its make-believe gave wings to the imagination, making the stage one of the most enduring, beguiling, inspiring, and socially incisive of all the arts.

With a fine cast: Jean Hersholt, Ricardo Cortez, Lena Basquette, and Rosa Rosanova, we made Fannie Hurst's play—*It Is to Laugh*—about a social-climbing super-Jew who denied his parents—into a half-talkie film. We called it *The Younger Generation*. The first half we shot silent at Columbia, the second half in sound at a "sound stage" on Santa Monica Boulevard, somewhere. While many big shots mulled about sound, or tried exorcising it with incantations of "fad!" "won't sell!" some sharpie wangled priorities in sound equipment, hung horse blankets on the walls of a "barn," and had himself a rental sound stage with customers waiting in line.

Shooting your first sound picture was an étude in chaos. First of all, no one was used to being quiet. Shooting of silent scenes had gone on with hammering and sawing on an adjacent set, the director yelling at actors through a megaphone, cameramen shouting "Dim the overheads!" . . . "Slower on the dolly!" . . . while everybody howled if the scene was funny.

Suddenly, with sound, we had to work in the silence of a tomb. When the red lights went on, everyone froze in his position—a cough or a belch would wreck the scene. It was like a quick switch from a bleacher seat at Ebbett's Field to a box seat at a Wimbledon tennis match. To the nervous snit of the non-stage silent actors—over having to memorize lines for the first time—the funereal hush added the willies. They shook with stage fright.

Then there were the cameras. In the silence they whirred like ancient sewing machines—some rat-tat-tatted like the pieces of cardboard kids fixed against the spokes of their bicycle wheels. To kill the camera noise, our wonderful mobile, moving cameras were mummified and entombed in thick padded booths—a soundproof window in the front, a padded door in the back. Of course, the cameraman was stuffed into the booth *with* his camera, and, of course, he couldn't hear a blessed thing about what was going on outside. But who cared about hearing when he was suffocating? There was more air inside the cameraman's lungs than there was in the booth. A two-minute stay in that padded vault and he was ready for the oxygen tent.

Our sound cameraman was Ben Reynolds—a five-and-a-half foot, three-hundred-pound veteran of the silents. He looked like a whisky barrel walking on two fire plugs. One shouldn't expect to see a neck on that build—but it *was* startling not to see his ears. Ben could sleep upright sitting on a stool, which he did regularly for ten-second intervals while you talked to him, after which he would open his eyes and ask, "What'd you say?"

Well, it took two huskies to shove Big Ben into the airless booth and sit him next to his camera, but it took half a dozen to pull him out. As soon as the camera-start bell rang, and his booth barred shut, Ben went peacefully to sleep. It didn't matter much to the scene because his camera was pre-set and locked into position. But it meant Ben's life to get him out in a hurry at the *end* of the scene—and snatching three hundred pounds of limp, stuck flesh out of that hot box wasn't easy.

After much fanning, Ben would open his eyes and say, "All right, fellas, I'm ready. Let's shoot the scene."

Then, too, there were the hellish, hot lights—with sound, hotter than the hinges of. Silent films ran through the cameras—and projectors—at a speed of sixteen frames per second; actors on the screen moved normally. But sound-track film was speeded up to *twenty-four* frames per second through the sound recorders. That meant *camera* film had to run at twenty-four frames through the synchronized cameras—50 percent faster than in silents. (That is why old silent films—shot at sixteen frames per second, but now projected at twenty-four frames—look so fast and jerky.) But speeding up the film demanded about twice as much light exposure on the actors, which generally meant about three times as much heat. Already sweating from the new excitement of speaking lines, the poor actors just melted. Sweat-soaked clothes were changed almost hourly.

But these were small annoyances. The *big* gremlin was the new Wizard of Oz, with his awesome earphones plugged into black boxes of magic—the *sound* man.

Our sound man *seemed* to be a level-headed, non-flappable technician— that is, until he started twiddling the dials on his "mixing" panel during a scene. Then he became unsoldered. Time after time, during a scene, he would push the "cut" bell button, then rush in to bawl out the actors.

"No! No! No! How many times do I have to tell you, Mr. Hersholt, you've got to talk directly into this mike in the flowerpot. You can't turn away and look at Mr. Cortez. And you can't talk between this mike and the one hidden in the desk drawer until you *get there* . . ."

At first I tried to reason, even humor him—then I had to lower the boom. "See here, sound man. Don't you dare stop another scene unless I tell you to. And don't *ever* walk into that set and talk to actors. Is that understood?"

"But you don't want bad *sound*, do you?"

"I've got a bigger 'don't want'—bad *scenes*. Now, you'll solve your problems if you keep all the mikes open—"

"But there'll be echoes, reverberations—the manual says so—"

"Not enough to matter. Just *try* it my way. Keep all mikes open, set all the dials, then keep your fingers *off* all of them—"

"But I've *got* to use the dials—to lower the loud words and bring up the soft ones."

"No, that's the *last*—never mind. Let's take the scene."

Slowly, link by link, chain by chain, the shackles of sound—that had set back filmmaking thirty years—were removed. Eastman Kodak researchers came up with faster emulsions needing far less light—the actors were freed from unbearable heat. The cumbersome microphones hidden all over the set—with dead spots in between—were replaced with one sensitive mike on the end of an overhead movable boom, which followed actors everywhere, freeing them from static immobility. The Mitchell Camera people made a "silent" camera usable *outside* that prehistoric "fixed" monstrosity—the camera booth. May it rust in pieces. Once more the camera was as free as a bird; Ben Reynolds was not doomed to drown in his own air.

And it certainly freed the director. When the kinks were ironed out, sound gave him the additional, magnificent tools of dialogue, sound effects, and *music*! Now we could put our *own* music on the picture sound track rather than depend on the random, "individual scoring" of eccentric organ players, player pianos, or barroom ivory ticklers.

Selecting background music for the first time was a thrilling forward step. Just one year and seven pictures ago I had been a discouraged two-time "loser" back in Sennett's Tower. Now I was putting the haunting themes from Anton Dvorak's *New World Symphony* into a talking picture —which, by the way, I think we "stole" from a symphonic record. For me, sound was lagniappe from the "Three Princes of Serendip." But what was it to be for my old boss Mack Sennett? Sound opened an ink bottle, and out came a powerful genie—the animated cartoon!

In his delightful book about Mack Sennett, Gene Fowler said finis to the Golden Age of Comedy in two cryptic lines:

Who killed Cock Robin?
"I did," said Mickey Mouse.

With the release (March, 1929) of the half-talkie *The Younger Generation*, "word" infiltrated major studio parapets that because of my science background I had handled sound like an expert. And because, at that odd time, a science background was more in demand than Garbo's Swedish accent, offers from other companies to "borrow" me were brought to Harry Cohn— and what sweet music they were to his ears. Normally, they wouldn't ask him the time of day. "Not available," Cohn proclaimed to the trade papers. "Capra will make nothing but 'specials' for Columbia from now on. Our stock is listed on the Big Board now—and going up fast." Let me add here that, to the major studios, Columbia "specials" were about on a par with the Blue-Plate specials the majors dished up at their extras' lunch counter.

The next "special" we looked for would have to be confined to interior sets—because our cameras were still entombed in those god-awful fixed camera booths. We chose a play—Owen Davis's whodunit, *The Donovan Affair*—in which nearly all of the action took place in one big house. And who asked to play the lead part of the detective? That old granite face right out of a Grant Wood painting—Jack Holt. And who knocked on dressing room doors and said "No make-up!" to Buster Collier, Jr., Wheeler Oakman, Eddie Hearn, Hank Mann, and Fred Kelsey? Correct: Jack Holt! Jack and I had become good friends. The rock-ribbed native and one of the "huddled masses yearning to breathe free" had found a common bond—love of America. Besides, I had removed a thorn from his psyche: his fear of flying.

In 1929 two history-making events took place—each involving an egg: Wall Street laid one; all the Muses got together to hatch one. During the shooting of *The Donovan Affair* at a rental sound studio, George Seid, Columbia's exuberant laboratory man, buttonholed me, bursting with excitement about a piece of film he insisted I see that night after the rushes.

"You've got to see this," he said, "it's like nothing you've ever seen before!"

That night, after shooting past dinnertime, my crew and I dragged our tired tails around the corner to a hole-in-the-wall projection room to see the previous day's work. Seid was waiting, eyes sparkling.

"Frank, meet Walt—" I didn't get the last name of the scrawny, nondescript, hungry-looking young man, wearing a two days' growth of beard and a slouch cap, who stood up and said, "Hi!"

At the end of our rushes I was so tired I got up to leave. Seid pushed me back into my seat. "Frank, you *promised* to see this man's film."

"Oh, yeah! Okay, but please hurry it up."

When the lights dimmed again I started to close my eyes, but as the picture flashed on the screen I opened them wide as saucers. This was something *new*—an animated cartoon! A bright, perky mouse—with a saucy, squeaky voice—was burlesquing a piano recital, banging on the piano with his hands, his feet, his nose, even with his tail. And picture and sound were beautifully synchronized. The tired crew howled with laughter. This was new and wonderful entertainment. As I remember, the cartoon was only four or five minutes long. But when it was over I forgot my fatigue and plied the trampish-looking man with excited questions. He answered them humbly:

"Yes, I was a cartoonist in Chicago . . . No, this mouse character is a new creation . . . I call him Mickey Mouse . . . No, that's my voice he talks with . . . No, we record the sound first, then time the animation to it . . . Yes, I'll be happy to have you show it to Harry Cohn . . ."

"For chrissake, it's just a lousy cartoon," grumbled Cohn when the film started.

"Lousy, hell—it's terrific! You'll flip . . ."

Cohn more than flipped. He called in the hungry-looking cartoonist and wheeled and dealed him into a contract to produce *Silly Symphonies* for Columbia release.

A genius was born—Walt Disney. But Disney the man-child and Cohn the vulgarian spoke different languages. Cohn mistook sensitivity for weakness.

Crudely, and stupidly, he badgered and bulldozed until he lost Hollywood's richest gold mine. The man-child took his enchanting films to RKO for distribution. And later, as all true geniuses must, Walt established his own production and distribution set-up. The modern wonder of Disney's magic flowered. The world and its children smiled.

It was *sound* that made Disney's wizardry possible. What Gutenberg's printing press did for the written word in the fifteenth century, sound did for the spoken word in the twentieth century: Actors' voices, music, and sound effects were stored or "canned" on film emulsions—later on magnetic tape—to be recalled and reproduced at will for hundreds of millions in the world's movie theaters.

In *The Donovan Affair* I again experimented, mixing comedy with another "sure-fire" ingredient—a whodunit. It worked beautifully, critically and commercially. Making *The Donovan Affair*, I believe, was the beginning of a true understanding of the skills of my craft: how to make the mechanics —lighting, microphone, camera—serve and be subject to the actors; how to ease the tensions of performers, calm their "butterflies." A style of my own began to jell—comedy in all things. Laughter was the disarmer, the friend maker. Entertain them, and audiences would accept most anything.

And making *The Donovan Affair* also marked the beginning of a secret ambition that would soon aggravate into a manic obsession: win the Academy Award for best film director. In 1929 the Academy membership consisted mainly of important Brahmins under contract to major studios. They had all the votes. Winning an Oscar in Poverty Row would be as easy as telling the sex of a fly. Nevertheless, I would have an Oscar on *my* mantelpiece, or bust.

Cohn, too, had a strong, personal ambition: to break into the elite inner circle of major studio Rajahs who had the production and distribution— and, in some cases also the exhibition—of films sewed up tight. Outsiders could feed on the crumbs from their lucrative table, but if they tried to muscle in for a "seat" they were thrown out through unopened doors. Nevertheless, Cohn was determined to crash the feast of the majors. He used me as his battering ram. I used his ambition to get control of my films.

But there was *one* control on which Cohn stood like Gibraltar: No Columbia director *could order more than one "take" printed* of any scene, regardless of how *many* takes the director had shot. This saved film raw stock costs, of course, but it gave the director a problem. Having, say, shot a scene five times (takes 1 to 5), he could circle only *one* take number for printing and viewing. Remembering the shadings and nuances of five different takes of the same scene is difficult without viewing them on the screen. Likely as not the director would circle an inferior take for printing, leaving the best to be forever locked in film vaults.

I couldn't budge Cohn on this, but I managed to outwit him, and in doing so I stumbled upon a most valuable directing tool. Take numbers—on slates—are photographed at the beginning of each take. Without stopping the

That Certain Thing, my first Columbia film—written, produced, and directed for $1,000. Story: disowned son and plebeian fiancee bring crusty rich father (chain restaurant owner) to his knees by inventing the box lunch. The girl (Viola Dana) and boy (Ralph Graves) show the boy's whipped father (Burr McIntosh) their box lunch factory. Aggie Herring looks on.

An early Columbia, So *This Love*, with Shirley Mason an Buster Collier (seated).

"Harry Cohn, I want nothing from you but complete and total control of my films—"

The Younger Generation, a story about a social-climbing Jew who disowns his parents (Jean Hersholt and Rosa Rosanova), who have toiled and starved to educate him. Shown here—Rex Lease and Lina Basquette.

The Donovan Affair (from a play by Owen Davis), my first all-talkie. A whodunit, starring Jack Holt, Dorothy Revier, and William Collier, Jr., and featuring John Roche, Agnes Ayers, Alphonse Ethier, Edward Hearn, Wheeler Oakman, Ethel Wales, Hank Mann, and Fred Kelsey. Shown here: Alphonse Ethier and Jack Holt.

camera I would quickly call back the actors to redo the scene once, twice, five times—*and all on one take number*! Now I could not only screen five *separate versions* of the scene (without breaking studio rules), but I also saved about twenty minutes of shooting time it would have taken to photograph five *separate takes* of the scene. Cohn screamed out of habit. But he had no rejoinder to my bland reminder, "Time costs more than film, Harry."

And, interestingly enough, this maneuver brought out *better performances* from the actors. Invariably, between takes, the "powder-and-comb brigade" would swarm onto the set like locusts to preen and polish the actors. Invariably, cameramen tinkered with lights, sound men repositioned microphones, prop men shifted the furniture, and someone told a long, stale joke—all of which caused actors to lose the mood of the scene.

But now, when I ordered, "Keep the cameras *running*! Come back in, *everybody*—do the scene over again!" the surprised actors had no chance to lose the mood. In the excitement of running to take their places they lost their superficial aplomb. By the third replay of the scene they began sweating, mussing their hair, rumpling their clothes. Gone were the well-curried store-window "dummies"—forgotten the minutiae of cues, direction of looks, position tapes on the floor, which was their "best" facial side. They became real human beings playing real scenes—and *believing* it. This is exactly what every director tries hardest to achieve.

Long after I became important enough to order a *dozen* takes printed, I still ran actors back and forth redoing a scene several times without a camera break—especially when dealing with stylized or "wooden" performers. As far as I know, I have been the only director to use this unorthodox method of "upsetting" actors into better performances.

New Year's Day, 1929, Harry Cohn and I attended one of the great shows of our time—the Rose Bowl Game. California was playing Georgia Tech before some ninety thousand rabid fans. Late in the game, with California leading 7 to 6, Georgia Tech fumbled deep in its own territory. In the wild scramble, a California lineman, Roy Riegles, picked up the fumble, became confused, and took off like a charging rhino for his *own* goal line. Ninety thousand shouted, "You're going the wrong way!" California's fleet backs raced to overtake their runaway lineman. But the mighty roar of the crowd put wings on Riegles's lumbering feet. With a last supreme effort he shook off a tackler and plunged into paydirt to score a safety, two big points—and win the Rose Bowl Game for *Georgia Tech*!

Half the crowd booed, "Oh you idiot!" The other half moaned, "Oh, the poor guy." In the excitement I shouted to Harry Cohn, "That guy goes into my next picture—'wrong-way' Riegles—he'll never live it down . . ."

Ralph Graves and I had been working on another Holt-Graves opus to follow up *Submarine*. I told Graves about "wrong-way" Riegles. Graves lit up. "That's the story of my life. Let's open *Flight* with it." And that gave us the plot for *Flight*, a story of Marine Corps flyers.

The plot wasn't new, but the flying was spectacular. The Marine Corps put all the facilities and personnel of their Marine Base at North Island, San Diego, at our complete disposal—including a squadron of nine Curtis fighter bombers, two-seater open-cockpit jobs with a machine gun in the nose, another for a rear gunner, and half a dozen trippable small bombs attached to the fuselage. The pilots were the crack hot-shots of the Marine Flying Corps, including Lieutenant Bill Williams and Lieutenant Jerry Jerome— later Major General Williams and Lieutenant General Jerome.

Our cameras, freed from their padded isolation booths, now literally took wing for the aerial photography in *Flight*. We had no "process shots" then, no trick photography in which actors are photographed in studio planes against aerial backgrounds. We got our air shots the hard way, and as the rear gunner, Jack Holt took the heftiest punishment. To blast away with his machine gun he had to stand up in the rear cockpit exposed to the fury of the prop wash—which pushed his facial features into a contorted, quivering, gargoylish mess back where his ears should be. And pulling up out of sharp dives overloaded his shaky legs with three G's—three times his own weight. Yes, indeed. Jack had lost all fear of flying—except on one occasion. It made me sure he had regressed to his phobia.

We needed some close-ups of Holt standing up in the cockpit, firing his machine gun. He was in one plane; Elmer Dyer—a no-nerve aerial cameraman who would hang by his toes on a wing to get a shot—was in the camera plane; I was in the director's plane. Leaving North Island we flew around San Diego County looking for rocky, wild hills that might pass for Nicaragua. We found them in the foothills above La Mesa. After several rehearsal runs—to position the planes below the tops of the hills—we dove down for the shooting run. I signaled, "Camera!" to Elmer Dyer, and waved at Jack Holt to stand up and fire.

All I could see of Jack was his little head sticking out of the cockpit—it was shaking a vociferous NO!! I waved back, "Get up! Get up!" "No! No!" he shook back. I got his pilot's attention, gestured to him to make Holt stand up. The pilot turned to Jack, motioning him to rise. Jack shook his head. No talking was possible in that noise and wind that flapped his face from side to side. The pilot turned to me and shrugged. The hills had gone by us. We pulled up and wheeled for another shooting pass. This time I unhitched my safety belt from the sitting to standing position. I stood up, waved my hands, sang, danced—did everything but stand on my head to show Jack "it was nothing!" His head was on a swivel. It never stopped shaking "No!"

Disgusted, I waved all planes back to base. "If that yellow so-and-so has gone chicken again," I thought to myself, "we're sunk." My plane landed first at North Island. I was *waiting* for Holt, as his plane pulled up alongside ours on the ramp, waiting to blast him with every dirty name I could think of. Holt jumped out of the plane white-faced and trembling. Behind him he was trailing a tail of yards and yards of white parachute silk. Walking up to me, speechless, he showed me his hands. They were frozen stiff in a clutching position—the insides of his fingers cut and bleeding!

Just before our photographic run he had rehearsed pulling the parachute pull ring on his chest. He rehearsed too hard. The chute he was sitting on popped *open*. White silk fluttered below. Grabbing the edges of the metal seat with both his hands, he "sat" on the popped chute with a death grip—and shook his head violently against orders to "stand up!" Had but a few inches of that fluttering silk flicked up into the prop blast, the parachute would have ripped Holt out of the cockpit and smashed him to death against the aircraft's tail. The whole Marine Base gave Jack a "well done!" party. And we tied a red ribbon on Holt's pull ring whenever he flew again.

Anyone who thinks making movies is all glamour and fun would be rudely disenchanted if he had to spend a rugged week on location with a picture like *Flight*. He would experience nothing but grime and sweat, tormenting physical hardships, a back-breaking schedule of eighteen hours a day, and the nerve-racking battle of logistical planning against time. Our day started at dawn: an hour and a half's ride to our jungle location in the back country, the assembling of a Marine battalion, and hundreds of "Nicaraguans" —local Digger Indians from Ramona, St. Ysabel, and Pala—and the landing of a squadron of planes on the jungle landing strip.

Then a full day's shooting of guerrilla warfare: hand-to-hand combat, rifle fire, bombs, strafing by planes. After dark, back to the Coronado Hotel, dog-tired and ready to drop. At 8 P.M., dinner with all the key people. Between bites a hundred details: wardrobe, film, cars, lunches, extras, planes, Marines, Navy, complaints, injuries, sickness, weather. After dinner, written schedules for actors, crews, and military—when and where to be with what and whom tomorrow. At 11 P.M., all key people hopped into company cars, took the ferry to San Diego, and entered a local theater—right after the last show—to see our film rushes: yesterday's work. Then back to our cars, racing to make the last ferry to Coronado. One A.M.—to bed. Six A.M.— up and at 'em for another day's grind. Was this any way to make a picture? You bet it was. We loved it—and I had a very special reason for loving *Flight*.

One midnight, after seeing our rushes in the San Diego theater, the crews left for Coronado while I stayed on to see a film test of a new actor Harry Cohn was interested in. My assistant, Buddy Coleman; his wife Alyce, a fun-loving, freckle-faced French gal; and a girl friend of hers saw the test with me. Leaving the theater we found two company cars waiting for us.

"Frank, we're too late for the ferry," said Buddy. "We'll have to go round the bay and drive up the Silver Strand. Why don't you take Lucille with you?"

I looked at Lucille. She was a smallish, attractive, exquisitely dressed young lady with short, dark hair and perky bangs on her forehead.

"Hi, Lucille. I'm Frank Capra. Think you could stand riding with me the long way round?"

"Oh, I'd love it. My name's Lucille Reyburn." What a lovely voice, I thought—and what lovely ankles as she stepped into the car. Coronado was just a couple of miles across the bay, but now we had to go thirty miles to get there. But there was a full moon—and this gentle, sweet-smelling young lady sitting next to me.

"Old friend of Alyce's, are you?"

"Yes. We went to Berkeley together."

"You—just get down here today?"

"Oh, no." She chuckled. "I've been here with Alyce for a week now."

"You've been here a *week*? How come I haven't seen you?"

"I don't know. I've had dinner with you every night."

"Dinner with me?"

"Well, not exactly with you, Mr. Capra—at your table, with many others."

"I don't believe a word of it, and the name is Frank, and I would have noticed a lovely girl like you in a mob scene."

"Thank you."

"Thank you what?"

She looked up at me curiously, enigmatically—then she smiled. "Thank you—Frank." My heart began to pound.

It was beautiful—unearthly beautiful—driving up that sliver of white sand between the quiet bay and the restless surf. We were alone in an unreal world—our car was a cloud floating in the moonlight. I held her hand. On her side the full moon was mirrored on the bay, so close it unrolled a shimmering, welcome-aboard carpet of moonlight right up to our car, inviting us to walk to the moon. On my side the surf rose, curled, broke into long traceries of rolling phosphorescence, and spread over the sands in delicate patterns of foamy moonlight.

I walked her through the bougainvillea-scented grounds of the Coronado Hotel, that nostalgia-rich spa built by Stanford White—its moonlit towers and flutings "alternately seemed framed of ebony and ivory." I walked her to her door. I kissed her. I knew. She knew. A romance began that has lasted thirty-eight years.

Flight opened at the George M. Cohan Theater in New York in September, 1929. Harry Cohn was so sure he had a hit he defied superstition and opened it on Friday the thirteenth. He was so proud, he copied the big hoopla openings of the major studios: searchlights, crowds, Navy bands, marching Marines, V.I.P.'s, and—in person—the stars, Holt and Graves, and the director. For the first time, all of New York's important critics came to see one of my pictures. Well, to my utter confusion, some burned incense to it, others threw stink bombs—or, as Winchell might say—orchids and onions.

What was the name of the game with these double domes? Was *Flight* a good picture, or a poor one? From the reviews, you pays your nickel for a paper and takes your choice. It was my first inkling that among the upper reaches of criticism there was disaccord—just as there had been among the Olympian gods. The "immortals" were as mortal as fishwives.

Well, until I became more sophisticated, I would just put my faith in the combined appraisals of the commoners who saw my films—the audiences. I'd read what the gods wrote, but I would listen to what mortals said. After all, there were more of us.

Arriving back in Hollywood, Harry Cohn remained glued to the telephone listening to rosy bulletins of *Flight*'s box-office figures—and to rosier tidings from his stock broker. The "market fever" ran rampant in Hollywood. Top executives installed ticker-tape machines in their offices; secretaries relayed the latest gyrations to the shops and stages. The virus hit the working stiffs. Extras pooled their dimes and dollars and plunged for a few shares on margin. Studio lunchrooms turned into shouting marts; boasting "bulls" bellowed their profits. Pet stocks were touted; few knew whether the firms made peanut butter or pile drivers—and nobody cared. All stocks were going up, up; *everybody* was getting rich. It was carnival time in Filmland—with red balloons and pie in the sky.

Singularly enough, I remained untouched by the speculative frenzy. Not because of occult powers, but because I was born into a family that worshiped, first, the Crucifix, and second, a coffee can stuffed with cash, preferably gold. God was our faith, but cash our security. I inherited the caution. My salary went into a modern coffee can—a safe deposit box—not one, but several. And just in case the world went to hell in a breadbasket, I kept a little nest egg hidden around the house.

"Sucker!" Harry Cohn repeatedly called me. "Get in on it. I'm making ten thousand a *day*."

"But if you win ten thousand, somebody's got to be *losing* it."

"Oh, what a nebb. Nobody's losing, we're in an expanding economy. Everybody's gaining—"

I succumbed just in time—(October 1, 1929) and for the whole bundle. "Harry, buy me thirty thousand worth of stocks—" Cohn leaped for his telephone. "Get me Felix Juda at Sutro's . . ."

He bought me one hundred thousand dollars' worth of Goldman Sachs, or Lehman Brothers, I forget which—on a 30 percent margin. Daily the stock went up, up. In a few weeks my investment doubled. Where had I been all this time? To celebrate my new wealth Al Roscoe and I went to our favorite getaway spot: the primitive Halfway House on the Mission River in Baja California. When Wall Street laid its egg, Al Roscoe and I were having a high old time shooting ducks and quail, and prying tasty abalone off sea-sprayed rocks at low tide. We were out to disprove the old saw that "no one can eat a quail a day for thirty days." The world was far away—so far we didn't hear of black October 29 until a few days later. I rushed to Ensenada to call Harry Cohn.

"Bottom fell out of the market, kid. Sutro's tried to find you for margin 'cover money.' When they didn't, they sold you out."

"Oh, no. How much did I lose?"

"You lost it all for chrissake. Just like the rest of us."

In Search of the Holy Grail

YOU MEET PEOPLE EVERY DAY; you forget their names, forget their faces. Occasionally, you meet persons; you remember their names and faces. A few times in your life you meet rare individuals you immediately want to marry. In the making of *Ladies of Leisure* I fell in love with not one, but two such fellow creatures—an actress and a writer. First, the writer:

The common lack in all studios was—and still is—good writers. Most studios put their faith and cash in "name" authors. Cohn came up with another idea. He had his New York office dig up a batch of fresh, young writers—mostly new playwrights. They were given short-term contracts and shipped to Hollywood on "trial." Four of them turned out to be bonanzas: Robert Riskin, Jo Swerling, Sidney Buchman, and Norman Krasna.

As was my common procedure with scripts, I sent a rough draft of *Ladies of Leisure* to all of Columbia's creative people for reading—and comment later in a conference in Cohn's office. I also sent copies to all the neophyte New York writers that had just arrived. It is difficult for creators to read someone else's script objectively. But I wasn't looking for objective criticism or praise. In the conferences I listened for the little "hints" that were dropped unconsciously, hints that would reveal their honest subjective reactions; such as:

"Yeah, I know the leading man's an idealist, but to me he's sappy in spots" . . . "The girl doesn't ring a bell in this scene" . . . "I dunno, but the last sequence left me flat." Those offhand first impressions were more valuable to me than ten-page critiques.

About fifteen of us gathered in Cohn's office for a conference on *Ladies of Leisure*. The fledgling New Yorkers were easily spotted by their superior, "slumming" attitudes—endemic to all East Coast writers who came to Hollywood. One of them attracted my immediate attention: a squat, heavy-set, seething young man, furiously chain-smoking strong White Owl cigars—which he carried loose in his pockets. His thick glasses so enlarged his watery blue eyes he looked like a mad white owl himself. One got the odd impression the cigar was smoking the man.

"Just to fill in you new boys," said Cohn, "Capra doesn't want to hear what you *like* about the script. He's looking for knocks. Understand?" Up jumped the White Owl man.

"My name's Jo Swerling. But you don't have to remember it, because I'm going back to New York just as fast as I can. You want knocks, Mr. Cohn? That's my cue. I don't like Hollywood, I don't like you, and I certainly don't like this putrid piece of gorgonzola somebody gave me to read. It stunk when Belasco produced it as *Ladies of the Evening*, and it will stink as *Ladies of Leisure*, even if your little tin Jesus does direct it. This script is inane, vacuous, pompous, unreal, unbelievable—and *incredibly* dull. If this is the kind of drivel you expect me to write, Mr. Cohn, I'm leaving on the Chief tonight. End of statement."

Harry Cohn was speechless. But I beamed. This outspoken gent might have something I could use. "Jo?" He turned to me ready to fight. "Jo, you're a breath of fresh air. Really. Great entrance speech. Can you back it up?"

"What do you mean?" he snapped.

"I mean, think you can write a better script than the one in your hand?"

"With the little finger of my left hand. If I couldn't, I'd go back to the East Side and push a cart."

"Fine. You've got the ball—for three days. Go ahead."

"Be seeing you." He rushed out, leaving a smoke screen of White Owl exhaust fumes.

He came back in three days with forty pages. They were magnificent—human, witty, poignant.

"Jo, this is wonderful. You've got to finish it. But remember the theme. It's all in two words: 'Look up!' That's what the boy *must* say to this tart—'Look up at the stars!'. . ."

Then there was Barbara Stanwyck, destined to be beloved by all directors, actors, crews, and extras. In a Hollywood popularity contest she would win first prize hands down.

I had assembled a fine cast for *Ladies of Leisure*. Ralph Graves, Marie Prevost, Lowell Sherman, George Fawcett, and the stage star Nance O'Neill. All we needed was a leading lady to play the "party" girl. I wanted a certain actress, but Harry Cohn dragged his feet about signing her. He asked me to talk to an ex-chorus girl who had made a hit in the stage play *Burlesque*. He had a hunch about her. I was annoyed. I had a girl already set. But respecting Cohn's hunches, I asked Barbara Stanwyck to come in for an interview.

She came into my office, sullen, plainly dressed, no make-up. Obviously hating the whole idea of an interview, she sat on the edge of her chair and answered in curt monosyllables. I didn't want her before she came in, and what I saw of this drip now made me sure of it. After about thirty seconds of the usual inane questions—"What plays have you been in?" . . . "Have you made any movies?" . . . "Would you make a test?"—she jumped to her feet and snapped, "Oh, hell, you don't want any *part* of me," and ran out.

I phoned Cohn. "Harry, forget Stanwyck. She's not an actress, she's a porcupine."

A half-hour later, Frank Fay, her sarcastic, comedian husband was on the phone.

"Look, fella, what the hell did you do to my wife?"

"Do to her? I couldn't even talk to her."

"Well, she came home crying and upset. Nobody can do that to *my* wife."

"Listen, funny man. I don't want any part of your wife, or of *you*. She came in here with a chip on her shoulder, and went out with an ax on it."

"Frank, she's young, and shy, and she's been kicked around out here. Let me show you a test she made at Warner's."

"A test?"

"Yeah, a scene from *The Noose*. About three minutes long. You gotta see it before you turn her down. I'm coming right down with it . . ."

The test flashed on the screen. Nothing in the world was going to make me like it. After only thirty seconds I got a lump in my throat as big as an egg. She was pleading with the governor to pardon her convicted husband. Never had I seen or heard such emotional sincerity. When it was over, I had tears in my eyes. I was stunned.

"Wait in my office," I said to Fay and rushed off to see Cohn.

"Harry! Harry! We've got to sign Stanwyck for the part . . ."

"What're you, nuts? Half-hour ago you told me she's a kook."

"Yeah, yeah—but I just saw a test of her. She'll be terrific. Frank Fay's in my office. Sign her up. Don't let her get *away* . . ."

Thus began my long personal and professional association with Barbara Stanwyck. Underneath her sullen shyness smoldered the emotional fires of a young Duse, or a Bernhardt. Naive, unsophisticated, caring nothing about make-up, clothes, or hairdos, this chorus girl could grab your heart and tear it to pieces. She knew nothing about camera tricks: how to "cheat" her looks so her face could be seen, how to restrict her body movements in close shots. She just turned it on—and everything else on the stage stopped.

But then, after a few scenes, I discovered a *vital* technical lack—one that shook us all up: Stanwyck gave her all the *first time she tried* a scene, whether in rehearsal, or in long shots which served only to geographically orient the audience. All subsequent repetitions, in rehearsals or retakes, were but pale *copies* of her original performance.

This was a new phenomenon—and a new challenge; not only to me, but to the actors and crews. I had to rehearse the cast without her; work out the physical movements without her. The actors grumbled. Not fair to them, they said. Who ever heard of an actress not rehearsing?

And the crews had problems. I had to take the "heart" of the scene—the vital close-ups of Barbara—first, and with multiple cameras so she would only have to do the scene once. Multiple cameras aggravate the difficulties of lighting and recording in geometrical progression, i.e., four times as complex with two cameras, eight times with three cameras.

On the set I would never let Stanwyck utter one word of the scene until the cameras were rolling. Before that I talked to her in her dressing room, told her the meaning of the scene, the points of emphasis, the pauses. Her hairdresser Helen had become her confidante. I let Helen give her the cues from the other actors. I talked softly, not wishing to fan the smoldering fires that lurked beneath that somber silence. She remembered every word I said —and she never blew a line. My parting admonition was usually this: "Remember, Barbara. No matter what the other actors do, whether they stop or blow their lines—you continue your scene right to the end. Understand? Good girl."

It is true that directors often fall in love with their leading ladies—at least while making a film together. They come to know each other so intimately—more so than some married couples—and their relationship is so close emotionally, so charged creatively, it can easily drift into a Pygmalion and Galatea affinity; or, as true in some cases, it can slip into a hypnotic Svengali and Trilby association. I fell in love with Stanwyck, and had I not been more in love with Lucille Reyburn I would have asked Barbara to marry me after she called it quits with Frank Fay.

Ladies of Leisure hit the theaters in March, 1930. A new star was born. The public loved her; critics hailed her; fan magazines pulled all the stops. For example: "A NEW STAR RISES! *Ladies of Leisure* was unrolling. Halfway through, the audience choked up. Something was happening . . . a real, beautiful, thrilling wonder had been born . . . and we are proud to cry her welcome."

But there was *one* disadvantage in working at Columbia that galled my ego. Neither the picture, nor Stanwyck, nor Swerling, nor I was mentioned for an Academy Award. The major studios had the votes. I had my freedom, but the "honors" went to those who worked for the Establishment. I wanted awards as well as independence.

From my lowly base in Gower Gulch I mapped out a guerrilla campaign for recognition. First: wangle an invitation to join the Academy by attacking as a howling minority; second: call it "unfair" to independent producers; third: steam up Harry Cohn into raising a "stink" with the majors about "inadequate representation" on the Academy's board of directors. The ploy worked. On May 8, 1931, I received a letter from Fred Niblo, Academy Secretary: ". . . the Board of Governors cordially invites you to Academy membership . . ." Then a letter from Executive Secretary Lester Cowan; Directors' Branch Executive Committee wished me to serve on Nominating Committee "to nominate one candidate for the Board of Governors . . ." Ten days later our Nominating Committee met and—"strangely" enough—unanimously selected *me* as the candidate. No election was necessary. On September 18, 1931, I became a member of the elite Board; William C. De Mille was President, Conrad Nagel Vice President.

Casually, at my first Board meeting, I asked for enlightenment about the awards voting procedures. I was disappointed. The voting was "kosher"—if you belonged. The Academy was made up of five branches: Producers, Actors, Writers, Directors, and Technicians. Membership in the branches was by invitation only—for meritorious accomplishment. This was the voting procedure for awards: By secret vote each branch selected five nominees for their respective Oscar. For example, only directors who were Academy members voted to select the "best" five directors of that year—then *all* Academy members voted on which one of these five received the Best Director Award. The trick was to get *nominated* by the clique of major studio directors who had achieved membership—and these Brahmins were not about to doff their caps to the "untouchables" of Poverty Row.

Later on I was instrumental in democratizing these silk-stockinged voting procedures. But, as of 1931, if I, a director for a minor league studio, wanted to win an Oscar—and that was my Golden Fleece—making good films was not enough. I would have to gain status with big name directors to get them to nominate me. That would not be simple. I had yet to make the acquaintance of a single major studio director. Two status-building maneuvers were open to me: One, to become an officer in the Academy—perhaps President—and preside over the world's most glamorous event, an Academy Award Banquet. The other—and more practical scheme—was to make a "loan-out" picture at a major studio where I could meet and hobnob with the Brahmins, clink glasses with them. But the best-laid plans oft fail to hatch.

Major studios had tried to "borrow" me from Columbia. Cohn held out for a trade: Capra for a big star. Forget it, they said. No director is worth a star. But Cohn was a bully—and all bullies have other bullies. The man who could make Cohn jump through hoops for an approving nod was Louis B. Mayer. Mayer wanted me because Mayer wanted everything—but no trade for a star—just a purr from Leo the Lion. I went on loan-out to MGM to make a comedy with Karl Dane and George Arthur for Executive Producer Harry Rapf, a man with such a prodigious proboscis, wags said "he could smoke a cigar taking a shower bath."

It was the first time I had set foot in a major studio. I walked in wonder in this Bagdad of Filmland. Its galaxy of stars paled the heavens: Greta Garbo, Norma Shearer, Joan Crawford, Marion Davies, Gloria Swanson, Marie Dressler, Myrna Loy, William Powell, Ramon Navarro, Wallace Beery, Clark Gable, Robert Montgomery, Lionel Barrymore.

Equal in brilliance to the stars in Mayer's Caliphate were his satraps: Thalberg, Selznick, Mannix, Rapf, Stromberg, Franklin, Wanger, Weingarten, Lewin, Thau, Cummings, ad infinitum. All were paid from three to ten times the salary of the President of the United States. Under their suzerainty seventy-five elite scriveners plied their pens, and some twenty crème-de-la-crème directors steered their star-spangled productions—among them Sidney Franklin, Robert Leonard, Clarence Brown, Victor Fleming, Jack Conway, George Cukor, W. S. Van Dyke, Sam Wood, Edmund Goulding. Names to conjure with. I didn't get to hobnob and clink glasses with them, but I did get to drive on the same parking lot where their names were emblazoned on reserved spaces.

Oddly enough these great filmmakers were worshiped in Hollywood but remained unknown to the public. They were "organization" men, as anonymous as vice presidents of General Motors. Here the slogan was not "one man, one film." It was "many films, many assembly lines." A sign on Eddie Mannix's desk warned: "The only star at MGM is Leo the Lion." Well, maybe I was wrong. They were all millionaires.

The Dane-Arthur comedy script was finished. I liked it. Executive Producer Harry Rapf liked it. It was Friday. Shooting would start the following Monday.

"Meantime," asked Rapf, "would you kindly shoot a retake tonight for me, for the last Dane-Arthur show? We previewed it and we need a laugh badly in one spot."

"I'll be glad to," I answered, anxious to please.

He handed me a script scene. Polly Moran (playing a hoity-toity rich dame, wearing a dressing gown over her "unmentionables") rings for the hotel maid to help her get into her corset. George Arthur comes in disguised as a maid. In his embarrassment he trusses her up with the corset backward, or something (I've forgotten), and runs out.

Simple, I thought, as I waited for the actors in a hotel set. At nine that night they showed up, tired from having worked all day, and fuming over having to shoot a retake at night. I told them the scene.

"Oh, you think so?" roared Polly Moran. "You will like hell put a corset on me."

I explained it was not my scene, it was Mr. Rapf's.

"Young man. I'm not taking off my dressing gown—and show my harness —for Mr. Rapf or for Mr. *God!*"

"Harness? What harness?"

"*This* harness!" She let down her dressing gown to show me a strap arrangement, around her shoulders and all, that held up her breasts. "Don't you see? If I take this harness off my shelves will drop down to my *knees.*"

"Oh, Miss Moran—I'm sorry—" I turned red, pink, purple. I stuttered, apologized—

"Oh, so we can't do the scene, huh?" cried George Arthur. "Great. Good-night—"

"Wait a minute! Mr. Rapf just needs a good laugh here. If we can't use the corset gag I'll figure out something else. It'll only take a few minutes—"

I shot about four different gags, matching Arthur's entrance and exit as per the written scene, and dismissed them. I went home elated.

Next day (Saturday) I drove out to the Rancho Golf Club to play alone and plan Monday's shooting. I was in the big time and I wasn't going to blow it. A caddy came running with a message: They want you at MGM—right away! Entering my office, I found a blue envelope on my desk. In it was a terse memo from the office of Harry Rapf: "Report back to Columbia Studio immediately." I grabbed the phone and called Mr. Rapf.

"Mr. Rapf is busy," said the honey-butter voice of a secretary. "He left word that if you called, I was to tell you the memo was self-explanatory."

Fired! Like that. With a memo. I blew it. But how? I picked up a few things off the desk, said good-bye to my steno-pool girl, and walked behind a wall of film vaults—where I could be alone, and let the hot tears flow. In between sniffles I heard a happy whistling coming around a corner. Fearing it was someone who knew me, I dropped my head and half-ran to get by him. I practically collided with a tall cripple shuffling on two canes.

"Good morning," he said cheerily. "Fine day today, isn't it?"

He resumed his whistling. Slowly, inch by inch, he dragged one foot after the other with the aid of two stout canes gripped in shaky, white-knuckled hands. So trying was the effort, sweat poured down his face and stained his back and armpits. Steel braces bulged his clothes from neck to knee. Yet he whistled. My blues evaporated. It it was a fine day for *him*—what did I— Turning down the main street leading to the gate *I* began to whistle. Loud. Loud enough, I hoped, to be heard by Mayer, Rapf, and all the other fat-assed MGM executives.

"Who's that crippled fellow on canes, that goes around whistling?" I asked the gateman.

"Oh, him. Quite a guy. That's Lieutenant Commander 'Spig' Wead. Ace Navy pilot, one of the first to land on an aircraft carrier."

"Did he crash?"

"Well, yeah. But not in a plane. Story is he got drunk, fell down his house stairs, and broke his neck. Didn't move a toe for six months."

"Hm. What's he doing here?"

"A writer. On Navy films, you know. Real guy."

Back at Columbia Cohn opened up on me.

"What the hell did you do down there? Rapf called me. Said MGM didn't need fresh, know-it-all punks like you. Said he gave you a simple retake to make and you threw it in the ash can and shot four or five crappy gags of your own. WHY?"

I told him about Polly Moran, her harness, her "shelves." "What should I have done, Harry?"

"Just what you *did*. Those silly bastards. That Rapf is all nose and no brains. The next time Mayer wants you it's gonna cost him fifty thousand —and a star." He had his crystal ball with him.

"Well, come on," Cohn growled. "Let's get back to work. Swerling's written a first draft on *Rain or Shine*. Joe Cook and his stooges can come out any time. And Briskin's got a hooker on a circus tent. Get right on it. And, oh—New York's hounding me about another Holt-Graves. What about that Navy air thing you had? With the dirigible?"

"Great. I got just the man to help us write it."

"Who?"

"Lieutenant Commander 'Spig' Wead. Ace Navy pilot. Got drunk, fell down the stairs—and broke his neck."

I first met Myles Connolly at a party I gave for the cast and crew of *Ladies of Leisure*. As usual, Al Roscoe was the factotum of convivialities. He had invited Connolly, a hard-nosed, sentimental sophisticate who was to burn his lasting brand on my professional and personal hide. Al had described Connolly as a hulking 230-pound, six-three, black-haired, blue-eyed, gum-chewing Irishman, with the mien of a dyspeptic water buffalo.

"Boston Irish," Al went on, "a hard-boiled newspaper reporter, one of the few to interview Coolidge, a violent Catholic, and a protégé of Joe Kennedy—"

It seems that Joseph Kennedy—besides siring a future President—had dipped long fingers into all sorts of enterprises, such as politics, whisky, and movies. As owner of Hollywood's FBO (later RKO) Studios, Kennedy talked Myles Connolly into leaving the Boston *Post* to take a fling at films. And, according to Al Roscoe, Connolly was the Admirable Crichton, St. Patrick, and Cyrano all rolled into one; a writer of short stories and author of a poetic gem, *Mr. Blue*; a slayer of dragons, a crusader against all that was mean, vile, and raunchy; a scorner of the petty who played life's cards close to their vests. Roscoe introduced us at the front door.

"Oh, hello, Myles." I grabbed his hand. "Al here has told me all about you."

"Nobody can tell you all about *me*," he answered.

"I'll buy that. How about a drink? Bet you could use a drink—"

"No, thanks," he mumbled through bored lips. "I brought my own liquor." Was this bloke for real?

"Well," I said, steamed a little, "can I offer you a *glass* for your liquor?"

"Yea-ah—I'll take a glass." I led him through the crowd to the bar, handed him a glass.

He reached back in his hip pocket for a pint of bourbon, poured a stiff slug. "Know a good toast?" he asked.

"In the right company."

"Uh, huh—" he raised his glass. "Then I'll give one:

> From quiet homes and first beginning,
> Out to undiscovered ends,
> There's nothing worth the wear of winning,
> But laughter and the love of friends.

"Like that?"

"Yeah—Hilaire Belloc liked it, too."

He drained his glass; then, with a big arm, he put a crunching hammerlock around my head.

"You lousy, stinking director—I've seen your puny pictures. There's a glimmer. Let's go out in the kitchen and get drunk."

We did. That's how I met my great friend and critic—just when I needed him.

Connolly's capacity to hurt was only equaled by his capacity to drink. Here's a typical sample of our many arguments:

"Oh-h-h!" he would sarcastically exclaim, pacing the room with a drink in his hand. "The big *thinker* now . . . He's read Coué and Louella Parsons . . . got his *name* up in lights . . . makes big speeches on the radio . . . *Who* is man? *Why* is man? Specious little questions . . . asked by every high school intellectual nitwit who wants to pose as a man of *profundity!*"

"Your hair shirt is showing, Myles," I'd quip, trying to cap the head of wrath this Irish Socrates was building up. "You're being insulting again."

"The truth is never insulting—except to weaklings. I heard you on the radio . . . spouting that pap about *brotherhood* . . . and *happiness* . . . You sounded like one of those oily apostles of comfort . . . Brotherhood is *not* just saying 'Good morning' . . . it's sacrifice. And happiness is not just a new suit of clothes and a shoe shine. It's getting down on your knees to beg God for mercy, and knowing that He *hears* you."

"Okay, okay. Let's have another drink. 'From quiet homes to first beginning—' "

"You've got a great, native, peasant talent. You're the best director in Hollywood. But you've got a puny, calculating, little mind. Your films are picture post cards when they could be Sistine Chapels and Mona Lisas. Why?"

"Because I'm not the garret type. I *like* success. You don't. To you success is failure. I've seen the little 'message' films you produce for Joe Kennedy . . . so dull they don't even play the arty shoe-box houses. Mine play to standing room. They make money. Money! And the minute they don't, this peasant's going back to civilization—"

"Then stick to your picture post cards. Why do you ask, 'Who is man? Why is man?' I'll tell you. There's something inside your peasant soul hurting to come out . . . and you're scared. Before you know who man *is* . . . you've got to *be* one."

"Meaning what?"

"Meaning put your manhood where your mouth is, and *commit* yourself. Open up your mind to the immortals—the prophets, the poets. Yes! The saints and the martyrs. Meaning get the hell away from stinkpot Harry Cohn—"

"You're nuts. Harry Cohn gives me complete freedom. I make what I—"

"Harry Cohn owns you. You're a slave—"

"What slave?"

"Cohn has already sold your next three pictures, hasn't he? Without you even knowing what the stories will be—"

"So what?"

"So you have to deliver films like sausages—on time, on schedule—and *hits* they gotta be, to carry the rest of Columbia's junk."

"That's my *business*, Myles—making and delivering hits—"

"Business, huh? You got it all added up in little numbers. What happens to your business if you deliver two *flops* in a row?"

"I have no intention of delivering even *one* flop in a row. And I don't care *what* the story is. I can shoot the *phone book* and make it entertaining."

"O deliver us, God, from the arrogance of minnows! The great Capra 'touch' I'm going to hear about. Know what you are? A juggler. Fancy. In red pants. You keep so many colored balls in the air, audiences can't see the drivel."

"What's wrong with that?"

"Nothing. Nothing at all—if you want to remain a juggler all your life. And that's all you'll *ever* be until you shake Harry Cohn off your back—"

"Get this through—your—thick—skull. I *want* to be at Columbia. I *like* Harry Cohn—"

"Sure. Why shouldn't you? You *like* being a monkey on a string."

"Oh, will you please go to *hell*!"

Obviously our relationship was a hate-love affair. We were either embracing or snarling. Months-long periods of not speaking were followed by slobbering reunions—until the next go-to-hell hiatus. He resented my writers, insulted my friends, hated Cohn. He wanted to be my only guru; my Edgar Bergen. I resented being anyone's Charley McCarthy.

And yet—his words seared like branding irons: "a puny, calculating mind . . . an oily apostle of comfort . . . your films are picture post cards . . . there's something inside your peasant soul hurting to come out . . . you're scared . . . a juggler . . . colored balls that hide the drivel . . ."

Connolly hurt because he was right. I feared total dedication to films. A logical little imp inside me kept warning: "It's all a pipe dream, man. Use your brain. Artists aren't concocted out of accidents and chemical engineers. When midnight strikes you'll wake up among your test tubes again. So have a ball, and make a pile, while it lasts, man."

"I can't spend that kind of dough," shouted Cohn at me. Musical comedies cost a *fortune* to produce!"

"Not *Rain or Shine*, Harry. I'll *throw out* all the musical numbers."

"Throw out the *numbers*? Then what the hell are we buying?"

"We're buying *Joe Cook*. He's mad, Harry. He's unique—the darling of the literati, of the Algonquin Round Table! Percy Hammond calls Cook 'the funniest man in America'; Brooks Atkinson says he's 'one of the greatest comedians of our times!' And we're buying two *other* great comedians in

Rain or Shine—Tom Howard and Dave Chasen. *Rain or Shine* will cost us *peanuts*, Harry. I'll shoot it all in a small two-ring circus tent. No other sets. No music, no chorus dames, no Busby Berkeley, no nothing. Just wild comedy—"

"Dago, you're bats. *Rain or Shine* is a smash Broadway musical! It's a sacred cow with the critics. Take out the numbers and the New York papers'll murder you. 'That's Hollywood for you!' they'll yell . . ."

"Buy it for me, Harry. I've got a hunch."

Logically, a hunch makes as much sense as saying, "All horses have tails; therefore, all tails have horses." But in the zany world of films you don't explain hunches—you just live and die by them. Harry Cohn bought *Rain or Shine*.

The hunch proved correct. *Rain or Shine* was a modest film with a spectacular box office. In addition, many of the New York critics called it much funnier than the original Broadway hit. In show business, tampering with sacred cows sometimes yields cream—and I bragged about my successful hunch to my acerbic friend Myles Connolly.

"What are you proud of?" he needled. "Any idiot would have thrown out that *Rain or Shine* music. It was *bad* music."

"Okay, okay. I'm still proud. After only nine years I've come full circle —from complete control in the ignoramus world of *Fultah Fisher's Boarding House,* to complete control in professional Hollywood. Not many can say that, huh?"

"No. And I'll go right out and shoot off firecrackers. But mull this around in what you are so pleased to call your mind. You're not an artist. You're a professional trickster. Artists die and live again, die and live again. You go through your gaggy pictures without a nosebleed . . . And remember this, my cocky friend: Harry Cohn is a pig. And those who root with pigs grow a snout."

"Oh, go to hell!"

No two motion pictures are alike in the making. Each film is living a piece of your life in a small unreal world with its own character and integrity; its own new set of memorable experiences and incredible happenings. You begin to love and adapt to its strangeness. Dreams harden into substance. Values seen "through a glass, darkly," come into focus. You wish it would never end. But the film does end. The dream world vanishes like mist before a rising sun; part of you vanishes with it. And back you land in the real world with a thud—fagged, uneasy, jittery, difficult to get along with. There is only one cure. A new film. A new, small, unreal world; new visions, experiences, incredible happenings. Again you love it, adapt to it, wish it would never end. But end it does. Another part of you vanishes. That is filmmaking.

Some of the strange experiences are not photographed—this cockeyed scene in the filming of *Dirigible* was not in the script:

Flag ceremony inside great naval hanger at Lakehurst, N.J. Hangar is so big it often condenses its own rain within it.

"South Pole" as actors see it. Blankets on cameras are to keep them quiet, not warm. On this set I came up with "sensational" stunt—dry ice-in-the-mouth to make breath show—which cost veteran actor Hobart Bosworth three teeth and part of his jawbone.

Camera view of our "South Pole." Critical eye should pick out two anomalies: actors' shadows are too short and their breath doesn't show.

At left, Jack Holt is making time with Fay Wray. At my left, Ralph Graves doesn't like what he sees. (Notice that as late as 1930 our "soundless" cameras were still too noisy to use without stuffing them inside padded "blimps.")

Rain or *Shine*. Three theatrical sports from Old Broadway join a film sport from Poverty Row. Left to right: Musical comedy star Joe Cook, his equally famous theatrical stooge Dave Chasen, and agent Leo Morrison.

It took place in the Lakehurst, New Jersey, hangar, so huge—230 feet high—it made its own rain! Within the hangar, the last of the great airships, the seven-hundred-foot-long *Los Angeles,* rolled imperceptibly. A half-dozen non-rigid blimps were tethered alongside the *Los Angeles* like fat little piglets feeding on their mother.

Captain C. E. "Rosy" Rosendahl's staff offices occupied one corner of the cavernous hangar. One of these concrete offices was our photographic headquarters. Sam Briskin and I stood bug-eyed outside our office door listening to the crunch of thudding fists, snarling oaths, and crashing of chairs on thick skulls. More than a dozen of the toughest union leaders in the East were locked in a knock-down, drag-out Donnybrook in our office.

"Hope those bums don't bust up our cameras," said worried Briskin. "Oh, oh! Here comes the Navy."

Captain Rosendahl, apostle of the dirigible—now fighting a last ditch battle to keep lighter-than-air alive—came rushing at us followed by subordinates. He was breathing fire. Violence threatened the peace and safety of his helium-fed "babies."

"What in God's name is going on here?" His voice echoed and re-echoed.

"It's okay, Captain. We'll pay for the furniture," Briskin placated.

"What furniture? Who's fighting in there? Open that door!"

"It's locked, Captain. Just two unions fighting for jurisdiction . . ."

Hastily we explained to the irate captain. Arriving at Lakehurst we found six New York union bosses waiting to lay down the "law": we had to hire a New York technician for every crewman we brought from the Coast; body for body, wage for wage—plus two-way transportation from New York, time and a half after 5 P.M., "golden time" after midnight—and no New York "stand-by" to move a chair or *leave the hotel!* Or else, you don't *shoot!* Forty additional men to hire—just to eat, sleep, and play cards. Blackmail against Hollywood, of course, imposed by "authority" of the fist and club. We argued but agreed. It was the custom.

Next week, in walked six new "enforcers"—*New Jersey* union leaders! *They* had jurisdiction over New Jersey, they said, and *demanded* we hire forty additional *New Jersey* stand-bys—topping it all by insisting on *back pay* for the five days we had been there. Briskin spewed lava.

"Why you chiseling thieves," he raged, "not one goddam red *cent* will I pay you."

"Oh, yes you will. My men need *bread!*" the New Jersey man menaced. He had hair growing out of his ears, and a lot of white in his eyes.

I ran to the phone to tell the *New York* head man what was going on. "I'll be right over," he said. In a few minutes he walked in, followed by eight of *his* big henchmen. Their coats bulged.

"What's the problem?" asked the New York leader.

"Problem's *yours,*" said Briskin fuming. "We'll pay *one* set of stand-bys, but not *two!* Let's get out of here, Frank. Let these burglars figure out who gets the gravy."

We told all this hastily to Captain Rosendahl, hoping he wouldn't make it a federal case. The sounds of battle abated. It was all over. The door opened. Out came the bloodiest beat-up group of men I ever saw—cursing, limping, holding arms, holding heads. Were they from New Jersey or New York?

"Well, come on, you guys. Who *won*?" asked Briskin gleefully.

"Fuck you!" snarled the nearest bleeding "enforcer."

"New *York* won, Mr. Briskin! Yahoo-o!"

The New York leader stood in the doorway, rubbing bruised but victorious knuckles.

"You, sir—from New York!" There was an edge to Captain Rosendahl's voice.

"Yeah? What can I do you for, Colonel?" grinned back the victor.

"You and your men have assaulted New Jersey citizens. How would you like me to call the New Jersey police?"

The victorious boss panicked. "*Jersey* police?! Aw, *no*, General. We're New Yorkers. We wouldn't like that at all!"

"Very well. Next door there's a room full of mops, buckets, soap and water. I want that office and this whole hangar floor washed *clean*. Now!"

"Can do, can do, General—"

In amazement we watched the fat-cat union victors, black eyes and all, swabbing our office. I heard a laugh. It was Briskin.

"Frank," he chortled, "I haven't had so much fun since the pigs ate my little brother. How about a drink?" He rarely imbibed.

"Can do, Admiral, can do," I replied.

This next off-stage scene had a ludicrous, painful ending.

"It just doesn't look *cold* enough, fellows," I complained to my assembled crew as I inspected our three-acre exterior set of the Antarctic ice cap we had erected in the San Gabriel Valley.

"Mr. Capra, this is the most realistic set we've ever built," countered the art director. "Three inches of salt that'll ripple and blow in the wind, that 'iced-up' plane looks cold enough, and so does that jumble of glacial ice. And that backing of snow mountains alone cost us five thousand to paint."

"And I've got a dozen wind machines and tons and tons of cornflakes for snowstorms," added the special effects man.

"I know, I know. And the actors wear parkas and all. But there's something missing. We don't *look* cold standing here. I've got it! Our breath doesn't show. If we could make the actors' *breath* show—"

"Mr. Capra," cut in the cameraman, "I'm no magician. In ninety-degree weather—"

"I know. But wouldn't it be wonderful?"

"It would be magic."

"No, Joe—not magic. Science."

I put the problem up to some of my old professors at Caltech. Professor Lucas came up with a thought.

"Dry ice, Frank. In the actors' mouths. That'll make the breath condense. Put a piece of dry ice in a tiny wire cage and stick it to——"

I ran out shouting "Eureka!"—ran straight to my dentist.

"Doc? I want the breath to show. Make me a dozen little wire cages . . ." He thought the idea was stupid, unworkable, and dangerous—but he built me my little cages. In his office I stuck one to the roof of my mouth with false-teeth "glue." It felt as big as a bird cage. I mumbled and slobbered my words. Oh, well. If Demosthenes could talk with rocks in his mouth, *my* actors could do it with bird cages in theirs.

The first scene on the ice cap was the planting of the flag at the South Pole by Hobart Bosworth, Ralph Graves, Clarence Muse, and three others. Each had a cage full of dry ice in his mouth. They mumbled like punch-drunk fighters—but their *breath* showed! I swore everyone to secrecy about my great discovery.

"Camera!" I shouted triumphantly. Hobart Bosworth, a noble actor of the old, old school, unfurled the grand old flag, stuck it in the ice, and eloquently announced: "In the shname of the Shnooni—Stoonited—" Suddenly he stopped, clawed the cage out of his mouth, and shouted: "Keep the cameras running. You want breath? I'll give you breath. But not with this bloody contraption in my mouth." True trouper that he was, he flung away the cage—and plopped the square piece of dry ice into his mouth as he would a big pill.

"Ready again!" he said. "In the name of the United States of—AH-H-H-H!" He fell to the salted ground groveling and screaming. We ran to him. We couldn't open his jaws! In a panic we rushed him to the emergency hospital in Arcadia. The intern quieted the moaning Bosworth with a shot of something.

"Dry ice in his *mouth?*" said the shocked intern. "MY GOD! Nurse! Some hot compresses and call the nearest dentist."

The dentist arrived. His verdict—"Mr. Bosworth will lose three lower back teeth, two uppers, part of his jawbone, and much dead tissue. Tongue's okay. He'll act again."

Returning to the Antarctic set I found a sign on my director's chair: "For sale—DRY ICE—Cheap." In front of the sign, a paper cup full of my wonderful little cages.

"I'm holdin' on to mine, Mr. Capra." It was Clarence Muse, my pet actor. "Cameraman says breath shows up fine against my black face. Ought to be good for some close-ups, eh, Chief?"

"Deal, Clarence, deal."

Which led a critic to ask this pointed question: "How come Clarence Muse got more close-ups in *Dirigible* than the stars?"

Would you believe dry ice?

On the night of April 18, 1931, searchlights lit up Hollywood's sky. *Dirigible* opened at Sid Grauman's Chinese—the zenith of recognition in Filmland. I sat through the picture in-between two special friends, Lucille

Reyburn and Myles Connolly. At the end, the full-dress audience broke into spontaneous, prolonged applause.

I can't begin to describe the euphoria—when long months of hard effort are finally applauded by a theaterful of people—perspiring relief, exaltation, racing heart, wet eyes, a fixed idiot smile. There is nothing, but *nothing*, so satisfying as accomplishment.

I looked at Lucille. She was wiping her eyes. I looked at Myles. Chin in hand, chewing gum, he looked straight ahead—glumly. I finally had put him in his place, I thought. The general applause died down, but a small group persisted. I looked around. In the center aisle Harry Cohn was receiving a standing ovation. He caught my eye, raised clasped hands over his head in the victory sign. I acknowledged with the same sign. Harry Cohn had made Hollywood's big time—a successful opening at Grauman's.

We left the theater through an alley exit. If there was any doubt that Cohn had it made, the loud speaker dispelled it: "Mr. Harry Cohn's car! A blue Rolls. Mr. Harry Cohn's car!" We pushed our way through the crowd—to my Buick in the parking lot. Probably half the audience would go to Cohn's victory party at his house in Fremont Place. I wouldn't be there. Life was possible with him because of an unspoken understanding: I wouldn't stand in his spotlight, for it was impossible for him to stand in mine. Doesn't make sense, does it? Or does it? Anyway, we were going to Jo Swerling's house. *My* friends would be there—Al Roscoe, Tim Whelan, Stan Imerman, Bob Riskin, Ralph Graves, their wives, and Swerling's friends. And before the drinking was over Connolly would sock Doc Imerman because he was the only one big enough to sock.

Bumper to bumper we eased our way out of the parking lot. Lucille sat between us in the front seat, wiping off running mascara. "Oh, Frank, darling. I'm so happy for you. Myles, did you ever hear such applause?"

"It was okay," he answered apathetically. "But you saw who took the bows, didn't you?" I felt the needle.

"Come off it, Myles. This'll make Columbia a major studio. It's Cohn's night to ride the white horse."

"The white horse is a jackass by the name of Capra."

"Here we go again," I said. "I know. Success is sinful. By the way—as if I didn't know—what'd you think of *Dirigible*?"

"Oh—bigger and better sound effects, that's all. Ten reels of noise without a single idea. Money today, forgotten tomorrow."

Damn that Irishman and his "ideas." Wasn't *success* the biggest idea of all?

Ideas! Ideas! I'd show that needling Connolly I could handle an idea. My next picture would deal with the most controversial idea I could think of— religion! I asked Harry Cohn to buy me *Bless You Sister*, a satirical play inspired by Aimee Semple McPherson, and written by Robert Riskin, the brightest of the "young Turks" Cohn had imported from New York.

"Frank, you're nuts. Religion is dynamite!"

"Harry, *The Miracle Man* was dynamite at the box office. We'll call ours *The Miracle Woman*. Perfect for Stanwyck."

"But you can't *kid* religion. The Christers'll murder you. Think about it for another day."

"I won't kid religion, Harry. I've thought about becoming a priest many times."

"Well, why didn't you?" He set me back with that one.

"Okay, I'll think about it."

As a boy I had begun to equate religion with peasant superstition. In our neighborhood only the poor went to church to confess sins. Why? Was poverty the big sin? Anyway, peasant stuff was not for me. At Caltech I found a new cause—science. The beauty, the clarity, the logic with which Galileo and Newton formulated their brilliant laws of mass and motion were all that a man needed in his quest of truth. Besides, I met a silvery blonde who sang in a Presbyterian choir. So Sunday after Sunday, instead of going to Mass, I sang and held hands with my blonde—except for the Christmas and Easter Masses.

On those two holy days I sneaked into a Catholic church to *kneel*; to smell the incense, hear the angels sing, and be lifted out of my shoes by the passion and resurrection of Christ. It may happen to you only once in a hundred Masses—but it will happen. You walk back from Communion with the Host on your tongue—a nobody. You kneel, drop your head in your hands. Slowly the wonder of it fills you with joy—the dissolving Host in your mouth is the living Christ! The priest, the church, all the bowed heads around you, disappear. You hear nothing, see nothing, feel nothing. Your mind empties itself of all thought, your body of all substance. You are a spirit suffused in a glorious Light. And out of its glory a word infuses your spirit: "Courage!" You have glimpsed the Eternal! The Light fades. Thoughts re-form in your mind; substance returns to your body; bowed heads around you materialize. You hear the priest say, "Go. The Mass is ended." You leave filled with the urge to shout it to the whole world—"Courage! Courage!" The urge gets lost in earthier urges. You go back to your math and your blonde. Man is not a simple animal.

I phoned Cohn. "Buy me *Bless You Sister*" was my verdict. He did.

Miracle Woman, the film version, had a most powerful opening sequence —a promise of greatness. A stiff-necked country congregation had replaced their aging, old-fashioned pastor with an up-and-coming "modernist." Sunday morning the villagers gather to yawn through the old man's last sermon. Instead, his daughter comes out, eyes flashing with hate. She mounts the pulpit. In a nutshell, this is what she says: "My father is not able to preach his last sermon. He just died in my arms. And you killed him. For thirty years he tried to touch your stony hearts with the mercies of God—and *failed*! Why? Because you don't *want* God. And you're right! There *is* no God . . ."

From here this bitter, disillusioned young lady should have decided *on her own* to give the stupid unwashed the religion they "want": a potpourri of happy sermons, brotherhood, sisterhood, and sex—all in the glittering trappings of "Xmas" paper and musical comedy. She wows them. She gets rich. *Variety* reports her weekly "take" in its show-biz columns. Then the Miracle—and her return to God. One woman's life in three acts: disillusion, venality, conversion.

Is this what we did in the film—after that opening scene of great promise? No. I turned chicken. The thought of a wicked evangelist deliberately milking poor, adoring suckers for money in the name of Christ was just too much for my orthodox stomach. I weaseled. I insisted on a "heavy" to take the heat off Stanwyck the evangelist. *He* cons her into it. *He* gets wealthy. She becomes his flamboyant stooge. Did she or did she not herself believe those "inspiring" sermons delivered in diaphanous robes, with live lions at her side? I didn't know, Stanwyck didn't know, and neither did the audience. And finally, in my confusion, I ended it all with the cheapest trick in dramaturgy: When a character bollixes up your story—let him get hit by a truck. My villain, fearful of exposure, sets fire to the tabernacle. He dies. But Stanwyck is saved "spiritually" by the love of an adoring "convert."

I dove into the pool of powerful ideas—and came up with a can of claptrap and corn. I had the feeling everyone at Columbia was secretly gleeful I had fallen on my face. Cohn? When I sat in his office and said, "Harry, I muffed it," he answered, "Forget it, will you? Get going on your next one."

The man I really dreaded to meet was Connolly. Would *he* pour it on! I could just hear him say, "I told you you were a juggler in red pants. Sure, gags just rattle off the top of your head. But for ideas, you dig deep in your guts—if you've got any."

So be it. I looked him up, told him about *Miracle Woman*.

"Uh huh, uh huh," he said. "Could be the greatest picture you'll ever make."

"What're you talking about?"

"I'm talking about failure. Failure's growth if you don't let it castrate you. Try again . . ."

Oh, sure. Try again. Simple—for spiders and William Jennings Bryan. But there is a gag line in Hollywood: "Buster, you're only as good as your last picture."

Make a blockbuster—you're the lion of the cocktail circuit. Make a bomb—you buy your own drinks. Make *two* bombs—aye, there's the rub. What if I failed *again*? Connolly had earlier warned: "Wait till you make *two flops in a row* for Cohn!" Would the fair-haired boy be fired—walk the streets again? Better men had hit the skids—D. W. Griffith, Mack Sennett. Play it safe, fool. Stick to melodrama—better yet, to comedy. To hell with "idea" films. They burn you at the stake for spouting ideas. Read your history.

Ladies of Leisure—and a star is born, Barbara Stanwyck. Here she is watching Marie Prevost "grinding it off."

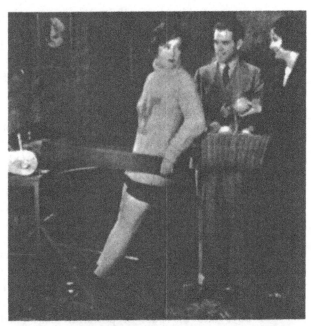

Miracle Woman. Barbara Stanwyck and David Manners after her tabernacle burned down. Stanwyck played a female Elmer Gantry role. Considered extremely radical for its time, *Miracle Woman* was my first Columbia film to lose money—mainly because film was banned throughout British Empire.

Forbidden. Barbara Stanwyck and Adolphe Menjou in a soggy story I wrote for myself.

BELOW LEFT

Platinum Blonde, a comedy starring Jean Harlow, Loretta Young, and Bobby Williams (a new comedy sensation). Here the Platinum Blonde is "luring" a lassoed, but nervous Williams into playing house. After this film, Harlow's breastworks burst their silken confines from magazine covers and pin-up walls. Had not Williams died shortly after *Platinum Blonde*, he surely would have become one of Hollywood's bright stars.

BELOW RIGHT

Harlow plays the scorned woman when she finds Williams smooching with his sob-sister pal, Loretta Young.

I played it safe with an out-and-out comedy—*Platinum Blonde*. For a story, Jo Swerling and I stole a column from *Front Page*, a big hit play. As a back-up I asked Robert Riskin to write the dialogue. We loaded the picture with gags and a great cast: Loretta Young, Bobby Williams (a new comedy sensation), and—for sex—we added Jean Harlow, the reigning Love Goddess. How could I miss? I didn't. And Harlow's breastworks burst their silken confines on magazine covers and pin-up walls.

Platinum Blonde recharged my cockiness. The less-than-miraculous *Miracle Woman* was the only entry in my Columbia "loss" column. I demanded a rematch with "ideas." But this time, by George, on *my* terms. I would write my own "idea" film. I fancied I could write, anyway. So, with a very large assist from Fannie Hurst's *Back Street*, I wrote an "original" story, *Forbidden*. I should have stood in bed.

I had yet to learn that drama is not really just actors weeping and suffering all over the place. It isn't drama unless the *audiences* are emotionally moved. Actors' crocodile tears alone can't touch their hearts. But courage, faith, love, and sacrifices for others will—if believable.

In spite of scriptwriter Jo Swerling's valiant efforts to write in some "bones," *Forbidden* ended up as two hours of soggy, 99.44% pure soap opera. Some critics moistened their reviews with tears, most burned them with acid. *Forbidden* was saved from the "loss" column by one or two directorial "gems" (sic), and the fine believable performances of Barbara Stanwyck, Adolphe Menjou, and Ralph Bellamy (one of his earliest films).

It was after the filming of *Forbidden* that it happened with Lucille Reyburn. We had been dating steadily for about two years. Not a word about marriage until—

"Frank, darling, I'm twenty-nine. I can't just go on dancing and partying all my life. I need to get married. Have a home. Have children."

The word "married" stopped me quicker than a rattlesnake buzz.

"My mother and dad are moving up to Santa Maria. I'll have to go with them, unless—"

"Lu, I've never said a word about marriage, have I? Besides, your black Republican father thinks all foreigners and Catholics have leprosy."

"You wouldn't be marrying him, Frank."

"Lu! I can't get married. I'm broke again. I lost all I had in Richfield Oil—"

"I've got two dollars for a marriage license."

"Lu, what I'm trying to tell you is that I don't *want* to get married. Never again!"

I told Al Roscoe about it, told him she didn't cry, didn't fuss—just left for Santa Maria. "Marry her, you chump!" was his comment. I was so angry I nearly took his head off. "Okay, okay, don't yell at me. I got another idea. Let's go around the world. You and I. Got dough enough for that?"

"Al, you're a *genius*. Let's pack!"

I had crossed the Atlantic once in the black steerage hold of a German ship. Twenty-eight years later I was recrossing it in the best stateroom of another German ship—the *Europa*.

Seldom were Roscoe and I more than arm's length from the bar. We toasted the world—the Depression, the breadlines, Herbert Hoover, Cohn, Lucille Reyburn. We drank to sin, sex, freedom! Yippee! We vowed to wallow in the dives and fleshpots of every capital from London to Tokyo. Husky German stewards half-carried us to our staterooms, but not till we made them sing "My Gal Sal" with us.

In London did we visit Westminster Abbey or marvel at Sir Christopher Wren's churches? We did not. We went pub-hopping from Piccadilly to Soho, paid streetwalkers to hear their funny talk, then paid them double to leave.

Laughs, hangovers, boredom. On to Paris! We gawked at the Lido "shows," double-gawked at the ingenious "exhibitions" in 32 rue Blondel. We roamed Montmartre, the Left Bank; watched men dance with men, women with women. Frenchmen sneered at us in their street argot. We sneered back in accents from Brooklyn to Biloxi. Those who understood some English we shook up with pig latin. Headaches, hangovers—and homesick. But on to Rome!

While we were packing, the concierge came to our room with a cablegram. "Al," I shouted happily, "listen to this from Lucille! 'Frank, marrying Dr. Brown in Santa Maria next month. Lucille Reyburn.' Yoo-hoo! I'm free!"

"Oh, oh!" muttered Roscoe, breaking off packing.

"What're you oh, oh-ing about, stupid? Best thing that could've happened to me. I'm free! But who the hell is Dr. Brown? Why didn't she *tell* me about him?"

"She just did," laughed Roscoe.

"Oh, yeah? Well, I'm going to send her the nastiest cable I can think of."

At the concierge's desk I scribbled out a "nasty" cable: "MEET ME HOTEL WALDORF NEW YORK IN ONE WEEK. BRING WEDDING CLOTHES AND TWO DOLLARS. ANSWER PRONTO. FRANK.

"Send this toute vite!" I said to the concierge.

"Send *this* toot vite, too!" It was Roscoe.

"Al! What're you doing?"

"Frankie boy, Confucius say—wise man always keep spare sucker up sleeve. I'm cabling Wally Beery to see if he wants to go fishing."

On a cold, snowy morning—February 1, 1932—Lucille and I were married by Judge May in his Brooklyn courtroom. She was radiant. With the five thousand dollars I borrowed from Harry Cohn we honeymooned a week in Lake Placid—seeing the Winter Olympics with Benny Rubin and Ted Husing—then honeymooned some more in all the bridal suites in Canada between Montreal and Vancouver. And to this day I have never asked Lu if there ever was, or was not, a Dr. Brown in Santa Maria. That is *her* secret—and I don't care to know it.

CHAPTER 8

Bitter Times and Bitter Tea

THE MOTION PICTURE industry was among the last American enterprises to feel the Great Depression. Films were the cheapest—and for many, the *only* form of entertainment. Moreover, for the wind-chilled job seekers who pounded the pavements the movie theater was the only convenient, catchpenny comfort haven for resting their feet and warming their bodies. And, although a ten-cent movie seat had to be the devil's own torture to sleep in, all-night houses were crowded with homeless snorers.

By 1932 many people couldn't even afford dimes for entertainment *or* comfort. Breadlines replaced box-office lines—the so-called "golden era of extravaganzas" turned sickly green, then went into the red. Two major producing companies, Paramount and Fox, had to go into receivership; others retrenched, pruned, and lopped off employees right and left. A fatuous shibboleth, "Don't you know there's a depression on?" was handed out with the pink slips. Hollywood hit the panic button.

Before 1932 I made only fictional films—without basis in reality—"escapist" the critics called them. Now I took a hard look at life from the eye level of the hard-pressed Smiths and Joneses. It was not the same rosy life we saw—and copied—in each other's Hollywood movies. The *real* lot of American citizens in 1932 was stark, bleak, and worsening. Despair was the prevailing mood.

There are now almost two generations of Americans with no personal memory of the Great Depression. Those who lived through the tragic thirties remember them dimly because of man's tendency to forget the unpleasant. But in 1932 they faced not unpleasantness—they faced disaster!

Earlier, many in the low-income groups had considered the crash as a good joke on the speculative rich. They lost their millions and mansions—ha ha! But now working people were losing jobs, and homes, and farms—and fast!

In those days, picturemakers on Poverty Row, lacking the money, stars, and facilities of the major studios, had to compete in the film marts with "gimmick" films featuring the bizarre, the outré, the risqué, the flamboyant —yellow journalism, if you please. Was there some film "hay" to be made out of the Depression? Of course—the "sob" angle: wealth versus "ideals"; Big Money against little people. Opportunistic as Hearst reporters, Riskin and I concocted a wild story about a bank president (Walter Huston) who is filled with youthful optimism and a cheerful trust in men. He is bitterly opposed by both his own directors and other banks for his "unsound" and "dangerous" practices of making loans on faith. Riskin wrote the screenplay, marking the beginning of a Capra-Riskin collaboration that was to last for years. We called our first effort *American Madness*.

But there was no madness in the casting of the actors: Walter Huston, Pat O'Brien, Kay Johnson, Constance Cummings, Gavin Gordon, and a dozen superb supporting players would have put punch and believability into even a weak story. *American Madness* might have erred a bit on the "gee-whiz" side, but it was not weak. In truth, it was one of the first Hollywood films to grapple directly and openly with the Depression's fears and panic. In our film story, bank president Huston has a theory: Money is something you can't eat, wear, or plant. But you can put it to work. And the harder the times, the harder it must work.

"Unemployed money leads to unemployed men," he argues with his ultra-conservative bank directors. "Business firms and factories are going bankrupt. Why? Because people have no money to buy their goods. Why? Because they're out of work. Why? Because stores and factories are closing down. It's a vicious circle—old Hard Times chasing his own tail. The answer is bank money; fuel to start industry's wheels turning again. Hoarding money in vaults makes as much sense as pouring oil back into oil wells.

"But, you say, banks should lend money only to those who can put up material assets as collateral. Well, gentlemen, it isn't news that the Depression has pretty well wiped out people's material assets. But it hasn't yet destroyed what Alexander Hamilton called America's *greatest* asset—CHARACTER! We must have faith in character, make *loans* on character . . ."

Idealist Huston is doing fine with his "character" loans to small businesses, until the unexpected happens: an event that pits doubt and panic against his faith. The in-debt cashier (Gavin Gordon) is forced by gamblers to engineer an inside bank robbery of one hundred thousand dollars. Rumors spread like wildfire. A bank switchboard operator tells another switchboard operator. She calls another. Shopkeepers whisper it to customers. The bank loss keeps pyramiding. A depositor hears the rumor. He calls other depositors, who call other depositors. The loss is now up to five million! Someone on the inside is the thief.

The bank run starts slowly; then, as in a dry gulch hit by a cloudburst, it swells into a rampaging flood. Huston calls other banks for aid. Smugly they decline: "It would be throwing good money after bad." Huston's directors refuse to put up their own assets, taunting him with, "Where's your faith now?" The bank has insufficient funds to meet the surging run. It is doomed. But not yet.

An assistant cashier (Pat O'Brien), a former convict whom Huston trusted, calls all the small businessmen Huston had loaned money to on character. They come running to the bank to deposit all their available cash. Both depositors and withdrawers storm the bank windows. Doubts and faith rack the panicky crowd. The odds are still a hundred to one against the bank, until Huston's directors, moved by the strange sight of Huston's "borrowers" returning faith for faith, throw in their considerable assets and raise other millions. The bank is saved—lending on character pays off!

American Madness was a shocker to the public. It created controversy among critics and bitter contention in financial circles. Some called it "New Dealish" . . . "impractical star-gazing" . . . "fuzzy thinking." Others said the thinking was no fuzzier than the "thinking" of financiers which created the boom and the crash.

But what impressed me most about *American Madness* was not that some referred to it as a "gee whiz" film, but that American filmmakers had the artistic *freedom* to make a motion picture about American "faults" and have it freely shown throughout the world. Which impels me (after forty years of filmmaking) to make personal comments on both gee whiz and artistic freedom:

There is a type of writing which some critics deploringly call the "gee whiz" school. The authors, they point out, wander about wide-eyed and breathless, seeing everything as larger than life. If my films—and this book—smack here and there of gee whiz, well, "Gee whiz!" To some of us, all that meets the eye *is* larger than life, including life itself. Who can match the wonder of it?

Despite his lean, bare prose, Hemingway was a gee-whizzer. The adrenals of all his characters were oversized—as were his own. He lived, wrote, and died in a fireworks display. Gauguin was a gee-whizzer. He painted the South Seas not as he found them, but as he *wanted* to find them. He created his own South Seas. Homer's heroes were super-heroes—Paris, Helen of Troy, Achilles, Hector, Odysseus. Plutarch's *Lives* were super-lives. And what of the prophets and apostles of biblical times—Moses, David, Peter, Paul? Those were men to match anyone's mountains.

We, the gee-whizzers, euphemistically say we are of the "up-beat" school, in contrast to the "down-beaters" whom we non-euphemistically relegate to the "ashcan" school, because their films depict life as an alley of cats clawing lids off garbage cans, and man as less noble than a hyena. The "ash-canners," in turn, call us Pollyannas, mawkish sentimentalists, and corny happy-enders.

These are the Hollywood filmmakers: Mr. Up-beat and Mr. Down-beat—

one hopes to be righter than right, the other righter than wrong—and in the middle is Mr. In-between. Yet we all respect and admire each other because the great majority freely express their own individual artistry, unfettered by subsidies or strictures from government, pressure groups, or ideologists.

In film vernacular, "pace" is the apparent speed of the flowing motion of "living" shadows across the silver screen. If scenes are photographed at twenty-four frames (still photos) per second, and projected at the same twenty-four frames per second on theater screens, the pace of the scenes in theaters *should* be the same as their pace at the time of photography. But is it?

It was in the making of *American Madness* that I made a rather startling discovery about pace. A scene that, to me, was normal in pace during its photography, or when viewed by a few people in a small studio projection room, seemed to *slow down* when I saw the same scene projected on a large screen before a theaterful of people.

At first I attributed this "slowing down" in theaters to my own jitters when seeing my own films with an audience. But then I seemed to sense a slower-than-normal pace in other filmmakers' pictures I saw in theaters. Was this an illusion? Did the brain of the viewer sort out the audio and visual stimuli from the screen with greater speed because the actors were magnified five times their normal size? Was it the gigantic *bulk* of the actors that made their speech and physical movements *seem* slower?

Or, did a thousand pairs of eyes and ears, reacting together to the same stimuli, fuse together into one huge, *quicker-reacting* pair of ears and eyes?

I discussed the subject casually with some sound men. "Impossible!" they said, looking at me as if I had dropped a marble or two. "There is no scientific basis for such phenomena." I changed the subject, but not my mind. Although not much research had been done on group behaviorism, I just *knew* that an individual's reactions were more exaggerated when he was elbow-to-elbow in a crowd than when he was alone. I sensed this phenomenon in baseball bleachers, parades, and political conventions. And since *American Madness* dealt with crowd reactions to rumors, panic, and faith, I decided to counteract the apparent "slowing down" of a film's pace in theaters by artificially quickening the pace during photography.

First, I cut out long walks, such as prolonged entrances and exits of actors. I "jumped" the performers in and out of the heart of the scenes.

Second, I cut out "dissolves." It was a fad of the day to indicate "passage of time" or "change in locale" by slowly overlapping one scene into another; for instance, an actor entering an elevator at the eighth floor "dissolves" into the actor coming out at the first floor; or, a blossom-covered tree "dissolves" into the same tree covered with snow. It was a show-off photographic gimmick that pleased filmmakers but bored audiences. I did away with dissolves by "straight-cutting" from the eighth floor to the ground floor, and from tree blossoms to snow.

Third, I overlapped speeches. To facilitate the editing of sound tracks, it was customary for actors to finish their lines completely before other actors responded with theirs. This is contrary to real-life conversations in which people talk "over each other" all the time. Try listening to three women talk sometime. In *American Madness* the actors interrupted and over-lapped their lines at will.

Fourth, and this was the radical change, I speeded up the *pace* of the scenes to about one-third above normal. If a scene played normally in sixty seconds I increased the actors' pace until it played in forty seconds. During photography the speed of the scenes seemed exaggerated—in fact, it *was* exaggerated—but when *American Madness* hit the theater screens, the pace seemed *normal*! Moreover, there was a sense of urgency, a new interest, that kept audience attention riveted on the screen.

This deliberate "kicking up the pace" was a most important improvement in my own technique of filmmaking. Except for "mood" scenes, where urgency would be a jarring note, I used this speeded-up pace in all my subsequent films. Critics have continually commented on the "pace" and "naturalness" and "interest holding" of my direction, but they have never guessed how it was accomplished. There are, certainly, other producers and directors who have made this discovery for themselves, although I am aware of only one who seems to *consciously* exaggerate the pace: Jack Webb, in his *Dragnet* television series.

Because of these innovations, I secretly thought *American Madness* would at least be nominated for an Academy Award in some category: acting, screenplay, or—assuredly—directing. The film was timely, controversial, realistic: the run on the bank was so real many viewers went straight to their banks to withdraw their money. But no! Critics said it was not Academy Award material. And although critical appraisals were light reading for the public, they were gospels for highbrow Academy voters. When I griped to Harry Cohn about awards, he said: "Forget it. You ain't got a Chinaman's chance. They only vote for that arty junk."

How could I forget it? I dreamed about Oscars. I *had* to get one. Okay. If the Academy voted only for arty films (not true), I would make the artiest film they ever saw—about miscegenation! That ought to stir up some arty votes.

Walter Wanger happened to be preparing a Columbia picture from Grace Zaring Stone's novel *The Bitter Tea of General Yen*. It was a strangely poetic romance between a Chinese warlord and an American missionary. Represent-atives of two cultures as far apart as the poles, clash and fall in love. To me it was Art with a capital *A*. Edward Paramore was writing the script for Wanger. I pleaded with Wanger to let me make the picture. He consented, provided he received screen credit as the producer.

There were three major roles in *Bitter Tea*: a young American missionary woman, a powerful Chinese warlord—General Yen, and his diabolically clever American financial adviser.

The missionary was a well-bred, straightlaced New England young lady, externally frigid but internally burning with her "call." Casting this part was easy—Barbara Stanwyck.

I pictured Yen's financial adviser as a fat, hard-drinking, wheezy cynic who sells his Machiavellian shrewdness to the highest bidder. But, strange even to his larcenous soul, he had acquired a lasting loyalty to General Yen. In a New York play I had seen my man: Walter Connolly, one of the ablest character actors on Broadway.

General Yen was the big casting problem. I knew what I did *not* want—a well-known star made up as an Oriental. I looked for a tall, overpowering, real Chinese. But there were no tall Chinese in casting directories, or even in laundries; most Chinese-Americans were short Cantonese. After many interviews we settled on a not-too-well-known Swedish actor, Nils Asther. He was tall, blue-eyed, handsome; spoke with a slightly pedantic "book" accent; his impassive face promised the serenity and mystery of a centuries-old culture.

But how could we make a Swede look Oriental? His blue eyes would photograph steel-gray in black-and-white film. That was an unusual plus. But what about the *slant* of his eyes? The prevailing method of "changing" Caucasian eyes into Oriental ones was to stretch and tape the outer ends of the eyes back toward the ears, fooling practically nobody. Besides which the actors looked more hideous than Oriental. There must be a better, more natural way. There was.

Closely studying Chinese features, I noticed two major differences between Oriental and Caucasian eyes: One, the upper Oriental eyelid is smooth and almost round, lacking the crease, or fold, of the Caucasian eyelid; and, two, Oriental eyelashes are much *shorter* than Western eyelashes. We followed up the two clues: The make-up man covered Nils Asther's upper eyelids with smooth, round, false "skins," and clipped his eyelashes to one-third their natural length. Without adding any other make-up we made photographic tests of Asther's face. On the screen he looked strange—unfathomable. The stiff, upper eyelids kept his eyes in a permanent, half-closed position. Of a certain he was *not* a Caucasian—and his face looked natural, uncontorted! Bedecked in rich Mandarin costumes, and a fez-like, black, tall skullcap for added height, Asther could pass for an awe-inspiring warlord. I added one final touch: an eccentric walk—long slow strides with both his long arms moving back and forth together— in parallel—with each stride. By keeping the camera low to accentuate height, Nils Asther became General Yet—ruthless, cultured, mysterious, and devastatingly attractive.

The Bitter Tea of General Yen lost money—mainly because it was banned in Great Britain and in the British Commonwealth countries, due to the shocking implications of a love affair between a yellow man and a white woman. It was thirty years ahead of its proper time. Nor did it receive any Academy Award mentions. Damn those Academy voters! Couldn't they recognize a work of art when they saw one? Nevertheless, *Bitter Tea* will remain forever as one of *my* pet pictures. And it *was* chosen as the film to open Radio City Music Hall.

There were two, what might be called, amusing—had they not been most painful—incidents that happened in the making of *Bitter Tea*. In clipping Nils Asther's eyelashes, we forgot that long eyelashes protected Caucasian eyes against harsh light. The first day we exposed him to the glare of studio sun arcs he came down with the worst case of eyeburn (klieg eyes) studio doctors had ever seen. He was ordered to remain locked up in a dark dressing room between shots, and to wear dark, red glasses during rehearsals. Only during actual photography did we expose his unprotected eyes to the sun or studio lamps. Despite these precautions, Asther suffered constant acute pain throughout the whole picture. Fearing for his eyesight, doctors attended him night and day, administering poultices, eyedrops, and pain killers. Yet the gallant Swede gave a performance that one has to call an elegant tour de force.

But it was Walter Connolly who—well, Connolly was very stout and slightly asthmatic. The slightest physical exertion started him wheezing and panting. He had never been in a plane or in a film. His first experience in each was slightly more than memorable.

We were shooting the night scenes of the ambush of Yen's freight train by a thousand enemy soldiers, when I suddenly got the notion that Walter Connolly should be in one of the box cars. His deal called for his remaining in the New York play until we needed him on the West Coast. I phoned a New York Columbia executive, told him to put Connolly on the midnight plane to L.A. to be here ready for work tomorrow night. Forget his baggage and clothes—send them later.

That night, on his way to his theater dressing room after the final curtain, two Columbia executives grabbed Walter and rushed him out to a waiting limousine. Before his portly body was halfway in, the limousine roared away with a police escort wailing its sirens. Racing through the New York traffic, methodical, sedate Walter began to pant and sweat with excitement. He still had on his make-up and stage clothes. The cavalcade thundered to a stop on the airport ramp. The two executives ran bewildered Walter to the waiting plane, hoisted him up the steps, shoved him inside and yelled: "Lots o' luck, Walter!"

Stewardesses hustled him to a seat. Before they could lengthen the safety belt to fit his ample stomach, the plane taxied off with a roar. It was his first plane ride. He clutched the arm rests, broke into a cold sweat—and prayed. Before the wheels thumped up into the fuselage he got airsick. The stars were against him. During the twenty-hour flight the plane was storm-tossed most of the time. He could neither eat, nor sleep, nor stop retching or praying.

At the Los Angeles airport two assistant directors pulled the limp Walter out of his seat, ran him down the stairs, ran him to another waiting limousine —and another police escort with sirens wailing. Poor Walter had no desire or breath left to ask questions. He just panted with his mouth open. They raced him to our San Fernando Valley night location where Walter saw and heard his first pandemonium—the chaos of lights, trains, and a thousand shouting extras. The car skidded to a stop in front of a tent. Everyone shouted. Wardrobe men pulled him out of the car, dragged him into the tent, stripped his clothes off, poured him into riding breeches, boots, riding coat and hat, then rushed him through the milling Chinese mob over to me.

I was behind a camera alongside the freight train, revving up a big complicated scene.

"Here's Mr. Connolly, boss!" shouted one of the two assistants holding him up. I took a quick look at him. Sweat had eroded streaks down his made-up face. His eyes had the haunted look of a man who had just seen the world go nuts. His big belly heaved back and forth like the flanks of a steer dodging cars on a freeway.

"Fine, fine!" I shouted. "Mr. Connolly, we're about to take a shot. Run down to that third open box car, climb in it, and when the car comes by this camera, jump out and fall right in front of us. Okay?"

"Do-o-o w-w-what?" he gasped.

"It's okay—all soft sand here. Sam! Send two guys with Mr. Connolly, to help him in and roll him out. Get going!"

"Gotcha, boss."

Two huskies each grabbed an arm and carried Walter to the box car. His feet left no footprints—just dragged furrows. The men heaved and shoved and rolled him into the box car.

"All ready? Roll 'em! I shouted. "ACTION!"

Bedlam broke loose—machine guns, rifle fire, a thousand yelling Chinese. The train started with a rattling jolt. As Connolly's box car neared the camera, two unseen men rolled him out. He fell as limp as a dead horse—fell and squashed and lay writhing in pain. He had broken a leg!

"Stand-by ambulance!" The shout was passed along. Two white-coated attendants rolled him on to a stretcher, shoved him into the ambulance. For the third time in twenty-four hours Broadway star Walter Connolly roared off with sirens wailing. Only this time he lay peacefully on his back—not running or vomiting, but with a broken leg.

Was Walter through in the picture? I should say not. In less than five hours he was back on the set with a cast on his leg, hobbling on crutches. We even managed to get him into a couple of long shots. He walked on crutches through the rest of the picture. Brilliant actor that he was, he used them to add a wry dimension to his character.

At dawn we wrapped up the shooting. I went looking for Connolly, found him sitting next to a stove in a tent, staring vacantly at nothing. "How do you feel, Walter?" I asked inanely.

"How do I feel? Jesus CHRIST!"

An ace sports writer, Damon Runyon, doing a little moonlighting with his portable, found he had a second, more lasting, talent: Knocking out short stories about ragtag muggs scrounging for crumbs in the twilight zone between the underworld and the supposedly decent upperworld. With his unique, slangy, journalistic idiom—dubbed "Runyonese"—featuring outrageous metaphors and constant use of the present tense ("He win easy"), he contributed his own delightful chapter to the lore of American humor.

Some eggheads dismissed Runyon's style and his beggary *Guys and Dolls* —petty mobsters, pickpockets, molls, grifters, touts, pool hustlers, and panhandlers—as another Broadway passing fad. But knuckleheads loved the fey antics of Louie the Lug, Harry the Horse, the Lemon Drop Kid, Dave the Dude, the Weasel, Butch, Madame La Gimp—all of whom considered honest work a human catastrophe.

An "art" film had won me no Oscar. (There he goes about an Oscar again, as if it were the Holy Grail. Well, it *was* my Holy Grail.) My ploy to wangle a nomination from the "inside," by crashing the Academy's inner priesthood, also fizzled. In the six years of the Academy's existence its award voters had not been impressed by "service." Even old master Cecil B. De Mille, a founder and continuing pillar of the Academy, had never been nominated. Nor were they awed by names: Greta Garbo, acknowledged "queen of queens" among actresses, never won a Best-acting Award in her whole career. There was a mystique about Academy voting that confounded trends, predictions, and logic. Some years the awards were paradoxical.

But those that grabbed off little statuettes didn't give a hang *how* they got one. They just knew an Oscar tripled their salaries and zoomed them to world fame. Salary increases didn't work up my appetite. But world fame— wow! I salivated morning, noon, and night.

All right, then, use your noggin. Go for the paradox. *Bitter Tea* had a cool, blue tinge. Why not try the other end of the story spectrum—the warmer, red end—by filming one of Runyon's muggy Cinderella tales? Who knows? At least the British Commonwealth couldn't ban a fairy tale. Harry Cohn hadn't let me forget that "that arty drek" had lost him money, "and," he superstitiously nudged, "it broke up your winning streak, you louse."

So, while others bid hundreds of thousands for best-selling novels and hit plays, I bought Runyon's "Madame La Gimp" for a measly fifteen hundred dollars. And then began to worry.

It is bizarre, makes no sense, but film studios and filmmakers, like baseball teams and players, have their unexplainable "slumps" and "hot streaks." A studio on a winning streak can't seem to make a mistake. Film after film piles up the long green in box-office tills. Everyone, from president to doorman, reeks with the "sweet smell of success." Salaries rise; the stock soars in the market. Everybody laughs all the way to the bank.

Then, for reasons nobody can fathom, that same studio, with the same successful personnel, suddenly goes into a slump. All their films smell "from herring." They can't buy a good picture for love or money. The result is panic. New York executives come flying out. Bankers tighten their purse strings. The stock takes a nose dive. Meetings, meetings, meetings! Blood pressures hit 200 as white-faced men accuse each other through foam-flecked lips. Usage dictates that heads must roll. But *gar nicht helfen.* The slump cannot be shouted away.

Then, some little-known studio producer or director, out of the panic's jet stream, calmly makes a small picture that is a hit! Magically the gloom dissipates. Western Union's lines heat up with congratulatory messages. Success rides again!

The classic example of this yo-yo phenomenon happened at MGM. During one of its slumps—while the moguls were tearing each other apart—a minor producer, Carey Wilson, was casually making a low-budget "B" picture with unknown teen-agers, which (fortunately) the brawling executives didn't know was being shot. It turned out to be *Andy Hardy Gets Spring Fever.* It made stars out of Mickey Rooney and Judy Garland, broke MGM's slump—and executives popped vest buttons again.

Similar cold and hot streaks plague individual filmmakers. My very long lucky streak at Columbia had become the talk of the town. But critics and friends both warned: "Your slump's coming, bub. Just wait." But so far, my batting average would have made news in baseball: thirteen straight hits— mostly infield singles and beat-out bunts—before striking out with *Miracle Woman*; then, three walks before a bases-loaded strike-out with *Bitter Tea.* Was this last untimely whiffing the beginning of the slump pundits predicted was long overdue?

Harry Cohn must have thought so. He had induced a name director, Howard Hawks, to make an exceptionally fine picture, *Criminal Code.* Capra was no more the lone "gem" in Columbia's diadem.

Besides, while I was striking out, other name directors had made a row of blockbusters: Edmund Goulding—*Grand Hotel*; King Vidor—*The Champ*; John Ford—*Arrowsmith*; Sidney Franklin—*The Guardsman* and *Smiling Through*; Rouben Mamoulian—*Dr. Jekyll and Mr. Hyde*; Clarence Brown—*Emma*; George Cukor—*A Bill of Divorcement*; Howard Hawks— *Scarface*—all made from important novels or plays, and loaded with stars. Was I smart in laying my wavering status on the line with "Madame La Gimp," a fifteen-hundred-dollar short story about an old beggar woman? And where would I find an old star? There was only *one* Marie Dressler— and Louie Mayer wouldn't "loan out" Dressler if you made him Ambassador to Turkey. No, I was getting cold feet on "Madame La Gimp."

Was I losing my cocksureness? At thirty-five? Sure, my curly locks were falling out by the handful; no longer did I sneak narcissistic glances into mirrors. But I was still sure I could direct pictures better than those name directors—or was I? I called Myles Connolly for some encouragement. He gave out with this curved needle: "Frank, pride creates its own banana peels. Step on one, it's a lesson. Step on two? Well, it couldn't happen to a nicer peasant." And hung up.

Then came an unexpected incident that made me a pariah to my fellow filmmakers, and caused a near-fatal event at home.

In March, 1933, Hollywood reeled under the shock of Roosevelt's Bank Moratorium. Most studio executives were in agreement that talent was overpaid. Their cupidity—and stupidity—lured them into the delusion they could use the crisis to effect pay cuts. Studios notified employees: "No salaries till banks reopen." Invoking the "national emergency" clause, Universal suspended all contracts. Studio heads met to discuss closing down. "Help!" they begged of the Academy of Motion Picture Arts and Sciences, the only intra-structure organization in Hollywood.

The Academy made the mistake of its young life. It appointed an Emergency Committee to meet with an Employers' Committee. The committees agreed to graduated pay cuts (up to 50 percent) for a period of eight weeks, or less if banks reopened during the eight-week period. All hell broke loose. "Traitors!" the company heads called us (the Academy officers), for not making the pay cuts permanent. "Stooges!" cried the wrathful actors, writers, and directors as they resigned from the Academy in droves to organize their own guilds. Conrad Nagel resigned as Academy President. Darryl Zanuck guttily resigned as production head of Warner Brothers, when that company refused to reinstate pay cuts after banks reopened.

Academy haters said it was not seismic waves that caused the disastrous earthquake of 1933. It was the roof falling in on the producer-controlled Academy. At any rate, it was just before a meeting of the Academy-Company committees that the earthquake hit. I was having my hair cut in the basement barbershop of the Hollywood Athletic Club, when the building rumbled and rolled. In two seconds I was outside with dozens of others, watching its tall tower swaying and cracking. Swallowing my heart I went back in for a steam bath to calm my jittery nerves. In the foggy steam room I found a lone occupant, calmly reading a paper: a tall, dour-looking bloke with a black patch over one eye. I looked at his legs to see if he had a peg leg, à la Long John Silver. No peg leg.

Then I recognized him—my idol! The fabulous John Ford. To start a conversation, I remarked, "Some earthquake, huh, Mr. Ford?" "What earthquake?" he muttered sourly without looking up from his paper. To ease into introducing myself, I said, "You've heard about the big pay-cut meeting the Academy's holding with the—" Still reading he cut me short: "That's all a lot of horseshit." On that neat appraisal I sneaked out.

An hour later some thirty Academy officers, producers, and lawyers had locked horns on the top floor of the Roosevelt Hotel when the after-shocks came. Angry, shaking fingers froze in mid-air during each tremor. Finally some honest man said: "Look, you guys. I'm no hero. Let's get the hell off this top floor." There was a rush to the elevators. Hardly had we resumed our brouhaha in a corner of the lobby when a sharper shake started an enormous chandelier swinging over our heads. As one man we rushed outside, to reconvene our harsh bickering in an open parking lot under the street lights. We were just revving up to some good name-calling when police cars trundled by with loud speakers blaring: "ALL AMERICAN LEGION MEN TO LONG BEACH! EMERGENCY! ALL AMERICAN LEGION MEN TO LONG BEACH——"

We all froze, then raced to our cars. I suddenly thought of my wife and mother-in-law (an invalid). Sweating for their safety, I raced for Malibu and found Lu hysterical with fear and worry. Our chimney had fallen through the roof and lay in a heap of rubble on the living room floor. It had just missed killing Lu's mother in her wheelchair!

My distraught wife had just recovered from *another* traumatic experience: losing her first baby in a six-month miscarriage. No, sir. The bluebird was not singing in early 1933. Any soothsayer worth his sooth would have said: "A near tragedy in an earthquake, losing your first baby, stooging for producers in the pay-cut mess, flopping with an important film, and losing confidence in your next, add up to a confluence of untidy omens that augur 'condition red' in show biz—a slump."

"Listen, Dago" roared Cohn (he had reverted to calling me that), "*you* wanted to buy that old-lady story, *I* didn't. You wanna make all the decisions around here, then don't gimme no maybe's. For three thousand a week I want *pictures* outta you, not excuses. Now get your ass outta here and get goin'."

"Frank, don't be a damn *fool!*" said Bob Riskin in my office. "We can make a hell of a show out of "Madame La Gimp." I've got a new name for it, *Lady for a Day*. Hit you?"

"*Lady for a Day?* Hey, sounds great."

"Come on, Frank. Screw Cohn. Let's go out to Palm Springs where we can work on the script, and where I can beat the pants off you in tennis."

"Bob, you're a shot in the arm. I'll call Lu to pack—"

There are writers who work for groceries, writers who work for big money, and writers who work for the love of writing. There are writers who write for fame, and others who write for causes: to reform the world, upset the world, own the world. You name the reason for writing, Hollywood will furnish the writer—and his frustrations. Because writing—for whatever reason—is a personal expression. You write *alone*. Except in Hollywood, where writing is *not* a personal expression. You write for, and sometimes with, producers, directors, stars. Often a writer finds himself writing a script with one, or even several, other writers. It can be a galling, ego-bruising, unspotlighted experience. But not always.

If serendipity smiles, a writer may team up with a man who makes his own films. If the team-up is symbiotic and successful, the experience can be *very* rewarding: artistically, economically, and as lagniappe for the ego.

Such was my long team-up with Robert Riskin. It took a war to break us up. Bob was a fine writer, a simpatico man. Natty, witty as they come, he loved life, sports, and women—and vice versa. We had many things in common, but two stood out: (1) our skulls vibrated to the same hair-lady's massager (we spent fortunes on nostrums to cure baldness—and made a startling discovery: cueballs have no dandruff), and (2) our funnybones vibrated to the same tuning fork in humor.

We worked together on scripts, sparking and building on each other's ideas. We were both creators and audiences. In general, I stayed ahead of him, thinking up the next batch of scenes which, when agreed upon, he would put into dialogue script form. And never was there a better "ear" for the spoken word than Riskin's. We worked long and hard on the minutest details. Yet we both knew that scripts are only the basic guidelines to what eventually goes on the screen; that casting, acting, staging, music, and editing are component parts of the overall authorship of the film.

In six weeks we banged out a script; hopefully, a warm, funny "saga" about Apple Annie: a filthy, drunken, apple-selling harridan who bossed the beggars of Times Square. Hidden in the deepest recess of her tatters, Annie nursed a secret of secrets—cabalistically shared only with fellow pan-handlers who swore the beggar's blood oath—Apple Annie had an illegiti-mate daughter! Sh-h-h! A daughter she had been secretly educating (since infancy) in a convent in far-off Spain by extorting "taxes" from the lame, the halt, and the blind who worked her "territory"; in return, she knighted them "godfathers."

A letter came from Spain. Her daughter (now seventeen) has fallen in love with a Spanish nobleman's son. The count wishes to meet *her* family before consenting to the marriage. On the next boat they are arriving to meet her mama—Mrs. E. Worthington Manville.

Apple Annie panics; gets sozzled; heads for the river. But the Big City has a heart—besides which, gangster Dave the Dude has to save the old bag because her apples are his "luck pieces."

So the Dude engineers the craziest of all hoaxes: Beggars, hoods, cops, the mayor, the governor, and half of the "400" conspire to palm off Apple Annie as Mrs. E. Worthington Manville on the Spanish count.

The miracle works! Apple Annie's daughter marries nobility; Dave the Dude saves his lucky apples; the "conspirators," from governor to pan-handlers, grow an inch or two in tolerance.

But who could play Apple Annie? As mentioned before, there was only one major, aged film star: Marie Dressler. But King Mayer would sic Leo the Lion on you if you mentioned her name. In desperation, I made one last pitch to Harry Cohn for Marie Dressler. I found him bedded down with the flu in the boudoir that adjoined his office. A Catholic priest was soothing him.

(This did not surprise me. Whenever Cohn got the slightest ailment, it was a royal crisis! Immediately he commanded the presence of a nose-and-

throat specialist, a heart specialist, a chiropractor, an osteopath, a surgeon—
and for back-ups—a rabbi, a priest, and a Christian Science practitioner.
"Just copping all bets," he would say, "one of 'em might know something.")

"MARIE DRESSLER?!" Cohn shouted, leaping out of bed as if I'd given him
a hotfoot. "You think I want Louis Mayer's fingers in my eyes? The world's
lousy with old dames. Go dig one up!"

I don't remember who made the suggestion, but it was a good one: May
Robson, the seventy-year-old stage star. We sent for her. That grand old lady
was as humble and excited as an understudy subbing for the star. I asked her
to read a few lines from the script. My heart sank. She boomed out the
lines in a voice that could be heard in the next county! A *stage* voice,
muscle-bound by fifty years of throwing it over the footlights.

How could I tell that dear old performer her voice wouldn't *do*, without
offending her or dousing her enthusiasm? And, would she accept the criticism? I tried a little white lie.

"Miss Robson, I forgot to tell you. There are two detectives who suspect
you're not on the up-and-up. They follow you and eavesdrop. And you *know*
it, see. So try the same lines in a hoarse whisper, so they won't hear you.
Understand?"

"Oh, I see, I see. Of course, of *course*. They mustn't hear me. Let me try it
again—"

She reread the lines in an anxious sotto voce that conveyed urgency,
dread, a despairing fear that she would fail her daughter. God bless all the
fine actresses in the world—she was perfect.

The part of Dave the Dude would, of course, have been perfect for James
Cagney (in my book *all* parts would be perfect for Cagney). But he was a
Warner Brothers star. Cohn had as yet nothing to trade for a star. Therefore, on Gower Street, casting was limited to performers "going up" (not
yet contracted), and those "going down" (contracts canceled). From this
free-lance pool we selected Warren William to play Dave the Dude. He was
rugged, handsome, wore clothes well—and played the part beautifully.

For the Dude's moll and fellow conspirator—a Texas Guinan, "Hello
sucker!" night-club-owner type—we only looked as far as Bob Riskin's girl
friend: Glenda Farrell.

The Spanish count could have been played by hundreds of run-of-the-mill
actors. All the count had to do was look distinguished and appear slightly
confused by strange Americanos. But who pleaded to play the "stick" part of
the count? That star in his own right—Walter Connolly! I tried to talk him
out of it, but he countered: "Frank, it is *not* a 'stick' part. I've sneaked a
script, I *know*. The count is the butt of the whole hoax. But he should be
intelligent enough to wonder if everything is kosher. One *slip*, and his
Spanish pride will burn the wings off your fairy tale. Frank, this part has
grace and humor—that pool game with the judge for the dowry is a dream
scene—and it's got *menace*. I don't care what Cohn pays me, LET ME PLAY
THE COUNT."

Lady for a Day, my first big hit, is toasted by the cast. Left to right: Nat Pendleton, Glenda Farrell, Guy Kibbee, Barry Norton, Jean Parker, May Robson, Warren William, Walter Connolly, Hobart Bosworth, Halliwell Hobbes, and Ned Sparks. (EDITOR'S NOTE: This film was first of eleven straight big hits in a row—an unheard of phenomenon in show biz.)

Barbara Stanwyck, Nils Asther, and Walter Connolly in *The Bitter Tea of General Yen* —a strangely poetic love story between members of different races. In 1932 miscegenation was far, far out. So far out, the British Empire banned it, making it my only other Columbia film that lost money.

Banker Huston begs his depositors not to panic. *American Madness* was one of the first Hollywood films to deal realistically and head-on with the contemporary hang-ups of the average American. My concern for the pushed-around little guys was beginning to sprout.

He was so right. Walter played the part with grace, humor, and a gentle but *real* menace that hung over anxious hearts like a sword of Damocles dangling on a silken thread. As the only sane man in the story, he was the rock that kept the fairy tale from flying off into the ridiculous.

The rest of the cast was selected from Hollywood's great storehouse of talent—those wonderful "bit" actors—who "make" many a picture. "Ned" Sparks—he of the dead pan, bleak mien, and parched voice squeezed dry of all compassion—played "Happy," Dude's unhappy henchman. Guy Kibbee was "The Judge": the pompous, threadbare pool shark who hustled yokels in oratorical Harvard lingo. Other casting: Barry Norton and Jean Parker as the young lovers, stumble-bums from "Cauliflower Alley" as the hoods, and real street beggars as the panhandlers.

I looked up one beggar in particular, "Shorty," a man with no legs at all. The bottom of his short torso was covered with a leather pad, on which he sat selling pencils in front of Jeffries' Saloon on Spring Street, when I sold papers there. I used to whizz around on one skate, while he propelled himself with his hands grasping the handles of small wooden blocks—they looked like Mama's irons, only wood—which he used as very short crutches to lift his torso and swing it forward. I used to laugh when he showed his bare leather bottom as he inched along. It reminded me of the bare behinds of monkeys in the zoo.

One day he grabbed me as I skated by him. "Hey, Frankie, lemme see that skate." My skate off, he lifted his torso onto it and pushed himself around with his wooden blocks. He moved fast, with little effort.

"Hey!" he laughed. "By golly, I got *wheels* now!"

"Shorty! Lemme get you a wood block to sit on," I said. It was a miracle to Shorty. Sitting on a block nailed to that skate he could whizz around on one skate as fast as I could.

I found Shorty. He had moved up in class to a "stand" in front of Lyman's Cafe. He looked grayer, better dressed, but still "rode" on a block with one skate under it; only now he took curbs on the run and skittered through traffic like a scared little bug. I introduced myself, told him I was now a movie director and wanted him to play a part in my movie. His answer: "Look, fella, take a walk, will ya?" I had to describe his first skate caper in detail before he was convinced I was Frankie, his newskid pal. And then: "Well cut off my legs and call me Shorty!" (his favorite gag line). "Things *do* happen, don't they, Frankie?" He played one of Apple Annie's panhandlers.

The first sneak preview of *Lady for a Day* sent Harry Cohn high-tailing back to his office to wake up New York executives. "Fly out, you criticizing bastards. I got me a blockbuster!" To me, he said, "You little son-of-a-bitch, you can make shit taste like pineapple," his *ultima Thule* in praise.

The news spread. My newfound—and lifelong—friend, Russian composer Dimitri Tiomkin, beat the drums in fractured syntax. For the press preview Cohn invited—and got the attendance of—most of Hollywood's V.I.P.'s, including that seldom-seen genius, Irving Thalberg. After the showing, one of the greats, Ernst Lubitsch, pumped my hand. Needling Myles Connolly pushed congratulators aside to smother me in a tear-stained bear hug. For the first time, the spotlight was on me—not Cohn.

On September 7, 1933, *Lady for a Day* was booked in the Radio City Music Hall sight unseen (as the Music Hall's head man, Mr. Van Schmus, had promised to book *all* my future pictures; "because," he said, "your *Bitter Tea* was lucky. Since it opened our Music Hall we haven't had a losing week.").

Robson was hailed as a new film star—the equal of Dressler. And glory be to all the saints, Academy voters nominated *Lady for a Day* in four major categories: Best Picture, Best Writing, Best Directing, and Best Actress! And, I became impossible to live with.

In the interim between the nominations and the final voting for the Oscars, I was shooting another comedy at Columbia, but my mind was on those Oscars. Day by day I kept persuading myself that I would win *four* awards for *Lady for a Day*. I looked up the records. No picture had ever won *four* major Oscars. It would set a *record*. Hot damn! I wrote and threw away dozens of acceptance speeches; practiced shy humility before the mirror; rehearsed emotional breaks in my voice at just the right spots. I ordered my first tuxedo—from a tailor, yet; rented a plush home in Beverly Hills—to be "seen," sway votes in bistros. I drove everyone nuts. But Lu kept calm. She was in the ninth month of her second pregnancy.

The world's most publicized event—resplendent with white ties and the newest in cleavage gowns, reported by six hundred flacks—the Academy Awards banquet was held at the Biltmore Hotel. (Another good omen: My old friend Will Rogers would hand out the Oscars. I couldn't miss.) Lu couldn't attend; so, to share my glory, I invited ten intimate friends: Mr. and Mrs. Myles Connolly, Dr. and Mrs. Stan Imerman, Mr. and Mrs. Jo Swerling, Mr. and Mrs. Al Lewin, and Dimitri Tiomkin and his wife, Albertina Rasch. Bob Riskin had his *own* table of nail biters.

During the technical awards given out by good old Will, my head swam through hot and cold flashes. I applauded like an idiot as each winner squeezed through celebrity-crowded tables to the small dance floor, where a spotlight picked him up, escorted him in glory to the dais where he clutched his coveted Oscar—and grinned like another idiot.

Then came the first of the major awards—Best Writing—the first of the *four* I expected to sweep. I looked over at Riskin's table. Bob *seemed* calm, but half of his cigarette disappeared with each puff. Will Rogers announced: ". . . and the winner for Best Writing is . . . [opens envelope] . . . Victor Heerman and Sarah Mason for *Little Women*! Come up and get it!"

I was stunned, but not overcome. "Guess I'll have to settle for *three*," I said inanely to my friends. A vague fear flitted over our table. It was immediately dissipated by Will Rogers. The next award was for Best Directing! While Rogers read the nominations, I sneaked a last quick look under the tablecloth at my wrinkled acceptance speech. But I couldn't even hold it, let alone read it.

Rogers said a few nice words about directors, then: ". . . and the best director of the year is . . . the envelope, please . . . [he opened it, and laughed] Well, well, well, what do you know! I've watched this young man for a long time . . . Saw him come up from the bottom, and I *mean* the bottom. It couldn't happen to a nicer guy. COME UP AND GET IT, FRANK!"

My table exploded into cheers and applause. It was a long way to the open dance floor, but I wedged through crowded tables, "Excuse me . . . excuse me . . . sorry . . . thank you, thank you . . ." until I reached the open dance floor. The spotlight searched around trying to find me. "Over here!" I waved. Then it suddenly swept away from me—and picked up a flustered man standing on the *other* side of the dance floor—Frank Lloyd! The applause was deafening as the spotlight escorted Frank Lloyd on to the dance floor and up to the dais, where Will Rogers greeted him with a big hug and a hearty handshake. I stood petrified in the dark, in utter disbelief, until an irate voice behind me shouted, "Down in front!"

That walk back—through applauding V.I.P.'s yelling "Sit down! Down in front! Sit down!" as I obstructed their view—was the longest, saddest, most shattering walk in my life. I wished I could have crawled under the rug like a miserable worm. When I slumped into my chair I felt like one. All my friends at the table were crying.

The rest of the evening compounded the hurt. For Best Actress—*not* Robson, but Katharine Hepburn for *Morning Glory*. For Best Picture—*not* *Lady for a Day,* but *Cavalcade*.

Sneaking out of the Biltmore, shame soured into bitter, galling anger. I recalled reading Oscar articles to Mama, as she blessed me and cried for joy; sending clippings to my brothers and sisters about my four nominations— which they innocently mistook as *winning* four awards, and sent back "Bravo! Bravo!" letters. Yeah, some Bravo. Big *stupido*—running up to get an Oscar dying with excitement, only to crawl back dying with shame. Those crummy Academy voters; to hell with their lousy awards. If they ever *did* vote me one, I would never, never, NEVER show up to accept it!

Back at my house we all got drunk fast. Al Lewin fell in the goldfish pond; Myles Connolly socked Doc Imerman; Imerman socked Connolly; I passed out in a laughing jag. But Lu kept her cool and smiled—smiled as only happy, pregnant women and Mona Lisa can smile.

A couple of weeks later, on the morning of March 20, 1934, our first child was born. Dr. Vruink insisted I watch the birth. "A boy!" said an excited nurse. "Say hello to Frank, Jr.," said Dr. Vruink, holding a writhing, crying, red little creature up by its hind paws. My heart sank. It wasn't human. Its face was a wrinkled onion, and its head was curved and pointed like a banana. I ran out of the delivery room to where Dimitri Tiomkin was waiting for me. "Dimi! Dimi! It's got a banana head . . . It's Zip . . . the missing link . . ."

"Papichka, you need big drink . . ."

An hour later, Tiomkin practically carried me back to Lu's hospital room. And there she was, holding her newborn, wearing a smile that rivaled the sunrise, and doing the first thing all new mothers do over and over—counting the little guy's fingers and toes. I embraced her and glanced at our firstborn. I couldn't believe my hard-to-focus eyes. "Lu! Where's its banana head? That's the most beautiful baby in the world!"

"Course it is, darling. He looks exactly like you—"

PART II
Struggle with Success

CHAPTER 9

Winning the Grail

IRVING BERLIN said it all in one line: "There's no business like show business." But had he worked at Columbia Studio in 1934 he might have been tempted to add three words: "except film business."

Shortly before I made such a public ass of myself, knocking people down when Will Rogers cried out, "Come up and get it, Frank!" another picture of mine had opened at Radio City Music Hall. It opened quietly with no great beating of drums or bating of breath (Columbia needed all its breath to cope with the deliriums of "Oscaritis" fever).

So quietly did the picture open, it failed to merit the usual second-week holdover at the Music Hall: a black mark against future business. That was disappointing, but no great surprise; two previous "bus-trip" films had recently rolled off Hollywood's "trend" lines, and both had run into box-office trouble. Trend devotees were jubilant. They predicted this third "bus" picture would never get out of low gear.

The critics, too, were caught with their adjectives down. Kate Cameron, the Delphic priestess with acknowledged prophetic powers to feel the picture-public's pulse, appropriately rated films with cryptic stars at the head of her column: one star—a Bronx cheer; four stars—hallelujahs. She dismissed this latest bus opus with two and a half stars (she had given *Lady for a Day* a "rave" three and a half stars). *Newsweek* called it "diverting," *The Nation* pontificated, ". . . entertaining," but "to claim any significance for the picture . . . would of course be a mistake."

Then—it happened. Happened all over the country—not in one night, but within a month. People found the film longer than usual and, surprise, funnier, much funnier than the usual. But, biggest surprise of all, they could remember in detail a good deal of what went on in the film and they found that everybody else did and that it was great fun talking about this and that scene. And let's go see it again and take the Johnsons. The quietness burst into the proverbial prairie fire. Theaters sold out for weeks and weeks. Critics went back for a second look, a third, a fourth—and wondered how such excitement could be generated by such routine material. The picture was *It Happened One Night*.

Astonishingly enough, the *news* about *It Happened One Night* was not that it made the "classic" ranks, but that it ever got made at *all*. A film about the making of *It Happened One Night* would have been much funnier than the picture itself. It would have furnished comical proof of two Hollywood adages: The only rule in filmmaking is that there *are* no rules, and the only prediction is that *all* predictions are by guess and by God until the film plays in theaters. And who would have it any other way? *Uncertainty* is the fun of it all; the door that can't be locked by film rajahs against adventuresome newcomers.

Anyhow, this "film history" comedy was conceived, quite by accident, in Palm Springs during the script-writing of *Lady for a Day*. Waiting in a barbershop, I picked up a *Cosmopolitan* magazine and scanned through a short story, "Night Bus," written by Samuel Hopkins Adams. It had the smell of novelty. Riskin read it. He agreed. I asked the studio to check out the asking price. "Buttons!" came back the answer. "We can buy it for five G's." "Buy it," I said—and promptly forgot about "Night Bus."

Climbing down off cloud nine wasn't easy after the hoopla previews of *Lady for a Day* but, as Cohn often said, "You count your blessings, I'll count your pictures. Get going!" Riskin and I reread *Night Bus*; wondered why we bought it. Oh, well, Palm Springs had been lucky for us once; we'd give the desert another go with the *Night Bus* script.

"Like hell you're going to Palm Springs!" roared Cohn in between flailing his riding crop and barking into telephones for the benefit of his captive audience. (Cohn now sported the super-status trademark of the film mogul: hamming it up for a constant "audience" in his office, usually a pretty starlet and a faceless young man acting as a "beard" or stand-in to divert suspicion from hanky-pankies.) "You're going to Culver City—to MGM again."

"What?! I wouldn't go back to MGM if you—"

"See what I mean about running a big studio?" This, raising eyes to heaven, he addressed to the starlet and the "beard." Both shrugged sympathetically. "I *made* this director, picked his name out of a hat, own him body and soul—and he won't go to MGM, hah! I could send him to Hitler's UFA, God forbid!" Then, back to me, "Listen, fat head, Irving Thalberg has offered me a fifty-thousand-dollar bonus *and* the loan of one of his *stars*, if you make a picture for him."

"Not unless I can produce my own show, as I do here."

"That's not in your contract."

"I don't read contracts. Besides, what about *Night Bus*?"

"Forget bus pictures. People don't want 'em. MGM and Universal just made two bus operas and they both stink."

Back I went to MGM; this time not as a scared "B" director, but as a protégé of Vice President Irving Thalberg, the thirty-five-year-old guiding genius of Metro's films, loved by all actors, writers, directors, producers —but hated by Vice President L. B. Mayer.

But, protégé or not, MGM always gave me the queasy, uneasy feeling I had entered a strange world that denied rationality. For instance, I always thought that a house divided against itself cannot stand. It didn't go for the citadel of MGM. Its fortunes were guarded by a figurative paradox: a Janus with two hostile heads, Mayer and Thalberg, who snarled and ruled with equal power. Yet the last roar was Leo the Lion's.

Divided, MGM stood. Concerning aesthetic values, I always felt the world cannot fall apart as long as free men see the rainbow, feel the rain, and hear the laugh of a child. But at MGM there was little room for freedom in its stratified class structure, and what seemed to inspire each class was not beauty, but the opulence, arrogance, and pot bellies of those above them. Nevertheless, MGM was the Mecca of filmmakers. It beat me. Probably all wild imaginings anyway, evoked by an innate peasant envy of the upper crust. Besides, it was no skin off my nose *what* these uncouth big shots did to each other. They could have my end of the rat-race as soon as I made my pile.

Anyhow, I didn't envy or scorn Irving Thalberg. Like everybody else I fell in love with him—and he with me. From the dozen scripts he had me read I chose *Soviet*, a strong melodrama about an American engineer hired to build a super dam in Russia. Thalberg promised me a "dream" cast: Wally Beery, Marie Dressler, Joan Crawford, and Clark Gable—wow!

Nearing *Soviet*'s starting date, frail Thalberg had to go to Europe for health reasons. Left in sole command, Mayer couldn't wait to harpoon Thalberg's pet projects. He canceled *Soviet*, sent me packing back to Columbia, but he still honored Cohn's bonus and loan-out of one of MGM's stars. Without Mayer's hatred there would have been no *It Happened One Night*.

Back at Columbia, I sailed into Cohn: "Going to MGM was the first thing you've made me do against my—"

"Quit yapping. So you *didn't* make the picture, but I got me a *star*. Go beat that for a deal." I couldn't. His values were slipperier than quicksilver. At any rate, I declared my next film would be a comedy—*Night Bus*! Trends or no trends. Riskin had written an outline; I liked it; we were going back to lucky Palm Springs to write the script, and that was that. "Go where the hell ever you want. But get that word 'bus' outta the title. It's poison."

Thus, in the fall of 1934, we were back at the Desert Inn. Lu watched our firstborn, six-months-old Frank, Jr., rattle toys in his playpen (she was in her chronic condition—pregnant again), while Bob and I, in shorts, worked at bridge tables in the sun and annoyed the neighbors no end with explosive laughs at our own gags.

Finishing the script, we changed the title from *Night Bus* to *It Happened One Night*—as a sop to Cohn—and took it back to the studio for "conferences." Cohn read it; played it cagey; his lone comment, "Well, I'm glad you took that lousy 'bus' outta the title." But following Parkinson's Law, success had inflated both the numbers and the heads of Cohn's supervisory personnel. Aping the god-like omniscience of MGM's supervisors, Columbia execs attacked with critical jeremiads.

"It's nothing," they said . . . "froth, trivia" . . . "just another bus picture" . . . "no suspense" . . . "no heart" . . . "no oomph!" . . . "besides, that mile-long title, *It Happened One Night*—how you gonna get it on the marquee?" . . . "winter's coming" . . . "it's all exteriors" . . . "the weather'll murder you" . . . "shelve it, Harry."

Cohn just listened. Lately, his boasts about "owning" me were cooling off; Iago whispers warned him he was building up his Frankenstein's monster. The all-too-common phrase in the gossip columns—"Capra is Columbia"— would have galled a studio head of one-tenth Cohn's ego. So, while his front office cabal blasted the script, he eyed me closely for some sign of weakness. Riskin watched the byplay with an impish grin.

"Well, genius," said Bob in his office as he fell into a chair and began laughing, "how does it feel to play a game of darts with you as the dart board?"

"Darts? I thought they were throwing knives. What's with this Cohn guy? It takes a genius to stay *even* with that self-made son-of-a-bitch. He's out to kill this picture, Bob. Why?"

"Naw-w," said Riskin, "he's out to put a crimp in your halo. Nothing wrong with Cohn that a Capra pratfall wouldn't cure."

"You know what, Bob? We're going to make *It Happened One Night*."

"Positively, Mr. Gallagher?"

"Absolutely, Mr. Shean."

At the next general conference, Cohn threw me the ball. "Well, Frank, let's get off the pot. What about this bus picture?"

All eyes focused on me. The prestige of Cohn's producers, supervisors, and private kibitzers would soar if they could make me turn tail. I lobbed the ball back to Cohn.

"Harry, I've listened to all the comments. I'm grateful for them. But I don't agree with them. I like the script, and I want to *make* it—as is."

The eyes turned to him. He stared back at me. I stared back. His jaw stuck out; his cheeks twitched; his nose widened. I knew then that man would hate me. I also knew it was folly to step too hard on a general's toes. "But Harry, *you're* the president of Columbia. In my book the man that puts up the money makes the final decisions."

Cohn relaxed. He had saved face. He stood up, banged his crop, and said: "All right! We've screwed around enough with this bus thing. If Capra wants to make it, that's good enough for me. What about the casting? Who can play the girl?"

I spoke up. "Harry, since MGM owes you a star, my first choice is Myrna Loy. If we get her—"

"What d'ya mean, *if* we get her? Course I'll get her."

We sent the script to Myrna Loy. And lo and behold! She turned it down. I was under the impression stars were dying to get into my pictures. Not Myrna Loy. "Papa" Mayer unctuously backed her up: "Harry, you know I *never* ask one of my little girls to play a part she don't want."

We sent a script to Margaret Sullavan. Maggie said, "No, thank you." Cohn called a top-level meeting. The opposition smirked. "We told you so. Turning down *It Happened One Night* is becoming a trend. If it gets out in the papers, you'll *never* cast it."

We resorted to clandestine approaches. A friend of a friend casually slipped a script to Miriam Hopkins. The friend of a friend returned it, hinting Miriam was insulted. "Not if I *never* play another part," she was reported as saying.

Riskin and I stopped laughing. The situation was not only getting ridiculous; it was ominous. We reread the script. It didn't read that bad to us. Another top-level strategy meeting. Let me say this about Harry Cohn. His faults may have been legion, but as a studio head he had a rare, uncommon virtue. When he decided to back you, he'd back you to the hilt—even if he'd rather see the hilt sticking out of your back.

We decided to approach the next actress-candidate personally, rather than through agents or go-betweens. We found out that Constance Bennett was vacationing in Palm Springs—and available. Sam Jaffe was then a Columbia executive, assistant to number two man Sam Briskin. Jaffe knew Connie Bennett well.

"Jaffe," said Cohn, "take this bus script to Connie Bennett at Palm Springs and for chrissake *sell* it to her. And don't you come back till that Bennett broad agrees to play the part—and not a dime over thirty G's. Hear?"

Sam Jaffe was a very smart man (later a big agent), a friend of mine and next-door neighbor at Malibu. But he sincerely despised the *It Happened One Night* script and said so. "Harry," pleaded Jaffe, "Connie's a dear friend. How can I sell her something I don't like myself? If she asks my opinion I'll tell her not to take the part."

"Goddam it, Jaffe!" exploded Cohn. "Who you working for, Columbia or the Salvation Army? Get your ass down to Palm Springs."

Jaffee took his derrière down to Palm Springs, but not his enthusiasm. As he expected, Constance Bennett told him to go fly a kite. "But," he triumphantly reported to Cohn, "Connie offered to *buy* the script and have it rewritten for *her*. And she'll pay a small profit over what we got in it. It's a great out, Harry." Other executives agreed.

"What d'ya think, Frank? We can get rid of this bus megillah at a profit."

"I think Connie Bennett has more brains than all of you put together. She's buying a Capra-Riskin script for peanuts. If she makes a hit out of it you'll be the laugh of the town . . ."

"Look, big shot. We been *weeks* trying to cast this thing."

"A couple of more weeks, just a couple of weeks. Then you can sell it."

Unknown to Cohn, Riskin and I had been secretly rewriting the script to fit an all-important change suggested by my critical friend, Myles Connolly.

"Frank, it's easy to see why performers turn down your script," said Myles after reading it. "Sure, you've got some good comedy routines, but your leading characters are non-sympathetic, non-interest-grabbing. People can't identify with them. Take your girl: a spoiled brat, a rich heiress. How many spoiled heiresses do people know? And how many give a damn what happens to them? She's a zero. Take your leading man: a long-haired, flowing-tie, Greenwich Village painter. I don't know any vagabond painters, and I doubt if *you* do. And the man I don't know is a man I'm apt to dislike, especially if he has no ideals, no worms, no dragons to slay. Another zero. And when zero meets zero you've got zero interest.

"Now. Your girl. Don't let her be a brat because she's an *heiress*, but because she's *bored* with being an heiress. More sympathetic. And the man. Forget that panty-waist painter. Make him a guy we all know and like. Maybe a tough, crusading reporter—at outs with his pig-headed editor. More sympathetic. And when he meets the spoiled heiress—well, it's THE TAMING OF THE SHREW. But the shrew must be worth taming, and the guy that tames her must be one of *us*."

This was Connolly at his very best—a story editor. I told Riskin. He said, "What chumps we are!" and we rewrote the whole story in a week. Cohn was amazed. "Now, Harry, if we can cast a good man star first, it'll be easier to get a girl. MGM has a great light comedian, Robert Montgomery."

Out went the script to MGM again. Back it came. Bob Montgomery turned it down.

Then came the first break in "The Perils of *It Happened One Night*." Cohn was crying his eyes out to L. B. Mayer on the phone. "But Harry," soothed Mayer, "Montgomery says there are too many bus pictures. And Herschel, no offense, stars don't like changing their address from MGM to Gower Street. But Herschel, you caught me in a good mood. I got an actor here who's being a bad boy. Wants more money. And I'd like to spank him. You can have Clark Gable."

"Louie, 'spose *he* don't like the script?"

"Herschel, this is Louis Mayer talking. I'm *telling* you to take Gable."

"Clark Gable?!" I said incredulously to Cohn. "I've only seen him in *The Last Mile*. He played a tough killer."

"Walyo, it's Gable or nothing, understand? He's on his way over to see you."

I understood only too well. Whenever Mayer sneezed, Cohn took aspirin. Cohn *had* to make *It Happened One Night* now because Mayer wanted to punish "bad boy" Gable by forcing him into a Poverty Row picture—exile to Siberia for hoity-toity MGM stars.

I knew it was Gable when I heard someone stumbling up the dingy stairs that led to my dingy office on the second floor of the dingy inner courtyard. My open doorway darkened; tall, square-shouldered Gable stood there swaying, hat rakishly tilted over his eyes. Evidently, he had stopped at every bar between MGM and Gower Street.

"Is thish *Mishter* Frank Capra's office?"

"Yes, Mr. Gable. I'm Frank Capra. Come in, please, come in."

"Gla-ad to meet cha. Likewise." He headed for a kitchen chair and plopped himself on it. I held my breath. The chair groaned, but didn't break. Oh, was he loaded! Through bleary eyes he tried to focus on my early period furniture—early Army camp. He cleared his throat with a disgusted belch. Then he focused on me.

"Well-l, what's the poop, shkipper—besides me?" He was not only boiled, he was *steamed*.

"Well, Mr. Gable, I—"

"That son-of-a-bitch Mayer," he cut in. "I always *wanted* to see Siberia, but damn me—I never thought it would *smell* like this. Blech-h-h!"

My insides were curdling. I picked up a script and riffled it. "Mr. Gable, you and I are supposed to make a picture out of this. Shall I tell you the story, or would you rather read the script by yourself?"

"Buddy," he said in his tough-guy drawl, "I don't give a fuck *what* you do with it."

There being no handy rebuttal to that conversation stopper, I mumbled something about *my* Siberia being MGM, tucked the script under his armpit, and suggested he read it between drinks. He swayed to his feet, looked down at me, and giggled drunkenly, "Hee hee-e-e! Sez you." He wobbled out the door, hit both sides of it, then stumbled off singing, "They call her frivolous Sa-a-al; a peculiar kind of a—hey, you guys!" this last to some Columbians in the courtyard, "Why ain't you wearing *parkas* in Siberia—"

That was my first meeting with Clark Gable and, I hoped, my last. I told Cohn what I thought he wanted to hear: that Gable wouldn't show up again; that I was fed up with all the lousy actors and actresses who turned down the lousy script, fed up with "bus" trend pictures that wouldn't sell, and that he and his supervisors were right—we ought to shelve the whole damn thing. Surprisingly, Cohn pulled a switch. He said he was committed to Mayer to make the picture, that Gable would *have* to show up or never play in another film, and now that we had a leading man, how about the leading girl? I told him I was fresh out of leading girls.

"But I'm not, stupid. I gotta brainstorm—Claudette Colbert."

"Colbert? She's under contract to *Paramount*."

"Yeah, yeah—but she's taking a four-week vacation. And I hear that French broad likes money. Why don't you and Riskin go see her personal?"

Riskin and I went to her house personal. The first thing that happened— as a maid let us in—Colbert's big French poodle sneaked up and bit me in the tail. Feeling my torn pants, my hands came up bloody. "We're in!" quipped Riskin. "You've drawn first blood. Oh, oh—wipe your hands, here comes Froggy—"

Froggy was in a French tizzy. She said it was all a mistake, she shouldn't have made the appointment, she was in the middle of packing, Bill and Edie Goetz were waiting for her in Sun Valley, she was leaving in half an hour, would we please excuse her. As the words tumbled out of her I could see her as perfect for the part of the rich heiress: spoiled, bratty, lovely. We wouldn't let up on her; followed her around while she packed; double-teamed her in extolling the script. Exasperated, she turned on us.

"Can't you understand? I'm tired. I'm leaving for Sun Valley. I don't want to *hear* any story. I don't want to hear *anything*. Paramount pays me twenty-five thousand per picture. You *double* that, and finish with me four weeks from today?—which you can't—so please leave me *alone*."

"Harry?" I said to His Crudeness on the phone. "You're right. She likes money. She wants fifty thousand—"

"Fifty G's? That's *double* her salary."

"That's just for openers. We've got to finish with her in four weeks."

"Can you do that?"

"No." There was a long pause. Decisions, decisions.

"Look, goddam you, you started this jinx thing. You finish her in four weeks—and I'll double her salary—"

"Deal, Claudette! Fifty thousand for four weeks! Okay?"

"Oh, for God's sake!" she cried, stunned at the offer. Now she *was* in a tizzy. Lovely and feminine as they come, Claudette had a mind as bright as a dollar, and a French appreciation of its luster. She held the last bottle of oxygen that would keep *It Happened One Night* alive. Would she give? It wasn't easy. Colbert still remembered that her first film, *For the Love of Mike*, was a stinker—and that Frank Capra made it.

"All right, damn it! I'll do the picture." But she added one proviso: Come hell or high water she would leave the picture December 23 to spend Christmas with the Goetzes at Sun Valley. As we stood there it was already November 21!

"Deal, Claudette," I said. "We start the show this week. Your wardrobe is simple: one ordinary street dress and a wedding gown. I'll send you a script. Thanks."

As Riskin and I got into our car I couldn't help saying, "Tough dame, that lovely frog." "Tough?" he snickered. "Wait'll she sees that blood you dripped all over her beautiful carpet."

Much has been said and much more written about the "meanings" and importance of *It Happened One Night*: a "classic" of modern cinema; the precedent setter of a "new wave"; will go down in film "history." Forgive me, but read, if you will, this purple blurb (if you understand it you are one-up on me):

Take Stew Smith of *Platinum Blonde*, Jones (Walter Connolly) of *The Bitter Tea of General Yen*, the gangster from *Lady for a Day*, cut, add, and blend well, and you have the newspaper man Clark Gable of this film—the classic "Picaro" rogue. Take the tough little adventuress of *Ladies of Leisure*, the phony evangelist of *Miracle Woman*, and the brave girl of *The Bitter Tea of General Yen*, stir well and you have the spoiled heiress Claudette Colbert. Take the class clash of *Platinum Blonde* and *American Madness* with an . . . improved version of the mass-hero from the latter, plunge them into the swift, broad river of Life—the open road— and you have a new *Canterbury Tales* and a new *Don Quixote* with Frank Capra as Cervantes and the venerable Don at the same time. It (*It Happened One Night*) was the Picaresque adventure of its era—the classic framework basically the same as Chaucer's . . . a busload of people . . . experience adventures together . . . our hero romances the snobbish heroine and does battle against the wind-mills of bourgeois chivalry . . . the mass-hero or hero-mass human-ized in its true place: the Picaresque tale.

I assure you I never anticipated—nor was I capable of—putting such esoteric "meanings" in *It Happened One Night*.

In fact, I was so dog-tired from all the road-work and shadow-boxing and suspense involved in putting this on-again, off-again project together, I felt like the overtrained fighter who left his fight in the gym. All I wanted to do was to get the bloody film over with, hampered as I was with a $325,000 budget, a four-week schedule, and winter exterior shooting.

So I shot scenes fast and unworried, much like Julius Boros shoots golf: walk up to the ball, hit it, laugh, and walk on without losing stride. Relieved from the onus of studio "expectations," we slammed through the film clowning, laughing, ad-libbing. Furthermore, Columbia's excitement— and mine—was being inflamed by trade-paper speculations as to how many Oscars *Lady for a Day* would win at the upcoming Academy Awards Banquet. All else fades into the background when "Oscaritis" fever strikes.

But two "happenings" during the shooting of *It Happened One Night* may be worth noting. One: Colbert fretted, pouted, and argued about her part; challenged my slap-happy way of shooting scenes; fussed constantly about making her date at Sun Valley. She was a tartar, but a cute one. In the well-known hitchhiking scene in which she proves her leg is greater than Gable's thumb, she refused to pull up her dress and show her leg. We waited until the casting director sent us a chorus girl with shapely underpinnings to "double" for Colbert's. When she saw the double's leg, she said, "Get her out of here. I'll do it. That's not *my* leg!" And it sure wasn't. There are no more luscious gams in the world than Colbert's—not even Marlene's.

In the titillating "walls of Jericho" scene (Colbert and Gable in twin beds

It Happened One Night shook the Oscar tree. It is, so far, the only film to make a clean sweep of the five most publicized Academy Awards: Best Picture, Best Actor (Gable), Best Actress (Colbert), Best Writer (Riskin), Best Director. Here, Gable and Colbert look for cars to flag down. In this scene, Colbert proves that in hitchhiking, her leg is mightier than his thumb.

It Happened One Night was mostly shot in real locations: buses, highways, byways, coffee shops, and among the new phenomena that had sprung up on the American scene—motels.

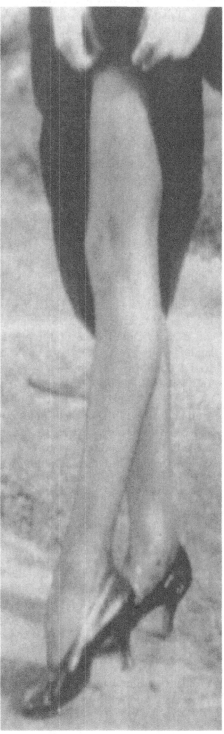

separated by the "walls"—a blanket over a clothesline), Claudette refused to even partially undress before the camera. She wanted to feature her acting, not her sex appeal. This led to a much sexier scene: Gable watching her undies being draped one by one on the "walls of Jericho."

But all her little tantrums—motivated by her antipathy toward me—were rehearsals for the picture. All she had to do was to bug Gable *on* camera as she bugged me *off* camera. And she was wonderful in the part—even though, after she joined her friends at Sun Valley, she was quoted as saying, "Am I glad to get here. I've just finished the worst picture in the world."

And, two: The metamorphosis of Clark Gable, the "bad boy" exiled to Siberia. It took him a day or two to get over his "burn," but when he did he had the time of his life. I believe it was the only picture in which Gable was ever allowed to play himself: the fun-loving, boyish, attractive, he-man rogue that was the *real* Gable.

As an example of our slap-happy ad-libbing I should mention the song "The Daring Young Man on the Flying Trapeze." To add color to our heterogeneous busload of people, we casually wrote in a hillbilly duet rehearsing a number to relieve the monotony of a driving rainstorm the bus was plowing through. In taking a close-up of the two hillbillies rehearsing, I noticed adjacent passengers spontaneously joined in the singing. It gave me a hint. Ordering several more cameras, I covered all the passengers simultaneously with long, medium, and close shots (to get one "master" sound track for all camera angles) and told the people: "No rehearsals. Just join in the singing in any way and at any time you feel like it."

Truculent Gable and "brat" Colbert sat next to each other, but intense mutual dislike still kept them poles apart. I asked them to slowly "unfreeze," and if the spirit moved them, to join in the gang song.

Well, after shouting "Action!" I just sat back and laughed. One by one the passengers shed their inhibitions and became nutty showoffs. They sang, danced, made up their own verses. But all joined as one in the chorus, holding on to the "Oh!" until their faces were blue.

> "O-o-o-o-o-o-o-o-o-oh, he flies through the air
> with the greatest of ease—
> This daring young man on the flying trapeze—"

Gable lost his truculence—he joined the singing. The "brat" dropped her brattiness—she joined in the fun. I sat in my chair watching that busload of singing strangers shed more than their taboos. Now it was a mass striptease of their autumn years. They were children again, romping and rollicking like lambs in springtime. And Gable and Colbert rollicked with them. But how was I going to end this gang-song frolic? I needed a topper.

Fishing for an inspiration, I saw the sourpuss bus driver—annoyed at his busload of nuts—turn away from his rain-swept windshield and add *his* raucous "O-o-o-oh!" to the bedlam. Sure. That was it. Let his turning away cause the bus to veer off the road into a muddy ditch, piling up the passengers into a laughing, happy mass of human bodies.

The picture got finished on time and on budget, and Claudette made her Christmas date in Sun Valley. Since Columbia's New York office clamored for another "Capra film," film cutter Gene Havlick and I hurriedly strung the scenes together into a long, two-hour version, and we previewed it before an audience. I thought the preview went well, but it didn't raise the Hollywood huzzahs that followed *Lady for a Day*'s previews. Cohn held the usual post-preview conference in his office. The Cassandras who had prophesied doom for *It Happened One Night* didn't give up.

"Much too long, Harry" . . . "no comedy can stand two hours" . . . "it's not Ben Hur" . . . "it's just a longer *bus* film" . . . "theaters will lose one show" . . . "know what that means in revenue?" . . . "cut it down" . . . "cut out half an hour and what schmuck will know the difference?" . . . "cut it down, Harry!"

Cohn turned to me. "Whatta ya say, Frank?"

"I'm sick of it, Harry. Ship it."

"Ship it!" said Cohn to his head film editor, then quickly: "All right, you muzzlers. I'm laying even money Columbia cops at least *two* Oscars next week for *Lady for a Day*—" You know what happened.

But at next year's Academy Award Banquet, February 27, 1935—wow! *It Happened One Night* grabbed all *five* major awards: Best Picture, Best Actress, Best Actor, Best Writer—and Best Director!—through 1970, the *only* picture so honored.

It was a dizzy night. All my same friends who had suffered with me last year through the *Lady for a Day* debacle were again at my table—and leaping deliriously out of their minds, as—but let Lyle Abbott, of the Los Angeles *Herald-Express* describe the scene:

> Claudette Colbert! Clark Gable! They were crowned last night . . . as the outstanding actress and actor of 1934.
>
> And, to complete the picture, their film, *It Happened One Night*, . . . received the accolade as the major production of the year . . .
>
> . . . Irvin S. Cobb, incomparable humorist, tried, like any good master of ceremonies, to keep his audience keyed to the mood of surprise (as he opened envelopes). But he soon failed.
>
> "You guessed it," he shouted over the loud speakers. "It is something that . . ." ". . . Happened one night!" vociferated the audience. At tables, in aisles, crowding the entrances, the guests at the dinner took up the refrain . . . "Happened One Night!" . . .
>
> Hidden at one of the obscure tables was Miss Colbert . . . in a tan sport suit. For Miss Colbert was going east. Her train was about to leave. An ardent coterie of studio attendants had dragged her to the Academy dinner—"just in case."

George Lewis, Los Angeles *Post-Record*:

> . . . There was a taxi waiting and a great mixup of men briskly clearing each other aside to provide a lane as [Miss Colbert] in traveling clothes, accepted the award from Irvin S. Cobb and kissed him, and tripped out, gold statuette in hand like a kewpie doll she won at a carnival, to catch a train . . .
>
> Yet she hesitated in flight from the Biltmore, half ran back to the microphones, and in a flutter of enthusiasm, said: "I owe Frank Capra for this."

My friends sloshed me and each other with champagne. When we got back to my house, Lewin fell into the fish pond again, Imerman socked Connolly, Connolly socked Imerman, Tiomkin banged out Chopin Ballades, his wife Albertina toe-danced, I passed out on the lawn clutching my Oscar. Lu? She kept her cool and smiled her Mona Lisa smile. She was in the seventh month of her third pregnancy. Dizzy night.

I had scaled the Mount Everest of Filmlandia. Nine years after my first childish gags for the *Our Gang* kids I had knocked off all my challenges. What should I do for an encore? What *could* I do for an encore?

All roads from Everest led downward. As overnight Mr. Bigs discover, success creates its own new challenges—subtle, powerful, soul-testing inner challenges that measure a man for what he *is*, not for his medals. I had licked poverty and ridicule; I had yet to lick a bigger enemy: myself. Externally, I accepted the laurels with a show of grace. But inwardly, I had become a pillar of jello; haunted by fear that my next picture would fail. In short, I made the major leagues—and choked up.

Show business is brutal to has-beens. Those pushed off the top are rolled into the valley of oblivion; often into degradation. I saw it all around me: D. W. Griffith—a forgotten man; Mack Sennett—walking unnoticed in the city he once ruled as King of Comedy; old stars pleading for jobs as extras; champ fighters, reduced to stumble bums, babbling for handouts. Cheers on the way up, piranha bites on the way down. That was not for me. Quit while you're ahead.

But how? I had a contract for two pictures a year with Columbia. They sold their whole program of low-budget films on the strength of two Capra films. I had to hit a home run every time I came to bat to keep them out of the cellar. Atlas carried only the world—I was carrying Harry Cohn on my back. And all the story material I had read since the *It Happened One Night* awards sounded trivial. This was slavery all over again. Success, fine. But who needed the torture of constantly *proving* he was number one. One failure, one flop picture, would knock off my crown. I felt sorry for all the kings in the world. No. I would quit. Go to South America, start over again—anything but make another picture. But how?

Then it came to me—a brilliant out! Burnish my halo with martyrdom—get sick!

I began the secret malingering campaign at the studio—complaining of tiredness, sitting through conferences like a Buddha with glazed eyes. I carried my charade home, neglected my usual romping on the floor with one-year-old Frank, Jr.; headed for a couch instead of embracing Lu. She asked me if I felt ill.

"No, no, darling. Just tired, tired." Should she call Stanley (our family doctor)? "No, it'll go away. It's nothing, nothing."

My worried wife invited Dr. Stanley and his wife, Connie, over for a bridge game. I played like a fatigued snail.

"Hey, stupid," Dr. Imerman remarked after a silly play, "you forgot to follow suit."

"Don't pick on him, Stanley. He's too tired," said Lu.

"Tired, huh? What's the matter, genius, those Academy Awards getting too heavy to carry around?"

"I think he's mad they haven't put his picture on money yet," kidded Connie Imerman.

"Oh, funny, funny." I threw my cards down and went to the bathroom. Stanley followed me in with his black bag.

"Just kidding, chum. How long've you been feeling tired?" he asked.

"Couple of weeks," I answered as he poked a thermometer in my mouth and took my pulse. In silence he read the thermometer; then examined my nose, throat, and ears. Closing his bag he said: "Nothing, Frank. Temperature and pulse slightly up. Take a drink and go to bed."

As Connie and Stanley were leaving he turned to my wife. "Lu, take his temperature every day at noon, will you, doll? And call my office."

My wife reported my noon temperature daily to Imerman: 99.6—100—100.5. The plot was working beautifully. I was such a good director I could even make the thermometer do what I wanted. Imerman sent me to a Beverly Hills nose specialist, who poked, stuffed, and irrigated my nose and sinuses. "Sinusitis," he pontificated, "bug going around." I laughed to myself on the way home: "How stupid can doctors be?"

But Imerman was worried about my continuous temperature. "Go to the radiologist at the Cedars of Lebanon Hospital," he ordered me, "and get your chest X-rayed. I've arranged it for you."

The plot was thickening. X rays now. Beautiful. Peering into my chest the radiologist puckered his face sourly and began to make clucking noises: "Oh, me . . . Tsk, tsk, tsk . . . but it's curable . . . tsk, tsk, tsk . . ."

"*What's* curable?"

"Don't worry, don't worry. Dr. Imerman will tell you. Now, we'll take the X rays. Tsk, tsk, tsk . . ."

What was going on here? This was all supposed to be a charade.

Back home I told my wife what had happened. I saw the worry in her eyes as she bent over her large stomach in covering me up in bed. Wonderful girl. I hadn't rubbed her bigness for so many nights. It was a happy ritual with us. She would lie on her back in bed while I rubbed her tight skin with lanolin to keep it from cracking. But what thrilled us both into happy titters was feeling the little knees and elbows kicking around inside her. She glowed; as all pregnant women glow—in wonder at the great miracle of new life inside them.

Late that day Dr. Imerman came by. Without saying much he took my temperature: 101.

"Chum," he said quietly, "the X rays show a spot on your right lung."

"What's that mean?"

"I'm not sure yet. I'll need a sample of your sputum."

"You worried about the old rale?"

"Could be. Tiredness, temperature, and spots—I've ordered a couple of nurses, to make it easier for Lu."

"Stan, wake up. There's nothing wrong with me. I've been kidding."

"TB isn't kidding. Stay in bed. No visitors, no phone calls. I asked the nose guy to treat you every day just in case. Spit me some in this bottle."

"Oh, boy," I said gleefully, "Harry Cohn'll have a fit."

"I called him already. He screamed bloody murder. Said I was trying to ruin him. Said that Dago sells all his pictures. Threatened to sue *me*."

"Good old Harry." I handed Stan his bottle. "Did you tell Lu?"

"Yeah, on the way in. She didn't believe a word of it. Great gal. See you in the morning."

That night the sweats hit me; the first of many "all night" sweats that were to reduce me to a broomstick. The daily cycle had a definite pattern; sleep, slight temperature in the morning; sinuses irrigated at noon; fever at about 2 P.M., rising steadily to about 104 at 9 P.M.; then sweats by the bucketful, and bed-changing every few hours.

About the fourth day of this bizarre performance of fakery turning into reality, a new doctor showed up on the scene—Dr. Verne Mason, the famed diagnostician who had done for Howard Hughes what all the king's men couldn't do for Humpty-Dumpty: put him together again, after the famed flyer had crashed an old plane in a movie stunt.

Verne Mason was one of those rare birds who looked and talked like a neighborly country farmer while secretly sizing up your ailments with the scientific clairvoyance only great doctors possess. A frantic Harry Cohn had hired him to find out what was wrong with his meal ticket. Day after day this eminent diagnostician would sit at my bedside, cross his long legs, study the charts, thump my chest, take sputum tests—and never stop talking about the wonderful prize bulls his son was breeding in New Jersey. Never a word about sickness. A week passed before he spoke of it directly. "Mr. Capra, I just told Harry Cohn I hadn't the slightest idea what to treat you for. Imerman says tuberculosis. The X rays support him. But the sputum is sometimes negative, other times positive. If you *have* TB, with your high fever it would have to be what we call a 'galloping TB'—and you should be dead by now. So I told Mr. Cohn you probably have a 'California pneumonia,' which is what I call any sickness that baffles me. Right now I can only suggest patience and courage until I find out what causes these abnormally high fevers and sweats. I know they are punishing and worrisome, but remember, Mr. Capra, our bodies are tough. They are beautifully and wonderfully made. And speaking of bodies, here's some pictures of heifers my son got by crossing Brahma bulls with Hereford cows . . .''

So that's the way it was. My malingering had maligned on me. I had talked myself into a disease that baffled the experts. It figured. Being an extraordinary person it was fitting that I die from an extraordinary ailment. Maybe the gods plan it that way for their favorite sons. My imaginings rose with the fevers. Look at Valentino, Keats, Guynemer, Joyce Kilmer, Alexander the Great—they died young; not steady flames that slowly burned brighter when fueled with the wisdom of age—no. They were meteors that flashed through life and left their auric afterglow; young soaring rockets that exploded into star dust rather than fall back into senility. Certainly. Live it all in one bright flash. Dramatic. Heroic. Prudent. Meet St. Peter while you're the champ.

Only one outsider was ever allowed into my bedroom—pleasant, smiling Max Winslow, a song-publishing partner of Irving Berlin. He would sit, suck his gurgling pipe, and gab about music and songs—even sing Berlin's latest with the gravelly voice of the song-plugger. I admitted to Max that I was going to die. His answer was to turn my radio on to a news broadcast.

About the tenth day, when I was fading fast, Max came in early in the morning to tell me there was a gentleman in the library to see me.

"Max, look, I've got three doctors already."

"No doctor, Frank. Just a man."

Max and his wife, Tillie, spent a great deal of time with Lu while I was in bed. They were dear persons. Lu loved them. We went fishing with them in the St. Lawrence River every year. But they were both Christian Scientists and I kidded the pants off Max about it.

"Max, if it's one of your voodoo guys, throw him out, will you?"

"Frank, he's just a nice gentleman. See him for one minute, just for my sake."

"Okay. For your sake, and for one minute. Bring him in."

"He won't see you in bed."

"What?!!"

"He's just across the hall in the library. Get up."

"Max! Are you crazy? I'm dying. I can't stand up."

Max helped me out of bed, put a robe on me, and pushed me toward the door.

"Max, hold me up. The room's swimming."

"You can make it. Go on. I'll sit here and play the radio."

I was so mad I could spit. But I was also intrigued about a voodoo treatment. I made it across the hall and into our second-floor den. A little man rose from a chair; completely bald, wearing thick glasses—as faceless a man as you will ever see. There were no introductions. He simply said: "Please sit down, sir."

I sat down, weak as a cat, and just as curious. The little man sat opposite and quietly said: "Mr. Capra, you're a coward."

"A what?"

"A coward, sir. But infinitely sadder—you are an offense to God. You hear that man in there?" Max had turned on the radio in my room. Hitler's raspy voice came shrieking out of it. "That evil man is desperately trying to poison the world with hate. How many can he talk to? Fifteen million—twenty million? And for how long—twenty minutes? You, sir, you can talk to *hundreds* of millions, for two hours—and in the dark. The talents you have, Mr. Capra, are not your own, *not* self-acquired. God gave you those talents; they are His gifts to you, to use for His purpose. And when you don't *use* the gifts God blessed you with—you are an offense to God—and to humanity. Good day, sir."

The little faceless man walked out of the room and down the stairs. In less than thirty seconds he had ripped me open with the truth: exposed the fetid pus of my vanities.

I don't know how long I sat there, fighting back hot tears of shame, before I angrily stormed back into my room on rubbery legs. Hitler was still ranting. Max smoked his pipe.

"Turn that damn thing off . . . and Max, get Lu up here, right now. Please."

"Sure, Frank." Max smiled. He understood.

Searching for underwear in my dressing room, I saw myself in a tall mirror: a skinny old man. I jumped on the scales: I had lost thirty-four pounds.

When Lu came in I was pulling on my trousers. The sight of her drawn, lined face was like a knife thrust.

"Lu, get packed. We're going to Palm Springs."

Palm Springs was a three-hour drive from Beverly Hills. Every half-hour I stopped to pant and rest. The perspiration literally poured out of me. Lu and I spoke quietly, fearful of breaking the spell. She had stood up gamely through weeks of living hell. But deep worry lines had etched her pretty face and anxiety had haunted her eyes as she felt the bigness of life within her grow bigger, and watched her husband waste away with consuming fevers. But now her eyes were moist with gratitude. For, from the moment I tottered feebly, supported by her shoulder, into our Desert Inn cottage, the fevers never returned. And, glory be, I began to gain a pound a day. What had happened? Who was that faceless little man who told me I was a coward and an offense to God? I didn't know, never would know, never *wanted* to know.

As the rubber in my legs stiffened, I walked and walked over the purple sand dunes. Spring had come to the desert. To honor its coming, the dunes unrolled verbena carpets of royal purple; ocotillos raised their thorny spears tipped with heads of hallelujah scarlet. I walked and walked. Startled jackrabbits leaped twice, then stood upright eyeing me curiously. Those clowning birds—the road-runners—peeked around the sage inviting me to play hide-and-seek.

I walked and walked over the purple sand dunes—then walked into the confessional of the local church, fearing the padre would disbelieve my wondrous cure. I ran into a no-nonsense Irish priest. "Nothing wondrous about it," he said sharply, "and for penance—say twelve Our Fathers and get back to *work!*"

Harry Cohn was shocked at the change in me when I walked into his office. Max Winslow was with him.

"Christ, you're a scarecrow! Max—he looks ten years older—"

"I'm a hundred years older, Harry. Hi, Max." Max and I had a secret—the little man.

"Forget it, Walyo," said Harry rubbing his hands, "I've got news that'll make you young again—" Then he told me I was never to leave Columbia; that he was tearing up the old deal and offering me a new six-picture contract at one hundred thousand dollars a picture, *and*, 25 percent of the PROFITS! "Okay, Harry," I said.

"O-KAY, for chrissake? Name me one director that's got a *better* deal." I couldn't. Then he went on to fill me in about *It Happened One Night*—the reviews, the box office, the medals; a hundred feature stories in big-time mags; how Mayer had to triple Gable's salary; how haberdashers screamed because Gable started the fad of wearing no undershirt—and so on, and so on, until his voice faded away as I relived yesterday's scene in the delivery room of the Good Samaritan Hospital, where I witnessed the birth of our second child, little John; heard the most joyously thrilling of all human sounds—the first triumphant cry of a newborn babe—"I am! I am! Unique, individual; a miracle born of time and star dust. Gangway, world! My name is John"—saw the nurses temporarily forget the mother to praise and adore the wonder of the new life Dr. Vruink held up by its squirming little red feet . . .

That night I went to the Connolly house for dinner with Myles and his recent bride, Agnes, a Nashville socialite and noted pianist (Madame Alda's accompanist). I found Myles mixing a huge pitcher of martinis. He greeted me with the usual needle. "Well, come in, come in, famous. Where's the bagful?"

"Bagful of what?"

"The clippings from *It Happened One Night*, the box-office figures! I can take it—after a couple of drinks."

"Myles, you know that picture's an accident. I made the damn thing because everybody said it shouldn't be made. Any credit for it belongs to you. You made the big story change."

"Agnes, come out here, *quick*. We've got a new Capra. A *humble* Capra, God help us!" A mellifluous Southern accent echoed from the hallway. "Myles, you let Frank alone, hear? We saw Lu and little John today, Frank. He's darling."

Throughout dinner I said very little. In fact, since my brush with death—and the little man—I had been practically tongue-tied. Perhaps friends could loosen my tongue. Connolly was a friend, but not the soothing kind, like Max Winslow. Max could enthuse and encourage by holding your hand. But give Connolly a hand to hold and he'd drop a hot poker in it. During dinner I knew he was heating up the poker. Later, at the bar, he handed it to me.

"You've been pretty quiet for a big shot. What's the matter? Halo too tight for you?" The poker singed.

"Myles, I came here hoping to talk. And if you laugh at me I'm going to climb this stool and punch you right on your Boston nose."

"Uh-huh, uh-huh. Good start. Go ahead, I'm listening."

"I don't give a damn whether you listen, or whether you think it's corny. But directors have the power to speak to hundreds of millions for two hours, and in the dark. Okay. But this director doesn't know what the hell to say. Am I going to give up entertainment and bore people stiff with 'message' films? You know what Howard Hughes said: 'When I want to send a message I use Western Union.' Well, what am *I* supposed to preach to people for two hours and in the dark? God, country, brotherhood, mother love? Jesus! They're tired old clichés."

"Well, well, well! You're growing up—a little. But you've got a long way to go. Many great plays and books have been written about those tired old clichés, *and* about greed, ambition, bigotry, hypocrisy. It all depends on who writes them. Read Shakespeare, Tolstoi, the Old Testament. You remember me saying to you once that there was something in your peasant soul hurting to come out, but that you were too scared to let it out? Well, I'm no peasant. I don't know *what's* hurting inside of you. But let it out. Not as preachment, you fool, but as *entertainment*.

"You say *It Happened One Night* is an accident. That picture's no accident. It's *you*. Letting something out without thinking. And you know what else you've done with that picture? No, I'm sure you don't. But you've started a new form of entertainment. You took the old classic four of show business—hero, heroine, villain, comedian—and cut it down to *three*, by combining hero and comedian into one person. And the public's eating it up. So stop worrying about saying something 'big' to people for *two hours* and in the *dark*. That would scare the hell out of *anybody*. Just tell your simple tales about the Johns and the Janes, and the Henrys and the Harriets—with comedy. That's your forte. And you'll unconsciously stick in some kind of a 'message.' Because you can't help it now—you're growing up."

Shortly after, Lu and I went bass fishing for a month with Max and Tillie Winslow, in the beautiful St. Lawrence River where it flows through the

Thousand Islands between New York and Ontario. The Winslows owned a summer house on the river just a few miles from the once magnificent Gay Nineties spa, Alexandria Bay. I took along a valiseful of reading matter from which to select my next film story.

Anchored in warm river bays, surrounded by piny wooded islands—many of them crested with the ruins of ornate palaces built by "robber-barons" in their halcyon days—I read all kinds of stories. In particular, I read and reread Tolstoi's *Anna Karenina*, Dostoevski's *Crime and Punishment*, Maxwell Anderson's *Valley Forge*, and Clarence Buddington Kelland's *Opera Hat*. The two Russian stories fascinated me, but I laid them aside; primarily because, as an American director, I felt incompetent to direct Russian characters. So I concentrated on the two American subjects: *Valley Forge* and *Opera Hat*.

So in love was I with *Valley Forge* that Cohn had already bought it for me. It is one of the most inspiring plays in American literature: the story of the tortures suffered by George Washington during that bleak, bleak winter when freedom's light was down to its last flicker. But, as with the Russian classics, I felt *Valley Forge* was beyond my competency. I wanted a story closer to our times; about people that I knew.

That left *Opera Hat*, laced with Kelland's usual theme-line: Country boy out-slicks city slickers. Longfellow Deeds, a homespun boy from Mandrake Falls, suddenly inherits twenty million dollars and, an Opera House in New York City. Reluctantly, he goes to the Big City to claim his inheritance, only to get all fouled up in the hyper-frenetics of the opera crowd. The opera stuff was just "too-too" for me. But—what would country-boy Deeds do with *twenty million dollars*? In the middle of the Great Depression? And with grouchy distant cousins conspiring for a cut of the kale. That *did* interest me. I wired Cohn to buy *Opera Hat* and asked for Riskin to write the screenplay.

Fishing and living with Max and Tillie Winslow was pleasant, easy, comfortable for Lu and me. At the time, our closest friends were the Connollys and the Winslows. Myles and Agnes were militant Catholics. Each had a sister who was a nun. Later, Mary, one of the Connolly daughters took the vows. But Max and Tillie were devoted Christian Scientists. We accompanied them to the Christian Science Church in Alexandria Bay on Sundays; went with them to testimonial meetings on Wednesday nights. We learned that Christian Scientists believed that sin, disease, crime, and all other forms of evil were simply errors of the "mortal" mind, incompatible with the perfection of the "immortal" Mind—as expressed by Christ: "Be ye therefore perfect, even as your Father in heaven is perfect." I read Mary Baker Eddy's *Science and Health*, became a subscriber to one of America's great newspapers, *The Christian Science Monitor*. There is no doubt that "Science" greatly influenced my life, even long after I ceased attending its churches.

Max Winslow was a tactful, understanding—though unlettered—man.

Gary Cooper's innate integrity was so strong, so sincere, that it surmounted bad scripts, bad films, and directors who had to stand on curbs to look him in the eye.

"Mr. Deeds" became a household name, "doodling" and "pixilated" went into the dictionary, and Jean Arthur—with the voice that broke into a thousand tinkling bells—finally became what she should have been all along: a great star.

Mr. Deeds Goes to Town.
My first all-out indictment of the inhumanities of our times. The above great cast made it possible for me to win another directing Oscar. Seated, from left to right: George Bancroft, Lionel Stander, Gary Cooper, the director, Jean Arthur, Douglass Dumbrille, H. B. Warner.

Memorable Occasion—The Master returns to Hollywood! In 1935, my first year as Academy prez. Talent guilds threaten Awards dinner boycott. Seeking Banquet attraction, find D. W. Griffith living in oblivion. Belatedly, Academy honors man who invented film art. On dais: president, The Master himself, Jean Hersholt, Henry B. Walthall (star of *Birth of a Nation*), Frank Lloyd, C. B. De Mille (presented Award), Donald Crisp.

Luise Rainer accepting congratulations from Academy president and George Jessel (Banquet M.C.) for winning second consecutive Best-Acting Award (1936, *The Great Ziegfeld*; 1937, *The Good Earth*). After second Oscar, Rainer mysteriously dropped out of films.

Neither he—nor I—ever mentioned our "little man." (There are some things in everyone's life that are so precious, so fragile, that if you touch them they vanish.) Winslow's career began as a honkytonk song-plugger of Tin Pan Alley's tunes (an early ancestor of the disc jockey). He crossed saloon doors with singing-waiter Irving Berlin; became Berlin's partner in a sheet-music firm. Later, Winslow was the secret "matchmaker" in one of the most widely publicized, Sunday supplement heart-throb stories: the love affair between socialite Ellen Mackay—daughter of gruff, Croesus-rich (Virginia City mines, Postal Telegraph) John William Mackay—and Russian-born, ghetto-raised Isador Baline (Irving Berlin), writer of ditties and singer in Bowery saloons.

Papa Mackay was horrified. He exiled Ellen to Europe for a year, during which time Berlin wrote some of his greatest love songs for her: "Always," "Memories," "All Alone." The exile over, the lovers met clandestinely in Max's house. He arranged their elopement and marriage—a marriage that is still a love affair.

After Berlin bought out Winslow's partnership interest, Harry Cohn asked Max to join Columbia Studio as its musical "adviser." (Winslow's wife, Tillie, was the sister of Cohn's wife, Rose.) For a year Max bugged Cohn to make an operatic picture with opera star Grace Moore. His constant argument: "A picture with six of the biggest song hits in the world has *got* to be a hit all over the world." He was right. *One Night of Love*, starring singer Grace Moore, directed by musical Victor Schertzinger (*Marcheta*), was a *smash* hit all over the world. Max Winslow was elevated to producer status at Columbia—and I acquired a second "guru"; patient, calm Winslow, in contrast to impatient, irascible Connolly. Between these two guiding lights—one red to mark the shoals, the other green to mark the havens—I launched my first of a series of social-minded films: *Mr. Deeds Goes to Town* (née *Opera Hat*), in which I presumed to "say" something to audiences for two hours, and in the dark.

And what I had to say better be worth saying, because *Mr. Deeds* was the first film in which I achieved filmdom's highest status—I had forced Cohn to feature my name above the title: Frank Capra's *Mr. Deeds Goes to Town*. All my subsequent films were to bear the same possessive trademark.

How powerful is the quality of honesty! Honest men, of any color or tongue, are trusted and loved. They attract others like magnets attract iron filings. An honest man carries with him his own aura, crown, army, wealth, happiness, and social standing. He carries them all in the noblest of all titles: an honest man.

Such a man was Longfellow Deeds of Mandrake Falls, a simple man with a small business and two hobbies: playing the tuba in the town band, and composing corny jingles for the greeting-card trade.

And who in Hollywood could play honest, humble, "corn tassel poet" Mr. Deeds? Only one actor: Gary Cooper. Every line in his face spelled honesty. So innate was his integrity he could be cast in phony parts, but never look phony himself.

Tall, gaunt as Lincoln, cast in the frontier mold of Daniel Boone, Sam Houston, Kit Carson, this silent Montana cowpuncher embodied the true-blue virtues that won the West: durability, honesty, and native intelligence. What is native intelligence? I don't know. I thought I knew when I was eighteen. Professor Judy, Caltech's stimulating English teacher, used to test our precise logic with written exams on deceivingly simple subjects: "Why is a woman?" . . . "Describe health" . . . "What is intelligence?" On the last subject I turned in this "brilliant piece":

> Intelligence is the constant of man's mind, just as the speed of light is the constant of the physical universe. *Knowledge* is the variable in the progress of man. Intelligence *never* varies. The intelligence of the modern scientist, with all his accumulated knowledge, is no greater than that of the cave man whose knowledge was limited to fire, the wheel, and the club. To parallel Einstein's equation of the universe, $E = MC^2$, I propose Capra's equation of the mind: $P = KI^2$—PROGRESS equals KNOWLEDGE times INTELLIGENCE squared. In clear, precise English that means: A tiny increase in knowledge will produce a tremendous increase in progress—the intelligence remaining constant. Q.E.D.

When I got the paper back it was graded with a big fat "O"—plus a scribbled note in red ink: "Zero is also a constant. And it will be your constant grade until you learn to read English. The question was, What *is* intelligence? If I asked you, What is the Gulf Stream? would your answer be, it has a constant speed of four knots? Judy. P.S.—enjoyed your equation. Prove it and they'll give you *two* Nobel Prizes."

Constant or not, it didn't take *any* intelligence to cast Cooper as Long-fellow Deeds. He *was* Mr. Deeds. But the girl? Who could play the mercenary, wise-cracking reporter posing as a bewildered sweet young thing lost in the heartless Big City—just to be near hayseed Deeds and write comical "exclusives" about him? He falls in love with her, and she with him—slowly—while still writing her ribbing "Cinderella Man" articles. That would take believable acting. And when Deeds finds out *she* has been making the whole city laugh at him, what actress could cross the impass-able hurt-gap she had opened up between them?

None, evidently, as far as I was concerned. Many leading ladies asked to play the part—reversing the turn-down trend of *It Happened One Night*—but I couldn't make up my mind. We started shooting the Mandrake Falls section of *Mr. Deeds Goes to Town before* we had cast the heroine. I was hoping for lightning to strike again; another Stanwyck to walk into my office. Well, she didn't walk into the office, but she *was* working on the stages of Columbia Studio—right under my nose.

I never could resist poking my head into a studio projection room when-ever I heard someone else's rushes being run. I stepped into a dark projection room. A Western scene was on the screen, an off-beat quiet love scene between Jack Holt and a girl—something about a ring as I remember. I had never seen the girl before. No, not a girl; a lovely young woman; simple, real, vibrant. And that voice! Low, husky—at times it broke pleasingly into the higher octaves like a thousand tinkling bells.

"Who's the girl?" I asked the film cutters sitting in the dark.

"Jean Arthur," answered one. "Good, isn't she?"

I ran up to Cohn's office. "Jean Arthur?" he rasped out of the corner of his mouth. "D'ja ever hear of her?"

"Well, no—"

"There you are. Three times she's left Broadway to crack Hollywood. And nothing." I wouldn't back off. Arthur had the quality I wanted. "Okay, listen," said Cohn, flipping intercom keys, "let's get some opinions."

He bounced Jean Arthur's name from Briskin, Riskin, to Nod—and some others. The responses: "Good actress, but—she's worked at Paramount, Fox, Selznick's." "Nobody's signed her" . . . "she's cuckoo" . . . "been around" . . . "no name."

"What'd I tell you," said Cohn, "no name."

"But she's got a great voice, Harry—"

"Great voice? D'ja see her *face*? Half of it's angel, and the other half horse."

"Joe Walker's camera'll fix that. We had a face problem with Colbert. Sign her, Harry. I've got a hunch." I turned to leave.

"Don't *you* go saying nothing to her," yelled Cohn, "her agent'll up the price—the *goniff!*"

Placing a last-minute bet on a claiming-race filly proved I was loaded with horseshoes. In the feature *Mr. Deeds* she "won easy" going away. They upped her in class to the big stakes. Jean Arthur became a star after years of "being around."

Jean Arthur is my favorite actress. Probably because she was unique. Never have I seen a performer plagued with such a chronic case of stage jitters. I'm sure she vomited before and after every scene. When the cameras stopped she'd run headlong to her dressing room, lock herself in—and cry.

When called for another scene she would come out looking like a mop; walk aimlessly around muttering a torrent of non-sequitur excuses for not being ready. And it wasn't an act. Those weren't butterflies in her stomach. They were wasps. But push that neurotic girl forcibly, but gently, in front of the camera and turn on the lights—and that whining mop would magically blossom into a warm, lovely, poised, and confident actress. Like "a cockroach what turned into a butterfly!" as the low comic said. The scene over, back she'd rush to her dressing room to vomit. (Years later, she ran out on the lavish Broadway production of *Born Yesterday* on the road. Had the producers chased her, dragged her back, and kicked her out on the stage for just one show, she would have given them an outstanding performance.)

In a conference in Cohn's office, about the *Mr. Deeds* script, Joseph von Sternberg—then directing a Columbia picture with Grace Moore—articulated his comments logically and gracefully:

"Frankie," he said to me, "it doesn't make sense to have your leading man, your *hero*, Gary Cooper, keep on playing the tuba nonchalantly after they tell him he's inherited *twenty million dollars!* Your hero becomes an idiot. And you can't degrade him by letting him chase fire engines like a village half-wit, or have him feed doughnuts to a horse just to see how many he will eat before the horse asks for a cup of coffee. Heroes must be noble, not imbecilic—"

The once-powerful head of Paramount Studio, B. P. Schulberg, then on his way down the ladder, had temporarily paused on a lower rung to produce some pictures for Columbia. "Frank," he argued patiently and sincerely, "you *can't* have your hero being accused of insanity. It'll kill him. The audience may start believing it—"

But I had learned what all committed filmmakers learn—to go for broke on your own gut judgments, for gut decisions are of a piece with your talents. And talents are not self-acquired, but gifts from on high. When that unknown, faceless little man rescued me from the river Styx, the few calm words he uttered served as a chrism to totally commit my talents— few or many—to the service of man. I knew then that down to my dying day, down to my last feeble talent, I would be committed. That I have not always succeeded is proof that the flesh is weak.

Did this new "dedication" affect my picturemaking, or my relationship with other creative minds? Yes, it did—drastically.

Beginning with *Mr. Deeds Goes to Town*, my films had to *say* something. And whatever they said had to come from those ideas inside me "that were hurting to come out." No more would I accept scripts hurriedly written and count on my ability to "juggle many balls in the air" to make films entertaining; no more would I brag about my powers to "shoot the phone book" and make it funny. From then on my scripts would take from six months to a year to write and rewrite; to carefully—and subtly—integrate ideals and entertainment into a meaningful tale. And regardless of the origin of a film idea—I made it mine; regardless of differences with studio heads, screenwriters, or actors—the thought, heart, and substance of a film were mine.

Was this a new form of arrogance, perhaps a superior form? Many fellow workers thought so. But, believe it or not, it was a change in the polarity of goals: from "using" films, to serving them; from "what is good for Capra," to what is good for the profession.

But to keep an idea from being influenced to death by other creative minds—no two of whom would make the same film out of the same idea —demanded a stubborn isolation that was grating to many.

For me, it was the "one man, one film" concept nearing fruition; at a time when the power-structure of executive control was at its zenith. I was the maverick demanding total control. That meant total responsibility. I accepted it. If a film failed, I failed. If too many failed, I was through. Okay. When any artist decides to serve man and the Almighty instead of the "picture business," he accepts the consequences.

My new "look" affected, of course, my harmonious relationship with my friend, screenplay-writer Robert Riskin. He contended, and rightly, that he had contributed greatly to my former films—which he had; and that he deserved additional credit on the screen, as my collaborator or something. I discouraged that strongly. Then he spoke of becoming a director— to fashion his own ideas in films. I encouraged him, spoke to Harry Cohn about it. In a little more than a year he got his first opportunity.

Meanwhile, Riskin did a brilliant piece of writing on *Mr. Deeds Goes to Town*, keeping what I wanted to "say" intact. And what was the great "message" of *Mr. Deeds?* Nothing earth-shaking. Just this: A simple honest man, driven into a corner by predatory sophisticates, can, if he will, reach deep down into his God-given resources and come up with the necessary handfuls of courage, wit, and love to triumph over his environment. That theme prevailed in all—except two—of my future films. It was the rebellious cry of the individual against being trampled to an ort by massiveness —mass production, mass thought, mass education, mass politics, mass wealth, mass conformity.

Curiously enough, one might expect such a serious theme to adversely affect the entainment value of *Mr. Deeds*. On the contrary, it enhanced it. Many said *Mr. Deeds* was funnier and more entertaining than *It Happened One Night*. Why? Because Longfellow Deeds was not just a funny man cavorting in frothy situations. He was the living symbol of the deep rebellion in every human heart—a growing resentment against being compartmentalized. And when Mr. Deeds routed the mass predators, using only his simple weapons of honesty, wit, and courage—audiences not only laughed, they cheered! Longfellow had struck a mighty blow for their *own* individual dignity and divinity.

Even my own fears that *Mr. Deeds* would be too provincially American —too "apple pie"—proved unfounded. "O-filling," "doodling," and "pixilated" were as rib-tickling in Ulan Bator as they were in Allentown, Pa. Evidently what rings true in one heart will toll the same bell all over the world.

In Hollywood *Mr. Deeds* sowed the seeds of change. In the silent days a few directors—they owned their own companies—Griffith, Ince, De Mille, Chaplin, were billed over the picture and stars, for instance D. W. Griffith's *Birth of a Nation*. But, if memory serves, I was the first American "working" director to achieve Frank Capra's *Mr. Deeds Goes to Town*, and to be featured over the picture and stars in marquee lights. The "one man, one film" idea took hold, grew slowly—against stormy opposition from entrenched executives—and today many directors have a box-office value as big, or bigger, than the stars.

Mr. Deeds became a public favorite, and the Academy nominated the film in four major categories: Best Picture, Best Actor, Best Director, Best Writer. I was certain *Mr. Deeds* would win all four of these Oscars. But the competition was formidable: *Anthony Adverse, Dodsworth, The Great Ziegfeld, Romeo and Juliet, San Francisco, The Story of Louis Pasteur, A Tale of Two Cities, My Man Godfrey.*

At the ninth annual Academy Award Banquet (February, 1937) the Best-Picture Award went to *The Great Ziegfeld*, MGM; Luise Rainer won Best Actress for the same film; *The Story of Louis Pasteur* won Best-Actor honors for Paul Muni, and Best-Writer Awards for Pierre Collings and Sheridan Gibney. I saved a shut out for *Mr. Deeds* by winning my second Oscar as Best Director. My elation was tinged with disappointment. If ever anyone deserved Oscars for *Mr. Deeds* it was Gary Cooper and it was Robert Riskin. But—Academy, thy name is capricious. While on the subject of the Academy, allow me to relate some of the back-stage efforts to keep that glamorous organization alive.

Late in 1935 (during the preparation of *Mr. Deeds*), the Board of Governors of the Academy of Arts and Sciences bestowed on me the dubious honor of electing me President. I say "dubious" because it would be presiding at a deathwatch. The Academy had become the favorite whipping boy of Hollywood; its membership down from six hundred to forty; its officers dedicated but discouraged; its hired staff reduced to loyal, underpaid, executive secretary Margaret Herrick—the Academy's alter ego. With few dollars in its treasury—and fewer in sight—the odds were ten to one the Academy would fold and Oscar would acquire the patina of a collector's item.

Why? Because the polyarchic Academy—governed by management, technicians, and creative talent—was caught in the middle of Hollywood's first labor war between management and talent. The producing companies did everything short of asking for the National Guard to prevent actors, writers, and directors from organizing into guilds. The guilds *were* organized. But their siege of company ramparts was to last five long years— years of strife and strikes—before management capitulated and accepted the guilds as the bargaining agents for talent.

But in 1935 the labor war was in full cry. Actor Ronald Reagan, writer John Howard Lawson, and director King Vidor led the fight for their respective guilds. Part of talent's strategy was to wreck the Academy in order to deny management the box-office promotional values of the Oscars. Oddly enough, short-sighted company heads couldn't care less—the Academy had failed them as an instrument of salary cuts during the bank-closing crisis. They withdrew their memberships and financial support, leaving the derelict organization in the care of a few staunch Academy-oriented visionaries dedicated to the cultural advancement of the arts and sciences of filmmaking, and to the continuance of the awards—the most valuable, but least expensive, item of world-wide public relations ever invented by *any* industry.

It is an honor to name the few unsung idealists who crossed all economic battle lines to prevent the destruction of Hollywood's lone bastion of culture: *Writers*—Howard Estabrook, Jane Murfin, Waldemar Young, Edwin Burke; *producers*—David O. Selznick, Darryl F. Zanuck, Sam Briskin, Fred Leahy, De Witt Jennings, Graham Baker; *actors*—Clark Gable, Lionel Atwill; *technicians*—Nathan Levinson, John Arnold, Van Nest Polglase; *directors*—Cecil B. De Mille, Frank Lloyd.

This group elected me to lead them in the Academy's fight for survival. Six months before, I would have told them to go fly a kite. I had gotten *my* armful of Oscars. Let the others sweat. Before meeting "the little man," the theme "get mine, get mine!" had been an article of faith in my credo.

But, since I had been shocked into realizing that serving self is small potatoes compared with the value of serving man, I had begun to care about the dreams of others.

Well, when the dedicated officers of a dying Academy asked me to become its President, what motivated my instant acceptance—pride or service? I am not sure. But I *was* sure that the upcoming Academy Awards Banquet of March, 1936, loomed dark and discouraging; that things *could* get worse before they got worser. Boycott rumors were rife. Officers of the Screen Actors and Screen Writers guilds sent telegrams to all members urging them not to attend the Academy dinner, and not to accept any Oscars.

To spur attendance, we countered by persuading the giant of all filmmakers, D. W. Griffith, to come out of his retired oblivion and to accept from the Academy a special statuette for his legendary pioneering in films. Griffith's name was magic. The boycott fizzled. Bette Davis was present to receive her Best-Actress trophy for *Dangerous*; Victor McLaglen was there to clutch a Best-Actor Award for *The Informer*.

But neither John Ford nor Dudley Nichols showed up for their Best-Directing and Best-Writing Oscars awarded *The Informer*. Ford accepted the trophy later. Nichols did not. He was quoted in a trade paper as having said: "To accept it would be to turn my back on nearly a thousand members of the Writers Guild . . ."

By prayers and incantations, and the Board members putting up their own money for the statuettes, plus some fancy begging on my part—each year I had to plead with the officers of the talent guilds to allow me to mail Academy ballots to their Guild members—the Academy deathwatch kept the grim reaper away until 1939.

Then came a massive transfusion of new blood. The writers and the actors—having signed their newly won basic agreements with management —returned to the Academy fold practically en masse. The Academy was reorganized into a self-supporting institution dedicated solely to cultural goals.

In late 1939, after the Academy was breathing again, and healthy enough to hold elections, I stepped down as its president—having held that office for five years—only to receive a signal honor from my fellow directors. They elected me president of the Screen Directors Guild. I think they needed a new arm-twister to force producing companies to sign their first basic labor agreement with directors.

CHAPTER 10

Burn the First Two Reels

IT IS FASCINATING to dwell on the sources of ideas for films: plays, books, the Bible, short stories, news items, dreams, arguments with your wife—the complete story of what I think is my best motion picture came from a Christmas card. And it is equally engaging to recall how ideas came to your attention, for example, the next story after *Mr. Deeds*.

Just before photography on *Mr. Deeds*, Harry Cohn invited a studio group to go to a Stanford-U.S.C. football game in Palo Alto. Browsing in the Union Station's newsstand for something to read on the train, I saw a book that Alexander Woollcott had praised on the radio, *Lost Horizon*, written by the English writer James Hilton. I read it; not only read it, but dreamed about it all night, particularly about a passage between Robert Conway, the kidnapped foreign secretary of Great Britain, and the two-hundred-year-old High Lama of Shangri-La, an inaccessible Tibetan lamasery where persons of various origins lived to incredible ages—and dreamed the impossible dream!

In this compelling passage the High Lama explained the dream and purpose of Shangri-La, and why Conway, the brilliant, sensitive intellectual, had been particularly chosen and kidnapped from the world to, hopefully, succeed the dying High Lama in making the dream come true.

The High Lama said he saw all nations strengthening—not in wisdom but in vulgar passions and the will to destroy. He saw their machine power multiplying until a single-weaponed man might match a whole army. He foresaw a time when man, exultant in the technique of homicide, would rage so hotly over the world that every precious thing would be in danger; a time when every book, every treasure, would be doomed to destruction. Anticipating the holocaust, Shangri-La had, for nearly two centuries, been accumulating the treasures of the mind and the wisdom of the ages.

"You, my son," says the High Lama to the astonished British leader, "you will live through the storm. You will conserve the fragrance of history, and add to it a touch of your own mind. You will welcome the weary stranger, and teach him the rule of age and wisdom. And when the survivors, weary, bewildered, and helpless, begin their search for solace and understanding, they will find them *here*—in the outstretched arms of Shangri-La!"

Does that theme sound modern?

Next morning, during breakfast in the Lark's dining car, I handed Harry Cohn the *Lost Horizon* book, told him it was the darndest tale I had ever read—a fantastic mystery melodrama about Tibet—and to buy it for me quick, please. He listened and said he'd take Stanford and six and a half points. I went on to tell him there was only one actor in the world to play the lead, Ronald Colman, and that the film would probably cost two million dollars. He dropped his fork.

"TWO MILLION? For chrissake, that's half our whole year's budget!"

No Columbia picture had as yet cost more than one-fourth that amount. But my enthusiasm for the book ran so high Cohn placated by saying he would buy a six months' option on the story and wait until he saw what *Mr. Deeds Goes to Town* would do at the box office.

Mr. Deeds went to town in a Brinks' money truck, so Cohn crossed all his fingers, kissed the mezuzah, and went for the two million—proving him to be half-mad, but all gambler. Two million dollars!—five times the cost of *Mr. Deeds*—to spend on a far-out fantasy the like of which had no precedent, no trend to back it up? Columbia's New York executives thought Cohn was half-mad and all *nuts*.

But Cohn had a bigger hunch about *Lost Horizon* than I did—though he never read the book. But that's the way films got made in Hollywood: Back the hot crapshooter who had rolled four sevens in a row—let the winnings ride on his fifth roll. My hand shook as I rattled the dice.

To plan the script, Bob Riskin and I went back to our lucky desert. We rented a red-tiled, adobe cottage at the beautiful La Quinta Hotel, a cool-green oasis nestled between the rocky roots of Santa Rosa Mountain, where they plunge—bare and pink—under the hot white waves of the desert sand dunes. This inviting spa, near Indio, was to be *our* Shangri-La for script-writing in the coming years.

Leaving Riskin to write the script, I began a prodigious research on Tibet: lamaseries, lamas, monks, people; customs, costumes, food, furniture; animals, vehicles, weapons, musical instruments.

We were most fortunate in acquiring the services of Harrison Forman —famed explorer, writer, photographer, of little-known Tibet—as our technical adviser. Pinning hundreds of Forman's photographs on the walls of two rooms, we spread out before us a whole pictograph of mysterious Tibet whose people lived in the snowy fastness of the isolated roof of the world, at an average altitude of fifteen thousand feet.

The photos revealed the ecology and ethology of Tibet; the strangeness of its cultural, religious, and ethnic mores; its prayer wheels, chortens, and ferocious deities. It was ruled by two high priests: the Dalai Lama (reincarnated from Tibet's original ancestor), and the Panchen Lama (reincarnated from the original Buddha of Light). Upon the death of either, his spirit passes directly into the body of an infant just born.

It was a land of rugged physical demands: goods were moved on the backs of porters and pack trains braving blizzards and icy blasts as they slogged single-file over cloud-shrouded passes; and of more rugged religious demands: the prayer *"Om mani padme hum!"* (Ah! the jewel is indeed in the lotus!) was repeated endlessly.

The first order of business was how to re-create and photograph Shangri-La, a magnificent lamasery that overlooked, from its perch on a cliff, the warm, verdant Valley of the Blue Moon; an earthly paradise so secluded, so isolated, so protected from the world and its cold winds by a ring of high peaks that time—unruffled and unmeasured—offered life its richest savor. The inhabitants of this cloistered Eden observed a sunset as men in the outer world heard the striking of a clock, and with much less care.

Shangri-La was hidden in the uncharted Himalayas—a thousand miles from nowhere. For those who might accidentally stumble into its trackless vicinity, admittance was purchased at the expense of inching and clinging to a miles-long narrow trail hacked in the rock and ice of cliffs so high, so steep, and so exposed to raging blasts of icy winds, that the entrance to the Valley (a secret crevice in the mountains) was never guarded.

We re-created the mountain-locked Valley of the Blue Moon—its peaceful village by a peaceful stream, under the tranquil primacy of the lamasery on a cliff—in miniature.

We built the exterior of the lamasery full size on the Columbia "ranch" in Burbank—its sunlit walls splayed with gnarled, centuries-old vines that dripped with fragrant blossoms; its broad, pink stairway that beckoned to the great portico; its acres of flat white roofs that shimmered in the sun at various levels. Shangri-La, where time stood still; where voices were as murmurous as the dozy amblings of a fly in summer; where flowers incensed their fragrance to peace, and rainbow-haloed fountains hummed in harmony to the evanescent ariel music of circling white pigeons—each pigeon with a tiny bamboo flute tied to its leg, from which the wind of flight evoked winged melodies.

Stephen Goosson, the art director, did a superlative job in designing and building the settings for *Lost Horizon*. His colorful sketches and paintings of Shangri-La and its people still adorn the walls of art lovers.

From Harrison Forman's photographs it was simple to design Tibetan costumes. But where would we find the people to wear them? Tibetans are Orientals, but taller, rangier than Chinese or Japanese. Again we had recourse to our non-Chinese but Oriental stand-bys—Pala Indians from the San Diego mountains. (Years later, I was a guest of Indian film director Chetan Anand, at his Juhu beach home near Bombay. He asked where, in Tibet, had I shot his favorite picture, *Lost Horizon*. He was astonished to hear that I had never set foot in Tibet. But those were real Tibetans, he insisted. No, I said, they were American Indians. He upheld his unbelief by asserting vehemently that, while visiting a certain Tibetan lamasery, he had read all about the making of *Lost Horizon* in its "secret books.")

Then, too, we would have to show some yaks. What the burro was to American sourdoughs of the West, the yak is to Tibetans. To badly simulate yaks, we covered yearling steers with long-haired, hoof-length blankets. To better simulate small Tibetan horses, we "haired up" the legs and chests of Shetland ponies.

Tibetan musical instruments would have stumped us, had not Mr. Henry Eichman, a California collector of rare, authentic Tibetan trumpets and horns, generously offered the use of his unique collection. Some of the trumpets were as long as eight feet; one rare, battered horn came from the sacred temple of Lhasa.

Now, to the casting of actors. Had the High Lama been able to scour the whole world for a man to carry on his vision of Shangri-La, he would have selected Ronald Colman. Beautiful of face and soul, sensitive to the fragile and gentle, responsive both to poetic visions and hard intellect—cultured actor Ronald Colman was born to play the kidnapped foreign secretary who "understood" his kidnapping.

The passenger-actors in the adventure-filled plane—bound for England, but hijacked to Tibet—were: Ronald Colman; his jingoistic younger brother—"there'll always be an England" type—John Howard; a fussy paleontologist—Edward Everett Horton; a brassy American industrial tycoon—on the lam from the law for embezzlement—Tommy Mitchell; and a pitiful but tough American prostitute—thrown out with the garbage from Shanghai's waterfront dives, only to be washed up as flotsam in Hong Kong, dying of tuberculosis—Isabel Jewell.

These actors were all *known* faces, and rightly so, because they represented characters from our known world. But actors in Shangri-La, figuratively out-of-this-world, should be *unknown* faces, if possible.

In casting the two girl parts we were lucky. One—the elegant Shangri-La white girl, romantically joined with Ronald Colman—was played by a Barnard College young lady, a stage actress whose exposure in films was limited to a couple of minor parts—Jane Wyatt. Two—the villain of the piece, a youthful Shangri-La maiden of mixed parentage who looks twenty but lies about her real age (in the late sixties) in order to escape with Colman's brother, John Howard. Her lie destroys Colman's faith in Shangri-La. He leaves with them. But later, when the three are lost in the

First movie set in a practical ice house. To the utter amazement of our five freezing Europeans (Ronald Colman, John Howard, Thomas Mitchell, Edward Everett Horton, and Isabel Jewell), a rescue party with food and warm clothes materializes out of nowhere.

BELOW
The professionals—left to right: Harold Winston, F. C., Margo, Ronald Colman, and John Howard—listen while rookie Jane Wyatt tells how it feels to be in her first film.

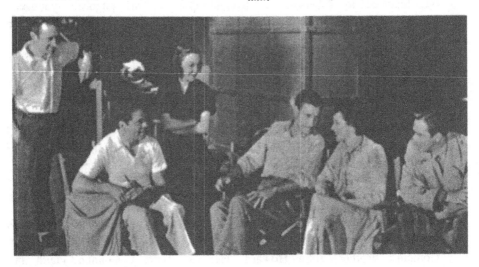

Finally, young (38) Shakespearean actor Sam Jaffe played the two-hundred-year-old High Lama. And, when day is done—a coke. But no carbonated drinks while shooting. Wide-open microphones (to pick up High Lama's dying whispers) would also pick up gurgles in nearby stomachs.

Climbing a steep, tortuous pass, the rescue party leaves the icy blizzard and enters warm gardens of the Lamasery of Shangri-La, in the uncharted Valley of the Blue Moon.

trackless wastes of the "outside," the girl suddenly, and dramatically, grows old and dies before their very eyes. In horror, John Howard leaps to his death over an icy precipice. But Colman's faith is restored, and on and on he stumbles through raging storms, trying to find his way back to Shangri-La. That young girl who turned old was brilliantly played by a young Mexican dancer with practically no film experience—Margo.

However, the casting of the High Lama gave us fits. What unknown face could believably play that ancient visionary—a Belgian priest who had stumbled into the Valley of the Blue Moon two hundred years ago?

Our first thought was to find some very old and forgotten stage star whose face had never been filmed. We found one, in nearby San Gabriel Valley. We took the ninety-year-old ex-stage star to the studio for a photographic test: to read one of the High Lama's speeches to Ronald Colman. Next morning we saw the test on the screen. He was perfect. Just as he was. No make-up. We phoned his home to announce he had been chosen. His house-keeper wept with joy. An hour later she called us back. She wept in sorrow. The old gent had died—right after he heard the news. Died peacefully, with a smile on his face. The long hoped-for Hollywood call had come. He smiled, and died.

The next candidate was Henry B. Walthall, the Little Colonel of *The Birth of a Nation*. Frail and failing, he died before we could test him.

The search for a High Lama went on. Stage actor Sam Jaffe had caught my eye in the Broadway productions of *The Jazz Singer* and *A Doll's House*. He had also played with the Ben Greet Shakespearean Company. But Jaffe was only thirty-eight. Could hated make-up make credible his having lived over two centuries? Even without make-up his skull had an aura of the biblical prophet about it: prodigious brow, suffering face, long Semitic nose, wild eyes, and wilder hair. Snowing up his wild hair and adding a layer of parchment to his face, we made a test of Jaffe as the High Lama.

By using only a portion of his upper lungs, as a weak bellows for his voice, Jaffe made his words almost inaudible; so inaudible, in fact, the wide open microphones picked up stomach gurgles from surrounding crew members. We would all have to go on a no-gurgle diet. Jaffe's words were weak but the zeal behind them was strong—the last words of a prophet passing on his vision. We knew instantly we had found our High Lama.

For the number two Lama, who parried such questions as, "Why were we brought to this God-forsaken place?" with wit and great good humor, we used that fine actor of courtly grace—H. B. Warner. His acquisition completed our major casting. Now, to solve the story construction of *Lost Horizon*—the "attack."

Lost Horizon was essentially a morality play, a poetic saga. But poetic sagas can be dangerous. If audiences get a hint of what you are up to before they are "conditioned"—they may resent it and shy away. That is why films about Lincoln, about saints, about Christ, are dangerous. Producers approach them with too much awe. Actors begin wearing halos long before they've earned them.

I would guard against that. All my "pre-halo" scenes should be photographed with a stark, documentary reality. Everything must smell real, *be* real: The burning of Baskul, the escape of the plane from rioting Chinese, its refueling by Mongolian tribesmen, its long freezing climb over the snow-capped Himalayas, its out-of-fuel crash on a glacier, followed by the torturous, lung-searing climb to Shangri-La through blinding blizzards— all must look real to audiences. The ice, snow, mountains, storms, and in particular—the *cold*—must not be phony. That meant the actors' *breath* MUST SHOW. That meant shooting the scenes in below 20-degree weather. Where?

I had a brainstorm that was too embarrassing to discuss with any one. Assistant director Art Black and I made a secret trip to the industrial heart of Los Angeles to check it out. There we found it: a cold storage warehouse—*insulated*; its dimensions: 150 feet long, 75 feet wide, and 25 feet high—a small sound stage with a perpetual weather of zero!

Gaping warehousemen passed the two movie nuts on to higher-ups. We got to the head man. Would it be possible to rent that ice house as a movie studio for a few months? Well, hardly, the man laughed. There is no power for lights, no ventilation for humans, and besides, it is half-filled with frozen swordfish stacked like logs. "And the other half," he added, "we need to store our artificial-snow machines—"

"Artificial-*snow* machines? What are they?"

"Big machines that grind up ice blocks into fine snow and blow it out over the fish—"

Hallelujah! Real snow! I could see it—real *falling* snow, real *blowing* snow.

It cost us plenty, but we rented the ice house and converted it into a working studio. For six weeks we shot all our "cold" scenes (about 20 percent of the picture) in sub-freezing temperatures, while outside it was a broiling 90 degrees or higher. But we ran into a nightmare of technical hang-ups. Cold film rolling through the cameras developed static electricity that fogged the film. We had to cover film magazines with electrically heated "overcoats." New cold-resisting lubricants had to be found for cameras and motors. The extreme range of temperatures from "on" to "off" cracked light sockets and shattered bulbs. Rubber electric cables stiffened, cracked, and short-circuited. Electricians' hands froze on the cold metal. Actors feared pneumonia going in and out of temperatures between 90 and 15. Yes, there were problems. But in that li'l ol' ice house we shot all the interiors of the plane, its crack-up, the treks, the blizzards, the avalanche that engulfed the porters, Margo suddenly turning into an old woman, John Howard's suicide leap, and Colman's super-human wanderings in quest of his lost Shangri-La.

With wind machines, snow machines, and back-projection machines we conjured up the Arctic rigors of the Himalayas. The snow the actors crunched through *was* snow; the fluted outcroppings of glacial ice shimmered real because they *were* real. The breath-showing puzzle—ludicrously "solved" once by dry ice in actors' mouths—was cracked by an ice house. The key to misty breath, red noses, and frosty eyebrows was so obvious it had been overlooked—lower the temperature, fool.

The musty studio projection room was packed solid with friends, Cohns, and Landsmen—two-deep in the seats and three-deep along the walls. They had come to bury or to praise Caesar Cohn for having spent two million dollars on one film (equaling the combined cost of Columbia's other twenty pictures made that year). The air was so thick with hopes and doubts you could finger-write your name in its smog.

The lights dimmed. The main title, *Lost Horizon*, flashed on the screen. Everyone took a deep breath. The chips were down in the ever-bitter feud between hunch-playing President Cohn and his more conservative New York partners. If *Lost Horizon* was a bust Cohn the Crude would get the old heave-ho.

Curiously enough, my biggest sweat was not the film. It was the musical scoring. I had given the job to a composer who had never before scored a film—Russian-born, ex-concert pianist, Dimitri Tiomkin. To a man, studio executives had railed against such an unnecessary, perhaps stupid, gamble. But a little bird told me that Tiomkin would come up with new, fresh, novel music. The nervous Russian pleaded with me to hear and approve his themes for the picture. I refused. I wanted *his* music, not mine. But I copped a bet against possible disaster by hiring Max Steiner—Warner Brothers' great music composer—to conduct Tiomkin's score. I knew that if wise old Steiner thought the score inadequate, he himself would step in to rewrite it—fast.

Curiosity had forced me to sneak unseen into the music-scoring stage to overhear Steiner's first orchestral rehearsal of the main-title music. I left with stars in my eyes. And after sitting for over three hours in that packed projection room, I still had stars in my eyes. Tiomkin's music not only captured the mood, but it darned near captured the film.

The lights came on. The packed audience remained hushed and still for what seemed like an eternity. Finally Dorothy Howell, my first Columbia scenarist, broke the spell: "If that isn't the greatest picture I ever saw, I'll eat the film inch by inch." That triggered the verbal tom-toms. A relieved Cohn barked out a typical Cohn-ism: "I got news for you lousy experts. In three hours I didn't wiggle my ass once." The crowd guffawed. All knew that Cohn judged films by the seat of his pants. His tail was his guru. Whenever it got bored and scrunched around, it told Cohn the picture was a bust.

Cohn immediately commanded Columbia's New York executives and board members to fly to Hollywood for a confess-your-sins seminar. I'm sure he told them to bring their noses so he could rub them into their criticisms. The cowed big-wigs would arrive Monday morning. But cagey Cohn —covering against the possibility of *Lost Horizon* being a studio "morning glory" (what the name trainers call a horse that looks like Swaps when racing against stop-watches, but stops and watches when racing against horses)—arranged for a top-secret Sunday night preview at a swank Santa Barbara theater. "If *Lost Horizon* can knock off those Santa Barbara snobs, I got those New York guys right in my pocket."

It was cold and raining hard in Santa Barbara as Lu and I, and Cohn and his new wife, Joan (a lovely young Columbia contract actress), stepped out of Cohn's Rolls Royce to mingle with the big crowd hurrying into the theater. In my excitement I left my hat and overcoat in Cohn's car, but who cared? I welcomed the rain as a good omen. In practically every picture I've ever made there are scenes in the rain—especially love scenes. It's a personal touch. Rain, for me, is an exciting stimulant, an aphrodisiac. It probably stems from my father's peasant farmer's happy hullabaloo whenever the rains came: *"L'aqua veni! L'aqua veni!"* (The rain is coming!)

Opposite the theater the hands of a big four-sided street clock pointed to eight fifty-five. Over the marquee a large banner announced: MAJOR STUDIO PREVIEW TONIGHT! "Damned right it's major," I smirked to myself.

Preview audiences never knew the title of the film, nor the name of the producing company. But experience had taught them to anticipate a film's quality by the heralding symbol that first flashed on the screen: for instance, Leo the Lion's roar, or Paramount's star-circled mountain, usually evoked anticipatory applause—probably because these companies brought their own large claques. When *Lost Horizon* opened with Columbia's Torch Lady trademark, our two wives and Cohn clapped like crazy but their applause was lost in the moans from the audience. The Torch Lady still presaged mediocrity. But we were used to that—and determined, in our time, to change those opening moans into applause.

The Santa Barbara audience sat quietly through the first ten minutes of the film. Then—it began to titter, where no titters were intended. The titters swelled into laughs, where no laughs were intended. I broke out into a cold sweat. The seat of Cohn's pants wiggled so hard his chair creaked out loud. Aghast with confusion, I crawled over people and rushed to the foyer for a drink of water. A well-dressed Santa Barbaran had the same idea.

"After you, sir," I said to him at the drinking fountain. Leaning down for a drink he looked up at me and said: "Did you ever see such a goddam Fu Manchu thing in your life? People who made it should be shot."

I shot out the front door into the rain. The hands of the big clock pointed to nine twelve. Cold with sweat and rain, I walked to Cohn's car for my hat and overcoat. The car was locked. I walked down the deserted street in a daze, my mouth filled with cotton. A lighted drugstore loomed in the rain. I entered, slumped on a fountain stool, ordered a Coke.

It had to be a bad dream. Why should my beautiful poetic saga—which took a whole year to make—exactly the same film that inspired and thrilled us in the studio projection room—be ridiculed in Santa Barbara?

I don't remember how many times I walked around the block, or came back for Cokes, or thought of climbing that pitiless street clock to push its mocking hands around to twelve fifteen—but finally, what was left of the audience poured out into the rain and ran for their cars. Their loud, jeering comments about *Lost Horizon* (to paraphrase Ring Lardner) fell like clods on my coffin. The preview was a shambles. *Lost Horizon* was an unshowable, unreleasable motion picture.

For the next two days I walked and walked and walked in a dark trance. Over and over I mentally reconstructed the film—scene by scene, look by look, word by word—seeking the elusive psychological key that made *Lost Horizon* appealing when seen by a few, ridiculous when seen by many.

On the third morning I drove fast to the studio, rushed to the cutting rooms, ordered Gene Havlick, my film editor, to take the main title from the beginning of the *first* reel of the picture and splice it onto the beginning of the *third* reel. No other change. The picture would now be some twenty minutes shorter; its opening sequence: the burning of Baskul. Then I rushed up to see Harry Cohn. He had black pouches under his eyes. I told him about the one change I had made, and that I wanted another preview in a theater—that very night.

"Frank, I can't *hide* another preview from my New York guys. They smell a rat already. Let's show them the picture here in the studio—"

"No, Harry. We *know* a small group will like it. The test is a big crowd in a big theater."

"Goddam you, you know what another disaster like Santa Barbara'll do to Columbia?"

"Yes! It'll wreck Columbia, and it'll wreck you—and *me*."

"What makes you so damn sure throwing away the first two reels will *work*?"

"I'm *not* sure it'll work. But it's the only change I could think of in three days without sleep. Let's preview it again. Invite your New York partners."

Cohn paced behind his desk like a caged tiger. The decision was tough. But he had no alternative. Little flecks of foam whitened the corners of his twisted mouth as he stopped, and said: "You son-of-a-bitch—if this doesn't work—"

There was more than Columbia's hierarchy riding in five limousines to the Wilmington Theater in San Pedro that evening. The mocking Fates were unwelcome hitchhikers.

The same *Lost Horizon*, the same turkey that had laid a catastrophic egg in Santa Barbara, flapped its wings again on the screen in San Pedro—but *without the first two reels*. For Columbia: the moment of truth, as they say in bull rings . . . There was not one laugh or titter in the wrong place! Not in the first ten minutes, not in the whole three hours. The audience was spellbound.

Our dread of disaster vanished like mist before the rising sun. Color and arrogance surged back into Cohn's leaden face. Cohn was Cohn again —in spades.

One small, seemingly insignificant change had turned an unreleasable, unshowable picture into the *Lost Horizon* that was welcomed by the world; a picture about which thousands of fans were to later say in their letters: "I have seen it as many as twenty times."

Unconscious of the sub-rosa drama of the last three days, the New York executives were jubilant as we all arrived back at the studio for a victory celebration—even though they realized that Cohn again had them "right in my pocket." But before I celebrated I had a chore to do. I ran up to the cutting rooms, took those blasted first two reels in my hot little hands, ran to the ever-burning big black incinerator—and threw them into the fire. Being nitrate film, they flamed up with a whoosh that lit up the night sky.

My rather astonishing and, for me and Columbia, almost ruinous experience with *Lost Horizon* points up a facet of motion pictures very few understand—especially the film critics. When an author writes a book, his aim is to communicate with one single individual reader at a time; one book, an audience of one. A motion picture is aimed at communicating with hundreds, or, hopefully, thousands of viewers at each showing; one film, an audience of many.

The line between the sublime and the ridiculous is rather wide and indefinite to an audience of one; thinner and sharper to an audience of many— the larger the audience, the thinner the line. That is why big-time film critics are wrong in insisting they view a film alone in private projection rooms— with drinks and snacks at their elbows. Their judgments, when seeing a film as an audience of one, will not always coincide with judgments they might make if they had to view it with an audience of many.

Critics say the theory behind private viewings is that they can be more intelligent, more subjective, in their critical reviews if they are not influenced by the crowd reactions of the great unwashed. But crowd reactions are precisely what the film was made for in the first place, and no proper judgment of a motion picture can be made without the vital "third dimension" of a large audience being present.

And, may I add, the collective opinion of a large group of normal individuals is generally saner and more correct than the opinions of individuals, singly or in small groups. In short: "The audience is always right" is a safe bet. The audience was right in ridiculing *Lost Horizon* in Santa Barbara; it was right in welcoming it in San Pedro. When something goes haywire with a film, try burning the first two reels.

Lost Horizon was Columbia's first expensive "class" film, on a par with any major studio super spectacle. The film's high cost called for high-level selling and drum-beating. This important chore was assigned to Columbia's "class" vice president—wealthy, bridge expert, and art collector—bon vivant Nate Spingold. The result: brilliant exploitation aimed at the world's literati, resulting, among other things, in boosting the importance of American films and raising the stature of film directors who espoused the "one man, one film" concept.

It was probably Spingold's literate and tasteful exploitation of *Lost Horizon* that finally put Poverty Row on the map. It also brought to the attention of the world's film buffs the emerging fact that there were now two distinct filmmaking methods in Hollywood: Columbia's "producer-director" way, pioneered by Capra; and the "committee" way of the major studios, pioneered by L. B. Mayer. In short, the individual versus the committee, or, in personal terms, Capra versus Mayer. And, because my way had produced five home runs in a row, other committee-hating directors were attracted to Columbia, namely John Ford, Leo McCarey, and George Stevens. So while many fine directors contracted to major studios still remained anonymous under the committee system, Cohn was assembling a powerhouse of much-talked-about independent producer-directors who turned out such hits for him as *The Whole Town's Talking, The More the Merrier, Love Affair,* and *Here Comes Mr. Jordan.* Cohn's star was rising fast, and fellow directors began calling me the director's director.

The Common Bond

ALL OVER THE WORLD the human spirit was at a low ebb. The fog of anxiety blanketed the globe. Like an enormous leech that wouldn't be shaken off, the Great Depression still sucked up our hopes. And there was war in Spain! Hitler was arming, Stalin was arming, Mussolini was arming. Free nations shivered, sighed, and tried to wish it all away.

The world was hungry for a lift; hungry for quickening examples of how individuals overcome the dreads of their environment. Such examples could best be dramatized in motion pictures: "You can speak to hundreds of millions for two hours, and in the dark." That was my needed job: Lift the human spirit.

No, I didn't choke up again, didn't worry about my films being hits or misses. I simply asked the Almighty for the wit and courage to do my job well—and left the rest up to Him.

Film critics took things up from there. They called *Lost Horizon* everything from a "Capra fairy tale," an exciting mystery melodrama full of "harsh clamor and surging movement," to a potpourri of "poetry, fantasy, and philosophy (the last somewhat indigestible)." But *Lost Horizon*'s utopian theme evidently touched a universally exposed nerve because pundits couldn't stop writing about it: second thoughts, essays, "think" pieces, editorials. Its anti-war "propaganda" stirred up a hornet's nest of political comment from the far right to the far left.

One of London's Fleet Street reviewers gave the film this pithy summation: "Freud, not Marx, is its father."

Another London reviewer, John Ramage, wrote this jocular, nostalgic comparison of Shangri-La to "Merrie England":

By heck, brothers, this *Lost Horizon* is a mighty picture. It is as
mighty as "Merrie England" (1894) when you and I were twenty.
Now, what in the name of almighty heck, you ask, has an up-to-the-
minute Hollywood super-sensation made by that Italiano, Frank
Capra . . . got to do with old Bob Blatchford [English journalist] of
the days of long ago?

Just this, brothers . . . You remember how Bob showed things as
they might be in this poor, dirty dump of an island, showed us in
rainbow lines above the slag heap where heaven hung, if only enough
of us would put the ballot crosses against the right name? . . .

Ballot crosses for a ladder to the rainbow! You laugh, maybe; but
you dream still, brothers, for you and I will never end our dreaming. And here in "Lost Horizon" the dream takes form. Miraculously
we believe again . . .

Hitler's goose-stepping propagandists sneered at *Lost Horizon*. One Nazi-
oriented paper referred to it as "decadent drivel from a decaying democracy." On the contrary, Mussolini's milksop press praised it as a masterpiece. Later, I discovered why. Mr. Strut had commanded the film be
"duped" in the Italian language, using voices of Italian actors—and the
fine Italian propaganda hand had twisted *Lost Horizon*'s utopian philosophy
into a deification of Il Duce's fascism. Viva Machiavelli!

London's freewheeling film critics had written so vigorously about *Lost
Horizon*'s press showing that Joe Friedman, head of Columbia's London
office, urged Cohn to send me and Bob Riskin to London for the film's
formal opening at the Tivoli. It seemed that whenever anything big happened to me, something far bigger happened to my wife. She was again
pregnant when the three of us left New York on the *Normandie* for London—
and some unexpected adventures.

Our first adventure was with the British press. We found their reporters
and critics highly literate, shockingly frank, and wide-ranging in their
spectrum of thought. But they had one virtue in common—good writing;
far more learned writing, in general, than their American counterparts.

Naturally their questions got around to the ideals of Utopia. We discussed the reasons why so many writers had tackled utopian novels—and
their popularity: In a Utopia the author can not only criticize contemporary
social evils, but also outline vast revolutionary reforms without the necessity of detailing the means by which the changes can be brought about.
Thus, authors can be inspirational without being practical; or, as poet
O'Shaughnessy wrote:

> We are the dreamers of dreams . . .
> The movers and the shakers
> Of the world for ever, it seems.

Obviously, I profited the most from my encounter with the British press. England may have lost the global Empire she fashioned with the sword, but I doubt she will ever lose the intellectual imperium she gained with the pen. An Englishman may appear to be overly reserved and unemotional. However, put a pen in his hand and he'll go to town in a mini kilt.

Our second adventure took place not in England but in the Soviet Union. It had its genesis in Hollywood. A few years before, Russia's great film director, Sergei Eisenstein (*Potemkin, October, Old and New*), had come to Hollywood for an extended visit. We met and talked films. He invited me to visit Russia. Later, as president of the Academy, I played host to a visiting delegation of Soviet film V.I.P.'s, headed by the minister in charge of all Soviet film activities, Mr. Shumiatsky. He said my films were seen and studied in the Moscow film school: "You must some day visit us in Moskva."

So, while arranging for passport visas in New York (on our way to London), Riskin and I requested visas for the U.S.S.R., never expecting anything to come of it. About three days after arriving in London—just before the big opening of *Lost Horizon* at the Tivoli—the concierge at Claridge's gave us a message from the Soviet Embassy: Our visas to Moscow were approved and ready to pick up.

So leaving Lu in the tender care of two dear friends, Miriam and Tim Whelan (a former gag man on my Langdon comedies, now directing British films), Bob Riskin and I hopped the Orient Express and headed for Belgium, Germany, Poland, the U.S.S.R.—and the archaic fences fearful nations had erected at their frontiers.

It was twilight when we pulled into Moscow's massive, noisy, teeming terminal—our chief bugaboos: Where would we sleep, how would we get there? (No one on the train spoke a word of English.) But as soon as we stepped off the car our worries vanished. A welcoming delegation surrounded us, embraced us, kissed both cheeks—photographers, four officials of the Film Workers Union, an Intourist woman interpreter, and a jovial but turgid government official who looked like Guy Kibbee (having forgotten his name I will call him "Guy Kibbee" from now on).

And—because film is one of the three universal languages (the other two: mathematics and music)—on that station platform in Moscow I first became aware of a most significant humanism inherent in filmmaking. Regardless of frontiers, regardless of national, political, or ethnical differences, filmmakers all over the world are united by a common bond: apprenticeship in the greatest of all the art forms—FILM.

We all have the same artistic and technical problems; all create entertainment responsive to the same human emotions, and all respect our peers and adore our betters. In a sense, we are an international band of gypsies bearing an undefined but real allegiance to our profession that equals—and at times surpasses—our allegiance to national powers.

So Bob Riskin and I were not just two American capitalists venturing into the forbidding bastion of communism. We were two American film-makers being embraced by brother Russian filmmakers. From the moment we arrived we were their guests. More, we were instant friends.

We couldn't spend a ruble. If Bob or I tried to pay a check one of them would slap our hands away—"You paid for your rubles, we make lots!" —and out would come a roll of rubles that would choke a hippopotamus. For Soviet film people were—and still are—the elite of the intellectuals and opinion molders; the government respected them, feared them, con-trolled them tightly, but paid them handsomely.

Film director Trauberg was our constant host in Moscow, picking us up at the Metropole Hotel in the morning and depositing us back at night. He took us to the Moscow Film School, where Riskin saw his scripts in the library; to theaters, ballets (then the best in the world), restaurants, and to Mosfilm Studio. He walked us through the teeming streets of Moscow where, night or day, restless swarms of gray ill-clad Muscovites (a tie on a man was a rarity, make-up and silk stockings on women non-existent) surged through the city between gray, massive buildings of mongrel archi-tecture. (And, of course, *always* with us was our English-speaking official bodyguard, jolly Guy Kibbee.)

But mostly we wined and dined with directors, writers, actors, cameramen. What did we talk about? Films, of course—our films; their films; British, French, Italian films; to our embarrassment they knew them all. How did we communicate? We used entangled English, fractured French, but mostly a German jargon. When these failed we tried Yiddish; when all else failed we resorted to good old-fashioned gestures, hand signs—and laughs.

Riskin and I got two distinct impressions out of these "vodka-klatches": one, Russians admired American films, and American people in general; and, two, because of their vitality, boastfulness, and lusty humor Russians re-sembled Americans more than either resembled other European nationals. One could sense that two possible fates awaited the driving forces of the United States and Russia—cooperation or conflict.

Guy Kibbee, our official escort and interpreter, fascinated and wor-ried us. With a white beard and a red suit he could have played a "Ho! Ho! Ho!" Santa Claus. In the midst of want he was fat, and come hell come Stalin he intended to stay fat. In restaurants he drank and ate everything in sight, but the check always blinded him. While someone else picked up the tab, he picked up all the leftover bread rolls and stuffed his pockets full— good for extra kopeks at his apartment house. His motto: Workers of the world lose your chains—so I can sell them for junk.

To save us time and red tape (he said), he obligingly exchanged our dol-lars for rubles at official money-exchange places (he said). Anyway, he brought back official exchange slips—needed at the border to account for our declared dollars.

Guy Kibbee's badge of the bureaucrat was a celluloid collar with a black, stringy tie. When we left on the night train for a week's visit in Leningrad, he came along without a bag or a suitcase. When asked why, he laughed, pulled a small paperbag out of his pocket, and said: "All I need for one week I put in *this* bag——" He showed us an extra celluloid collar and a toothbrush. "But you forgot the toothpaste," said Riskin. "No, no!" he chuckled, "I use toothbrush to wash dirty collar when I change it."

It was on that overnight train to Leningrad that I had one of those rare wonderful experiences one never forgets. Riskin had been paired with Guy Kibbee in one compartment. The conductor motioned me toward the other end of the car and, since I understood one might be paired with a stranger of either sex, I wondered what I would do if——but the suspense was over. There was a *man* sitting in one of the chairs of my assigned compartment.

Lifting my bags and cameras onto one of the berths, I looked the man over. He was about fifty; coatless; his graying hair cropped close; his clean-shaven face lean and tanned. He wore a clean white shirt with a neat black tie. He hadn't looked up once from his book since I had entered. I glanced at his book——and did a double-take. On its cover I read the title——in English: *Anna Karenina* by Leo Tolstoi.

"Sir?" I said, "you must speak English."

"Yes, some," he said as he looked up. His voice was as pleasing as his face. "You must be an American."

"Yes, sir——" Then I introduced myself. He said his name was Captain Smolyavitch of the Soviet Navy; he read *Anna Karenina* at least once a year, and he somehow liked it better in English than in its original Russian. And then he astounded me with this bit of information: He was the captain of the world famous icebreaker, the *Krassin*; he was on his way to Archangel to board the *Krassin* and begin his yearly breaking of the Arctic ice from Archangel to Nome! What a man. I insisted he tell me every little detail of the ice-breaking. My enthusiasm must have pleased him for he smiled and said: "If you have some film for those cameras, and six weeks to spare, would you like to be my guest on the *Krassin*, and photograph the trip?"

"Oh, my God! You mean——could I?"

"Of course. I am the captain of my ship. The food is good, the wine is better, the ice is always a challenge, and we could have some good talks. What's more, I will take you back to your country and land you at Nome, Alaska."

Holy tomato! Breaking the ice from Archangel to Alaska!

"Captain, I'd give anything to go with you. I'll notify my wife from Leningrad——"

First thing I did when we entered the Astoria Hotel was to send my wife this cable: DARLING. HAVE WONDERFUL OPPORTUNITY GO ON ICE-BREAKING TRIP ARCHANGEL TO ALASKA AS GUEST OF CAPTAIN OF ICEBREAKER SHIP KRASSIN. OKAY? CABLE IMMEDIATELY. LOVE FRANK.

The answer came back so fast it scorched the wires: FRANK ARE YOU CRAZY? NO REPEAT NO. LU

The first "no" killed me. The second one was kicking a corpse. Ninety-nine times out of a hundred marriage is wonderful. But not when I wanted to go ice-breaking from Archangel to Nome. I nearly cried when I called Captain Smolyavitch.

Film director Ermler was our volatile, fun-loving guide and host in Leningrad. He reminded me of my close friend—American director Bill "Wild Man" Wellman. Communicating with Ermler—in our common smattering of German plus an uncommon mixture of Slavic and Wild West hand signals—was laughable. In a sightseeing government limousine (on our way to see the wonders of the Hermitage museum and the Winter Palace) Ermler began smoking a little old burned-out pipe with its broken stem patched with adhesive tape. Ermler's pockets may have bulged with rubles, but the few things he could buy with them did not include a new pipe.

I pulled out one of the new Dunhill pipes I had just bought in London. Ermler's eyes popped at the sight of it. He recognized the white Dunhill dot on the stem. "Ah! *Sie rauchen ein Doonhill*—" I took out another brand new Dunhill pipe and offered it to him as a present. Big Brother Guy Kibbee pompously announced that Soviet people could not accept gifts from capitalists. Ermler ruefully tried to hand me back the pipe. I refused to take it, saying that out West in our country it was an offense to refuse to smoke the pipe of peace. The small international situation was broken up by Riskin. He took out his fountain pen, handed it to Guy Kibbee, and haughtily said: "And you can put that in writing with this brand new fountain pen."

Guy Kibbee's cupidity got the best of him: a new fountain pen was like gold. "Oh, of course, of course. We could not think of offending *anybody*." He pocketed the fountain pen. Ermler and I exchanged knowing winks and burst out laughing.

"In Hollywood," Ermler quipped, *"Sie sagen*, 'Print it!' Okay?" "Okay!" I said. Ermler was as pleased with his new pipe as a boy with his first pair of skates—and friendship reigned again between communism and capitalism.

The Lenfilm Studios was a dilapidated, reconverted ancient building; technical facilities and stages much more primitive than the better equipped Mosfilm Studios in Moscow. But the film artists had more spirit, more daring, in keeping with the ferment of intellectual dissent Leningrad was noted for. The workers revolt of 1905, Kerensky's overthrow of the Romanovs in February, 1917, and the Bolshevik overthrow of Kerensky in October, 1917, all were spawned in Leningrad.

Compared to Moscow (the Chicago of the East), Leningrad (the Paris of the East) was a spacious city of classical beauty designed by Italian and French architects commissioned by Peter the Great. Leningrad film people boasted they had more artistic freedom than their confreres in Moscow because Leningrad was the intellectual and cultural center, Moscow the center of politics.

In Leningrad we were privileged to meet and mingle with the city's artistic elite in a special, semi-private building, a sort of an academy building, where film artists met among themselves and with poets, painters, and musicians to discuss art and politics. It was there that they plied us with searching questions about the United States. It was there that we learned about Soviet films: their genesis, growth, and advancement in artistry and technique from 1920 to 1937.

We asked about Eisenstein and, as in Moscow, we got vague answers: "He is in the Crimea" . . . "in Kiev" . . . "he is not well" . . . "nobody has seen him" . . . We also asked about head film man Shumiatsky and got even vaguer answers.

Returning to Moscow again, we found a telephone message from Eisenstein at the hotel, and a phone number to call—at a certain hour of the day. We called. Eisenstein answered.

"Fronk," he said cautiously, "you vant to see me? Vy?"

We told him how disappointed we'd be if we were to leave Moscow without paying our respects to one of the world's great picturemakers. He gave us an address to hand to a taxi driver and, if we could shake our escort, to come now. We slipped out of the Metropole lobby to a taxi without jovial Guy Kibbee seeing us.

We found the great Eisenstein sitting alone in a broken-down booth of a broken-down Georgian cafe in one of Moscow's broken-down sections. Making sure we were alone, he asked us to sit down and have a hot glass of tea with melting butter floating on it. He looked drawn, depressed.

"Fronk, Bub," he said smiling wryly, "I am in the dog house." We laughed at his American slang. "I can no make pictures, I can no go in studios, no movie workers can talk to me. I am in the dog house."

Then he explained: The Kremlin had asked him to make a film trilogy on the life of Ivan the Terrible. "I make Part One; the Kremlin bosses see it— they give me big medal. Good. Soviet hero! I make Part Two; big shots see it —they take back my medal. Stalin say no Part Three, no more films; say I make big political mistake. Soviet bum! Three months now I'm in the dog house. You like?"

We didn't like. Then we told him we had been trying to pay our respects to Mr. Shumiatsky, the Soviet minister in charge of the Soviet delegation to Hollywood. "No use look," he said, "he's in dog house, too. Maybe—" He shrugged and said no more.

We commiserated with that wounded giant for about an hour, then left for the Metropole shocked at the iron discipline Soviet film creators had to contend with. (The Kremlin's iron grip on Soviet artists of all kinds was to relax substantially after Stalin's fall from grace.)

Back at the Metropole we found jovial Guy Kibbee about to go out of his mind over our disappearance. We calmed his fears by telling him we went for a taxi ride—and never left the taxi. That relieved his fright, but not his pouting. So we salved his hurt feelings by handing him fifty dollars to exchange for us in rubles—quite sure he'd never go near the official money-exchange window, but would come back and hand us a sheaf of his own rubles—and a phony receipt.

While we were away in Leningrad, Trauberg (our Moscow director-host) had achieved the impossible: two stadium tickets for the big parade in Red Square for Riskin and me—out of a total of only three thousand allotted for all spectators—foreign embassies, Communist dignitaries from sixteen Soviet Republics, and "piece-work" champions from Minsk to Omsk.

On May 1, 1937, Trauberg, Riskin, and I left the boarded-up front of the Metropole Hotel at dawn (all business fronts in Moscow were padlocked and boarded for the parade), for the long, slow trek to Red Square. We walked between continuous lines of Red soldiers, through great canyons of red flags; through roadblocks of secret police for checking, stamping, and frisking—the closer to Red Square the longer the checking. The silence of the great city—flying its flags at red alert—was eerie, ominous, defiant. The choleric color reflected from eyes, from faces; sparked fire from bayonets. Red was the city, red the mood.

Two hours later we were ushered into concrete bleachers that jutted out from the sides of Lenin's tomb like wings of a monoplane from its fuselage. In each of the bleachers there was standing room for only fifteen hundred—there was no space and no place for anybody to sit. Directly behind, the massive Kremlin wall dwarfed us; on our right, the more massive Kremlin gate, surmounted by a clock tower and its red star-tipped spire, intimidated us; but the desecration of St. Basil's Cathedral—its famed gilded Byzantine domes and spires now hidden under dirty brown paint—incensed us.

The buildings across the Square were a mass of red flags and huge, but huge, faces of Stalin and Lenin that looked down on the living expression of their power—Red Army regiments standing at attention.

To me, the huge blood-tinted Square was a monumental outdoor stage; a gigantic setting for a strange animistic ritual—a solemn High Mass to be offered up to Marxist gods on the massive altar of Lenin's tomb. Over-whelmed, we spoke in whispers.

Several hundred foreign diplomats and attachés, nervously twiddling with cameras and notebooks—anticipating the unveiling of new weapons—chit-tered like jittery jays in the first two rows of our concrete bleachers. We were huddled somewhere in the middle, stomping our feet with all the rest to keep warm. Welcome swigs from a vodka bottle passed around by two friendly, fur-capped Mongolian Communists from across the Urals helped fight off the cold.

Shortly before ten o'clock, the uneasy calm was shattered by the booming of distant cannon. At ten sharp, Stalin suddenly materialized on top of Lenin's tomb, flanked by about a dozen gray-overcoated, bemedaled bigwigs (over half of whom were to be jailed or liquidated within a year).

Bugles sounded; the Kremlin gate opened; military chief Voroshilov pranced out on a white horse to read the oath of allegiance to each regiment. The Red soldiers pledged their allegiance with a mighty yell—it sounded like a college "Rah-h-h!" Then came the Red speeches—loud, angry, defiant —pledging destruction of all their enemies. To which the assembled soldiers shouted "Amen" in a long continuous "Rah-h-h-h!" The mighty yell moved like a wave to unseen military contingents all over Moscow until the city trembled to the thunder of the male roar. It was hair-raising.

Then the parade! Soldiers, soldiers, marching, marching; cannons, tanks, cannons, rockets, cannons, motorcycles—the rumbling of the motored might was deafening!

Foreign attachés feverishly took pictures and made notes. I just took pictures, not of the Red Army, but of faces, faces; of Stalin raising his right hand up and down like a toy automaton. And still they came. Trucks—fleets of them filled with helmeted, statue-like soldiers—rolled by ten abreast.

Then came the people—thousands of them, tens of thousands—a river of people flowing bank to bank across Red Square, holding up flags, placards, and massive head photos. The tag end of this parading mass sucked in the spectators. We found ourselves floating out of Red Square on the people's river, between banks of elbow-to-elbow soldiers.

Far out in the outskirts of Moscow the police lines suddenly ended. The sun was setting. Ahead of us we saw a great cloud of dust in an open field. The marchers in front of us broke ranks and raced for the cloud. Riskin, Trauberg, and I raced with them. And there, inside the gloom and dust of that protecting cloud, the greatest mass urination of all time was taking place.

It was dark before the three of us stumbled back into the Metropole Hotel as grimy, exhausted, and vacant-eyed as the Forty-Niners who made it across Death Valley. Trauberg shoved us into the cafe, ordered beakers of vodka and pounds of caviar. By the second drink we could talk again, by the third one we laughed, after the fourth we were in hysterics.

Departing from our Soviet film friends was an emotional wrench. We had been their constant guests for three weeks. Not once had we been near the American Embassy, nor had we met any Americans. As a last gesture of friendship, about a dozen directors and writers escorted us to the train and filled our arms with gifts—boxes of candy, stacks of Russian sheet music, packages of long Russian cigarettes, small bottles of vodka, and flowers. And finally, there were the warm embraces and sincere good-byes.

On the train, Riskin and I traded impressions of the big country we were leaving. Riskin couldn't forget the rusty, leaking plumbing, the broken toilet seats, and that god-awful toilet paper—newspapers and wrapping paper cut up in little square sheets. I couldn't forget the shocking irreligious window displays in public squares—atheistic mockeries of God, Christ, and the virgin birth—with their ever-present slogan: Religion is the opium of the people. And, of course, right next to the religious caricatures, Papa Stalin was displayed dispensing gifts to the happy Soviet workers.

We talked about Stalin's iron censorship of films. Some film artists, the party members, had speciously argued it was not real censorship; that within the framework (the "window" they called it) of the Kremlin guidelines artists were completely free to develop their own film style. It was like saying a prisoner in a cell had complete freedom of movement within the cell. What would become of the artist's right to dissent, lampoon, rebel against corrupt power—if power wrote the guidelines? Could communism disprove Baron Acton's warning that "power tends to corrupt and absolute power corrupts absolutely"? Disproving that would quail the gods.

"Working for Harry Cohn is tough enough," said Riskin, "imagine what it must be like working for Stalin." I couldn't. But somehow I felt that the spirit, verve, and artistry of directors like Eisenstein, Trauberg, Kozintsev, and Ermler couldn't be held down forever by any power.

Yes, Riskin was disappointed. He had expected more of socialism's vaunted Utopia—more welfare for the people rather than great military parades. He was a sincere pacifist. But I, who had expected little, came away more impressed than I had anticipated.

I could not forget the priceless art treasures in the Hermitage, bought by the Tsars—with tax money wrung from the illiterate "dark people"—to give a Romanov recluse something nice to look at on the walls of her cloistered palace.

I could not forget the vulgar display of diamonds, emeralds, and rubies—gems as big as walnuts—in the crucifixes and coats-of-arms encrusted on the Romanov tombs that lay in a private crypt of their private cathedral. Fantastic jewels that would pay off many a national debt. A sacrilegious waste of wealth that would evoke atheistic thoughts in the most pious—let alone in the newly emancipated serfs whose welts from the cossack's lash still scarred their backs.

Nor could I forget the Russian people's passion for work, passion for education, passion for tractors, concrete, and steel to rebuild the shambles left by three catastrophic national disasters in quick succession: a World War, a Revolution, and a Civil War.

Being peasant born, I could sense the drive, the will, the necessity for the stricken peasant colossus to lift itself out of the depths by its own bootstraps, not necessarily by the democratic methods I revered, but perhaps by harsher means more seasonable to its bleakness of circumstance and havoc of history.

At any rate, I left Russia with a liking for its people, and a prayer for the betterment of their hard life.

There had been one jarring note: Guy Kibbee, our wily official guardian, had relieved me of all my exposed movie and Leica film the day before we left. I argued that I had asked his permission for every shot that I took, but he said he couldn't vouch completely for the innocence of the film until he had it developed and passed by the censor, then he would ship it to me with his own hands. I had a hunch the artful old boy had his hand out for a few last-minute dollars, but my movie friends had warned *never* to offer gratuities to a government official.

As a result, there was a big to-do about the missing film at the Russian border. Officials there said they had signed me into Russia with so much film, and where was it now? I explained that I had shot it all myself, with permission, but that our escort had taken it away from me. They finally believed my story, but they also said I should have brought the film to them for *their* approval of what might be taken out of the country. Now their red tape had been fouled up.

I never did get the film from Guy Kibbee; my many subsequent inquiring letters went unanswered. Perhaps the jolly old boy was enjoying a long overdue vacation in some Siberian spa.

There is no denying our relief in breathing free air again as we crossed into Poland. The presence of newspapers from all over the world on Polish newsracks dramatized the Russian people's isolation. During our three-week visit in the U.S.S.R. we had not read one newspaper, heard one newscast, nor even one word-of-mouth news item from the outside. Now in Poland we grabbed up half a dozen French and British papers and, for the first time, learned that the dirigible *Hindenburg*, loaded with passengers, had tragically gone up in flames several days ago, while attempting to dock at the Lakehurst mast—the same mast we used for docking the *Los Angeles* during my filming of *Dirigible*.

CHAPTER 12

"If You Could Only Cook"

BACK IN LONDON, two Britishers well known in Hollywood, Charles Laughton and Alexander Korda, not only introduced Lu and me to the film elite, but also to Members of Parliament, to editors, publishers, bankers, and to artists of other disciplines. Much to our surprise, film people were not merely accepted by the upper echelons of British government and British culture, they were welcomed—professionally and socially. British films were part of Britain's culture.

How different things were in the United States, where, despite the fact that the American films were far and away the best of all salesmen for American goods, products, ideas, mores, and customs, despite the fact that the American film was "Americanizing" the world—the entrenched poobahs of our Eastern seaboard still looked down on Hollywood as a cesspool of cheap exhibitionists and crackpots. It was—and still is—a pity that American filmmakers are better known, more admired, more appreciated in foreign countries than they are in their native land.

Indicative of the attitude was President Kennedy's list honoring thirty or more of our most distinguished contemporary American artists. That list included the names of hair stylists, fashion designers, and interior decorators—but not one film name!

It was Hungarian-born producer-director and financial wizard Alexander Korda who put British films on the map in a big way, with such notable achievements as (Academy-Award winning) *The Private Life of Henry VIII*, *Catherine the Great*, *The Scarlet Pimpernel*, and *The Ghost Goes West*. I believe he was the first filmmaker to be knighted by British royalty, and undoubtedly the first to charm British bankers into investing important money in films.

Tall, handsome Korda was not only a superb conversationalist—twice superb because of his million-dollar accent—but a big-time visionary with the wheeler-dealer shrewdness of a rug peddler. These advantages, coupled with his exotic glamour as a luxury-loving Sybarite, gave him uncanny persuasive powers with unromantic bankers. Wherever Korda operated, there was sure to be excitement, glamour—and aspirin pills.

(A year later, in Hollywood, Korda, David O. Selznick, and I formed a partnership to buy United Artists. We had visions of making millions by distributing our own films and those of other independent producers. The deal was all set. But Korda's irresistible charm ran into Selznick's immovable ego on the question of which one should be the new president of United Artists. I sat in the bleachers, while Korda made long impassioned speeches favoring Korda, and Selznick wrote equally impassioned, but longer, letters in favor of Selznick. It was really a titanic tilt of the tonsils, for Selznick dictated his marathon letters to shifts of stenotypists as he paced a ditch in his office rug deep enough for Junior Laemmle to fall into. As the oratory waxed, the deal waned—then died for lack of a president. But the Duel in the Sun continued long after there was any presidency to vie for. For the Korda-Selznick debates were not for a vulgar prize—such as the Lincoln-Douglas debates on slavery, or the Huxley-Bennett wrangles about whether science or the humanities were best for man. No, indeed! The film titans were untainted purists arguing the ideal of supremacy for the sheer love of simon-pure logic: "My father can lick your father, so there!")

It was at a luncheon—and a film showing—given by Korda at his Denham Studio that Alex introduced Lu and me to the Man. The Denham film center was near the village of Hounslow in Middlesex. The studio was a reconverted fish hatchery, "The Fisheries," which once raised fish for London's streams. Korda's London Films headquarters were in a grand old mansion that had survived the renovation.

Just before the luncheon, Korda gave us the fifty-cent tour; we met Vincent and Zoltan Korda, the Boulting brothers, Korda's head film editor, Bill Hornbeck (an old friend from Mack Sennett days), and Hornbeck's assistant film cutter, David Lean (later, director of *The Bridge on the River Kwai, Lawrence of Arabia, Doctor Zhivago*).

For the luncheon, Alex had invited two other guests, both English, both wore the dark coats and wing collars that seemed to denote importance in Britain. But, as usual, I didn't catch their names. One was a grayish, blandish man; not unlike one of the well-dressed, inconspicuous extras in Hollywood that directors choose—because of their low-key charisma—to back up stars in close-ups.

But no director in his right mind would ever use the *other* Englishman as a backdrop for stars, for he immediately caught your eye with his extraordinary vitality and boldness. Some call it presence; others prefer leadership, magnetism, personality, or what have you. Film directors describe this quality as one that, "jumps right out of the screen at you." It is a quality that one is born with. All great stars have it. In fact, all great leaders, be they heroes or villains, have it. I don't know what "it" is exactly, but that John Bull character, sitting across the luncheon table, sure had it to spare.

His bulldog face with its jutting jaw was certainly familiar. At first I mentally put him down as some well-known English character actor whose name wouldn't come to me. He had the voice of an actor, too—like an organ, except for a slight lisp. But when he and Korda traded witticisms, Alex kept calling him "Winnie." I knew of no British actor by the name of Winnie—at least not important enough to have lunch with Korda. So I decided the two English gentlemen were financial "prospects" being exposed to Korda's glamour pitch.

The luncheon over, we stretched our legs before the film showing. Korda escorted me to the washroom, where I asked about his two English friends, expecially the witty one who looked like John Bull. "At first," I said, "I thought he was an actor, except that I couldn't think of any actor by the name of Winnie."

Alex leaned his head back and roared with laughter. "Oh, my God, Frank, you're joking. Winnie! An actor?"

"All right, all right. But if he's a pigeon you're fattening up, he's going to be a hard man to shave, I'll tell you that."

Korda let out a bigger roar. "Oh, I'll tell him you think he's a hard man to shave. He'll love it. His name is Winston Churchill."

Everyone who was anyone in London would, sooner or later, be taken to one of Sir Louis's and Lady Stirling's lavish open-house Sunday parties the Stirlings gave in their elegant stately mansion. Lady Stirling was to the manor born, but Sir Louis was an ex-American Jew from Manhattan—knighted for his enterprising development of the "his master's voice" (Victor) phonograph in Britain.

The Stirling bashes were entertainment in the grand style; only one slight obligation for the guests: Those who played ping-pong (table tennis in England) were "commanded" to play against Cissie Stirling. And very few could beat the gay hostess—or did.

Lu and I quickly cottoned up to the Stirlings on discovering that they, too, were enthusiastic collectors of rare books. I'll have to admit that we book collectors are a tight-knit, snooty lot. We feel superior to the average book lover because we delve into the history of books—the vagaries of the printer, the gambles of the publisher. And, above all, we know that a great book is probably the most precious gift man can leave to posterity. And, say we book collectors, a good way to become privy to the author himself is to collect his first editions. For in tracking down first printings, one often opens the dossier on the writer: his botched beginnings, shattered hopes, dark dreams, frustrations, endurances; what drove him to write the book; what made the book a collector's item.

You probably have read Milton's *Paradise Lost*, and loved it. But wouldn't you love it more if you knew that the first edition of this classic—with the title page reading: *Paradise Lost* by JOHN MILTON—was a complete failure? And that when the disgruntled publisher grudgingly printed a second edition, he lower-cased the author's name to *John Milton*? And that when the second edition moved as slowly as the first, the name on the third edition was further diminished to *J. Milton*—and to just *J. M.* on the fourth edition? But then the book began to sell. On the fifth edition the intials expanded back to *John Milton*, and by the sixth printing the author's name was restored to the upper-case glory of the first edition: JOHN MILTON.

If you yawn, and ask *why* that bit of trivia should make you love *Paradise Lost* more than you do, well, now—that's what makes us book collectors so snooty—nobody understands us.

It was at the Stirling's bar that a British actor volunteered his opinion of Jean Arthur: She was his favorite American actress, and *he* could go for her whether she could cook or not. Failing to see the point of his "joke," I smiled vacuously. The actor left me to seek brighter company.

Driving back to Claridge's with the Whelans, I repeated what the English actor had said about Jean Arthur, and confessed my bafflement with English humor.

"Oh, he wasn't joking," laughed Miriam Whelan, "he was talking about your last picture with Jean Arthur that's playing London now. The one about if she could only cook—"

"Now *you're* trying to be funny. My last picture with Arthur was *Mr. Deeds*—and she didn't even boil water."

"I don't blame you for trying to disown it, Frank," kidded Tim Whelan, "what'd you do, make it between taking bows?"

"What bows? What're you talking about?"

"Your Columbia picture—the one called *If You Could Only Cook.*"

"I never heard of it."

"Come on, Frank. You got your name all over it—on the screen, in the ads—"

Next morning I phoned Joe Friedman, head of Columbia's London office, to ask about *Lost Horizon.* He said every performance was a sell-out. Then I casually asked how *If You Could Only Cook* was doing. Without hesitating, he said it was cleaning up because British theaters paid the highest prices ever for Capra productions, and he wished I'd give him two or three more each year to sell.

Well, somebody must be crazy. I hurried to Friedman's office on Wardour Street, asked to see the film's press book. And there, in that huge folder of press clippings, was the whole story: paid ads, reviews, and comments about a modest little film, *If You Could Only Cook,* a Frank Capra Production, produced by Frank Capra. The reviews were so-so—the tenor of most: "not up to Capra's standard."

I couldn't believe my eyes. A picture I never heard of was being advertised and sold in England as a Capra film, and at the highest terms. Friedman readily allowed me to take the press book to the hotel, so the deception could not have been his. But who in Columbia Pictures, now presumably a responsible international corporation, would commit such an obvious, bald-faced fraud? One name flashed to mind—but no. Harry Cohn couldn't be that stupid. Or could he? I cabled a friend: Check if my name was on the film in the U.S. The answer: No.

I had one more chore to do in London: An interview—under the hottest of all lights, in front of a long black square tube they called a television camera—at the British Broadcasting Corporation's pioneering television studio on Savoy Hill off the Strand.

That done, I took Lu (and the press book) to Paris and to Cap d'Antibe; then to Florence, Rome, and Naples where we met Riskin again. Then back to New York on the liner *Rex* and, without a stopover, went straight to Hollywood and into Harry Cohn's office with the press book under my arm, to ask: "Harry, what do you mean by putting my name on a film I never saw, and selling it as a Frank Capra picture?"

The Crude One brazened it out. "Oh, *that*, for crissake. Some brain in the New York office got a wild hair about making a few more bucks in England. Does it kill ya, for crissake, to see Columbia make a few more bucks in England? Maybe we can cut you *in* for a slice—"

"Cut *me* in—"

"Get smart," he lectured, "cash in—like everybody does. I'll put your name on two of my cheaper pictures each year—and we'll split the profits. *If You Could Only Cook* can be the first one. Who's gonna know the difference?"

And when he finally asked, "What d'ya say, Walyo? Deal?" all I could sputter was, "Why *goddam* you, Harry. I never thought I'd call you stupid. But that's what you are. Stupid! If you think for one minute that I'd put my name on someone else's films—for a *price*."

"Oh, price my ass. What are you, the Pope or something? What about the price you've made Columbia pay? Full control of your pictures. Producer-director. Critics even write you up that *Capra* is Columbia, instead of Cohn. So what the hell is wrong with playing ball with *me* a little? Is it a deal, or isn't it a deal?"

It was an ultimatum—more in tone than in words. Mafia-like, he was out to incriminate, then own me—knock off my halo, make me "sing his song, if I ate his bread." If I refused, there was the veiled threat that I would lose my precious authority over my films.

Time and again, during Columbia's upward scramble from Poverty Row, we had practiced brinkmanship in similar climactic confrontations. Each time, my final ultimatum—"my way, or I leave"—had made Cohn back down because he needed me. And each time, the pressure gauge of his resentment shot up a notch.

And now that Columbia had scaled Mount Success, Cohn felt strong enough to choose the time, place, and conditions for another confrontation. His ultimatum: "*My* way from now on. Play ball, or else."

The battle was on. But I sensed a desperateness in his attitude. Could it be he had put his tail in a crack by putting my name on *If You Could Only Cook* before I agreed to it? Was he backtracking—forcing me into a deal—to cover up his boner? At any rate, I threw him a curve of my own: "Harry, if you will cancel my contract, give me my freedom—I won't sue you for *If You Could Only Cook.*"

"Are you nuts!" he bellowed. The curve was right over the plate.

"Nope. Just doing you a favor. I'm checking out of Columbia, Harry. Good-bye."

"You do," he yelled after me, "and you'll never work again! I've still got you under contract for three more pictures—don't forget *that!*"

I went to my office, cleaned out my desk, and walked out of Columbia Studios—forever, I hoped.

What I needed, of course, was a hard-boiled agent to represent me. It was almost ten years ago that my first agent, Demmy Lampson, dismissed me as a liability. One year later, the Small Agency dismissed me for having negotiated my first deal with Columbia without consulting Morris Small. Since then I had done very well without the ten-percenters, so who needed them now?

I did. But having turned so many agents down lately, my ego balked at seeking their guidance. Besides, I considered my case against Columbia so righteous that surely virtue must easily triumph over Cohn. Thus, in lieu of an agent, I hired a young, inexperienced lawyer, and filed suit against Columbia and Harry Cohn, charging "fraud," "embezzlement," and a half-dozen other juristic phrases meaning "you dirty skunk"; demanded one hundred thousand dollars damages for the libelous use of my name; further demanded the cancellation of my contract on grounds of moral turpitude, or something.

Cohn countered by cutting off my salary and sending me legal notice that my contract was suspended until I returned to Columbia and reported for work on my assigned duties.

It was a time when studios had united to discipline contracted artists whose noggins had inflated. Warners had suspended James Cagney, Bette Davis, and Olivia de Havilland for insubordination. Not only were they off salary, but their exclusive iron-clad contracts—with continuing options—precluded them from working for anyone else. They either knuckled under or were through in pictures.

Olivia de Havilland stuck it out. She sued for cancellation of her "slavery" contract. She won—and achieved a milestone court decision against involuntary servitude: No person could be held under an exclusive personal service contract for longer than seven years—including all suspensions.

That ruling hardened the attitude of the Motion Picture Producers Association (MPPA) against contract jumpers. They tacitly agreed not to "raid" each other's talent, nor to talk to, approach, or negotiate any present or future agreements with any other company's suspended contract personnel. I knew all this, but I had an open-and-shut case. All any judge had to do was to read the London press book of *If You Could Only Cook*—and Cohn would be parboiled. Besides, no other producing company would dare stick with Cohn on a bare-faced fraud. So I naively announced in the trade papers that—for serious personal reasons (a hint to nosy reporters)—I had severed connections with Columbia; then sat on the sands of Malibu waiting to be inundated with offers from other studios. Wasn't everyone saying I was the most sought after director in Hollywood?

Day after day I waited. Not a single phone call. Month after month I waited, biting my nails. No phone calls. I was the one sinned against. Did that make me a pariah—like Eisenstein in Moscow? One word from Stalin had put Eisenstein "in the dog house." Evidently, one word from Cohn had branded me an "untouchable" to all other studios. Was the Kremlin's political dictatorship too much different than Hollywood's economic autocracy? And did the power to blacklist extend to control of the press? Not one reporter called me to find out what's what. I simply ceased to exist. Okay, I'd put my money on the law to free me from Cohn.

After months of waiting, my suit came up for a preliminary hearing in a Superior Court at Los Angeles. "Never mind any legal shenanigans," I whispered to my lawyer as we entered the courtroom, "just put me on the stand and let me open this press book to the judge. That's all. We'll get a judgment in two minutes."

In the courtroom I saw a well-dressed group of spectators; wondered who they were. I didn't wonder long—they were all Columbia lawyers.

The judge entered, called up the case. Before my lawyer could open his briefcase, the battery of Columbia barristers read what they called a "demurrer" to His Honor. They claimed that whereas: Columbia Studios, Hollywood, was a mere facility of Columbia Pictures, Inc., of New York; therefore; Columbia Studios could not be sued or held responsible for actions of the New York parent company. The judge asked a question or two, then ruled: "Demurrer granted. Case dismissed."

I jumped to my feet. "Your Honor, the president of the company, Harry Cohn, is in Hollywood. He is responsible for this. If you'll just look at this press book—"

The judge banged his gavel. "Demurrer is granted. Clear the courtroom!"

After waiting months, it took minutes for my lawsuit, my lawyer, and me —with my precious press book under my sweaty arm still unopened—to be thrown out of court. Round one was Harry Cohn's before I could get my gloves on.

"I boo-booed," said my brilliant barrister, "we should've sued in New York." Now, he tells me. I sent him East to file a second suit, this time against Columbia Pictures, Inc., of New York—while I took Lu to the Good Samaritan Hospital to have her third baby. On the same day, Gary Cooper brought his wife, Rocky, to the same hospital to have her first child.

Like a Mutt and Jeff team, tall Gary and I paced the maternity halls, gave passing nurses anxious, pleading looks. They ignored us. He-man "Coop" became unglued. He had a room next to Rocky's, but he cowered in the halls and fire escapes where he could chain-smoke.

Finally, a bulletin: Lu beat Rocky to the delivery room—a beautiful baby girl (Lulu) was born blue. Sticking his fingers down her throat, Dr. Vruink spanked her into redness. Like two idiots, Gary and I gitchy-kooed at little Lulu through the baby window. Next day, Rocky gave birth to her beautiful baby girl, Maria. I helped Gary gitchy-koo at little Maria. Lulu and Maria, born one day apart, were to grow up as inseparable as Siamese twins until their college days. They are still fast friends.

My lawsuit? I called my lawyer in New York almost daily. With the legal aid of an expensive New York firm, he had again filed suit and was waiting for a date to be set for the preliminary hearing. "No sweat, Frank," he kept pacifying me, "we'll knock Columbia off this time. But it may take weeks. So relax. Go fishing—"

Relax, yes. Might as well tell a grizzly caught in a bear trap to relax. Here I was—at the very top of my career—when each picture was better than the last; when I figuratively bubbled with new ideas; when I sensed a mastery over my tools: making actors believe what they are doing, even extras; making dull plot scenes entertaining; discovering the secret trick of making back-projection scenes look like the real McCoy, a secret even my own cameramen couldn't fathom; developing a sixth sense of "pace" (to move dialogue faster—don't raise voices, lower them); but most important of all, just when I *felt* I was becoming a real artist, perhaps a great one—I was banished from films, for God knows *how* long. Why? For refusing to lend my name to a fraud.

As weeks of idleness and misgivings stretched into months, my essential buoyancy, enthusiasm, and sunny idealism gave way to hard-bitten, cynical thoughts about the law, the Hollywood rat-race—and my friends. For, surprisingly, my best friends took a very mild attitude toward what I considered a heinous crime.

Max Winslow, for instance—a clean, good man whose joy was fanning the spark in others—fretted from the day I walked out of Columbia. "Frank, for God's sake come back to work. You're going strong. Five big hits in a row already. Don't let a stinking argument with Cohn cool you off. You'll blow your *momentum*—"

Then there was Myles Connolly, now an important contract writer at MGM. I regaled him with my tale of woe, asked him to riffle the pages of the *If You Could Only Cook* press book for corroboration of my actions. I expected a violent anti-Cohn tirade. Instead, he chewed his gum impassively and muttered "Uh-huh, uh-huh . . ." Then he suddenly closed the press book. "Yep. It's par for Cohn all right," he said, blowing out some air.

"*Par* for Cohn?" I exclaimed, "why that's the dirtiest trick he's *ever* pulled—"

"Frank—little shenanigans like this are played every day—in sports, politics, business. Yes, in making out your income tax. Little barnacles they are —on free enterprise. Frank! You ask me, you made a helluva mistake in leaving Columbia. It's like leaving your wife after you've had twelve kids—"

"Myles! I left Columbia because of a fraud—"

"Okay, fraud. But you're part of it. Why did you keep signing contracts with Cohn for ten years? You *knew* he wasn't St. Francis of Assisi—and you weren't either. You signed with Cohn to *use* him—to become a big producer-director. You said so yourself. So when Cohn tries to use *you* a little, why all the fuss?"

"For God's sake, Myles. Are you telling me *I'm* in the wrong?"

"No, no, not wrong—but not smart, either. You're playing Cohn's game. What with lawsuits and appeals he can keep you out of work for years—"

"Wait a minute! Should I connive at a fraud just to keep a job? I asked you down here for encouragement. I believed you when you kept preaching that evil is evil no matter how many pink ribbons you tie around it; that truth is *absolute*. And that I was a small calculating mind—a juggler, a compromiser. Now you tell me I *should* play games and compromise with barnacles. What the hell's happened to you down at MGM? Has some of that phony gloss rubbed off on *you*?"

He jumped up and paced. His jaw tightened; his nostrils widened. I knew he'd like to punch me in the nose. "Look, Frank," he said suppressing his anger, "nothing phony *ever* rubs off on me. I'm working with two of the greatest guys I ever met, Joe Pasternak, and a director by the name of Henry Koster—who's got everything you've got, plus more heart and more taste—"

"Which means—he agrees with you more than I do. Right?"

"Oh, go to hell!" He strode for the door.

"Remember, Myles, *commit* yourself. Open your mind to the immortals. You know—the poets and the prophets, and throw in the saints and martyrs. Have fun at MGM."

He turned at the door. "I'm committed, fella. And I'm working at it, while you're bellyaching, sitting down here on the sand eating your guts out; doing just what stinkpot Cohn wants you to do. Don't forget, Columbia's a big studio now. Cohn doesn't need you as much as he used to. Why he'd give his right arm to prove to everybody that Columbia *isn't* Capra. And you're making it easy for him. You're *stupid*."

He banged the door, leaving me with a head full of pounding woodpeckers, and a belly full of knots.

I might as well tell you that when a film director is kept from directing, he is a twitching, worrisome thing—that stares but doesn't see, listens but doesn't hear. If he talks at all, it's in little barks. Like a man with the hives he is never still. He goes, comes, sits, stands, twirls key chains, jingles pocket coins, whistles through his teeth. If a door sticks on him he tears it off the hinges.

"Darling," said my intuitive wife, "before you start beating up the children—why *don't* we go fishing?"

We raced up to Silver Lake in the High Sierras—where Wally Beery, Al Roscoe, and I used to fish and do crazy things with Beery's plane. We found that Beery's two-story lake cabin had been smashed into kindling by a hurtling avalanche of snow. But lake fishing proved too slow—too much time to think between strikes.

We went fishing for the fighting steelhead in the Klamath River, near the Oregon border, staying at "Van" and Esther Van Pelt's Lodge on Orleans Bar.

But it wasn't *fishing* I wanted, or reading, or playing the piano. I wanted to work, to make films, to wake up in the morning knowing I was needed somewhere.

Oh, those happy, rousing, exciting, exasperating days of shooting a film! Those wonderful mornings that challenged you with a dozen insoluble bafflers, some of which you solved with kicks in the groin, some with insults, others with blarney, but most with the chutzpah to slash Gordian knots with the sharp blades of YES! or NO!—not certain yourself which blade you should have used. Happy days of cheer-ups and foul-ups, when stars would bitch about their parts, writers howl about mayhemming their dialogue, and cameramen say "No *way* to light this set under two hours!"—and I would give them twenty minutes. When a sweat-dripping boom man, manipulating a mike over a fast-moving actress, would wildly wave his arms and shout, "Muffed it, boss! I *muffed* it! In rehearsal she turned the *other way* to tell the guy to shove it!" Days when wise-guy bit actors would try you on for size by lousing up late afternoon scenes so they'd *have* to be called back for another day's work; when all of yesterday's film would be ruined by a lab breakdown; when a white-faced studio head would burst into the middle of a scene waving falling box-office receipts and scream, "Finish by Tuesday or the company's BANKRUPT!" Oh, happy days! When Father Time breathed constantly down your neck and honed his scythe on your nerve ends. Happy, unforgettable days when your blood pumped furiously, and tender unforgettable scenes would bloom in bedlam. Were they gone forever?

Film is a disease. When it infects your bloodstream, it takes over as the Number One hormone; it bosses the enzymes; directs the pineal gland; plays Iago to your psyche. As with heroin, the antidote for film is *more* film. Withdrawal from junk tortures a mainliner's body. But kicking the film habit wracks a filmmaker's soul—his essential nature.

I sought peace and forgetfulness through fatigue and exhaustion. Furiously I plunged into Academy matters as its president; loudly I argued with friends; feverishly I prayed in churches. I walked fast, ate fast, drove my car at top speed, hoping to outrace the devil doubts, to shake off boredom.

But there were occasional pleasant interludes with my Russian friend, composer Dimitri Tiomkin, that helped to pass many a dragging hour. Acclaimed for his *Lost Horizon* musical score, he was now in great demand. Together with his wife, Albertina Rasch (once a famed ballet dancer, then an operator of ballet schools), Tiomkin began giving gay, lavish parties—food, wines, decor, music, and guests were as schmaltzy and waltzy as old Vienna and Strauss.

Tiomkin was one friend who didn't try to advise me about my battle with Columbia. "Fronk! You got big bore, yes?" he would ask on the phone—in such fractured English he broke you up. "I come to you. Give you maybe good laughs, no? Ooh, Fronk! I got big gossip—joocy gossip [he was the world's greatest at gossip]. Und Fronk! Listen me, babushka. Maybe music lesson I give you, yes? No! No! Not on piano. You play soch a stinking piano my ear it kills me. We *talk* music. Nacherly. I come now—"

On the beach, on long car rides, he taught me "talk" music. "Now, papitchka, vat is notes to C major?"

"Let's see—C—E—G—C."

"Goot. Vat is dominant of C major? . . . G seventh, goot! Und vat is the notes? . . . Da! Vat is C major quarta chord? . . . F major, goot . . . Vat is the little dominant? . . . triad? . . . augmented fifth? . . . C diminished? . . . relative minor?—"

And so it went. Mentally, without going near any instrument, he taught me the note combinations of all the possible chords in all of the twelve keys. Then, in reverse order, he called out the notes; I had to identify the chord and the key. Nobody ever had such an illustrious musical composition teacher—free—and with irreverent jokes about filmland's aristocracy thrown in as lagniappe. Not only were these lessons fun—and time-killing; they gave me the yen to write simple themes. But there was one small hitch: After writing out the notes, I couldn't play them back on the piano—I couldn't *read* music. And the world lost another Puccini.

And there were a few other bright interludes in that dark year that helped to keep me reasonably sane. After *Lost Horizon*, Lu and I had become intimate with Ronald and Benita Colman and often attended their famed and charming sit-down dinners at their palatial Beverly Hills home. In addition to visiting English celebrities—Bertrand Russell, Laurence Olivier, Vivien Leigh, James Hilton, and many others—the most frequent guests were Charles and "Pat" Boyer, Richard and Jessica Barthelmess, Lady (Sylvia) Ashley, Brian Aherne, and Mr. and Mrs. Bart Marshall and Mr. and Mrs. Warner Baxter.

Ronnie and Benita were probably the handsomest couple in Hollywood, and both loved all in life that was sensitive, fragile, and beautiful. But, much to their sorrow, they were childless. I had once made up an on-the-spot formula for the begetting of offspring that amused Ronnie no end. At times he would ask me to hold forth on the subject for the entertainment of his guests.

"If you will all listen," he would proclaim, "Dr. Capra has some profound Boccaccian advice for those who would beget but are unsuccessful. Give out, Doctor."

"Well," I would begin pontifically, "sex is not merely a biological phenomenon. It is primarily a wild emotional and psychological experience, the wildest, perhaps. It is fundamentally a three-act play, consisting of: the Desire, the Chase, and the Ravishment. Each act is a prologue to the next. Without the 'yen' there is no chase, without the chase—no climax. Played well, in natural sequence, you score a bull's-eye—new life. Played badly, with interruptions, intellectual discussions, habitual approaches; or tamper with its natural construction by introducing new "business," new gimmicks; or change the sequential order of the acts—and you end up with a series of bad rehearsals; no wild beauty, no new life.

"Now what happens after a blushing bride and a handsome groom take their nuptial vows—particularly if they are intellectuals? Well, they want to 'plan' their family—perhaps not have a child for three years. In addition they have separate bedrooms. Tradition and conformity dictate they must do their love-making at bedtime, which could be after midnight when they are worn out with working, or partying—and when, biologically, their vital forces are at the lowest ebb.

"Now comes the routine of going to bed. If the husband has any yen left, he makes civilized little passes at his wife; a pet, a squeeze, a pat on the fanny. Loving him, she responds—lets him know she'll be with him in a minute. Does the husband pursue the chase? No. He gets into bed with his yen and waits, and waits, and waits. No chase. No second act of the life play.

"What does the wife do? She undresses, takes off her make-up, takes a bath, puts on cold cream—and then proceeds to make the climax meaningless by fiddling around with libido-killing contraceptive gimmicks for another ten minutes. Perfumed, lovely, and 'prepared' against accidents, she floats into her husband's bedroom—and finds him snoring; not realizing that even a hot potato gets cold in less than an hour. Frustrated, perhaps slightly insulted, the wife flounces back into her room, un-gimmicks herself and goes to sleep. Not even a bad rehearsal.

"But let us presume that the husband, by intense concentration on his wife's charms, did manage to stay awake, and that they did wangle into a climax of sorts. But now the hot body juices are stopped cold by the contraceptive gimmicks. And after several years of continuous frustration the body juices get the idea—it's just a game called Love's Labour's Lost.

"And so, when after three years the couple decide they want a child, the wife throws away the contraceptives, but nothing happens. Their body juices are living cells with a memory. Memory tells them all previous sexual acts have been frustrating so they don't respond—contraceptives or not.

"So what is the cure? The cure is to restore the natural order of yen, chase, and ravishment. The cure is to go home for lunch—when your wife is not expecting you—then grab her, tear off her clothes, her panties—and ravish her! Right where you catch her: on the floor, in the kitchen, on the stairs. The excitement and the ecstasy will shock the body juices out of their contraceptive syndrome—and they'll respond again.

"That's my formula, gentlemen. You want children? Then go home for lunch and rape your wife."

There is a happy ending. Within a year or two, assuredly by coincidence, the Ronald Colmans and the Charles Boyers (also childless for years) both had lovely children.

Yes, I am indeed grateful to Tiomkin and the Colmans for having brightened some of the days and evenings of my exile. But then came the nights—brutal nights—when the weary body and brain cried out for sleep— as Cleopatra cried out: "Give me to drink mandragora . . . That I might sleep out this great gap of time . . ."

But sleep was a stranger. I paced and paced, with arms held tight against the hard lump of pain in my belly which Dr. Verne Mason, time and again, laughingly dismissed as an "out-of-work director's stomach." But the lump grew larger; the nausea more constant; and the urge to vomit continuous. But strain as I would the lump held fast. The best I could puke up was an occasional explosive belch which sucked up in its wake vile, burning lava that stuck in my throat. I could not eject or swallow the fetid stuff. Oh, God let me vomit—just once. God had no comment.

And then the wild vengeful brooding; holding Harry Cohn's head under water, chopping him to bits with an ax. Had it not been for the cheery optimism of my darling wife, I would have most assuredly blown my stack.

The first night she discovered me pacing the living room she nearly laughed out loud. "What're you doing, darling—picketing?" My director's instinct pigeon-holed the line—I used it later in *It's a Wonderful Life*. But at the moment, Groucho Marx couldn't make me laugh.

She tripped down the stairs with a robe. "Here, put this on before you freeze to death. Did the same wonderful idea wake you up too?"

"What wonderful idea?"

"Sit down, darling. I'll make some coffee and scramble some eggs." She hurried out into the kitchen, turned on lights, clattered pots and pans, kept on talking: "It's about that beautiful piece of property we bought a year ago in Brentwood, near the Wellmans'—that you said your father could make into a paradise of fruits and flowers—and that Mr. Coates [Roland Coates, the famous architect] designed such a beautiful house to build there—"

"You know I stopped all that nonsense when my salary stopped at Columbia—"

"Yes, and you stopped living. Let's build the house *now*, darling. And *you* plant the home orchard. It's in your blood, I *know* it is."

"You're insane. Have you forgotten we've got *nine* mouths to feed now? Nine. Count 'em—you and me, three kids, a cook, a nurse, a driver—and Joe the gardener on your Brentwood property. Wait a minute—it's *ten* mouths. No, it's ELEVEN!—what with taking care of Mama and my sister Ann. Build a big *house*? What'll we use for money?"

"Nerve, gall, *insolence*," she replied. "It'll kill Harry Cohn to know he can't stop us from living."

Within two months, the foundations of our new home were poured, and I —with my spanking new little red tractor—had cleared, plowed, disked, and manured two of the eight acres for what was going to be the best damned home orchard since Papa planted his in Sierra Madre. Grape cuttings, potted berry plants, and one hundred and fifty balled fruit trees (of all kinds) had been delivered by the Armstrong Nurseries.

"Plant new trees when they are two years old," Papa used to say, "the weak ones will have shown up by then. Plant them in late October, give them the winter to fall in love with their new homes. Then, when spring comes— they will take off happy." Surely, Papa was more poet than gardener—or are they synonymous?

At any rate, while Lu and the children "supervised" the building of our new Brentwood home, I planted trees like a madman, and discovered what Papa knew—and all those who work with soil know—that nothing cheers the human spirit quite like digging an earthy womb, implanting a seed or the balled fetus of a tree, and puddling the womb with a fecund mixture of manure, water, and good earth.

And, for the moment, the sweat of the soil had eased the lump in my belly. Mopping my face I turned to Joe, the Mexican gardener. He was staring with unblinking Aztec eyes, chin resting on hands propped on a shovel handle. To Joe, there were but two realities: the rich and the poor. The poor worked hard; the rich rested and enjoyed life. I owned this big estate. Ergo, I was el patron, rich. So why wasn't I lying back in a hammock with servants fanning me?

"Nothing like good dirt, huh, Joe?" I said, mopping my face.

"I no believe you big movie man," he said, without moving an eyelid. "Why you work with shovel, like me, poor gardener?"

I don't know why, but that remark cracked my shellac. "I'll tell you why, Joe." I threw my shovel down at his feet, yanked the newly planted tree out of the ground, ball and all, and smashed it in the dirt. "Because I'm crazy, Joe. Up here, loco!" and walked off.

From the unfinished house Lu had kept an eye on me—lately she kept a constant eye on me—and saw me kicking clods. Hastily she gathered up Vivie (our young nurse) and the three little ones, hustled them into the car.

"Hurry up, darling, we're just in time for a swim," she said as I came ambling up.

"Swim. Yeah, great."

I got in the car, slammed the door. "When are those lazy goons going to finish that lousy house? They're eating us up." This had the makings of a long day. It was. An unforgettable day.

The sun was low in the west (October is the most beautiful month at Malibu). We were all in bathing suits. Vivie watched chubby, two-month-old Lulu discovering new wonders in the wet sand on her fingers; Johnny (two and a half years) ran back and forth like a little shore bird—chasing the retreating edge of the sea foam, squealing with delight when it chased him back; I was out knee-deep, mechanically teaching Frankie (three and a half) how to body-surf, my mind a long way off. Lu sat on the sand watching me closely. She knew, and I knew—something had to happen. Soon!

A shout came from our picket fence (not over one hundred feet away). It was Rosa, our Danish cook: "Telephone! From New York!"

I leaped out of the water. "Hot damn, Lu! It's our lawyer—the lawsuit in New York. Wish me luck, hon—" Dripping wet, I raced into the house, to the library phone—and to the shock of my life. To again paraphrase Ring Lardner—the words of my lawyer fell like clods on my coffin: "Case dismissed . . . alleged offense took place in foreign country . . . U.S. courts have no jurisdiction . . . I boo-booed again . . ."

I don't know how long I sat motionless in my red library chair, but Lu came in, took one look at me, paled, stifled a whimper, then ran upstairs. A loud whirring sound made little impression on my numbed brain. Rosa shouted from the kitchen, "Telephone!" I picked up the receiver. My "hello" was a croak. It was Bob Riskin.

"Tough luck about your lawsuit, pal. Cohn's broadcasting the news on the telephone. He's laying eight to five you'll come crawling back to the studio in a week—"

"Yeah, Bob—yeah—" I hung up. Panic hit me. I had to run, hide, think . . . I raced out to the beach; my little boys spotted me. I headed away from them. Frankie ran after me followed by toddling Johnny. "Wait for us, Daddy, wait for us!"

Furiously, I turned on them. "Get away from me! Get back to the house. Beat it!" The little fellows stopped in their tracks, terrified. The lump in my belly was as big as a football. A neighbor's collie rose from the sand—came barking at me. "Eight to five you'll come crawling," it barked. I pelted that damn dog with curses and wet sand. The dog ran. I heard Frankie's voice: "Daddy?" He and Johnny stood side by side like frozen little statues. "You still here?" I shouted. "Get the hell away from me. Beat it, dammit. Get *away!*"

My two little boys turned and ran away terror-stricken, screaming, "Mommy! Mommy!—" That finally blew my pent-up stack. Choking with nausea and shame, I ran toward the far cliffs where the houses ended. Running, I picked up a gnarled piece of driftwood, held it up as a weapon: "Come on, all you bastards of the world!"

I reached the cliffs, clambered over rocks to a secluded cove. A flock of startled gulls rose, circled low over me, cawing: "Eight to five you'll come crawling—" I flung my stick at them; hurled wet rocks till my arm hung limp; then fell on my knees, beat the sand with my fists, and finally—vomited.

My childish tantrum against defeat ended ludicrously in that lonely, surf-beaten cove. The retching over, I looked at the sour fetid stuff—and laughed.

Here was the president of the Academy, winner of awards, apostle of the "one man, one film" school, squatting on hands and knees spewing out his choleric distempers like a sick dog . . .

The annoyed gulls landed again to resume their interrupted conclave. I rose, kicked sand over my mess—a burial, I thought, of defeat and indecisions. Then I scrambled back over the rocks to the deserted beach, and ambled homeward slowly, calmly—for I had made a decision: no surrender, no compromise, no crawling back to Cohn.

And there in the fading gloam was our picket gate, and our home all warm and glowing, and my wife and my children were in it, and I could sing as I ran to them.

I sneaked in through the front door. It was feeding time for the small fry, but all was silent; then Rosa's voice: "Mrs. Capra, Frankie and Johnny won't eat a thing." "It's better if they *don't*, Rosa." There was a sting in Lu's voice. I winced. How could I apologize?

Still wet, with sand sticking all over me, I tiptoed to the piano, pressed a heavy foot on the loud pedal—and belted out the kids' favorite ditty: "Three blind mice, three blind mice—"

The dining room exploded with happy squeals—"It's Daddy! It's Daddy!" They all came a runnin' and a singin'—Lu, Rosa, Vivie (a bottle stuck in Lulu's mouth), the two boys—"They all ran after the farmer's wife, did you ever see such a sight in your life—" Frankie clowned a war dance, Johnny toddled an imitation—"as three blind mice—" I leaped on Frankie and Johnny, rolled on the floor with them, kissed them, tickled them. Through their squirming legs and arms, I spotted Lu's wet eyes. "And *you!*" I commanded, "you run right upstairs and put your best dress on. We're going to Chasen's for dinner." The kids chorused: "They all ran after the farmer's wife—" The Capra zoo was normal again—a bedlam of happy noises.

As we drove along the beach highway, marveling at the great semi-circle of twinkling lights that Santa Monica Bay proudly wears as a tiara of sparkling jewels, I had much to say to Lu—but couldn't find the words.

As a delaying action, I filled in with small talk about our good friend Dave Chasen—recalling how his world-famed eating place had had its humble, humorous genesis in the fireplace of our Malibu living room.

Dave Chasen—his wild mop of frightened red hair (standing on end) paradoxically surmounting the gentle happy smile of an idiot—was the darling of Manhattan's literati when he played Joe Cook's stooge in our film version of *Rain or Shine*. Soon after, Parkinson's disease struck down Joe Cook's brilliant career and, as a ricocheting corollary, it practically ended Dave Chasen's stage future.

As for his working in films (you may find this incredible), in the cheerless years of Hitler, film censorship had taken a reverse, ironic twist: Jewish comedians were barred from American films by Hollywood's Jewish film moguls *themselves*. "So as to not give Hitler more fuel for hate," some lamely reasoned. Others: "Jewish comics and their dialect depict Jews in a bad light." The careers and the laughter of some of our greatest comedians were wantonly sacrificed on the altar of Hitler's hate. Not all appeasers carried umbrellas. How hate doth scar the souls of both haters and victims.

At any rate, discouraged and penniless, Chasen gave thought to opening a small eatery. He asked permission to practice barbecuing spare ribs in our fireplace. For weeks he knelt, sweaty and sooty, in front of hot coals—barbecuing himself as well as countless batches of pork and sauces. We, our neighbors, their dogs—and even the sea gulls—were the guinea pigs of Dave's culinary experiments. We ate spare ribs till they came out of our ears. Some smart gulls learned to break the bones to get to the succulent marrow—by flying high and dropping ribs on rocky ledges.

With financial aid from a few friends—principally Harold Ross, editor and publisher of *The New Yorker* magazine—Chasen opened a hole-in-the-wall, six-stool counter at the corner of Doheny and Beverly Boulevard, gave it the grandiose name: THE SOUTHERN BARBECUE PIT. The lone item on the menu: barbecued spare ribs, if you please. And believe it or not, from opening night on, the PIT was a hit—what with our wives and several starlets waiting on Dave's customers and washing his dishes. In a few years the PIT boomed into Chasen's—patronized by the leading lights in films, the theater, sports, politics, letters, and industry.

It was well past midnight before Lu lost her patience and brought up the subject I had so far avoided. We had turned off the beach highway, checked in with the guard at the Malibu Colony gate, and were bumping slowly over the "thank you ma'ams"—concrete risers across our back road (to protect our children from speeders)—when Lu upped and asked: "All right—what happened this afternoon after you barked at your children and ran up the beach waving a stick?"

"Oh, that. Well, nothing much. I made some startling discoveries, that's all."

"Like what?"

"Like discovering I wasn't God." I turned into our garage, shut off the motor. "Lu, do you realize that in spite of collecting Academy Awards for *It Happened One Night* and *Mr. Deeds, and* making the cover of *Time*, when I turneth my face from the iniquity of Columbia—you know what? Not one single wall falleth down in Poverty Row. Shall we get a whiff of the kelp beds before we turn in?"

Quietly we walked along the narrow brick walk that separated our house from the Schulberg fence, sauntered past our glassed-in ping-pong table and out to the moonlit beach. It was low tide. Washed-up seaweed glistened in the pale light. Obeying a childhood impulse, I slipped out of my shoes and socks and began stepping on the little air-filled balls that are attached to kelp stalks. They popped like firecrackers. Lu sat in the sand and watched.

"What other startling discovery did you make?" she asked.

"Well—that I'm not Garbo." I popped a kelp ball. "If Garbo walked out on MGM she'd stop the presses. Other studio heads would break their necks and all their secret anti-raid pacts to sign her up. Oh, would they. But when I announced I was airing Columbia—it had all the impact of an autumn leaf falling in a wet sand trap. Ergo: I'm not Garbo. Nice to know these th·ngs, isn't it, hon?"

"·Peachy. Who else did you find out you weren't?"

"·Clarence Darrow I weren't. Columbia's fraud took place in England, right? So I sue in America. Smart. So—while you were dressing for dinner tonight—I called London. Woke up Tim Whelan at three in the morning. Asked him if he had a good English lawyer handy. He said Miriam objected to having English lawyers in bed with them, and all that rot. But he'd scour the pubs in the morning for one."

"Another lawsuit? In England?"

"Yes! Another lawsuit in England. What do you want me to do—just sit around and go nuts?"

"No-o. But—what if it pans out like the other two—"

"I don't *know* what. But I'll tell you one thing. Not all the Cohns in the New York phone book can make me crawl. So what the hell. I'm only forty years old. We'll blow this stinking Hollywood. I've got you and the kids, haven't I? What else is there?"

She embraced me tightly, and wept. I kissed every spot on her lovely wet face. It had been a long, miserable day.

It was about six weeks later—November 11, 1937, to be exact—that an unexpected wave of excitement shook up our Malibu household. It began when our cook, Rosa, answered the kitchen phone. It was Bert, the guard at the Malibu gate (who knew what was going on in every home in the Colony).

"Rosa?" exclaimed the guard, "I just checked in Mr. Harry Cohn in his limousine. He's coming in to see Mr. Capra—"

Rosa jumped out of her skin. The guard might as well have said Adolf Hitler was coming. In fact, around our house, Harry Cohn *was* Hitler. She ran through the house shouting, "Mr. Harry Cohn is coming!" Vivie, the nurse, picked it up. "Oh, my God!" She ran out to the beach where Lu was reading stories to the children. "Mrs. Capra, Mrs. Capra—Harry Cohn is coming!"

I was a half-mile away buying meat at the general store. The butcher hung up the phone. "Frank! Your wife wants you back at the house. Right away!"

Heart attack, riptide, fire—raced through my head. I was glad our first editions were in a fireproof safe. My head hit the top of the car as my Buick bucked over each concrete riser on the back road. I saw a long black limousine parked at our gate. Little Frankie was waiting for me. "Daddy! Daddy! Mr. Cohn is in the house!"

"What Mr. Cohn?"

"I dunno. He brought flowers—"

I walked into the kitchen. Rosa and Vivie were in a dither. "He's in the living room, Mr. Capra—" they said together.

"*Who's* in the living room?" I knew, but couldn't believe it.

"Harry *Cohn!*" they whispered excitedly.

What in hell was Harry Cohn doing here? I couldn't recall his ever being in our house before. Suspicious, wary, nerves atingle—I walked into our living room. Lu was putting long-stemmed roses into a vase on the piano. And sitting uncomfortably on the edge of the sofa, twirling a gray derby in his hands—was the man himself. Harry Cohn.

"Look at these beautiful red roses Harry brought me—" There was a stridency in Lu's voice that betrayed her calm. "I'll get some water—excuse me, Harry."

We were alone. "Hi, Harry," I said, flatly.

"Hi, Frank," he answered quietly, his eyes fixed on his twiddling derby. I slouched in a chair opposite him. There he was—my benefactor, my ogre, my enemy, my friend—averting his eyes like a bad boy caught with his hand in a cookie jar. He was a little fatter, the pouches under his eyes were a little darker. Small beads of sweat glistened on his half-bald head. Telltale wet spots darkened his arm pits. The Crude One was sweating out something big. But what? Conjectures raced through my head—and also a warning: This guy's got more tricks than Houdini. Don't tip off that you're glad to see him. So I sat back smugly—like a poker player who has just paired his hole card —and waited.

"I would've called before coming," he finally said without looking up, "but I was scared you'd blow out of town." I said nothing. Then he looked at me with a crooked congratulatory smile. "Well, you little dago bastard —gotta hand it to you. You finally put me and Columbia behind the eight ball."

He took in a deep breath, puffed his cheeks, then blew it out. He rose, paced. He missed his riding crop. Without its whacking he was a castrated bull. I noticed a large sweat patch on his back. "Yep," he went on, "Joe Friedman and his Columbia guys in London are screaming bloody murder. They say that if you win that libel suit in London—and Friedman thinks you're a lead-pipe cinch—he and his top boys, innocent or not, will be clobbered with stiff fines for selling a non-Capra film for Capra prices. And maybe even have to serve some time if they draw a tough judge."

At long last, I scented the sweet smell of victory. How sweet it is—over a tough nut like Cohn. He went on quietly, subdued. "The hell of it is, Frank— and maybe you didn't even think about it—if you prove your libel case in court, the English theater chains will certainly sue Columbia for refunds— and maybe even refuse to book future Columbia pictures. You know those limeys. If that happens, the roof will fall on Columbia. The bankers and stockholders will throw me, my brother Jack, and all other Columbia officers right out on our ass. And they should! Understand?"

Wait a minute, before you go smelling victory, boy. Is Cohn admitting defeat? or putting on a crying act? He went on: "Frank—you stand a good chance of wrecking all us guys that put Columbia together. And there's a helluva chance you'll collect a potful of dough in the English courts. But—about breaking your Columbia contract? You haven't got a prayer. British courts have no jurisdiction over American deals. And any *new* management at Columbia, believe you me, they've *gotta* hold you to your Columbia deal. Or *they'll* be out. Understand?"

"Come off it, Harry. I'm stupid, but not *that* stupid. One measly nickel phone call—telling me *you'd* cancel my contract if I canceled the lawsuit—would have saved Columbia from all those catastrophes you're moaning about."

"You're a hundred percent right, dago. You got Columbia over a barrel with a libel suit, Columbia's got you over a barrel with a contract. So we trade barrel for barrel—and *everybody* would be happy. Yeah. Everybody but *me*."

"Oh-h-h, so that's what's eating you." I should have known it was a personal vendetta with him. "Everybody'd be happy with the settlement—but *you*. You won't be happy till you run me out of pictures, will you? Even if it wrecks Columbia. Well, let me tell you something, Cohn. You'll *rot* before I walk into your studio again. And if you came out here to weep crocodile tears over what my lawsuit will do to your company—well cry your frigging eyes out and be damned."

His face whitened and contorted. Foam flecks appeared in the corners of his mouth as he suddenly turned on me with unexpected fury. "You think this is easy for me, you goddam dago? Yes! I'm crying! I started Columbia with spit and wire and these fists, made one-reel comedies with no money to pay bills. I stole, cheated, beat people's brains out to build Columbia; got known as a crude, loudmouth son-of-a-bitch. But I built Columbia. Into a major studio. Yes, you helped. But I picked you out of the gutter and backed you. Now you wanna leave Columbia. It's dreck to you. Poverty Row. But to me, goddam you, Columbia is—is—not just my love. It's my baby, my *life*. I'd die without Columbia!" He paused to get his breath and wipe his foamy lips.

"*You* know those bastards on the board of directors in New York have been giving me the shaft—trying to force me out as president, the jerks. So —when I flew to New York and hinted we *should* cancel your contract if you canceled your suit, they had me right by the balls. They ganged up and laid it on the line to me: 'Money lost in lawsuits is bad enough. But if Columbia loses Capra, our big breadwinner, because of your stupid stunt with that *Only Cook* picture—it's your head as *president*, Harry. And we've got the votes!' they bragged."

He paused, groped for words. "Yeah, YEAH! It's my head, for chrissake. After all I've done. So that's why I came out to see you. But I ain't begging, and I ain't crawling, you goddam dago. *You* want my head? If you do—I'll cancel your contract. Right now! You gotta cigarette?"

I gave him a cigarette. He sat down to light it. His match hand shook. He smoked only on the rarest occasions. I knew what he had said was true. With one word I could have this monster's head and my freedom. I went to our library bar to pour myself a stiff drink. I gulped the drink and banged the glass on the bar. I could kill that son-of-a-bitch in the other room. He was out of sight, so I shouted: "Damn you, Cohn. You know what you're asking me to do? Lose a year's time, a year's salary, ten thousand dollars in attorney's fees, forget a year of eating my guts out, and come back to the studio as if nothing had happened. Just to save your neck. Is that what you expect me to *do*?"

A quiet, resigned answer came from the other room. "Yes, Frank. That's what I'm *asking* you to do."

I took another drink. I had him on the ropes, defenseless. But a disarmed giant has one final weapon that only giants have the derring-do to use: "Go ahead—shoot!" Few are the trigger fingers that are not paralyzed by that supreme challenge. I took another drink. Then: "Harry, if you'll get the hell out of this house right now, without letting me see you, I'll call off my suit and report back to the studio in the morning."

There was silence. Then he appeared at the library door. "Jesus Christ, Frank," he said gratefully. "Pour me one of those, will ya?" I had never seen him take a drink. He gagged on half the drink and put it down. "Dago?" he said with the old Cohn bravura. "Tell you what I'm gonna do. I'm gonna call my New York partners and tell 'em to approve paying you for one of the contract pictures as if you had made it. That leaves you only two. I'm gonna tell 'em to approve buying that play you're nuts about, *You Can't Take It with You*, for two hundred thousand—that last year I told you I wouldn't pay two hundred G's for the second coming. And if my partners *don't* approve—I'm gonna tell 'em to go fuck themselves." He turned and strode out of the house.

Disgust and admiration swirled through my head. I had Cohn right up to the gaff, then let him off the hook. He disarmed me with my own specialty: sentiment—Capra-corn. With my inverse binocular eyes—which looking inward, magnified; looking outward, minified—I had grossly underestimated the size of Mr. Harry Cohn. He was one of the film giants, with an enormous helping of what all film giants have in common—guts, imagination, and a passionate love of films. In some ways he topped them all. He was the only one to grab a fly-by-night, Poverty Row outfit by the scruff of the neck and lift it to the most continually successful major studio in Hollywood. He forced entrenched moguls to shelve their precious "committee" system and adopt maverick Cohn's "one man, one film" method of producing films. Producer-directors all round the world owe a megaphonic salute to Harry Cohn.

And when, next morning, I reported for work at Columbia Studios—to receive the equivalent of a returning hero's ticker-tape parade from doormen, messengers, secretaries; cameramen, electricians, sound men; producers, writers, and directors—I was a happy man. The dingy courtyard was the courtyard of St. James; the rickety flight of steps to my office was the grand staircase to my Shangri-La. And I thanked the Almighty for my membership in that exciting, close-knit, creative, zany, sloppily sentimental world called a movie studio.

CHAPTER 13

You Can't Take It with You

MY FIRST FORTY YEARS WERE OVER. Forty years that could only happen in America; that began with a childhood hate for America. With a child's eyes I used to look up at Mama. There she was, standing all day on blistered feet I knew wouldn't heal; standing all day in the miasmic steam of the olive plant—ten hours a day for ten dollars a week—her flying hands pasting labels on cans she rhythmically snatched from a line without end: cans, cans, cans, jiggling by on a witch's cackle of clanking, clanking, chain belts.

I'd look up at Mama's face, her strong peasant face, now wet with strain; nodding, nodding, nodding; a robot chained to the monster's rhythm, no time to brush stringy hair from her eyes—lest she break the spell of the deadly monotony. And Mama looked like a witch to me. A Halloween witch. And I'd run off, and bite my lip, and clench my fists, and curse America.

Then there was the blinding heat of the glass factory; a roaring hell of fiery furnaces where the condemned, half-naked bodies gleaming, made bottles, bottles, bottles. There was a hierarchy in the skills of the damned. On top, the bellows-lunged blower arced his tube—tipped with a white-hot blob— from furnace to form; then into the tube, gargoylish cheeks ballooning, he blew and blew and blew.

Below the blower—the form-man. He trapped the blob in jaws of iron, then untrapped, red-hot, the bottle. Next down the totem pole—the short-paddler. With bottle on paddle he fed the hot mouth of the annealing oven. Below them all was the long-paddler. Papa was a long-paddler.

I brought him lunch as a child and watched him running, like a pole-vaulter running, back arched backward; running, bare-waisted, sweated to the bone, clutching one end of a twenty-foot paddle balancing the weight of six dull-red bottles.

My heart ached for him. Papa, illiterate Papa, ignorant of language and laws; running, dreaming of farms; running, lungs burning, from oven to oven; ten hours.a day six days a week, a long-paddler running—for twelve lousy dollars. For this he came to America?

In town I sold papers to big fat businessmen, wearing big fat coats; bit fat necks overflowing tight white collars; entering big fat limousines through doors held open by big black chauffeurs. How I resented them. "All going home to big fat dinners," I'd think to myself. "Meat they'd eat. Big fat meat. Damn them!"

No meat at our house that night. Not unless Papa's nickel investment paid off. Dog-tired and dirty he'd rush home from his job to be met by Mama, holding shotgun and shell. "Remember, Turiddu. Five cents the cartridge cost. Must be two rabbits or four quail. Hear?" And off he would lope to the Elysian Park hills.

Sentry-like, on the street corner, Annie and I awaited the news. From a long way off, even in the dark, Papa's walk flashed the binary signal—meat, or no meat. At times, I'd shake a fist at little Ann's nose.

"Some day, Annie. *Some* day it's gonna be different."

"What different?"

"Aw, shut up!"

In my fortieth year, things *were* different. Quite different. Mama was aging happily, proudly, in her own home. No beggar or panhandler ever knocked and left hungry. Sister Ann had married Folmar Blangsted, a Columbia film cutter. They quickly adopted two newborns, David and Jo Anne.

I had reached a lifetime goal: Making something out of nothing; a nobody became Mr. Somebody—and I made the world like it. What began as a gleam in my eye (the "one man, one film" concept) in Ball's San Francisco laboratory fifteen years before, was now a successful Hollywood reality: A film director's name spelled box office. Marquee lights featured "Frank Capra" above the title of the film and the names of the stars—the first hired director to wrest that distinction from the Hollywood Establishment. Today, it is commonplace.

Yes, indeed. Things *were* different. All the honors and glory a film director could hope for—were mine at the age of forty. I even made the cover of *Time* without suffering its legendary kiss of death. What would the *next* forty years bring?

During my year of banishment I had had time to think, to get back to my roots. Remember those little Joes that helped push you over steep hills? Remember the day you started up that glory road? That Fourth of July when you were six years old, and Mrs. Vignolo, the Castelar Street schoolteacher, picked *you*—out of hundreds of little dagos, niggers, cholos, and Japs—to lead the school in the pledge of allegiance? And proud Papa bought you a new sailor suit and a sailor hat with a ribbon? And how Mama and Papa cried after, but you didn't, and bragged it was nothing?

Take another look at the country that gave you a road to climb. Drink in

Five directors with egg on their faces. New Oscar "stunt" backfires. In presenting Best-Directing Award for 1940, I called the five nominees to the dais so the losers could congratulate the winner before the whole world. Smart money being on Hitchcock (*Rebecca*) or Wyler (*The Letter*), I disregarded John Ford's (fifth nominee) being in England. Whose name popped out of the envelope? Right. John Ford! This photo snapped just as four yet-to-win directors (Hitchcock, Cukor, Wyler, Conway) realized from my idiot's stare that the "man who wasn't there" had won his third Oscar (*Grapes of Wrath*).

As Directors Guild prexy I had great honor of presenting D. W. Griffith (first and greatest "one man, one film" maker), and our legal counsel Mabel Walker Willebrandt with life memberships in our Guild. Kibitzing directors (left to right): John Ford, Frank Strayer, Rouben Mamoulian, J. P. McGowan, W. S. Van Dyke, Willie Wyler, Leo McCarey, and George Marshall.

Director Frank Capra makes the cover of *Time* Magazine.

TIME

The Weekly Newsmagazine

DIRECTOR FRANK CAPRA

Volume XXXII   Number 6

The superlative *You Can't Take It with You* cast that won for the man with the pencil his second Oscar for Best Picture, and his third for Best Directing.

its spirit; breathe deep its freedom. And take a special look at "We the People" who made this country great; people to whom weary souls can return again and again to commune and to draw, like Antaeus, another tankful of their courage and faith.

I had no idea what the next forty years would bring to me. But I knew what I would try to bring to them: films about America and its people; films that would be my way of saying, "Thanks, America."

I would sing the songs of the working stiffs, of the short-changed Joes, the born poor, the afflicted. I would gamble with the long-shot players who light candles in the wind, and resent with the pushed-around because of race or birth. Above all, I would fight for their causes on the screens of the world. Oh, not as a bleeding-heart with an Olympian call to "free" the masses. Masses is a herd term—unacceptable, insulting, degrading. When I see a crowd, I see a collection of free individuals: each a unique person; each a king or a queen; each a story that would fill a book; each an island of human dignity.

Yes, let others make films about the grand sweeps of history, I'd make mine about the bloke that pushes the broom. And if this bloke is a skinful of conflicting contraries; if his physical genes impel him to survive, to devour his neighbor, while his reason, will, and soul urge him to *love* his neighbor —I thought I could understand his problem. That was the kind of film material I looked for; literature in which "Love Thy Neighbor" collided head-on with social disorder. I found it.

In flying trips to Broadway to catch the new plays, film directors could see parts of three plays in one night by theater-hopping: one act of three different plays in three different theaters. If a play or a performance sparked them, they would return next night to see the whole show.

While in New York for the Music Hall opening of *Lost Horizon*, I had slipped into the rear of the sardine-packed Booth Theater to catch the first act of Kaufman and Hart's Pulitzer Prize-winning play, *You Can't Take It with You*. Its witchery was so entrancing wild horses couldn't have dragged me away before the final curtain.

The show was about a happy-go-lucky family of rebels—and some outsiders who joined them as "family"—living in perfect concord, finding happiness in individual expression: doing the things they had always *wanted* to do, even though they did them badly.

Thoreau's dour observation that the big city was "a mass of people being lonely together" did not apply to the Vanderhof family's private merry-andrew Shangri-La, just around the corner from Columbia University. For here this heterogeneous group of "happies" found the courage to do what most Americans secretly wished *they* could do: Consign to oblivion the hammer blows of crisis headlines—depression, wars, Hitler, Stalin—and more important, to escape from the modern rat-race which pressured the average American into a lifetime of accumulating wealth and living standards he could never take with him.

You Can't Take It with You had to be my next film. But—producer Sam Harris's asking price was staggering: two hundred thousand dollars! Harry Cohn's squeal blew out phone fuses. "Tell that goniff Harris I wouldn't shell out two hundred G's for the second coming!"

Then came the year of exile and lawsuits—Cohn bought me *You Can't Take It with You* for two hundred thousand dollars! The record price made theatrical headlines.

Why this mania to film Kaufman and Hart's play? Because it was a laugh riot? A Pulitzer Prize play? Of course. But I also saw something deeper, something greater. Hidden in *You Can't Take It with You* was a golden opportunity to dramatize Love Thy Neighbor in living drama. What the world's churches were preaching to apathetic congregations, my universal language of film might say more entertainingly to movie audiences, *if*—it could prove, in theatrical conflict, that Christ's spiritual law can be the most powerful sustaining force in anyone's life.

The conflict: devour thy neighbor versus love thy neighbor. The weapons: a bankful of money against a houseful of love. The stakes: the future happiness of two young people, a Kirby son and a Vanderhof granddaughter; and more important, the viability of a lamb when confronted by a lion.

But, you may ask, can a defenseless lamb cope with a lion armed with fangs and claws and a willingness to use them? He can. And how he does was, for me, a new dramatic format that I used in practically all my future films.

As has been stated, the classic four in dramatic construction are hero, heroine, villain, comedian. In my comedies, critics said, I had reduced the number to three by combining, in one character, the hero and comedian. This resulted in a different, and perhaps more human, type of comedy.

If mankind, as I have previously conjectured, is in the early stages of an evolution from the brutal past to the compassionate future, it must follow that the more advanced—the good guys—are kinder, more merciful, and more peaceful than the evolutionarily arrested or retarded—the bad guys.

But since none of us has reached the ultimate peace of Nirvana, the inner battle between brutality and compassion agonizes the spiritually advanced, yes—but it racks and tortures the spiritually retarded. That's why villains are often more sympathetic than heroes; why the biblical father rejoiced and killed the fatted calf to celebrate the return of his prodigal son, much to the annoyance of the "square" brother who had never wandered; why the shepherd loved the one lost sheep he found and saved more than the ninety-nine that had not strayed.

And so, in *You Can't Take It with You*, I again tampered with drama's classic four. I combined the villain and the hero; changed Kirby, Sr.—the play's two-dimensional, cardboard bad guy—into the film's *villain-hero*. Furthermore, I threw out the play's third act, reduced the Tony-Alice love plot to "counterpoint," and elevated the philosophical conflict between the lamb (Grandpa Vanderhof) and the lion (Kirby, Sr.) to the "point" of the story. The "new" plot was, in reality, a love triangle with Kirby's son at the apex, and the lion and the lamb at the other two angles.

How did it work out? Fine. Brutality is humbled by love. The lion climbs a rung on the spiritual ladder. Love thy neighbor wins the day—and the film wins the Best-Picture and Best-Director Academy Awards for the year 1938.

There has been no mention of the actors and actresses in *You Can't Take It with You* because, first, I wish to doff my director's cap to the whole art of acting. Acting has been waggishly called the second oldest profession. But it would not be too wild to call it the first, since Mrs. Warren's profession entails a certain amount of ecdysial theatrics. I'll settle for a tie in timing, and for the fact that both began as amateur beguilement.

And certain it is that entertainers (paid or not) have improved the quality of the day for men, women, and children since the first caveman acted out how he felled his first stag with a rock. If St. Peter asks my opinion of Thespians, I will say: "God bless them all! From stars to extras, from hams to shams, bless them all!"

The patriarch of the addlepated household, Grandpa Vanderhof, was played by Lionel Barrymore whose memory, as an artist and a man, I shall always revere. In any actor's Hall of Fame, Lionel Barrymore's name deserves top billing among the immortals. Yet he was the humblest, most co-operative actor I've ever known.

When I interviewed him for the Grandpa Vanderhof part he was crippled with arthritis. His hands, elbows, feet, and knees were as stiff and knobby as old oak roots. He couldn't walk or pick up a spoon; needed hourly shots to ease the killing pain. His body was a mess. But not his verve. "I'll play the part on crutches," he said with a laugh. "Just put a cast on my foot to alibi them. That'll do it."

To play Alice—the only sane member of the genial idiots—I called on the finest actress of that day, Jean Arthur; she of the husky voice that broke into a thousand tinkling bells.

I had seen Jimmy Stewart play a sensitive, heart-grabbing role in MGM's *Navy Blue and Gold.* I sensed the character and rock-ribbed honesty of a Gary Cooper, plus the breeding and intelligence of an ivy league idealist. One might believe that young Stewart could reject his father's patrimony— a kingdom in Wall Street.

Then there was Ann Miller. She played Alice's sister Essie, the awkward Pavlova; played her with the legs of Marlene, the innocence of Pippa, and the brain of a butterfly that flitted on its toes.

And to play the threadbare Russian, Kolenkhov, there could be no one gloomier than the fallen-faced, picture of doom itself—Mischa Auer. His saturnine opinion of Essie's dancing, the Bolshevik Revolution, or of the world in general: "Confidentially, eet steenks!"

The most aptly named actor I know of was Donald Meek (he played Mr. Poppins). If the Meeks must inherit the earth—may they all be Donalds. All that was humble was rolled into one little—but talented—bald-headed man, so shy his voice would crack into the embarrassing trebles of childhood.

Lillian Yarbo played Rheba, the wise-cracking half of the Negro branch of the family. The other half, Donald, was expertly played by laugh-getter Eddie Anderson—Jack Benny's deflater (Rochester) in Benny's radio shows.

The part of Penny—the pixie, moon-struck mother of Alice and Essie, who typed unfinished plays, was difficult to cast. At first I wanted Fay Bainter. Unavailable. Then, as so often happens, we found the perfect Penny right under our noses—Spring Byington. Spring was so delightful in the part, she won an Academy nomination for the Best-Supporting Actress Award.

Samuel Hinds played Penny's husband, the fireworks expert, and Halliwell Hobbes (the perennial butler) played Mr. de Pinna, the iceman who delivered ice and just stayed.

That left just one more daffy part to cast—Ed, Essie's xylophone-playing husband. I was interviewing xylophone players, when in walked a merry oaf wearing a perpetual infectious grin as big as a sunburst. Sweat drops gleamed on his receding forehead.

"I'm Dub Taylor, suh. And I kin play the xylophone." His very presence evoked laughter. "Have you ever played in a picture, Mr. Taylor?" I asked. "No suh, I ain't. But I played in the Rose Bowl on the Alabama football team." His Southern accent dripped hominy grits. I asked him to play the xylophone I had in the office.

"I'll play you a love song, Mr. Capra. I'll play you 'Dinah.' " The uproar he raised on the xylophone would wake up the dead. He made "Dinah" sound like four "anvil choruses." The louder I laughed the louder he played. I cast him on the spot.

And now, Mr. Anthony P. Kirby, the villain-hero of the show. He was the drama, the guts of the film. I wanted only one certain actor, and I postponed the picture two months to get him—Edward Arnold. Arnold had the power and presence of a J. P. Morgan. He could be as unctuous as a funeral director, or as cold and ruthless as a Cosa Nostra chief.

Furthermore, he had a laugh as unique and as phony as a three-dollar bill. It would wind up in pitch like the flywheel starter of a fighter plane, then explode in choked-up pops like its motor.

Edward Arnold was anathema to directors. In take after take he would blow his lines and shrug it off with that phony laugh. Other actors could wring his neck. They would have to give their all in take after take, just in case Arnold *didn't* blow his lines. The result: Arnold got all the attention. Distraught directors would okay *any* take that he finished, regardless of how the other tired-out actors fared.

But, if you could put up with that—and I gladly did—Arnold was a powerhouse on the screen. His performance as the jungle king of Wall Street, who walked away from his throne for the love of his son, was the philosophical clout an otherwise farcical comedy needed to make *You Can't Take It with You* the acclaimed Best Picture of the year.

However, if actors are the roses on the film bush, writers are its roots. Robert Riskin wrote a great script for *You Can't Take It with You*, but not without some persuasion. During my year of isolation Riskin had directed his first film—a Columbia picture, *When You're in Love*, starring two big box-office winners, Grace Moore and Cary Grant. To everyone's surprise, Riskin's film was disappointing—especially to him. And for some strange reason our intimate relationship was never quite the same again.

I knew what was bugging Riskin. He thought I was getting too much credit for the Capra films, and he, too little. We discussed it. "Bob," I would say to him, "make your own films and you'll get all the credit." He made his own film, and found there was a fine-print proviso to the "all the credit" clause: "all the blame" if the film did not come up to snuff.

Riskin was brilliant. He had all the required talents of a filmmaker. What he lacked was not talent but a native drive—the ability "to get things done under stress." The bedlam of film production got to him. Evidently he was his sharpest and most creative when writing alone in the quiet of his thoughts. And I realized there was something more to film directing than talent. To be a director one needed the capacity to do one's best under pressure; to be alive, tingling, and sharp in the confusion of fielding a dozen questions a minute. And that was why I loved being a film director—I was at my best in a crowd.

While on the subject of film directors, I'd like to make a comment or two about film directing. First, let me assure everyone that I lay no claim to having climbed the film director's Mount Sinai and come down with the tablets on directing. De Mille may have been tempted. But he wisely resisted and told himself to "Get thee behind the camera." To which a voice from above answered, "Whenever you're ready, C. B."

Film directors are the filmmakers; no two work alike. For instance— Willie Wyler and George Stevens. Both photograph a scene over and over again, but for different reasons. In shooting a scene several times from the same angle, Wyler is waiting for that magical change—that bit of human "chemistry" to happen—that lifts an ordinary scene into one he feels is great. That is Wyler's way. And his credentials are fantastic: *Dodsworth, Jezebel, Wuthering Heights, The Little Foxes, Mrs. Miniver, Best Years of Our Lives, Ben Hur, Funny Girl.*

George Stevens will photograph the same scene from many *different* angles—another method of shooting several takes of the same scene. But, in addition, Stevens's method gives him the option of using the best parts of different angles of the same scene. In the cutting room he cannily integrates the bits and pieces.

Wyler is at his best when he films a script or play that has been completely worked out by someone else. To make sure actors fully understand the nature and character of their parts, Wyler digs and probes into their minds, using the gibe, needle, or compliment with equal versatility.

On the other hand Stevens, having learned his ABC's in the inventive school of slapstick comedy, works hard and long with his writers on story and script. He is not averse to making script changes during the shooting. In contrast to Wyler, he is inarticulate; at times, it is difficult for actors to understand what he is after. For George is given to periods of meditation during filming, often walking alone behind the sets smoking his pipe for as long as an hour, while his actors wait in suspenseful silence. Returning to the set he may make a complete change in the scene, or just sit in his chair and laconically announce, "Let's take it again"—leaving the actors to wonder what in the world he's been thinking about.

Well, what *was* George Stevens thinking about, walking alone and smoking his pipe for an hour? As a fellow director I think I know. He was mentally reviewing his whole picture—scene by scene—from beginning to end; analyzing the characters, their growth, their degradation, their effect on each other. Did the preceding scene (shot or unshot) logically build to the one at hand? And would the present scene lead logically to the ones that followed? Was the scene he was shooting necessary? Why? Which character (or characters) should it most affect? Did it ring true? Did he believe it? If not, why? Should he pitch the girl's emotions higher? Could the leading man's reaction be more effective if played silently, or should he make more of his spoken lines? All gut decisions the director must make for himself.

Having concluded he should make no changes, he must take another look at the scene to check his gut decision. So, "Let's take it again." This, too, is directing—à la George Stevens. And his batting average is very high (*The More the Merrier, A Place in the Sun, Shane, Giant*).

At comedy, no one was better than Leo McCarey (*Laurel and Hardy, Love Affair, Going My Way, The Bells of St. Mary's*).

Leo would at times play the piano for hours during filming—noodling or trying to compose tunes. Yet while he played he pondered, reviewed, analyzed, invented, just as Stevens did while walking and smoking.

All directors must ponder and meditate in their own way. For they all have this common problem: keeping each day's work in correct relationship to the story as a whole. Scenes shot out of time and context must fit into their exact spot in the mosaic of the finished film, with their exact shadings in mood, suspense, and growing relationships of love or conflict. This is, as one can imagine, the most important and most difficult part of directing, and the main reason why films, perforce, are the director's "business."

The meteor Gregory La Cava (*Symphony of Six Million, Stage Door, My Man Godfrey*) was an extreme proponent of inventing scenes on the set. Blessed with a brilliant, fertile mind and a flashing wit, he claimed he could make pictures without scripts. But without scripts the studio heads could make no accurate budgets, schedules, or time allowances for actors' commitments. Shooting off the cuff, executives said, was reckless gambling; film costs would be open-ended; no major company could afford such risks.

Films are a peculiar dichotomy of art and business, with executives emphasizing business. But not La Cava. He stuck to his off-the-cuff guns. Result: fewer and fewer film assignments for him—then none. The flashing rocket of his wit was denied a launching pad because he wouldn't, or couldn't, conform. So he mixed his exotic fuels with more mundane spirits, and brooded himself into oblivion—his rebel colors still flying. La Cava was a man out of his time—a precursor of the "new wave" directors of Europe. Pity he didn't live long enough to lead them.

Ernst Lubitsch (*Lady Windermere's Fan, The Student Prince, The Patriot, The Long Parade, If I Had a Million, Trouble in Paradise*) was the complete architect of his films. His scripts were detailed blueprints, replete with all the required sketches, drawings, and specifications. Every scene, every look, every camera angle, was designed in advance of photography and he seldom, if ever, deviated from his blueprints in the actual shooting.

His direction of his cast was strictly Lubitsch. Waving his ubiquitous cigar, this humorous, magnificent imp showed each actor exactly what to do and how to do it. His stamp was on every frame of film from conception to delivery. For high-styled romantic comedies and spicy musicals he set a standard that may never be equaled. The Lubitsch "touch" was unique.

John Ford is The Compleat Director (*Arrowsmith, The Informer, Stagecoach, The Grapes of Wrath, The Long Voyage Home, How Green Was My Valley, The Quiet Man*), the dean of directors—undoubtedly the greatest and most versatile in films. A megaphone has been to John Ford what the chisel was to Michelangelo: his life, his passion, his cross.

Ford cannot be pinned down or analyzed. He is pure Ford—which means pure great. John is half-tyrant, half-revolutionary; half-saint, half-satan; half-possible, half-impossible; half-genius, half-Irish—but *all* director and *all* American.

Henry King, the most underpublicized filmmaker in Hollywood, belongs on anybody's "First Five" list. An inventory of his great pictures is the history of films—*Tol'able David, Fury, The White Sister, Stella Dallas, The Winning of Barbara Worth, Lightnin', Over the Hill, State Fair, Lloyd's of London, Alexander's Ragtime Band, Jesse James, Stanley and Livingstone, The Song of Bernadette, Wilson, A Bell for Adano.*

Still flying his own plane in his seventies, this lean, tall, handsome, urbane, but unflamboyant model of a corporation president makes film hits so easily, so efficiently, and so calmly that he is not news in a community of blaring trumpets, crashing cymbals, and screaming egos.

Legends have grown up about directors. For instance, this one about Al Rogell, who had a tendency to wax apoplectic:

Rogell was setting up a love scene in the stern of a yacht in San Pedro harbor. The sea was flat, the sky leaden. Very unromantic. "Granucci!" yells Rogell in a voice as raucous as a prison break. "I got no background for my goddam love scene. Bring me some sea gulls!"

Prop man Granucci tears open a couple of box lunches and throws bread upon the waters. Here they come! All the sea gulls in the harbor. The air behind the lovers is filled with birds and squawks. Rogell leaps to his feet. "Granucci! You son-of-a-bitch! Your goddam sea gulls are stealing my love scene! Bring 'em in one at a time, one at a time!"

Then there was the horse-opera director who was dying to graduate from Westerns. Myles Connolly was telling him about his tender, poetic love story, *Mister Blue*. The Western director listened and cried. The story finished, he leaped to his feet and sobbed: "Myles, it's so beautiful. Let me direct that for you. I promise you, I'll kick the shit out of it!"

What distinguishes great directors from the pack is their ability to entice optimum performances from actors for each individual scene, each a bead on the string. A well-matched string of real pearls is more valuable than a string of mismatched synthetic ones.

This is the artistry of the film director: convince actors that they are real flesh and blood human beings living a story. Once actors are themselves convinced, then, hopefully, they will convince audiences. This self-convincement of actors applies with equal force to those playing the smallest of parts. Does a star, paying his hotel bill, pay it to a bit actress or to a *real* cashier? A bit actress, perhaps hired for one day, will be just a bit actress to herself and to audiences.

But let the director give her an identity—an only daughter worried about her mother in the hospital, a wife anxious about her husband losing his job, or a woman in love going to a party that night with the man of her life—and that bit actress becomes a woman. She may not say a single word in her brief appearance on the screen, but her "identity" will fix her mood, her thinking, her attitude. And audiences will sense her as a real person, not an actress. Very important, this.

Extras walking on sidewalks as backgrounds to a scene can walk through as a flock of sheep or as real pedestrians, depending on the wit of the director. He must give each one an identity. One extra is late for a dentist's appointment, another is looking for the address of his wife's lawyer. That one is going to a poker game. This woman is shopping for her kid's shoes. That young one has a lunch date, that other one hopes men will notice her new hairdo. It doesn't matter who the director tells them they are, as long as they are *somebody* as they walk through the background. One simple detail changes the scene from ersatz to real.

Directing requires a passion for believability. On the lintel of the entrance to the Directors Guild Building, these words should be inscribed: THERE ARE NO BAD ACTORS, ONLY BAD DIRECTORS.

Another distinguishing mark of top directors is the absence of obvious camera moves. Undisguised camera tricks are the mark of beginners who fall in love with bizarre camera angles and hand-held moving camera shots. Wrong. Fall in love with your actors. All else is machinery, and director's vanity. The audience must never become aware that there is a camera within a thousand miles of the scene. Mood scenes? Fine. Necessary. But establish moods subtly, suggestively. Don't let your cameras hang up figurative signposts giving mileage and directions. Audiences cannot both feel and think at the same time. If they notice your "show-off" camera, the mood goes out the window. Stanley Kramer's 360-degree pan shot in the courtroom of *Judgment at Nuremberg* served only to distract attention from his tense drama.

Therefore, young directors, forget techniques, forget zoom lenses and subliminal cutting; remember only that you are telling your story not with gimmicks, but with *actors*!

I have heard an extra ask the assistant director (he generally handles groups of extras in crowd scenes): "Who am I supposed to be in this scene?" To such a question, vital to all actors in all scenes, the sweating assistant is apt to answer: "Who the hell cares *who* you are, lady? Just sashay through the scene, will ya?" That assistant will never make a director.

There is a certain type of actor—not too rare—who shows up on the set and brays: "Well, you lucky people, here's the body. What do you want done with it?" That ham will always be salami. But the background extra who asked, "Who am I?" lit a bulb toward her name in lights.

My wife once remarked that all directors look alike, but writers looked different. Lu is very feminine, a very good listener, never tries to compete with men—which accounts for her popularity with the male sex. Consequently, her generalizations about directors and writers interested me. "How can all directors look alike, when they come in all sizes and shapes?"

"I know," she said, "but directors all seem to be satisfied with what they are doing. Writers don't." Writers can take it from here.

Without make-up, an actor is normally a nice guy, perhaps even a shy hem-and-hawer. But put make-up on him and he becomes something else, something exclusive, above and beyond. It's fascinating to watch an actor put on grease paint. The metamorphosis from a human being to an actor takes place before your very eyes. The ham takes over, the libido blooms, the ego puts its tail up. In make-up all actors become Barrymores and Garbos. Make-up is their armor, their Excalibur, their Red Badge of Courage. Wearing make-up they are a race of nobles; they drink out of the Big Dipper. Grease paint is Max Factor's LSD. It comes in tubes.

Extras who *know* they'll work a block away from the camera, come on the set fully made up. They've put on their pancake, mascara, and eye shadows at home in order to get attention on buses and streetcars. That's their pay-off, their Shriner pin, their Croix de Guerre. They're in show business!

Take the grease paint off an actor's face, he comes down to earth with the rest of us; just as a motorcycle cop in uniform stands out as something special, but in "civvies" he's just another guy.

Anyway, the rule was "no make-up" on my set. Ah, but I made exceptions to that rule. We live by exceptions. If water did not grow lighter and "float" as it approaches its freezing point, there would be no life on earth. So—though I ordered stars to take off their make-up—I never had the heart to order extras (not working close to the camera) to take off theirs. I'm no dream killer. Who knows what keeps extras ever hopeful—talent, or the hashish of grease paint?

There is another element of the Hollywood magic that is more synonymous with Hollywood than grease paint—Sex.

Sex is mental, elusive, mysterious. It is a chemistry of desire of one sex for the other. Whistle girls are not necessarily sexy. Men whistle at girls mostly to show off their own libidos. When they are really hooked they don't whistle. They suffer.

A masseur, Claes Adler, who specialized in walking on your back in his bare feet, insisted I meet one of his clients—an unknown actress he said had great possibilities. I agreed to meet her, thinking he was paying off a promise to some girl friend. I met her. She was plenty curvaceous. But in black floppy hat, cheap brown suit, and an almost complete inability to communicate, I paid little attention to her. Her name was Marilyn Monroe.

Adler had asked me to pay particular attention to her breasts. Breasts she had. And a wiggly figure. But to me sex is class, something more than a wiggly behind. If it weren't, I know two-hundred whores who would be stars. But how could I have passed up Marilyn Monroe? I've been worried about that ever since.

It Happened One Night has been called a very sexy film but, believe it or not, Gable and Colbert never even touched hands. Sex was so much in their minds, it charged the atmosphere. That gave audiences more of a kick than if they had romped in the hay. Desire is the key, not fulfillment. The chase, not the catch.

Actual sex scenes between young people are so embarrassing they are funny. Between older people they are ludicrous, even offensive. That is why sex scenes are difficult to write or play. They are better left to the audience's imagination. I usually had a spectator viewing a love scene. He triggered the audience to laugh naturally. Or, I would break up love scenes with gags to relieve the embarrassment.

When I had Gary Cooper read Jean Arthur one of his love poems, I knew I was playing with fire. It was a good bet the audience would laugh *at* it. To release the laugh purposely, I had Gary run away and fall over a garbage can.

One of the sexiest (and funniest) love scenes ever staged occurred in *The More the Merrier*, between Jean Arthur and Joel McCrea, and directed by George Stevens. Joel was pawing all over Jean while talking serious government shop talk, while Jean kept taking his hands off her, and answering him in shop talk. Their lips were speaking gobbledygook, but their hands and bodies and minds were talking hanky-panky. It was great.

Straight love scenes were murder for me to stage. I usually approached them obliquely through argument, idle talk, or complete silence. The idea was to charge the minds and atmosphere with hot desire, stringing out the fulfillment as long as possible. Actually, the bringing together of two people in love can be as suspenseful as a Hitchcock thriller.

Frank Lloyd once asked me to see one of his big films which had had a disappointing preview. We viewed it together in a studio projection room. In the first meeting the hero and heroine started biting each other's necks. Then the hero spent the rest of the film wooing her. "Frank," I said to him, "I think you've shot your wad in the first reel. Once they slobber all over each other, what can you do for an encore? Try cutting out that first love scene." He did, and his next preview was far from disappointing.

August 23, 1938. A day circled in red on the memory calendar.

The sneak previews of *You Can't Take It with You* had been so filled with promise that Cohn and the Columbia hierarchy decided to shoot the works with an unusual exploitation stunt: an international press preview. Not only for the six hundred resident scribes and lensmen who inundated the world with "news" from Hollywood's publicity mills, but also for several hundred personally invited pundits, sages, and critics from this country and abroad—Columbia picking up the tabs.

The studio's largest stage was draped and decorated and special projection equipment installed. Flowers, favors, and engraved programs for the guests graced the half-acre of luncheon tables and, of course, two bars were set up to quench journalism's pre-prandial thirst. There was a name band to beguile the newsmen during lunch, and then—*You Can't Take It with You* would try to spin a magic web that would capture and hold a thousand pairs of critical eyes. And Harry Cohn would sweat off ten pounds.

Critics poured into Hollywood from around the globe—Canada, Europe, South America, India, Japan. On the morning of the press preview my wife and I; Vivie, our nurse; and little Johnny, our number two son (now three and a half years old) came tootling into Hollywood from Malibu.

We had a little chore to attend to before I made my welcoming speech to the critics of the world in the Columbia stage at noon. A surgeon was going to take out little Johnny's tonsils, so (doctors said) he'd be freer from colds. Johnny had been slow in learning to talk, but lately he'd found his tongue and wanted to show off. He so seldom had us all to himself that he made the most of it. He jounced up and down between Lu and me on the front seat, and every time I started to tell Lu about the big press shindig Johnny would clap his little hand over my mouth and say: "Lissen me! Lissen me!" Then he'd point to passing objects and triumphantly shout: "Car!" . . . "Bus!" . . . "Lady!" . . . "Bicycle!" . . .

The little cuss had us in stitches all the way into town. The more we giggled the harder he performed. We giggled when we walked into the Children's Hospital on Sunset Boulevard, near Vermont. We giggled when he ran backward in front of us as the nurse ushered us down the long hall and around a corner to the room reserved for Johnny. We exploded when the partly gowned surgeon walked into the room and Johnny pointed and shouted: "The doctor!"

"The little ham has just found his tongue and he's showing off," I apologized. "Well," chuckled the surgeon, "wouldn't it be nice if everybody walked into hospitals as gay as you all are? All right, nurse. Get him ready and bring him up."

Lu and I waited outside while Vivie and the nurse undressed Johnny. But we could still hear him calling out: "Bed!" . . . "Window!" . . . "Wheel!" . . .

In a few minutes the nurse wheeled him out on a surgery cart. Johnny was sitting up and going strong as we dashed for the elevator. At the elevator, I hung back. "Lu, I'll be in the waiting room going over my speech. Be a good boy, Johnny." " 'Bye, daddy. Elewaitor!"

An hour later—I was so busy rehearsing it seemed like minutes—Lu and Vivie walked into the waiting room, all smiles. Tears of relief trembled in Lu's eyes. "He's just fine, darling. He's back in his room. You want to see him before you leave?"

We hurried down the long hall, turned right, and into Johnny's room. There was the little ham in a crib, lying on his stomach, face toward us, one little fist tucked under his chin; asleep, breathing normally. We kissed his wet brown locks. The surgeon came in, still gowned. "Everything went smooth as silk, Mr. Capra." He gave us the okay sign. "No problems. He'll sleep for about an hour, then you can take him home. Why don't you all have some coffee?"

Lu escorted me to our car. "You run along, darling. Vivie and I will have something at the drugstore." "Okay, hon. The moment the picture starts, I'll sneak out and come back to pick you all up. Okay?" "Don't hurry, sweetheart. This is your big day. Good luck!"

Columbia Studios was about a ten-minute drive down Sunset to Gower. Yes, it was a big day for me. Driving along, I added things up. Fifteen years ago I was developing film in Ball's Laboratory for board and room. Today, one thousand of the world's elite correspondents would appraise my latest film. I knew that *You Can't Take It with You* would be my sixth straight smash hit—an unheard of feat in Hollywood. I had been president of the Academy for three years.

Yes, sir. I was taking this town apart, just as I said I would when I first drove out to McGowan's house to ask for a gag man's job on the *Our Gang* comedies. There *are* some things you can take with you—your accomplishments, the love of your wonderful wife and three beautiful children. In my elation I imitated our little ham Johnny. I pointed a finger at passing things and shouted, "Car! . . . Milk truck! . . . Dog! . . ."

The gate to Columbia's back lot opened on Bronson. Motorcycle police had closed the street to all traffic except for cars with stickered invitations. Music blared from loudspeakers and "Frank Capra's *You Can't Take It with You*" emblazoned from banners and posters. I inched through rubbernecking crowds, through the police barrier, and swung into the festooned gate.

Mac, the gateman, was on the phone in his glassed-in cubicle. He raised an arm to stop me. A last-minute message from Cohn, I thought. I could see the large open door of the preview stage. A hundred or so newsmen milled around in the doorway holding champagne glasses. I recognized pint-sized Sidney Skolsky, and Harrison Carroll, and Bill Wilkerson of the *Hollywood Reporter*. Sticking my head out of the car window I waved and yelled at them. They couldn't hear me. The gateman's voice at the passenger window interrupted my waving. "Oh, hi, Mac. What's the good word?"

"Mr. Capra—uh—they want you back at the hospital—right away—"

"Hospital? Who wants me?"

"It was a lady's voice. She said to tell you to please come quick—"

"Oh, my God. Now what?" I backed out, the police opened a lane through the crowd; I turned right and raced back up Sunset Boulevard. My fears raced ahead of me. Maybe it's Lu . . . a car hit her . . . Maybe it's Johnny—he woke up and they can't handle him . . . Maybe—

I ran from my parked car to the hospital door, turned left down the long hall, then right—there they were, a silent group—Lu, Vivie, the surgeon, two other doctors, two nurses. My throat closed tight. I walked up to Lu. She threw her arms around my neck and whispered the dreadful words. "He's dead, Frank. Little Johnny's dead." I drew her trembling body closer, looked questioningly at the others. Vivie twisted a wet handkerchief. Tears trickled down the surgeon's cheeks.

I broke away from Lu, rushed into Johnny's room. There he was, in the crib, just as I last saw him, lying on his stomach, face turned toward me, a little fist under his chin. But his color—my God, his color! He was white, like a sheet. His eyes were half-open. Only the whites showed. I touched his cheek. He was ice cold. He was dead. (A massive blood clot in the brain, the autopsy showed later.)

There were no tears in our car as we drove slowly homeward, just heavy, silent grief. The tears would come later. We drove past Columbia Studio. The crowds, police, and banners were still here. Somehow they didn't mean much now. Lu reached for one of my hands. I knew she heard it, too—little Johnny's happy voice: "Lissen me! Lissen me! . . . Car! . . . Bus! . . . Lady! . . ."

If You Have to Think About It, Forget It

"MARLENE DIETRICH? She's poison at the box office. I wouldn't put a quarter in her," said Cohn to me in his office.

"Come on, Harry. It's lousy *pictures* that are poison at the box office, not actors. Anyway, Dietrich plays George Sand—or forget the Chopin picture."

"Okay, forget it."

I was raging when I slammed into my office and barked at my secretary: "Get the gang up here. Quick!"

The gang: Joe Sistrom, Harold Winston, Chester Sticht. Joe Sistrom's hair was black, bushy, and untamable; his glasses so thick they could have been cut out of inkwells. A brilliant Stanford intellectual, a whiz at math and science, Joe was a wunderkind who never grew up. As a "think" man in films he *knew* everything but *did* nothing. "I don't have to lay an egg to know how the hen does it," was his motto. As a purist in thinking he was my invaluable number two man, as he had been for Stevens and McCarey, and would later be for Wilder.

Harold Winston was a refugee from the New York footlights, now serving as my dialogue coach. Winston was a gentle, sensitive soul who loved all that was beautiful, loathed all that was shoddy. As a purist in aesthetics his taste could discriminate between what was artistic and what was merely pleasing or utilitarian.

Chester Sticht was one of two younger brothers of my college roommate and best friend, Robert Sticht. Their parents were wealthy owners of the Queenstown copper mines in Tasmania. After World War I the copper market crashed; the Sticht parents died suddenly, almost penniless. Robert, my roommate, remained in Australia as chief chemical engineer for a fertilizer firm; the two younger brothers, Chester and Hadmar, came to the States. Hadmar went on with his schooling, became head of the Geology Department at College of the Pacific, Chester went to work for me as my secretary and man Friday.

These were my "needlers three"—Sistrom, Winston, Sticht. Their jobs: gadflys, deflaters, goaders. Their purpose: to keep me from being satisfied; nothing I did was good enough—I could do better. Their virtue: a fierce loyalty to me and my films.

"What's going on, for Pete's sake?" asked Sistrom as I cleaned out my desk. I told them. The Chopin film's off; I'm leaving Columbia; they better look for another job.

To my surprise they seemed pleased. "Chopin's off—that's great!" said Harold Winston to the others. "The timing's beautiful," said Sistrom. He handed me two typewritten yellow pages. "Read this, Frank, before you blow a tube."

"It's another *Mr. Deeds*," chimed in Chet, "perfect for Gary Cooper and Jean Arthur."

I read the first yellow page. Before I got to the second page I leaped up, began pacing. Ideas leapfrogged so fast I couldn't keep up with them. "No. Not Gary Cooper and Jean Arthur," I spluttered in short bursts. "No— Jimmy Stewart and Jean Arthur—this is a young senator—Boy Scout leader —naive, idealist. Joe! Where'd you get this idea?"

"I read an out-of-print book, *The Gentleman from Montana*. That's a two-page synopsis. You haven't read the last page—"

"I don't have to. I can see the whole story. Joe, can you buy it?"

"For a lunch at the Brown Derby."

"Buy it. Quick! In my name. Chet! Call Wasserman at MCA. See if Stewart and Arthur are available. Harold, make some copies of this synopsis—and don't pass 'em around! Hey—we'll call it not *Mr. Deeds*, but *Mr. Smith Goes to Washington*. We'll make it here, or for my own company. Hot damn, Joe, thanks. I'll be back in five minutes—"

That's the way things happen in studios. You sit around for months in the doldrums, then suddenly you're in the eye of a hurricane.

In two weeks, script writer Sidney Buchman (Bob Riskin was now at Goldwyn's) and I set out to "explore" Washington, D.C. With us were cameraman Joe Walker to shoot backgrounds, and a still-photo crew to photograph the thousand and one details of the Senate—walls, doorknobs, chandeliers, etc.—with a yardstick in each shot as a dimension parameter for the studio set builders.

And, of course, Art Black came with me. Art Black was my long-time assistant director. Without him around I was as helpless as a basket case. There are extraordinary men in the world that perform extraordinary feats in obscurity. There are first sergeants, for instance, who can extract the utmost from men in agony—and yet the men love them.

Such a man was Art Black. An assistant director's enemy is the clock. His prime function is to anticipate and magically produce on the set the myriad of details it takes to keep the director shooting without delay. At this, Art Black, an uneducated, gravelly voiced Irishman had no peers. But his chief asset was his constant line of unique chatter—mostly ad-lib malaprops—that disarmed, amused, and revivified the most exhausted actors and crews.

The first thing we did in our Capital City—Sidney Buchman and I and the whole crew—was to go rubbernecking in a sightseeing bus. We wanted to see Washington just as our dewy-eyed freshman Senator from Montana would see it: the Capitol, the Supreme Court, the White House—our trinity of liberty, three in one and one in three—the godhead of freedom on earth; the memorials to our great Presidents Washington and Lincoln; the statues of our founding fathers who established the rule of "we the people"; the stately crosses, row on row, honoring the bravery of men who died for freedom, the sentinel trees in Arlington Cemetery flying autumn colors in their honor.

These were the sights that were certain to unglue the freshman Senator from Montana, just as they did this little old country boy from California.

While Art Black photographed monuments and buildings, Sidney Buchman and I searched for a knowledgeable expert to serve as technical adviser on Senate procedures. During interviews with two local movie critics, Jay Carmody and Andrew Kelley, they recommended an expert by the name of Jim Preston. "Where can I find him?" I asked Carmody. "Just ask anybody. Preston's as well known as the Capitol dome."

I phoned an old friend, Bill Henry, probably the most factual, down-to-earth political reporter in the country; his Washington column, in the Los Angeles *Times*, was a must for California readers. Bill and I had known each other since 1912, when he started reporting sports for the *Times* and I started stuffing papers—inserting one section of the Sunday edition into another—on Saturday nights. He kidded me about making a film about the Senate, saying I was either very brave or very innocent, and that the Senate—the most exclusive club in the world—was very touchy about any commoner poking his nose into their uppity bailiwick, especially a Hollywood nose.

I asked Bill about Jim Preston. "He's your man, Frank. As superintendent of the Senate press gallery for forty years, old Jim has wet-nursed about three generations of reporters and Senators. Good thinking, Frank. Jim Preston might help cool off any senatorial ire that may singe your curly locks."

"Where will I find this indispensable paragon, Bill?"

"Look him up in the archives."

"Archives? Is he dead?"

Bill laughed, and said something about Preston being easier to "find" if I wore white gloves and a monocle—then invited me to lunch at the National Press Club.

For an hour or more Sidney and I soaked up the details of the tradition-rich club and its members. Buchman's ear was cocked for any bits of characteristic dialogue, which he jotted down, while I zeroed in on visual particulars— clothes, uniforms of attendants, table covers, paintings, wall decorations— details for the press club we'd build at the studio. And finally we got around to Jim Preston.

George Brown, head of Columbia's Washington office, made the appointment with Jim Preston to show us through the empty Senate chamber (Congress was not in session). Preston led us through the old Supreme Court Chambers, through maze after maze of pillars and vaulted hallways to an unmarked elevator; up several floors; through narrow archways to a locked door. "The Senate press room," he said, unlocking the door and plunging in, "all the wire services and major dailies." I remember many phones, many booths. He unlocked another door. "Senate press gallery," he said, leading us down a short, but steep, flight of stairs to the front row of balcony seats. And there, in a voice reserved for reading the Dead Sea Scrolls, Jim Preston announced: "The chamber of the Senate, the Upper House of the Congress of the United States of America."

I'm a silly goose about things patriotic, so it was a natural—I got a bad case of goose pimples. There it was, spread out below me, as silent and awe-inspiring as an empty cathedral—the Senate! Right in front of us was the Senate clock. We could touch it. Beneath the clock, the Vice President's dais, and fanning out from the dais, the ninety-six desks.

And suddenly—I saw those empty desks filled with angry, tired, shouting Senators. And I saw Jimmy Stewart on his feet in the back row, hoarse, haggard, barely able to stand.

"Great. Mr. Preston, you're on salary as of now. Five times what anybody else is paying you. First thing, I want you to arrange for our crew to come in here and photograph all the details—inkwells, pencils, stationery, everything down to the hole the Union soldier kicked in Jeff Davis's desk the day Jeff walked out to join the Confederacy. Later on you will come to Hollywood and help me select ninety-six actors to fill those desks—that look like *real* Senators—"

"The composite model of a United States Senator is fifty-two years old, five feet eleven inches tall, weighing one hundred and seventy-four pounds."

"I could kiss you, Jim."

Our story was a duplication of *You Can't Take It with You*'s villain-hero format. Once again the drama was keyed on an agonizing inner conflict. Our villain-hero—Montana's senior Senator, silver-haired Joseph Paine— once cared, then cared less, and finally ceased to care at all. For which he paid a degrading price. Our plot: Montana's number two Senator, a party hack, dies in office. The Senate's White Knight flies home to confer with Boss Jim Taylor and Governor "Happy" Hopper. The Willet Creek Dam appropriation is neatly tied to the Deficiency Bill; the Governor must appoint an absolutely "safe" man to the Senate.

Now the Governor is a Pontius Pilate with the sweats. Boss Taylor orders him to appoint a hack, Horace Miller. Governor demurs. At home he has eight outspoken children who ride him ragged for being Taylor's stooge. At dinner the barrage hits him: "Don't be a stooge, Pop!" . . . "Miller's a trained seal" . . . "Appoint a good man for a change . . ."

"QUIET! Perhaps you know-it-alls could suggest a better man—"

They don't suggest, they shout: "JEFF SMITH!"

"Who?"

"Jefferson Smith, head of the Boy Rangers!" . . . "Biggest expert on rocks and animals!" . . . "Put out a big forest fire!" . . . "Can recite everything George Washington said by heart!" . . .

In a moment of rash independence, Governor Hopper appoints pet-shop owner Jefferson Smith as interim Senator. Boss Taylor rages: "You bubblehead! A squirrel chaser—to the United States Senate?"

"Listen, Jim—the simpleton of all time! A big-eyed patriot—stood at attention in my presence—collects stray boys and cats—"

The White Knight beams at the choice. "Jim, Jeff's a fine boy. His father was an old law partner. Fine boy—"

"Joe, I don't trust guys in knee pants that wave flags," growls Boss Taylor. "Can you handle him in Washington?"

"A young patriot, who recites Jefferson and Lincoln? Turned loose in our nation's Capital? I can handle him—"

And so the young idealist, Jefferson Smith, goes to Washington as a worshipful disciple of the White Knight; discovers he has feet of clay; desperately tries to convince Senators the White Knight is a fraud (in a filibuster) and that his appropriation rider to the Deficiency Bill was outright graft for the pockets of Jim Taylor, his political boss; only to be crushed and flattened by the Taylor machine's steam roller, until . . . Well, until gutty ideals, the words of Lincoln, the wit of Jean Arthur, plus a one-man filibuster, and the conscience of the White Knight—all drive relentlessly toward an emotion-packed climax.

It happened to me on every film. As P.P. (principal photography) Day approached, enthusiasm's bubble would suddenly burst—and I'd get a bad case of film fright. At Columbia it would generally happen when Lionel Banks, the art director, took me on a stage to show me the first set being erected.

The story may have cost two hundred thousand dollars, a three-thousand-dollar-a-week writer may have been on salary for months, high-priced actors could have been signed and the weekly cost sheets indicate half a million had been charged to the picture. But these kinds of figures made no sense anyway. They were fantasies, paper dollars that hadn't bought anything you could pick up and carry off. So I'd toss the figures aside and go back to concocting make-believe scenes with my writer, or to discussing actors with anybody who listened. It was fun talk, free as the wind. We'd argue, laugh like children.

But when the art director showed me dozens of real carpenters hammering real nails into real boards, by grannies they meant business. Reality clunked me on the head like a dropped sandbag. All our airy fun talk suddenly hardened into nails and boards and bricks and mortar—bought with real money. My first instinct was to fly to South America, get lost, drop dead. But now I was hooked, trapped, committed to spending two million dollars—on what?

I'd rush back to my office, lock the doors, read the story and script. It was drivel. Imbecilic drivel! The panic was on. I'd rush to my Brentwood orchard and hoe weeds till I dropped, or race to the Tennis Club, bat balls till my eyes popped. And gradually, you'd remember that you were a pro; that all art demanded an iron discipline of form; technique. You'd remember that making films is making decisions. "Is it good or bad entertainment?" If it hits you right off, it's good entertainment. If you have to think about it, forget it. If neither alternative lights a fire, throw them both away. Start over. And you plunge into the picture wearing the strait jacket of discipline. Ten thousand decisions? Don't think. Count as good only those that strike you immediately. And the film gets made. Talent—art? God knows. Discipline? Yes.

So it was par for the course when panic hit me in Washington. This time reality's sandbag dropped on me from a very high source. While my crew was busy photographing and script writer Buchman was honeying details out of Jim Preston, I leaped at Bill Henry's once-in-a-lifetime invitation to attend a White House press conference with him.

The White House! America's hallowed symbol of the people's power to elect one of their own to the world's mightiest office. And let me shout it from the housetops and publish it in Gath: Be you a hard-boiled cynic or an insensitive ox—the White House will get under your skin.

Some fifty accredited White House pressmen waited silently in a lower hallway outside the Oval Room. I huddled close to Bill Henry, still as a mouse. Bill had had some difficulty clearing my admittance with Secret Service men; three of them still eyed me furtively. "You look a little pale around the gills, Frank," chuckled Bill Henry. "My God, Bill, my knees are shaking," I whispered, "my first gander at F.D.R's bailiwick." "Isn't it something? I've been in here a hundred times, and I still get butterflies in the old pazzaz."

The door opened. Newsmen squeezed through for advantageous positions. Bill and I were in the tail of the surge. "Let's stay in the back," he whispered to me. "Old Franklin D. has an elephant's eye for faces."

Through three rows of standing reporters I caught glimpses of F.D.R. He sat back confidently, regally, against his high-back chair. A long cigarette holder tilted up rakishly from his massive face as he scanned the reporters with a roguish, challenging smile. My first thought: He is *not* crippled. (Not from the waist up, he wasn't). My second thought made my heart skip. I was standing not more than fifteen feet from Franklin Delano Roosevelt, President of the United States of America! Foreign-born Americans more fully appreciate the awesome aura of that title.

I became aware of questions. Would Mr. President care to comment on Prime Minister Chamberlain's "peace in our time" statement after he returned from appeasing Hitler in Munich? . . . Would he comment on Hitler's statement that he was satisfied with his gains in Czechoslovakia? . . . Would he press Congress to revise the neutrality laws so that belligerents could purchase munitions? . . . Are we still selling scrap iron to Japan? . . .

And panic hit me. Japan was slicing up the colossus of China piece by piece. Nazi panzers had rolled into Austria and Czechoslovakia; their thunder echoed over Europe. England and France shuddered. The Russian bear growled ominously in the Kremlin. The black cloud of war hung over the chancelleries of the world. Official Washington from the President down, was in the process of making hard, torturing decisions.

And here was I, in the process of making a satire about government officials; a comedy about a callow, hayseed Senator who comes to Washington carrying a crate of homing pigeons—to send messages back to Ma—and disrupts important Senate deliberations with a filibuster. The cancerous tumor of war was growing in the body politic, but our reform-happy hero wanted to call the world's attention to the pimple of graft on its nose. Wasn't this the most untimely time for me to make a film about Washington?

Outside the White House I thanked Bill Henry and hailed a taxi. Where was I going? To the memorial built to honor Abe Lincoln, another lanky hayseed who came to Washington—and saved the Union with his ideals; to the fountainhead of moral courage where our own Jefferson Smith would go for a refill of inspiration after the political steam roller had flattened him.

And there, in the most majestic shrine we have in America, sat the colossal marble figure of our greatest man—rumpled, lanky, homely—his eyes daily filling the hearts of thousands of Americans with the deep, deep compassion that seemed to well out from his own great soul; eyes that seemed to say: "Friend, I have seen it all. It is good."

Along with dozens of tourists, I read the words that were carved on the Memorial wall, the words of Lincoln's Gettysburg Address. I heard the voice of a child reciting the words. There, next to me, an eight-year-old boy was holding the hand of a very old man—whose body and sight were failing— and reading him Lincoln's inspirational words in a voice as clear and innocent as a bell. And the old man smiled to himself, nodded proudly after each sentence. I looked up at the marble face of Lincoln. Only imagination, of course, but I was sure he smiled.

Then the boy led the old man to the opposite wall and read him the carved words of the Second Inaugural Address. Never had Lincoln's impassioned, moral indictment of slavery sounded so eloquent, so moving, so powerful as when that young boy read it to his grandfather. That scene must go into our film, I thought. We must make the film if only to hear a boy read Lincoln to his grandpa.

I left the Lincoln Memorial with this growing conviction about our film: The more uncertain are the people of the world, the more their hard-won freedoms are scattered and lost in the winds of chance, the more they need a ringing statement of America's democratic ideals. The soul of our film would be anchored in Lincoln. Our Jefferson Smith would be a young Abe Lincoln, tailored to the rail-splitter's simplicity, compassion, ideals, humor, and unswerving moral courage under pressure. And back we went to Hollywood to get to work on *Mr. Smith Goes to Washington*. The panic was over. It is *never* untimely to yank the rope of freedom's bell.

We returned to Columbia Studios from Washington about November 1, 1938, and before the next November rolled around I was to experience enough exciting events to last me a lifetime.

First, there was the bedlam-against-the-clock, pre-production phase of our film. I have no wish to magnify the drudgery of being the last word on the million and one details involved in launching a project as big as *Mr. Smith Goes to Washington*. Nor do I wish to minify the nagging suspense as to whether all the details would coalesce in time for the big day—the point of no return—when the director is scheduled to shout "Roll 'em! Action!" But this statement I do wish to stress: To lower the odds against a film being "quality"—there is no substitute for intensive attention to pre-production details. And to insure the quality of these details—there is no substitute for back-breaking drudgery.

The work all begins with the "word," of course. We had to digest the piles of Washington notes and incorporate them into a script that had a theme, made sense, told a believable story and, above all, was entertaining. And that is a very large order to complete in two months, as any playwright or novelist can tell you. And here Sidney Buchman and I were alone, especially Buchman. Here not even an army of technical advisers can be of use. Only God can help you, and sometimes He has to. For script-writing is a lonely job of inventing and creating something that did not exist before—two hundred pages of dramatically constructed, imaginative, entertaining scenes that will justify spending two million dollars to film them. And do these scenes come out of a spigot, like tap water? No, indeed. They are created. By a talent. Yes, an extraordinary talent. But also they are created out of writing and rewriting, out of sweating and head-banging, out of the endurance and stamina that mark a decathlon champion. And Sidney Buchman came through with a gold medal performance in the writing of *Mr. Smith.*

Then there was the art director, Lionel Banks. From ancient blueprints dug out of the Capitol's catacombs, and thousands of photographs, his department of magicians was asked to conjure up, in one hundred days, exact replicas of what had taken one hundred years to build. In reconstructing the Senate chamber, seen by countless eyes and hallowed by a thousand traditions, even the omission of historic scratches on a desk might betray the imitation. In addition, other exact duplications crowded all of Columbia's stages—cloak rooms, committee rooms, press club, hotel suites, monuments, even a midwestern Governor's mansion.

Then there was the long arduous task of casting the players. I say arduous because I insisted on personally interviewing every last performer who appeared on the screen. I had a very unorthodox thing about casting. There were no big or small parts. All parts were star parts, even if they lasted but five seconds. And this was a cardinal rule for me: Each time-increment of a film (however short) is as necessary and important as any other time-increment (however long).

There were 186 speaking parts in *Mr. Smith Goes to Washington,* and hundreds more "atmosphere" parts, extras. The casting department and my "needlers three"—Joe Sistrom, Harold Winston, and Chester Sticht—would call in four or five actors or actresses for each part. That meant weeks and weeks of personal interviews.

I seldom, if ever, made any screen tests. I thought they were idiotic and certainly unfair to the players. I selected my cast solely by instinct. When interviewing, I didn't see the candidates as actors. I tried to visualize them as human beings who were part of our story. If they didn't ring a bell right off, I'd thank them and dismiss them. But if something inside me jumped up and said "That's your man for the doctor" . . . "That's her—that's your secretary," those players would be signed up on the spot; no further arguments or interviews. And soon I was able to visualize the whole film as a real story about real human beings whom I knew. If there is any merit to the credit bestowed on me for the natural acting in my films, it is due to this attitude: No matter how small the roles, I treat all actors as stars.

For the main roles of the story there was little interviewing. I knew the performers I wanted and went after them with the zeal of Harpo Marx pursuing blondes. Jimmy Stewart and Jean Arthur were a made-to-order natural team—the simon-pure idealist, and the cynical, fed-up-with-politics Washington secretary with a dormant heart of gold. They were signed up at the very inception of the project.

But who could play the gutty role of the senior Senator, the White Knight, the villain-hero of our show? We leafed and leafed through the Players Directory, poured over names in the lists of clients agents sent us. None raised blood pressure until one of my henchmen casually remarked: "I just thought of an actor that'd *look* like a Senator—Claude Rains." Boing! Of course. Not only could that distinguished British actor add grace and luster to any nation's Upper House; he had the artistry, power, and depth to play the soul-tortured idealist whose feet had turned to clay.

Casting the part of the powerful political boss was practically automatic —my favorite villain with the wind-up laugh: Edward Arnold. And to play the role of the bumbling, vacillating, "They can't do this to me!" Governor —who else but pop-eyed, diaphoretic Guy Kibbee? And for the Governor's eight roughneck children who rode him ragged for being Boss Taylor's stooge, Joe Sistrom hit pay dirt: "Let's get the younger two-thirds of the Watson tribe—they'll drive anybody nuts." (Pa and Ma Watson and about a dozen freckle-faced little Watsons all worked in pictures.)

It took weeks to find the right actor for the part of "Diz," the poet-quoting reporter who wouldn't cross the street to see Lady Godiva unless the horse had bucked her off into a cactus patch. Diz was the constant pal and faithful admirer of "Saunders" (Jean Arthur). He proposed marriage twice a day when sober, and twice an hour when he recovered from sobriety. Gallantly he vowed that—in the words of Lamb—Saunders would be his "fine lass to go a-gypsying through the world with."

To my "needlers three" I insisted that Diz be played by a left-handed actor. "Why?" they challenged. "I don't know. But southpaws are immediate 'characters'—full of surprises. Like doors that open the wrong way, clocks that run backward. Look at 'Lefty' Gomez. I'll bet 'Wrong Way Corrigan' was a lefty. Anyway, Diz is left-handed."

Sistrom, as usual, came up with the answer. "Best southpaw actor I know is the guy you always rave about—Tommy Mitchell." Bells rang. Everyone shouted his version of "Eureka!" Tommy Mitchell was heaven's answer to our prayer. In fact, he was soon to become heaven's answer to many a director's prayer—including John Ford's.

I must tell you about casting the Vice President's role, because it reveals a Thespian's psychological quirk. In our film the Vice President had little to do except sit on his rostrum. But he was the anchor that saved the Senate from foundering when filibustering winds began to blow.

We were all agreed that a distinguished character actor, Mr. Edward Ellis, would make a fine Vice President. I called his agent. "Frank," said the agent in a take-it-or-leave-it voice, "Mr. Ellis does not discuss or read parts unless it's a firm offer. His salary is twenty-five thousand flat for six weeks of his time. Pro rata after that."

A firm offer meant he was guaranteed the part *before* he accepted or rejected it. "Firm offer," I said. "I'll send a messenger with the script."

Several hours later, the agent himself returned the script. He found me, and cameraman Joe Walker, studying the partly built Senate through viewfinders. "Frank," said the agent, handing me back the script, "Mr. Ellis says he's never been so insulted in his life. He demands an apology. Says a third-rate bit actor wouldn't play that part. Not over twenty words in it."

"My friend, it's my lucky day. My apologies to Mr. Ellis, and thank him for refusing the part."

It was Sistrom again: "For Pete's sake, we don't *want* a big actor, because, number one, no big actor will play a twenty-word part. We want a face—a strong American face." We scanned the Players Directory for strong American faces—and one rugged Yankee puss zoomed up at us: Harry Carey's. Let that veteran cowboy actor tell it himself, in an interview he gave Douglas Gilbert of the New York *World-Telegram*:

> When my agent told me Capra had a part for me in *Mr. Smith,* I never rode a nag faster than I took off for Columbia Studios. "Will you play a Vice President for me?" asked Capra. "I don't know. I never even saw one in the newsreels." "Good," he said. "You're my Vice President." And what do I do but damn near muff the part . . . Me, who's been in pictures since 1908. In my first scene I have to administer the oath of office to Jim Stewart. It was no good and I knew it. Capra ordered a retake, and again I muff it. Another retake, another muff.
>
> "Print it," Capra said (meaning it goes). But I knew it was terrible, and so did he, because he left the camera set up exactly as it was while we went to lunch . . .

I had called lunch because that horse-opera actor was losing face in front of all the fine actors who surrounded him. Back from lunch I casually said to him. "Harry, while the cameras are still set up, let's try the scene again. This time, remember this. The people of America have elected you as their Vice President. You are just one heart tick away from the White House. Forget Harry Carey the cowboy actor. Swear this new Senator in as Harry Carey the Vice President of the United States."

His shoulders squared back, the tenseness of his weather-beaten face relaxed into a quiet dignity. "Go ahead, Frank. The Vice President is ready," he said quietly. And he was. The critics mentioned Harry Carey's warm performance almost as often as Jimmy Stewart's tour de force.

So far, three major pre-production tasks have been mentioned: research and script-writing, set construction, and casting. But there are others: Selection and design of wardrobe for each player; interior decorations for each set (the Capitol furniture was exactly duplicated and fashioned by hand); hand props (to be current with the film's time, special issues of appropriate magazines and newspapers had to be set up and printed). The budget sessions were tedious, torrid, and long. Shooting schedules were constantly being laid out and changed.

There was one movie-making quirk that might be easily overlooked—but if you did you'd suffer many a headache later. And that was to design the sets to fit the stars. Yes, you read it right. For example: One side of Jean Arthur's face was much more attractive than the other; in fact, her "bad"

"Repeat after me," says Vice President (Harry Carey), "I, Jefferson Smith . . ."

". . . do solemnly swear that I will faithfully execute the Office of Senator of the United States, and will to the best of my ability, preserve, protect, and defend the Constitution of the United States."

"Jefferson Smith, as a leader of our great American youth, will you accept the great honor of representing our great State as a Senator in the great Senate of these our great United States of America?"

"Get up there with that lady that's on top of this Capitol dome—the lady that stands for liberty—and you'll see the whole parade of what man's carved out for himself after centuries of fighting for something better than just jungle law—"

"I accuse that man of character assassination. He stood on the Senate floor and insinuated that I am sponsoring a Bill to line my own pocket. I demand that this Committee expel him—"

side made her look like a different person. Thus the sets had to be constructed so that Jean Arthur's "entrances" showed only the "good" side of her face. Otherwise, she'd be forced into cumbersome, unnatural crossings and turns to maneuver her "good" side to the camera. Jean Arthur's problem was far from unique. Very few stars, and very few commoners, have perfectly symmetrical faces.

Then came music conferences with composer Tiomkin. "Now, Dimitri! Forget Borodin and Moussorgsky. Only native American themes, hear? Folk songs, Stephen Foster, Sousa, W. C. Handy—"

"Fronk, vat you theenk, I'm like children? Papichka, in my head is notes like apple pie so American—"

And then I'd rush to montage sessions with the master of montage—Slavko Vorkapich; to second-unit and insert layouts with Charles Vidor—a bright young director import from Vienna. Oh, yes. To an innocent bystander all this feverish pre-production activity might appear to be an eight-ring circus in an insane asylum—with the inmates doing the stunts. But it wasn't. There was a methodology to this madness. And it was this mastery of an apparent chaos—involving the highest of artistic and technological skills—that had made Hollywood the world's number one film center.

And if preparing *Mr. Smith* didn't keep me busy round-the-clock, preparing for the upcoming Academy Awards Banquet took up the slack—arrangements for the balloting, invitations, guest stars; the press, magazines, radio people. This was my fourth year as president of the Academy. Moreover, to make certain life didn't become too boring, my fellow directors had recently elected me president of the Screen Directors Guild. Viva yo!

When suddenly, at the height of the *Mr. Smith* preparations, a clash of events—and of egos—shot me into the front lines of a labor-management war which climaxed in my hurling a directors' strike ultimatum at the crowned heads of the Motion Picture Producers Association, and in my plotting the disruption of the Academy which I had labored so long to preserve.

The seeds of this unexpected crisis had been planted a year earlier when, as president of the Academy, I appeared before the Directors Guild Board to make my annual plea for their cooperation in the Academy Awards voting. I pointed out that the officers of the other two talent guilds—Actors and Writers—had dropped their active opposition to the Academy and were allowing their members to cooperate freely.

King Vidor, Directors Guild president, said Academy cooperation was of little consequence when the Directors Guild was fighting for existence. Sure, the Actors and Writers guilds could now take an interest in industry-wide affairs. They had won *their* four-year battle for recognition; they were in business. But the directors hadn't gotten to first base. All the company heads were dead set against recognizing our Guild as the bargaining agent for directors and assistants. The producers would meet with Howard Hawks's negotiating committee, which included Rouben Mamoulian and Eddie Sutherland, then suddenly break off negotiations. Months later they'd repeat the process.

"Our Guild's in trouble, Frank. Some directors, Bill Wellman for instance, are resigning in disgust. Others think it's ridiculous for important directors to join a union in the first place, a few rabid ones call us all a bunch of Communists. You're a member of our Guild, Frank. Why don't you come in and help out your fellow directors instead of spending all your life promoting the Academy?"

That led to my filling a vacancy on the Directors Guild Board. At the next general meeting of all the directors, Guild officers nominated me for president. In the hope that anyone who could revitalize the Academy might add some ginger to the Guild, I was elected. I accepted the challenge with pleasure. I was itching to roll in the dirt with the movie moguls that had ganged up to keep me out of work for a year.

My first meaningful action as the new president was to acquire the wisdom, experience, and brilliant legal talents of that great lady of the law, Mabel Walker Willebrandt.

Being wise to the ways of Washington (where she practiced law), Mrs. Willebrandt arranged a date for a Guild hearing before the National Labor Relations Board. One week before the scheduled hearing, Sam Goldwyn contacted me. He advised that we not wash our dirty linen in public, and gave his word that, if the Guild appointed a new negotiating committee, he would guarantee meetings with a small committee of producers to work out our problems in private until a deal was negotiated.

We discussed this new proposal with a grain of salt. Twice, during the preceding year, opposing negotiating committees had met and practically arrived at a final deal—only to have the producers arbitrarily break off negotiations. It was obvious to us that Joe Schenck, president of the Producers Association, was playing a game of meet and stall, meet and stall, until directors got sick of the Guild idea. But we had great respect for Sam Goldwyn's integrity.

Besides, I had a yen to beard Joe Schenck with the bullfighter's "*mano a mano*" challenge. We called off our hearing before the National Labor Board and opted for a third try at negotiations. I appointed myself as chairman of a small committee of directors, informed Mr. Schenck that we wanted to meet immediately with any officially appointed committee of producers.

On January 3, 1939, Joe Schenck informed our Guild by letter that he had appointed the following committee: Joe Schenck, Sam Goldwyn, Harry Warner, Eddie Mannix, Y. Frank Freeman, and Harry Cohn.

On February 9, 1939, the two committees met. Mr. Schenck opened the meeting by announcing the committee would not negotiate with the directors unless they threw the assistant directors out of the Guild. Another stall. We walked out.

Next morning Joe Schenck phoned the Guild offices requesting a private meeting with Mr. Capra, and would Mr. Capra please stand by for a call from Mr. Schenck. I stood by all day. No phone call. Next morning I phoned Mr. Schenck for an explanation. He apologized and asked me to come to his office at 3 P.M., alone. At 3 P.M. I reported at Joe Schenck's office. Mr. Schenck was not in, the secretary informed me. He had left for the Santa Anita racetrack at noon. My hackles rose. He was trying me on for size. Okay. To hell with *Mr. Smith Goes to Washington* for a while. The racetrack would be a fine place to let Schenck know I could carry the weight. I leaped in my car and raced for Santa Anita.

I knew that Joe Schenck, in spite of his soft-spoken thick accent, was all brain and iron. Bald, inscrutable, massive and craggy of face—he looked for all the world like a Buddha with a perpetual hangover. But his looks were deceptive. He was easily the sharpest poker player in Hollywood's high-stake games, and an equally good poker player in Hollywood's power struggles. Yet, he was well-liked and respected. His loyalty had become legendary. When Willie Bioff, the hoodlum head of the Chicago I.A.T.S.E. (the A. F. of L.'s International Alliance of Theater and Stage Employees), got control—through his stooge pal George Brown (president of the I.A.) —of the Hollywood local and proceeded to shake down Hollywood studio heads with threats of strikes and personal violence, the courts established Schenck as the pay-off man. Because he refused to reveal the names of other supposedly victimized company heads, Joe Schenck, head of Twentieth Century-Fox, served a year in jail.

Joe Schenck understood power and the timing of its use. I knew he would be impervious to pressure—unless I had an ace-king showing.

At Santa Anita I worked up quite a head of steam tracing Mr. Schenck to his private box. He greeted me expansively. "Well, well, look who's here. Frank Capra. Come in, come in. Be my guest. I've got at least seven tips to give you on the next race." Play it cool, boy. Give him the shaft gently, then walk away.

"No, thank you, Mr. Schenck," I said casually. "I just drove out to give *you* a tip. The next time you ask me for an appointment, I'll be there. And so will *you*—with your hat in your hand."

I called a special meeting of our Board. The Academy Awards Banquet was slated for February 23—eight days away. I acquainted the Board with the sequence of insulting episodes with Mr. Schenck. The Board members were furious. I warned them that Schenck would only yield to power; that we must move quickly, gamely, and lethally—or forget the Guild. We discussed possible power moves. Some members were for calling an emergency meeting of all directors and asking for a strike vote. Others warned we shouldn't start anything we couldn't finish; that top directors under contract might be sued if they walked out. I agreed. I suggested a more immediate power play: disrupt the upcoming *Academy Awards Banquet.*

I explained that previous Academy boycotts by the talent guilds (to put pressure on management) had failed because producing companies didn't care who killed the Academy after it refused to play ball on the pay cuts. But today, they cared. The Academy lived. It is strong again. It is management's number one publicity stunt for their films. Next week's Academy Awards Banquet was a sell-out. The program was set—music, stars, visiting celebrities, four hundred press people. "I know," I explained to the astonished Board members, "because as master of ceremonies I've made all the arrangements. Now, here's a plan that's pretty sure to put management's tail in a crack.

"First, I will immediately resign as president of the Academy, and withdraw as master of ceremonies. Reason: the rude, contemptuous attitude of the Motion Picture Producers Association toward the Screen Directors Guild and its officers. The Academy's hot news. This accusation will make the world's front pages.

"And second, call an emergency meeting of *all* directors."

George Marshall made the motion (seconded by Rowland Lee, and unanimously approved) that an emergency membership meeting be called for the following night, Thursday, February 16, 1939, at the Hollywood Athletic Club. Urgent telegrams were immediately sent to all directors. We leaked news of the mass meeting to the trade papers. They played it up big.

Over 250 film directors assembled at the Hollywood Athletic Club. Their mood was angry. The officers reported in detail the humiliating on-again, off-again negotiations with the producers; that management was stringing us along with the old carrot-stick treatment; that their real aim was to smash our Guild. When a Board member told them their president had to chase Joe Schenck out to the Santa Anita racetrack after being stood up on two appointments, the directors exploded.

One member asked for the floor, gained it, and moved we take a strike vote. The motion was immediately seconded. As the chairman, I tried to calm the meeting down, but then realized that a strike vote, *and* the Academy boycott would give me a one-two punch—the ace-king showing that might force Schenck to throw in his hand. The vote to strike—at the discretion of the president—was approved unanimously. Also approved unanimously were my resignation from the Academy and a boycott of next week's Awards dinner.

The approved plan of action: Give management twenty-four hours to sign an agreement recognizing the Guild as the bargaining agent for directors and their assistants. Our attorney, Mrs. Willebrandt, would send the ultimatum by telegram to Mendel Silverberg, the attorney for the Producers Association. If there was no positive response within twenty-four hours, the Guild president was instructed to release the ultimatum to the press, and proceed with the "or elses."

I didn't sleep much that night. A boycott of the Academy would be unpopular enough. But a strike would be a declaration of war. It would be asking dedicated filmmakers to be more loyal to their union than to their films. Would I walk out on *Mr. Smith Goes to Washington*? God knows. After all, what was at stake? Not much more than bruised egos, really. But I imagine more wars have been loosed by trodden toes than by trodden rights.

Next morning, Friday, February 17, Joe Schenck called the Guild office to say that he and several company heads were in Palm Springs; a sandstorm was raging. Would the Guild give them a day's extension on the time limit. The answer: NO!

That afternoon, about 4 P.M., I received a personal call from Joe Schenck. All the company heads and their attorneys were meeting in his office, he said, and would I please come to the meeting alone. Facetiously, I asked, "Would it save time if I went directly to Santa Anita?"

He chuckled. Schenck would chuckle if he broke the stock market or the market broke him. "In my board room," he said, "as a personal favor, please come out, Mr. Capra. I remember about the hat, too."

I was ushered into Twentieth Century-Fox's large executive room. A dozen of Hollywood's high-and-mighties and their attorneys slouched with flushed faces; some were coatless. They greeted me with harsh stares and harsher questions: "You've got your nerve" . . . "Who do you think you are —sending us ultimatums?"

"Gentlemen," I answered, as pious as Mark Twain's Christian who held four aces, "I am a servant carrying out an order from Hollywood's film directors: Come back with a signed agreement with the Producers Association by eight o'clock tonight, or boycott the Academy and call a strike. I'm here for an answer, not for more stalling."

"Mr. Capra," called out Joe Schenck, "we are not stalling, just procrastinating." I was beginning to fall in love with Joe Schenck. "Wait in my outside office, please. And maybe we can procrastinate something out of this."

I spent a couple of shaky suspenseful hours waiting in his office. Having watched Schenck play poker with the big boys, I knew he was never more dangerous than when he was amusing.

At 6 P.M., Schenck came out of the meeting and handed me a two-page letter of agreement, addressed to me as president of the Screen Directors Guild, and signed by Joseph N. Schenck, president of the Association of Motion Picture Producers. It was all there: The producers concurred in Guild shop, arbitration and conciliation, and the Guild was to be the sole bargaining agent for directors and assistants. In fact, they agreed to all points in our submitted platforms except two: salaries and working conditions for assistant directors and film-cutting time for directors. These would be further negotiated at the convenience of the Guild.

"Is it okay, Mr. President of the Directors Guild?"

"It's very okay. There'll be no Academy boycott, and no strike, and you're looking at a very happy man, Mr. Schenck."

"I'm happy, too. And you can make me happier if you'll answer one question: Were you, or were you not, bluffing?"

"Mr. Schenck, what really matters is that you thought I was *not* bluffing. Courtesy requires me to agree with your conclusion."

"Smart boy. I congratulate you." He escorted me to the door. "Frank, I admire people who know how to get things done. When you finish at Columbia, Twentieth Century-Fox is going to offer you the best contract any director ever got."

I'll have to admit that when I brought back that signed agreement to a waiting Guild Board we all went out and got pifflicated.

A good idea has more lives than the proverbial cat. Ideas such as freedom, equality, charity, the Olympic Games, fall but rise again. Hollywood had originated two ideas that seemed to defy death. One was the United Artists concept (a distribution outlet for independent films first conceived by Pickford, Fairbanks, and Chaplin). That idea was so necessary, so sound, it survived many disasters. The other was the Academy idea, a "homage to quality" organization of the film people, by the film people, and for the film people. The Academy survived the idiotic—and abortive—attempt of management to use it as a stooge for pay cuts.

It survived the subsequent retaliatory wholesale resignations of the talent groups; survived the resignations and withdrawal of financial support of the Producers Association; survived four years of pauperism during which loyal Academy members paid for the Oscars. And it would have survived my resignation as its president, and my withdrawal as the master of ceremonies, on the eve of the world's premier glamour show: the Academy Awards Banquet.

These were the thoughts that raced through my head in the Biltmore Bowl as the stirring strains of "The Star Spangled Banner," sung by Meliza Korjus, died down, and Basil Rathbone introduced me as the Academy president and the master of ceremonies. And as I stepped to the rostrum and faced the brilliant assemblage—twelve hundred of Hollywood's finest —all beautifully gowned and carefully groomed, and four hundred of the world's press, I never felt prouder—or more grateful—for being the head of this beloved Academy which, only days ago, I had conspired to disrupt.

This year I was free from any personal suspense about winning awards for *You Can't Take It with You*. Since the New York Critics Award, often the harbinger of Academy voting, had not included *You Can't Take It* among its top ten, and since last year my high hopes for *Lost Horizon* had been deflated (it was voted very few nominations, and only one Oscar—film editing). And since being loyal to a distressed Academy had earned me brickbats from the talent groups, I had to assume that future Oscars would be hard to come by. And so I was free to concentrate on making this 1939 Awards Banquet more glamorous than ever.

The first celebrity I introduced was Jerome Kern. He was applauded vociferously as he opened envelopes and awarded Oscars to Ralph Rainger and Leo Robin for their Best Song, "Thanks for the Memory." Next up was Irving Berlin. He awarded Alfred Newman the Best-Scoring Award for *Alexander's Ragtime Band*, and an Award to Eric Korngold for the Best Original Score for *Adventures of Robin Hood*.

Then I introduced a surprise that brought down the house. Child-star Shirley Temple presented child-man Walt Disney with a Special Award for his creation of *Snow White and the Seven Dwarfs*, an elaborately designed two-foot trophy symbolizing the characters in Walt's first full-length cartoon masterpiece.

I beamed from the sidelines as celebrity after celebrity handed out statuettes. Bob Hope cracked jokes in presenting the Short-Subjects Awards. Distinguished author Lloyd Douglas (*Magnificent Obsession, The Robe*) presented Oscars to Dore Schary and Eleanore Griffin for Best Original Story, *Boys Town*, and to George Bernard Shaw for Best Screenplay, *Pygmalion* (British Consul Francis E. Evans accepting for Shaw).

Then another laugh riot: Edgar Bergen and Charlie McCarthy handed Deanna Durbin a special trophy in the interest of Hollywood's "youth movement," and when Mickey Rooney didn't show up for a similar trophy, Mortimer Snerd accepted it for him.

Next, I introduced one of the original conceivers of the Academy idea, veteran director Fred Niblo. He was to present the Best-Director Award. The pundits and the "smart money" had made Norman Taurog (*Boys Town*) and King Vidor (*The Citadel*) the favorites. Imagine my utter consternation when Niblo opened the envelope and announced: "And the winner is Frank Capra for *You Can't Take It with You!*"

My third Oscar for Best Directing left me so stunned, I remember little of my "thank you" mumblings. The rest of the program was a blur. Vaguely, I remembered Spencer Tracy being honored as Best Actor for his performance in *Boys Town*, and that Spence's thanks to Boys Town's Father Flanagan were the high spot of the evening; and also that Bette Davis thanked director Willie Wyler for her Oscar-winning performance in *Jezebel*. But when Jimmy Roosevelt opened the Best-Picture envelope and broke the suspense with: "And the best picture of the year is: *You Can't Take It with You!*"—my poor numbed brain tail-spinned into total amnesia.

The crazy events of the past week: Chasing Joe Schenck to the racetrack; the strike vote, my resignation and boycott of the Academy; the last-minute producers' agreement that called them off, that put the Directors Guild in business; the whole wonderful Academy Banquet that climaxed in my third Best-Director and my second Best-Picture Oscars—these were events that simply reaffirmed a lifelong belief: Everything that happens to me happens for the best.

In later years that feeling was to be strained a little, but it was still strong when I finally made it back to Columbia, put on my ringmaster's hat and cracked an eager whip over the eight-ring circus that was shaping up into *Mr. Smith Goes to Washington.* During the last two weeks prior to the beginning of principal photography I began the process of shutting out the world and concentrating on visualizing the whole film, scene by scene, much as a pole vaulter stands for minutes at the end of the runway shutting out all external stimuli, concentrating on a mental picture of every move of his vault—his sprint down the runway, the thrust of the pole into the socket, the spring, the upward leap, and the catapult over the bar—seeing every move in his mind before he starts his vault.

By the time I began my vault (April 1, 1939) I had a mental picture of the entire film and had conditioned myself to close my switches to all stimuli not directly connected with *Mr. Smith Goes to Washington.* Once filming began I never left the set, never took phone calls, never heard or saw anything unless it pertained to the scene we were shooting. I was a tuning fork that vibrated only to the wave length of *Mr. Smith.*

Film Power vs. Freedom of Film

THE SHOOTING of *Mr. Smith Goes to Washington* presented one unusual problem. The Senate chamber was a boxed-in, four-sided set surmounted by a continuous rectangle of gallery seats, which in turn was backed up by four niched walls containing the marble busts of all twenty ex-Vice Presidents. In short, our Senate was a deep well filled with several hundred people. Story action took place almost simultaneously on three levels: the floor of the chamber, the rostrum, and the press gallery. How to light, photograph, and record hundreds of scenes on three levels of a deep well, open only at the top, were the logistic nightmares that faced electricians, cameramen, and soundmen. Had we tried to photograph the Senate with the usual single camera, "jackassing" tons and tons of heavy equipment (lights, sound booms, camera platforms) for each single new set-up—we might still be there.

But enthusiastic, resourceful men such as cameraman Joe Walker, head electrician George Hager, and sound engineer Ed Bernds stayed young by licking such challenges. Together, we devised and diagramed a multiple-camera, multiple-sound-channel method of shooting which enabled us, in one big equipment move, to film as many as a half-dozen separate scenes before we made another big move. I mention these technical details because it was out of this in-depth study of camera-sound relationships that I came up with a simple solution to a problem that had bugged directors since film had evolved its larynx: how to improve our ridiculous, inadequate, horse-and-buggy method of shooting close-ups.

Let us assume that Jimmy Stewart, Jean Arthur, Claude Rains, and Edward Arnold are playing a dramatic scene. First, we take a "master shot" of the complete scene; it includes all four actors. In a way, this master shot is a micro-play. Next we usually take individual close-ups of each performer replaying the scene—to punch up dramatic high spots in the little play.

Now read carefully and you will understand why the standard procedure for shooting close-ups is for the dodo birds. Let us place Jean Arthur about seven feet in front of the camera. She will be surrounded with lights; her movements are restricted because at close range the lens focus is critical. Black "ears" with white chalk marks on one or both sides of the camera will fix her looks geographically toward where the other actors were in the master shot.

Technical details approved, Jimmy Stewart, Claude Rains, and Edward Arnold are called in to stand or loll behind the lights and feed their off-stage lines to Jean Arthur. But important actors are too busy, too tired, or too bored to accept this mechanical drudgery. So bit actors or stand-ins read the off-stage lines. At times, the script girl may monotonously read *all* the feed lines.

And what do the close camera, the chalk marks, the strange voice mechanically reading cues, do for poor Jean Arthur? Nothing but make it almost impossible for her to exactly match the mood, tempo, tension, and the voice pitch she used in the master shot—that was taken hours, or even days, ago. The usual result: When her close-up is cut into the master shot, it is a badly shaped jigsaw piece that won't fit into the puzzle. The result in theaters: Audiences are jarred by her uneven performance.

So, when I "invented" a way to surround Jean Arthur in her close-up with the exact reality that had surrounded her in the master shot, I thought it was the best thing that had happened to the close-up since D. W. Griffith invented it.

What did I do that was so great? I used the actual *sound track* of the *master shot* to feed Jean Arthur the off-stage lines for her close-up. The sound of the master shot was recorded not only on film, but *on a record* as well. When the master shot was approved, the sound department rushed the record back to the set and put it on a playback machine. Attached to my chair were a volume-control dial and a push button with which I could cut in or cut out the playback's loudspeaker at will.

Now back to Jean Arthur's close-up. No actors, stand-ins, or script girls mouthing insipid feed lines. Just Jean Arthur and the playback. Rehearsal. I let the playback play continuously. Whatever Jean Arthur said in the master shot's playback, she'd mouth in her close-up. This put her back into the mood of the master shot. Camera! Just before Jean spoke a close-up line, I'd cut off the playback. In between her lines I'd cut it back in, so she could react silently to what Jimmy Stewart, Claude Rains, and Edward Arnold were saying in the master shot. Result: Arthur's close-up fitted beautifully into the jigsaw puzzle.

The next time you see *Mr. Smith Goes to Washington*, observe how all the close-ups meld and flow with the longer shots as smoothly as if they were photographed simultaneously. In a sense, they were. It is too late to patent the idea now. Furthermore, since I've never heard of another director stealing the new, improved "Capra close-up" I doubt the royalties would have put me in Paul Getty's income bracket.

Jimmy Stewart had to be hoarse for the final hours of his filibuster. He found it difficult to fake hoarseness, particularly when called upon to project his voice from the back row of the Senate floor. We called in a throat doctor. "Doc, we know you can reduce hoarseness, but can you *in*duce it?" "That's a switch," he laughed. "Yes, I think I can."

Twice a day Jimmy's throat was swabbed with vile mercury solution that swelled and irritated his vocal cords. The result was astonishing. No amount of acting could possibly simulate Jimmy's intense pathetic efforts to speak through real swollen cords.

On another day we were filming a scene on the Vice President's rostrum. Suddenly the courtly, unflappable Jim Preston (our Washington technical adviser) leaped in front of the camera wildly waving his long arms. "Stop it! Stop everything, you'll have to throw it all away! I'll be the butt of all Washington!"

"Whoa, Jim! What's wrong?" I asked.

"What's wrong? The *clock* is wrong!" he shouted, pointing frantically at the big Senate clock over the rostrum. "It's my fault, all my fault! You can't *use* this film—I'll get the horselaugh in the Press Club. There's no *lock* on the clock!"

After calming him down he explained that recently a lock had been put on the clock to keep Senators from opening it up and advancing the clock hands—so they could adjourn in time to go to the ball game. And everybody in Washington knew about the senatorial dido.

To pacify Preston's fears, I promised to put on the missing lock and to take a close-up of it big enough to be seen from the top of the Washington Monument. "Shall we paint the lock red, Jim?" I asked with a straight face.

"No, no, no! It's a small brass lock, don't you *understand*?"

However, the real news about *Mr. Smith* was not made in the filming, but in the tragi-comic, nearly fatal—

One day in July, 1939, a letter came from Washington. It came while film editor Gene Havlick and I were comparing the last two preview tapes of *Mr. Smith*. What's a preview tape? Well, that was another superlative invention of mine that I also forgot to patent—mainly because it would have publicly exposed my recently acquired yellow streak. I hated to admit it, but the traumatic experience with our disastrous first preview of *Lost Horizon*—on that black Sunday night in Santa Barbara—had turned me into a driveling coward. In fact, after *Lost Horizon*, I never attended a single preview of my subsequent films. I'd have preferred being thrown into a cement mixer. And so, out of cowardice, came another brush with immortality.

To the first preview of my last film (*You Can't Take It with You*) I had sent a host of spies—while I stayed home and sweated. But no two of them

New way of shooting close-ups. No tired actors feeding her tired, off-stage lines. Arthur plays her close-up against the full impact of the "master shot's" sound track being played back for her.

Fierce debate between freshman Senator Smith and veteran "Silver Knight" is photographed simultaneously with three cameras—one camera on Jimmy Stewart, one on Claude Rains, a third on Harry Carey (Vice President).

reported back identical accounts of how the film went with the audience. In general, they agreed; but in details, they were at sixes and sevens.

Then it struck me—as it should have struck a ten-year-old mind: Persons with a stake in the success of a film lose their objectivity at a preview. Surrounded, as they are, by a subjective audience, they, too, become subjective. I was reminded of Mack Sennett's caveat to gag writers: "No 'think' gags. When the audience is thinking they can't be laughing." Evidently the reverse of this coin is also true: "When the audience is laughing they can't be thinking." My preview spies were laughing *audiences* rather than objective reporters.

But previews were trial runs to expose the "bugs," to collect reliable data for further film editing. But how to collect objective, recallable data? Selah! A tape recorder. *Tape* the preview. Record, simultaneously, both the sound from the screen and the sound from the audience.

That was it for me. Let Cohn take a hundred wise guys to the preview. I sent one man with a tape recorder. Then in the quiet of my office, away from the flushed-face hysteria of curbstone conferences, the tape told me the detailed story, foot by foot, scene by scene, of exactly what happened at the preview. Where the film was interest-grabbing, the audience was silent, hushed. Where it was dull or long, I heard coughs, shufflings, rattlings of peanut bags. The laughs—from giggles to guffaws—were measured exactly in length and volume. To our surprise some gags were funnier, others less funny, than expected. Some good lines were lost in the over-laughs. We picked up many added laughs by lengthening the film between gag lines. And so, like tailors tearing apart and rebuilding a coat to their chalk marks, we re-edited our film to the tape.

Another preview; another tape. Comparing the two, we assessed our corrections. For some unaccountable reason this scientific method of film editing did not spread through Hollywood like a prairie fire. In fact, it did not spread at all. In fact, they laughed at it. What executives would trade a rousing, shouting post-mortem preview party at Chasen's—where they "save" the film with hunch editing and champagne—for the cold logic of my little old tape recorder? And so again immortality passed me by.

Anyway, a very interesting letter came to me from Washington.

Scripps-Howard Newspaper Alliance
Washington, D.C.
July 7, 1939

Mr. Frank Capra
Columbia Pictures Corporation
1438 North Gower Street
Hollywood, California
Dear Mr. Capra:

As chairman of the entertainment committee of The National Press Club I am writing to ask if our Club could have the privilege of sponsoring here the premiere or preview showing of your new picture *Mr. Smith Goes to Washington.*

. . . Our idea would be to make the showing a kind of tribute to our beloved friend, "Jim" Preston . . .

We would plan to invite all the newspaper people of Washington, all members of Congress, and other notables in Official life. . . .

> Yours sincerely,
> Fred W. Perkins

My answer:

My dear Mr. Perkins:

Thanks for your kind and generous offer to sponsor *Mr. Smith Goes to Washington*. . . .

Will you forgive me if I delay giving you an answer for a few weeks until we see whether the damn thing is worth sponsoring?

Please hold your offer open, and accept my kindest regards.

> Sincerely yours,
> Frank Capra

Mr. Fred W. Perkins replied (on UNITED STATES SENATE Press Gallery stationery) that he would be glad to hold the offer open.

By mid-September our preview tapes told us *Mr. Smith* had been edited to fit hand-in-glove with audience reactions. Now for the always suspenseful press preview. Press appraisals would determine my answer to the National Press Club's request. Next day there was dancing in Columbia's non-ivy halls. The trade critics had flipped their adjectives:

Variety:
The most vital and stirring drama of contemporary American life yet told in films. It is screened with superlative artistry.

Dean Owen, *Billboard*:
The great American picture!

Edwin Schallert, Los Angeles *Times*:
Mr. Smith Goes to Washington and Frank Capra goes to town in probably the most hair-raising adventure along political, social and patriotic lines . . . ever conceived for the movies.

Hedda Hopper, Esquire Features, Inc.:
Not since Edison discovered motion pictures fifty years ago have we realized their possibilities until Frank Capra made *Mr. Smith Goes to Washington*. To me it is as great as Lincoln's Gettysburg speech.

I knew Mr. Lincoln's great heart would forgive Hedda's sacrilegious analogy as just another gushing show-biz blurb. And I also felt he might be pleased if the premiere showing of a film he had inspired would be held within sight of his memorial. So I urged Columbia's New York executives to honor the National Press Club's request, with this proviso: The Press Club's officers must view the film *before* they accepted sponsorship.

On October 3, 1939, the Press Club's entertainment chairman, Fred Perkins, accompanied by Club president Arthur Hachten and Walter King, correspondent of the Newark *Evening News*, arrived in New York. At 8:30 P.M. Columbia executives escorted them to a private preview of *Mr. Smith* at the Dyckman Street Theater in the Inwood section of New York City.

Enthusiastically, the Press Club delegation accepted full sponsorship and full responsibility for all the arrangements of the Washington premiere —invitations in the Club's name, protocol seating, entertainment, publicity, cocktail parties, the works.

Columbia executives gleefully rubbed their hands in anticipation: This would be Hollywood's most prestigious exploitation coup. In a few days those same hands would be wringing in agony.

October 16, 1939, was declared "Mr. Smith" day in Washington. Natives said nothing like it had hit the nation's Capital since the British sacked the White House. The day began with a formal dinner and cocktails given by the National Press Club in honor of their dear friend, Jim Preston, within the inner sanctum of the Club itself. Press guests came from as far away as Boston. In celebration of the momentous occasion the exclusive Club declared a social amnesty—for the first time in its history it allowed women to pass through its sacred portals.

A military band played rousing patriotic marches; then the Press Club's glee club sang nostalgic songs. My wife and I sat at the head table with Jim Preston, the Club's officers, and prominent guests. For some reason or other, "Happy" Chandler, ex-Governor of Kentucky, also sat with us— hoping he'd be called on to sing "My Old Kentucky Home."

Then came the speeches. First, about the grand premiere that night of *Mr. Smith Goes to Washington* at the D.A.R.'s Constitution Hall; that it would out-Hollywood Hollywood; that half of Washington would be there, and the other half was clamoring for tickets; that the Washington *Times Herald* was printing a special National Press Club edition, giving over its front page to the showing of *Mr. Smith.*

And finally, speeches and toasts to Jim Preston by the pillars of the Press Club. When called upon, I paid my sincerest tribute to Jim, saying: "Without Mr. Preston, there could have been no *Mr. Smith.*"

And when the chairman introduced Jim Preston, the old boy got a standing ovation. "Chamberlain" Jim choked up a little as he thanked his news friends; said it was the crowning day of his forty years of service to the press and the Senate; said he hoped they would like *Mr. Smith* as much as he had liked working on it. Lu was misty-eyed, so was I, and so was the Washington press corps. "Mr. Smith" day had begun with a love feast.

Later, Press Club president Arthur Hachten and Mrs. Hachten called for Lu and me at the Willard Hotel to take us to Constitution Hall in their limousine. It seemed as if every limousine in town, filled with correctly groomed officials and their gorgeously gowned wives, was headed for Constitution Hall. "How do you feel, Frank?" asked Arthur Hachten, grinning from ear to ear. "I'm having a beautiful dream, Arthur. Don't wake me up."

And it was a great dream come true. How I wished Papa could have lived to see the day when America's leaders would honor the work of his youngest son. I grinned and grinned, blew my nose, and took surreptitious handkerchief swipes at my eyes. There they were—army searchlights; their beams playing tag among the low-scudding clouds. Constitution Hall was a fairy palace of splendor. A Marine band belted out the pulse-stirring strains of "Halls of Montezuma"; huge throngs of roped-off bystanders cheered their favorite government dignitaries as they stepped out of their low-license-numbered official cars. How Sid Grauman would have envied the pomp and pageantry of this opening night.

Inside, the great Hall glittered with all the opulence of a new season's opening at the Met. Supreme Court Justices, Cabinet officers, Senators, Congressmen, generals, pundits, and Georgetown's social aristocracy—four thousand in all—buzzed, chatted, and waved at each other. Mr. and Mrs. Arthur Hachten escorted us to a center box in the rear. They introduced us to Senator and Mrs. Burton K. Wheeler and their teen-aged daughter. Mr. Smith, in the film, allegedly came from Montana, so it was thought fitting that Montana's Senator Wheeler should sit in the official box with us.

A short distance away I spotted Columbia's box, occupied by Harry Cohn, his brother, Jack Cohn, sales head Joe Brandt, and their New York guest James Farley. Harry Cohn's group was as boggle-eyed as I was. Harry caught my eye, raised his hands palm upward, and gave me an astonished shrug, which meant: "Can you beat this?"

When the lights dimmed a spotlight hit our box. Mr. Hachten nudged me to stand up. There was a thunderous applause. Good Lord. I stood up, took a bow, and sat down. Columbia's Torch Lady flashed on the screen. Another thunderous applause at the title: "Frank Capra's *Mr. Smith Goes to Washington*." I crossed all my fingers and prayed a little that nothing would go wrong.

I hadn't prayed hard enough. About twenty minutes into the film, during an early scene between Jimmy Stewart and Jean Arthur, their voices abruptly changed into machine-gun fire. I knew exactly what had happened: The film had jumped a sprocket wheel, the sound track had shifted sideways, and the sound pick-up was broadcasting the running sprocket holes.

I leaped out of the box and ran for the projection room. "Upstairs!" pointed the ushers. I ran up to the balcony. "On the roof!" said the ushers, pointing to a ladder. I raced up the ladder, emerged on the roof. The night was black, a fine rain was falling. I spotted the eerie glow of the projection booth. It had been built on the ancient curved roof as an afterthought. A catwalk led to it, under a maze of overhead ventilators. In my haste I banged my head on a steel pipe. Down I crumbled on the catwalk. When the stars stopped whirling I made it to the projection booth, flung open its door. The startled projectionist resented my intrusion. "Keep your shirt on, Mac," he rasped, "I got it, I got it."

Faintly, I heard Jimmy Stewart and Jean Arthur speaking normally again. I apologized and turned back. My head throbbed with pain. There was a lump on my noggin the size of an egg. Blood trickled down behind my right ear. I sat down on the wet catwalk, swabbed my head with a handkerchief dipped in puddled rainwater. The distant Washington Monument and Lincoln Memorial glowed fuzzily in the drizzle. A strange business, making movies. But the strangeness had just begun.

It was a soggy, rumpled mess of a film director that crawled back to his box. "Where've you been?" whispered Lu anxiously. "What's that on your collar?" "Nothing. I hit my head on a pipe." "Oh, Frank!"

The ominous signs that strike terror into the hearts of filmmakers—whispering and fidgeting—became evident about two-thirds of the way into the picture. Walk-outs would confirm the omens. There was the first one—a couple rose, headed for the exit, the man making thumbs down motions with his hand. Another twosome followed suit, then a foursome. The scaffold was being erected—and I had a box seat.

When Jimmy Stewart started filibustering, the whispering swelled into a provoked buzz. To me it was the rolling of distant tumbrils. Mrs. Wheeler and her daughter withered us with hostile glances, then whispered into Senator Wheeler's ear. Arthur Hachten, chief sponsor of the film, dropped his twisted program, ran a finger around the inside of his wilted collar as he watched his guests move like picket lines toward the exits—flaunting furs instead of placards. Flying words, such as "Outrage!" "Insult!" must have zinged into him like ice-tipped arrows. My wife, Lu? As a descendant of Lord Nelson she, too, could stand on her bridge and say to the world: "Victory, or Westminster Abbey!" As for me, when doom looms for certain, only the trifling irritates—the swelling bump on my head was growing a point; would I look like Zip, the missing link?

By the time *Mr. Smith* sputtered to the end music, about one-third of Washington's finest had left. Of those who remained, some applauded, some laughed, but most pressed grimly for the doors. The Wheeler family, having courteously stuck it out, now rose and huffily left our box; but not before Senator Wheeler had thrown me a polite, but curt, over-the-shoulder "Good evening." He was not amused.

I looked for Harry Cohn's party. Their box was empty. Lu and I sat alone and exchanged wry grins. Then we mixed in with the exiting tail-enders, hoping to sneak off to the nearest bar without being noticed.

Outside, newsboys hawked the National Press Club "Special Edition" of the Washington *Times Herald*. The full-page banner headline: "4,000 WELCOME 'MR. SMITH' TO WASHINGTON." Beneath the headline a panoramic photo of the Constitution Hall audience stretched across the whole front page; beneath that was a three-column photo of Mr. and Mrs. Arthur

Hachten entering the Hall with Mr. and Mrs. Frank Capra. Luckily no photographer was there to catch Mr. and Mrs. Capra trying to sneak off through the crowd coming *out* of the Hall.

But it wasn't to be. The bizarre day had to be played out to its fantastic end. A Press Club official caught up with us. "Mr. Capra, you're expected at the Press Club's victory party. You know—supper and cocktails. Mr. Hachten asked me to pick you up—"

And sitting in the back of one of the Press Club's restaurant-bar booths, with my good wife next to me, I took the worst shellacking of my professional life. Shifts of hopping-mad Washington press correspondents belittled, berated, scorned, vilified, and ripped me open from stem to stern as a villainous Hollywood traducer. For—much to my surprise—I was accused of double-sinning in *Mr. Smith.* Sin number one was just a mortal sin: showing that graft could raise its ugly head in the august Senate chamber. But sin number two: depicting one of their own Press Club members as being too fond of the juice of the grape—Well! That was *heresy*; punishable by being burned at the stake in the fires of their wrath.

It didn't make sense. The average reporter I knew would have laughed at himself under the circumstances. But these gentlemen were not average reporters. They were demi-gods, "byliners," opinion makers. What they wrote was instantly printed in hundreds of newspapers at home and abroad. They not only influenced government policy; at times, they made it. They were the real "power" of the press before whom Senators—even Presidents—quailed. Their irrational attack on *Mr. Smith* was not an attack against entertainment, or against me personally. It was an attack against a new, perhaps superior, power invading their empire—"film power."

They could make or break Senators, they could influence elections, they could expose graft in high places. But let Hollywood dare to suggest that one Senator was a trained seal for a political machine, or dare to publicly depict one of their own Washington press corps as something less than a paragon of virtue and wisdom, and Hollywood would suffer the full fury of their majestic rancor.

Clearly, the National Press Club envied and feared film as a rival opinion maker. Clearly, they detested *Mr. Smith Goes to Washington* because it was the first important film to muscle in on their private Washington preserves. Clearly, their own officials had been tricked into sponsoring a Trojan horse. So resentful were those Olympian cuff-shooters that they could take this hypocritical stance: Holding a Martini in angry fingers, they looked me right in the eye and said, "There isn't one Washington correspondent in this room that drinks on duty, or off duty!"

My wife was the first to lose her cool. "*Mr. Smith*'s a great picture, Frank. Don't take any more insults." "I won't, hon." But hemmed into the back of the booth, my only way out was to start swinging and hope I could bloody a Press Club nose or two before they carried me out.

Fortunately, sympathetic friends came to our rescue. Most of New York's

Times Herald gives *Mr. Smith* an unprecedented front page welcome. It was printed just before film was shown.

Mr. and Mrs. Hachten and Lu and I sit in box with Senator Wheeler from Montana and his wife and daughter (left). The film infuriated them.

Vice President Barkley to Speaker Rayburn: "A gross distortion, Sam—"

Many famous Washington columnists ask for my autograph—that is, *before* they saw *Mr. Smith*. Afterward they ran me out of town.

important film critics had been invited as guests. Sensing an ugly scene, Frank Nugent (*Times*), Howard Barnes (*Herald Tribune*), Eileen Creelman (*Sun*), and I think Archer Winston (*Post*) and Bill Boehnel (*World-Telegram*), slipped into our booth and set up a shock-absorbing barrier. All had written reviews lauding *Mr. Smith* as one of the year's most impressive films. Now two proud disciplines of the fourth estate—art and politics—stoutly argued the merits of *Mr. Smith*.

The crazy scene had to end with an unexpected topper—one which I couldn't have cooked up in my wildest days as a gag man. Our attention was arrested by a clamorous voice, loud enough to be heard over the tumult. It came from the direction of the two-deep bar.

"Where's that Hollywood jerk! Where is he?" roared a distinguished, well-dressed, gray-haired gentleman—now a disheveled drunken gentleman. He was fighting off restraining hands. "No! The hell with you. I want to meet the son-of-a-bitch that made that goddam picture. Where is he?" Someone pointed to our booth. Someone else whispered he was the editor of a Washington daily. Mr. Editor fixed glassy eyes on our booth, tore away from his friends, stumbled and zigzagged to our table, and grabbed it with both hands to keep from falling.

"Oh, there you are, you Hollywood jerk!" he snarled. "Where do you get off telling the world that all reporters are drunken bums? I'm gonna bust you—" He made a wild pass with a hand and sprawled flat on his face on the table, sending drinks and flying glass all over us. Friends straightened him up and pulled him away. But he kept on shouting: "I want that two-bit movie punk barred from every press club in the country. I want all the officers of National Press Club *fired*—for sponsoring that piece of shit! Fifty years, they've set us back. Fifty years—"

In the uproar Lu and I made our way to the elevator; then ran like fugitives to the Willard Hotel. What a daffy day. At dinner we had been toasted, honored, and welcomed by the National Press Club. At midnight we had been roasted, dishonored, and given the bum's rush by the same club. There is no dizziness like show dizziness.

The afterclap of that Constitution Hall showing was to rock Hollywood, rile Congress into punitive legislation, shake up the State Department, agonize our American Embassy in London, and precipitate arguments about patriotism that were to fill columns and editorial pages for some time to come.

There are two freedoms that have created more headaches for the Supreme Court than all others put together—freedom to enforce freedom; and freedom to flout it, or advocate its destruction.

The import about *Mr. Smith* was not its box-office or artistic success. (The *Hollywood Reporter*'s annual Critic's Poll reported that the nation's film critics had voted 10 to 1 for *Mr. Smith* in the following categories:

Best Picture, Best Directing, Best Writing, Best Acting, Best Photography, and Best Musical Score.) The significance was the unprecedented number (in the hundreds) of editorials and columns which blasted or praised the film as a service or disservice to our American ideals of democracy.

But lèt America's press voice its own opinions. First, an interview with Senator Alben W. Barkley:

> The *Christian Science Monitor*
> By Richard L. Strout
> Washington, October 27, 1939
>
> In the midst of his cares as Majority Leader piloting the neutrality debate through Congress, Senator Alben W. Barkley (D) of Kentucky stopped long enough in a corridor of the Senate to express his views forcibly and at length about *Mr. Smith Goes to Washington*. . . . He declared he spoke not only for himself but for the entire Senate in his condemnation. The picture, he declared, was a "grotesque distortion" of the way the Senate is run. . . . "As grotesque as anything I have ever seen! Imagine the Vice President of the United States winking at a pretty girl in the gallery in order to encourage a filibuster! Can you visualize Jack Garner winking up at Hedy Lamarr in order to egg her on?"

Other correspondents tried to turn attention to the neutrality debate, but Senator Barkley was not to be distracted. He continued: . . .

> . . . "And it showed the Senate as the biggest aggregation of nincompoops on record! At one place the picture shows the Senators walking out on Mr. Smith as a body when he is attacked by a corrupt member. The very idea of the Senate walking out at the behest of that old crook! It was so grotesque it was funny. It showed the Senate made up of crooks, led by crooks, listening to a crook . . . It was so vicious an idea it was a source of disgust and hilarity to every member of Congress who saw it."
>
> "Didn't some of the members praise it?" asked the reporter.
>
> "I did not hear a single Senator praise it," said Senator Barkley. "I speak for the whole body. The vote was 96 to 0—and no filibuster."
>
> Senator Barkley's statements seemed to be echoed through Congress.
>
> He declared that Senator Burton K. Wheeler (D) of Montana, who shared Mr. Capra's box at the premiere, felt as he did.
>
> Senator James F. Byrnes (D) of South Carolina called the picture "outrageous . . . exactly the kind of picture that dictators of totalitarian governments would like to have their subjects believe exists in a democracy. . . ."

Detroit *News*
October 31, 1939
Solons Lick Wounds Left by *Mr. Smith*
Fearful Studios Look for a Legislative Reprisal
By Harold Heffernan

More fire than smoke flares behind the scenes of *Mr. Smith Goes to Washington* . . . Insiders here look for an early and smashing retaliation. Passing of the Neely anti-block booking bill, a back-crusher to the present distributing set-up of the film business, is predicted for early January . . .

Philadelphia, Pa., *Inquirer*
By John M. Cummings

. . . Now and again you hear it said that foreign countries interpret life in America from what they see in American-made pictures. They're going to get a fine idea of the United States Senate when they take a squint at *Mr. Smith Goes to Washington*. They're going to get the idea that we reach into jails for our Senators and into the insane asylum for our reformers. . . .

Pete Harrison, the respected publisher of *Harrison's Reports* was exhorting exhibitors to urge their Congressmen to pass legislation that would permit theater owners to refuse to play films that were "not in the best interests of our country"—meaning, of course, *Mr. Smith*.

Jimmy Fidler, a well-known Hollywood radio commentator, broadcast the startling announcement (from reliable sources) that the "big producing companies were offering Columbia $2,000,000—as reimbursement for film costs—if Columbia would withdraw *Mr. Smith* from circulation. Purpose of the two million offer was an appeasement gesture to Congress, lest it inflict punitive legislation on the industry."

It is important to note that *Mr. Smith* opened in October, 1939, a few weeks after all hell had broken out in Europe. On September 1, Hitler had invaded Poland; two days later England and France declared war on Germany. On September 17, Soviet Russia raced into Poland to claim its half of the carcass. In less than a month Hitler destroyed the Polish armies, bombed Warsaw into rubble. Poland was obliterated. The speed and might of Hitler's blitzkrieg terrified the free world. German subs prowled the high seas, sank ships without warning. Hitler screamed the supremacy of his Herrenvolk, scorned the decadence of democracies, laughed at our soldiers maneuvering with wooden machine guns, our air corps dropping flour sacks instead of bombs.

Our nation was divided between those who urged, "Join the fight against the Nazis!" and those who exhorted, "Stay the hell out of Europe!"

And in the midst of this chaos a young idealist comes on to our screens to put up a one-man fight, not against Hitler or his Panzers or his superman theory, but against corruption in our own high places. Again we are divided. Some say, "Jeff Smith is a subversive idiot; he's proving Hitler right." Others, "Jeff Smith is a patriot. He's showing us we have something dear and precious to fight for."

Columbia executives were on the horns of a dilemma. *Mr. Smith* was gold in the box office, but gall in the industry. The big producing companies feared punitive laws; the pressures mounted. Then came a crusher with the clout of authority.

I was called to Harry Cohn's office. He was pale as he handed me a very long cablegram, stamped "urgent and confidential." After reading it, I was paler than Cohn. The cable was from Joseph P. Kennedy, the American Ambassador in London.

In it he said that he had viewed *Mr. Smith Goes to Washington*; that he had been dismayed; that it ridiculed democracy; that it would be a blow to the morale of our allies; that it would do untold harm to America's prestige in Europe; that it might be construed as propaganda favoring the Axis powers. Therefore he earnestly and urgently requested Columbia Pictures Corporation to immediately withdraw the film from European distribution and exhibition. . . .

I have not been able to find a copy of that cable, so I am relying on my memory. I am not certain, but I think he also mentioned no publicity and that copies of the cable had also been sent to the White House, State Department, and the Will Hays office.

Harry Cohn paced the floor, as stunned as Abraham must have been when the Lord asked him to sacrifice his beloved son Isaac. It was some time before I could advise Cohn not to panic. "Harry, no ambassador has the right to censor films. Besides, he's mistaken. I *know* he is. Even if the Pope sent that cable I'd still say that we are what we are, and Mr. Smith is what he is —a shot in the arm for all the Joes in the world that resent being bought and sold and pushed around by all the Hitlers in the world."

"Oh, great! Speeches he gives me."

"Yes, speeches. Why the hell is it that once they get a political job, smart guys like Joe Kennedy stop trusting the people? Why do they try to sweep freedom under a rug? Don't they know that America is the envy and the hope of Europeans, Asians, and all the other kicked-around people, *because* we can make "Mr. Smiths" and show them to the ordinary citizens? Don't they realize that that's why the dictators hate us most of all?"

"All right, already! How do we answer this? I can't duck it."

"*You* don't answer, Harry. Let public opinion answer. Let the voice of the people tell the Ambassador he's mistaken . . ."

It took us a day or two, but we assembled a sheaf of hundreds of opinions, editorials, and comments—including a few Canadian and British responses to the idealism of Jefferson Smith, and airmailed them to Ambassador Kennedy in London.

Here are some random samples:

Kansas City *Journal*:

. . . The bewildered young Senator Smith symbolizes those figures who arise occasionally to challenge the dragons. Those they would dethrone brand them as radicals and eccentrics and seek to discredit their motives. There is a distressing amount of evidence that without them, there would be government of, by, and for boodlers.

Pittsburgh *Press*:
By Florence Fisher Parry

. . . The Freedom of the Press has used its liberties to the hilt in printed denunciations which would make *Mr. Smith Goes to Washington* taste like orange juice to arsenic . . . Let him go again and again, say I, and rip the Capitol Dome wide open, if it gives us pictures like this latest of Frank Capra. . . .

Cincinnati *Post*:

The high privilege of being an American citizen finds its best and most effective expression in *Mr. Smith Goes to Washington*.

Time:

. . . Its real hero is not calfy Jeff Smith, but the things he believes, as embodied in the hero of U.S. Democracy's first crisis, Abraham Lincoln. Its big moment is . . . when Jefferson Smith stands gawking in the Lincoln Memorial, listening to a small boy read from a tablet the question with which this film faces everyone who sees it: "Whether that nation or any nation so conceived and so dedicated can long endure."

The National Board of Review, October 20, 1939:
By the Committee on Exceptional Photoplays

Never before has he [Capra] touched upon anything closer to what Americans should take a vital interest in than this story of the adventures of Mr. Ordinary Citizen in the legislative halls of the nation. . . .

Los Angeles *Times*:
By Philip Scheuer

It says all the things about America that have been crying out to be said again—and says them beautifully. . . .

Spokane, Washington, *Spokesman Review*:
By M. B.

. . . For the first time the screen has become eloquent in relation to the significance of our times.

Cleveland *Plain Dealer*:
By W. Ward Marsh

. . . Best of all, it deals with "us," with our "lives," with "our form of government"; it is exciting, patriotic, and hard-hitting all the way through . . . Time after time Mr. Capra stresses that only in America could one man fight this lone battle and win. . . .

New York *Daily Mirror*—Editorial Page:

There is a great movie at the Radio City Music Hall . . . *Mr. Smith Goes to Washington* . . . That respect for the traditions of democracy, that persistent overtone of the spirit that fired every great American in history, is not present in this movie by accident. One man is responsible. . . .

Frank Capra does with a movie what Sinclair Lewis does with books, what Arthur Brisbane did with a column, what Will Rogers did with his wit. He "holds the mirror" up to America . . . [His] achievement in translating America onto film is all the more remarkable, because . . . he was born in Sicily.

Let his simple devotion to America be an example to the Browders and the Kuhns.

London *Observer*:
By C. A. Lejeune

. . . Mr. Smith presents one of those dazzling simple revelations of human values in which Mr. Capra excels. His creed has always been, blessed are the meek for they shall inherit the earth. Homely kindness, shy good sense, and just a touch of dogged reverence, are always for him the panoply of heroes. Chesterton's little Father Brown could have walked and talked with such men, and shared their silences, and loved them. . . .

Glasgow *Herald*:

. . . hits the European world of today with a breath of refreshing west wind. . . .

London *Daily Herald*:
By H. Swaffer

". . . Frank Capra attacks democracy," I saw one critic wrote . . . The truth is that democracy can stand any attack upon its weaknesses. . . .

Irish *Times*:

. . . One weapon remained to him, to go on speaking . . . And there he stands, reads, talks for nearly two rounds of the clock, to vindicate himself. And, as the radio commentator says—to vindicate democracy.

I could not wish a better theme. . . .

How did Ambassador Kennedy respond to this outpouring of praise from Vox Populi? He was somewhat mollified, but still dubious. His concern— expressed in the following letter to Harry Cohn—was, and still is, the concern of many other thoughtful Americans about the inherent power of the American film.

EMBASSY OF THE
UNITED STATES OF AMERICA

London, November 17, 1939

Dear Mr. Cohn:

. . . I am afraid that we are looking at [*Mr. Smith*] from different eyes. I haven't the slightest doubt that the picture will be successful in America and I have no doubt that, financially, it will be successful here and will give great pleasure to people who see it. It is my belief, however, that . . . it will give an idea of our political life that will do us harm. . . .

. . . For instance, today I am disgusted, in reading all the English papers, to see Al Capone's release from the penitentiary receives front page notice, while only one paper gives an obituary notice concerning a man who has given many years of his life to service in the Supreme Court of our land—Mr. Justice Butler . . . it is amazing, the impression they have about our Country being run by gangsters and crooked politicians.

. . . I have a high regard for Mr. Capra . . . but his fine work makes the indictment of our government all the more damning to foreign audiences . . . I feel that to show this film in foreign countries will do inestimable harm to American prestige all over the world.

I regret exceedingly that I find it necessary to say these things . . . The fact remains, however, that pictures from the United States are the greatest influence on foreign public opinion of the American mode of life. The times are precarious, the future is dark at best. We must be more careful.

Sincerely yours,
(signed) Joseph P. Kennedy

Three years later—in direct contradiction to Ambassador Kennedy's concern about American prestige, to angry blasts from Senators, and to vilifying screeds by National Press Club pundits—my wife sent me (I was in the army) this heart-warming report which made it all worth while:

The Hollywood Reporter, November 4, 1942

Last Cheers of French Audience for *Smith Goes to Washington*

Frank Capra's *Mr. Smith Goes to Washington*, chosen by French theaters as the final English-language film to be shown before the recent Nazi-ordered countrywide ban on American and British films went into effect, was roundly cheered . . .

Full text of the report, dated Berne, October 22, reads: "Some idea of the deep disappointment with which Frenchmen received the news of the recent ban of all English and American films throughout their country is given in a private and presumably uncensored dispatch to the *Basler Nachrichten* today from the unoccupied zone.

"When the ban became known," the *Nachrichten*'s correspondent reveals, "the French people flocked to the cinemas to get seats for the last showing of an American film. In many provincial theatres Frank Capra's *Mr. Smith Goes to Washington*, in the original English version, was chosen for the occasion and a special farewell gala performance was staged."

Storms of spontaneous applause broke out at the sequence when, under the Abraham Lincoln monument in the capital, the word "Liberty" appeared on the screen and the Stars and Stripes began fluttering over the head of the great Emancipator in the cause of liberty.

Similarly cheers and acclamation punctuated the famous speech of the young senator on man's rights and dignity. "It was," writes the *Nachrichten*'s correspondent, "as though the joys, suffering, love and hatred, the hopes and wishes of an entire people who value freedom above everything, found expression for the last time . . ."

Amplifying on this defiance of Nazi oppression, the Army News Service sent me word that one theater in a French village in the Vosges Mountains played *Mr. Smith* continuously during the last thirty days before the ban.

No indeed, Mr. Senators, Ambassadors, and other public officials—as *Mr. Smith* said: "Liberty is too precious to get buried in books. Men ought to hold it up in front of them—even on the screen—every day of their lives, and say, 'I am free—to think—to speak. My ancestors couldn't. I can. My children will.' "

Five Endings in Search of an Audience

Mr. Smith ENDED MY CONTRACT with Cohn and Columbia. It was time to leave. David O. Selznick offered me office space at his Selznick-International studios in Culver City. I accepted and moved out.

Thirteen years before I had entered Columbia's Poverty Row doors as a bitter, discouraged run-of-the-mill Sennett gag man. Now I was leaving Columbia's major studio doors as Hollywood's acclaimed number one film-maker. My first year's salary at Columbia—for producing, writing, and directing five feature-length films—was under ten thousand dollars. My last year's salary (plus percentage profits) was over three hundred thousand dollars for making *one* film. Time to strike out on my own. But I needed a partner—a gambling, sympatico, creative spirit—to join me in my independent film company. Robert Riskin was a natural. But he was off making a name for himself with Sam Goldwyn.

Before making a move I don't consult astrologers, fortune tellers, or Ouija boards. And yet, as I have noted before, whatever happens to me seems to happen for the best. The rose-tinted glasses of a super-optimist could be one explanation—"Ill wind" . . . "Silver lining" . . . "Bright side" . . . ad nauseum. Another, the rationalizing of a super-ego; unwilling to admit defeat. When you're a combination of both, you say, "It always happens for the best"—implying you are the pet protégé of some benign mystic power.

Whatever it is, I recommend it highly; for when I approached Bob Riskin about a partnership, I expected a turn down. But no. He agreed, joyfully. Even though, as the major stockholder, my word would be final. Creatively, as well as socially, there was a psychological affinity between Riskin and me, an afflatus that quickened creative impulses, stirred up wavelets of sympatico ideas that reinforced each other's crests rather than canceled them out.

And so, in August, 1939, the State of California issued incorporation papers to Frank Capra Productions, Inc. (F.C.P.). Riskin owned one-third of the stock, I owned two-thirds. Expenses and initial investments were shared proportionately. My long cherished dream—in business for myself —was a legal reality. "Good luck!" messages poured in; some sent rabbit feet. Harry Cohn was a hold-out. His telegram: "You'll be back."

The team of Capra-Riskin was a one-two punch with negotiating power. Offers from major studios came fast—financing, profit-splitting, three-picture deals; six-, ten-picture propositions. The most tantalizing proposals came from the prominent independents. Samuel Goldwyn wanted the Capra and Goldwyn companies to join up with Howard Hughes in a new produc-tion-distribution set-up. David O. Selznick proposed a similar combine: Selznick-Hughes-Capra. But neither Riskin nor I wanted any part of long-term contracts again. What we demanded were one-picture-at-a-time arrangements, first come first served, with any major distributing outlet, and no profit-splitting or outside approvals of subject, cast, or budget. These were hard terms. The offers cooled off.

But there was one nonconforming, irrepressible spirit among the studio heads—Jack Warner. Jack was a jokester, a self-confessed wit who was loved and laughed at more for his garrulous non-wit. But beneath his "jokes" Jack Warner ran a taut, well-disciplined major studio. The first to introduce sound, the frère Warners were among the first to develop a stable of great stars, including Bette Davis, Humphrey Bogart, Edward G. Robin-son, James Cagney, Olivia de Havilland, Errol Flynn, Paul Muni, Ronald Reagan, Kay Francis, Ann Sheridan, Jane Wyman, and Rudy Vallee.

By reputation, Jack Warner was a martinet, not noted for giving aid and succor to independent mavericks. Hence, eyebrows raised all over town when Jack offered us a one-picture proposition on terms far better than any previously imagined. In essence, this was the deal: Warner Brothers would advance all costs for production, prints, and advertising and—providing Capra and Riskin donated their time and invested one hundred thousand dollars in cash—Frank Capra Productions would own the film—and *all the profits!* Only Seward made a better deal when he bought Alaska. It had to be one of Jack Warner's unpredictable whims. Perhaps he wanted to find out if there really was a Frank Capra, and if there was, he wanted to see how he made pictures. Oh, I forgot his most important concession: He asked for no approval of story, budget, or cast. Riskin and I swallowed, blinked, and asked Jack Warner, "Where's the pen?"

And what film story would we choose for our first independent produc-tion? We toyed with Rostand's *Cyrano de Bergerac* and with the *Life of Shakespeare.* I say toyed, because I had raced my motor many times before about filming some costumed, historical classic, but when time came to put it in gear my instinct said: "Whoa! Charlie. Contemporary Americana is your blue-plate special."

Well, up popped a story as American as baseball. One day in November, 1939, while sitting in my office in David Selznick's Culver City studio (two months before our deal with Warners), a writer friend, Robert Presnell, walked in with a long treatment he had written with Richard Connell. They called it *The Life and Death of John Doe*. I read it. A bell rang. Riskin read it. A carillon chimed. We bought it before Presnell left the office.

In a matter of days, Riskin and I headed for the desert and lucky La Quinta where the muses were kind and mockingbirds and linnets darted in and out of smoke trees and flowering bougainvillea. Lu came along with little Lulu; Frankie remained in school at the Urban Military Academy. But Riskin was alone—still the most eligible bachelor in Hollywood; his recent romance with wonder-gal Carole Lombard had phffft! as W. W. would say.

Outside our red-tiled adobe bungalow, sitting in shorts, at card tables strewn with yellow pads, Bob and I hammered out scene after scene. Enthusiasm bubbled; ideas outraced pencils. Each new film was a new Arabian Nights adventure. Each evoked its own moments of hot excitement.

In one of those moments I said to Riskin: "For all the tea in China, Bob—this'll be the greatest film we ever made."

"Down, boy, down!" he laughed. "We haven't got a finish yet."

"We'll find a finish. And when we do, a few highbrow critics are going to eat under-done crow."

"Oh, oh. Now I'm worried," said Riskin. He hummed Cole Porter's "I've Got You Under My Skin."

Were critics getting under my skin? Well, let us say that because I had not come into films via the footlights I had no preconditioned reverence for the elegant cognoscenti. In fact, I thought they were getting by with murder.

In the United States a newspaper is a private enterprise in a free country. So is a restaurant, department store, Ford agency, or theater. Each sells a specific commodity to the public. Now let's take New York City. What metropolitan daily dares run a daily column which tells its readers: "Stay away from the Twenty-One Club, the food is lousy," or "Macy's dresses shrink in the rain," or "the new Ford is a pile of junk?" None.

But just seven drama critics can close a theater on opening night if a majority of them publicly print thumbs-down ukases which state, in effect: "The new show at the Winter Garden stinks. Save your money."

Later in life I became a fishing pal of Harold Ross, publisher of *The New Yorker* Magazine. "Harold," I asked him, sitting around a fire, "why do you hate Hollywood?"

"I don't hate Hollywood. But who reads our magazine? Mostly the horsy set of the East. It tickles their vanity to read that your Hollywood heroes are really spavined bums."

"Harold, how would you like it if I had an actor, on the screen, pick up your magazine in a dentist's office then throw it in the waste basket, saying: 'That's the crummiest magazine I ever read?' "

He laughed merrily. "I'd probably sue the hell out of you. But go ahead and do it, and I'll print why you did it."

Did I ever shoot the scene? No. I realized that if there were no critics, show business would have to create them. For the manic outbursts of squealing joy or tearful despondency with which we "read our notices," are the very heart of the mystique of the theater. We caress the notices, save them, press them in clipping files, to read them later to our children in pathetic attempts to impress them that we, too, were once somebody.

No, it wasn't the existence of critics that really riled me. It was their supercilious attitude that got under my skin. I had made seven smash hits in a row. Had I performed that feat on Broadway I would have been canonized. Shubert Alley would have been renamed Via Capra. As it was, not one of my last three films—*Lost Horizon, You Can't Take It with You,* and *Mr. Smith Goes to Washington*—had made the New York Critics Annual Poll of their selected "ten best" films.

So I can truthfully say that it was the box-office customers who made Frank Capra whatever he was or is. I was not invited into motion pictures, nor did I enjoy special favor of finance, nepotism, or critical influence. I simply did my thing with films and the people responded.

And yet, and yet—an ego like mine needed—nay, required—the plaudits of sophisticated criticism. Childlike, creativity thirsts for the heady wine of the connoisseur's acclaim. The "Capra-corn" barbs had pierced the outer blubber.

And so, *Meet John Doe,* my first completely independent film venture, was *aimed* at winning critical praises.

Hitler's strong-arm success against democracy was catching. Little "führers" were springing up in America, to proclaim that freedom was weak, sterile, passé. The "new wave" was Blood Power! Destroy the weak, the Jews, the blacks; destroy Christianity and its old-hat commandment "Love thy neighbor." Arriba the Herrenvolk!

Riskin and I would astonish the critics with contemporary realities: the ugly face of hate; the power of uniformed bigots in red, white, and blue shirts; the agony of disillusionment, and the wild dark passions of mobs. We would give them a brutal story that would make Ben Hecht sound like Edgar Guest.

Becoming president of my own company meant shedding some extracurricular jobs. The presidency of the Academy took the most time. In December, 1940, I announced my retirement and called for the election of a new Board, the first administration change in five years. The new Board chose Walter Wanger for the Academy's new president. Wanger was an ivy leaguer, a producer of tony films; he had class, savvy; wore a white carnation in his buttonhole.

My last Academy actions before retiring as president were to appoint Darryl Zanuck head of the Academy Research Council (a group of volunteer technicians doing basic research for the whole industry), open up all categories of Academy Awards to foreign films made in the English language, and produce the first Academy promotional film—a thirty-one-minute theatrical short, *The Cavalcade of Academy Awards.*

Walter Wanger took over the upcoming Awards dinner with a bang by inducing President Roosevelt to address the banquet from the White House. After chairing five Awards dinners from the rostrum, I would again be sitting with my wife and friends in the audience—sweating it out with all the other nominees.

Mr. Smith had been nominated in nine categories, including: Best Picture, Best Actor (Jimmy Stewart), Best Supporting Actor (Claude Rains), Best Directing, Best Original Story (Lewis Foster), and Best Screenplay (Sidney Buchman). But it was a year of great films, such as: *Gone with the Wind, Goodbye Mr. Chips, Dark Victory, Ninotchka, Love Affair, Wuthering Heights, Stagecoach*; and of great performances by Bette Davis, Irene Dunne, Greta Garbo, Greer Garson, and Vivien Leigh—all up for the Best-Actress Oscar. The Best-Actor candidates were Robert Donat, Clark Gable, Laurence Olivier, Mickey Rooney, and Jimmy Stewart.

In a normal year Stewart's performance would have surely been voted an Oscar, and *Mr. Smith* would have been even money against the field in many other categories. But Jimmy Stewart, the American Senator, ran against Robert Donat, the British teacher (Mr. Chips); academe won by a bloomin' 'ead. In other categories *Mr. Smith* tried to outstunt Selznick's *Gone with the Wind* and got bounced around in its slipstream.

So, the Awards Banquet of February 29, 1940, was, as Bob Hope quipped, "a benefit for Dave Selznick." His film of Margaret Mitchell's great novel was almost a sweep; Best Picture, Best Actress (Vivien Leigh), Best Director (Victor Fleming), Best Screenplay (Sidney Howard). When that beloved Negro performer, Hattie McDaniel, received her Best-Supporting Actress Oscar for *Gone with the Wind*, there was a wet-eyed demonstration that lasted for minutes. Hattie sobbed her gratitude, clutched the statuette to her breast, and sobbed her way back to her seat through a standing ovation—one of the Academy's great moments.

The *Gone with the Wind* table glittered like the inside of Fort Knox; of the seventeen possible awards, ten of the golden Oscars were won by *Gone with the Wind*. And only yesterday the film had been known as David's Folly!

What happened to *Mr. Smith*? With the exception of one surprise winner, Lewis R. Foster for Best Original Story (*Gentleman from Montana*), *Smith* ran second-best right down the line—close, but second. Moral: Don't make the best picture you ever made in the year that someone makes *Gone with the Wind.*

At any rate, I was relieved of the presidency of my beloved Academy. I also gave thought to giving up the presidency of the Screen Directors Guild. But film directors were my new love; as long as the Guild needed me, and wanted me, I would continue to serve it.

However, I could give up another presidency that took time and money. In this case the word "presidency" was a laugher—we were about as well organized as Thanksgiving turkeys. I was a lodge member of a do-it-yourself, unsubsidized "Research and Development" outfit, a poor man's (very poor) precursor of the Rand Corporation, and the Bunker-Ramo group. Our "personnel staff" was a secret tribe of three: two Chiefs (my cameraman Joe Walker and I), and one Indian (a machinist skilled in tools). Our "industrial complex": a one-room rented store on Santa Monica Boulevard. No signs on doors or whitewashed windows, but behind the blank facade—a roomful of drawing boards and small precision tools.

Here Joe Walker perfected and patented the first zoom lens for cameras. Here we scrambled radio impulses for the guidance of pilotless bombers. The *Motion Picture Herald* (December 2, 1939) carried this item: "Frank Capra is revealed as part owner of a patent just granted by the Patent Office in Washington for a remote-control system for guiding airplanes and releasing their bombs by radio. . . ."

Here we invented a selenium-celled grid through which antiaircraft gunners could sight and "see past" the blinding light of flares German bombers dropped below their planes. Here we designed one-way "wind cups" that would start an aircraft's landing wheels spinning as the pilot lowered the gear for a landing—eliminating the fiery "burn-off" of rubber when non-revolving tires smack the concrete runway. These last two ideas we gave to Howard Hughes for transmittal to the military without charge.

But our chef-d'oeuvre was in crytography—a code machine, not much bigger than a portable typewriter, which it resembled. At considerable expense (my own investment was twenty-five thousand dollars), we made many models, took out many patents, and offered the code machine to State and all the military services. The constant answer of their intelligence experts: No comment.*

So I withdrew from "research and development" for lack of cash, and mortgaged my home to finance *Meet John Doe*. How could I have been short of cash if my year's income was three hundred thousand dollars? Simple but painful. That year I paid the second highest income tax in Hollywood —two hundred and forty thousand dollars. Only L. B. Mayer paid a bigger tax.

---

* Three years later, I happened to mention my interest in code machines to the army's Chief Signal Officer, Major General Ingles. He smiled; asked if I had been through Colonel Friedman's hush-hush Signal Corps Communications Center in Washington. When told I hadn't, he dropped the subject. But he did suggest I see a secret training film on the "M-102." Later, I saw the film in Hawaii. The "M-102" was a code machine—a twin brother, I thought, of our own code machine. All you inventors in the poor house—move over.

Bob Riskin and I were now movie tycoons. We had hocked our shirts to form our own company—Frank Capra Productions. Our first wholly owned film: *Meet John Doe.*

Actual night shooting of Convention in Wrigley Field ballpark. Note rain-makers, and track for camera boom.

I love rain scenes.

At a roadside beanery. "Colonel!" says Long John. "I feel so good I'll treat you to a sugar doughnut." Cameraman George Barnes at left.

"You fainted, Buster. How long since you've eaten?" "Guess I better get outta here," says the tall derelict.

There was another fascinating interest I had to, regrettably, withdraw from for lack of time. I had approached Howard Hughes to join me in erecting a much-needed, non-profit Hobby Shop; a large building, equipped with power tools, and perhaps a hundred cubicles where artisans, tinkerers, and gadgeteers could come and fashion things with their own hands, free of charge. We would supply technical and patent experts. If any patents proved profitable, Hobby Shop would split profits with the inventors. Howard Hughes—supreme flyer, playboy, financier, mystery man—is, above all, an engineer. "Good idea, Frank. Cost it up; find a location, draw up some plans, sketch out a building. You do the leg work and I'll put up the money." Unfortunately, the John Doe film hobbled my leg work; Pearl Harbor killed it.

Making a film out of *Meet John Doe* proved to be as full of surprises as breaking a half-rogue wild stallion to the saddle. Precisely when I thought it would make one of the world's great show horses, it would leap and buck and throw me over the fence. It was still untamed when, with blinkers on it, we shoved the maverick into a theater for its opening night.

However, in the beginning it had been docile and full of promise. For instance, seldom does a filmmaker ever assemble his dream cast—his druthers for every role from the world-wide firmament of stars. That rarity happened in *Meet John Doe*. For the part of "John Doe"—a lanky hobo, an ex-bush league pitcher with a glass arm—I had but one choice: Gary Cooper. I wouldn't have made the picture without him. But I had no script for him to read when I asked him to play the part. Surprisingly, he said: "It's okay, Frank. I don't need a script." His wife, Rocky, put it this way: "John Ford sent Gary a script of *Stagecoach*. Gary was on the fence about it. I read it, and advised him to turn it down. *Stagecoach!* It made a star out of John Wayne, but we turned it down."

Moreover, all the other star names in my first-choice dream cast— Barbara Stanwyck, Edward Arnold, Walter Brennan, James Gleason, and Spring Byington—were available and signed for the film. And, as with Cooper, they all accepted their roles before reading the script—which is about the highest compliment a director can be paid.

Long before we began principal photography, *Meet John Doe* had stirred up world-wide press speculation; primarily for two reasons: First, it was news when a writer and director put their own money into a film; most of the film scriveners called it "brash," "reckless." And second, we made news because we wouldn't tell the press what the story of John Doe was all about.

As for being reckless, all Riskin and I could lose was our shirts, but that was small disaster when film company presidents stood in line holding fur coats to cover our backs. But making the press privy to our story was another matter. Not that we played hard-to-get as a publicity gimmick, or stole a nook from Garbo's seclusion ("I vant to be alone") bit. *John Doe* was a secret to the press because it was still a secret to *us*. To admit it publicly might give Jack Warner and the Bank of America second thoughts.

Our story problem was self-inflicted. To convince important critics that not every Capra film was written by Pollyanna, and that I could handle hard-nosed brutality with the best of the groin-kickers, Riskin and I had written ourselves into a corner. We knew we were loaded with entertainment; we had a startling opening and a powerful development that rose inexorably to a spectacular climactic wow. But—we had no acceptable SOLUTION to our story. The first two acts were solid; the third act was a wet sock.

We had abandoned our usual formula—a sane, honest "man of the people," thrust into a confrontation with the forces of evil, wins out with his innate goodness. This time our hero was a bindle stiff, a drifting piece of human flotsam as devoid of ideals as he was of change in his pocket. When the forces of evil tempt him—fine; no skin off his nose if they call him John Doe, the "Messiah of goodness," in exchange for steaks and fancy clothes. But—discovering he is being used to delude and defraud thousands of innocent people, he rebels. When he tries to tell the deluded people that he had been a fraud, but now believes as they do, the people turn on him, try to tear him limb from limb. So far so good. But now, what happens to John Doe? to the thousands that believed? to the forces of evil? We didn't know. Up to there the story wrote itself; beyond that point, it balked.

We called in Myles Connolly, my friend and severest critic—but also my ace-in-the-hole story constructionist. Connolly suggested several possible endings but admittedly, he, too, was stumped. We called in Jules Furthman, Hollywood's most sought after story "doctor." Furthman—a noted rare-book collector, he inoculated me with the bug—was in demand not for his inventive originality, but for his encyclopedic memory of past authors and their story plots. Filmmakers would tell him their story hang-ups; nine times out of ten, without recourse to research, Furthman would say: "Oh, that plot was used by Shakespeare"—or Chekhov, De Maupassant, Sheridan, Goethe, Kipling, Stevenson, Conrad, Cooper, or one of a host of other authors—"and this is the way *he* solved it." Plagiarism? We like to call it borrowing.

Anyway, "Doctor" Furthman listened; then hemmed, hawed, dredged the fathomless depths of his recall for a plot like ours—novels, plays, poems; legends, myths, sagas; the New Testament, the Old, the Apocrypha; Egyptian writers, Sumerian, Sanscrit; hieroglyphics, cuneiform, the Rosetta Stone. Nothing. Annoyed, "Doc" Furthman fell back on quackery. "Hell, it's simple," he declared. "You guys can't find an ending to your story because you got no story in the *first* place."

Riskin, Connolly, and I threw him out on his ear. His diagnosis was enough to put us all in the hospital. The picture was cast, we had a starting date, our own money was on the line—and he tells us we've got no story in the first place.

Meet John Doe's inside joke was on the bizarre side—"The Mystery of the Unsolved Ending," we called it. It is astonishing, but true; *Meet John Doe* missed becoming a lasting film classic because *we couldn't end it!* For seven-eighths of the film, Riskin and I felt we had made The Great American Motion Picture; but in the last eighth, it fizzled into The Great American Letdown.

It was mea culpa, of course. From the first day of script-writing, Riskin fretted about the ending. I didn't. "Stop worrying, Bob. The picture will dictate its own ending."

"But Frank, it's murder to start shooting a picture without knowing how it's going to end."

"Haven't you heard? Everything happens for the best. Wait and see."

Bob waited, but didn't see much. In desperation—setting some kind of a pointless record—I was to photograph five different endings, and then try them out on theater audiences; all collapsed like punctured balloons. Why? Why did the hundreds of scenes integrate into a jigsaw puzzle that had greatness written all over it except for one gaping hole no last scene would plug up? I never found out why.

Of course, the press had a field day with the new phenomenon of playing musical chairs with film endings. Jay Carmody (Washington *Star*) wrote: "Mr. Capra, whose 'rightness' in disposing of his magnificent little people . . . has been one of the miracles of the screen, finally has landed in the middle of a hornet's nest . . . When his *Meet John Doe* opens at the Earle . . . it may have any one of four endings . . . a new world's record in indecision . . ."

And Beau Broadway quipped in his New York *Telegraph* column: "The new giggle around town is this:

"Do you know why today is so refreshing?"
"Why, because the sun is out?"
"No. This is the day Capra isn't shooting a new ending for Doe . . ."

How did *Meet John Doe* finally fare? With some reservations, it finally won me what I long had coveted: acclaim from the intellectual critics.

Kate Cameron (New York *Daily News*) gave it her rare top rating— "Four Stars." William Boehnel (*World-Telegram*) called it: "The finest film Frank Capra ever made, bar none . . ." Howard Barnes (*Herald-Tribune*): "The full power of the screen is unleashed in Frank Capra's *Meet John Doe* . . . With an artist's fine perception he has gone to the heart of the issues which are troubling us so profoundly these days . . . It is a testament of faith as well as brilliant craftsmanship . . ."

Those words, "an artist's fine perception," had seldom been applied to my work before. And Bosley Crowther (*The New York Times*) upped my rating: ". . . eloquent with love for gentle people . . . it marks a distinct progression in Mr. Capra's—and the screen's—political thinking . . ."

The hard-nosed *Variety* seldom used unpragmatic phrases of this sort: "A showman's pride . . . Much comedy, much humor, much sly wit and broad fun . . . Pictorially and technically, the picture is a masterpiece . . . the dramatic narrative is one of the literary milestones of the screen."

Archer Winston (New York *Post*) felt as I did: ". . . [They] have made seven-eighths of a great and timely film . . ." Leo Mishkin (*Telegraph*) echoed the appraisal: "At least one may say that the first half of *Meet John Doe* is undeniably . . . one of the great pictures of any year . . . You'll never see anything better . . ."

But the audiences, my John Does, about whom and for whom I made my films, they left the theater somewhat disappointed—no matter which ending they saw. This was shrewdly predicted by movie critic Edwin Schallert (Los Angeles *Times*) when he first saw the film: "Frank Capra's *Meet John Doe* . . . an admirable challenge to the spirit of life today, is a picture that should make history and give a new turn to the thoughts of the nation, if— and the IF is very large, indeed—it does not die abornin' . . . [because] it lacks the inspiration of a great ending."

And then—after the film had been playing a couple of weeks in six major cities—I received a letter signed "John Doe." It read: ". . . I have seen your film with many different endings . . . all bad, I thought . . . The only thing that can keep John Doe from jumping to his death is the John Does themselves . . . if they ask him . . ."

A large bell rang. I called back all the cast and shot *Ending Number* FIVE!

I called back all the outstanding prints of the film and spliced on ending number FIVE. And that finished our crazy game of "Five Endings in Search of an Audience."

That last ending was the best of a sorry lot, but *still* it was a letdown. Was an acceptable ending *ever* possible for *John Doe*? I still don't know. Perhaps readers will. I do know that at the time, I was much harsher on the film than the critics. I *knew* Riskin and I had written ourselves into a cor- ner. We had shown the rise of two powerful, opposing movements—one good, one evil. They clashed head on—and *destroyed each other!* St. George fought with the dragon, slew it, and was slain. What our film said to be- wildered people hungry for solutions was this, "No answers this time, ladies and gentlemen. It's back to the drawing board." And the people said, "Oh, nuts!"

But whether Cooper jumped or not, we were not prophets without honor in our own filmland. A sample telegram: David O. Selznick—"ONCE IN A BLUE MOON A PICTURE COMES ALONG THAT MAKES ONE PROUD TO BE IN THE PICTURE BUSINESS . . ."

And while we struggled with make-believe endings at the studio, life was writing its own beginnings and endings at home. On February 12, 1941, Lu gave birth to another boy—little Tom. He was to fill the great void left by the death of little John.

My mother was being wheeled into surgery at the Cedars of Lebanon Hospi- tal when she got the news of little Tom's birth. She smiled. She was eighty-

COOPER: **Number nineteen just went by. Give up, Colonel?** BRENNAN: **Funny. It worked for Claudette.**

"Listen to me, John Does! You're the hope of the world—"

One of five endings in search of a finish. Back in the ice house.

"Oh, yes—that's a good face. They *will* believe anything you say—" Ex-comedy star Hank Mann is the photographer.

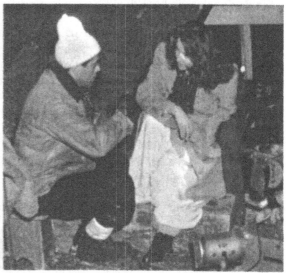

ARNOLD'S VOICE: "Do you no good to jump, fella. My men will pick up your body and get rid of it before you can say John Doe—"

"You climbed out of a sick bed and ran up fourteen flights of stairs. You're weak, drained, dizzy, hurt, in love. Throw your arms around him—say, 'John! John!' And go limp—"

one. Through a small square window I watched Dr. Stanley Imerman ampu-
tate her blue thrombotic leg. The stump had begun to heal when, a week
later, pneumonia struck. Lu and my two brothers and three sisters were in
the room. I held Mama's calloused hand, heard her rattles grow fainter and
farther apart. One more—then silence. The great heart, strong arms, un-
shaken faith, and fierce courage that had conquered her days one at a time,
had finished their job. Like a candle, Mama gave out light and warmth, but
consumed herself in the process. Now Mama's light was no more. All that
she was had been spent for us. And Mama was dead. In peace, in pride, in
dignity. Her seed, and the seed of millions like her, created the American
dream.

When Bob Riskin and I blithely formed a corporation and cheerily went
into business for ourselves, we didn't fully realize we were taking on a
silent partner, an uncle, who couldn't write, act, or even sweep out the office.
But he could eat like a lion. In fact, so voracious was Uncle's appetite his
lion's share had to be delivered to him far, far, in advance of mealtimes.
Uncle Sam, we all called him.

Six weeks after *Meet John Doe* opened in major cities, Warner Brothers
did some extrapolating, and reported to us the good news: The picture
would make our corporation a profit of nine hundred thousand dollars!
We were ecstatic. So was Uncle. He sharpened his pencils and said to us:
"Frank, Bob, it's amortization time!"

"What's amortization?"

"It means that a goodly portion of every dollar the box office takes in
now, is an 'estimated profit,' see? Furthermore, in your case, since you are a
new company, all your profits are taxable as 'excess' profits. Understand?
Therefore, you owe me *now*, over 50 percent of the estimated profit on every
ticket being sold in the world."

"Uncle! You've got to be kidding. Why must we pay taxes on profits we
can't expect for a couple of years—if ever?"

"Simple, nephews. I demand it."

"But where do we get the money to pay you taxes in advance?"

"Boys, if you can't stand the details, stay out of the kitchen," I always
say.

So Bob Riskin and I got the hell out of the kitchen—and dissolved our
corporation. After a year and a half of working without salary, and after
borrowing to pay corporation taxes in advance, and paying personal income taxes on our divided assets, this was the score: Uncle Sam—ninety
cents out of every profit dollar; Riskin and Capra—ten cents!

In June, 1941, almost on the same day Hitler's armies attacked Russia,
David Selznick had all the legal papers drawn up: He and I, as a team,
were to join Pickford, Chaplin, and Korda as 20 percent owners in United
Artists. My new agent, Phil Berg, would study the deal.

I met Phil Berg in his office for his verdict on the Selznick partnership deal. His partner, Bert Allenberg, joined us. Natty Phil, every blond hair in place, stood (as always) when he talked.

"Here, Frank. It's just a matter of how well you hit it off with David, that's all. Otherwise, it's a great deal. You'll own a good chunk of United Artists, and that could mean millions! But, here!" His pale blue eyes began to sparkle. "Bert and I've got a much *better* deal for you! Haven't we, Bert?"

"Joe Schenck!" said Allenberg. "Joe Schenck will give his right arm to get you at Fox. Unbelievable, Frank—terms he wouldn't give to Garbo! Any picture you want to make, your own boss—two-fifty a film and 50 percent of the profits—"

"Phil, Bert—I'm dizzy . . . Have you guys heard Ed Murrow's 'This Is London!' broadcasts? Have you heard what that Luftwaffe's doing to London?"

There was a pause. Phil Berg broke the silence. "Here, Frank. As your agent I've got to tell you. You'll never again in your life be offered what Selznick and Schenck are offering you. Believe me. But I can stall them for a week or two. And if the Navy calls me up, Bert here knows all the details."

I boarded a plane for Washington. Sy Bartlett (a Hollywood writer recently commissioned in the air corps), introduced me around.

From what I saw and heard, we were so woefully unprepared for war that Army chiefs dreaded our possible involvement. They hinted that our troops only slightly outnumbered Washington's Continentals—and were as badly trained and ill-equipped. I asked to head a field Photo Company; the Signal Corps offered me a major's commission. Now I knew the Army was hard put. I signed papers; was told to stand by for a call. I was forty-four.

Now for one last stunt: make a cheap film for a fast buck to keep my family going. The way *we* lived, a major's salary of $250 a month wouldn't pay the phone bill. It cost us forty thousand dollars a year, tax free, for living expenses and mortgage payments on a ranch we had bought in Fallbrook. By closing up Brentwood, firing the house help, and sending Lu to the ranch to live with her parents, expenses might be cut to twenty-five thousand dollars. But how to make that much while in the Army?

Howard Lindsay and Russel Crouse had a sell-out hit playing on Broadway, *Arsenic and Old Lace*. I had seen the play, knew it could be filmed cheaply and quickly (along with most film directors, whatever I saw or read I translated into film terms). In New York I caught Howard Lindsay back stage in between acts. "Howard, I've got a yen to film your great show. Any hopes?"

"It'd be great, Frank. But we've already sold it to Jack Warner—" And he added that the film version couldn't play movie houses until the play closed on Broadway. Which could be "three, maybe four years—the way advance tickets are selling." Ouch! Never mind. Talk to the cast.

I think I offered twenty-five thousand dollars each to Josephine Hull and Jean Adair, and fifteen thousand dollars to John Alexander for four weeks of their vacation time in Hollywood, and warned them the deal was "iffy" and that any advance publicity could kill it.

Then I rushed back to the West Coast to weave the rest of the plot. And plot it was. Nobody could expect Jack Warner, or any other studio head, to sink a barrel of money in a film and then lock it up in vaults for four years. There were risks: wars, depressions, changes in fads and clothes. Members of the cast might die, or fall into disfavor with audiences. Interest on the tied-up money would up the film's cost.

But I counted heavily on Jack Warner's quixotic strain. He was a sucker for the unusual. If I could bait the trap with a lure that was both complete and compelling—he might just go for it.

Next on the scheme's agenda was a star. Cary Grant was Hollywood's greatest farceur. He was also one of its greatest box-office lures. And he wanted one hundred thousand dollars to make the picture.

I had a quiet meeting with the Warner Brothers production staff. "Boys, Jack Warner doesn't want this to leak out. Make me a quick budget estimate of the below-the-line costs for *Arsenic and Old Lace* (the costs of story, director, and cast were called above-the-line). Here are the details: an all-Warner crew—camera, sound, lighting, editing. Lay the picture out on a four-week schedule—"

"Frank! You're gonna shoot a picture in *four weeks?*" asked an art director.

"Please, will you? The schedule is four weeks, and not a day over. Now. There'll be no extras, no locations, no transportation costs—except for round-trip fares for three actors from New York, and fifty bucks a day each for living expenses. Got that? Now, here's the news! The whole picture will be shot in the studio, on one stage, in *one set*—a spooky, two-story, old Brooklyn house next to a cemetery. Here, these are some sketches, exterior and interior.

"Build the front and left side of the house wild, so we can shoot inside and out. Some broken down tombstones in the foreground, see? And diminish them in the distance. Far off we see the two-dimensional profiles of the skyscrapers in Manhattan's skyline. It's night. Lights in the windows, glow over the city, colored neons that blink, and a couple of scrims in front of the skyscrapers to make them look far off. In back of the old house, build a fast-diminishing, three-quarter-angle miniature of the Brooklyn Bridge, with little miniature trains and cars that move. Got it?

"The backing is a night sky. Paint some wispy clouds in front of a full moon—you know, ghostly, Halloweenish. And allow for bags and bags of autumn leaves to blow around the house and tombstones. Oh, yes—and three silent wind machines. Any other details you want?"

"Is all the shooting at night?"

"All the exteriors are at night. There'll be a few day scenes inside the house. And oh! In the living room, under the left window, figure in the cost of a window seat with a creaking lid, and big enough to hold a body. And don't forget the creaking door and the steep stairs down to the dirt cellar where the old ladies bury the bodies. Anything else?"

"Shall we allow for camera booms?"

"Yes. The 'A' camera will never be off a Chapman twenty-foot silent boom. The 'B' camera will be wild. Okay, fellas. And never mind padding the figures for 'emergencies.' If you come up with a below-the-line cost of more than four hundred thousand—you're cheating."

"What're you doing, Frank," kidded production manager Steve Trilling, "going back to your Poverty Row quickies?"

"Yep. For a refresher course. See you."

If I am making all this sound too easy, it's because success *is* easy—if you know the magic word. Psychologists may pontificate that success is "intellectual challenge buttressed by emotional courage." That's flashy talk, but pippy-pock. Success depends on nothing more than doin' your l'il ol' itty-bitty, nitty-gritty homework. Clyde Beatty studied his cats; Casanova pored over his women; Ulysses Grant poured out of his bottle. Homework! Yessir. That's the magic word.

And my homework on Jack Warner unearthed this warning: Though Jack likes his laughs, never try to clown him into a deal. Many who tried had felt the heft of his follow-through as they went flying out the door. So, armed with facts and figures, but no gags, I stepped into his office.

In less than a week preparation wheels began spinning for *Arsenic and Old Lace.* My script writers—those talented, fun-loving twins, Julie and Philip Epstein—went racing to New York to see the play. My cameraman was that reliable old pro, Sol Polito; my assistant director was Jesse Hibbs; my film editor, Danny Mandel.

To the already imposing cast of Cary Grant, Josephine Hull, Jean Adair, and John Alexander we added these high-powered performers: Raymond Massey, to play the maniacal killer (played by Boris Karloff on the stage); Peter Lorre, to play Massey's partner-in-murder (a shy, idio surgeon); Priscilla Lane, for Grant's new bride; Jack Carson, for the dumb cop who writes plays; and my favorite character actor, Jimmy Gleason, for the tough-detective role. And to round out an all-star cast of scene stealers, we engaged Edward Everett Horton to play the huffy keeper of the "rest home" who comes to pick up the "girls," but instead picks up "just a pinch" of arsenic in his elderberry wine.

Less than two months after I had broached the idea to Howard Lindsay back stage, we were shooting the first scene of *Arsenic and Old Lace* on a Warner stage. And I couldn't have been happier. No great social document "to save the world," no worries about whether John Doe should or should not jump; just good old-fashioned theater—an anything goes, rip-roaring comedy about murder. I let the scene stealers run wild; for the actors it was a mugger's ball.

The fun had one more week to go, when it was brutally interrupted by—PEARL HARBOR! Next day, Monday morning, December 8, two Signal

"He's our number eleven, Mister Spinalzo. We keep the poor dear in the window seat until we can give him a decent Christian burial in the cellar."

"This had bloody well be funny, chum." "Yes, Mr. Grant."

Magnificent Studio Set in *Arsenic and Old Lace*. View from window of Brewster home in lower Brooklyn—graveyard, bridge, and Manhattan skyline—is classic example of achieving three-dimensional effect by perspective and foreshortening craftsmanship. From front tombstone to back building: forty feet.

Cast was pretty good, too. Starting third from left: Peter Lorre, Jean Adair, John Alexander, Josephine Hull, Cary Grant, Priscilla Lane, Raymond Massey, James Gleason, Edward Everett Horton, Jack Carson, and Edward McNamara.

Corps officers came to the studio stage to swear me in. I was in the Army. I asked for, and was granted, six weeks' leave of absence to finish, edit, and preview *Arsenic*. Nights, a tailor fitted me for uniforms. A little frightened by it all, I entered an Army-Navy store to try on caps and buy some major's leaves and Signal Corps crossed-flags insignia. I had no idea how to put them on, and neither did the tailor. On February 5, I received this telegram:

> MAJOR FRANK CAPRA . . .
> YOU WILL PROCEED ON FEBRUARY ELEVENTH TO
> WASHINGTON DC REPORTING CHIEF SIGNAL OFFICER
> FOR DUTY
>
> ADAMS ADJT GENL WASHN DC

That's a pretty cheeky order, I thought. Not "Please proceed," or "Kindly proceed," but "*You will proceed . . .*" I suppose it was in my blood to resent arbitrary authority. For some four thousand years Sicilian peasants have suffered through so many capricious capers from so many idiot tyrants, their respect for all authority has seldom risen above the fecal level of the four-letter word. The epithet *sbirro* applies either to a policeman or his informer. Call a man a *sbirro* in Sicily, and pardner—you ain't gonna get off with just a smile.

Why, then, was I joining the iron dictatorship of the military? Why give up family, personal freedom, and my name blazoned in marquee lights above the names of the biggest stars? And why turn down a partnership with David Selznick (which would have made us part owners of United Artists) and the once-in-a-blue-moon contract from Schenck—either of which would have guaranteed my joining the multi-millionaire class? Why trade all this fame, glamour, and wealth for a number stamped on dog tags that hung round my neck—the number 0900-209?

Patriotism? Possibly. But the real reason was that in the game of chance and wit that is motion pictures, I had climbed the mountain, planted my flag, and heard the world applaud. And now I was bored. I'm an uphill man. When my motor races uphill, my interest rises. When it idles on the flat, I'm bored.

Furthermore, I had a guilty conscience. In my films I championed the cause of the gentle, the poor, the downtrodden. Yet I had begun to live like the Aga Khan. The curse of Hollywood is big money. It comes so fast it breeds and imposes its own mores, not of wealth, but of ostentation and phony status. The result: It turns one into an insufferable something one never was, or ever thought he could be.

John Mosher, in *The New Yorker* Magazine, had opened his critique of *Meet John Doe* with this sentence: "Mr. Capra's love of the common man, the average man, the dope, the punk, passeth all understanding." That statement has two meanings: How great, or how phony, is the love that passeth understanding. In my case I had the disturbing feeling the meanings were merging. The cynical hobo in *Meet John Doe*, Walter Brennan, would have warned, "The Heelots are closin' in on you."

Yet—one may argue with pride, rather than with guilt, that one's fame and lavish living have been self-earned with sweat and toil, so what is wrong with enjoying them? Nothing is wrong with enjoying lavish living if you can endure the boredom, and stomach the inanity of the "fast set."

So the Army was a welcome out for me; a clean, respectable way to turn down enslaving million-dollar contracts that form, courtesy, acclaim, and forward momentum were forcing me to accept. Besides, it gave one a superior aura of patriotism and self-sacrifice—qualities one rarely has the chance to flaunt in the faces of his peers.

Then, too, the Army loomed as another formidable mountain. That thought had evidently also crossed the mind of my lovely wife. On the evening of February 11, 1942, after she had driven me up from the ranch and deposited me at the teeming entrance to the Union Station, she gave me one last kiss and one last command: "Darling, now please! Please! Don't go trying to *direct the Army*! Promise?"

It all felt so theatrical, like a scene from one of my own films.

And as I waved good-bye to my departing wife, I was struck with the humdrum way a Hollywood champ was departing for the wars: No photographers or reporters; no Marine band or welcoming generals; no studio limousine filled with assistants and flacks; no delegation from the Academy to see me off, or officers from the Screen Directors Guild (of which I was still president) to wish me luck.

I knew that neither press nor trade papers would mention my departure because 95 percent of Hollywood's "news" originates in studio publicity departments, or with the dozens of private publicity firms, neither of which I had going for me at the moment. I had never employed a personal press agent on the rather pure but unrealistic and theatrically wacky theory that "If I was good—everybody would know it. If I was bad—I didn't want anybody to know it."

Moreover, Hollywood's trade papers, tom-toming the major companies' drive to hang on to their artists and technicians, editorialized against the Hustons, Fords, and Capras who had offered the government their services. "Any job that Capra could do . . . in war service," declared Billy Wilkerson in his *Hollywood Reporter* Tradeviews, "could be filled by a brain that could not contribute to making film entertainment . . . We believe that the government's answer will be: STAY WHERE YOU ARE, WORK HARDER AND WORK MORE . . . TO CREATE ENTERTAINMENT, FOR THIS IS A MOST NECESSARY CONTRIBUTION IN OUR BATTLE FOR FREEDOM. We further believe that the government will soon announce, as it did . . . in World War I, that motion pictures are a NECESSARY INDUSTRY . . ." Meaning, of course, exempt from the draft. No such announcement was ever made.

So Lu supervised the putting on of my first uniform, packed a folding bag with about sixty pounds of uniforms, shoes, shirts, whisky flasks, vitamins, medicines, cold nostrums, enema bags, jars and jars of candies, jams, cookies, and lump upon lump of lumpy things all wives knit for their men in uniform. And, like millions of other wives in the world, she supervised my kissing good-bye of the children, then drove me to the station to see me off.

And being close to middle age, we were too embarrassed to emulate younger couples who stood entwined in ten-minute soul kisses like little islands while humanity smiled and flowed around them. So I waved to Lu till she disappeared in the night traffic, knowing that soon she would be dissolved in tears, and turned to look for a redcap to carry my bags. None came near me, even though I knew them all by first name. I noticed that all men in uniform carried their own bags. I picked up mine. I had been introduced to a sickening fact of life all our armed forces know: An American in uniform is a second-class citizen!

As Mr. Frank Capra, film producer, I used to arrive at the station in a limousine and be greeted by porters and station officials; Station Master Mendenhall would escort me through the tunnel and up the ramp to the shiny Super Chief. The spick-and-span Pullman porters standing at their car entrances would "Mr. Capra" me all over the place as we traded little jokes. The station master would take me to the lounge car, where a steward (Mac or Herman) would take over, and prepare martinis just the way I liked them, and the maître d' from the dining car would suddenly appear with his menu and recite a list of tasty, toothsome specials for dinner. Then a porter would appear: "All your bags are in car C, drawing room A, Mr. Capra." And I'd hand him a ten-dollar bill and order another martini.

But the night I left in uniform I was met by no porters, no station attendants, and no Station Master Mendenhall. I made my way through the crowded station walking lopsided, carrying a sixty-pound bag in one hand and a ten-pounder in the other, and at the same time tried to keep an oversized officer's cap from wobbling off my head—because I had bought it *before* clipping my bushy hair to a military crew cut.

And when I made the long trek to the sleeping car next to the baggage car and threw my bulky bags in through the curtains of an already made up lower berth, I was faced with the brand-new torture of coping with a Pullman berth. For believe it or not, I was like the Arab who had leapfrogged a whole century by going directly from the camel to the jet. I had leapfrogged this upper hand lower-berth business by going directly from the clatter and clank and straw of the box car to the soft music, tinkling ice, and downy pillows of the drawing room.

As Film Director Frank Capra I used to look forward to the four-hour layover in Chicago in between trains. There would be photographers and interviewers and a limousine to take us to the Pump Room for a long, leisurely luncheon and pleasant interviews with Irv Kupcinet and Irene Thirer.

As Major Frank Capra, I dragged my seventy pounds of bags to the taxi entrance, where angry passengers fought for cabs that raced in throwing angry roostertails of dirty snow behind them. "You, Captain!" yelled the

angry starter, shoving people into cabs. "You for the Twentieth Century?"
"No! The B and O—"

"Drop dead," he muttered and waved the taxi out. "Better start walkin',
Captain. Ain't no hack gonna pick up a fare for three blocks."

I picked up my bags and slushed through the snow. My arms were coming
out of their sockets, the cold and sweat blinded my eyes. But how wonderful
it was to feel the pain and ache of physical effort against something; fighting
something, beating something, even if it was just the weight of your bags.

"Is Mr. Swazey in?" I asked the clerk at the Carlton Hotel in Washington.
"If it's about reservations, sir—" "No. Just tell him Frank Capra from Hollywood would like to say hello."

Frank Swazey materialized behind the counter, 150 pounds of handsome,
wisecracking, courtly pleasantness. "Well, well, Frank Capra. What is this,
Mr. Smith *Returns* to Washington? Is that a uniform you got on or a dis-
guise against the Press Club running you out of town? How about a cup of
coffee—you look like all those other poor bastards around Washington."

"What poor bastards?"

"The big wheel Army and Navy guys. They're all skin and bones and
beards. They come into my cocktail lounge at five and fall asleep before
they finish one drink, the poor bastards. Hon!" We had entered his managerial suite. "Friend of yours wants a cup of coffee." His very pretty wife
greeted us. (I had made friends with the Swazeys while shooting *Mr. Smith.*)
Mrs. Swazey fixed me up some ham and eggs to go with the coffee.

"Frank," Swazey went on, "chances are the Signal Corps won't keep you
in Washington, but if they do, the only sure way to find a place to sleep is
to shack up with a secretary that's got an apartment. Just kidding, hon!
Frank, nobody's ever seen anything like it. The old Capital is the new
Klondike. Every jehu from Maine to Hawaii that owns a tool kit is here in
Washington getting a government contract. There's fifty of them sleeping in
my lobby every night waiting for guests to be kicked out. There's even a
new law: If I let anyone stay in a hotel room more than five days I get
thirty days in the poky."

"Swazey, you're breaking my heart, but I'm leaving my bags in your
hotel. And unless you and your beautiful wife don't mind a third party in
bed with you, you better fix me up with a broom closet or something."

"You'll be sorry. I'll give you my unlisted ace-in-the-hole for one night.
Room three-oh-eight. It's FFO, for friends only—when I find them in the
gutter."

"Why just for one night?"

"Because after one night, friends prefer the gutter."

On my first Pentagon visit I was lucky. After much asking and pointing,
and what seemed like miles and miles of hallways and stairways, I aimlessly turned a corner—and there it was! The Signal Corps' APS (Army
Pictorial Service), Colonel Schlosberg commanding. Army Pictorial was

beautiful; suites and suites of sumptuous offices. I passed several "Projection Room" signs. I peeked into one—red-cushioned chairs, and the latest in modern equipment. Great.

I passed a door sign which read: "Lieutenant Colonel Darryl Zanuck." I felt right at home. Zanuck had been commissioned to supervise the production of training films, and now he had been granted leave of absence from his job as vice president and production head of Twentieth Century-Fox to devote full time to the Signal Corps Army Pictorial Service. He was Hollywood's head man in the Signal Corps.

Colonel Schlosberg was one of the Signal Corps officers who had signed me up in Washington many months before, and when his secretary said the Colonel would see me, I walked into his office full of excitement. Colonel Schlosberg was a heavy man whose weight seemed to settle at the bottom, like an inverted top. In fact, everything about the good Colonel was bottom heavy. He had the humor of unleavened dough, the charm of a bag of cement, and the tact of a Mack Sennett rubber mallet. But he knew he was sitting on the throne of a film empire that was to rival Hollywood itself, and he wasn't about to help any outsiders muscle in on him.

"Capra," he laughed gruffly, "never mind taking off your coat and hat. You've been assigned out of the Signal Corps."

I froze with one arm out of my overcoat. "I've been *what*?"

"As of today you're permanently assigned to that newfangled service some bright civilians thought up, the Morale Branch. General Osborn asked for you to help him think up ideas for morale films which, if approved topside, the Signal Corps will produce for him. The Chief Signal Officer approved, so here's your published orders: You are to report immediately to the Morale Branch, Brigadier General Osborn commanding, in Temporary Building H, right off Pennsylvania near the Navy Building. Any taxi driver will—"

"Wait a minute, Colonel. My racket is films, what the hell do I know about morale? I volunteered to serve in the Signal Corps, where the action is."

"Capra, you can't pick and choose like you did in Hollywood. You're in the Army now. You're just another body the Chief Signal Officer can send any place he wants to."

"Colonel Schlosberg, you signed me up. How would you like me to hang this brand new uniform up in your office as a souvenir?"

"You Hollywood big shots are all alike, all a pain in the ass. If you can't get what you want, you cry!"

"That's right, we cry when somebody gives us the shaft. The truth is you don't *want* me in the Signal Corps—am I right?"

"One Darryl Zanuck around here is enough. You Hollywood guys just won't fit in with the Army way of producing films."

"You mean I won't fit in with that dull crap you turn out as training films—that's what you mean."

"Yeah, dull crap to you. But serious war training to us. Anyway, here's your orders: Major Frank Capra, Oh nine hundred two oh nine, Signal Corps, is assigned to detached duty to the Morale Branch—"

In a sleazy, paperboard Temp Building H—it had been a temporary building in World War I—I found the Morale Branch. Its name had just been changed to the Special Services Branch. It was a rat's nest of officers, papers, and cheap desks. I was ushered into the office of Brigadier General Frederick H. Osborn— six foot nine, newly uniformed, polite, bewildered, intellectual, gentlemanly.

Osborn was a Princeton Phi Beta Kappa, who had finished his graduate work on anthropology at Cambridge University. He was first called to Government service in 1940, to head the civilian Army-Navy Commission on Welfare and Recreation. He caught the eye of Chief of Staff George C. Marshall, who commissioned him brigadier general and asked him to organize the Morale Branch.

General Osborn expected me. Conscious of his towering above me as we shook hands, he politely sat down and introduced me to his executive officer, Colonel Livingston Watrous, an all-gray man in his seventies. "Yes, Mr. Capra," said the gray man with a gray smile, "you see the Army fights on paper. So they've de-mothballed hundreds of us old retired colonels to teach you newcomers how to win the paper war." Just my luck, I thought, to get stuck with the tallest general in the Army, and the oldest colonel. Reading my thoughts General Osborn politely asked me to report to my immediate superior, a Colonel E. L. Munson, Jr., "head of the information services," he said, "made up of sections for news, radio, pamphlets, and film."

"And all in one room until we move to the Pentagon," laughed the de-mothballed colonel as he led me into a room bursting with desks and officers. He introduced me to Colonel Lyman Munson, a smallish, compact man. "He's a West Pointer!" proudly emphasized the gray colonel. We shook hands. Chairs scuffed the floor as officers turned to inspect a live Hollywood character.

"You're the head of the whole film section, Major," said Colonel Munson expansively (giving me the first inkling that most West Pointers are witty, salty, articulate). "In fact, you *are* the whole film section. And that's your office," pointing to one of six beat-up pine desks, "and don't ask me what you're supposed to do because I'm a son-of-a-bitch if I know yet."

Well, I thought to myself, these Morale jokers have a sophomoric enthusiasm about them. At least I hadn't met any lead ass colonels sitting on nests trying to hatch empire eggs. But I was still so resentful against Schlosberg that *anybody* in uniform was a bastard.

"Colonel Munson, as a fool who's turned his back on Camelot, I don't feel like jumping up and down over heading a one-man Film Section, in a one-room Morale Branch."

"Well, welcome to fantasy land," he said with a twinkle. "Here, have

some coffee and meet the other Mad Hatters." First man he introduced me
to was squatty, glowering, "Slam"—Major S. L. A. Marshall, Detroit
News—who was setting up the Army News Service. Then I met Lieutenant
Colonel Frank Forsberg, Madison Avenue slick-magazine publisher. He was
pasting together a new Army magazine called *Yank*. And Major Paul Horgan, writer of Army pamphlets telling G.I.'s how to behave in foreign countries, "and to remember," said Munson, "that every gal is somebody's sister." Then a Dr. Sam Stauffer—"I still haven't figured out what the hell *he*
does"—followed by a Harvard educator by the name of Major Francis
Spaulding—"heads the ivory tower group, research," said Munson.

"Research?" I asked. "About what?"

"Where'd you come from, Hollywood?" smirked Colonel Munson.
"Haven't you heard of the 'Id'? Attitudes, psychology questions—that's the
new thing."

"Look, Colonel Munson, not from the looks of these officers, but from
their titles—am I in the propaganda headquarters of the U.S. Army?"

"If it is," Colonel Munson answered wryly, "Goebbels will fall on his
face laughing. We are Special Services, morale builders. We will supply
the draftees with entertainment that'll prove to them what chumps they are
to have left home—bands, pin-up girls in person, movies, comic books,
bean balls, and don't forget the seven kinds of Jello. You know, morale
builders—and how's yours?"

"Never lower."

"Bully! And now, Major Frank Capra, important man from Hollywood,
do you know Tom Lewis?"

"I know *a* Tom Lewis—married to Loretta Young."

"That's the man. We think he's the best candidate to head up our radio
section. How well do you know him?"

I didn't think my spirits could sink any lower, but they did with that
remark. All in one morning I had been thrown out of the Signal Corps,
ordered to join overaged Boy Scout leaders whose goal was to play bean
ball with enlisted men, and now I was being asked to pimp for them—
recruit big entertainment names into the Morale Branch. Yessir. A battered
desk, a telephone, and I; Morale low, Morale high, we fought the battle of
Sigma Chi. A queazy tide rose in my throat. I headed for the door. "Excuse
me, Colonel. Which way is it?" Munson pointed to the right.

There were more officers in the hall than there was hall, and down the
hall there were more officers going into the men's room than were coming
out. I crowded in; larger men surrounded me; I was trapped in a uniformed
well of steamy, sweaty men pouring out ammonia-rich urine excreted by
tight tense nerves.

At the Special Services hall door, Colonel Munson and another officer
about his size were waiting for me. Both had on caps and overcoats.

"Frank," said Munson, "meet Jack Stanley. His racket's charm. Got him
through West Point."

I nodded and shook hands. "Jack, Frank was about to tell us how well he knows Tom Lewis."

"Colonel Munson, let me give it to you straight. I know Tom Lewis well enough to tell him to stay the hell out of uniform unless he wants to become another 'body' to be kicked around by some jerk superior. Well enough to warn him not to get sucked into becoming head of another one-man section in a one-room Morale Branch. You see, I'm a lousy pimp, Colonel Munson."

They seemed astonished. "Lyman," said Jack Stanley, "something wrong here. This can't be the guy we had all those meetings about."

"If it isn't I'll take the hook out and throw him back. Get his cap and overcoat, Jack."

"A pleasure." Stanley ducked into the Morale offices.

"Major Capra," said Lyman sharply, "you're getting your first order from your jerk superior. You will let me buy you *lunch*." Stanley came out with my coat and cap. "Turn around!" Lyman put on my coat, then buttoned it. Jack put on my cap. It was too loose. "Hey Lyman," he laughed, "here's a switch. This guy's head's too *small* for his hat. I'll fix that." He took a memo from his pocket, tore it into strips which he stuffed inside the sweatband. Then he put the cap on my head. It fitted. "And as your head swells take out the strips one at a time. Ready, Lyman?" "Ready."

Each took an arm. They practically carried me out to lunch.

In the basement part of the Old New Orleans restaurant, they bought me a couple of drinks and a three-hour lunch. They didn't drink before the sun set over the yard arm. Jack Stanley opened the briefing session.

"Frank, *you* may think that Schlosberg kicked you out of the Signal Corps, and *he* may think so, but you're both wrong. You were commissioned into the Signal Corps, and assigned to Special Services, at the personal request of one General George C. Marshall, Chief of Staff of the whole shebang."

"Let me back up a minute, Jack," said Colonel Munson. "Frank, you know as well as we do that 'propaganda' is a dirty word to the American public. And you know that Congress has always been mistrustful of any 'managed' news, any so-called propaganda being fed to the captive audiences of *millions of troops in uniform.*

"But to the everlasting credit of this man's army—" and Lyman went on telling me that young Americans will not only want to be well fed and well taken care of, they will want most of all to know WHY the hell they're in *uniform.* "And behind the innocent facade of 'morale building' the Army is going all out with modern communications media—newsprint, radio, film— to *tell* them why."

And to insure objectivity, Lyman went on, the top brass selected a Republican, a man of high civic standing and impeccable character, to head up the brand-new Morale Branch, General Osborn.

"And," said Jack Stanley, "to make it acceptable to mossback Army

diehards, the brass chose a West Pointer—and the son of a West Pointer—
Lyman Munson, here, to be in direct charge of Army information material;
journalism, radio, and films."

Then Munson warned that for printed stuff and radio they could acquire
personnel and equipment and write up new tables and manuals without
stepping on other Army toes. But films are something else. Photography
and all its derivations have been written into the Signal Corps' charter ever
since the Civil War. And they're jealous, they're tough, and they're big.
They won't sit still for any other Army unit fooling with film.

But—and here's where I came in—Osborn and Marshall didn't think
Signal Corps' Army Pictorial Service capable of producing sensitive and
objective troop information films. "But when months ago *you* volunteered
your services," interjected Stanley, "you were the answer to the General's
prayer," and Marshall, Osborn, Munson, everybody, said "that's our
man!" A take-charge guy. And that it was Marshall who said, "Let the
Signal Corps commission Capra, then get him assigned to Osborn, so that
Capra can have direct access to me." "You see, Frank," said Munson, "this
idea about films to explain 'Why' the boys are in uniform is General Marshall's own baby, and he wants the nursery right next to his Chief of Staff's
office."

They both let that statement sink in; then: "Still think you're being asked
to pimp for fun-and-games guys in short pants?" asked Munson.

"Fellas, can I have another drink?" I said, holding up my glass to the
red-coated waiter. "Lyman . . . Schlosberg told me I was to write up ideas
for morale films, then turn them over to Schlosberg for production. From
then on the films'll be a Signal Corps show, not mine, not Osborn's, nor—"

"That's why we chose you. Osborn thinks that anyone that can lick the
Establishment in Hollywood can lick it in the Army."

"Oh, for God's sake, Lyman. Not again! Not in the Army—"

PART III
The Great Struggle

Why We Fight

IT WAS DIFFICULT for me to keep up with Lyman Munson as he led me through the labyrinthian ways of the Pentagon. He was a hard driver, a jet-like man always ahead of his sound. In fact, just standing still Munson seemed to create a whirlwind. I'll never forget the way he put on his tunic, on the run. Grabbing its collar with both hands he would fling it high overhead, deftly let both sleeves slide down his upright arms—and the tunic was on without Munson losing his stride.

Lyman *had* to be on the run to act as warden, nurse, and Boy Scout leader to dozens of touchy civilian egos he had straitjacketed in uniforms: high and haughty Harvard professors who spoke to neither the Cabots nor the Lodges; mulish newsmen who thought "channels" were for greased swimmers; Madison Avenue ad men who stressed, "If the bottle is pretty enough you can sell sea water"; authors whose every word was gospel; and Hollywood "names" who wouldn't step on a carpet unless it was red.

And now Munson was escorting me to the office of the Chief of Staff. General George C. Marshall had sent for me. He wanted to talk to me alone. Not being a military man I didn't fully realize that this was tantamount to a private audience with the Pope.

We stopped at a hall door with the sign CHIEF OF STAFF over it. "Give your name to the guard inside, Frank. When he says go in, walk into Marshall's door without knocking. And *don't salute*. If he's busy, walk over to the chair at the right of his desk and sit down. Shoot straight, Frank, and with few words. See you."

Left alone I made for a nearby drinking fountain. But even water was a poor antidote for a cottony mouth. Suddenly I felt fear, homesickness—an uncontrollable urge to fly home to my family, to hide in the loving warmth of my wife and kids. But my feet wouldn't move, as they won't in a bad dream.

Officers passed me by without a glance; their faces drawn, unshaven. I leaned over the fountain, let the water cool my hot, dry lips. Then I walked to the door marked CHIEF OF STAFF.

There he sat behind a desk, gray, spare, undistinguished, quietly checking off items on a list. "Don't salute!" Munson had warned. Had I tried I would have fallen flat on my face. Without moving his head his pale blue eyes flashed me a quick look. "Major Capra, sir," I heard my voice saying.

His eyes returned to his papers. Yep, I thought to myself, he could be cast as a sad-eyed Oakie watching his soil blow away. There was the chair at the right of his desk. I walked to it, sat on its edge, clamped cold clammy hands on my twitching knees—and waited.

I was impressed by the intense concentration of this quiet man; he seemed to give the blue-cone tip of his mind to each item he checked off. Scribbling something quickly, he turned to me, smiling faintly—but only with his eyes.

"Good morning, Capra. You know, it's a constant inspiration to realize how many of our fine minds are giving up careers and family life, and putting on uniforms. Yes, in a total dedication in this terrible emergency." His eyes held and searched mine. "And that's fine. That's America. Mr. Capra—allow me to call you that for a moment—you have an opportunity to contribute enormously to your country and the cause of freedom. Are you aware of that, sir?"

I knew my answer was important to him. But all I could blurt out was, "Well, General Marshall, I—I mean if you're asking me does it scare the heck out of me, I'll have to say, yessir. It does!"

The fine lines of a smile radiated from his straight mouth and joined the crinkles round his eyes. I knew I could fall in love with this man.

With utter frankness he talked for about an hour. He told me we were raising a very large army—around eight million—and that we were going to try to make soldiers out of boys who, for the most part, had never seen a gun. They were being uprooted from civilian life and thrown into Army camps. And *the reason why* was hazy in their minds.

"Within a short time," he said, "we will have a huge citizens' army in which civilians will outnumber professional soldiers by some fifty to one. *We* may think this is our greatest strength, but the high commands of Germany and Japan are counting heavily on it being our greatest weakness.

"Our boys will be too soft, they say, too pleasure-loving, too undisciplined to stand up against their highly trained, highly indoctrinated, highly motivated professional armies. They are sure the spirit, the morale of their individual soldier is superior to ours. He has something to fight and die for—victory for the superman; establishing the new age of the superstate. The spoils of such a victory are a heady incentive.

"Now, how can we counter their superman incentive? Well, we are certain that if anyone starts shooting at Americans, singly or collectively,

Americans will fight back like tigers. Why? Because Americans have a long record of survival when their skins are at stake. What *is* in question is this: Will young, freewheeling American boys take the iron discipline of wartime training; endure the killing cold of the Arctic, the hallucinating heat of the desert, or the smelly muck of the jungle? Can they shake off the psychological diseases indigenous to all armies—boredom and homesickness?

"In my judgment the answer is 'Yes!' Young Americans, and young men of all free countries, are used to doing and thinking for themselves. They will prove not only equal, but superior to totalitarian soldiers, *if*—and this is a large if, indeed—they are given answers as to *why* they are in uniform, and *if* the answers they get are *worth* fighting and dying for.

"And that, Capra, is our job—and your job. To win this war we must win the battle for men's minds. Osborn and I think films are the answer, and that you are the answer to such films. Now, Capra, I want to nail down with you a plan to make a series of documented, factual-information films —the first in our history—that will explain to our boys in the Army *why* we are fighting, and the *principles* for which we are fighting."

"General Marshall, it's only fair to tell you that I have never before made a single documentary film. In fact, I've never even been near anybody that's made one—"

"Capra," he said, with a slight edge to his voice, "I have never been Chief of Staff before. Thousands of young Americans have never had their legs shot off before. Boys are commanding ships today, who a year ago had never seen the ocean before."

"I'm sorry, sir. I'll make you the best damned documentary films ever made."

He smiled. "I'm sure you will. We are all being asked to do what we never dreamed we could do. I'm asking you to tell our young men why they must be in uniform, why they *must* fight. These films are a top priority. I'll send you and Osborn a directive to that effect. Take charge as you have in Hollywood. Any serious hitches, report them back to me. Any questions?"

"Plenty, sir. But I'll find the answers," I said, rising. He gave me a sharp, quick look. "Thank you, Capra."

In his fleeting glance, before returning to his papers, the pale blue eyes of that quiet, severe man burdened with awesome power, revealed the loneliness of his soul—the constant yearning for guidance in the secret depths of those who must make decisions.

Leaving General Marshall's office I walked into a washroom to lock myself into a cubicle; to be alone; to think things out. The simple but enormous thrust of the assignment was bewildering. "Tell our young men *why* they are in uniform, *why* they must fight—" Yes, and why many will be blown to pieces. Always the young, the flower of youth. Did not Jehovah require young Isaac as a sacrifice from old Abraham?

I hadn't the foggiest idea of how to make a documentary film. To me, documentaries were ash-can films made by kooks with long hair. I was no expert on the reasons and causes of war. I had no organization, no money, no plan. But I did have a direct order from the Chief of Staff, and a desk in a small room with five other desks, and a painted sign: MAJOR FRANK CAPRA, ORIENTATION FILM SECTION. I was the section.

Shortly after General Marshall ordered me to make the *Why We Fight* films for our servicemen, I saw Leni Riefenstahl's terrifying motion picture, *Triumph of the Will*. The film was the ominous prelude of Hitler's holocaust of hate. Satan couldn't have devised a more blood-chilling super-spectacle.

Using the facilities of the Nazi-commandeered UFA film empire, Leni Riefenstahl (a woman producer) made the classic, powerhouse propaganda film of our times. It was at once the glorification of war, the deification of Hitler, and the canonization of his apostles. Though panoplied with all the pomp and mystical trappings of a Wagnerian opera, its message was as blunt and brutal as a lead pipe: We, the Herrenvolk, are the new invincible gods!

Triumph of the Will fired no gun, dropped no bombs. But as a psychological weapon aimed at destroying the will to resist, it was just as lethal.

The film's opening was a master stroke of god-building. In an aura of celestial music, an invisible, mystic camera photographed Hitler's invisible spirit descending toward earth from the clouds and stars of Valhalla, and gliding lower and lower over the beautiful German countryside.

As the messiah of malice brushed unseen wings over chimneytops, multitudes of waving, cheering, hysterical Nazis hailed the visitation with ovations of HEILS!—offering up the incense of bedlam in adoration of "his coming."

The music crashed out its *Götterdämmerung* to the gods of freedom; the supernal specter touched down on an airport runway; glided to a full stop; then—silence.

Magically, a plane door opened; its mystic frame dark with mystery. Then, god the spirit materialized into god the Führer—uniformed, resplendent, stigmatic with swastikas. He stepped forward, clicked his heels, blessed the chosen with the Nazi salute—and Thor loosed its thunderbolts. A Valkyrian roar of SIEG HEIL! ruptured the silence and rolled in thundering echos. The Nuremberg Congress of supermen had opened! A hundred thousand storm troopers—booted, armed, swastika-draped—stood rigid row on row, as Hate walked alone to his altar of microphones.

The Voice of Hate shrieked from millions of radios: "We are the master race!" "SIEG HEIL!" amened a hundred thousand throats. "Today, Germany! Tomorrow, the world!" "SIEG HEIL!" . . . "SIEG HEIL!" . . . "SIEG HEIL!" . . .

Then Hitler walked among his supermen who stood rigidly at attention. Blond, booted, helmeted Siegfrieds—swastika flags billowing—their faces shone with pagan madness as Hitler gripped each right arm in the warrior's clasp, forearm to forearm, and eyes met eyes in a wild hypnotic troth—vowing the blood oath of obedience.

Mass murder of innocents is beyond human understanding. But a viewing of *Triumph of the Will* should have predicted it—to any mind that could have remained unshriveled by horror.

Yes, the message of the film was plain and brutal: "Power is ours! Unbeatable power! Surrender, all ye weak babblers of freedom! The meek shall inherit only the earth to fill their graves. Surrender!"

That film paralyzed the will of Austria, Czechoslovakia, Scandinavia, and France. That film paved the way for the Blitzkrieg. That film practically paralyzed my own will as I walked slowly back to my battered desk to sit alone and unnoticed in a roomful of officers, each engrossed in his own inadequacies to meet the challenge of war.

I sat alone and pondered. How could I mount a counterattack against *Triumph of the Will*; keep alive *our* will to resist the master race? I was alone; no studio, no equipment, no personnel. Commandeering a Hollywood studio for this effort seemed out of the question. Could I plan idea films and turn them over to the Signal Corps for production? Did they have the creative brains to cope with such propaganda blockbusters as *Triumph of the Will*? No. The Signal Corps was geared to training films: how to fire machine guns, build trenches, clean rifles—the "nuts and bolts" type of visual aids to explain the "hows" of war, not the "whys." The struggle for men's minds was too new, too highbrow, too screwball for old-line colonels who still referred to soldiers as "bodies."

Earlier, I had dropped in on the poobah of Signal Corps films, Colonel Schlosberg, to tell him about my directive from the Chief of Staff. He was impressed, not with me, but with the growing importance of his film empire. Yessir! Producing films for the high command! He could visualize that new star, perhaps two stars, on each shoulder.

"Why that's fine! Fine!" he said, each word a heavy pat on my head. "See? I told you Morale was the right spot for you. You prepare the scripts, get them approved, then bring them over here to me. If I think they're feasible I'll give them a project number and forward them to Colonel Gillette in Astoria, Long Island."

I played it low key; pleaded, reasoned; appealed to his God, his country, the emergency. "Allow me to make just these *special* General Marshall films at Astoria. On my word, I won't interfere with any system you and Colonel Gillette have set up—"

"You bet your ass you won't. Because if I let *you* get away with it, every Tom, Dick, and Harry in the Army'll wanna come in to make their own films—medical, transportation, ordnance, what have you. No! Only the Signal Corps can handle or touch film. It's in our charter and nobody, but *nobody*, can change it. Not even your Chief of Staff."

Well, here we go again. Another battle against entrenched stupidity. "Colonel Schlosberg, I know this war is wrecking a lot of little sand castles.

You should see what it did to mine. But you're in a civilian army, now. And all we civilians want is to get the hell out of uniform as fast as we can, nothing more. Now the Chief of Staff gave me an urgent job to do, and charters or no charters, *I'm going to do it*. Understand, Colonel? So why don't you cooperate before the going gets rough for all of us?"

"Are you trying to threaten a superior officer?"

"Oh, balls. No, sir. I'm the village idiot trying to save the neck of a superior officer."

Was it Fate that decreed that my life should be a continuous battle against the Establishment, in the Army as well as in Hollywood? Or was I creating my own environment in my obsession to become number one in any job I tackled? Was I building up Colonel Schlosberg into a villain that barred my way, a Goliath that had to be overcome—like Harry Cohn or L. B. Mayer? In fact, isn't Fate just the apothecary that fills out the life prescriptions we ourselves prescribe?

Did I *need* villains to do my thing? If there had been no Harry Cohns, or L. B. Mayers, or Colonel Schlosbergs in my life, would I have had to create them?

It would have been stupid, if not disloyal, to allow the inspirational *Why We Fight* films to be made by Signal Corps colonels to whom soldiers were "bodies"; colonels who were automatically hostile to the power of ideas; colonels dumb enough to have earlier refused to admit me to a "secret" showing of *Triumph of the Will* because *I was not yet cleared by "security."* The expert who was commissioned to fight enemy propaganda was not "cleared" to see an enemy propaganda film. No wonder dictatorships of *all kinds* are doomed to fail.

But more important than how or where I would produce answers to *Triumph of the Will* were the answers *themselves*. What *were* the answers? What *were* the antidotes to the poisonous ideas of a master race—be it blond or yellow?

I needed one basic, powerful idea, an idea that would spread like a prairie fire, an idea from which *all* ideas flowed. I thought of the Bible. There was one sentence in it that always gave me goose pimples: "Ye shall know the truth, and the truth shall make you free."

Did it also mean the truth would make you strong? Strong enough to stop Hitler and Tojo? What *was* the truth about this World War? Well, it was obvious to me that the Nazis of Germany, the warlords of Japan, and the Fascists of Italy were out to deliberately take over the free nations by force, so they could stamp out human freedom and establish their own world dictatorships. If that statement was the truth, free men everywhere would fight to the death against it.

But how did *I* know that statement was true? Who proved it to *me*? Why the enemy *himself* proved it to me, in his acts, his books, his speeches, his films.

That was the key idea I had been searching for—on my feet in Pentagon halls, on my back in bed, and on my knees in pews. Let the *enemy* prove to our soldiers the enormity of his cause—and the justness of ours.

Colonel Munson startled me out of my brown study by sitting on my desk and quipping that I was getting paler and paler since seeing *Triumph of the Will.* I assured him my paleness was nothing—inside I was getting greener and greener.

"Come on, Frank, you need some air. Let's go home and see what the wife's got for dinner."

In the car Lyman told me that General Osborn and General Surles, Army Public Relations head, had had some powwows with Lieutenant General Somervell, chief of G-4 (Service of Supply), about forcing the Signal Corps to cooperate in the production of Special Services films. The Signal Corps, Lyman said, had breathed dragon fire on the talks.

Munson also chewed me off for having given Pathe News in New York my personal check for three thousand dollars for the historical newsreel footage I had ordered because only the Signal Corps could buy film and they had disapproved buying it for me. So I was out three thousand clams. But he said he had approved my hiring of Edgar Peterson, a local Washington documentary film man, as a Civil Service assistant, and that I had permission to hire other film people as Civil Service employees.

Lyman Munson, a West Point general's son, and his wife, "Jimmy," a West Point general's daughter, lived in a small Army duplex in Alexandria, Virginia. Theirs was the typical barracks romance of army brats. Both were born and raised in army barracks. They met and fell in love in army barracks. And they got married and lived happily ever after in nothing but army barracks.

While Lyman Munson was mixing drinks and Jimmy Munson was conjuring up salivating smells in her kitchen, we were joined by Lyman's number two man, Jack Stanley, and his very beautiful wife. With them was— surprise!—a red-mustached American captain with a British accent; a Yorkshireman whose unruly shock of dark red hair seemed as full of mischief as his sharp, ferret-like eyes. He was Eric Knight, the author of *The Flying Yorkshireman,* the *Sam Small* stories, *This Above All,* and *Lassie Come Home.*

For me it was love at first sight with Eric Knight. He had all the talents that could be compressed into a single writer: Wit, compassion, sensitiveness, an intriguing style, and a great, great love for human beings. He had Keats's: "mighty idea of beauty in all things." But this above all—Eric was a rollicking boon companion; one of the three most charming men I met in the service, the other two being his good friends novelist Paul Horgan and painter Peter Hurd.

After dinner, while the wives washed the dishes, the four of us—two West Point men, a noted British author, and a Hollywood film director, all American Army officers—talked about what we could never stop talking about: psychological warfare against paranoids who had, psychologically and on the field of battle, just about convinced many nations in the world, and a good many people in our own country, that it was useless, and perhaps senseless, to struggle against the power structure of the master-race trinity: Hitler-Tojo-Mussolini.

I told them of my hunch: Use the enemy's own films to expose their enslaving ends. Let our boys hear the Nazis and the Japs shout their own claims of master-race crud—and our fighting men will *know* why they are in uniform. Eric jumped to his feet. "Frank, if you never get another bloody idea you'll still be way ahead. It smacks of Thomas Aquinas's pet debating ploy; discuss all your opponents' main points—then powder them."

Munson and Stanley were equally enthusiastic. "Okay," I said, "but I've got to have a film set-up of my own. And more important, I need the enemy films. Who's got them all?" They looked blank.

"Lyman," I butted in, "I'll lay ten to one the Signal Corps is too dumb to think of grabbing up propaganda films. There's got to be a big cache of enemy newsreels somewhere, and with your permission I'm starting out at dawn on a one-man film hunt. And if I get my hands on any, I'm setting up my own film unit to make General Marshall's films, even if I have to make them in the broom closet I sleep in at the Carlton—room 308."

Jimmy Munson poked her head in the door to announce: "Lousy news on the radio, fellas. The Japs drove MacArthur's men off Bataan. They're holed up in Corregidor, the poor bastards. Anybody want a drink?" No answer. She withdrew to the kitchen.

"Frank, what if Schlosberg has already nailed down those enemy films?" asked Munson quietly.

"Aw, come off it, Lyman. Frank's got a rare champion spirit, man. Why don't we back him up? Sure, the Army snipers'll take pot shots at him. But you know bloody well the weapon isn't made that can shoot down ideas."

Eric Knight was to tragically prove his point in less than a year.

Edgar Peterson, a bright young ivy leaguer who knew his way around Washington's film alleys, was my first Civil Service employee. He increased the personnel of my film section by a whopping 100 percent. I really hired him to find me a place to store the thirty cans of nitrate (dangerously flammable) newsreel film I had bought (with my own money) from Pathe News. He said every dinky film-cutting room in Washington was rented, but he knew of a little-known government film set-up that was practically moribund. Only one problem—it belonged to Secretary of Interior Ickes, and Ickes was a hard man to shave. He took me to see it.

A square service building called the "Cooling Tower" stuck up in the middle of the inner court of the North Interior Building. It housed the heating and cooling machinery for Ickes's multistoried Department of Interior. But the first two floors were all occupied by Interior's 16 mm film set-up—cutting rooms, projection facilities and storage vaults. It also had two old-fashioned 35 mm projection machines. Obviously some of the privileged help saw movies there. We found two old Civil Service retainers trying to look busy. One, Mr. Dame, was the Chief; the other, Walter West, was obviously the Indian. They looked frightened as they watched an Army officer case their little empire. I told Pete to get a set of keys and set up a little office for us and make an inventory of the equipment. He was in the middle of inventory-taking when I walked into the Cooling Tower the morning after dinner at the Munson's and said: "Pete, you're a pretty good film hound. Bring your smeller and let's try to track some down."

We tried smelling for enemy films at the State Department. They sent us to the FBI, who sent us to the Treasury Department, who said, "Try the Alien Property Custodian," who referred us to Mr. Samuel Klaus, a special assistant to Treasury's General Counsel. The trail ended. For us, Samuel Klaus—a small, baldish Jew—was Santa Klaus.

"What can I do for you, Major?" he asked curtly, without rising.

"German and Japanese newsreels, Mr. Klaus."

"What about 'em?"

"General Marshall has asked me to make films that'll show our boys what kind of bastards they are fighting—and *why*."

His eyes lit up. But his voice was still dry and flat. "Sit down, Major. Or should I call you Mr. Deeds or Mr. Smith?" I bowed and gratefully sat down. "Yes, Frank Capra, I've got *warehouses full* of German and Japanese films; all their newsreels for the past twenty years. But you're a few days late. Here's a request from the Chief Signal Officer to turn all this film over to the Signal Corps."

My heart almost stopped. "Mr. Klaus, I'm talking to you now as one American citizen to another. Telling our soldiers why they are being drafted has got to be our number one priority. If these enemy films get buried in Signal Corps channels it'll take me months just to get to see them. I need these films *now*."

He looked at me for a long time as he pulled on his lower lip. Then he leaned forward on his desk and said: "Frank Capra, are you telling me that you, an Army officer, handed me a formal written request *five days ago*, asking the Alien Property Custodian to deliver all enemy films in his possession to you, for the purpose of making information films for the Army at the direction of the Chief of Staff—"

Peterson and I walked away on air. We had found the great cache of enemy films—and it was ours! Now to officially get the Cooling Tower. We ran to it, barged in, and announced to the old retainer that the Army was commandeering half of his quarters to store important Army films.

I raced to Temporary Building H to tell Munson and Osborn of our good fortune—leaving out the pre-dating part to avoid implicating them in any official conspiracy. Munson said: "Nice going." General Osborn, a man of character, was worried. His Special Services Division had no right to accept the responsibility for such films. I reminded the General that I had signed for the films personally and as a Signal Corps officer, and not in the name of his Special Services.

The good general was still worried; he abhorred gutter-type infighting. But I was no gentleman. I hated war; hated to dignify it with rules of conduct. I hated being a second-class citizen; hated having to get an okay to make a long-distance call, or send a telegram; hated having to remain within fifteen minutes of Washington without an approval from the Adjutant General —which took about five days. I hated having to swallow the galling figment that someone else's opinion was superior to mine because he outranked me. But I hated becoming a slave of a master race even more. At least my wife and children were free. And I would resort to the dirtiest kind of infighting to keep them free. So come Army charters, or clod-pated colonels, or gentlemen generals, I would make films that justified this war to our soldiers.

The final confrontation took place in a small conference room in Special Services' new quarters in the Pentagon. In a private meeting demanded by them, a livid Colonel Schlosberg and a very uncomfortable Colonel Darryl Zanuck, handed me an official ultimatum: "Turn over all films in your name to the Chief Signal Officer, or face court-martial. And that's a direct order from the Chief Signal Officer."

I told them exactly what they could do with their ultimatum *and* the Chief Signal Officer; reminded them that I was given a direct order from the Chief of Staff to make the *Why We Fight* pictures. And that if I was stupid enough to turn that responsibility over to pompous asses like Colonel Schlosberg, I deserved to be shot, not court-martialed.

I warned the Colonel to stop trying to bury me, because whether he liked it or not, in the world of film—in Hollywood, in the Army, or in the toilet —wherever I sat was the head of the table. And if he didn't believe it, he should ask Darryl Zanuck about the contract his Twentieth Century-Fox company offered me, which I turned down to join the Army.

They left, making dire threats—against Special Services as well as me.

Munson and Osborn were deeply concerned about this inter-Army jurisdictional squabble. They thought I should go to General Marshall about it. I said the Chief of Staff was too busy running a global war. Besides, he had said, "Capra, take charge." I urged General Osborn to take the offensive against the Signal Corps; accuse, protest, challenge. If that didn't work I could always scrounge enough equipment from my friends. And we could always hire more civilian personnel. I already owned the Cooling Tower and its measly equipment. They said I *didn't* own the Cooling Tower. The Secretary of the Interior could throw me out anytime. I pointed out that Ickes wouldn't dare. There's a war on! And anyway, what with the mountains of captured film I had in the Cooling Tower, Ickes wouldn't have enough trucks to throw me out.

It all began to sound like comic opera—"The Great Celluloid War" between the Know-It-Alls of Hollywood and the Got-It-Alls of Pentagon—while MacArthur's men died inch by inch at Corregidor.

And then—the unexpected and unfunny happened. It murdered our confidence. When my seven writers (volunteer Hollywood civilians) turned in their treatments—each had been assigned a segment of the historical decade between Manchuria and Pearl Harbor—I was aghast. The outlines were larded with Communist propaganda.

I huddled with Osborn, Munson, and Watrous. They were shocked. Special Services was already in difficulty with the Congressional Appropriations Committee; the chairman was suspicious about orientation films for the Army. "What the hell is this 'orientation' business—a new word for propaganda?" If the slightest hint were leaked to the Committee that the scripts contained pro-Communist stuff—Zap! Our necks would be out a mile, and the Signal Corps was waiting with the ax. The outlines were classified "top secret" and the writers were quietly dismissed.

We all realized the project was so sensitive it could only be carried out with controllable men in uniform. General Osborn must ask for power to enlist and commission his own film personnel, or ask that his Special Services Division be relieved of the responsibility for carrying out General Marshall's directive. Quiet waters run deep. Gentle General Osborn gave me a lesson in high-class infighting. On May 2, 1942, a memo directing the Chief Signal Officer to "establish a Signal Corps (film) Detachment under the Jurisdiction and Direct Control of the Chief of Special Services," went out from the Office of the Commanding General, Services of Supply—namely, Lieutenant General Somervell.

The 834th Photo Signal Detachment was born. Jubilation reigned. I immediately signed a year's lease on a large house in Bethesda, and phoned Lu to bring the children and Rosa the cook and Kelly the nurse.

Meanwhile, Anatole Litvak, Tony Veiller, Robert Heller, and Leonard Spiegelgass (pending their induction into the Army) and I went to work on the *Why We Fight* scripts, on which we would base the following seven fifty-minute "must see" one-hour training films (ten minutes allowed for filling and emptying theaters):

1. *Prelude to War*—presenting a general picture of two worlds; the slave and the free, and the rise of totalitarian militarism from Japan's conquest of Manchuria to Mussolini's conquest of Ethiopia.
2. *The Nazis Strike*—Hitler rises. Imposes Nazi dictatorship on Germany. Goose-steps into Rhineland and Austria. Threatens war unless given Czechoslovakia. Appeasers oblige. Hitler invades Poland. Curtain rises on the tragedy of the century—World War II.
3. *Divide and Conquer*—Hitler occupies Denmark and Norway, outflanks Maginot Line, drives British Army into North Sea, forces surrender of France.

4. *Battle of Britain*—showing the gallant and victorious defense of Britain by Royal Air Force, at a time when shattered but unbeaten British were only people fighting Nazis.

5. *Battle of Russia*—History of Russia; people, size, resources, wars. Death struggle against Nazi armies at gates of Moscow and Leningrad. At Stalingrad, Nazis put through meat grinder.

6. *Battle of China*—Japan's warlords commit total effort to conquest of China. Once conquered, Japan would use China's manpower for the conquest of *all* Asia.

7. *War Comes to America*—Dealt with who, what, where, why, and how we came to be the U.S.A.—the oldest major democratic republic still living under its original constitution. But the heart of the film dealt with the depth and variety of emotions with which Americans reacted to the traumatic events in Europe and Asia. How our convictions slowly changed from total non-involvement to total commitment as we realized that loss of freedom anywhere increased the danger to our own freedom. This last film of the series was, and still is, one of the most graphic visual histories of the United States ever made.

These were the seven *Why We Fight* films that were to revolutionize not only documentary filmmaking throughout the world, but also the horse-and-buggy method of indoctrinating and informing troops with the truth. Primarily made by the Army for the Army, they were used as training films by the Navy, Marine Corps, and Coast Guard. The British, Canadians, Australians, and New Zealanders used them as training films for their armed forces. Translated into French, Spanish, Portuguese, and Chinese they were shown to the armed forces of our allies in China, South America, and in various parts of Europe and Africa.

One film was shown to the American people in theaters. By an order from Winston Churchill *all* were shown to the British public in theaters. The Russians showed *Battle of Russia* throughout all their theaters. And in the chaotic months of occupation after the war, American Embassies played the *Why We Fight* series in enemy countries, charging ten cents for admission. The State Department has stated that these showings enriched our treasury by more than $2,500,000—a sum six times greater than their original cost.

Thus, the *Why We Fight* series became our official, definitive answer to: What was government policy during the dire decade 1931–41? For whenever State, the White House, or Congress was unable, or unwilling, to tell us what our government's policy had been (and this happened often) I followed General Marshall's advice: "In those cases make your own best estimate, and see if they don't agree with you later." By extrapolation, the film series was also accepted as the official policy of our allies.

Thus, it can be truly said that the *Why We Fight* films not only stated but, in many instances, actually created and nailed down American and world pre-war policy. No, I won't say it. Yes, I will say it. I was the first "Voice of America."

About May 10, 1942, Mrs. Capra came to Washington with her brood: Frankie (eight), Lulu (four), Tommy (one), and Rosa the cook and Kelly the nurse. We moved into a two-story, four-bedroom house in Bethesda, Maryland, surrounded by a spacious lawn and large black-trunked trees. And surprise! We all saw our first fireflies and just couldn't believe them. The kids put them in bottles and, squealing with excitement, used the bottles as sparkling flashlights to explore the house and garden with.

The fireflies were delightful—but not the servants' quarters in the concrete basement: two ugly, cramped, uncarpeted cubicles shot through with exposed steam and sewer pipes—designed with malice to keep the Negro in his place. In fact, I was informed that most houses around Washington were all magnolia and Southern hospitality upstairs, and all skunk cabbage and bigotry in the cellar.

I moved out of room 308 at the Carlton, but refused to give it up. For the next four years it would be my sometime home and tiny eddy of quiet in the Washington millrace for the scores who came to work for us a few hours or a few days. Even while living in 308 I allowed others to use it in the daytime. Some days as many as three shifts of sleepers occupied the room. Visiting wives kept trysts with uniformed husbands. Visiting celebrities like John Gunther or Charles MacArthur simply asked Frank Swazey, the hotel manager, for a key and shacked up with me for a day or two.

Leonard Lyons wrote this item about room 308 in his New York *Post* column:

> Marc Connelly will write a movie for Frank Capra's film-division of the Army . . . Connelly reported for work in (congested) Washington. In Capra's office he met Kurt Weill, the composer, and Maxwell Anderson, the playwright . . .
>
> "Capra was thoughtful enough to reserve a little room for me," Connelly told Weill. "Were you able to get a reservation, Kurt?" . . . "Yes," the composer replied, "I'm in Room 308, at the Carlton." "But that's the room I'm in," said Connelly, "and I suppose that bag I saw in the corner of the room was yours." . . . "No, it isn't," Weill added. "That bag is Maxwell Anderson's."

Playwright Charles MacArthur, now Major MacArthur, an aide to the commanding general of the hush-hush Chemical Warfare Service, had never been a fan of my films. Too corny for that hard-nosed ex-reporter. But as we hit the sack in room 308 one night, he poked me with a stubby finger and asked: "I want to know something. My general told me a guy by the name of Capra did a helluva piece of research at Caltech twenty-five years ago: Spontaneous combustion of liquid carbon disulfide saturated with silicon-hydride gas, to burn holes in enemy masks. Was that you?" "Charlie! You speak the lingo good—" "Was that *you*?" I nodded. He pumped my hand. "You're nothing but a goddam Dago, you know that?" he said, and turned off the light.

Room 308, unlisted and unrentable, was exactly seven feet wide and twelve feet long. But it had a three-quarter bed, an open clothes closet, a three-drawer bureau below an oval mirror into whose wavy glass one could look darkly and see mysterious sunsets. And it had one chair, and one dirty screened window which tamed the zeal of the sunniest day into the anemia of twilight.

One person could negotiate the obstacle course of boots, bags, bed legs, and Peter Hurd's guitar without breaking toes—if he wore his shoes. Two persons had to walk sideways like crabs. If a third person came in, traffic was paralyzed. But at times we were as many as eight, sprawled on the bed and wedged on the floor, shouting in bull sessions, or listening to Peter Hurd, Paul Horgan, and Eric Knight sing folk songs. And a delight it all was for my next-door neighbor, wise old Barney Baruch, who occasionally —when he wasn't advising F.D.R. and Cabinet members, or sitting in a park trading Socratic ironies with fellow bench warmers—joined our goings on. Room 308. A broom closet. But never such a wonderful broom closet.

And now the Cooling Tower had figuratively shrunk to another broom closet. Much like hungry viruses invade a bacterium and multiply by eating their host, Edgar Peterson and I had invaded the Cooling Tower and multiplied into the 834th Photo Signal Detachment of eight officers and about twelve enlisted men. All were Hollywood professionals—directors, writers, and film editors. In addition, some twenty civil service personnel performed various duties.

Working like disciplined and tightly packed ants we attacked the making of the *Why We Fight* series. One group of translators (supplied by Iris Barry, film curator of New York's Museum of Modern Art, and by Army intelligence) rephrased the German and Japanese films into English. Another group catalogued and cross-filed the film scenes—a tedious, backbreaking job. Our main group worked on research and the scripts.

As the executive producer I outlined the scope and thrust of each of the seven fifty-minute films, Tony Veiller and I did most of the script-writing, although we had considerable help from some fair writing talent, namely, authors Eric Knight and James Hilton, screen writers Alan Rivkin and Leonard Spiegelgass, and newsmen William Shirer and Bill Henry.

At the very outset I assigned teams of assistant producers, writers, film editors, and research men to work more or less concurrently on each film. But the truckloads of impounded enemy film came rolling, came rolling, until there was no room at Ickes' Inn for even one team.

Furthermore, Paul Horgan would soon need a shooting crew for his *Officer's Candidate School* script, and Undersecretary of War Patterson was pressuring us for a Negro film to buck up the morale of our black soldiers. The Undersecretary put me in touch with his Negro adviser, Truman Gibson. Gibson opened up a thick dossier of sickening acts of discrimination against Negro troops in the South. Exaggerated? The Secretary of War didn't think so. There were too many reports equally incredible. He ordered Special Services to give the highest priority to a Negro soldier film, and assigned us a young Negro writer, Carlton Moss, to collaborate on the script.

Besides these urgent outside requests, I was anxious to launch my *Army-Navy Screen Magazine* and another series of orientation films: *Know Your Ally, Know Your Enemy.* So I asked permission to move the film section to Hollywood where we belonged in the first place. Osborn and Munson agreed—especially if I could also find a set-up for Tom Lewis's Armed Forces Radio which desperately needed the broadcasting talent and facilities on the West Coast.

Before my wife had finished unpacking at our rented house in Bethesda, I told her to start packing again while I rushed out to Hollywood for help. And I knew exactly who to go to for help—Colonel Darryl Zanuck. Zanuck knew my situation. He had been present when Schlosberg threatened me with a court-martial.

The old Western Avenue Twentieth Century Studios had been abandoned years ago. It was now a pile of run-down buildings—a ghost studio. I asked Darryl to let me have it for my film section and for Tom Lewis's Armed Forces Radio. He said, "Of course, it's all yours." He'd have it cleaned up and painted for me.

There was a Signal Corps procurement office in Hollywood. I officially requested that office to furnish and equip my new base on Western Avenue. Request turned down.

I quietly contacted friendly back-lot department heads in various studios; asked for any worn-out furniture and equipment they could spare. They dug me up old typewriters, desks, chairs, filing cabinets, and even old Movieolas and cutting-room tables and bins.

That sub-rosa operation "scrounge" moved George Stevens to join our unit. He was shooting a picture at Columbia Studios when he spotted me on one end of a beat-up desk that Ray Howell (Head of Props) and I were lifting into a studio truck. I was in uniform. "Frank! What in hell are you doing here, moving furniture?" "Sh-h-h. Make out you don't know me. I'm stealing this stuff." "You? You need an old desk? I thought you were chief of something." "George, in the Army you've gotta be an Indian to get something done." "Well, Frank, I'm part Indian. Can you use me?" "My God, yes. Come over to Western Avenue. The old Fox studio—"

George Stevens came over. He was a major before he could raise his hand

and say "How!" He asked to head a group of combat photographers. He did. In Europe until after the surrender.

The only equipment I couldn't "borrow" were sound projection machines. Old 35 mm projectors were at a premium because the military had priority on the new ones. So I ordered the two vintage projectors at the Cooling Tower to be secretly torn out of their concrete bases and shipped West to our new headquarters. We also practically shanghaied the Cooling Tower's civil service projectionist, Walter West, because Walter was the only man in the world that could coax the old machines to work. Since the projectors were non-synchronizing, he would run *picture film* on one machine and *sound track film* on the other, keeping picture and sound in sync by braking one machine or the other with his thumbs.

The whole *Why We Fight* series, the *Know Your Ally, Know Your Enemy* series, the *Army-Navy Screen Magazine, The Negro Soldier in World War II* were all made in that falling-apart borrowed studio with scrounged furniture and equipment, and those two horse-and-buggy projection machines we hijacked from Interior that had to be kept in sync with braking thumbs.

In wartime one learns to get around the lead-tailed colonels who squat on empires. In our case necessity was not a mother but a distressed maiden who brought many additional professional Hollywood knights to her rescue—in uniform: Anatole Litvak, Tony Veiller, John Huston, George Stevens, Willie Wyler, Sam Briskin, William Hornbeck, Leonard Spiegelgass, Merrill White, William Claxton, William Lyon, Henry Berman, Ted Geisel, Claude Binyon, Carl Foreman, Stu Heisler, David Miller, Bill Mellor, Joe Biroc, Joe Valentine, Eric Knight, and Meredith Willson and his great Santa Ana Air Force orchestra. And out of uniform: Walter Huston, Lloyd Nolan, Robert Stevenson, Bill Henry, Robert Flaherty, James Hilton, Alan Rivkin, Joe Sistrom, Edgar Peterson, Dimitri Tiomkin, Alfred Newman, plus the sound, music, and dubbing departments of Twentieth Century-Fox, Paramount, MGM, and (of utmost importance) the personal talents of Walt Disney and his best animators in making our animated maps artistic as well as informative.

The war information films were made in spite of the heavy-handed opposition of entrenched colonels. They had warehouses full of unwrapped equipment and facilities to spare. But we had the brains, the talent, and the desire. With these, and our industry's cooperation on a no-profit—often on a no-cost—basis, Hollywood professionals made film history in a field strange to them—documentary films, the private preserves of intellectuals.

In October, 1942, just three years after I took *Mr. Smith* to Washington and was run out of town, I took another picture to Washington for its premiere showing: *Prelude to War.*

General Osborn described the Chief of Staff's reaction to our first *Why We Fight* film, in a letter Osborn wrote to Lu:

Dear Mrs. Capra:

"Your husband's film, *Prelude to War*, was shown to General Marshall yesterday . . . When the lights went on there was complete silence in the room for two minutes or more. Then General Marshall turned, looked about until he saw your husband and said, "Colonel Capra, how did you do it, that is a most wonderful thing." Then he called him over and talked about it part by part in detail with him. . . . It was a moving occasion. . . .

(signed) F. H. Osborn

The day the White House showing of *Prelude* was scheduled General Marshall invited me to lunch alone with him in his office. He was most friendly and most pleased that his idea of troop information films had started so auspiciously with *Prelude to War*. He asked me if all the film was authentic. I said it was. Our only re-creations were newspaper headlines and, of course, the animated expository war maps. He asked where the enemy film came from. I told him I had possession of all German, Japanese, and Italian newsreels made in the last twenty years. And also most of their propaganda documentaries made before and during the war.

Then he wanted to know how I obtained the film. "General Marshall, it's a long, boring story. Point is, I've got all the captured enemy film, I'm negotiating for Russian war film, T. Y. Lo of the China News Agency has promised me all their Chinese film, and Donovan's O.S.S. is stealing current enemy newsreels for me in border countries . . ."

I was hoping he wouldn't bring up the next subject, but he did. "Osborn has hinted that you've had problems with the Signal Corps. Have you?" "No real problems, sir." "Frank, these *Why We Fight* films are of enormous value, for us and for our allies. Any delays from any source—and you come direct to me." "General Marshall," I said jokingly, "I'll make you a deal. I'll let you stick to winning the war, if you let me stick to minding the film store."

He grinned. He liked people who knew they could get things done. He then said Secretary Stimson wanted to make certain that all policy statements made in *Prelude to War* had been checked for accuracy. "Have they?" he asked. I answered that all policy questions had been checked with State, OWI (Office of War Information), and Presidential advisers such as Lowell Mellett. To most questions we got clear-cut answers; to some, elliptical answers or none at all. On these matters my staff and I stood back and did what the General himself had advised: made the best objective guesses as to what our policies had been.

Again he beamed at my answer, and said he would have Osborn run the films for State, OWI, and for congressional leaders. Only then did it dawn on me just how far General Marshall was sticking his neck out in having the Army make information films (propaganda his detractors would call them) for captive Army audiences. Only his great faith in the belief that free men are better fighting men when they are well informed could make this great soldier step into a political and psychological arena where civilian angels feared to tread.

In the next couple of years I was to enjoy many such talks with General Marshall, especially during dinners with him alone at the Chief of Staff's house, "Quarters Number One," the large, comfortable, two-story red-brick building at Fort Myer, Virginia, across the Memorial Bridge. Only a Filipino enlisted cook would be with the General. Between seven and seven thirty we would have two stiff, bourbon old-fashioneds which the Chief liked to mix himself.

There would be talk of course, but absolutely no war talk. That day he probably had had to make decisions that affected the fate of nations; tomorrow he would face problems equally crucial. But that evening he would be calm and unworried as he listened to my chatting. Once, I asked him how he stood up under the strain; he answered: "I've had to train myself never to worry about a decision once it's made. You worry before you make it, but not after. You make the best judgment you can about a problem—then forget it. If you don't, your mind is not fit to make the next decision."

At exactly seven thirty the Filipino would serve dinner at a small table, and for the next hour and a half I would answer questions about all the techniques of motion pictures: acting, photography, sound recording, animated cartoons, musical comedies. Or, I would tell him about my early years, or Papa's green thumb; how he could make mature orange tree limbs grow roots, then saw them off and present them to friends as full-bearing orange trees; how he sprinkled ground-up minerals around the roots of rose bushes and changed the colors of the roses.

And when he found out I owned a large fruit ranch he wanted to know all the details, and being a compost buff himself, he flipped his top when I described to him our large concrete compost pits and the machinery for making and turning the compost. This in turn would inspire the General to talk in glowing terms about his Dodona Manor in Leesburg, Virginia, where he hoped to retire and plant all kinds of fruits, vegetables, and flowers. And I would plead with him not to use any poisonous sprays.

His eyes shone as he spoke of working with soil. But they shone brightest when he talked of his experiences in commanding CCC boys' camps in Florida and the Pacific Northwest. For in those camps he first met the frail, anemic, poverty-stricken youths of the Great Depression. In those camps he first decided to bring young men back to health, courage, and manhood through education—feeding the mind as well as the stomach— teaching them to acquire abilities that would make the most of their born-with capacities.

It was his experience with the CCC boys that led him to conceive and add a new and revolutionary concept to the American Army—a Morale Division which catered to the welfare of the mind and soul of a soldier. For the first time a heart was implanted into a military system that had referred to service men as "bodies" and "numbers." One result of that new

concept: the *Why We Fight* series of Army information films. Another result: my lasting friendship with one of the great men of our century,
George Catlett Marshall.

To those who knew and loved G.C.M., it was no accident that Chief of
Staff Marshall, the architect of military victory in Europe, should, as Secretary of State Marshall, be the architect of the Marshall Plan to help Europe
recover from "hunger, poverty, desperation, and chaos." Nor did it surprise
us when he was honored with the Nobel Peace Prize.

CHAPTER 18

F.D.R., Mr. P.M., & W.W. II

"Capra!" said General Sommervell as we rode from the Pentagon to the White House in a staff car flying three-star flags, "Have you ever met the President?" "No, sir." "Have you ever seen the Grand Canyon?" I nodded. "Well, meeting F.D.R. is like seeing the Big Hole the first time—you feel puny."

Franklin Delano Roosevelt was not the largest man in the world, nor even the largest President. Taft was. But F.D.R. made you feel *he* was. At least he loomed large to me as I shook his hand with all the aplomb of a man standing on his first pair of ice skates. His head was the biggest, his face the widest, and his smile the most expansive I had ever seen. By every measure he was a big man—including time; he had occupied the White House longer than any other President, and gave not the slightest indication that he was about to call a moving van.

As Secret Service men wheeled him into the middle of the front row of chairs, the President introduced us to a woman guest who sat down next to him—Duchess "somebody," from Luxembourg or "some place"—"and," he said to me, indicating two other guests, "you must know these two jackanapes." I nodded to Harpo Marx and Alexander Woollcott.

"Sommervell!" called out the President, sky-writing with a lighted cigarette on the end of a very long holder, "an Army picture, tonight, right? Well, how about briefing us with some of the gory details—and don't forget the meaning of the word 'brief.'" His laugh was big, too, and truly infectious—in spite of the noblesse oblige to laugh at Presidential "jokes." General Sommervell laughed the loudest. Apparently, he and F.D.R. were old friends, used to guying each other. The President turned to Woollcott.

"Alex, there was a play about brief—brief something—" "*Brief Moment,*
Mr. President, by Sam Behrman—"

"That's it. Come forward, Sommervell! And enjoy your brief moment."
(It always shocked me to witness the monkeyshines of national leaders in
wartime, not realizing how desperately they needed occasional release from
nerves rubbed raw by worry.)

The General stepped in front of F.D.R. He seemed to relish the horseplay.
"Instant brief, Mr. President. All you need to know about this film, in
five little words: It's a Frank Capra film." Harpo Marx guffawed and led
the applause.

"Touché, touché!" applauded the President. Then he turned back to me,
"Take a bow, young man, take a bow—" I rose, bowed in all directions.
Evidently, you either got off on the right foot with F.D.R., or you didn't get
off at all. Harpo gave me a big Mack Sennett wink of approval.

I waved to the projectionist to roll the film. The lights went out. General
Sommervell sat down on my right, and suddenly a wraith-like man slipped
into a chair on my left. "Frank Capra," he whispered, "I'm Harry Hopkins.
Welcome." I shook the soft hand and looked into the soft doe eyes of
F.D.R.'s lean, lanky, hatchet man whose name and ulcers had become inter-
national items.

The day was on the verge of becoming too much for my trick stomach
when the opening chords of Alfred Newman's magnificent music made us
all sit up. (Newman had composed, arranged, conducted, and recorded the
score of *Prelude to War* at Twentieth Century-Fox without charge.) On the
screen our Liberty Bell tolled its paean to freedom. Over the ringing bell
these titles appeared,

The U.S. Army
presents
Prelude to War
Produced by
The War Department

followed by a written statement over General Marshall's signature, declar-
ing that this film and subsequent films in the series were made by the War
Department to "acquaint members of the Army with factual information as
to the causes, the events leading up to our entry in the war, and the principles for which we are fighting . . ." (No names of any individuals were
ever mentioned or credited in any of our Army information films.)

Franklin Roosevelt was not one to yield the floor lightly to any person or
any thing. But after the first five minutes of being "on"—chatting to those
around him and to the screen—he settled into a statue-like stillness. Harry
Hopkins nudged me, and whispered: "Congratulations, Frank. You've got
him. And he's the world's biggest ham."

The film ended on the faces of marching citizen-soldiers of all free na-

tions. Superimposed over these young men was this Draconian statement
of their task:

> "No compromise is possible and the victory of
> the democracies can only be complete with the
> utter defeat of the war machines of Germany and Japan."
>
> G. C. Marshall
> Chief of Staff

When the lights went on, F.D.R. triggered an applause that sounded very
sincere. "Every man, woman, and child in the world must see this film,"
he asserted over the din.

Both Harpo Marx, a favorite of the Eastern "in" clique, and Alex
Woollcott, one of the clique's bellwethers, shook my hand profusely. That
was holy oil from the intellectual curia.

"Frank Capra," said the President, "will this—what's the title—yes,
Prelude to War. Will it be shown in theaters?"

"No, Mr. President. Only in Army camps."

"Why? Civilians need to see it as much as soldiers."

"Mr. President," I answered, in defense of our industry, "movie houses
are privately owned. If they play one government information film they
fear a flood of others. And they say the public will resent dull official
films. Besides that, Mr. President, I acquired some free film and free
services on condition the film plays only in Army camps."

"Well, isn't that all just too bad," said Mr. President with biting sym-
pathy. Then he ordered Harry Hopkins to see Elmer Davis, head of the
Office of War Information, and Lowell Mellett, Federal Coordinator of
Films, about persuading theater owners to show the film.

Later on as we all sat in a small library-like room having highballs, and
enjoying the President's trading quip for quip with us, I began to understand why that rich Harvard-bred extrovert had become the patron saint of
the downtrodden. Charm he had, and charisma to spare. But his greatest
asset was the way he made you—no matter who or what you were—feel
important. He did it mostly by being a great listener.

He knew that the overpowering presence of the President of the United
States could turn strong men weak, and weak men imbecilic. So with a big
friendly smile, and the glint of intense interest in his sparkling eyes, he
would encourage you to talk about yourself, your family, your work, anything. "Well, I declare!" he'd exclaim after you'd made some inane statement. By little laughs, and goads, and urgings such as "Really? Tell me
more!" . . . "Well, what do you know!" . . . "Same thing's happened to me
dozens of times!" . . . "Oh, that's fascinating" . . . his warmth would
change you from a stuttering milquetoast to an articulate raconteur. And
you would remain forever in his debt. And who knows? You might also walk
down the sawdust trail and join the forever-Roosevelt faithfuls. He almost
converted me into becoming a Democrat.

I was about to leave for the Coast when Colonel Munson, my boss, confronted me with an urgent message to report immediately to Colonel Fitzgerald, Office of Internal Security, Military Intelligence. A suspicious Munson asked me what the call was all about. "Oh," I answered, "G-2 has probably dug me up another half-dozen translators for our Japanese films. I'm going to hit them for Russian translators now. Back in five minutes."

I found Colonel Fitzgerald deep in the "off limits" section of G-2. With him sat a young major with an opened file, and a male, faceless, civilian stenotypist.

After inspecting my ID card the colonel, a sober man with glasses, made a solemn statement to the effect that I was under military arrest, and that I was being held incommunicado pending an inquiry. He also warned me that anything I said could be used against me, and that I had the right to have a counsel of my own choosing present, or the Adjutant General's office would automatically provide one. If I chose to be represented by counsel, a more formal inquiry would be held. But if I chose not to have a counsel present, he would proceed with an informal interrogation.

"Colonel Fitzgerald," I asked, "will you please tell me what in hell you are talking about?"

He leaned forward. "I'm talking about a major breach of the Articles of War, a breach that in wartime can be considered a capital offense." I could easily guess what the breach was, but I had to play it dumb.

"My dear Colonel," I said, "I have never read the Articles of War and never intend to. All I know about military rules is that you salute and say 'Sir!' to superior officers. Now what's this big breach that I can hang for?"

He handed me an 8 by 11 photograph. It was a grainy, extremely long-focus shot of me whistling and standing in front of a doorway with my hands in my pockets. "Hey, that's me, Colonel, standing in front of the Soviet Embassy. By golly, you must photograph everybody that goes in and out of embassies. That's a pretty smart trick, Colonel," I said in open admiration.

The unflappable colonel had a queer look on his face. His aide, the major, put a hand over his mouth. The sad sack stenotypist remained an unblinking replica of Kelly the Clown.

"Then you admit this is your picture at the Soviet Embassy?"

"Of course it is. And I twice had lunch with Ambassador Litvinov and Mrs. Litvinov. She used to be an English lady, Ivy Low. Wait a minute! Are you worried that I may be a spy for the Russians or something? If you are, you're out of your mind. And dammit, Colonel, if you'll please keep your nose out of this for another week, I'm sure I can persuade the Russian Ambassador to give us something of great value to us in the future—films of our lend-lease material being used by Soviet soldiers. Understand?"

"By whose authorization did you consort with representatives of a foreign power?"

"By my own authorization. General Marshall gave me a job to do, and

I'm—Look, Colonel, I'll spell it out for you . . ." I gave him the whole story; the *Why We Fight* films; the lengths I'd gone to to get Russian war films, and the greater lengths to get photographic proof that our aid had helped the Soviets fight off the Nazis. "Now if that's treason," I summed up oratorically, "fine! Take me to your stockade and hang me. But if it isn't treason, then let me get the hell out of here and get back to work!"

Colonel Fitzgerald sat back, speechless. I could tell that his life was being shortened by stupid uniformed civilians who didn't "follow the book." But around the eyes of the young major a faint suspicion of a smile flitted on, then off. Sad sack, the stenotypist, remained unblinking, but I knew he'd have one heckuva story to tell his wife that night.

"And damn it all, Colonel," I added with suppressed anger, "if you insist on keeping me from carrying out the orders of the Chief of Staff, I demand a certified transcript of this nonsensical interrogation. I'm sure Drew Pearson will print it verbatim."

It seemed to work as well in the military world as it did among civilians. The best defense is an unexpected offense. I know women will understand what I mean.

"I shall advise General Osborn," said the Colonel quietly, "to keep you available for further interrogation. You may leave."

In the hallway, beyond the "off limits" notices, I found Lyman Munson pacing. His tunic was wet under the arms. I joined him; we walked off silently. When out of earshot, I whispered: "Lyman, I owe you and Osborn a very big apology. I pulled a smart-ass stunt that backfired into a court-martial case."

The upshot: a verbal reprimand by my immediate superior officers, and an official meeting with two Soviet military attachés arranged in Colonel Fitzgerald's office. We exchanged memos with them about each country supplying the other with combat film. Then Colonel Fitzgerald asked them to sign a memo calling for Soviet cameramen to photograph our lend-lease war materials being used by Soviet soldiers. The Russian attachés looked blank. Then one said, "But Colonel, how is possible to photograph that which does not exist?"

Then back to something I knew about—back to our Western Avenue headquarters in Hollywood, where the success of *Prelude to War* was a shot of adrenalin for everyone, and where things were popping fast. There was the intense effort to finish *Why We Fight* films number two and number three—*The Nazis Strike* and *Divide and Conquer*. There was the high-priority Negro film which Carlton Moss and I were working on. Film director Stuart "Stu" Heisler was commissioned a major to direct the *Negro in World War II* film. When suddenly—

Rumors from Washington flew West on witches' wings: Old-line film colonels were being banished to Signal Corps Elbas. First to go was Colonel Schlosberg, the Dalai Lama of the Army Pictorial empire. Sad, really—a casualty to the myopia of his entrenched mind. A regent was appointed

until the stars could confirm the birth of a new Dalai Lama. The regent's
name: Colonel Kirke B. Lawton, a "safe" Signal officer, and friendly, too.
In his teletypes he asked: "Do you need anything? . . . Anything we can do
to help you? . . ." Our cheery, but smug answer: "No, thanks. We don't
need a thing."

But—as a rebuke to our arrogance—the very existence of the Capra unit
and the *Why We Fight* films was threatened anew from an unexpected but
powerful source. Here are excerpts from the February 11, 1943 issue of
the *Hollywood Reporter*:

> Mellett, War Dept. Clash Over *Prelude to War* Film
> Release to Public Cause of Dispute
>
> Washington—There's more than one controversy over the film,
> *Prelude to War.* Senator Holman thinks it's propaganda, a fourth
> term for Roosevelt, and urges an investigation of this and all gov-
> ernment films. But it develops there's another controversy between
> Lowell Mellett and the War Department over the question of
> releasing the picture to the general public . . .
>
> Mellett thinks Capra has pulled the stops and played too many
> notes of hate for general audiences . . . Mellett told the *Hollywood
> Reporter* yesterday that he welcomes [Holman's senatorial] investiga-
> tion . . .

At any rate, despite congressional harpoons, and Signal Corps road
blocks, the *Why We Fight* series was completed. And despite Lowell
Mellett's grave concern—that John Q. Public would learn the true nature
of the enemy, and that that learning would breed loathing—*Prelude to
War* was released to the civilian movie houses.

Tens of millions of theatergoers were exposed, probably for the first
time, to what the war was all about. Many were shocked. It was not only
hell, it was *real.* It hurt. It killed. It devastated. Most frightening—the
enemy leaders were madmen.

After an invitational showing at the Museum of Modern Art, John
Gunther commented: "I'm so used to documentary films, montages, flags
waving, in film sequences, that I doubted anything NEW could be done . . .
the picture was perfect—it did everything it should do—excite and
convince."

H. V. Kaltenborn added: ". . . a magnificent job. To my knowledge,
the first time a *true* historical documentation has been presented of the decade of aggression."

And even Harold Ross, editor and publisher of *The New Yorker* magazine, huffed a few words of praise: "Is THIS the picture that the Congressman picked on the other day? There's no propaganda in it! Just the TRUTH!"
Famed columnist Dorothy Thompson went so far as to call the film, "the
greatest novel of our times."

Our Army films were not only written about, but also honored. The

Academy voted *Prelude to War* an Oscar for the Best Documentary of 1942. The New York film critics annually vote their own highly prestigious "best" awards. One of my films, *Mr. Deeds*, and one of my stars, Jimmy Stewart in *Mr. Smith*, had received the coveted accolade, but I, personally, had never cut the mustard with theatrical films. But I did with Army films. In 1944, the *Why We Fight* pictures received the New York Film Critics Award as the Best Documentaries.

These awards were given to me as the head of my Army unit. But they honored, and belonged to, every last one of the forty-odd talented artists that worked their hearts out on our films. In particular, I want to share all honors with my five key men: film director Anatole Litvak, writers Tony Veiller and Eric Knight, my first employee Edgar Peterson, and head film editor William Hornbeck. Without them no one could have made the *Why We Fight* films.

The public theaters in Canada, Britain, Australia, unoccupied Europe, and South America played all seven of the *Why We Fight* films. And Russia? Let Leonard Lyons report it in his April 22, 1944, column:

> The Soviet Embassy sent word to Col. Frank Capra's Signal Corps unit that Stalin wanted to see the film on Russia (*The Battle of Russia*) the fourth in the Army's series. A bomber was about to take off for Russia, and so there was no time to have a Russian translation substituted for the English commentary by Maj. Anthony Veiller . . . Stalin saw it in a projection room. A Soviet translator stood behind the Marshal and translated each sentence . . . Stalin ordered 500 prints made at once, Russian captions were superimposed, and . . . the film was shown in every Russian movie-house.

When Major General William H. Harrison was investigating the whole Army film set-up, he impaled me with a direct question: "Capra! Are you trying to tell me what Harry Hopkins has said publicly, and Lyman Munson's hinted privately—that *you* should be running the Army Pictorial Service?"

"No, sir! My racket's film. What you need is an administrator who can mobilize and *use* our nation's film power to help win this damned war. Someone like Colonel Munson—"

But brilliant officers like Lyman Munson were not apt to be found lolling in Pentagon halls leg-watching shapely secretaries. In fact, the brass couldn't find another Munson anywhere. So it had to be Colonel Munson himself. And the Army film program caught fire.

Together with General Harrison and Lieutenant Colonel Sam Briskin, one of the ablest Hollywood studio executives (retired to civilian life because of a heart ailment), Munson reorganized the whole military film empire.

As expected, he found (already in uniform) many patriotic film talents to head the many film enterprises; Colonel Emmanuel "Manny" Cohn, a former head of Paramount studios, was put in charge of the important Photo Center at Astoria, Long Island; Lieutenant Colonel Robert Lord, a Hollywood writer-producer, became the producer of all training films; Major Kenneth MacGowan, Hollywood writer, took over the war production incentive films, and Lieutenant Colonel Anatole Litvak was left in command of our Hollywood Photo Center at Western Avenue. For his executive officer in Washington, Munson selected Lieutenant Colonel Buddy Adler (who later became production head of Twentieth Century-Fox Studios).

What would be my role in the reorganized film dynasty? I didn't know what Munson had in mind for me, but I knew what I wanted. I wanted to improve the status of the Army photographer. Field photo companies and combat cameramen were pigeonholed in the organization tables of the local Signal Officers—far, far removed from any contact with the theater commander and his staff. Orders from Washington were relayed down to them from Signal Officer to Signal Officer, most of whom couldn't care less about film or cameramen.

On the other hand, Army Public Relations men were in direct contact with theater commanders and their staffs. If I could pry the combat photographers away from the unsympathetic control and assignment of the local Signal Officers, and put them under Public Relations Officers, I knew the photo groups would be much happier, and the photo coverage be immensely improved. I also knew it would take an awfully big lever to do the prying —and lo! The lever was put right into my hot little hand.

In August, 1943, about the time the _Why We Fight_ series was nearing completion, and the ramparts of the old film dynasty were being torn down, colonel by colonel, a new force moved into the celluloid picture—Major General Alexander P. Surles, Chief of Army Public Relations.

General Surles was tall, thin, and ailing. He was the only man I ever saw that seemed to actually have a hole in his head. There was an indentation about the size of a five-cent piece in one of his temples, with seemingly no bone under its raw, scarred skin covering. I always thought it was a window the surgeons had left open so they could, from time to time, go back and see what was going on inside the man's skull. I imagine the Army had tried to retire him for physical disability. But, about the only disability that can retire West Pointers is rigor mortis. Besides which, few could equal the patient genius of Surles for chilling anti-Army beefs.

His latest beef was from _within_ the Army. The British army-produced film _Desert Victory_ was proving most popular in the world's theaters. Our Army brass asked: Why hadn't Surles and his Public Relations people made pictures like _Desert Victory_ about the American war effort?

And now the British were pouring it on. They had just finished a new film on the Allied landings and occupation of North Africa. They called it

Africa Freed. Reports reaching General Surles about the film said the British had given themselves the starring role in what had been a co-starring Anglo-American effort, with a bit part thrown in for the Free French.

Surles protested to Brendan Bracken (head of the Ministry of Information) about the British film minifying the American accomplishments in North Africa. Bracken said it was because American combat photographers had shot very little film. Surles said it was a bit ridiculous for both Britain and the United States to make separate versions of the campaign. He suggested a combined Anglo-American film. Bracken said he would be happy to discuss it, particularly if Lieutenant Colonel Frank Capra was the American producer. (The Ministry of Information people were admirers and boosters of our *Why We Fight* films.)

General Surles had me temporarily assigned to his Public Relations staff. "Capra," he said, "go over to London and see if a combined Anglo-American film is possible. If it is, make the best deal you can with the Britishers. I have an idea the President and the Prime Minister would like the world to see an Allied film release. Anyway, you handle it all for our side, will you?"

I knew the combined film version would deal with sticky high policy decisions involving dual command and national pride and prejudices. I was honored to be the fully empowered negotiator for the American armed forces. But I also sensed that this was the time to speak up for the combat photographer.

"General, I wangled a separate independent unit to make the *Why We Fight* films. Why can't you ask for a separate independent special film coverage Signal Corps unit, responsible only to you and to your PRO's all over the world?"

The ploy worked. I was relieved of my command of the 834th Photo Signal Detachment assigned to Special Services, and made CO of the Signal Corps' Special Coverage Section, on detached duty to Public Relations. My duties were to organize special coverage photo teams with the express approval of the commanding generals of the various theaters of war. (There was one proviso: I must complete *Why We Fight* number seven, and *The Negro Soldier* for General Osborn.)

The first men I brought into the new PRO Special Coverage Section were Stevens, Huston, Veiller, and two film cutters (White and Claxton) and their assistants (Dunning and Beetly). Our first job: go to London with our North Africa film, and make a deal with the British to combine our film with theirs in a joint Anglo-American release. Our second goal: request the approval of Lieutenant General Jacob Devers, commanding general ETO (European Theater of Operations), to include our Special Coverage teams in his invasion plans.

One night I saw Clark Gable in the lobby of the Grosvenor House. He was a captain in the Air Force. With him were several other Air Force officers, including his commanding general. Clark looked well, but he wasn't too happy to see me, or anyone else for that matter. When I asked his commanding officer how Clark was doing, the General opened up and couldn't stop: "How's he doing? He's scaring hell out of us, that's how he's doing. The damn fool insists on being a rear gunner on every bombing mission. Public relations, my eye! He's a hot potato! And I'm pulling every string to get him out of my command, tell you that. Guy gives me the willies. Know what I think? Gable's *trying* to get himself killed. Yeah! So he can join up with his wife."

In the blacked-out London it was easy to recognize American soldiers' voices in Piccadilly Circus, or in Grosvenor Square (nick-named "Eisenhower Platz"). A couple of times, listening to G.I.'s horse-playing around, I heard them shout: "Charge!"

Soon after, at the R.A.F. mess at Pinewood, several British flyers came running up to my table, brandishing imaginary cutlasses and yelling: "Charge!"

I pointed my finger at them and cried out: "You guys have seen *Arsenic and Old Lace*—right?"

"Righto! And we laughed our bloody heads off, we did."

Old softy Jack Warner had released my film *Arsenic and Old Lace* to all our armed forces a full year before he could play it in public theaters. Batty Teddy Roosevelt's *"Charge!"* up the stairs became a catchword wherever Americans wore uniforms. Later on the Los Angeles Dodger baseball fans took it up as a call to action. Other baseball fans followed, until today, *"Charge!"* is a familiar battle cry for home-team rooters in several sports.

You will probably remember the big plot to make *Arsenic and Old Lace* on a percentage basis so that I wouldn't have to dig into the old sock to keep my family going while I was in uniform. How did the plot work out? A disaster. The picture was not played in theaters until 1944. Then it made money so fast my first percentage check was for $232,000! Great! Oh, sure. The Federal and State income taxes on it added up to $205,000!

I think it was Sidney Bernstein, head of the film division of the Ministry of Information, who brought me the heart-stopping news: "The P.M. wants to see you in his office—"

I wangled a car and driver from Major Hugh Stuart, and rushed to 10 Downing Street.

It had to be the crowning moment of my life when Winston Churchill took my hand in both of his and complimented me so highly for the *Why We Fight* films. He told me how grateful he was to General Marshall and to me and my boys for the whole project, and that if I would bring a camera and sound equipment to his office I could photograph him speaking a foreword that he had written "to introduce your great films to a grateful British public—"

Before dawn next morning (September 29) a British crew and I were pushing cameras, cables, and mike booms over a wall, across a small garden, and into a rear window of Churchill's office at 10 Downing Street. Tony Veiller was hanging around hoping he could get a glimpse of England's greatest Prime Minister. I told him to go around to the front door and wait. I would try to sneak him in for the filming.

When I walked into the Cabinet Office through a back door, there was Veiller, seated in the Prime Minister's chair reading a paper. "How'd *you* get in here?" I asked. "Nothing to it," he said, barely looking up. "I knocked on the front door and said I was Captain Veiller, here to oversee the filming of the P.M. Are you ready, boy?"

We were all ready for the P.M. when he came through a side door with the Spanish Ambassador. My imagination, of course, but I was sure I could smell the P.M.'s brandy breath clear across the room. I introduced him to Tony Veiller. Veiller swayed but remained upright. Then the great man, in good mood, sat in his chair, set down his cigar, and took from his pocket a sheaf of hand written notes—his speech. The thickness of the sheaf worried me. The foreword must not be too long. I asked him for a voice test. He read the first line of his notes. I thought his delivery was too slow. The director in me got the best of me. I leaned over his desk and asked him to please speed up his delivery a little.

He looked up at me roguishly, over his glasses, and said: "Young man, I've been making speeches to audiences since before you were born."

It dawned on me that I was trying to tell the greatest orator of modern times how he should make a speech. I salaamed deeply and retreated. But as I reached the safety of behind the camera, I said: "Yes, Mr. P.M., but this audience is going to *pay* to hear you talk." With rare good humor he salaamed back at me, and we bowed to each other. His speech brought a lump to my throat, particularly the line: "I have never seen or read any more powerful statement of our cause . . ."

There is little doubt that Churchill's public praise of my Army films zoomed my personal stock with our own Army brass in Europe. Indoctrinating the high command to the value of film (not an easy job), and forcing drastic, upgrading changes in the whole Signal Corps system of field photography, became much easier when my personal reputation gained me ready access to Lieutenant General Devers, his staff, and the staffs of Air Force Generals Spatz and Doolittle. Of course, my standing needed no upping to Jimmy Doolittle. He and I had battled and respected each other since we were teenagers.

Tunisian Victory was released to American and British theaters in March, 1944. As a piece of entertainment, the *Hollywood Reporter*, of March 9, said of it:

> . . . Flaring from the screen with a titanic sweep . . . its impact is tremendous . . . The Academy-Award winning *Desert Victory* was a great picture. *Tunisian Victory* leaves it at the post . . .

Today's Cinema, London, called it a "remarkable picture . . . [of] historical importance . . . outstanding as a box office attraction . . ."

Readers will note in *Today's Cinema*'s closing paragraph, that we, the "recreators" of the capture of the Mojave Desert's "Hill 609," kept faith with our critics and audiences: ". . . The major portion of the action is actual shots from the battlefields, but a few scenes . . . which happen at night, or where it was impossible for cameramen to be present, have been reconstructed under supervision of men actually on the spot at the time."

General Surles arranged to show *Tunisian Victory* to the National Press Club members in the privacy of their august club rooms—from which I had been given the bum's rush five years earlier. The General asked me to introduce the film and say a few words about the problems of British-American co-production. I swallowed hard.

"General Surles, that's the worst thing that could happen to your picture. I'm banned forever from the Press Club. If I show up there, uniform or no uniform, they'll mob me and murder *Tunisian Victory*."

"Frank, you're all imagination and no brains. Come on."

The screen was up in the Press Club dining room. The room was packed. General Surles calmly introduced me as the American Army half of the co-production team. There was no applause as I walked out. But I knew exactly what I would do; pull the gag that had served me so well whenever I found myself in the kind of spots that led Quirt to snicker: "Think fast, Captain Flagg!" I would calmly stand on my head, and hold the headstand. The gag was so unexpected, so brazen, it would generally top any kind of opposition or soften any hostile audience.

But as I looked out at the serious faces of the Washington press, I forgot the headstand. I represented the United States Army. I stood at the mike and quietly scanned those potent faces with unblinking eyes. I had grown up. They sensed it. I saw some faces relax and smile. A few giggled. I broke into a smile, still looking them over. Titters, then laughs. The laughs swelled. I joined in. Not a word had been said. General Surles stepped out from behind the arch wondering about the uproar. I gave him the okay sign, then waited for the laughs to subside.

My years in the service seemed like a series of flat out hundred-yard dashes against the clock. But there were moments when time stood still:

The evening of January 14, 1943. Eric Knight was leaving for Cairo to open a new Armed Forces Radio station. Eric was charged up. He talked of Mr. Deeds, and of his Sam Small; of a better world after the war, and of how films could make it so. I carried his duffel bag from room 308 to the lobby. Lyman Munson invited us to the bar for one-for-the-road. It being the road to Cairo we needed five more drinks to cross the Sahara.

Eric gave toasts to himself as radio's newest sensation—Lord Hee Haw of the East. He asked for names for the new station. He got The Voice of

Cleo's Asp; King Tut's Womb; then, Nefertiti's Nities; which led, by alco-
holic acclamation, to *Always*titi's Nities. Then off to Bolling Field.

At the airfield I wanted to embrace Eric; to tell him what he had meant
to me, to Lyman, to life; to tell him that if he did for radio what he had
done for our films, all the world's downtrodden would clap hands. I didn't.

Munson and I were in twin beds in New York's Gotham Hotel. The phone
rang and rang. Munson groped for it. "Hello?" he growled. He leaped out
of bed. "It's Jack Stanley, Frank . . . Eric's plane is down in the Caribbean.
Shot down, they think. By a U-boat that mistook it for the plane taking
Roosevelt to Casablanca—no survivors."

He was Army. In a driving rainstorm, I photographed Supreme Allied
Commander Eisenhower delivering the commencement address to the 1943
graduating class at Sandhurst (British equivalent to our West Point). The
gist of his speech:

> Gentlemen, in the middle of a war, you have just graduated as pro-
> fessional officers in the profession of war. A profession, my fellow
> officers, that is the most archaic, brutal, senseless, destructive, bestial,
> de-humanizing profession ever invented by man. It should have been
> abolished long, long ago. But we have a job to do, a dirty, brutal job.
> There is an evil loose in the world that glorifies war; that would destroy
> by war all that we hold dear. It must not prevail!

He was Navy. He stood slim, straight, white-thatched. He was Commander
in Chief of the Pacific (CINCPAC). He stood alone in the doorway of his
office at Pearl Harbor. He was four-star Admiral Chester Nimitz.

I was coming downstairs from Admiral "Bull" Halsey's office. I would
have to pass right by Admiral Nimitz. Was he waiting for me? Would he
renege on the all-important Special Film Coverage directive I had written
for him, and he had signed? Had MacArthur nixed the order to integrate
all combat photography? Had the Air Force? The Marines?

I hesitated, then saluted, and walked by him.

"Oh, Capra! Can you spare a moment?"

I went limp. "Of course, Admiral."

Behind his desk, his back to me, he faced a window that looked out over
our sunken warships. "Sit down, please," he said, huskily. "I apologize for
calling you in here. It's just this—this—goddam sonofabitch of a *war!*"

His hands clasped and unclasped behind him as he rocked slowly back
and forth on his heels. Then, out of the depths of an overwhelming hurt, he
cried out: "They cheered me . . . Three thousand of them . . . Eighteen-year-
olds . . . Legs gone, faces gone . . . They cheered me . . . I sent them there
. . . They cheered me . . ."

Then he turned, sat heavily in his chair, and with tears streaming down
his face, he beat the table with both fists: "GODDAM SONOFABITCH OF A WAR!
GODDAM SONOFABITCH OF A WAR! What am I going to write to their parents?

What can *anybody* write to their parents? . . ." He grabbed his wet face in both his hands. He was sobbing now. A father weeping for all the sons in the world. "Eighteen-year-olds . . . kids . . . boys . . . three thousand of them . . . back from Kwajalein . . . I went to the hospital . . . legs gone . . . faces gone . . . They cheered me . . . I sent them there . . . they cheered me . . . GODDAM SONOFABITCH OF A WAR! . . . goddam sonofa——" His handkerchief was out now. Not once had he looked at me, directly.

I sat as if transfixed. Tears had started down my cheeks. The white-thatched admiral blew his nose, composed himself, then looking at me with a shy little smile, he said pleasantly: "Thank you, Capra. Thank you."

He had wanted to share his great pain with another human being—someone that was not Navy. I rose to my feet; tried to mumble something. I couldn't. So I smiled back and walked out. I had witnessed something rare. Something awesome—the inside of a tormented human soul.

It was Christmas morning at the Munsons' in their Alexandria apartment. At Christmas I see myself as I really am. And as I could be, if I weren't such a stinker. As the whole sick, weary, unhappy world sees itself as it might be, if it weren't such a stinker. Noel! Joy! Peace awaits. Killings, brutality, meanness is here. Cry world.

There were gaily-wrapped packages under Jimmy Munson's gaily decorated tree. Eggnogs were passed around. I needed one. Christmas away from home, and—I had just read this AP dispatch in the morning paper:

COMEDIAN HARRY LANGDON DIES
$7,500-A-WEEK, THEN $0

He had fat jowls . . . wide innocent eyes . . . a bewildered look . . . hands that spelled helplessness . . . for which the movies paid him $7,500 a week. Harry died yesterday . . . He starred in two-reelers and ended in them . . . He hired Capra as his director . . . created a cinematic sensation . . . decided he didn't need a director. Capra (now Lt. Col. Capra of the Signal Corps) went up the ladder . . . Landgon went down.

He never became bitter when his money was gone and he was earning $22 a week "some weeks," as he testified in one alimony suit . . . four wives divorced him . . .

Langdon hit the maximum: Greater than Chaplin. He didn't know why. Langdon hit the minimum: the lowest-paid bit actor. He didn't know why. Cry world.

Lyman Munson was playing Santa Claus. That's what I'd be doing if I were home. "Ho! Ho! Ho!" He gave me a little package wrapped in red, white, and blue. I opened it. Other officers present grinned in anticipation. A pair of silver eagles—a colonel's eagles!

"A Christmas greeting from General George C. Marshall," said Munson doing a bad job of being casual. "Frank McCarthy cabled from Australia that while flying over the Indian Ocean from Ceylon, the five-star man decided to personally promote his two pet Franks—McCarthy and Capra. And I've been saving these chickens just in case—"

Munson unpinned the lieutenant colonel's leaves from my shoulders. "There's an old Army saying, Frank: After the leaves have fallen, nothing remains between the eagles and the stars."

West Pointers can get quite maudlin over a small investiture in rank: "Them's eagles that am eagles, Frank." "Over a hundred years old and pure silver." "Know how long they've been in Lyman's family—" "Hold it, you guys!" said Munson. "This is my show. Capra! My grandfather pinned these on my father, my father pinned them on me, and now I'm pinning— for chrissake, hold still! There . . . Merry Christmas, Colonel Capra . . . Jesus, he's gonna blubber . . . Jimmy-y! Got her on the phone yet? . . . Come on, let's talk to Lu—"

A snowy day in January, 1944. Two hundred silent, skeptical Negro publishers, editors, and writers of Negro papers filed into the Pentagon projection room. They had come at the personal invitation of Secretary of War Stimson, to see the first public showing of my Army film *The Negro Soldier*. I could see it written in their faces: "Another snow job on black people."

To my knowledge, no documented film on the American Negro had ever been attempted. The subject was dynamite. If my film inflamed passions, or hardened existing prejudices, it would be shelved.

The Secretary of War's office had sent me a young Negro radio writer, Carlton Moss, to serve as script writer, researcher, and technical adviser. Moss wore his blackness as conspicuously as a bandaged head. Time and again he would write a scene, then I'd rewrite it, eliminating the angry fervor. He'd object, and I would explain that when something's red-hot, the blow torch of passion only louses up its glow. We must persuade and convince, not by rage but by reason.

The lights dimmed. The title flashed on the screen:

THE UNITED STATES ARMY
Presents
The Negro Soldier

For the next forty-five minutes I did not hear a cough or see a squirm.

The lights came on; still not a sound from the colored pundits. I stepped up on the dais in front of the screen and asked if there were any questions. That audience was stunned. Incredulity was written on their faces. Finally one asked: "White soldiers going to see this picture?"

I explained that it was a training film, that *all* soldiers—in camps in this country or reserve areas behind the battle lines—had to see it whether they wanted to or not.

Then another came up with this challenging question: "Mr. Capra, I know, and everybody else here knows about your films. What I want to know is, How come the Army—the tough, conservative Army that trains people to kill people—how come the generals let you make this kind of a film? Who's kidding who?"

I answered that the generals didn't *let* me make this film; they *ordered* me to make it. I said I didn't know about other armies, but in this Army I, a Hollywood film man, had been freer to say the things that needed saying than I had been in civilian clothes. I had found our Army chiefs to be human beings who care, as well as being generals who have to defend America.

Then General Surles stepped on the dais and took over. He said that chaplains had discovered that there were no atheists in fox holes, but the fighting men had also discovered that there was no color line in fox holes. He closed by telling them the Army hoped *The Negro Soldier* would get wide civilian distribution. It was available to civilian agencies without charge. "I hope," said General Surles, "that this body of opinion-makers thinks enough of this film to put the heat on the theater chains—"

The Negro press hailed the film. Reporter Herman Hill, of the Pittsburgh *Courier*, wrote:

> . . . An ultra favorable-opinion reaction by members of the fourth estate, indicated that the 45-minute picture might easily prove to be one of the most outstanding and factual characterizations of the Negro ever made . . .
>
> It is the writer's candid opinion that *if* the film—which by the way is available to movie houses free—is properly distributed throughout the nation, it will be worth its weight in gold . . .

And Abe Hill wrote in the New York *Amsterdam News*:

> . . . One cannot believe that such dignity and integrity inherent in the script would have ever been accomplished in this generation.
>
> When this reviewer saw a preview of the film a few weeks ago along with a group of Negro weekly publishers, he kept pondering this fact: Who on earth thought such a thing could be done so accurately—without propaganda, without sugar-coating and without the jackass clowning the movie acting Negro usually degrades himself to . . .
>
> The movie succeeds in proving that this is the Negro's war. He is too deeply rooted in the making of this great country—he has as much at stake in its destiny as any other waver of the red, white and blue. If any child, white, black, or blue ever wants to know what in the world the Negro has been doing in this country for the past 300 years, let him spend 40 minutes seeing this picture and he will have learned a life's lesson . . .

Cold generals reading cold, dread words from cold paper would not do. Boys and mothers deserved a compassionate explanation from *concerned* officers who *cared!* The upshot: I invented a Rube Goldberg *Teleprompter* out of toilet paper rollers and wire so that General Marshall could look straight into their eyes and hearts . . .

Lt. Col. Robert Presnell (author of *Meet John Doe*), Capt. Len Hammond, and I watch G.I.'s go through jungle training in Hawaii.

Negro Soldier in World War II.
First historical film on the American Negro, made by order of the Secretary of War. Critical comments were surprisingly good in both the white and black press.

One of life's most memorable moments. General Marshall—a great and good man—honors me with the Distinguished Service Medal on the day of my discharge.

"Young man," said the Great One with eyes twinkling, "I've been making public speeches since long before you were born." I bit my tongue, salaamed, and stumbled back to the camera.

Langston Hughes, the *Defender* columnist, wrote:

> The War Department has just shown to the press the most re-
> markable Negro film ever flashed on the American screen . . . It
> is distinctly and thrillingly worthwhile.

The white press was equally moved by the film. *Time* said in its review
that at sneak previews for Negro soldiers, "at first they froze into hostile
silence. But after 20 minutes they were applauding. For just about the first
time in screen history their race was presented with honest respect. Many
wanted to know: 'Are you going to show this to white people?' Asked why,
they replied: 'Because it will change their attitude.' . . . In 40 minutes
there has taken place on the screen . . . a brave, important and helpful event
in the history of U.S. race relations."

It was my first leave since donning a uniform. Major Bong, air ace of the
Pacific and Medal of Honor winner, was on the train. I saw a large crowd
outside the Chief as we slowed to a stop at the Los Angeles station. How
nice, I thought to myself, they're here to cheer Major Bong.

I saw Major Bong walk unnoticed through the welcoming crowd of chattering teen-agers, mostly girls. A mass scream scared the daylights out of
me. Frank Sinatra stood in the Pullman car door waving at his frenzied
fans.

Was Frank Sinatra an omen of an instinctive change in human females?
Was motherhood's age-old wisdom whispering intuitive instructions to these
frenetic teen-agers: "Girls, war is for the dodo bird. Give the brush-off to
bemedaled heroes who boast of killing and violence. Let the fathers of your
sons be gentle peace heroes who sing of sex sweet sex and the bluebird."

Lu cut short my epistemic vaporings by throwing her arms around me in
the station lobby. "Ten days, hon. We're going fishing—" "Oh, darling, I
hope so," she said anxiously, "but Pete Petitto wants you to call right
away."

I called from the station. "Yep," said Captain Petitto, our adjutant,
"Colonel Munson wants the Colonel to fly back to Washington
immediately . . ."

At 8 A.M. sharp, I walked into General Marshall's office. "Oh, fine. Good
morning, Frank. They're meeting now. A sergeant will take you there.
They're in a bind, Frank."

I followed the MP into one of the many secluded wings of the Pentagon.
I had no idea who "they" were that were in a bind. But I had learned to
decipher General Marshall's mind even when his words were cryptic. In
some strange way I had become one of his trouble shooters. He liked the
way I had won my *mano-a-mano* fracas with the Signal Corps.

The MP knocked on a nondescript door. Bolts unbolted, a shirt-sleeved,
unshaven colonel poked his head out. The MP introduced me. "Oh, yes.

Come in, Capra. We've been *waiting* for you." I got the hint. No welcome mat here.

I followed him into a large smoke-filled conference room. Walls and easels groaned under charts and diagrams as mystic as petroglyphs. About fifteen tieless, coatless, harassed, short-tempered professional soldiers— most of them wearing stars—sat or paced about the room. A three-star general, with a face like Bull Montana's, greeted me.

"Capra, if the smallest hint leaks out about what we're discussing, it could prolong this goddam war by as much as a year. You understand? "General Marshall thinks you can solve any problem in the world. Well, lots 'o luck. Grab a chair and listen and go nuts with the rest of us."

I think I dozed and half-listened to the acrimonious bickerings for two whole days before I caught the drift of their problems. Fortunately, I was not consulted on anything. The notion that a Hollywood film man could help them in any way had to be the idiocy of the year. For they were an elite committee selected and charged by the Combined Chiefs of Staff to come up with a piecemeal demobilization plan, effective on the day Germany surrendered. These were some of the hot potatoes they played catch with:

After V-E Day, some military forces could go home, others were needed in the Pacific until Japan surrendered. Now then, *which* troops should be considered surplus? What would the priorities be, and what weight should be given each priority, for instance: marriage, children, length of service, battle service, wounds, hardships, decorations? All Greek to me. And then . . .

I spoke up, "Gentlemen, may I ask a question?" All present froze in their tracks. "My god, it talks!" was plainly written on their unshaven faces. I went on: "It's taken me three days to make head or tail of what's going on. My question is, How will you communicate your complex solutions to the servicemen in the field?"

"By secret memos through the chain of command: theater commander, to corps, to divisions, regiments, battalions, companies—"

"Excuse me for interrupting, sir, but you might as well use French telephones. By the time your 'priority point system'—so complicated it'll stump a Philadelphia lawyer—by the time that filters down to the troops through memos and chains of command, your plan will snowball and distort in all directions like a runaway rumor. And I think you gentlemen know it."

There was a long silence before the general in charge asked: "What's on your mind, Capra?" "Just this, sir. I've been racking my lame brain trying to guess why General Marshall sent *me* in here—a dopey civilian. Now I know. Film. Communicate with film. Beats all other media. Put all your information in one film. Show that *same* film to *all* servicemen on V-E Day. Let the Chiefs of Staff explain things directly to the G.I.'s—and gentlemen, you will avoid the SNAFU of the age."

The idea hit pay dirt. One general asked, "How long will it take to make a film about this? The Allied High Command estimates the Germans could conceivably surrender by December 1."

Jeez! Sixty days! "It isn't *possible* to make a picture in sixty days!" I blurted out. "Half of it'll be animation . . . Maybe . . . if I could write a script by tomorrow night. I know Disney'll help. Well, what the hell. Let's try it . . ."

I sat down at a typewriter. "We'll call it *Two Down and One to Go* temporarily. Now. The separation plan. Will the surplus guys go home by unit or as individuals?"

"That hasn't been decided yet."

"Well goddam it—DECIDE! If you want a film I need answers NOW!" The urgency of a script got results. Arguments crystallized into decisions. By next afternoon an outline of the script was on General Marshall's desk. I got the green light, with one addition: The film must be shown simultaneously to troops and *to the public*, so that parents would get the same story as their sons.

I flew out to see Walt Disney. Yes, he could complete ten minutes of "line" animation on a twenty-four-hour schedule, *if* the film was in color —"Because, Frank, separate colors tell their own story quickly, like traffic lights."

Technicolor executives threw up their hands in horror. *One thousand* 35 mm Technicolor prints, and three thousand 16 mm prints of a thirty-minute film? Delivered in thirty days after they get the cutting print?

"Frank, you're out of your mind! We couldn't do that if we stopped all color work on all studio films, and doubled our output of raw stock, and tripled the size of our plant! It's impossible!"

I called Disney. Okay on color. It's "go" on the storyboards. Get me a bed ready in his classified area.

Having started wheels rolling in Hollywood, I flew to New York to ask the War Activities Committee to handle the civilian showings in public theaters. Prints were to be classified top secret and locked in the vaults of MGM's distribution centers. The alert would be a direct telegram from General Marshall.

Back in Washington I set up sound equipment and a Technicolor camera in one of the Signal Corps' secret conference rooms. Navy Lieutenant Al Kellogg of John Ford's OSS group was the cameraman. The first general before the camera was Marshall. I backed him up with the famed painting of Pershing. Generals are not trained actors, and the generals I had to shoot were much too busy to learn long speeches. But generals *reading* long speeches could be deadly. My generals *had* to look directly into the eyes of millions of tired, homesick, anxious G.I.'s and tell it to them like it was: Some *could* go home and some could *not* and why! They'd have to look into the faces of millions of heartsick, emotionally irrational parents (who wanted their sons home *now*) and tell them that many of their boys who escaped death in Europe would have to face death again in Asia. Those were tough tidings. Cold generals reading cold, dread words from cold paper would not do.

I thought of what studios call "idiot cards" for the generals—usually blackboards with words printed in chalk. But inexperienced persons reading from idiot cards, will look, on the screen, like what they are: idiots reading idiot cards.

If I could fashion some sort of "moving speech device"—From a washroom I stole two wooden rollers from the inside of toilet-paper rolls. With wire coat-hangers and pliers I made wire axles and a wire frame for the rollers. A stenographer found me a strange typewriter that printed letters in very large capitals. She typed General Marshall's speech. We pasted the typed pages end to end into a twenty-foot strip, and wound the strip on the bottom toilet-paper roller. By winding the top roller—I had invented the teleprompter!

Through the camera lens I watched General Marshall read a few lines. His eyes were obviously focusing on something very close, and not on audiences that would be at least one hundred feet away. I put on a long focus lens and backed the camera off about twenty feet. This corrected the close eye-focusing fault. But he still was not looking directly into the lens—or into a soldier's eyes from the screen. But, by lowering the camera and shooting *up* at the general—as if from the viewpoint of a G.I. in the middle of a theater—and placing the Rube Goldberg teleprompter just *below* the lens, I did achieve the illusion that General Marshall was talking directly to those in the first row nearest the screen.

And I might as well tell you that had it not been for that toilet-roller doohicky, *Two Down and One to Go* might not have convincingly justified the necessity that tens of thousands of soldiers—having won the war in Europe—might now lose arms, legs, and lives in the Pacific.

On May 9, 1945, General Marshall flashed this message to eight hundred national theaters, and to seven hundred Army installations all over the world:

RELEASE WAR DEPARTMENT FILM EF–I TWO DOWN AND ONE TO GO
AT NOON EASTERN STANDARD TIME TENTH OF MAY.

G. C. Marshall
Chief of Staff

To the Army message Marshall added "all detachments, no matter how small or isolated, must be shown film in shortest possible time."

EF-I swung into action. Army bombers and transports took off on special film circuits. Where fog prevailed, sedans and half-tracks crunched to outposts. EF-I was run in transports at sea, in hospital wards, in guardhouses, on lookouts atop mountain peaks. Whether G.I. audiences numbered two thousand or just two, each one got the same message from the highest officers—hard facts, given to them calmly, statistically, and personally. Americans can take hard facts. EF-1 cleared the air of a potentially stormy, nasty situation which might have blown up into demonstrations and riots.

Oh happy day! My terminal physical exam was normal. I had gone through the AGO routine of being declared surplus. Tomorrow, June 15, 1945, I would be on the inactive list. Good-bye Army, hello Hollywood, I was cleaning out my desk. A very sumptuous desk, in a very sumptuous office in the Army Pictorial Service—the very same office in which I had nervously reported to Colonel Schlosberg for duty three and a half years ago, only to be banished out of the Signal Corps and out of Army films.

Today I was leaving that office as the Assistant Chief of an Army Pictorial Service I had reorganized and staffed with professionals, and which I was leaving under the leadership of an officer with one of the most brilliant minds in the Army, Colonel—no, now Brigadier General Munson.

Last night, Munson had asked Tony Veiller and me to his apartment to celebrate my leaving the Army. When I walked into my sumptuous office, to begin cleaning out my desk, I looked like a wino who'd slept in the alley. But not even one of John Steinbeck's *Cannery Row* characters was as happy a wino as I was that morning. I had already kissed every secretary in our office.

Munson stuck his head in the door. "Frank, use my razor, quick. General Marshall wants to see you."

My blood froze. "Oh, no. What in hell does *he* want now? I said good-bye to him day before yesterday, when he sent me that thank you letter—"

"Come on. Don't race your motor," said Munson with a calming grin. "You're still a colonel in the Army. Take a quick shave and—you got another tunic? That one's spotted—"

"No, goddam it. I *won't* change my tunic, and I *won't* shave. Lyman, I'll never get out of this damned Army. First it was the *Why We Fight* pictures. Hurry, hurry, hurry! Then the Negro film. Gotta have it tomorrow. Then *Two Down and One to Go*. Gotta be all over the world in sixty days. Thousands of prints. Disney had to stop everything else. Technicolor did the impossible. Last month it was *On to Tokyo!* Morale in Europe's bad. Eisenhower and all the others generals want to answer G.I. questions on film. *Thirty* days to make *that* one! I'm pooped, Lyman! I'm dead! If that sonofabitch Marshall's got another hurry-up job for me—I'M GOING OVER THE HILL—"

I ran out of my office and high-tailed it to the Chief of Staff's suite. I burst into Frank McCarthy's office. "Frank, what the hell does the General want me for, *now?*"

"I dunno, Frank," said Colonel McCarthy jovially. "Sit down, sit down. Want a cup of coffee?"

"No!" I sat down. "Doesn't the Chief know I'm being discharged *tomorrow?*"

"Oh, you are? Lucky man. I'll see if the Chief's busy—"

McCarthy disappeared into Marshall's office. "That's the way with the whole damn world," I muttered to myself. "Nobody wants to hear *my* troubles."

McCarthy poked his head out. "You can come in now, Frank." He held the door open for me. I barged in, then stopped as if I'd been shot. It was a tableau. Right out of Graustark. General Marshall stood smiling behind his desk. Facing me, and standing at attention, was a line of beribboned generals—Arnold, Somervell, Surles, Barker, Osborn, Ingles (Chief Signal Officer), and my good friend—General Lyman Munson. All were grinning at me. Two Signal Corps photographers raised their cameras. McCarthy waited behind me—with a stretcher I hoped. What happened in the next five minutes was all in slow motion; a dream.

I remember General Marshall uncoiling a parchment from its binding ribbon and reading words, some of which I caught: ". . . United States of America . . . greeting . . . the President . . . Act of Congress . . . awarded the DISTINGUISHED SERVICE MEDAL . . . Capra . . . Signal Corps . . . meritorious . . . distinguished . . . duties . . . of great responsibilities . . . 1945 . . . Secretary of War . . ."

Then General Marshall picked up more parchment and read a longer citation of my Army efforts. But I was beyond hearing.

THE DISTINGUISHED SERVICE MEDAL . . . me! The highest award the Army can bestow outside of actual combat. General Pershing had received the Distinguished Service Medal, and General Eisenhower, and General Marshall.

And now General Marshall is coming over to pin that great honor on *me*. Camera bulbs flash . . . I look like a bum . . . I flush with shame. The General shakes my hand . . . other generals surround me . . . pump my hand . . . they are proud . . . I am limp . . . Munson embraces me . . . stand straight . . . don't break now . . . Frank McCarthy rescues me . . . leads me to his office and out into the hall . . . I walk down the hall . . . like a zombie . . . citations in one hand, medal box in the other . . . go into the first washroom . . . into a cubicle . . . lock the door . . . sit on the toilet seat . . . and cry like a baby . . .

PART IV

An Entirely New Ball Game, With Entirely New Rules

Give Me Liberty

THE FIRST SCIENTIFIC STATEMENT ever uttered by man is credited to an ancient Greek philosopher, who said: "Man can never step into the same stream twice." Similarly, directors can never return to the same Hollywood twice. After an absence of four years the turnover was astonishing. I hardly knew anyone. The new faces were younger, brassier, more flushed with success. It was most disconcerting to be introduced to an upcoming actress or director and have them ask, "Frank who?"

Four years ago Hollywood was my town. When I fiddled, people danced. I was president of everything. Now the pip-squeaks with L.P.'s (Learners' Permits) asked "Frank *who*?" Now the Berg-Allenberg Agency had no million-dollar contracts for me to sign. They had no contracts, period. Had my kind of filmmaker gone out of style?

As has been stated before, the war years were boom years—and booms in show biz are quality's bane. When it's raining dollars the question is not how pretty but how many. Hollywood film production was roughly divided into 20 percent expensive "A" films, and 80 percent inexpensive "B" films. Exhibitors paid a rental fee of around 50 percent of a theater's take for the "A's," and about 25 percent for the "B's."

When moviegoers shopped for films, *quality* pictures were in demand. Theater owners knew—despite higher rental fees—that one good "A" film would net them more money than half a dozen "B's."

But in the war years, *quantity* pictures took center stage. If a theater owner could stand them in line with a "B," why should he pay twice as much rent for an "A"? The Hollywood result: mediocre picture talent became as important as quality talent, if not more important. Thus, at the end of four boom war years, the "one man, one film" idea was practically dead.

Assembly-line products were manufactured not only cheaper and faster than the independent producers' quality films, but in addition (clap! clap!) they made more money. Executive vest buttons popped; cigars waxed fatter and longer.

Everybody made big money. Who cared whether one man or one hundred men made films? Your Uncle Elmo could make films. And many Uncle Elmos did. Oh, a few producer-directors turned out some fine pictures: McCarey made *Going My Way*, Hitchcock produced *Lifeboat*, and Wilder directed *Lost Weekend*. But the half-dozen blockbusters that used to make big news each year were lacking—and, seemingly, no one missed them.

Yet, the "one man, one film" precept was not only still present but still dominant with me. Whether it was a film that explained to fighting men the causes and reasons of war, or that dramatized to audiences the fact that life was wonderful, that film had to be my personal creation—my bag, my thing. I could never share the experience with a committee. Whatever art was in me demanded that I say, perhaps "an ill-favored thing, sir, but mine own."

Yet I would be stepping again into a Hollywood whose mainstream of film production had shifted back into its old "committee-system" channel. And that meant film directors were losing—or had lost—the right to have their names above the picture titles on theater marquees. Well, I decided it was high time the director's name went back up there where it belonged. I put it up there once. Could I do it again? The juices began to run. A new challenge was a new love affair. I had a plan.

The first news of the plan didn't set off any earth-shaking temblors along the San Andreas Fault, nor did the heavens sky-write it with lightning. It was not celebrated with an extra "Fire Fall" in Yosemite Valley; it did not make the front pages of the Hollywood trade papers. But hidden within the trades was a three-line item: "Incorporation papers were filed today (April 10, 1945) at Sacramento by LIBERTY FILMS, INC. The three incorporators were Frank Capra, Samuel Briskin, and attorney David Tannenbaum." I say the news was hidden because no one could have guessed that those Sacramento papers were to set in motion this train of events: (1) influence the course of Hollywood films, (2) make four former Army officers independently rich, and (3) virtually prove fatal to my professional career.

The idea for Liberty Films was born in the Army: unite producer-directors in service into a post-war independent combine of independent filmmakers. The prime candidates were John Ford, Willie Wyler, George Stevens, John Huston, Garson Kanin, and Frank Capra. Whether those pre-war stalwarts could immediately command their former prominence on re-turning to Hollywood was questionable. For, besides the major studios regressing to assembly-line production, the "anything goes" war years had spawned a novel group of "independent" producers: War profiteers seeking status, socialites seeking glamour, swishy "uncles" promoting handsome "nephews," big daddies buying star parts for blonde chicks, etcetera ad nauseam.

Nevertheless, a few months before my Army discharge, Briskin and I incorporated Liberty Films. A few months after my discharge, this item appeared in the New York *Herald-Tribune*:

> Hollywood's veterans are on their way back, folks. Uniforms are going into mothballs all over the land as the stars of pre-Pearl Harbor days prepare to face the cameras and competition once more.
>
> Comfortably ensconced at RKO are Colonel Frank Capra, Colonel Willie Wyler, Colonel George Stevens, and Colonel Samuel Briskin, who have just completed a little post-war deal with RKO whereby they will make nine pictures involving production expenditures in excess of $15,000,000. . . .

And so I did not return to Hollywood with my hat in my hand, but as president of Liberty Films, a company that provoked much comment and speculation in the nation's critical columns. We were a company whose officers—vice presidents Wyler and Stevens, and secretary-treasurer Briskin —were working film talents; a company which sought the affiliation of other leading filmmakers such as Leo McCarey and Victor Fleming; a company that was immediately offered deals by MGM, J. Arthur Rank of Britain, Goldwyn, Selznick, United Artists, and RKO. In short, we were something new in Hollywood: a company of, by, and for producer-directors only. The "one man, one film" idea was news again. Hot news. Today's news. Once again it threw down the gauntlet to the assembly-line "committee system" of the major studios.

Film aficionados may be interested in the modus operandi of Liberty Films. Stock distribution: 32 percent to Capra as president and organizer, 18 percent to Briskin, 25 percent each to Wyler and Stevens. But the voting rights were all equal. It took 3 out of 4 votes to resolve such major company decisions as hiring a star or buying a story. But once bought, the story was assigned to Capra, Wyler, or Stevens who from that point worked autonomously, functioning as producer-director without interference from others.

Our deal with RKO called for nine films, three from each producer-director. Wyler, Stevens, and Capra each received three thousand dollars per week from the day the RKO deal was signed. It was assumed (but not obligatory) that each producer-director would make one picture per year. Briskin received fifteen hundred dollars per week as business head for the whole company.

The financing: RKO advanced the cost of physical facilities—rental fees for offices, studio space, and equipment. Bank loans would cover all other production costs. We put up (proportional to our stock holdings) an initial sum of $150,000 to cover pre-production costs—our salaries and that of writers and office help. We had to pay ourselves three thousand dollars per week (upon which we paid 80 percent income tax) because the Internal Revenue Service had declared it unkosher for film artists to work for less than their going salaries when working for companies in which they were substantial stockholders.

Willie Wyler still owed Sam Goldwyn one picture on a pre-war deal, which he would make before moving into our Liberty offices at RKO. Goldwyn gave Willie a choice of three scripts. He chose *Glory for Me!* a script by Robert Sherwood based on a novel by MacKinlay Kantor about returning war heroes. The film was released as *The Best Years of Our Lives.*

Wyler was very high on Liberty Films, probably because he and his associates had matured professionally and personally in the war. In an interview Willie had with Tom Pryor, *The New York Times,* September 16, 1945, Pryor wrote:

> . . . To have missed or passed up the opportunity to personally assimilate "The greatest experience in history" was one of the biggest mistakes a film writer, director or producer could make, Wyler observed . . .

> The war has advanced the motion picture at least ten years ahead of its normal development . . . And Wyler thinks his new partner, Mr. Capra, who earned his colonel's chickens and a Distinguished Service Medal . . . has contributed much toward educating a new type of audience for the movies of tomorrow. "Frank's *Why We Fight* series . . . will live longer than *Gone with the Wind,* and will have greater effect on the development of the medium," he says. . . .

Liberty Films (its trademark was the same one we used on the Army films: our cracked Liberty Bell tolling our liberation) had moved into a private bungalow in the center court of RKO Studios. Stevens was still in the Army, and Wyler had to finish his Goldwyn commitment, so it was up to Briskin and me to make the first Liberty production. The publicity build-up about Liberty Films was overwhelming, and there was much snickering and laying of odds in the inner sanctums of the major studios that the four colonels—as cracked as their bell—would fail big.

There's no denying that butterflies began putting on their own private air show in my stomach. How would a Ruth, Gehrig, or DiMaggio feel if he hadn't swung a bat for four years and was suddenly asked to hit a home run in Yankee Stadium? Well, I was no Ruth, Gehrig, or DiMaggio—which made me all the more nervous.

"It's frightening to go back to Hollywood after four years," I said to Tom Pryor in a *New York Times* interview, "wondering whether you've gone rusty or lost your touch. I keep telling myself how wonderful it would be just to sneak out somewhere and make a couple of quickie Westerns— just to get the feel of things again . . ."

Okay, genius, what *is* your first film going to be about? I knew one thing

—it would *not* be about war. I sensed a growing revulsion among the world's people against brutality. I sensed that this would be bound to happen—and soon: Two nations will declare war, and no one will show up. No. I wanted no part of terrified women clutching whimpering children while bombs shook the world and chaos screamed; no part of G.I.'s bobbing face down in the surf of Omaha Beach. Who were they? Your brothers, your sons, your sweethearts?

The cataclysmic aftermaths of war—hunger, disease, despair—would breed gnawing doubts in man. Why? Why? Why did my wife and children have to be blown to bits? Where is God now? Why must I starve? Why must whole villages starve while fat American soldiers offer us chewing gum and ravish our women? Why? Why? . . .

"Because," the minions of Big Brother were beginning to say in films and books, "because, little man, of yourself you can do nothing to protect yourself from the fat exploiters. Wise up. You've been had. There is no God, no freedom, no democracy. Lies they are. Lies that cause wars. To hell with God and mother and your neighbors. Come over to Big Brother. He will feed you and protect you and give you peace."

The age-old siren song of the dictators: "feed you, protect you, give you peace." So will any prison warden.

No. My films will explore the heart not with logic, but with compassion. "The heart has its reasons which reason knows nothing of," wrote Blaise Pascal, the French scientist. I will deal with the little man's doubts, his curses, his loss of faith in himself, in his neighbor, in his God. And I will show the overcoming of doubts, the courageous renewal of faith, and the final conviction that of himself he can and *must* survive and remain free. For the only true revolutionary is the free man, and revolution is liberty, and liberty is revolution. And I will remind the little man that his mission on earth is to advance spiritually, that to surrender his free spirit to Big Brother's concentration camp is a step backward to the jungle.

As a filmmaker I will champion man—plead his causes, protest the degradation of his dignity, spirit, divinity. Because be he saint or sinner, rich or poor, coward or hero, black or white, genius or retarded, basket case or pole vaulter; be he lame, halt, or blind, each is of a piece with his Maker. Pat the head of a child, you are patting God; slay a man, you are murdering Goodness.

And finally, my films must let every man, woman, and child know that God loves them, and that I love them, and that peace and salvation will become a reality only when they all learn to love each other.

What story ideas did I have for our first film? None that rang bells. I owned *The Flying Yorkshireman*. During the war RKO had taken an option on it, hoping Barry Fitzgerald would play the Sam Small part. Fitzgerald refused: RKO gave up their option. I also had Liberty buy *It Happened on Fifth Avenue*, a comedy about a tramp who found the secret of living the life of Riley: He lives in rich men's homes in New York in winter, and in their Florida homes in summer. I was reading and rereading Alfred Noyes's novel *No Other Man*, and on the side was writing an original Western, *Pioneer Woman*. All these stories had one thing in common: I knew in my heart I'd never film any of them.

I was beginning to wonder why in the world I had ever started Liberty Films, when pleasant Charles Koerner, RKO's studio chief, stuck his head into our bungalow office, and enthusiastically asked: "Frank! You got your first film story yet? No. I can tell by your puss you haven't. I told my wife last night that I'd buttonhole you about *The Greatest Gift*, and that if you didn't make it, I'd cut my throat—" And Charlie Koerner proceeded to tell me about an original story he bought: that it was written as a Christmas card by Philip Van Doren Stern, and mailed to his friends. And that RKO had spent a fortune on three complete scripts by three great writers— Dalton Trumbo, Marc Connelly, and Clifford Odets; and that not one of the scripts did justice to the original story, and that—

"Charlie, stop racing your motor. You must have over half a million tied up in those scripts. Liberty can't handle that kind of—"

"Frank, give me your word you'll make the picture and I'll give you *The Greatest Gift* for what I paid for the original Christmas card—and I'll throw in the scripts."

I read the original idea—a few typewritten pages bound in Christmas covers. It was the story I had been looking for all my life! Small town. A man. A good man, ambitious. But so busy helping others, life seems to pass him by. Despondent. He wishes he'd never been born. He gets his wish. Through the eyes of a guardian angel he sees the world as it would have been had he not been born. Wow! What an idea. The kind of idea that when I got old and sick and scared and ready to die—they'd still say, "He made *The Greatest Gift*."

"Charlie!" I said barging into Koerner's office. "How much did you pay for the Christmas card?"

"Fifty thousand."

"It's a deal, Charlie, if my partners vote for it. That's the best idea I ever read—by light years . . ."

Later I read the three scripts by Trumbo, Connelly, and Odets. They were wide of each other and wider of the simple beauty of the original idea. I saved a few of Odets's opening scenes. I thought of Robert Riskin as the writer. Riskin was out. He had just incorporated his own independent company. And Sidney Buchman was out, of course. He had become Harry Cohn's fair-haired producer. During the war Buchman dusted off my version of *The Life of Chopin*, and produced it, in color, as *A Song to Remember*, Charles Vidor directing. It made a fine successful film. But the Hacketts (Albert Hackett and Frances Goodrich) were perceptive, human writers. I hired them to write a new script that stuck closer to Van Doren Stern's original concept. Then I worried about an actor to play the man.

Of all actors' roles I believe the most difficult is the role of a Good Sam who doesn't know that he is a Good Sam. I knew one man who could play it. From an enlisted private he had worked his way up to a colonel leading a squadron of B-24 bombers. Jimmy Stewart. He had just been discharged. I spoke to Lew Wasserman, the MCA agent who handled Jimmy, told him I wanted to tell Jimmy the story. Wasserman said Stewart would gladly play the part without hearing the story. But I insisted. If Jimmy was as scared as I was about making another film I'd like to know it.

A meeting was arranged in Sam Briskin's apartment. Lew brought in Jimmy. He was older, shyer, ill at ease. My butterflies fluttered. It was four years since I had last told a story to an actor. It was six years since Stewart had last heard a story from a director. Jimmy listened quietly—bored, I thought. The story evaporated into thin air, flew out the window; like one of those fragile, gentle things that "if you touch them they vanish."

Frustration hit me. I leaped to my feet. "Goddammit, Jim, I haven't got a story. This is the lousiest piece of cheese I ever heard of. Forget it, Jimmy. Goddammit, forget it! Forget it!"

Briskin and Wasserman tried to calm me down. "Frank! Jimmy'll sign without hearing the story—"

I remember going for a long ride. What kind of a crazy business is this where one day you've got a story as solid as *Les Miserables*, and the next day you're grabbing air?

Two weeks later Stewart signed for the part. The story came back to me, more beautiful than ever. The Hacketts were writing some bright, sensitive scenes but why didn't the scenes move me? I sat down and wrote some key scenes. The Hacketts melded them with their own. I had the script I wanted. Take it or leave it—things had to be done my way. Now to cast all the other parts.

For the part of the skinflint who owned half the town and coveted the other half I wanted Lionel Barrymore. No one else would do.

Without reading the script Barrymore wangled a loan-out from MGM. And MGM had the lass—Donna Reed—I wanted to play the solid, sensible country girl in whose life there could be but one man. Another loan-out from MGM. I also needed a village flirt, preferably a young blonde sex-pot. I asked Billy Grady, MGM's casting director if he knew of any.

"Do I know any?" he cackled. "For crissake I'm up to here in blonde pussies that've never been to the post. Let me show you some tests—"

The second test was that of a sultry, surly young blonde that seemed undecided whether to kiss you or knock you down. "Hey, Bill! Who's *that* dame?" "Who is she, for crissake? She's a star. But do you think I can get any of our jerk directors to listen? Two years she's been around here snapping her garters. You can have her for a cuppa coffee. Her name's Gloria Grahame." Another loan-out from MGM. And another star was born.

Except for a new young man to play Stewart's brother, Todd Karns, and two other important exceptions, the rest of the cast came from the Ford-

Capra stock company: Tommy Mitchell, H. B. Warner, Beulah Bondi, Ward Bond, Frank Faylen, Sam Hinds, Mary Treen, and Frank Hagney. The first exception—to play a brass-knuckled bartender—was a fine stage actor new to films: Sheldon Leonard. The second exception was sent by heaven itself to play Stewart's pixy guardian angel—a second-class angel who had yet to win his wings—Henry Travers.

I can't begin to describe my sense of loneliness in making that first film which we now called *It's a Wonderful Life*, a loneliness that was laced by the fear of failure. I had no one to talk to, or argue with. My former close associates, "the fiddlers three," had scattered. Joe Sistrom was a big producer at Paramount (*Wake Island, Star Spangled Rhythm*). Harold Winston had disappeared. Chester Sticht was still in the Army untangling the film mess we left behind. Riskin was busy writing the script for his own film—*Magic Town*. My old and dear friend Myles Connolly had resented it personally when I donned a uniform. I guess it finally convinced him that he didn't own me. At any rate I hadn't seen him for years. I finally hired my old writer Jo Swerling just to talk to him, but when he couldn't rewrite the whole script he left.

Of my Liberty partners, Briskin was up to his ears in bank loans and distribution contracts, Wyler had his own problems of preparing and casting *Best Years of Our Lives*, and Stevens—the last to be discharged—after two and a half years of photographing the European war from the invasion of Brittany to the gas ovens in Dachau, had the most difficult time of all finding his bearings.

Had it not been for my old friend and assistant director Art Black, and my film editor, ex-Lieutenant Colonel Bill Hornbeck of my Army unit, I might have come apart at the seams. For I was not only carrying the load of making *Wonderful Life* a successful picture. I had to make a success out of Liberty Films. We were the bellwether of the post-war independents.

Besides I had publicly gone out on a limb against the major studios' assembly-line system in an article I wrote for *The New York Times*, "Breaking Hollywood's Pattern of Sameness." It was printed May 5, 1946, and immediately reprinted in the *Reader's Digest*, the French *Carrefours*, and by our State Department in *America Illustrated*. The article's two key points: Hollywood films were being funneled through the tastes of half a dozen studio heads, and filmmakers began to get their ideas not from life but from each other's pictures. We were creating within walls of mirrors.

Then the article stated that we of Liberty Films had returned from the service with a firm resolve to break that "pattern of sameness," and that Liberty Films was being emulated by many other film creators who had grown tired of having their creative ideas squeezed dry of originality by being pushed through funnels.

As Billy Wilkerson said in the editorial column of his *Hollywood Reporter* of February 22, 1946:

Four ex-colonels, jittery from long absence from Hollywood, hock shirts and some wifely jewels and form LIBERTY FILMS, an independent company that became bellwether of independent film production.

The four: William Wyler, F.C., George Stevens, and Samuel Briskin.

"Is it *that* funny?"

With such a wonderful cast, it *is* a wonderful life.

"Wait a minute, here. Just who are you?" "I told you, George. I'm your guardian angel." "Yeah, yeah . . . Why don't people know me?" "Because you don't exist. You were never born . . ."

George took over the Bailey Building and Loan. No trip to Europe; no going to school. Instead, he gave his college money to his brother Harry. "Will I ever get out of this crummy Bedford Falls?" he wonders.

"Carriage trade, Ernie!"
George's best friends—Bert the cop (Ward Bond); Ernie the taxi driver (Frank Faylen).

On the same bridge where he tried to leave this life, he comes back to it. Bert the cop finds him. "George, where the devil have you been? The whole town's looking for you!" "Bert, look! Zuzu's petals. I'm alive again! . . ."

There are days when writer Jo Swerling and Jimmy and I know the whole damn film will stink.

The majors are worried about the defection of many of their important picture creators to the ranks of the independent units . . . The answer has to be written at the box office. If these defectors can crack through, then the defection *will* cut in heavily on the majors . . . The most important of these defections is the organization . . . under the Liberty banner . . .

On April 8, 1946, I began shooting *It's a Wonderful Life*. By coincidence, Wyler began principal photography on *The Best Years of Our Lives* on the same day. We wished each other luck on the phone and agreed that the last one to finish shooting was a rotten egg.

With my accelerator pushed to the firewall, all that I was and all that I knew went into the making of *It's a Wonderful Life*. The pace was that of a four-month non-stop orgasm.

To celebrate the advent of Liberty Films' first production, Wyler, Stevens, Briskin, and I invited all the stars and near stars we had ever used in our films to a dinner dance and a showing of *It's a Wonderful Life*.

Then we previewed *Wonderful Life* for the press. Some sprayed it with incense:

James Agee, *Nation*, New York:
. . . one of the most efficient sentimental pieces since *A Christmas Carol*.

Life:
. . . a masterful edifice of comedy and sentiment.

Newsweek:
. . . . sentimental, but so expertly written, directed, and acted that you want to believe it.

Time:
It's a Wonderful Life is a pretty wonderful movie. It has only one formidable rival (Goldwyn's *Best Years of Our Lives*) as Hollywood's best picture of the year . . .

But some other Manhattan critics sprayed it with bladder juice:

Bosley Crowther, *The New York Times:*
. . . for all its characteristic humors, Mr. Capra's *Wonderful Life* . . . is a figment of simple Pollyanna platitudes . . .

New Republic:
. . . Hollywood's Horatio Alger fights with more cinematic knowhow and zeal than any other director to convince movie audiences that American life is exactly like the *Saturday Evening Post* covers of Norman Rockwell . . .

The New Yorker:
>   . . . so mincing as to border on baby talk . . . Henry Travers,
> God help him, has the job of portraying Mr. Stewart's guardian
> angel. It must have taken a lot out of him.

But I didn't give a film-clip whether critics hailed or hooted *Wonderful Life.* I thought it was the greatest film I had ever made. Better yet, I thought it was the greatest film *anybody* ever made. It wasn't made for the oh-so-bored critics, or the oh-so-jaded literati. It was my kind of film for my kind of people; the motion picture I had wanted to make since I first peered into a movie camera's eyepiece in that San Francisco Jewish gymnasium.

A film to tell the weary, the disheartened, and the disillusioned; the wino, the junkie, the prostitute; those behind prison walls and those behind Iron Curtains, that *no man is a failure!*

To show those born slow of foot or slow of mind, those oldest sisters condemned to spinsterhood, and those oldest sons condemned to unschooled toil, that *each man's life touches so many other lives.* And that if he isn't around it would leave an awful hole.

A film that said to the downtrodden, the pushed-around, the pauper, "Heads up, fella. No man is poor who has one friend. Three friends and you're filthy rich."

A film that expressed its love for the homeless and the loveless; for her whose cross is heavy and him whose touch is ashes; for the Magdalenes stoned by hypocrites and the afflicted Lazaruses with only dogs to lick their sores.

I wanted it to shout to the abandoned grandfathers staring vacantly in nursing homes, to the always-interviewed but seldom-adopted half-breed orphans, to the paupers who refuse to die while medical vultures wait to snatch their hearts and livers, and to those who take cobalt treatments and whistle—I wanted to shout, "You are the salt of the earth. And *It's a Wonderful Life* is my memorial to you!"

And my kind of people saw the film. And it touched their hearts, and it moved them to write thousands of letters, half of them first-time testimonials.

Then came the great day. The renewal of the Academy Sweepstakes, the annual "run for the Oscars." Liberty Films had a one-two entry going for it in what looked like a strong field. Trainer Willie Wyler of Liberty Films had entered *Best Years of Our Lives* for owner Mr. Samuel Goldwyn. Trainer Frank Capra of Liberty Films had entered a strong contender, *It's a Wonderful Life.* It was owned by Liberty Films. Other strong contenders were *Henry V* (Laurence Olivier), *The Razor's Edge* (Twentieth Century), *The Yearling* (Clarence Brown).

In the elimination heats the Liberty team of Wyler-Capra had both placed Best Picture, Best Actor, and Best Director in the finals.

The morning line for the Oscar Stakes were, Best Picture—*Best Years*

8 to 5, *Yearling* 2 to 1, *Wonderful Life* 3 to 1, *Henry V* 5 to 1, *Razor's Edge* 10 to 1.

In the Best-Actor class, Capra's James Stewart was the heavy favorite (6 to 5), Wyler's Fredric March the long shot (4 to 1).

In the Best-Direction category, Wyler and Capra were co-favorites. Wyler had won the New York Critics' Award, Capra the Foreign Correspondents' Golden Globe.

When the finals were over and the Price Waterhouse judges had seen the photos, it was Wyler over Capra in all categories by a nose. *Best Years* had swept the field, even pulling in Fredric March as Best Actor over the heavily favored Jimmy Stewart.

But two ex-colonels from Liberty Films ended up one-two in the Best-Picture and Best-Director stakes. They had come back to show the stay-at-homes how to make films. Had George Stevens, another ex-colonel, made a picture that year, we bragged that Liberty's producer-directors would have come in one-two-three in the Academy Sweepstakes.

But only winners are awarded Oscars. And Oscars are the adrenalin shots that quicken a languid box office. Finishing second by a nose was not much more advantageous to *Wonderful Life*'s grosses than running out of the money.

"Frank, I'm worried," said Sam Briskin privately. "*Wonderful Life*'s opening soft in some situations. Just our luck if the gravy train slows down now."

The New York *Post*'s Samuel Grafton exposed the culprit that was flagging down the train:

> . . . The plain American is now shopping around for his entertainment. He can no longer be depended on to stand facelessly and docilely in line for hours, and pay big money, to see anything that happens to be on film . . . Sometimes the stubborn fellow goes home without seeing anything—a fate which during the war would have seemed to him worse than death.

To try to persuade Mr. Plain American that *It's a Wonderful Life* was a wonderful film to see, Jimmy Stewart and I accepted Bob O'Donnell's invitation to make personal appearances in his great chain of Texas cinema palaces.

One incident in Texas might bear relating. We were in Dallas. The mayor and city fathers of Beaumont were waiting for us with a brass band, a parade, and a City Hall reception. But Texas, between Dallas and Beaumont was socked in. No planes flying. The Beaumont mayor pleaded on the phone. We must come. All his plans will be spoiled if we don't. Get a charter plane. Veteran flyer Stewart nixed any charter flights. Even commercial airlines made him jittery.

But Bob O'Donnell and Dallas officials ganged up on us. They brought the local "Lindbergh" over to see us. No sweat, said "Lindbergh." He can fly his Cessna in any weather—blindfolded. I'm ignorant of such things but I like to fly. I talked Jimmy into it.

Flying very low and following the railroad tracks, our intrepid flyer stayed below all the nasty weather and got us to Beaumont on time. A huge throng greeted us at the airport. Behind screaming sirens we were paraded to the civic center passing under welcoming banners and by light poles festooned with large heads of Stewart and Capra.

On the City Hall steps a band belted out "Dixie" while hundreds of tall Texans in taller hats crushed our limp right hands. The mayor welcomed us to Beaumont. I found myself standing in front of an enormous blown-up picture of a head—my head. I felt like Stalin.

From the City Hall we paraded to the hotel. Drinks and drinks and lunch with the press. Then speeches and speeches and interviews with the press. Then to the airport with sirens and sirens and several hundred officials and pressmen who feel no pain, no pain. We piled into the Cessna and our "Lindbergh" took off right now.

It was getting dark. The overcast seemed lower. It *was* lower, said Stewart nervously. The plane flew closer to the tracks. "Will you give us some lights back here?" shouted Jimmy over the motor noise. "No lights," the pilot yelled back over his shoulder. "A fuse blew." "Your landing lights out, too?" asked Stewart. "No sweat. Won't need 'em at Dallas," assured the pilot. "How's the weather at Dallas?" "About the same, I guess." "Well, get them on the radio and make sure." There was annoyance in Jimmy's voice. "My radio's been out for a week. But no sweat." "Okay, turn around!" "What?" "I said get your ass back to Beaumont. It's ceiling zero ahead! Turn back! Now!"

We hedge-hopped over houses and trees, feeling for the airport. Taller tree tops disappeared in the haze. Street lamps and car lights were lit.

"Right below us, Mr. Stewart," said the pilot, pointing down. There it was, dark and deserted. The airport. The litter left by the welcoming crowd made it look emptier.

"Well, thank God," sighed Jimmy the squadron leader. "Buzz the hangar," he shouted, "make them turn on the runway lights."

"No lights on this airport. But no sweat, Mr.—"

"The hell there isn't. I'm *all* sweat. Make a flat approach and borrow the whole runway. NOW!"

"Lindbergh" gave him the okay sign. He circled the field without landing. Stewart has had it. "For God's sake, man, set 'er down while you can still *see!*"

"No sweat, Mr. Stewart. Will you pull open that floor door next to you?"

"Holy smoke! The landing gear?"

"Yeah. Just see if it's down."

Jimmy yanked open the door. A cold hurricane blew in.

"The wheels are NOT down!" shouted Jimmy, his voice cracking.

"No sweat. Just kick at 'em with your foot."

I sat in my seat, scared to death, but getting a bang out of watching tall, skinny Stewart wildly stomping the landing gear against a wind that was determined to blow his clothes off. From somewhere the pilot came up with a young sledgehammer. He had left the cockpit and stood alongside an aghast Stewart. "Let me give her a whap with this, Mr. Stewart." He kneeled down and whapped. There were some thumps. "They're down!" cried Jim. "Yeah. You see, Mr. Stewart, you gotta hit that knee joint just right—"

Now Jim ain't a swearing man. But he forgot himself. "Get this goddam plane down, you idiot, before you kill us. It's pitch black outside!"

Calmly the man put his hammer away, slipped into the pilot's seat, nosed the plane down and landed in the dark as gracefully as a gull.

When the man cut his engine our relief was so great that Jimmy and I looked at each other and burst into idiotic laughter. In between laughs Jimmy invited the pilot to dinner and some drinks. The pilot allowed as how that was mighty white of Mr. Stewart, and Mr. Stewart replied that it was "No sweat, friend, no sweat." That triggered another round of silly guffaws as we careened toward a highway crowded with traffic, walking over bits of Stewart's face from the torn up "Welcome Jimmy" posters.

Liberty Films could not count on any profits from *Wonderful Life* for at least a year. Meanwhile I had put down a hefty deposit on Lindsay and Crouse's Pulitzer Prize play, *State of the Union*, and had bought *Friendly Persuasion*, Jessamyn West's novel about Quakers. I had two writers on *State of the Union*, and another writer on *Friendly Persuasion*.

Each Liberty director had a secretary and three assistant producers on his staff. Our original ante of $150,000 had evaporated. Collectively we put up another $150,000. That meant hocking real property. We could not recoup any of this pre-production money until films went into principal photography. But neither George nor Willie was anywhere near principal photography on anything. That meant George, Willie, Sam, and I had to keep putting up our own money to pay ourselves $10,500 a week in salaries, of which we netted (after taxes) about 15 percent. On every go-round we lost 85 percent of our own money.

It was the fastest and most gentlemanly way of going broke ever invented. Unless three very famous producer-directors started making films fast, there would be three very hungry producer-directors in the breadlines.

As if this news was not bad enough, the box office suddenly laid an egg bigger than the one Horton hatched. War industries closed down, ten million service men were returning to civvies and a scramble for jobs. And Great Britain slapped a "75 per-cent-of-earnings tax" on American films showing in Britain. The war boom collapsed like a ripped balloon.

The *Daily Variety* of Hollywood called 1947 the year that:

will go down in the history of Hollywood as the year of the big
flood . . . there weren't enough crying towels available in the whole
studio area to sop up the overflow and by mid-summer you couldn't
enter a Hollywood executive office without sloshing ankle-deep
through the accumulated tears . . . The only construction that now
interests movie magnates in the erection of another wailing wall . . .

There was only one out for us—sell Liberty Films to some major studio.
Two of Liberty's partners, Willie Wyler and George Stevens, were violently opposed to calling quits on our wonderful independent set-up that all
the directors in the world were watching and hoping to emulate. Briskin and
I argued that collectively our talents might be worth a good deal to some
major studio, but if we held out until the bank foreclosed, they'd pick us off
one by one at their own price.

The big New York *Variety* of February 12, 1947, printed a few "I told
you so's":

> . . . The trek back to the major studios is already under way and
> is expected to develop to proportions of a rout within 6 to 12
> months.
>
> Bellwether on the trail back may be Liberty Films . . .

Furthermore, 1947 was the year the House Un-American Activities Committee's hearings in Hollywood stirred up the iguanas and touched off civil
wars in the Actors, Writers, and Directors guilds. Major film companies
were accused of setting up a sub-rosa "blacklist" of artists the Committee
labeled card-carrying Communists or fellow-travelers. Like the biblical
rain, rumors, suspicions, and secret accusations falleth on the just and un-
just. For me the year marked the beginning of an innuendo campaign that
was to climax in a Kafkaesque nightmare of humiliation.

It was also a year of hard political decisions for America; the year that
retired General Marshall, now President Truman's special peace Ambassador to China, returned from the Orient as a "voice in the Wilderness" crying "stay out of Asia." In-between planes he stopped at our home to mix
himself a couple of old-fashioneds and chat with Lu and the children. He
was terribly discouraged, he said, because arriving at a truth that was common to both Chiang Kai-shek's Nationalists and Mao Tse-tung's Communists was like dipping water with a sieve. He would strongly urge President
Truman to never, but never, commit even one American soldier on the Asian
mainland, because, said the General, it would suck us into pouring our
manhood and substance into a bottomless bog from which we might never
extricate ourselves with honor. That great public servant—architect of the
Marshall Plan for Europe's recovery and the only general ever to receive
the Nobel Peace Prize—was as prophetic as he was tireless in his quest for a
peaceful world.

It was also the year of my first head-on confrontation with a star. It was
on a Friday in May. Late afternoon. Come Monday morning I would launch

the principal photography of *State of the Union.* I was about to go into my pre-production cocoon that shut out the world. So far, everything had come up roses.

When RKO backed off from a budget of $2,800,000, MGM took on the picture. They had to. Spencer Tracy had his heart set on playing the leading role. And "after all," he joked in Bob Thomas's column, "I'm getting old, and I've never done a picture with Capra." Tracy's wants were practically commands at MGM. "Okay," they said. "We'll loan Tracy to Liberty Films, if Liberty makes their independent picture at our studio, and we release it as an MGM picture. That'll still keep Tracy under Leo the Lion's banner." "Deal."

And so here I was at last, in a large suite of offices on MGM's Director's Row, trying for the third time to make a film at fabulous MGM! I had a great script and a greater cast: The one and only Spencer Tracy; that sure-fire Adolphe Menjou; an irrepressible new star, Van Johnson; Angela Lansbury, the amazing British gal that could play anything and everything well; Lewis Stone, everybody's favorite; all my prize bit performers, and the best prize of all, Claudette Colbert to play the leading lady who would pit her wits and feminine courage against the hard-boiled Republican king-makers for the soul of the man she loved—her husband.

And here she comes into my office looking as cute and bright and stand-offish as she did fourteen years ago in *It Happened One Night.* She had matured into a real top star now; her price, two hundred thousand dollars per picture!

"Frank," she opened up business-like, "I just read my contract. You left out that I was not to work one minute after five o'clock on any day."

"What? You never mentioned five o'clock to me—"

"I must have. My agent puts it in all my contracts now. My doctor says I get too tired—" Her agent was her brother, and her doctor was her husband. "Claudette, this is a big expensive picture. I *can't* tie my hands to a seven-hour shooting day—"

"Frank, those are *your* problems. I have to quit work at five. And if it isn't in my contract I won't sign it."

"Meaning?"

"Meaning no contract no picture."

Her extensive wardrobe (fifteen thousand dollars) had been created and tested. It was late Friday. Monday morning she would be in the first shot with the other principals. There wasn't a prayer of replacing her over the weekend. It would cost Liberty Films tens of thousands—perhaps hundreds —to deny her a 5 P.M. quitting clause now.

"Okay, *sister,*" I said, implying a not-so-sib relationship. "No picture! And check in your wardrobe before you leave."

She rose, gave me a quick look, and walked out.

"Oh, my God!" blurted out Sam Briskin. "Everybody's on *salary!* Could cost us a fortune—"

Quickly he phoned L. B. Mayer and Eddie Mannix. Mayer said, "Call Spence before he reads about it." Mannix said, "Good for the dago!"

Sam called Tracy. Spence's first reaction was to laugh. "Put Frank on," he said. "Hey, you little bastard," he greeted, "I thought you were a nice guy. I may have to report you to the Actors Guild—"

"Spence, I blew my stack. Have you got any girl friends that aren't working? I mean, actresses?"

"Waaal, come to think of it, Katie isn't hamming it up at the moment—"

"Hepburn! Oh, no, Spence. You think she'd do it?"

"I dunno. But the bag of bones has been helping me rehearse. Kinda stops you, Frank, the way she reads the woman's part. She's a real theater nut, you know. She might do it for the hell of it—"

There are women and there are women—and then there is Katie. There are actresses and actresses—then there is Hepburn. A rare professional-amateur, acting is her hobby, her living, her love. She is as wedded to her vocation as a nun is to hers, and as competitive in acting as Sonja Henie was in skating. No clock-watching, no humbug, no sham temperament. If Katharine Hepburn made up her mind to become a runner, she'd be the first woman to break the four-minute mile.

And, as Tracy said, she is theater. On the phone, Hepburn wasted no words on contracts or salary or billing. A show was in distress. She was being asked to help. And help she did.

Monday morning at nine sharp, we shot our first scene with Tracy, Menjou, and Hepburn. For many of the cast and crew it was the first indication that Hepburn had replaced Colbert. There were no tears and no jeers. MGM crews were not easily impressed. They, too, had eaten of MGM's superman spinach. But *one* man on the set was impressed—the director.

To me, films were novels filled with living people. I cast actors that I believed could *be* those living people. Gary Cooper *was* Longfellow Deeds; he *was* Long John Doe. James Stewart *was* Jefferson Smith and George Bailey. But now I had Spencer Tracy who had "lived" and won Academy Awards as a priest (*Boys Town*), and as a Portuguese fisherman (*Captains Courageous*); who had "lived" as Dr. Jekyll and Mr. Hyde, Thomas Edison, the Show-off, A Guy Named Joe, a wino in *Tortilla Flat*, and as a pilot over Tokyo.

And I had Katharine Hepburn who "lived" in *The Philadelphia Story, Morning Glory* (Academy Award), *Alice Adams, Sylvia Scarlett, Mary of Scotland, Stage Door, Bringing up Baby*, and many other "lives." In short, I had the two champions of what Lionel Barrymore called the "oldest and noblest profession."

Tracy, the actor, had never manufactured even a hairpin, yet mentally, physically, and psychologically he *was* the very rich American industrialist who wanted to put his know-how and ideals about democracy into the service of better government. And Hepburn, the actress, *was* the very-much-in-love wife who saw the ideals and hopes of her strong, decent, patriotic husband being twisted, warped, and compromised into cheap vote-getting tricks by a gang of hungry politicos too long away from the patronage trough.

When Tracy and his "bag of bones" played a scene, cameras, lights, microphones, and written scripts ceased to exist. And the director did just what the crews and other actors did—sit, watch, and marvel. And the name Claudette Colbert, only days ago synonymous with disaster, now became associated with serendipity.

Shortly, I shall have less complimentary remarks to make about some performers, but in *State of the Union* my hardest directing job was trying to keep four other great pros—Adolphe Menjou, Van Johnson, Angela Lansbury, and Lewis Stone—from stealing too many scenes from the two champs.

In fact, my toughest job in *State* was not directorial but political. The film was a political satire, rather brutal at times. But the great majority of Americans (Republicans and Democrats) whose politics lie in the middle of the broad political spectrum, will laugh at political lampoonery if the lampooning is even-handed. However, the closer their political hue shifts toward either end of the spectrum, the more they lose their sense of humor. Those at the extreme ends—Communists or Fascists—never laugh. They can't.

The year 1947 was a time of vicious intra-industry political war; returned service veterans and others were trying to root out the entrenched reds. Bitter arguments, loud shouting matches, even blows filled the air. Whose bitch was witch? became a grisly game.

In a tense emotional big-money industry, governed by super-egos with super-thyroids, an industry whose history could be the plot of a Marx Brothers' farce, one might have expected that industry's politics to follow suit in kookiness. It did. In spades. It seemed that two-thirds of the picture people registered as breast-beating Democrats, but voted as coupon-clipping Republicans.

Only the Big Brother twins (one left-handed, the other right-handed) were grimly, deadly serious about Hollywood's politics. And for strong reasons. Hollywood had become not only a world center for entertainment and "news"; it was also the home of the world's richest Easy Marks. Since every day was Christmas Day for some lucky ones, these emotional suckers would contribute to anything and everything charitable—including some not easy-to-spot Big Brother Enterprises. Then, of course, what better propaganda than a party-line speech here and there by some popular movie hero to a listening audience of hundreds of millions?

In films—as in radio and press—Stalinites were more numerous, and certainly more popular, than Hitlerites. First of all the reds were our allies in fighting Hitler's Fascists. Second, Hitler's human barbecue ovens made even some of our own Kook Kluck Klackers pale under their hoods. But despite the presence and war-created popularity of reds in Hollywood, red propaganda in films had been miniscule in importance or dividends.

Another Hollywood political ana: Big Brother "Lefty" early glaumed on to the words "liberal" and "democracy" and "progressive" as slogans for his snake-oil; these words being normally in Big Brother "Righty's" lexicon of shibboleths. "Righty" had to be content with such less glamorous words (since the war) as "patriotism" and "conservatism" and—a word they wish they could eat—"reactionary." But still, Hollywood "gave out" as liberals, yet voted as conservatives. An example: In our filthy-rich residential section of Brentwood, a group of "bleeding-heart" liberal homeowners would regularly solicit for progressive movements. But one day they came to our house asking us to sign a community contract that pledged us all not to sell our homes to Negroes! Some liberals. My wife threw them out on their progressive ears.

But to get to my *State of the Union* set. Politically, my cast ran the gamut of "hue and cry" from Hepburn to Menjou. Wisecracking, witty, Menjou—a flag-waving super-patriot who invested his American dollars in Canadian bonds—had a manic thing about Communists. "Scratch do-gooders like Hepburn," he used to mutter, "and they'll yell *Pravda!*"

A crack like that might both anger and amuse Spencer Tracy, one of the captains of Hollywood's Irish Mafia (Pat O'Brien, Lynne Overman, James Gleason, Frank Morgan, James Cagney, George Murphy, Bill Frawley, and several others). "You scratch some members of the Hepburn clan," he said to me on the set, leering roguishly at Katie, "and you're liable to get an ass full of buckshot."

"Oh, Spence, not that old family bromide. You make it worse every time you tell it," said Hepburn, pouting and giggling.

"Gospel truth, Frank," said impish Tracy with a big wink. "First time I got invited to the Hepburn home in New England—home, hell! A palace! On half an island and facing a private fenced-off beach a mile long. Well, you know Madame Do-gooder, here. She'll donate to the Committee for the Protection of Fireplugs. She'll parade for the civil rights of the three-toed sloth. And you know what? Her family are all bigger fruitcakes than she is. You know—ultra-liberal New England aristocrats that work their ass off for the poor, poor folk, but never see one.

"Take her father. A big doctor. They won't let charity letters go through New England's mails unless his name's on the letterheads. And her mother helps Margaret Sanger with young girls that get knocked up—"

"Spence! You're awful," broke in Katie. "Mother helps with birth control—"

"Okay, Mother helps young girls from *getting* knocked up. And all the six grown Hepburn kids've got pet social rackets of their *own*. What a clan! Well, at dinner my head's this big. Can you imagine listening to *eight* Hepburns all talking at *once* about the Negroes, the slums, the Puerto

When Katie Hepburn talks
—which is almost always
—the garrulous listen . . .

. . . Wise guys learn . . .

. . . And idols adore.

Then, too, Hepburn has that divine quality of being a good audience — especially for Tracy. Here she laughs...

Luncheon day after preview with MGM officials and Vice President Barkley. To my utter surprise the VP praised *State of the Union*. Truman, of course, loved the film. Word came to us that it had encouraged the President to run for a second term.

Ricans, abortions, the homeless, the hungry? So I get up and say, 'If you don't mind, I'll step outside and lift the lamp beside the golden door.' So I go out on the porch for some peace and to watch the sunset.

"The beach was empty. Had to be empty with those barbed-wire fences on each side. And I see a guy, with a fishing rod, a little guy, crawling through the barbed wire about half a mile away, so far away he was a speck. 'Hey!' I yelled to them inside. 'Better put on another plate. Here comes a wretched one yearning to breathe free!'

"Old man Hepburn came out running with fire in his eye. 'Where is he?' I pointed to the fence. Mr. Hepburn took down a megaphone off the porch wall and ran out on the beach yelling, 'This is private property! You are trespassing! Get off this beach immediately or I will fill your tail with buckshot! Now, git!'

"The poor old fisherman dove through that barbed wire and gits for his life up the beach trailing barbed wire from his legs. Papa Hepburn hangs up the megaphone and says to me: 'Getting so a man can't enjoy any privacy any more. At least twice a week some nervy interloper tries crawling through that fence.' And he goes right inside and joins the hot family discussion about the rights of the poor—"

And so, in the interest of political peace, I closed off all sets in *State of the Union*, and established a tight security against visitors—especially reporters, who would like nothing better than to egg on a political donnybrook between Hepburn and Menjou. But one reporter managed to get to Menjou, or vice versa:

Los Angeles *Examiner*, November 15, 1947
MENJOU SEES NEW FILM RED EXPOSE
By Harold Heffernan
    In his first public utterance on the subject since returning from the House Un-American Activities Committee hearing in Washington, Adolphe Menjou predicted that resumption of the congressional investigation two weeks hence would "tear Hollywood wide open."
    Immaculately attired in dinner coat and black tie, Menjou sat on the sideline of the *State of the Union* set at MGM and resumed his explosive assaults on producers, directors, writers and actors who have reputedly become involved in subversive activities . . .

So right in the middle of my shooting a savage satire on American party politics, Congressman Thomas's Committee holds its "tear Hollywood open" hearings.

I had every logical reason to worry about *State of the Union*. Eight years ago Congress and the Washington press corps had practically crucified me for making *Mr. Smith Goes to Washington*. What would they do to me for *State of the Union*? Could this become my disaster film, the film all directors have nightmares about—the film nobody goes to see? It was that kind of year. Fear. Uncertainty. Panic.

In our film profession you may have Gable's looks, Tracy's art, Marlene's legs, or Liz's violet eyes. You may be voted Miss America or male model of the year. Talent, beauty, wealth, ambition, intelligence, luck, personality, and sex appeal haunt the studio gates. But these qualities, singly or in clusters, don't mean a thing without that swinging thing called courage. Courage is the sine qua non—the Knute Rockne hormone that drives all other hormones to kick, run, pass, and tackle.

I was not born to fear. I was not a man who measured the height, depth, or width of obstacles. The survival courage of my peasant ancestors was my equalizer against the richer, smarter, stronger. Courage kept my soul leaping higher, ever higher. Courage made me a champion long before I was a champion. But the world was full of *ex*-champions. What made them ex-champions? What did they lose? The year 1947 showed me what they lost.

My soul stopped leaping upward after I forced my partners to sell Liberty Films. Greatness had beckoned to the very last: "Keep going, laddie! To hell with failure and bankruptcy. Keep going! Greatness is yours. You proved it with *It's a Wonderful Life*. Keep going!"

But no. I hesitated—then traded the elan of courage for the safety of money. I pulled back—then became an uncertain Lord Jim. Would greatness pass me by?

"It's all arranged, Frank. A black-tie celebrity-night premiere for *State of the Union* at our Capital Theater," enthused Carter Barron on the phone. Carter Barron was Louis B. Mayer's popular ambassador in Washington. "And guess who's sponsoring the shindig."

"The House Un-American Activities Committee. Who else."

"Well, I gave them considerable thought, Frank. But I reached for more class—the White House Correspondents Association."

"Oh, no!" I groaned. "It's *Mr. Smith* all over again. Have they seen the picture?"

"No. They accepted sight unseen. 'If it's a Frank Capra picture,' Vaccarino said, he's the president of the White House gang, 'it's okay with me.' And Frank. Guess who else is coming?"

"The Queen of England, of course."

"You're warm. The President of these here now United States!"

"WHAT!? You're nuts! We've got Truman jokes all through the picture—"

"He knows it. Besides, his press secretary said old 'give 'em hell' will come invited or not."

"Okayyyy. Now guess who *ain't* coming—"

"Don't you dare! The President's your guest of honor."

To vulgarize Pascal, "show biz has its reasons that reason knows nothing of." How else explain my standing with White House Association president Ernest Vaccarino on the curb of a completely deserted street in front of MGM's Capital Theater (waiting for President Truman) on the opening night of *another* film that slashed and ripped at politicians? How many times would our Capital's press have to run me out of town before I took their hint: "Lay off Washington's politics?"

"Ten seconds!" said a Secret Service man with an earphone, from a car at the curb. Another Secret Service agent, standing behind "Vac" and me, nodded. And here they come—a White House limousine, followed by a Secret Service car, approaching quietly down the wet street. (By some ingenious, moving, no-traffic "wave," a twenty-second all-red hold on traffic lights, the Presidential car could roll inside the "wave" at a thirty-mile clip through streets empty of car or pedestrian traffic for two blocks ahead and one block behind it; and very few Washingtonians noticed it.)

No use trying to describe the diaphoretics induced by welcoming the President of the United States to a political satire that pulled politicians apart promise by promise. Let's just say that sweat poured down my face, back, and legs. Vaccarino and I were the official hosts and Presidential escort. "Vac," a Truman favorite, introduced me to the President and to his daughter, Margaret. Her eyes sparkled with excitement. Mrs. Truman did not come.

The Secret Service men gently but quickly nudged us toward the lobby doors—behind us, the street traffic was magically normal again. I made a mental note: What a neat trick, that red light, rolling "hold," for a bad guy's getaway.

Except for Secret Service men, here and there, the Capital Theater's ornate lobby was empty; the auditorium doors shut and guarded. The silence was eerie. I knew there were thirty-five hundred of Washington's government and social crème de la crème seated behind those doors. From hidden loudspeakers "Hail to the Chief" cracked the silence. "Well!" said President Truman roguishly as he glanced around with affected surprise. "Somebody must be coming in!"

Our group ascended a little-used stairway to a narrow darkened hallway that serviced the plush theater boxes—now curtained and guarded. At the front box two S.S. men, beckoning with small flashlights, held the curtain open. Truman entered the box. "Hail to the Chief" still blared from the speakers. The theater lights went on. The audience stood to applaud the President's entrance. He bowed. There was one standing occupant already in the Presidential box—my wife. I introduced her to Mr. Truman and Miss Margaret. Women are wonderful. Lu didn't bat an eye or drop a curtsy as she shook Mr. Truman's hand.

On the last note of "Hail to the Chief," the President sat down—Lu on his left (next to the wall), Margaret on his right (overlooking the audience). I had been rehearsed to sit directly behind the President to answer any questions. Vaccarino joined his own group in a box behind us.

The moment Mr. Truman sat down, the lights went out and Leo the Lion roared his jungle fanfare from the opening screen curtains. Leo's roar was too onomatopoeic. Hastily, I whispered to the nearest Secret Service man—he ran interference for me to the nearest washroom. Up came the butterflies and all their cocoons.

The Secret Service agents had briefed Vaccarino and me in dry runs that afternoon: how to escort the President in and out, what to do in case he was shot, or passed out, or was menaced by riots or fire. We were led through each of the three guarded exits to waiting getaway cars (one in front, two in the alley). Tiny, almost invisible, gold-colored clips were attached to our coat lapels to identify us in the dark to the agents, all of whom wore similar clips. (Each separate occasion calls for a different identifying clip.) My clip allowed me to walk around the theater at will. And, of course, I never did return to my seat in the President's box.

I walked upstairs, downstairs; I sat on the stairs. And every few minutes, like an arsonist drawn to his fire, I'd sneak to the back of Truman's box— and listen. At first the gimlet-eyed Secret Service men barely tolerated my quick look-ins. Then they greeted me with broader and broader smiles. "The Chief really likes this one, Mr. Capra," whispered the chief agent.

"How do you know?" I asked curtly.

"Oh, I've watched him enough. When he sees something on the screen that really excites him, he lifts himself up and down on his seat—like a small boy watching a chase. Watch him."

The picture was coming up to a remark about Truman. I held my breath. On the screen, Menjou brags to Hepburn about Tracy's chances: "He's going to be the next occupant of the White House." Hepburn's answer: "Do Mr. and Mrs. Truman know about this?" sent the President bouncing merrily up and down in his chair, while the whole house rocked and boffed.

Normally I should've felt like doing what Jimmy Durante did after every successful performance: Run to the nearest phone booth, put in a nickel, dial the letters *G—O—D*, say "Thanks!" and hang up.

But not now. I walked to the lobby, sat on a stairway, lit my umpteenth Melachrino. Secret Service men at the doors gave me congratulatory winks and "okay" signs. Explosive laughs from inside were increasing in length and frequency—from virtually the same audience that nine years ago had walked out on *Mr. Smith*. The same press that had boiled me in ink for *Smith*—a far greater film—would undoubtedly toast me in champagne for *State . . .*

When we left for Washington I had said to my wife: "Lu, pack lightly. We may have to make a run for the border." I was certain *State of the Union* would create angry repercussions, sure the House Un-American Activities Committee would not muff the opportunity to subpoena us all into a congressional spectacular called "Film Reds on Parade."

I sprawled back on the deep pile of the carpeted staircase, and listened. The laughs reminded me of the pounding surf at Malibu. I had finally captured the intellectual and political elite of Washington; captured them by making them laugh at themselves. But why couldn't *I* laugh?

Because I felt a visceral fear: *State of the Union* would be my last Frank

Capra film, my last burst of autumn colors before the winter of artistic slavery to the major studio hierarchy at Paramount Pictures. How ironic that I, who had started the cycle and beat the loudest tom-toms for the "one man, one film" principle, had probably negotiated the death of that glorious cycle —for cash!

I did not thrill or doff my humble cap when Senator Barkley and Speaker Rayburn, and dozens of other big-name solons who had pilloried me for *Smith*, now extolled me for *State*. I didn't glow like a firefly after reading in the *Motion Picture Daily* (April 16, 1948) that "President Truman is becoming a one-man sales-staff for *State of the Union*. He liked it so well he asked [MGM] to send a print over to the Presidental yacht *Williamsburg.* . . ."

Nor did I kick dirt with my toe and say: "Shucks! Twarn't nothin'," when the big *Variety* (January 5, 1949) carried an article titled "Film That Changed History?" by Charles Allredge (advance man for President Truman when Dewey was an odds-on favorite to oust him from the White House):

"The most important film of 1949—if importance lies in influencing people and events—was Frank Capra's *State of the Union*" . . . "In that film," Allredge goes on to say, "a presidential candidate beats the political bosses by going over their heads with a dramatic appeal to the people." Truman saw the film repeatedly, as Allredge points out, and at the climactic point in his (Truman's) campaign, he did exactly what the movie candidate did—he went to the people!

"At a dinner in the Capital," wrote Truman's advance man, "shortly after Mr. Truman returned from a whistle-stop trip to the West, he declared, 'There will be a Democrat in the White House in 1949, and you're looking at him!' A good portion of the audience, and they were Democrats, didn't believe him. But he never wavered . . . this writer believes the film confirmed his courage, determination not to quit, and firm belief that if you were on the right side and told the people the truth, you probably wouldn't lose. And that if you lost, you would lose the right way. . . ."

Well, maybe the film did give Harry Truman a timely kick in the pants to confirm his courage (a commodity that Mr. Truman had an ample supply of). But it served as the back of the hand to my moxie. For it was a lack of that wonderful commodity that led up to this sour climax: *State of the Union*, the picture that made world critics finally admit I was a filmmaker, that made them roll over and cry "Uncle!," was the film that was to be my last independent production. The film director who had dedicated his God-given talents to the service of man, had hocked those gifts in his finest hour. Witness these critical acclaims for *State of the Union*:

> Bosley Crowther, *The New York Times*:
>   . . . if anything, it is sharper in its knife-edged slicing of pachyderm schemers and connivers than was the original. . . .

Howard Barnes, *Herald Tribune*:

. . . No way of describing the sorcery which Capra can effect . . . a minor miracle of transmutation . . . into a fresh, eloquent, enchanting film [with] its own contours; its own compulsion . . . a film of heart, dignity, and great artistry. . . .

Scotsman:

. . . for more than a decade, [he] has used the commercial cinema as a pulpit from which to preach an articulate philosophy of human relationships. An artist who graduated from slapstick comedies— and there have been worse training grounds—[Capra] has never lost his talent for simple visual humors. On another level, he is the critic of materialism, the satirist of pretension, the idealist seeking a working basis for a capitalist democracy. His politics are what are generally described as liberal; his ethic—with occasional lapses— is that of Christian humanism. . . .

Well, this satirist of pretensions, this Christian humanist, this critic of materialism, now gave substantial trust funds to his three children, moved into posh offices at Paramount Studios—and slowly drank the hemlock of champions: the bitter, souring realization that part of what had made him great was dying.

Balaban's Law

IT IS MONDAY morning quarter-backing. It is not subject to absolute proof. It may all be just a slight case of looking back in anger. But I am sure my former Liberty Films partners, Willie Wyler and George Stevens, will agree with me in whole or in part when I say that the more or less continuous downward slide of Hollywood's artistic and economic fortunes that began in 1947 was triggered not by the advent of television, not by the intransigence of foreign governments. That slide was set in motion by our sale of Liberty Films to Paramount.

And lest anyone challenge the existence of a continuous slide, let him compare the world importance of Hollywood's major companies and the great films of the thirties and forties, with today's status of these same companies and their films.

Mighty MGM, the Bagdad of filmdom, once teeming with stars and radiant with glamour, is now a ghost city, inhabited by mocking winds that flap its once-gay tatters. Star-crowned Paramount is a write-off item in an industrial conglomerate. United Artists, the once "indestructible idea" (a releasing outlet for independent producers), is a stock manipulation ort in Transamerica's bag of "diversifications." And ancient and venerable Universal Pictures ekes out survival by moonlighting in tourism.

Furthermore, practically all the Hollywood filmmaking of today is stooping to cheap salacious pornography in a crazy bastardization of a great art to compete for the "patronage" of deviates and masturbators. If that isn't a slide, it'll do until a real avalanche hits our film Mecca.

In 1948 there was a historical confrontation between big company managements and the "one man, one film" independents. A major crisis had hit Hollywood. American theater attendance had dropped from a high of eighty million customers per week in 1946, to sixty-two million in 1948.

"The drop," the company heads argued, "is permanent; it is due to the expected post-war shrinkage in spending."

"The hell it is!" countered the independent producers. "It is a backlash against Hollywood's flood of lousy wartime pictures."

"But the loss of our foreign markets is permanent, too!" wailed the company presidents. "Therefore, our companies must tailor our costs to the diminished demand."

"Pfui!" said the independent producers. "There's no *end* to the demand for great films, and no *limit* to their box-office returns. We must spend more and more on fewer and better pictures!"

Then Barney Balaban exploded his shocker. Who is Barney Balaban? He was the president of Paramount Pictures. There was a Balaban "success mystique" within the industry. Paramount was, financially, the most solid of all the major film companies. Paramount stock was almost a blue chip; its "book" value far below its actual value. For example: The huge Paramount Theater Building on Times Square was carried on the books at one dollar. And everyone credited Paramount's solidity to Barney Balaban. A fine, upright man, they said. A financial wizard; a magician at analyzing box-office figures. Oh, yes. There was a Paramount board of directors. But Paramount was Balaban, and Balaban was Paramount—and Balaban came out with one of the slightly more than extraordinary edicts in theatrical history, to wit:

Based on the industry axiom "a film breaks even when its take reaches twice its cost," Balaban declared that his "figures"—which never lied—predicted that NO FUTURE BOX-OFFICE HIT, NO MATTER HOW GREAT OR HOW COSTLY, COULD EVER AGAIN TAKE IN MORE THAN THREE MILLION DOLLARS!

Therefore, THE PRODUCTION COST OF OUR TOP FILMS MUST NOT EXCEED ONE AND A HALF MILLION IF WE ARE TO SURVIVE!

"Amen!" shouted other company presidents, grateful to Barney for blaming company losses on shrinking markets rather than on shrinking visions. And they cited two recent examples: Frank Capra's *It's a Wonderful Life* and *State of the Union,* although acclaimed by critics and public, were both struggling to show a profit BECAUSE EACH HAD COST OVER TWO MILLION.

It became known as Balaban's Law. About the time Liberty Films moved into Paramount we found this decree, figuratively written on the studio halls: "No Picture Whose Budget Exceeds $1,500,000 by as Much as a Farthing Shall be Approved for Production! NO EXCEPTIONS.—Balaban"

I am not blaming Balaban for starting Hollywood's grand downward glide, for he was a real-estate man hostage to real-estate logic. But I can blame myself, for had I not persuaded my reluctant artistic partners into a sell-out of Liberty Films, the rush of other independent producers to return to the "security" of the Establishment's major studios would probably not have occurred. Liberty Films was the bellwether. When Capra-Wyler-Stevens-Briskin copped out, others copped out.

The *Hollywood Reporter* (August 8, 1949) reported:

> . . . that independent production faces practical extinction . . .
> at least 76 indie units have dropped from the "active" production
> lists . . . names like David O. Selznick, Mervyn LeRoy's Arrowhead
> Productions . . . the Cary Grant-Alfred Hitchcock unit, Leo Mc-
> Carey's Rainbow Productions, James Cagney Productions, Bill
> Dozier-Joan Fontaine, Frank Borzage, Douglas Fairbanks, Jr.,
> Robert Montgomery, Michael and Garson Kanin, Lester Cowan. . . .

Had Liberty Films gone ahead with independent films, the "one man, one film" idea would most certainly have proven Balaban's Law a new low in absurd showmanship. But as it was, business heads won the day, and when business wins the day in our profession, it sets motion pictures back for at least a decade.

What of my three ex-colonel partners? Sam Briskin was delighted with the sale of Liberty Films; he cashed in nearly a million, and wound up with a five-year executive-producer contract with Paramount.

George Stevens had been adamantly against the sale of Liberty Films. In fact, when negotiations started with Paramount, George had said, "Include me out," and left Liberty to join Leo McCarey's Rainbow Productions. But, to George's dismay, he found McCarey dickering to sell his Rainbow company to Paramount!

Back came Stevens to Liberty, and his first Liberty picture: *I Remember Mama*, for RKO release. The Paramount deal was on again. George argued, protested, set his heels against the sale. But finally, and glumly, he agreed. "Frank, Willie, Sam," he warned, "it's wrong, it's immoral to sell our independent company. It's a colossal sell-out of our artistic freedoms—"

Willie Wyler? He, too, objected strongly to giving up Liberty Films. But Willie is pure film director. Business and production details bore him. Willie wants and needs a producer to make the petty, nitty-gritty decisions. That worried me. In the end, I think Willie was not too unhappy to join Paramount and get back to pure film directing. Besides, he made over a million before he turned a crank.

And so, the "one man, one film" apostle became, for the first time, an employed contract director taking orders. I was tempted by a million dollars —and fell; never to rise to be the same man again, either as a person or as a talent. For, once I had lost (or sold) control of the content of my films and of the artistic liberty to express myself in my own way—it was the beginning of my end as a social force in films.

But it was not my end as a filmmaker. I had mastered the skills of the medium. I could still make a film on any subject—whether it cost ten thousand or ten million—as well as any director in the world, if not better. For

I was born with the determination to win any race that I ran. Coming in second was, for me, no better than coming in last.

But I was also born to function best as a free man. Deprived of freedom, the restraining bars and handcuffs irked me more than the restraining authority. Like a tethered eagle I fought the tether rather than the man who tied it. Imagine my inner boilings knowing that I was my own tether *and* the authority that had tied it. I began to act strangely, to look for "villains."

President Truman had appointed me an alternate delegate to the Third Session of the General Conference of UNESCO (United Nations Educational, Scientific and Cultural Organization), to be held in Beirut, Lebanon. The U.S. Commission for UNESCO held a preliminary meeting at the Hotel Copley Plaza in Boston, September 27–29, 1948.

Speeches were given by Milton S. Eisenhower, Archibald MacLeish, Donald R. Young, and Harlow Shapley. I was part of a panel discussion with Erwin "Spike" Canham, Representative Christian Herter, Walter H.C. Laves, Mrs. Anne O'Hare McCormick, Senator Margaret Chase Smith, and George C. Stoddard on "UNESCO in a Divided World."

Before the first day's meeting ended I had a disturbing feeling that America was being sucked into something. One of the stated objectives of UNESCO was world peace. Good. To achieve world peace UNESCO proposed to teach children—but only Western children, since UNESCO was not allowed behind the Iron Curtain—that "peace was more important than freedom," while the dictatorships indoctrinated their children with "death to American imperialism." Having just lost my own freedom I wanted no part of losing it for others. So I left the meeting, returned home, and resigned from UNESCO. It was a foolish move. I couldn't remember having ever walked away from a fight. I should have stayed with UNESCO and pressed home my viewpoint from its world forum. But no. I resigned. Didn't show up for the bell.

I found a more immediate villain at home—our library of rare books. Suddenly it became a symbol of a stodgy, snooty reach for status.

"Lu!" I informed my wife, "I've made arrangements with Arthur Swann of the Parke-Bernet Galleries in New York. We are auctioning off our first editions."

"Selling our wonderful books? Why, darling?"

"Because I hate 'em—that's why!"

I longed for the film director's refuge—the safety and privacy of shooting a film. For on the stages the director is King of the all-absorbing kingdom of Work.

My first Paramount film would be *Friendly Persuasion*, a Quaker story by Jessamyn West. If I could get Bing Crosby and Jean Arthur to play the two star parts, I would rewrite it specifically for them. Bing and Jean were *very* interested.

My second film would be *Roman Holiday*, a story about a runaway princess who gets picked up in Trastevere by an American newsman, and for which I had already contacted Liz Taylor and Cary Grant.

My third film would be either *A Woman of Distinction*, ideal for MGM's Katie Hepburn and Paramount's Ray Milland, or it would be the ubiquitous *The Flying Yorkshireman*. I had in mind Victor Moore, stage star of *Of Thee I Sing*, for the Yorkshireman part, and Gracie Fields to play his Xanthippish wife.

And so, I laid out a complete blueprint for my "short" assignation with the Establishment at Paramount: Complete the three scripts and sign up the casts for *Friendly Persuasion*, *A Woman of Distinction*, and *Roman Holiday* —then shoot the three pictures without a break in between. Allotting four months to each film, I could be out of Paramount in a year—and be free again to organize another Liberty Films type of independent company in which filmmakers of the "one man, one film" class could again find artistic freedom.

That was my blueprint, my dream, to recoup some of my lost self-esteem. But it wasn't Paramount's blueprint, and certainly not its dream.

Paramount's Hollywood studio was run by a troika of executives—Y. Frank Freeman, Henry Ginsburg, and Jack Karp—a trio that was completely autonomous in all studio decision-making—that is, in all decision-making involving costs of *less* than three thousand dollars. If an actor, a truck, or an office remodeling cost one dollar *more* than three thousand dollars, New York (Balaban) had to approve the expenditure in writing. From three thousand miles away, Barney dictated all policy decisions: stories, budgets, schedules; and all personnel decisions: writers, actors, directors, cameramen, film editors, musicians, etc. Thus, a "figure" man, who spent most of his time receiving, digesting, and analyzing the daily box-office returns from every theater in the world, based and made Paramount's creative decisions on "what the box-office figures tell me."

The compelling, often pathetic, craving of cool business heads to want to "tidy up" the production of films is one of the more abiding wonders of Hollywood. Scratch a successful businessman and you will find an incipient moviemaker, eager to yield to the lure of Circe the enchantress. Those who are tempted and fall, almost invariably leave Hollywood beaten, dazed, and bleeding.

In 1948, Paramount executives were determined to halt the downward plunge of the box office with common-sense arithmetic. However, reason and logic notwithstanding, common sense and arithmetic are two of the nostrums more apt to aggravate than to cure box-office anemia. The cure for all box-office ailments is, of course, fresh transfusions of great films that people must see. But money-wise and art-foolish president Balaban decreed a curious cure of his own: Shrink the cost of films to fit the shrinking number of ticket buyers.

And so, because I could not agree to make them for Balaban's limit of one and a half million dollars, Paramount turned thumbs down on *Roman Holiday*, *Friendly Persuasion*, *The Flying Yorkshireman*, *Woman of Distinction*, and my own story *Westward the Women* (a big Western with Gary

Cooper). They even turned me down when I offered to remake one of Paramount's great silent hits—*The Covered Wagon.*

PARAMOUNT: Capra, when *Covered Wagons* need remaking *we* will make them. We didn't pay you a bundle to pick plums from Paramount's tree, but to bring us fresh new stories and fresh new faces—"

CAPRA: Fresh faces? Great. Let me remake your own *The Trail of a Lonesome Pine.* In color. I'll use young unknowns, John Barrymore, Jr., for instance. I'll shoot the whole picture in the Kentucky hills, using real people, real scenery, real villages, real dialect. I'll photograph John Fox's sentimental tale like an idyllic poem, a native operetta, set not only to music, but to the moods and colors of the Blue Ridge Mountains. Like Murnau shot *Tabu.* Gentle beauty. Native, earthy beauty. It could make a timeless classic, perhaps! And at a cost of only HALF A MILLION! *One-third* of Balaban's limit!"

PARAMOUNT: Lovely. But from Capra we don't want "filler" films shot on location. We want pictures we can ballyhoo, and big name stars we can clobber the theaters with, for stiff terms—"

At home I was making everyone miserable, so much so that Lu lowered a wifely boom.

"Darling," she said with fed-up gentleness, "you are fighting your own windmills. You think that because you sold Liberty Films, you've sold out your fellow directors. Well, stop beating your breast, dear. Your fellow directors are still doing okay. In the last year Huston has made *Treasure of the Sierra Madre*; Litvak, *The Snake Pit*; Olivier, *Hamlet*; Rossen, *All the King's Men*; Seaton, *Miracle on 34th Street*, and Joe Mankiewicz has turned out *A Letter to Three Wives.* Pretty good for directors you sold into slavery.

"I know. Paramount's stepped on your pride. And you'll do anything to break Balaban's Law. But you're letting them break you, Frank. You, the number one pro who can make films better than anybody at *any* cost. So please, darling—either quit pictures altogether, or make three fast ones for Paramount and get out of there—"

That stopped me from sulking like a petulant messiah, and put me back into the business of using my native wit and back-alley cunning. I heard that Harry Cohn was interested in buying *A Woman of Distinction*, one of my Liberty-owned stories Paramount had turned down. A bell rang.

Only weeks after I had finished *It Happened One Night* in early 1933 (and months before it copped the five major Oscars in the Academy sweepstakes), I had made an entertaining film out of Mark Hellinger's short story about a man, a maid, and a Cinderella racehorse named "Broadway Bill." The man was Warner Baxter, the maid Myrna Loy, and Broadway Bill was a tame, tired plug because Warner Baxter was deathly afraid of horses—especially of those with their tails up. As a result, many warm scenes I had in mind between the man and his horse I could not do, and those I did photograph were disappointing because Baxter was terrified of being bitten or kicked. I vowed that some day I would do *Broadway Bill* over again with a man who *loved* horses.

Well, a man who loved and owned horses (they never won), and who was one of our biggest stars, had a dressing room right around the corner from my Paramount office. Der Bingle! Bing Crosby, a horse, and a maid— a *natural!*

I phoned Harry Cohn. "Harry, you want *A Woman of Distinction*, I want the remake rights to *Broadway Bill* and its negative film. Will you trade even-Steven?"

"Deal, Frank, if Paramount loans me Ray Milland for the *Woman* story."

"Gentlemen!" I said to Paramount, "I can trade a story you own but don't want to Columbia for the rights and the negative film of *Broadway Bill*. By using the expensive race sequences and other scenes from the old film, I guarantee Paramount I can make a new *Broadway Bill* with Bing Crosby for ONE MILLION AND A HALF DOLLARS."

Crosby fell in love with the idea. He pressured Paramount until Balaban reluctantly agreed, although Balaban's figures said remakes were longshots. I firmly believe that had it not been for Crosby's pressures, Paramount would have kept me out of work for years, as a proper punishment for leading the maverick rebel directors.

It would take my whole bag of tricks to bring in the film at the budget price. Time would be the worst enemy. And the best tactics to earn a draw with time are (1) using a cameraman that doesn't waste precious minutes fiddling with lights, and (2) hiring sure-fire, professional actors that can give you their best in "one take" scenes.

For a cameraman, no one was faster, or better, than George Barnes.

Since Bing Crosby was rated a super star, I could save money by using a relative "unknown" as the girl. We chose Colleen Gray, a gay, energetic, enthusiastic beauty of the "no make-up" school of newcomers. A big-name girl star would have cost at least two hundred thousand dollars. With the savings made by hiring Colleen Gray, I was able to put together one of the greatest collections of time-saving, sure-fire entertainers ever assembled in one film: Charles Bickford, Frances Gifford, Oliver Hardy, William Demarest, Raymond Walburn, James Gleason, Ward Bond, Clarence Muse, Percy Kilbride, Harry Davenport, Margaret Hamilton, Paul Harvey, Douglass Dumbrille, Gene Lockhart, Charles Lane, Irving Bacon, Dub Taylor, Willard Waterman, Marjorie Lord, Frankie Darro, Marjorie Hoshelle, Rand Brooks, with a performing rooster and a trained stallion, and Max Baer and stutterin' Joe Frisco th-th-thrown in f-f-f-for lagniappe.

Any director who couldn't entice two hours of great fun out of that marvelous aggregation of professional entertainers should be directing traffic in Vera Cruz at siesta time.

I knew very little about Bing Crosby except the thousand tittle-tattles bandied about that pinpointed Bing as a saint or a monster, a model father or a philandering Casanova, a miserly scrooge or the Church's "St. Money," a sipper of buttermilk or a tippler of corn juice, a disposition sweeter than Jimmy Durante's or meaner than a water buffalo's—take your pick.

I had noticed that Bing was one of the press's "sacred cows," about whom there "never was heard (nor printed) a discouraging word."

The most adverse scuttlebutt about Bing came from inside Paramount Studios—from hairdressers, electricians, assistant directors—especially from my assistant director, Art Black. Black was such a professional that he could perform his duties as ably for directors he didn't like—such as Charles Vidor and Joe Mankiewicz—as he did for those he loved; me, for instance.

But when Black learned that Bing would be the star in *Broadway Bill*, he threw up his hands and groaned. "Oh, Mr. Capra, just hearing his name gives me ulcers. He'll leave the set without a word· and go off and play golf with his army of ass-lickers, and not show up again for days. And he never comes in before ten or eleven in the morning, if he comes in at all. He'll kill you, Mr. Capra. There's nothing he likes better than to give the ephus to directors on a tight schedule . . ."

"Art! I never heard you talk like that about anybody before."

"It's just that I know you're gonna work your eyes out—and Crosby'll laugh and drive you nuts."

The first day of photography I gave a nine o'clock call to Clarence Muse, Colleen Gray, Skeeter the banty rooster, Broadway Bill the black stallion, and of course, to the Bingle.

Nine o'clock—no Bing. I calmly began shooting around him with the other actors, improvising many new scenes. At ten thirty Bing showed up and found us busily shooting. I didn't say a word about time.

"What's going on?" he asked me.

"Just another little old picture, Bing."

"I thought you said I was in the first shot."

"We'll take your first shot whenever you're ready."

Next day, same occurrence. The Cassandras chortled. Black shook his head, "Told you he'd drive you nuts, boss." Again Bing found me shooting scenes when he came in at ten thirty.

"Frank, if I'm in the first shot, what're you shooting before I get here?" he asked.

"Bing, I've got some forty days to shoot a mil-and-a-half picture. That's at the rate of forty G's a day, or five G's per hour. Only way I can do it is to shoot from nine to six—constantly. So I start shooting at nine sharp with any actors that are around. If no actors show up, I invent scenes with dogs, cats, inserts, or actors I pick up on the streets."

No words, no arguments, no recriminations. Bing was an actor-business-man; he respected persons who got the job done without fuss or feathers. Also, he realized that if he didn't show up on time I would shoot with other actors.

Next morning Bing was on the set a half-hour earlier. Then—at nine. No word was said about it. He asked me what time I got on the set. I told him seven thirty. "Why so early?" he asked. "To plan, rewrite, think of new 'business,'" He wanted to know when we ran the rushes. I told him the crews ran them at the studio at seven thirty in the morning, but I ran them alone at home in my projection room at 6 A.M. On many a subsequent morning Bing would knock on my front door at 6 A.M. to see the rushes with me.

Art Black's eyes bugged. I have found most actors to be cooperative. They take your lead, and love it. What actors hate most is to be called at nine, then have to sit around till eleven before they are used, or not used at all. "A fish stinks first from the head," is a Jewish adage, and in films the director is the head. There are directors who maintain discipline by running a taut ship (Ford, Van Dyke); others succeed by running a happy ship (McCarey, Lubitsch, Capra). But however you run your set, it's all-important to earn the respect, admiration, confidence, and, yes, the love of your cast and crew —then it's smooth sailing with cooperation from all, Crosby included.

Bing Crosby is not an easy man to know. In virtually everything he does— golf, acting, crooning, and, I imagine, necking—he is as relaxed as a cat stretched out in the sun. But if you let that lazy, old-shoe casualness fool you into thinking the Bingle doesn't know what's going on—you're living in a dream world. His wit can devastate you, and what's more, you can't see it coming.

In his coordination Crosby is in a class by himself. Most actors must stop everything they are doing with their hands, or with props, in order to deliver an important speech. Crosby can recite the Gettysburg Address while juggling three balls and listening to Hope crack toupee jokes.

Crosby is blessed with a photographic mind. He can learn a two-page speech by reading it twice. And usually whatever he changes or adds in the speech is better than what is written. For he is the master of the literary ad lib.

As a film director, one of my pet peeves was the general practice of allowing musical directors and song coaches to direct and pre-record the "musical half" of songs—this on the fallacy that music, one of the great arts, was too arcane to be included in a film director's ken.

The musical coaches would spirit the performers off to their inner sanctums of thick-doored musical stages, and stand them around mikes to get perfect musical recordings of the numbers. When the performers were returned to the film director he must take them to the film set and photograph, the "visual half" of the song numbers to playbacks of the pre-recordings—which, I assure you, is a nightmare to both directors and performers.

The actors must strive to synchronize their mouths with the blaring music from playback loudspeakers. By trying desperately to shut out all other senses, they force themselves into an acute stage of listening. Their eyes are glazed, expressionless; their faces fixed and vacuous. The singers aren't really singing, moods and lyrics become meaningless, all sense of naturalness is killed— because the *playback machine* is "directing" the performers. "To hell with your emotions!" says the machine, "just give me good lip-sync, that's all!"

In studios where the music department head carries enough clout to control the musical numbers, pre-recording is their moment of glory. But for the film director— it's frustration time. Except for pre-recordings of music for big dance numbers (in which dancers need only the rhythm from the play-back), or for long shots of song numbers (where lip-sync is unimportant), all close shots of singing should be not pre- but *direct-recorded* simultaneous with photography.

In *Riding High* we did an impromptu number in the dilapidated tack room of a beat up barn, which included Bing, Clarence Muse, Colleen Gray, a horse, and a bantam rooster. It was called *We Ought to Bake a Sunshine Cake* (by Sammy Cahn and Jimmy Van Heusen). The occasion was Colleen's joining the hungry Bing and Clarence to bake them a chicken. Bing picked up two spoons and played them like two bones in his fingers. Clarence played the guitar and kicked a large empty box, as the bass drum. Colleen danced, all three sang a three-part harmony. There was no off-stage background music, only the music they created for themselves from props that were handy. The number lasted over four minutes, replete with comedy, posturings, neighs from the horse, crows from the rooster. It had the prime essence of fun; impromptu gags and the wonderful charm of sounding as if the whole thing had been made up right on the spot. Of course, it had to be direct-recording because we had no way of knowing what we were going to do beforehand.

The music department had objected violently to direct recording; Bing would never accept it. He had always pre-recorded his numbers under proper musical directing and coaching. Bing came to me about it, slightly dubious. I told him not to worry. If he didn't personally like the number after we shot it I would agree to pre-recording, but until then I wanted no piano players, no musicians, no song coaches on the set. He was a bit worried about playing the spoons as a pair of bones, so we flew in Freeman Davis from New York ("Mr. Bones" himself), an artist who could make a pair of polished ebony sticks do everything but talk, to help out Bing with a pair of spoons off stage.

With the first rehearsal, Bing got into the spirit of the impromptu fun. Everybody had a ball; so much so, Bing, Clarence, and Colleen kept breaking each other up. We had five other musical numbers in the picture. All were recorded directly, even the song "Camptown Races" which Bing, Clarence, and Colleen sang on the street as they were taking Broadway Bill from the barn to the race track. I put a pre-recorded band record of "Camptown Races" on a loudspeaker a block away—as if the music was being played by the band at the race track—and recorded the actors' voices and the distant band at the same time with a two-camera dolly shot that took the actors from the barn to the race track, followed by a gang of kids who joined in the singing.

How did Bing like my fast shooting and faster direct recording of num-bers? Harrison Carroll columned (Los Angeles *Express*, April 11, 1949) that:

"Woodshedding" or working out moves of the song-dance number: "We Ought to Bake a Sunshine Cake." It was Crosby's first direct-recording on a set.

The finished number. Four minutes of fun as Bing, Coleen, and Clarence improvise on makeshift instruments, while Broadway Bill adds his whinnies; Skeeter, his crows.

Surprise of *Here comes the Groom* was Jane Wyman's singing ability. The song-and-dance number she did with Bing—the Oscar-winning "Cool, Cool, Cool of the Evening"—— was a delightful gem.

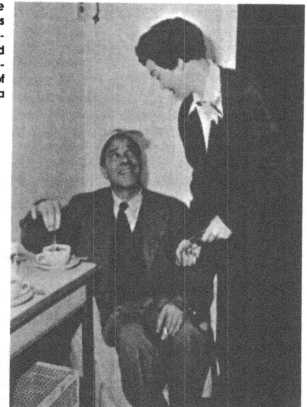

Here Comes the Groom. It gives you an inkling of how many it takes to put so few on the screen.

Bing Crosby was in a very gay mood when I visited the set of *Riding High.* He loves this remake of *Broadway Bill,* and loves working for Frank Capra . . . Bing is a great ad libber. He reads the dialogue differently almost every time. I asked Capra if this bothers him. "Not a bit," says Frank. "The things he says are better than what's written."

As for me, gone were my fits and frets over Balaban's Law and fatuous "figure men" boasting "we know what the audiences want." For regardless of how the picture would turn out, I was having the time of my life with actors, cameras, horses, roosters—especially roosters.

This little article I guest-columned for Edith Gwynn (Los Angeles *Mirror,* September 5, 1949) may hint at the picture's "fun":

Did you ever have to make a rooster crow? Now, that's a silly question. Of course not! Most sane, normal people would like to choke the silly so-and-so's when they start crowing in that fool neighbor's back yard. That's if you're sane and normal. But if you're a motion picture director, well—

Anyway, this is a little tale about how we made a rooster crow on cue, any time we wanted him to.

Now, chickens aren't noted for their high I.Q. For brains it's a toss-up between them and the worms they scratch up. So if you think it's easy to get a rooster to crow when you want him to, just try it some time. Especially when it's costing several thousand dollars an hour to wait around for him to crank up.

But we had to have a rooster and he had to crow, because you see, Bing owns a horse called "Broadway Bill," or rather, the horse owns him, because if the horse doesn't run Bing's a bum. And the horse won't run without his mascot Skeeter, the banty rooster. And what good's a rooster that can't crow? So there you are. No crow, no rooster; no rooster, no mascot; no mascot, no horse; no horse, no Bing; no Bing, no Paramount; no Paramount—what am I saying?

Anyway, when I asked Bill Hurley, the studio animal man, to find me a good-looking banty rooster, I told him to forget all about teaching him to crow, as I had a private way to do it which was a big secret. Many years ago I had made a banty rooster crow at will by letting him fight his image in a mirror, and then taking the mirror away. The little guy thought he had licked the other rooster and would immediately crow in victory.

So we started the picture and we used a very perky little banty whom we called Skeeter, with everybody on the set wondering how I was going to get him to crow on cue. When anybody asked me I looked smug and said nothing.

Came the day when we wanted Skeeter to crow in a scene with Bing and Colleen Gray and the horse. When the suspense was just right I raised my hand like a magician and ordered, "Bring me a mirror." Like magic a mirror appeared. Waving everyone aside I placed the mirror in front of Skeeter. The silence was deafening. Bing helped things out by cracking, "This better be good."

Skeeter took one look at himself in the mirror and ran for a dark corner of the barn. Prop men captured him and brought him back to me. "He's not mad enough," I said. Holding him in my hands I made some passes with him at his image, then put him down again. Skeeter ran for a darker corner. The onlookers stifled their laughs and I could have stifled Skeeter. "Get a hen!" I cried. "He's got to be jealous before he'll fight." I hadn't worked around pictures for nothing.

Out of nowhere a hen was produced. She took one look at Skeeter and chased him all over the stage. "Ferdinand, the rooster," laughed Colleen, but like Jimmy Durante I kept my attitude. "Get me a record with rooster crows!" I yelled. "This little guy never heard a crow."

You can't stump those magicians, the prop men. In no time at all we had a record-player on the set playing a record of rooster crows. By this time Skeeter was getting tired of it all. He listened to the record, then closed his eyes. The laughs were not stifled this time. With a magnificent gesture of surrender I turned to the grinning hyenas and said, "All right, wise guys. You make him crow."

Well, everybody had an idea. The gags started. The topper came when the still man, Bud Fraker, dug up a busty picture of Jane Russell and showed it to Skeeter. Skeeter didn't crow, but everybody else on the set did.

Hurley, the animal man, had watched all these shenanigans with a sour, disgusted look. When the laughs stopped and things began to look serious for us, he quietly stepped up to me and with thinly disguised irony said, "Mr. Capra, *I'm* supposed to be the animal trainer around here. Mind if I take over?" The voice of an authority made us all feel like spanked children. "Go ahead," I said. "Got to have him alone for ten minutes. O.K.?" "O.K."

Hurley took the rooster in his capable hands and disappeared behind the set. Then minutes later he came out and placed Skeeter on a chair. Skeeter shook himself, flapped his wings and crowed! Before the excitement had died down he crowed again, and again.

"Can you do it again?" I asked in an awed voice. Hurley repeated the performance. This time I put a stop watch on Skeeter. Sixteen seconds from the time Hurley let go of him he crowed the first time, and then five or six more crows at intervals of twenty-two seconds.

Eureka! All we had to do was time our dialogue accordingly and Skeeter could play scenes with actors. First crow, sixteen seconds, then another crow every twenty-two seconds.

Want to know how Hurley did it? So did we, because Mr. Hurley wasn't giving out, even though we were all dying to know. His stock answer was "With mirrors!"

The relaxed, easy-going behavior on our sets was partly due to the fact that *Riding High* was my first picture in years that did *not* deal with a social issue. But mostly it was due to Crosby's gaiety and whole-hearted cooperation. An example of his festal feelings:

"Frank, it's a capital offense to make a racetrack story without Joe Frisco in it."

"First degree murder! Where do we find our stuttering friend?"

"Wherever bookies bloom. Try Florida for openers."

We traced Frisco to Hialeah; sent him fare to come West. It was a mistake. He lost it on a show parlay.

Then we sent him an airline ticket. He came. He kept the whole company loose and laughing by holding racing-joke seminars. Of me he said: "Capra, if-f-f-f you had made this p-p-p-p-picture right the f-f-f-first time, you wouldn't ha-ha-ha-have to make it-t-t-t again."

An example of Crosby cooperation beyond the call of contract:

After ten days of location shooting at Tanforan race track (south of San Francisco) we were down to our last big sequence—the dawn burial of Broadway Bill in the infield. Present, to honor the gallant horse that broke its heart to win for Bing, would be thirty picked stakes-winning thoroughbreds, their owners, jockeys, grooms, stable boys in all their colors and finery, and judges, starters, and ticket sellers.

If a director averages shooting four to five script pages per day—that is *fast* shooting. Broadway Bill's burial covered thirteen and a half script pages, a good three full shooting-days. But to simulate dawn lighting (low sun and long shadows) the thirteen and a half pages were tightly scheduled into three late afternoon sessions between 6 and 8 P.M.—the two hours before the low western sun sank behind the Peninsula hills.

It was 3 P.M., Friday—the first day of our late afternoon burial photography. We had been shooting since early morning. Crew and cast were fagged out, particularly Crosby. It was race day. Bing had shouted himself hoarse, urging "Go, Bill, GO!" He had strained with Bill's every stride in the stretch, leaped with hysterical joy when Bill won—and froze with heart-stopping horror when the heroic horse fell dead. All had earned a welcome siesta before the late afternoon shooting began.

But the weather was working up to a theatrical mood to dramatize the burial of the Cinderella horse—a thirty-mile wind to flutter garments, tousle hair, whisk manes and tails, ripple banners and bunting, and alibi for tears that might have remained unshed; and the flat blue sky was quickened by small white scudding clouds gathering to pay their last respects to Broadway Bill. Would the wind, sun, and clouds hold steady till 8 P.M.? Would the nightly fog hold off? There was a chance.

But could we count on the same wind and clouds next *Monday* between 6 and 8 P.M.? And next *Tuesday*? Not likely. If I wanted to capitalize on nature's dramatic gifts—I would have to SHOOT THE WHOLE THREE DAYS' WORK IN THIS ONE WINDY AFTERNOON.

I found Bing resting in his portable dressing room. He heard me out. Then: "Holy Toledo! Thirteen script pages in two hours? Fire away! No Crosby ever flinched in battle—if I can drag my can off this cot—"

Vivacious Colleen Gray trilled, "Anything Bing can do I can do better." Assistant director Art Black: "No sweat, boss. I just put new batteries in my electric prod." Cameraman George Barnes: "All my gang's crazy, too. They're nodding 'Yes!'"

We did it. Ten minutes of film time (three days' work) in two hours! With thirty horses and 150 people, in a driving wind—a tribute to the loyalty and involvement of actors and crew, and to the extraordinary cooperation of the Bingle. And, much to the surprise of Paramount executives, *Riding High* was completed days under schedule and dollars under budget.

The fun and frolic of filming *Riding High* must have been infectious, for most audiences and critics were caught up in its gambols.

> The *Hollywood Reporter*:
> A joyous celluloid occasion that will be celebrated by ticket buyers with the same enthusiasm it is played . . .
> *Time*:
> . . . The most shrewdly effective show ever put together about horse racing . . .

Then, out of the slime, came this vicious racist smear by Manny Farber.

> *Nation*, New York, June 10, 1950:
> Having won more prizes and recorded more hits in thirty years than any other Hollywoodian, Frank Capra is rated a "cinemagician" whose "masterful comedies" reveal a "tender sense of humor, a quick sense of social satire, and a glowing faith in human nature." . . . Actually, the only subtle thing about this conventionalist is that despite his folksy, emotion-packed fables, he is strictly a mechanic, stubbornly unaware of the ambiguities that ride his shallow images . . .
> *Riding High* (from riches to nags with Bing Crosby) catches some of the jumpy, messy, half-optimistic energy seen around racetracks, but leaves you feeling that you've been taken like the carnival sucker. For instance, the movie drools with democratic

pride in Crosby's sugary relationship with his colored stableboy, displaying a sashaying Negro named "Whitey" whose happy slave personality, Sambo dialect (hallelujah), rapid expressions of unctuous love are derived from an old stencil cut from the deepest kind of prejudice . . .

But illustrating the viability of Emerson's Law of Compensation, the *Nation*'s malicious slur was balanced off by Lillian Scott's evaluation in Chicago's Negro publication the *Defender*:

> Paramount has a blue-ribbon winner in the new horse racing film *Riding High*, starring Bing Crosby, and famed director Frank Capra has allowed Clarence Muse to act without the eye-rolling and "Yassah, boss" approach he's previously had to use . . . Go see it and take the kids by all means.

How did *Riding High*'s critical huzzahs affect my brouhaha with Paramount? Apparently they strengthened Balaban's Law. For by maneuvering a maverick director into a shrunken budget, Paramount had gained a winning film and a much-needed glamour-polishing job for Bing. Ergo—restrict directors and you resurrect your stars.

To ballyhoo *Riding High*'s openings, Paramount sent me to New York, Detroit, and Chicago to stir up some hoopla with press, radio, and television interviews. Like trouble in Eden, trouble in Hollywood was news. Interviewers were all ears to hear my opinions on: "How does Hollywood feel about (1) soaring costs and dwindling box office, (2) growing popularity of foreign films, and (3) competition of television?" And as a footnote question (mostly from women critics), they'd throw this dart in the hopes of drawing a quotable retort: "And why is Bing so damned uncooperative with the press and fans?"

As to soaring production costs, Otis Guernsey, Jr., film critic of the New York *Herald Tribune* wrote:

> . . . when asked how things were in the film capital, Capra stated: "There is one word which describes Hollywood. It is: 'nervous.'" But the one sure cure for Hollywood's nerves, went on Capra, always has been and always will be the rustle of high-grade paper engraved with pictures of Presidents . . .
>
> What is Capra's solution? Cut out the in-between pictures. "Set ourselves a very low budget of $500,000 on a picture, forcing ourselves to think up new ideas and new techniques—like the multiple-camera television technique. Or, we should increase—yes, I said increase—our budgets and give the public whopping big shows . . ."
>
> In other words, Capra would compress pictures into smaller budgets until the pressure reacted in the form of artistic power, or build them up until audiences could not help looking at them in wonder and awe . . .

Concerning foreign films, the New York *Telegraph's* Leo Mishkin wrote:

> . . . Capra still has the deep abiding faith in the essential good-
> ness and decency of the average man, the theme he developed in
> both *Mr. Deeds* and *Mr. Smith.* And although he has great respect
> for such Italian films as *The Bicycle Thief* and *Paisan,* he feels they
> strike a note of despair altogether alien to Americans. "Those
> pictures all say, 'What the hell's the use? What must be must be,' "
> Capra points out. "We over here, still believe in the happy ending;
> it's as necessary to our way of thinking as automobiles and plumb-
> ing."

On the subject of Bing Crosby's intransigence—he seldom chatted with the
press—Lucy Kay Miller of the Chicago *Tribune,* wrote:

> "Crosby is often called uncooperative," remarked producer-
> director Frank Capra, "but he isn't. The trouble is—his *toupee.*
> Or 'my bowser' as Bing calls it—my assistant Art Black calls it
> 'Bing's brain doiley.' Bing hates to wear his brain doiley when not
> before cameras, but on the other hand, he hates to be photo-
> graphed in public *without* it. So rather than boorishly refusing to
> take off his hat, he tries to stay out of the limelight as much as
> possible."

But about television, I hemmed and hawed like everyone else. To Mae
Tinee of the Chicago *Tribune,* I gave a "Henry Ginsberg" answer:

> On the one hand, some exhibitors think they might as well close
> down willingly . . . but on the other hand, many believe television
> is a passing threat, of which people will soon tire, just as they tired
> of staying up half the night with head sets for the wonder of getting
> Peoria in the early days of radio.

Then, with the hope for the sententious and epigrammatic that springs in
the breast of all who speak for publication, I opined that television was but
a bigger, hungrier mouth voraciously devouring words. "Mr. Capra," wrote
Mae Tinee, "shrewdly pointed out the enormous consumption of various
forms of entertainment in the United States—hundreds of radio programs,
thousands of printed volumes . . . plays . . . films . . . and that all were
equally handicapped by a shortage of writing talent . . ." And having
shrewdly pointed it out, I shrewdly let it dangle.

And then I saw—from inside TV director Ralph Nelson's booth—a CBS
"Studio One" show being broadcast "live." I was astonished, then impressed,
then converted. No. Not converted. I was charmed, raped, and enslaved by a
monstrous wonder that was to charm, rape, and enslave the world. It was a
physical thing, a black box, born of Circe, fathered by Hertz, and reared by
Sarnoff; a black box crammed with life-in-a-hurry and picking up speed, a
box of a thousand genies all multiplying with computer haste. Was it a new

art form? No. Forms and molds of the past could not contain its power. Was it the ultimate medium of instant communications; all living, breathing people, from as far off as the moon, only a switch flick away? Was it the tearing away of the last veil of ignorance, revealing that the world is one, that we are one, and that all is now?

Had the new monster been all these things combined, it could astonish, perhaps frighten—but not charm, rape, and enslave. This monster is a new *god*! An enchanting god—giving rise to a new, raging mystique built on the twitching stimuli of zap, leap, flip, and break. All other gods are past, dead. "Perform" is this new god's name; his religion: "Exposure." On top of a pink, mushroom cloud, he sits enthroned on his Elysian Stage, under a proscenium of arching rainbows, surrounded by a thousand monitors that flash the world and its times.

And all the people of the earth—rich man, poor man, beggar man, hippie; doctor, lawyer, merchant, yippie—all fight to perform for a TV camera. Some wave and shout "Hello, Ma!" Others argue, talk, give opinions. Still others start new movements, promote personal causes. Militants use exposure as a weapon—they riot, demonstrate, burn, *only* when TV cameras are on them. For they know that a ten-second network exposure can make a national figure out of a genius or a nitwit.

And that is what the black box of a thousand genies means to the world: It has changed us all from people to performers. And all that goes on in the world today is a performance for television. "O my Children of Pleasure! PERFORM! PERFORM!"

The children of the poor are born with their eyes and ears open—and seeing and hearing much, they know all things before they can walk. But there is no advantage to this knowing unless one has the wit to escape from poverty. Well, I had made my pile and escaped poverty. But I was ready to give it all back to be free again; to once more have little, so I could again live well and do much—besides making Paramount's "sure-fire, priced-right" films.

I knew that without complete control of their content, I could make a hundred Bing Crosby comedies and never feed a hungry heart. I knew that filmgoers did not see my films just to enjoy comedy, pace, or other entertainment excellencies. They came ahungering for soul food. "God loves you, little man. Hang in there." Without that spiritual meat my films were, as stated before, just blue-plate specials.

At any rate, after finishing *Riding High*, I informed Y. Frank Freeman that unless I could make my kind of films I would leave Paramount and take the suspension that would legally keep me out of films for seven years.

Freeman listened till I ran out of profane gas. Then: "Frank Capra, you ain't never going to be happy any place but in your own l'il ol' cabbage patch. Now as a friend I'm talkin'. Irving Asher—you know him from London in wartime—Irving's got a story for Bing Crosby. Richard Haydn's

Riding High, a remake of Broadway Bill (1934). While Coleen Gray holds halter, ex-horseman Bing Crosby (now bored stiff managing a paper-box factory) examines Broadway Bill, a young pet thoroughbred Bing couldn't part with.

Bing, Jackie, and Thelma Ritter are pop-eyed as the director out-hams the hams.

Rehearsing "Whiffenpoof" scene. Bill Demarest, Raymond Walburn, the Groaner.

gonna direct it. I talked to Irving. He's willing to give up producer credit if *you* direct it. Grab it, and we'll call it the last two films you owe Paramount. Then you get outta here and grow your *own* cabbages—"

Prominent among desiderata in Hollywood is making quick decisions. "Mr. Freeman, tell Irving he's got a deal. I don't care *what* the story is . . ."

Here Comes the Groom was noteworthy to me because of a song, the launching of a fourteen-year-old Italian girl's career, and the charming chemistry that developed from the performances of Bing Crosby and Jane Wyman. First, the song.

Much to my delight I discovered that Jane Wyman—short nose, long legs, big heart, and all talent—had a rarely used flair for singing and dancing (in films she started in the chorus line, second row). I *had* to have a great song for Jane to do with Bing. But you don't just find great songs lying around on shelves. Oh, no? We did.

Joe Sistrom (one of my earlier "fiddlers three") said: "Frank, got just the song you want. Been in Paramount's dead letter files for years. Johnny Mercer and Hoagy Carmichael wrote it for a Betty Hutton picture I was going to make about Mabel Normand, till it got the Balaban ax. I'll dig it up for you."

Back he came to my office and put a small try-out record on my record player. A gravelly voice scratched out: "This is Johnny Mercer singing 'Cool, Cool, Cool of the Evening,' lyrics by Mercer and music by Hoagy Carmichael." Then Hoagy played the piano intro and Mercer sang: "In the cool, cool, cool of the evening,/Tell 'em we'll be there . . ."

That was it! Bing liked it, Asher liked it. It would be our big gag-comedy number. I hired my pal, dance director Charlie O'Curran (Patti Page's worse half), to work out a wild dance routine.

The news about "Cool, Cool" (it won the Academy Award for Best Song) was not that we recorded, simultaneously, the orchestra in the music stage and Bing and Jane on the live sets (with tiny radios in their ears to pick up the orchestra from antenna loops on the floor)—although *Film Daily* said we set a precedent: "Marking a first, Paramount's full orchestra yesterday recorded on the scoring stage while Bing Crosby and Jane Wyman simultaneously recorded Johnny Mercer's 'Cool, Cool, Cool of the Evening' blocks away on Frank Capra's shooting set . . ."

Nor was the news about the song the intricate technical job of photographing and recording Bing and Jane as they started their song and dance in a plush upstairs office, then, without a break, clowned and sang down a corridor, to the elevator, out the main lobby to the lighted street, and down the street to Jane's car. All in one take. All on one sound track—cameras and mikes in the office, the corridor, the elevator, the lobby, and the street, picking up actors as they came into view à la TV coverage—a distinctive bit of staging the actors and crews were deservedly proud of.

No, the news about the song was Jane Wyman—the way she traded in her crying towel for a glamour-girl's raiment, and became a dish to behold!

When a love story rings true on the screen, it catches up both audiences and players in its wonderment. An emotional chemistry happens between two people that transcends the film itself. It occurred to Clark Gable and Claudette Colbert in *It Happened One Night*; to Jimmy Stewart and Jean Arthur in *Mr. Smith*; to Spencer Tracy and Katie Hepburn in *State of the Union*. And now it happened again—in a wild comedy—between Bing and Jane. They fought, argued, and scratched. But when they were alone, the world didn't exist. They loathed each other, yet were one another's favorite entertainers and audiences. They were in love. And love, as we've all found out, bewitches and ennobles anything—even hokum comedy.

Then there was the fourteen-year-old Italian singer. I first heard her bell-like coloratura tones bring an audience to its feet in Ed Sullivan's Sunday night TV show. I had to have her—as a stinger to my soft orphanage opening, and as another "kitchen stove" to throw into my last Paramount film. And since I had made up my mind it would be my last film for anybody, I relished showing all the Hollywood bastards how to load a film with entertainment.

The girl with the voice was Anna Maria Alberghetti. When Bing contrived for her to sing the difficult but showy "Caro Nome" aria from Verdi's *Rigoletto* for prospective adoptive parents from America—in order to spring the blind fourteen-year-old war waif from a Parisian orphanage—it turned into a heart wrench that catapulted Anna Maria into stardom.

Then, too, we had to cast a French moppet of ten whom Bing adopts. Irving Asher found Jacky Gencel in Paris—after interviewing five hundred doting mothers who admonished their moppets to "kiss Monsieur and reecite 'Ze Three Little Bears.'" Having been born and reared in Parisian night clubs, Jacky was a one-man vaudeville show. He could sing, dance, juggle, do magic tricks, tell jokes, and imitate Robinson and Cagney. In fact, with his stringy hair, and a nose spread all over his face, Jacky was a miniature Cagney playing George M. Cohan.

On first meeting him I asked: "Jacky! *Es-tu un bon acteur?*" His laugh was infectious. "*Oui,*" he answered, "*si t'es un bon metteur en scène.*" ("Sure, if you are a good director.")

I took him home for a few days to improve his English with my son Tom —about Jacky's age. It only took Jacky one night to drive us all nuts. At dinner he wanted only pie and ice cream—and wine! Eight o'clock was Tom's bedtime. But Jacky was just cranking up. The little ham kept Tom up half the night teaching him to dance and to shoot craps and play cards. At midnight, Lu rescued our groggy Tom and dragged the lovable French jackanapes off to bed. But Jacky had to have wine to go to sleep on. And not just any old wine. Chevalier the Second knew his vintages as well as Tommy knew his box tops.

But Jacky was a stranger to English. However, with his super-sharpness he learned his English lines phonetically. Of course he had the world's highest-paid dialogue coach—Bing Crosby. Der Bingle and le gamin went for each other in a big way, their laughter filling the stage as they broke each other up with gags.

Then there was that most beautiful, stately woman—Alexis Smith. Because she was so beautiful, and there was so much of her—she was a six-footer—and because many of Plaster City's romantic heros were half-pints, Alexis was condemned to play only villainous roles. The more sympathetic parts went to the less beautiful, but more petite, clinging vines. Men don't even waste sympathy on six-foot Minervas.

But I thought she'd be fine as a comedienne. She was. For his own sly reasons, Bing took this magnificent hunk of wallflower beauty and changed her into whistle-bait. He taught her a sexy walk. "Just barge along babe, like an old bait-boat," and made her proud of her height—but let Alexis tell it as she told it to Aline Mosby of the New York *Telegraph*:

> "My height used to worry me terribly . . . I could stand up straight in long shots, but as I walked towards the camera I'd throw out my right hip and slump. That took inches off my height.
>
> "And for close-ups of love scenes, I've always had to take off my shoes. I got so I couldn't act with my shoes on.
>
> "All the directors would say 'Why can't you scrounch down a bit to look shorter?' You know that wonderful angle of a woman's throat when she looks up into the leading man's eyes? I've never been able to do that."

Alexis (or "Axle") acted with shorties like Charles Boyer and Humphrey Bogart and worried because if she took a deep breath she could tuck them under her chin.

Then, for *Here Comes the Groom*, director Frank Capra tried a switch.

> "In the very beginning of the movie, Capra had Crosby remarking about how tall I was—'You're the most gorgeous first baseman I ever played against!'—and wasn't it wonderful to be tall! Frank established a story point of my height. And from then on we didn't have to fuss about it."

Now Miss Smith doesn't worry about her tallness any more. "It's not that I'm too tall; it's the leading men that are too short."

I knew the thrill that must have been Axle's when she read Herb Stein's column in the New York *Telegraph*: "Two sneaks of Capra's *Here Comes the Groom* have preview audiences convinced there's a new career for Alexis Smith, who comes off as a slick comedienne for the first time."

After finishing *Here Comes the Groom*—on time, within the budget—my three-year stretch in Balaban's Brig was up. I was discharged with no time off for good behavior; a free man again, but drained. No matter where you thumped me, I rang empty.

Variety called the picture "a smash hit . . . a cinch to be one of the studio's biggest grossers . . . Capra at his best . . . a rapturous event for his final production chore at Paramount . . ."

But there was no rapture in Mudville. When they released the "one man, one film" apostle, they turned loose a brain-washed prisoner whose values had been branded with dollar signs.

Self-Exile

Six months had gone by since my release from Paramount, six months spent in divesting myself of anything that even smelled of Hollywood. I first got rid of story properties.

I sold *Flying Yorkshireman* to Stanley Kramer. Then Willie Wyler, needing a story for his fourth Paramount film, asked for my rights to *Roman Holiday*. I demurred. Willie pleaded. "Okay, Willie. It's my pet yarn, but you can have it. And if you like that one, come back and I'll give you *Friendly Persuasion*." Which is exactly what Willie did two years later. And he made two great films out of those stories. For years after, whenever Willie and I met, he would invariably laugh good-naturedly and jibe: "Hey, Frank! Got any more goodies for me stashed away in your trunk?"

That left me with *Westward, the Women*. And that brings me around to our very dear friend and neighbor, William "Wild Bill" Wellman, his beautiful wife, Dottie, who had stopped aging at twenty-one, and their seven wonderful kids—Patricia, Billy, Kitty, Timmy, Cissie, Mike, and Maggie. Our kids—Frank, Jr., Lulu, and Tommy—were with the Wellman clan practically every day, while Lu and I had dinner with Bill and Dottie at least twice a week. We were about as close as two families can be and not live under the same roof.

A former flyer in the Lafayette Flying Corps, Bill was an attractive hell-raiser before he married Dottie. After that he was still a most attractive man, but he confined his hell-raising to directing such films as *Wings, Public Enemy, So Big, A Star Is Born, The Ox-Box Incident, G.I. Joe, The High and the Mighty . . .*

One night at dinner, I told Bill the story of *Westward, the Women*. He flipped. And Dore Schary bought it for Bill to make at MGM.

But I couldn't break completely away from Hollywood while still living there. So I dismissed all the house help and moved the whole family down to our Fallbrook ranch, one hundred miles away. It was a wrench leaving the home we had built and the orchard and flowers I had planted. It was particularly hard on Lu and the children to part company with their friends. The day we left, I personally said good-bye to every tree and bush on our five-acre estate, I wished them well with all new owners, and told them I would plant trees and flowers just like them in Fallbrook.

Yes, sir! The commedia was finita! O happy day! From now on I would do nothing but sit around and enjoy the wonders of little things for a while. We took Lulu out of Westlake School for Girls and put her into Fallbrook Public High School, while Tom entered the elementary school. Frank, Jr., at seventeen, was living in one of Caltech's dormitories. Thirty-seven years earlier I was seventeen, and a freshman at Caltech, while Papa was farming the most beautiful lemon grove in California. Now another Frank was a Caltech freshman, and I would plant not only the most beautiful, but the biggest avocado grove in California on our eleven hundred-acre Red Mountain ranch.

And quit Hollywood forever? Of course. Quit while you're ahead. Before it makes a slave out of you. Before your own conceits commit you to slavery. Relax. Build big barbecue pits under those beautiful oaks; and big tables. Invite friends, cook whole steers. Dig up a mariachi band, olé! Castanets and Spanish dancers. And Leo Carillo will bring his horse and silver saddle. Sure. Big Sunday parties like Papa used to throw. Live like a Spanish Don, on a historic rancho, in historic San Diego County. Olé! Sleep late, Don Francisco. No more leaping out of bed at dawn, rushing to projection rooms, running to stages, fielding a thousand questions from actors and crews. Sleep late!

Sleep late? My problem was sleeping at all. The spirit of man is never lower than when he wakes up with nothing to rush to—with nobody to need him. I bitched around like an unfed ego, not realizing that the wackiest years of my life were still ahead of me. In fact, at Christmastime of our first year in Fallbrook, I was to receive a kick in the teeth that was to prove the bitterest and most humiliating experience of my life.

"Frank?" asked Dr. Lee DuBridge, suddenly injecting a serious note as we sat together having one of Caltach's austere lunches in the faculty dining room of the Athenaeum. "If you're free for a few months, could I interest you in doing a little chore for your country?"

"This chore," I asked the Institute's driving young successor to Dr. Robert Millikan, "does it concern films?"

"No."

"Important?"

"It's all-important to the Defense Department."

Shortly I became part of a most amazing development in American science

—Project Vista. Dr. DuBridge had been entrusted by President Truman and the Defense Department, with the hush-hush task of assembling scores of the country's top scientists, engineers, and psychologists, and esconcing them in a maximum security compound on the edge of the Arroyo Seco. Their mission: "Should the United States become involved in a global war, how would science fight and win such a war?"

Scientists were urged to let their imaginations soar. No strategy was too fantastic, no tactic too wild, no weapon too exotic. It was an ad hoc intellectual War College, with men of science supplanting the military planners. The revolutionary, almost science-fiction, ideas that sprang from Vista have kept the boggled Research and Development Departments of the Army, Navy, and Air Force hustling ever since.

Because of my war experience I was assigned to the Committee on Psychological Warfare, or PW. The chairman was Ernest Watson, Dean of the Caltech faculty. Also from Caltech was committee member Hallet Smith (English Department). The half-dozen other members were psychologists and kindred experts from important universities. Chairman Watson gave each of us a different facet of PW to write up and submit for committee discussion. My subject: "Content of Psychological Warfare."

I also wrote Dr. William "Willy" Fowler (Caltech astro-physicist on DuBridge's executive committee) a memo on the final presentation of Vista findings. It was labeled "A Photographic Report of Vista Conclusions," in which I suggested making a *documentary film* of Vista's work, with charts and animations; a visual aid to the written report . . .

Dean Watson thought so much of the film idea, he took a trip to Washington to try it on for size on the Secretary of Defense (Robert Lovett) and on the retired General George Marshall. While in Washington he checked on why my top-secret clearance had not yet come through.

The good Dean came away from Washington disappointed and worried. General Marshall was too ill to see him, the Defense Department took the "Capra Film Report" under advisement, *and* he got the impression my security clearance was in jeopardy.

I laughed. But Dr. DuBridge wasn't laughing. So I dispatched queries to Army Intelligence, the Army-Navy-Air Force Security Board, and a personal note to Secretary Lovett (whom I knew in war time as the Secretary for Air). Army Intelligence answered: "It is difficult at this time to estimate when your papers will be forwarded from Sixth Army . . ." Army-Navy-Air Force Security Board replied: "There is no indication in the records of this Board that your case has ever been presented for review . . ." Secretary Lovett answered: ". . . As you probably realize, the investigative machinery operates quite slowly . . ."

Good old Army red tape, I said to myself. Very annoying, of course, since lack of clearance had precluded me from attending top-secret discussions with other Vista committees for some three months. But worried? Ridiculous. Anyway, I had to take a few days' leave to attend a Washington meeting of the President's Advisory Committee on Information. I was a member and so were a score of press, radio, and television leaders. Our mission: to advise the State Department on how to best present the image of America on the "Voice of America" radio, and other information media. The chairman of our Advisory Committee was Erwin "Spike" Canham, editor of the *Christian Science Monitor*.

I came away from the meeting bewildered and agitated. So much so, I had to write Chairman Canham about it:

Dear Spike:

. . . I am sure something was bothering that group of illustrious Americans who sat in that committee room with you presiding. Something vague and inexpressible . . .

All expressed a desire for a symbol that would dramatize what we stand for and believe in. We have that symbol. That cause is Freedom! But its light must shine with the constancy and purity of the Eternal. If it flares up and dims, if expediency aims its beam now East, now West, or if we screw in a white bulb one day, a red one the next, men will lose faith in freedom. And when men lose faith, they lose hope . . . which is what dictators feed on . . .

Those shadows that we occasionally see obscuring freedom's light aren't real. They are our own shadows which we ourselves make as we jump this way and that.

Cordially,
Frank

On December 16, I reported back to Vista, happy in the feeling that here, at last, I was making a significant contribution to the needs of my country. The entrance guard stopped me from entering. "Sir, you are to report immediately to Colonel Miller's office—"

Colonel Miller was Vista's keeper of the keys. I entered his office whistling.

The Colonel rose. "Mr. Capra, I'm sorry to have to do this, but I am forced to relieve you of your identification card and all pertinent papers from your briefcase."

"What in hell are you talking about?"

"Haven't you received the refusal of clearance from the Security Board?" asked the Colonel.

"No. I've been in Washington."

"Oh. Well, it's probably waiting for you at Fallbrook. Here's a copy they sent for our information."

I read the copy. My blood froze. The letter quoted seven vague charges. Five of them applied to thousands of people in Hollywood. The other two were not only vague, I had no knowledge of what they were talking about.

"Colonel! This is crazy. You know what this means?" He fixed me with a cold look. There it was. Suddenly. Suspicion gulf a mile wide. His eyes zoomed away from the contemptible. Authority had spoken. Instant conviction. Traitor. "Jesus Christ, man! Me? An enemy of this country? Hell, I'd shoot myself first—"

The ninety-mile drive to Fallbrook was like a Kafkaesque nightmare. I must have pulled off the highway a dozen times, to think, pound my head. One review about *State of the Union* jumped out of the past. It was a libelous smear by movie critic Lee Mortimer, of the New York *Daily Mirror*.

Columnist Irving Hoffman commented on Lee Mortimer's review in the *Hollywood Reporter*:

> . . . President Truman, who certainly needs a laugh these days, would get one should he chance on Lee Mortimer's reflections in the *Daily Mirror*. The President—who enjoyed *State of the Union* so much—would learn from Mr. Mortimer that the MGM chieftains and Adolphe Menjou (both extremely conservative Republicans) had let communistic propaganda slip by them. The news should also interest the capitalistic Rockefellers—who are tenanting this attraction (at their Music Hall). Mortimer's schmopinion follows:
>
> . . . If you think Frank Capra isn't using his movie version of the hit Broadway satire, *State of the Union*, now at the Music Hall, to peddle some peculiar "advanced" political thinking, you had better take a second look. This artful trickster hawks his propaganda to audiences through two wonderful and irresistible salespersons, Katharine Hepburn and Spencer Tracy . . .
>
> This stuff slipped through the customers by one of the oldest dodges in the game, "Sure, I'm against communism, but—"
>
> . . . The indictment against this country, its customs, manners, morals, economic and political systems, as put in the mouths of Tracy and Miss Hepburn would not seem out of place in *Izvestia* . . .

But I had reacted quickly and strongly to that smear, as Lee Mortimer himself printed in his "Hollywood in Gotham" column in the *Daily Mirror*:

> CAPRA DEFENDS HIS *State of the Union*
> "Your review of *State of the Union* knocked me into a tailspin," writes Frank Capra, its producer . . . "If you've come to the conclusion I am a Communist manipulator or a Communist stooge, you are completely off your nut . . ."

But once a printed smear gets widely circulated there is no defense for it. Was the clipping filed against my name by Joe McCarthy's witch-hunters?

I told Lu. Tears of shame. She held me tight. "We must *do* something, darling. Quick. I know. Call Mabel. She'll know what to do . . ."

Mabel Walker Willebrandt. Lawyer. Friend. An unforgettable example of courage among the timid, integrity among the hypocrites, morality among the point-shavers—a lifelong one-woman lib movement with brains.

"Frank," said Mrs. Willebrandt on the phone, "this is your crisis. Fight hard, Frank. Fight with truth, but fight with passion. Get *mad*! Now, first. Tell all your children, they must not hear about it from some other source.

"Second. Work hard, work fast. Dig for facts and figures—all the figures; your donations, activities for the past twenty years. Who your friends are, a list of character references. And hit hard. Be wrathful. It's your world that's being destroyed, not theirs—"

I stood before my three children—Frank, seventeen; Lulu, fourteen; Tom, ten. No shame, no hangdog look now. I told them all. My children believed in me! There is no greater tribute.

It was December 18, 1951. For the next ten days, including Christmas Day, my secretary Chester Sticht and I locked ourselves in the ranch office and worked on a twenty-four-hour schedule, taking catnaps in shifts. We prepared a 220-page tome of facts, figures, names, and letters, which renounced and denounced all the charges, and sent it to Washington. The letters were character references from such friends as Mrs. Willebrandt, Y. Frank Freeman, Myles Connolly, General Lyman Munson, and John Ford.

"One moment, please, Mr. Capra," said the long-distance operator. "Mr. Turner Shelton of the State Department is calling from Washington."

Twelve days had passed since I sent my 220-page answer to the Security Board's charges. Twelve days of agonizing silence. Those sons-of-bitches in Washington sure knew how to worry you to death. And now the State Department calls.

"Frank?" said Turner Shelton in his big hearty voice. "How the hell are you? I hope you're well and can spare a couple of months' time because State's got a real honey of a job for you—"

"Turner, you tell State and all those bastards in Washington they can go to hell. Do you know what's happened to me?"

"I know all about it, Frank. Forget it."

"FORGET IT! Turner! That Army-Navy Board's murdering me. I still have no answer—"

"Frank, I can't talk about it, but it's okay. Trust me. Now listen. *India*, Frank. We want you to go to India—"

"India? I don't want to go to India. I won't even go to Glendale until you government jerks clear my good name and apologize. You hear?"

"Frank, listen. Chester Bowles, our Ambassador to India is worried. He thinks he smells a rat in the International Film Festival the motion-picture Indians are holding in a week. Bowles thinks the Festival is a Communist shenanigan of some kind, but he doesn't know what. Here's where you come in. Bowles has asked for *you*. 'I want a free-wheeling guy to take care of our interest on his own. I want Capra. His name is big here, and I've heard he's quick on his feet in an alley fight.' "

"Has he also heard the FBI and the military have branded me a lousy Communist spy?"

"Oh, for crying out loud, Frank. Forget it, will you? Nobody's branded you anything yet."

"Turner, somebody in Washington is out to get me. Who is it?"

"How should I know? But you've stepped on a lot of important toes in your life—Army, Congress, the press. But look, Frank. Can I tell the Ambassador you'll go to India?"

"No. Not unless I'm cleared for Vista—and with apologies to DuBridge."

"You know I can't make deals."

"And you know I can't go to India."

With that I hung up and simmered. What a government. The military's Board of Torquemadas kicks me out of Vista because I'm supposed to be a Commie lover; the State Department begs me to go to India because I'm supposed to be a Commie fighter.

The phone rang. It was Y. Frank Freeman. "Frank Capra, you know you can represent us in India better'n anybody in the world. They know you there. They like you. So why don't you stop being mad at everybody and go be our representative?"

"Mr. Freeman, how can I represent a government that's stamped me as disloyal and unfit to trust before DuBridge and all my other Caltech associates? How do I know our government won't ask Indian police to pick me up and ship me back as a bad security risk? No, Frank. They clear me, I go. They don't clear me—I'll be no good to anybody anyway—"

Two days later, January 14, 1952, Turner Shelton called from Washington to say that the Army-Navy-Air Force Board had given me top-secret clearance for Vista. DuBridge and I would be notified by air mail.

Well, the sun came out, the sky turned blue, and the flowers smelled again. Lu seldom cries. But she broke down that time. She cried and laughed, cried and laughed, and not even champagne could stop her. What a day. January 14. Suspended life began breathing again.

DIARY ITEMS

January 18, Washington

State (Turner Shelton, Frank Siscoe) briefed us on India. With me was Harry Stone (Eric Johnston office), and Dr. Floyd Brooker. Stone represents film industry; Brooker, film documentaries. I represent State . . . "Just play it by ear, Frank, and report to Ambassador Bowles" . . . America's festival film entry: De Mille's *Greatest Show on Earth*, plus some documentaries . . .

January 25, Bombay

Film Festival opened last night. Our plane late so we missed opening. But Mrs. Bowles flew down from Delhi to represent America. Ambassador on urgent trip to Nepal . . . I stay at famous Taj Mahal Hotel. Fantastic stairways climb inner court. *When the Rains Came* stuff. British architect designed it. Indians faced it wrong way. Architect jumped over stairway and killed himself when he saw what they had done . . . 3:30 A.M. Can't sleep. Boats, people, bells, birds, dogs, crows, shouting. My introduction to Orient: sound effects and smells.

January 26

Delegates taken to see old traditional Indian dances at theater. Much neck stuff back and forth, much eye and eyebrow movement. Music—an enormous guitar-like instrument, flute, drums (thumped with hands or fingers), and a harmonium which played one chord. No dominants or key changes. Only rhythm changes.

Sat in front of Russian and Chinese delegations. Photographers mostly around me. Reds in uniform. Fourteen Russians, about ten Chinese. No introductions. They want no part of me. Met Mohammed Fathy Bey, Egyptian delegate— Minister of Education. Was told privately by local Paramount film man that festival is brain child of M. Bhavnani, head of Indian government films. Commercial films not cooperating in festival. Press is riding the whole idea of festival. Why? And, why was *I* sent here? . . .

January 27, Sunday
To Central Studios again. A small stage was decorated with flowers, and lit by rows of lighted wicks set in small metal containers. They put flower garlands (like ropes) over our heads . . .

Delegates (guests) sat on the floor facing audience (hosts) who also sat on floor. Russians all dressed the same—dark suits. Chinese all in light-blue suits. They looked like a military organization. Speeches. Iron Curtain boys all needed interpreters. Odd thing, all delegates except Iron Curtain ones could speak English. Iron Curtain evidently keeps English out.

Each Red got up and spoke "peace" "peace" "peace." Workers—your workers —our workers—all must work together for peace.

Long live workers of China! Long live workers of India! etc., etc.

All had notes (including interpreters). All made same speech, as if one man had written them all. Boring.

My turn, second from last. Spoke less than a minute, then sat down. Loud applause. This must be a good angle.

January 29
So far, welcoming speeches by Indians slanted toward the Red group. Indian Reds and Russians and Chinese must have cozy interest in Festival.

Have yet to talk to Bowles. He is in Nepal. American Consul and USIA man shrug off questions about what worried Bowles. "When you find out, tell us."

Last night I found out. Dinner with Barbarau Patel, notorious owner and editor of movie mag *Filmindia*. A lurid, critical magazine, tears film stars and politicians apart. This fat but elegant egotist brags he blackmails ads out of film stars, because he "knows too much." Rich, beautiful wife, American secretary, French cook, fine wines; like Nero Wolfe never leaves home or his luxuries. Sardonically praises communism in his mag, "So they won't shoot me when they take over."

Anyway, this sybarite gives me first hint of what is bugging Bowles. Said Film Festival is Commie plot to break a law—film censorship law that keeps Communist films out of India on grounds too political and inflammatory. So local film Reds hatch festival idea to insure showing dozens of Russian and Chinese films on ten-week circus tour of four major cities—Bombay, Madras, Delhi, Calcutta. It's a direct appeal to people to breach India's film barrier, using Festival as Trojan Horse. Smart.

That was plot Ambassador Bowles hoped I might knock off. How? Two things going for me. One: I'm my own boss, free to speak and move—Reds are muzzled and haltered. Two: I'm only "name" foreign filmmaker; me good press copy. Me should have heap fun.

January 31, Thursday

Tell Bhavnani one more pro-Commie speech by any Indian and I take all American films and leave, after holding press conference to explain my leaving. Also will not appear at any more functions, symposiums, or meetings with any Iron Curtain delegates except the official opening in each city. If any group wants to meet me, they will have to meet me alone. I give this ultimatum and then send telegram to Embassy in Delhi to explain my actions.

Scheduled to appear tonight to meet film producers and directors for general discussion with all delegates. I refuse to attend. Producers' meeting canceled. Fine.

February 1, Friday

Reception by Mayor Patil in Corporation Hall set for 4 P.M. Again say to all concerned will walk out and go home if any Indian chairman makes pro-Soviet speech.

Mayor makes a speech. This time very pro-American—distinctly praises America and calls for eternal friendship between India and the United States. Well, this is different.

At end we got bouquets. My bouquet three times the size of all the others. Chinese so disgusted, they throw theirs back on the table refusing to carry them out with them. Now we're talking.

A Cine Technicians meeting and discussion has been set up for this evening. Bhavnani begs me to go. I said I would gladly meet with technicians night or day, but I must be alone. (Smell a big demonstration coming at one of these meetings—denunciations hurled at us, etc. All staged, of course.)

I again warned Festival officials I was not here to be suckered into any Commie plots. I was here to beat their brains out if I could and for no other reason.

The Cine Technicians meeting was also canceled at the last minute. It seems no meeting unless I attend. Well! Now I can call my own shots.

February 3, Sunday

All kinds of people at my door. I let them all in because they might be beggars or editors. They turned out to be both.

Picked up by film director Chatan Anand at 7 P.M. and taken to his home in Juhu. Took along Harry Stone, too. This Anand family has adopted me. Never met such friendly people.

Dinner—classic Indian dancer—danced both male and female parts. Fascinating to watch. Then four hours of native Indian music by best musicians in films.

(Guests sit cross-legged on floor, face musicians sitting on floor. Musicians vamp—like tuning up—until audience gets "with it." Each member of the audience closes eyes, lets music hypnotize him. When he shakes his head from side to side, and makes little audible humming noises—like the Jewish "quelling" —he's "ready." When audience all quelling, the musicians play for real. Great evening of strange music with friends who are becoming less strange.)

February 4, Monday

Four P.M. Tea with film star Surayia, one of the most popular stars—sings her own songs. Lives with mother and grandmother—all sleep in same room. They are Mohammedans. Most film stars here are Moslems, as Hindus think films far beneath them, and will not allow daughters and sons to join films. Odd, many film stars come from very low-class families; some can neither read nor write. Had charming time with Miss Surayia—pictures taken. She is a great fan of Gregory Peck.

Back to hotel. Nargis—she is the biggest film star, a very sensitive young lady—called to invite me, but couldn't find time. Will see her in Delhi.

February 5, Tuesday

Lunch with fifteen Indian directors and producers in my room at the Taj Mahal Hotel. I constantly pointed out they must preserve freedom as artists and that any government control would hinder that freedom. A totalitarian system—and they would become nothing but publicity men for the party in power.

One of the biggest interests: our Motion Picture Relief Fund. This taking care of our own seems to hit them very hard. Seems to them un-American that rich, crude Americans should take care of their people when they can't work any more.

Four P.M. Pen Club tea, arranged by Nino Messani (public relations head for Tata corporations). Some forty literary and other lights arrive to hear me speak.

Pen Club famous. Started by Tagore. Tried to dispel some of their odd notions about American films.

They all think some super-government or super-collection of individuals dictates all American pictures. Free enterprise is mystery to them. Somebody *must* control, either visible or invisible.

Since motion pictures all over world seen by masses, as they call them, all seem to think there *should* be some control as to what to show masses. Even intellectuals have no great understanding of liberty and freedom.

February 6, Madras

Very, very hot. Small reception for Stone, Brooker, and me. Newsreels, garlands. Indian garlands unlike Honolulu leis. They are larger, mostly flowers in woven wire, and very heavy. Also stain your clothes. Keep them on long enough, and you'll look like a Technicolor shot.

Chinese and Czechs who were with us on plane got larger Indian reception. Russian delegation had left Bombay four days ago. Since Madras in South India is a Communist stronghold, Russians came early to make hay at *political* rallies. Got to stop that.

Met by Needham and Sherbet, public affairs officers in our Consulate. Taken to Connemara Hotel . . . To Gymkhana Club for dinner. These famous clubs are in practically every city. Used to be clubs in which rich English got away from poor Indians. Now rich *Indians* own them and get away from poor Indians.

February 8

Had a press conference this morning. Expected tough arguments, and got them.

Press is a young, educated, intellectual group that needs expression of some kind. They would like to better themselves, but have no idea how. Democracy only a theory to them. They have no idea of service to others, of service to the poor. The poor are despised, in a sense. They want to raise their standard of living, rather than raise the poor's standard of living. Communism has made great play for these young intellectuals—probably promised them jobs. Not only jobs, but power.

Tried to be open and frank with all questions; to answer them as correctly as possible.

February 9

Called Paul Sherbet at 8 A.M. to verify Soviet delegates addressing fifty thousand people at political meetings. Will lodge official protest with the Festival committee.

At 4:30 P.M. went to the airport to meet Cesar Romero, Marie Windsor, Rod Cameron and his wife, William Berke (director), and producer Durgan. Clyde De Vinna (cameraman) too sick to come from Salem where they are shooting a jungle picture. Need them to add clout to our delegation.

At 5:50 P.M. we all assembled at Congress grounds for Cine Technicians official meeting. For once we had an American delegation. Capra, Stone, Brooker, Romero, Windsor, Cameron, Berke, Durgan, Hadley, Mrs. Cameron, Haughton, McEldowney. All introduced.

Before the meeting started, head of film technician's union wanted me to meet them after and talk privately to a large group of members. Said I would if they'd *meet me right after the meeting.* "At that hut over there," he said, pointing.

Reds made usual long speeches, only this time, they proposed something concrete—to send men and equipment into India to help Indians make pictures.

Then a rather amusing thing happened. We all spoke in alphabetical order, I being second from last, Russians last. In middle of Russian speeches about half the audience began to *walk out.* Very startling. Consternation among Iron Curtain delegates. Much buzzing and glaring. I didn't get it for a moment, then suddenly knew. Those Indians aren't walking out on the *Russian's* speech. They're hurrying to the hut where *I'm to talk to them* after the meeting. Well, how do you do. Maybe I could *arrange* to have Indians walk out on future Russian speeches by same trick of promising to talk to them privately right after meetings.*

February 12, New Delhi

Delhi is different kind of town. Like Washington, clean, people better dressed. Officialdom resides here.

Saw C. S. Rao, Deputy Minister of Information; told him about Russians addressing political rallies. Said he would bring it to attention of Prime Minister Nehru. I'm causing embarrassment, anyhow.

Met Davidas Gandhi, son of the famous Gandhi. He is the editor of the *Hindustani Times.* Saw him in his office and was interviewed by three or four of his men . . .

February 16, Saturday

Scheduled to visit Gandhi's Tomb (Rajghat) this morning. Wreath I order is scrawny. No flowers. So are wreaths of other Westerners. Not a flower in Delhi, I'm told. Reds bought them all up. Ho, ho. They wanna play games. Because of lousy wreath I refuse to go to Gandhi's Tomb. Reds will have mountains of wreaths and cameras there. Festival committee aghast. Colossal boner they say. Harry Stone and I meet with French, Italian, and Egyptian delegates. Pound

---

* I used same gag at least a half-dozen more times, all with "walkouts" reported prominently in the press. Russians never caught on. Must have driven them nuts.

heads. How to outsmart Commies? Stone suggests going to Tomb with couple of cute Indian children. Boing! Davidas Gandhi, editor of *Hindustani Times*, told me he has children. St. Gandhi's own *grandchildren.*

Stone and I rush to *Times* office. Mr. Editor is astonished, but will call wife. Mrs. Gandhi agrees. She will be at Rajghat at 4 P.M. I alert all the newsreels. This is news!

I set up six cameras behind trees that line walk to Gandhi's Tomb, a low, circular open-air tomb in Park. Four P.M. Limousine drives up. Lovely Mrs. Gandhi arrives with charming daughter of twelve, and handsome son of seven, all starched and pink. Each child has little basket filled with rose petals. How lucky can you get? While cameras roll we escort Gandhi family to tomb, watch discreetly while grandchildren strew rose petals on immortal grandfather's tomb. Great moment, very touching. We escort family back to car. Mrs. Gandhi said children never been photographed by newsreels. A big first. This should kill the Reds. (It did.)

February 20, Wednesday

Saw Ambassador Bowles at 10:30 A.M. Looked tired, having just come back from Nepal. Pleased with my report.

February 21, Thursday

Inaugural of the Film Festival in New Delhi. Nehru to open meeting in theater at National Physical Laboratory . . . All delegates on stage. Prime Minister Nehru comes in; they play the National Anthem. The Russian crowd comes in after Nehru.

I spoke about one minute. The Soviets spoke last. They got the biggest hand, in fact the biggest hand yet received in India. Surprising. They made exactly same boring speech they had made everyplace. Perhaps officialdom trying to bend backward, since officialdom is really very friendly to Americans.

This was my first look at Nehru. Ambassador Bowles thinks he is really a great man, has great fear he will be assassinated. Thinks country will be in chaos if Nehru assassinated, because no one to take his place.

February 22, Friday

Five P.M. To President of India's palace for the most beautiful reception yet. More than two thousand people in a great, enormous room. The President, Rajendra Prashad, is a kindly, tall man with a droopy mustache. Pigeons flying all over room. Most rooms in India are open to outside. Pigeons just flew in. Saw no accident, but worried.

The Festival has gained momentum here in Delhi. All the pessimists now think it's great success. Government invited movie stars from Bombay, Madras, and Calcutta. All here at President's Palace. This has never been done before, as government and film stars are at opposite social poles.

I asked Romero, Windsor, and Cameron up here from Salem. Clyde De Vinna came with them. To get here they had a five-hour trip by car, an eight-hour trip by plane. But they are big attractions, and the best good-will ambassadors the U.S. could send anywhere.

February 23, Saturday

Our biggest day in India. First a visit to the Prime Minister's home where we met Mrs. Pandit, Nehru's daughter [the Mrs. Indira Pandit Gandhi, Prime Minister of India today]. She used to be Ambassador to the United States. A lovely, charming, smart woman, educated in the States. She came home, ran for election to a seat in the people's House—like our House of Representatives—and won the election from her district.

In a very charming garden we sat around and talked of many things. Told her all that had happened between us and delegates from Iron Curtain countries. Told her how Russians were addressing political rallies. I knew it would get to Prime Minister. Got to keep the heat on our Red brothers.

Two P.M. Parade of stars at Sports Stadium. About fifty thousand people turned up. Indian movie stars on jeeps. Pulled cutie here. We got Romero, Windsor, and Cameron on a jeep to parade with the Indian stars. (Harry Stone's idea.) The Russians furious because they didn't get in on the parade. So our American stars parade along with Nargis, Raj Kapoor, Prem Nath, Surayia, Veina, Duga Khote, Moti Lal, and Sanser.

Government officials surprised at huge crowd. They look down on films, and have no idea of the popularity of stars.

Nehru was there. Saw how Raj Kapoor could be President today if he ran for office. Indian government has not realized power of films.

Four P.M. A delayed Washington birthday reception at the U.S. Embassy. Twenty-three hundred people show up.

Mr. and Mrs. Bowles charming and simple. They shake hands with everybody who comes in. President Prashad, Prime Minister Nehru, Mrs. Pandit, and all the embassies came. All except the Russian and Chinese.

Had long talk with Nehru. Charming, simple man; could be the most important man alive today.

Six P.M. A reception by the Delhi citizens to the film stars and delegates at the Imperial Hotel grounds. Mobs—stars—pictures—speeches. I think I've met everyone in India. Everyone in government, in business, the Maharajas, the beautiful women.

Nine P.M. Harry Stone and I organize a dinner that we ourselves give to selected guests. Sixty people at the Maidens Hotel. Guests: Mr. and Mrs. Pandit; Mrs. Sen; Mr. and Mrs. C. S. Rao; the Honorable Diwaker, Minister of Information; Sir Clifford Agarwala, chief censor; Davidas Gandhi, Editor *Hindustani Times*; Members of Parliament; and all the Indian movie stars.

This dinner was our biggest moment in India. In fact, it was a real accomplishment. We brought stars and politics together. While editors and businessmen looked on. It is absolutely unusual for film people and government people to sit down together. They are socially not on the same standing at all, and here they are—touching elbows, breaking bread together—united by the catalytic action of simple, crude Americans.

I kept the dinner most informal. Wanted them to take their hair down. After dinner got up and said something had happened today in Delhi—India would never be quite the same again. Two of the oldest professions in history had met each other. Show business and politics. Both were surprised, both should know each other better, for stars could swing public opinion almost any way they wished.

Have never seen humans quite as pleased as politicians and actors were to meet and know each other. I called upon each of them, indiscriminately. Tears and laughs. It was a love feast.

Communists had invited many delegations of Indian film artists to Moscow, feted them, sent them back with fur coats. Almost everybody in films had been to Moscow. Some were impressed, some not. But all were grateful for the attention.

But today, after we had helped win them social recognition from high government officials, the gratitude of the Indian film stars was all in our direction.

Moreover, after that dinner, quite a few government officials privately said to me that I had done a great service to India today. Big day. Bowles pleased.

February 25, Monday

Although Festival not over in Delhi, I decide to leave for Calcutta before it is over. I have a plan. If can go to Calcutta a few days ahead, I can take the cream off the welcoming committees, and perhaps by the time they do it again for other delegates, it'll be stale news.

The Festival committee notified the Calcutta people that I was coming ahead of time. Well, when I arrived at eleven thirty in the morning, there were mobs at the airport. Signs that read: LONG LIVE FRANK CAPRA. Was deluged with garlands. Consulate people tried to rescue me, but I winked at them and told them to disappear, that I was among friends.

There is quite a film industry in Calcutta, and practically everybody in films was at the airport to meet me.

A humorous note: The advance man for the Russians was on the plane, and he was knocked down by the mob that came to greet me. He gets up, brushes himself off, turns around, and gives me the dirtiest look of my life.

Bengali people are quite different from the rest of India. They are like the Irish, emotional, sentimental. All riots and revolutions start in Bengal. I can understand it. It took me an hour to leave the airport, what with the crowds and the photographers. These Bengalese had been getting ready to meet somebody for a long time, and here I get the whole heat of it.

February 26

Get-away day. At Dum Dum Airport Bhavnani thanked me from the bottom of his heart for helping him put over the Festival. Told me privately that the Russians would never get their pictures into India, at least not on this occasion. Since this is probably the main reason I came to India, I felt very good about it.

And when Ganju (Festival public relations man) said that after my end-around play in Calcutta the Russians and Chinese packed up their "Peace! Peace!" speeches and bolted India in the dark of the night, I broke out the bottle of Scotch I'd cadged from the Embassy and we drank toasts to us, them, and we.

In two days I was back in Fallbrook. In less than two weeks I checked into Washington to deliver my confidential India Report to State and to accept Secretary of State Dean Acheson's commendation for "virtually single-handedly forestalling a possible Communist take-over of Indian films." He also told me Ambassador Bowles had asked him to extend to me his personal congratulations and gratitude "for one helluva job."

I suggested to Mr. Acheson that he could best thank me by joining the Hollywood motion-picture producers in sponsoring a visit to Hollywood (and the United States) by some of India's film leaders. The notion was approved.

India's Film Festival was nine weeks of outdoor rallies before immense crowds in different cities. They were engineered by Russian, Chinese, and Indian Communists. Purpose: to arouse public opinion into forcing Indian officials to lift embargo on foreign Communist films. My purpose: to foil their purpose. Front row: C. M. Agarwala (film censor); Dr. Vinicio Marinucci, Italian delegate; Mohammed Fathy Bey, Egyptian delegate, and two members of Chinese contingent.

In Madras, I find stars of my own to buck up American status. Marie Windsor and Caesar Romero (first row), and Rod Cameron and his wife (second row), who were shooting an American film in local jungle, drove many miles just to come and sit on dais with me at rally.

While my six discreetly placed cameras grind out newsreel footage, we four Western delegates "help" Gandhi's grandchildren (right) strew rose petals over the ostentatious mountain of flowers the Russians and Chinese had left that morning.

On October 6, 1952, I found myself the toastmaster at one of Hollywood's most memorable occasions—a gala welcoming banquet by over three hundred Hollywood stars and other luminaries honoring the arrival of fourteen of India's top film celebrities.

The Indian delegation had already visited New York, Tennessee Valley Authority, Chicago, Denver, and Salt Lake City, and had had luncheon with Mrs. Franklin Roosevelt at Hyde Park, and dinner with Frank Folsom, president of RCA in New York. They had been banqueted in Washington by the motion-picture industry's representative, Eric Johnston, and been personally welcomed to the White House by President Truman. And now they were the guests of Hollywood, and never had the film capital been more gracious or more hospitable.

In the chandeliered Crystal Room of the Beverly Hills Hotel, the banquet began with the singing of both National Anthems—the American led by Katherine Grayson and the Indian by a very young and very beautiful guest, Surya Kumari.

"Between the two largest free nations in the world," I said in my opening speech, "there is a kinship of the spirit that can only mean good to all mankind. There are no strings attached to this visit, no 'deals,' no promises . . . Our guests from India are here so that we may know them better, so they may know *us* better."

Then I gave notice to my glamorous audience that we, number one in the film world, may be soon feeling some whiffs of exotic breathing down our necks. "Indian films are number two. And get this; their great stars are in *first* place in one category: They have more fans than any other film stars in the world. Let's meet our friends and you'll understand why . . ."

I introduced Nargis (India's reigning film queen), Surya Kumari, Arundhati Mukherjee, and Bina Rai; then Raj Kapoor (the most popular male star), Prem Nath, and David Abraham, the Jewish-Indian character actor; then producer Chandulah Shah, president of India Motion Picture Producers Association, and his writer, Miss Char; producer-exhibitor Keki Modi and Mrs. Modi; producer D. Subramanyam; cameraman B. P. Divecha, and sound technician Ninoo Katrak.

A welcoming speech by Frank Freeman on behalf of the motion-picture producers of Hollywood, a climactic learned tribute to India's cultural heritage by Mr. Movies himself, Cecil B. De Mille, and the stars of the East were surrounded and taken over by admiring stars of the West. Two very important ladies spent much of their time collecting autographs. Nargis harvested signatures of her American colleagues while Greer Garson made sure she got an autograph from every one of her new-found Indian friends.

For the next ten days the Indian delegation was wined and dined and welcomed by all the studios and all the guilds; by unions, technicians, cinematographers, and entertained privately by such celebrities as Greer Garson, Walt Disney, Cecil B. De Mille, Mervyn Leroy, and many others. I choose to think that the corollary ripples of unspoken good will are still moving outward, around, and through from heart to heart, from people to people.

Shortly after my return from India, a Don Jones of the N. W. Ayer Agency called from New York. Was I free to come to New York (all expenses paid) to meet with and advise (for a fee) Mr. Cleo F. Craig, president of A. T. & T., about a new television program on science the Bell Telephone System was contemplating?

President Craig was a large, sandy-haired, ruddy-faced man who evoked fleeting memories of Ivanhoe and Macbeth, lochs and firths, glengarries and bagpipes, and the stag that drank his fill on Monan's rill. I had been escorted into Mr. Craig's office by Harry Batten, a Philadelphia Mainliner and president of N. W. Ayer Agency, and by Jim Hanna, a skeptical dynamo and head of Ayer's TV and Radio Division. Tagging along was quiet, baby-faced Don Jones (who had first contacted me by phone). He seemed more the "books and plays" type than an ad writer for soap.

Naturally, my first reaction was to ask why I, abysmally ignorant of television, was being asked for advice on television programming.

"I can answer that, Mr. Capra," said President Craig. "I commissioned Harry Batten here, and Jim Hanna, to research the whole of show business for a man that was an expert in science and entertainment. And it seems that after you there is no second choice."

Jim Hanna spoke up. "Frank, you know as well as I do that science documentaries are a dime a dozen because they're all as dull as dishwater. But Mr. Craig insists that since science is what his company is selling, science is what the Bell System should sponsor. But as an agency that has to try to get the biggest audience for the client's buck, we recommend against a science show for A. T. & T.'s first entry into the TV rat race. And we're sort of hoping you'd agree with us."

Well, this was a new twist. A major advertiser strongly bucking for a program that the agency was strongly nixing.

I turned to Mr. Craig and readily admitted that Harry Batten and Jim Hanna were right in recommending against his pet idea because the "figures" and "ratings" were overwhelmingly on their side. But I never discount strong hunches. In one sense education was "discovery," I said. "And if the discovery of continents, planets, and man himself is dull, then men like Galileo, Newton, Magellan, Freud, Einstein, Fleming, and Alexander Graham Bell led lives as dull as dishwater. Which is not so."

Mr. Craig stood up. "Let's go to lunch. Our Board's meeting today. Mr. Capra, I'd like to introduce you to some of our officers and Board members—"

Salvatore Capra's youngest son—that feisty, ragged, snot-nosed newskid—sat down as the special luncheon guest of the president and the Board of Directors of A. T. & T., the world's richest corporation. Hot damn! I sent a silent message: "Papa! She won't believe it, but tell Mama about it anyway."

"Mr. Ley, if a national television network asked you to produce an hour-long program on the sun, what would you say, and how would you present it?" I posed the question to Mr. Willy Ley, the scientist-writer who had written several interesting books on rockets and space travel. We were having coffee in my suite at the Sherry Netherlands. "Write out your answer in a detailed treatment and I'll pay you five thousand dollars on delivery."

My next move would be to approach Aldous Huxley—all in accordance with a deal I had made with N. W. Ayer and Mr. Craig. I had advised them to quietly make a "pilot film" before committing A. T. & T. to the program. We mutually chose THE SUN as the pilot film's subject, because the sun was not only filled with science, it was also chock full of interest to every man, woman, and child in the world.

"Aldous," I said to the fabulous Huxley over a drink in the patio of his Kings Road home in Hollywood, "if a network like CBS asked you to produce an hour-long filmed program on the sun, what would you say, and how would you present it?"

Thus two famous people began writing treatments on the sun: Willy Ley, a scientist who could write, and Aldous Huxley, a writer who was Aristotle, Aquinas, Newton, Buddha, and P. T. Barnum all mixed up into one incredible character.

But I felt I also owed Mr. Craig a theatrical version of the pilot film. I remembered his admonition when, at the end of our meeting, he nudged me into an anteroom and said: "One reminder while we are alone. Anything second best is not acceptable to the Bell System. Please remember that, Mr. Capra." And I did remember. So much like my own credo: "Finishing second in a race is no better than coming in last."

Okay, a theatrical version. How would Irving Berlin write a show about the sun? How would Frank Capra?

Armed with research books on the sun—mainly Harvard astronomer Dr. Donald Menzel's book, *Our Mr. Sun*—I worked out a showman's treatment in play form, all in dialogue, with two principal live characters, Dr. Research and a Fiction Writer, and four principal animated cartoon characters, Mr. Sun, Father Time, Thermo the Magician, and Chloro Phyll.

When I received written treatments from Willy Ley and Aldous Huxley (both were excellent), I mailed N. W. Ayer all three versions with a notice that I considered my obligation finished.

In a matter of days Don Jones put in long-distance calls as if he owned A. T. & T. Mr. Craig must see me . . . the Scientific Advisory Committee must meet with me . . . all had unanimously chosen my "Showman's" version over Ley's and Huxley's.

There they were around the table. President Craig had introduced me to them: the Scientific Advisory Committee—a collection of minds that had to be among the most brilliant in the nation. Dr. George W. Beadle (biology), Caltech; Dr. John Z. Bowers (medicine), University of Wisconsin; Professor Paul R. Burkholder (bacteriology), Brooklyn Botanical Garden; Professor

Farrington Daniels (chemistry), University of Wisconsin; Dr. Maurice Ewing (geophysics), Columbia University; Dean George R. Harrison (physics), M.I.T.; Dr. Clyde Kluckhohn (anthropology), Harvard; Dr. Warren Weaver (mathematics), Rockefeller Foundation; Dr. Ralph Bown (engineering), vice president in charge of the Bell Research Laboratories.

All the talk had been centered on persuading me to produce their first pilot film. They had many flattering comments on my theatrical approach; one scientist said my use of talking animated cartoons of Mr. Sun, Thermo the Magician, and Chloro Phyll, to illustrate and explain the complex in terms of the simple, was as brilliant a device as Aesop's and La Fontaine's use of talking animals to illustrate human vices, follies, and virtues.

How could I tell these good gentlemen the verities of my profession? That show business is an existentialist "now" business with little tradition and no memory for its greats? Would they understand that in Hollywood "to be" is never conjugated beyond "I am, you are, he is?" and that for me to step down from theatrical films to TV documentaries would be like being sent down from the Yankees to Walla Walla? They would laugh if I said, "Count me out, gentlemen. Professional 'face' decrees I'm too big for the job." Couldn't each of these eminent men say, "I'm a pretty fair Mr. Big in my profession, too." And what about President Craig? Barring Truman and Stalin, he had about the biggest job in the world.

No, I needed a less hammy excuse to get me off the hook. By the end of the luncheon I thought I had found one.

"Gentlemen, I'm not your man," I said to the Committee scientists in the privacy of a Board room. "You gentlemen are scientists. A physical fact is your truth, your bible, your discipline. Well, to me a physical fact is boring, unless—it is illumined by a touch of the Eternal. So you see, if I make a science film I will have to say that scientific research is just another expression of the Holy Spirit that works in *all* men. Furthermore, I will say that science, in essence, is just another facet of man's quest for God."

There was a long pause. Finally Dean Harrison, the physicist from M.I.T., spoke up. "Frank Capra, scientists feel there is a gulf, a widening gulf, between science on one side and Mr. Average Citizen on the other. We have become members of this Advisory Committee in the hope that we can help you build a bridge across this gulf. An artistic bridge, a spiritual bridge if you will, that will open up a two-way traffic of understanding between scientists and other human beings. You build such a bridge, Frank Capra, and you will accomplish much for yourself and the Telephone Company, but much more for the nation and perhaps for the world."

Like a spent salmon, I made one last gasping flop to shake the hook. "Dammit, gentlemen, I guess I haven't gotten through to you. I'm not only religious, I am a Catholic!" I waited for the reaction. There was none.

"Yes?" said Dr. Kluckhohn.

"And not even a *good* Catholic," I went on, "not one that tailors his actions to the verbotens of Popes, bishops, and priests. I'm worse. I'm a Catholic in *spirit*; one who firmly believes that the anti-moral, the intellectual bigots, and the Mafias of ill will may destroy religion, but they will never conquer the cross. Don't you understand?"

"So?" It was Dr. John Bowers of Wisconsin.

"So? So I'm also a *wacky* Catholic. Do you know what just happened? My wife, a recent convert without me knowing it, talked me into being remarried by a priest. Silliest goings on you ever saw at the Pala Mission. With her brother and sister-in-law, and our three grown children kneeling behind us, Father Mondini says, 'I now pronounce you man and wife.' I tittered, my wife tittered, my children tittered, and even the dead-pan Pala Indians tittered." I paused for effect.

Again Dr. John Bowers asked a flat "So?"

Hollywood is impermanence, change; instant stardom, instant limbo. Streets are tilted stairways, now up, now down. All is motion. Fast beats the heart. Urgent, desperate run the feet. Winds shift and blow. Fierce winds. Hurricane winds. Blow you onward, blow you backward.

But every hurricane has its calm, peaceful eye—nature's most secluded hideaway. On the corner of Sunset and Doheny, safe from the winds in our underground workshop, we did our thing in Hollywood's eye.

In the next five years my name was scarcely mentioned in the movie columns.

Together with Frank Keller and Dolores Waddell, I was having the time of my life in our little Professor Santa's workshop, as Keller called it. Alone with typewriter and Movieola, the magic of film, and the freedom to create, the days passed like hours, the months like days. Once again I was living in the sensuous fires of enthusiasm. The years 1952–56 were as productive and as packed with achievement as the war years of 1941–45. But this time I was not revealing the ugly facts of war but the awe and wonder and fascination of nature to youngsters from eight to eighty.

Those four films about science, hand-woven with bits of celluloid, were sprightly patterns of poesy and fact; fresh ideas were their main charm, a rather elegant charm, we thought; much like the light-hearted but disciplined charm of a Mozart composition. By weaving together live scenes, fantasy, traceries of diagrams, animated cartoon characters, puppets, and—above all—humorous illustrative parables, metaphors, similes, and analogies, we reduced the complex to the simple, the eternal to the everyday. In short, though it took five years, I built a small bridge that spanned the gulf twixt scientist and commoner. Spanned it by making education as exciting and entertaining as any comedy, drama, or whodunit.

On November 19, 1956, almost five years after my first meeting with Cleo ("second best is not good enough") Craig, president of A. T. & T., *Our Mr. Sun* was televised nationally in color by CBS, at 10 P.M. It was followed (in four-month intervals) by *Hemo the Magnificent, The Strange Case of the Cosmic Rays,* and *Meteora, the Unchained Goddess.* The films were then rerun over the NBC network.

Jack Gould, TV critic for *The New York Times,* called *Our Mr. Sun* "a long forward step in the enlightened use of television . . ."

 Leon Morse, *Billboard*, Cincinnati
 A new and exciting dimension has been added to TV . . .

 Hank Grant, *Hollywood Reporter*
 . . . as perfect a blend of understandable information and de-lightful entertainment as we'll ever see on TV . . .

 San Francisco *Chronicle*
 Hottest thing on television . . . best of all, a few spiritual over-tones: "Measure the outside with mathematics, but measure the inside with prayer. Prayer is research, too." . . .

 Variety, New York
 . . . provided a glimpse of the amazing power of TV when it really decides to probe its potential . . .

 Variety
 Last Wednesday, Frank Capra's *Hemo the Magnificent* edged out *Kraft Theater* by 19.9 to 19.4 . . . and 'Hemo' . . . will be a recipient of one of the four 1958 Howard W. Blakeslee Awards given by the American Heart Association . . .

The "happening?" It shook us all up.

About a month after the *Hemo* telecast, a large, waist-high packing bar-rel arrived at our Sunset Strip office addressed to: "Frank Capra, Hollywood." The barrel was stamped "CHEM PLANT . . . FRAGILE . . . HANDLE WITH CARE!" My new secretary (Dolores had married a minister), Maggie Parker, and film editor Frank Keller and I opened the barrel. Digging into the packing confetti we uncovered the most amazing, and the largest, golden trophy I ever saw. A gold plate on the base heralded this etched inscription:

To
FRANK CAPRA
for
Writing and Directing
Hemo the Magnificent
a very fine program
SMILEY

No other name, or return address. Just "Smiley." Had to be a gag. A gold-plated gag. By Benny Rubin, maybe, or Harry Ruby. We stashed the enor-mous "Oscar"—enormous? I'll say. Midgets could play hide and seek on it. We put the "golden calf" in the cutting room—and waited for the practical joker to spring the laugh. Weeks went by. Luckily we had saved the packing barrel. Examining it, we discovered the "thing" had been packed by Karl Mouch Trophies and Jewelry, of Cincinnati, Ohio.

We air-mailed a letter to the trophy company. Back came an apology and an enclosed letter they had missed putting in the barrel. The letter:

> 1238 Rossmore Avenue
> Cincinnati 37, Ohio
> March 22, 1957

Dear Mr. Capra:

. . . I don't make a lot of money and I certainly have no claim to being a critic. But, I do have a good job and I know the value of the fine feelings your program stirred up in me. Please accept this trophy in appreciation of the best program which I have seen in television . . .

> Yours truly,
> (signed) Sam Smiley
> SAM O. SMILEY

We contacted Sam O. Smiley on the phone. He was a family man, an electrician. "Well," he said, "lots of times good programs like yours don't get awards. So I sent you an award from Smiley. . . ."

In one of my films some too-tired critic would have labeled Smiley as "Capra-corn."

In April 1969 I escorted a Fallbrook teacher and her group of sixth-graders around our Red Mountain ranch. From my jeep I pointed out historical spots. It was hot. The children were bored. I took them down to our cool basement playroom for cold drinks. The walls are plastered with pictures of movie stars. But neither Gable nor Garbo interested them.

Then—a boy spotted a picture of me holding a painted animation "cell" of Mr. Sun. "Hey! Look, you guys. Mr. Capra and Mr. Sun—together!" When they learned that I had made *Mr. Sun* and *Hemo* and *Cosmic Rays* and *Meteora*, I became an instant hero. They had seen them all. They gathered around me. They giggled. They worshiped. "Ooooh, Mr. Capra. Let me touch you—" "Groovy!"

They touched me, and I touched them. For, each year, twelve million such lively American and Canadian fifth- and sixth-graders still see my educational films and now call them "groovy." Film *is* a magic carpet.

Stars over
Hollywood

IT WAS 1957. I was sixty years old. For eleven of the last fifteen years I had been out of circulation in Hollywood—five years in Army information films, and now I had wound up six years of making educational films. Wonderful years they were, meeting fresh, vigorous minds—exploring minds that charged me up with new enthusiasms, new ambitions. Now I was itching to come out of hiding and do my thing; make the best films of my life.

I began searching for heroes for my film stories. What kind of heroes? Outsize men who conquer against odds—men who leave a wake of human progress.

The advents and epiphanies of heroes, the moments that set them apart— especially the "why, where, and *when*" their adrenals pump at the "furiest" —will always captivate the curious mind, and the movie audiences.

Dr. Carl Anderson, head of high-energy physics at Caltech, and Nobel Prize winner, gave me a fascinating hint about the magic age of this heroic "when."

Anderson said that since his discovery of the positron, dozens of other totally unexpected atomic particles had come to light, shattering the modern concept of the atom to smithereens—sending physicists into whiffits and snits. I asked what it all meant.

"I don't know," said Carl. "Right now we're yelling 'HELP!' But some student of twenty-six will give us the answer soon."

"Why twenty-six? Is that the most active age of the brain?"

"No-o," he answered, "but it's the age when the combination of knowledge and brashness is the most potent. At twenty-six a student is flush with up-to-date learning, yet is rebel enough—and full of beans enough—to defy the conservative scientific Establishment, and come up with some wild 'guesses.'

After twenty-six he acquires much more knowledge—but also becomes more conservative. He sees more trees but fewer forests."

Well, I thought that was one heck of a statement. I ran to a research library to check it out. Was I surprised. Here are a few items that spotlight the high-caloric age of twenty-six:

Einstein announced his Theory of Relativity—at the age of twenty-six.

Alexander began his conquest of the then known world—at twenty-six.

Napoleon took command of the French Revolutionary mobs—at twenty-six.

Yukawa, Japanese Nobel Prize winner, brilliantly predicted the existence of the meson before it was found—at twenty-six.

Marie Curie began investigating radioactive uranium—at twenty-five. (But women mature earlier—and prettier.)

Lincoln switched from wandering to politics and immortality (elected to State Legislature)—at twenty-six.

Shakespeare wrote first major play, *King Henry VI*—at twenty-six.

St. Francis exchanged finery and a gay life for rags and a saintly life—at twenty-five.

Marco Polo crossed Asia, the Gobi Desert; arrived in Peking—at age twenty-six.

Leonardo da Vinci proclaimed a "master painter"—at twenty-six.

Michelangelo called to Rome, executed his famous *Pietà*—at twenty-six.

Magellan started his first trip around the world—at twenty-eight.

Dante wrote *La Vita Nova*, his first prose poem, about his love for Beatrice—at twenty-seven.

Churchill, the "Man of our Century," was elected for the first time to Commons and to history—at twenty-six.

D. W. Griffith, the Leonardo of the Screen," took his first step toward film immortality by directing *The Adventures of Dollie*—at the age of twenty-seven.

And there are many, many more examples: Chaplin became a world star at 26, Orson Welles made *Citizen Kane* when just under 26, Eisenstein made *Potemkin* at 27, and pyromaniac Nero was about 26 when he fiddled to his Roman bonfire. But the idea is apparent—and startling.

Well, the first hero I ran into (after emerging from my science films workshop) was well over twenty-six. He was Frank Sinatra. Bert Allenberg —now with the William Morris Agency—brought us together. But not before Allenberg had spent days bringing me up to date on the astonishing things that had happened to my Hollywood.

"Frank," said Bert Allenberg, heaving a tired sigh, "it's not the Hollywood we used to know. It's not a director's business, but an actor's business now. They pick their own stories, and their own directors. So if you're thinking of making pictures again, you're gonna have to shack up with a star, or the banks won't lend you a quarter—"

What had happened? In the past half-dozen years, Hollywood had been rocked by a major shift in values. The revolution began with the withering of managerial confidence. In 1950–51, major studio executives looked out of their baronial windows, counted the ever-growing forest of antennas—TV crosses row on row—gasped, and decided the "fillum" business had had it. They took stock of their negatives, asked for real estate appraisals, and liquidated contracts with their stars. Hollywood abdicated to the idiot box.

That left a vacuum in film production. Now nature may abhor a vacuum, but Hollywood couldn't afford one—especially in the coffers of the two largest talent agencies: Music Corporation of America (MCA) and the William Morris Agency. (Ten percent of one star's salary wouldn't buy an Aleutian Island, but 10 percent of four hundred important clients was more than we paid for Alaska.)

Fighting disaster, William Morris and MCA—with the aid of some nervy banking—began packaging their out-of-work stars, writers, and directors into production units; and lo!: the beginning of wide-spread independent production. And lo! lo!—the "fillum" business wasn't dead. In fact, it was livelier than ever. The coffers of the two agencies once again ranneth over. And thrice lo! The stars rose over Hollywood.

The banks began financing independent productions directly rather than through the cowering major studios. But the banker—God bless his myopic, non-glassy eye—saw big-name stars as the safest insurance for production loans. Independent producers had to submit contracts with stars before they could get financed.

Stars became necessary not only as fine actors with box-office value, but, more importantly, as collateral for bank loans. No stars, no financing. Up went their demand. Higher went their salaries. The two chased each other up into the ionosphere. Actors who had received fifty thousand dollars per picture under major studio contracts now demanded—and got—two hundred, three hundred, five hundred thousand per film from independent producers. The major studios came out of storm cellars and offered actors ten times the price they paid the same actors under contracts to them only two years ago. Star salaries went into orbit when they reached one million dollars per picture! *One hundred thousand per week* for a ten-week stint. Supporting players hitched their salaries to the stars and went into orbit with them.

Are stars worth those unheard-of salaries? No. Not as actors *or* collateral. One can count the stars who have assured box-office value on the pitching hand of "Three-Fingered" Brown. Even these luminaries will play to empty houses in a bad picture.

Then why do hard-headed bankers (or perhaps their light-headed wives) finance only pictures with stars—almost certain to cripple the production if the lion's share of the budget goes to an actor or two? The answer: Stars' names are on the marquees, their faces dominate advertising and publicity. They are the glamour. To the eyes and ears of a layman, stars make the films. By osmosis, bankers absorb this canard and, believe it or not, so do the stars.

So they demand approval of director, writer, and cameraman; demand script changes to suit them; demand the red-carpet treatment—limousines, royal suites, and the hiring of their regal retinue of personal menials on the picture.

The Star-Agent-Banker Axis contributes heavily to the failure of many a good film in recouping its cost. But that is Hollywood—the only free enterprise, non-subsidized film-production center left in the world. We like it that way. If stars can destroy the "one man, one film" idea in a free system, the producer-directors are failing not only in their potential but in their duty to the great medium of the motion picture.

"Anyway, Capra, I can fit you right into a helluva package deal," said super salesman Bert Allenberg, "Sinatra, you, and Arnold Schulman, author of the play *A Hole in the Head* we bought for Frankie. All clients. Sinatra wants you to direct it, and Eddie Robinson, another client, to play the square brother. Here's how we can set it up. Your Frank Capra Company and Sinatra's company enter into a co-venture deal, with a fifty-fifty vote on all co-venture matters. The two of you appoint a third party to decide things that you and Sinatra don't agree on, understand? That third party will be Abe Lastfogel, head of William Morris. Keeps it all in the family, see?

"Now listen to this. Sinatra will give you a one-third ownership of the film, and his company will own two-thirds. That's it. Short and sweet. And a helluva deal for you."

"Does Sinatra know I make my own films, make all the decisions?" I asked, very much unimpressed with my role as a piece of a William Morris package. "He knows. 'Get me Capra,' he said."

I had met Frankie Sinatra fifteen years before, for the first and only time, when I was still in uniform. I was leaving a party Charlie MacArthur had taken me to (Harold Ross's birthday I think). It was 3 A.M. Walking up Fifth Avenue I ran smack into Jimmy Durante. We embraced.

"Caprastropic!" said Jimmy. "Coming round da corner I wuz jes t'inking. If had me cherce who on Fift' Avenoo would Durante go ta see another pretty good Dago's last show atta Copa wit? Speak a da devil and who should pop up? You. Come on. Let's catch Frankie boy. Mamma mia, wot a verce!"

I heard Sinatra sing at the Copa; heard him grab that night-club audience; heard him grab me. He knew the meaning of his lyrics and sang them to you, powerfully, dramatically. Vocal cords swelling out from his thin neck, face contorted with passion, blue eyes moist with meaning—that thin vibrant man sang like nobody of the time, like nobody of today. Durante introduced us in his dressing room. I mumbled something like, "Boy, you've got it. Don't throw it away—"

I met Sinatra again in his swank office in the William Morris Building on El Camino, Beverly Hills. He was a few pounds heavier, and many hairs lighter than the Copa Frankie, but much, much more charming—no. The word is fascinating. No. He's more than that. Fact is, it's difficult to describe a once-in-a-lifetime star. That's what Frank Sinatra was, and still is—a superstar. Brighter than he's ever shone. Bigger than he thinks he is—and it scares him; makes him mean at times. Champagne explodes when you bottle it in beer bottles.

"Cheech!" He winged it at me as I sat down. "Why don't you and I make *Hole in the Head* together? You do all the dirty work, while I smile and knock off all the broads—"

The deal was on. We exchanged letters of agreement and left the rest to lawyers. Then Allenberg threw me a change-up. "You got plenty of time to go fishing, Frank. Sinatra can't make the picture until November, 1958."

"What? That's a year and three months from now!"

"You're lucky. Most big stars are booked solid three years in advance. But we found a little hole in Sinatra's tight schedule—so we squeezed in *Hole in the Head*."

(There was a limerick there somewhere: "There once was a man with a hold in his schedule . . . Into which we squeezed a hole in his headule.")

"Bert! Why didn't you tell me *before* I agreed to the deal?"

"What's to tell? It's only a year off. Look. Harry Cohn's asking about you. Maybe he's got something you could be preparing while waiting for Lover Boy—"

It was all quite familiar, like revisiting the home you grew up in. Here's the baby grand piano near the door, there's the long walk to his desk, the Oscars in the glass case behind him. And behind the barricade of phones and squawk boxes there squats Harry Cohn puffing his cheeks in and out like a battered old bullfrog. Yes, he's tapping his desk with a stick—ah, a change. Not with a riding crop. It was a curved-handle cane. And knock me down! There's his usual audience—the ubiquitous broads. Whoa! These two ladies aren't broads. They're important women.

"Sonya! . . . Lillian!" I cried, giving each a peck on the cheek. One was Sonya Levien, the out-going scriptwriter with the infectious laugh. She wrote *The Younger Generation* for me, about the super-Jew who denied his parents. The other was producer-director George Sidney's wife, outwardly an attractive half-pint of bottled bossiness, but inwardly a good fairy. C. B. De Mille nicknamed her "Tinker Bell." "Frank, darling," she tinkled. "How these walls could talk. Harry told us it's eighteen years since you last stepped into this office."

"Yeah. Eighteen years!" said Harry, rising. "But Capra came crawling back. Just like I said he would when he left. Hi, Walyo!"

"Hi, Harry." He was old, gray; his bloated face sagged under the weight of its prison pallor. I offered my hand. He looked at it.

Like a pallid winter's dawn, a sardonic victory smile flushed his drooping jowls. "Come on!" he growled, waving his cane. "I didn't even shake hands with Mussolini. Sit down. You broke? You need some dough? [to others] You know this guy was once number one director in the world? When he worked for me? Look at you. The great Capra. Number one. You stupid schnook, leaving Columbia. Got any idea how much my Columbia stock is worth? Huh?"

"A billion dollars?"

"Oh, funny. Still the crappy gag man. No wonder you ain't made a picture in six or eight years."

"Oh, Harry," scolded Lillian Sidney, "Frank's been making those wonderful science shows for television—"

"Horseshit! Those TV things are *shorts*. I gotta short department. Maybe the dago wants a job in my short depart—where ya goin'?"

"Harry, I'd forgotten how much fun you were."

"Oh, balls! Lemme give you an office, Walyo. I may need some help on a script we're screwed up about—*Joseph and His Brethren*. Maybe you'll get hot pants about it—"

For the Christmas vacation I took my family to lucky La Quinta, and began to write a treatment on the best-loved tale in the Old Testament. In the desert air—always creative for me—the scenes came fast; treatment expanded into script. Seventy pages in ten days. I read them to Lu. She flipped. "Darling, drop everything else. This can be your greatest film—"

I heard it on the radio at our Fallbrook ranch: "Harry Cohn, sixty-six, the last of the 'one-man studio' moguls, died in an ambulance on the way to St. Joseph's Hospital in Phoenix, Arizona, only minutes after being stricken by a coronary occlusion at the Arizona Biltmore Hotel. His wife, Joan, was at his bedside. . . ."

And with him died an exciting era of new undertakings and courageous giants. He was crude, he was mean. He stirred controversy with a massive dirty-nailed finger. But he was the only buccaneer to grab his original runt-of-the-litter company by its ears and raise it kicking and scratching to Hollywood's top dog *major* film company.

After Cohn died, the New York executives took charge and—like Jack Sprat and his wife—they licked Cohns' platter clean. *Joseph and His Brethren* was canceled before Cohn's body was cold.

Now what would I do while waiting for that "little hole in Sinatra's schedule" into which we could squeeze *A Hole in the Head*? First, I went to Cambridge, Massachusetts, to see how M.I.T.'s Professor Zacharias's "five-year physics plan" was coming along, and to supervise a couple of the seventy twenty-minute color films I had helped Zacharias lay out. For film was becoming a magic carpet for teachers as well as for showmen.

Then, too, I filled in more time (waiting for the little hole in Frankie's schedule) by accepting Dr. Alfred Bauer's invitation to serve as a member of the eleven-man jury at the Berlin Film Festival.

If film festivals are a little-known and less-understood phenomenon to the general public, it is only fair to say they are only slightly better understood by participating Western governments. First of all, film festivals are not a "World's Fair of films" in which the world's filmmakers exhibit their wares and vie for prizes. It is a fair in which the *world governments* approve and select the entries, and campaign for prizes. For a film festival is only secondarily a showcase for artists; primarily it is an arena for competing ideologies.

And nobody appreciates this more than the Iron Curtain countries, or less than the United States.

The Soviet Union and its satellites have one very important purpose at film festivals: to propagandize the assembled world artists (and world press) into changing the meaning and import of art—from an aesthetic excellence to a social usefulness. This leads directly to the evaluation of art in terms of ideology: Good art is what promotes the Communist cause; bad art opposes it.

This is propaganda in the grand style; imaginative, visionary. For if communism could spread this new conceit, "Art is synonymous with socialism" among world art centers, the next logical thrust would be, "Art is synonymous with Communistic dictatorship." And therefore, communism is beauty. It is Truth. It is good; heaven; God.

Too farfetched? Mr. Khrushchev didn't think so when he assembled a National Congress of Artists, Writers, and Film Workers (1963) and reminded them that Stalin would have had them shot for straying from the Party line. "Why? Why do you insist on seeking the Truth, when the Party has already *told* you the Truth?" To Mr. "K" and to all other dictators, the "party line" is Truth.

Arnold Schulman had first written *Hole in the Head*—about a bush-league Florida wheeler-dealer (always broke today but gonna hit it big tomorrow)— as a TV comedy special. Garson Kanin asked Schulman to expand it into a play—which Kanin produced, directed, and opened on Broadway. It was a fair hit.

After Sinatra turned the Sinatra-Capra package over to me, Gar Kanin called to say that I *must* get Arnold Schulman to write the script. "He'll drive you nuts, Frank. He's such a cocky little bastard, but he's got the greatest ear for dialogue."

So we brought Arnold out from New York and I asked him down to the Red Mountain ranch for a first conference. I opened the door—and there he stood; five feet of fuming anger.

In the living room I asked him to sit down. "I'd rather not if you don't mind. I just came down here to get a few things straightened out. Now about the script of *Hole in the Head*, Mr. Capra. I've heard you rewrite your writer's scenes. That's out. O—U—T. I allow *nobody* to rewrite one word of my stuff."

He was now pacing the floor, and moistening his full lips with a darting tongue. Though small, he looked strong and full of moxie—a miniature Jim Londos. "Another matter that I won't stand for. Allenberg hinted you wanted to change the characters from Jewish to Italian, maybe because you're Italian. Well, I'm a Jew and I'm proud of it. My characters are Jews, and they're proud of it. And they'll remain Jews. And lastly, if I write the script, I will *not* end the story with the usual Hollywood hackneyed, stale, bromidic, banal, obsolete, senile happy ending. No critics are going to accuse me of going Hollywood and putting buttered Capra-corn in my show."

I laughed out loud at that one. "Arnold, you're wonderful—"

"Yes, well, I didn't come down here to be wonderful. I came here to—"

"To straighten me out on a few things, I know. Let's have lunch—"

The upshot of Schulman's outburst: We ended up good friends. He wrote a very funny script, I changed many scenes, we changed the characters from Jews to Italians, the film had a happy ending, and Arnold ended up with a young fortune from his share of the grosses.

But Schulman's attempt to end a comedy unhappily leads me to a few comments about comedy. Comedy may be many things to many people. But one thing it is not to anybody; it is not a tragic ending. That would be as anomalous and as ludicrous as putting a jackass's head on Man-O-War's body.

Comedy is fulfillment, accomplishment, overcoming. It is victory over odds, a triumph of good over evil. Tragedy is frustration, failure, despair. The evil in man prevails; there is mourning.

Comedy is good news—"How beautiful . . . are the feet of him that bringeth good tidings . . ." The Gospels are comedies: a triumph of spirit over matter. The Resurrection is the happiest of all endings: man's triumph over death. The Mass is a "celebration" of that event. Priests and parishioners "celebrate" a Mass. It is a divine comedy.

In social terms, comedy is a complete surrender of one's defenses. If you don't like a certain person—your defenses are up. No laughs. If a person acts superior, or if you fear him—your defenses are up. You won't laugh, with him or at him.

Therefore, before you can laugh you must surrender yourself—let your defenses down. Enemies, strangers, snobs, the sarcastic, the haters, the brutal, the fearful, the ugly, the dangerous, the unknown—no laughs.

But—you laugh easily among friends; you love them; you let down your defenses. And you laugh easily among the innocent; babies, for instance, whether human, animal, or bird. No fear.

You laugh at the playful antics of a lion cub—innocence. You don't laugh at his father—fear. Your defenses are up.

Dictators can't laugh. They hate. Hitler and Stalin were not funny to themselves or to you. Their defenses were up, so were yours.

What *is* laughter? . . . this sudden, explosive, salutary, almost involuntary release of happy energy? . . . this rippling, guttural, inarticulate cry of joy only *humans* utter and understand? . . . that dissolves hates, heals the sick, and binds humanity together in a common fellowship only *humans* can join?

Is it man's primeval, defiant cry against the demons of terror, hunger, sickness, and death? Is it man's way of saying to hell with sorrow, tears, and woes? Is it the God within reminding man he is a vain, foolish Narcissus?

Odd that five of the greatest humorists that made the world ring with laughter were priests—Rabelais, Sterne, Scarron, Swift, and Sidney Smith.

Man is the only animal that can laugh and has a soul. Are the two related?

It has been argued that man laughs because he has a memory, a sense of history; animals do not. Man remembers how things *should* be; when they are not, he laughs.

For instance, Napoleon reaching for a telephone and ordering his generals to capture Moscow would be funny. We know he had no telephone. Russians would laugh louder. They also know he didn't take Moscow. But animals wouldn't see the joke.

This theory of comedy has validity. Yet we smile and laugh at births, weddings, young people in love, harvest festivals, and many other normal events that *are* as they should be.

Furthermore, laughter is so tantalizingly fragile we cannot *will* it into being. Something pleasant, comic, or witty must trigger it. Not one of the world's great stage artists has ever fully mastered the trick of laughing on cue—convincingly. Well, then, what *is* laughter? I don't know. But hiding behind a screen of pretentious syllables—in hopes I may sound as abstruse as Bergman or as proleptic as Antonioni—I will venture a definition with all the assurance of Wally Cox: Laughter is the most pleasantly mysterious component of a much greater mystery—the human psyche. There. Now you know. Laughter, anyone?

Oh, cynics will try to confuse you by saying we laugh because all life itself is a joke; that the ogre masks children wear on Halloween disclose the real truth. And non-cynics may counter by saying mothers laugh at the masks because they are happy the ogre faces are *not* the truth.

But this much we all somehow know instinctively: Wit, humor, laughter are the hope, the promise, the sunlight, the flavor, the perfumes that enliven our days of pilgrimage on this earth. What a sour joke on God and man if the lamp of wit were to be extinguished, and the humorless Hitlers became kings.

As you may have guessed by now, ours is a sentimental family; sloppily so. We laugh easy, we cry easy. But we cry more easily at happy news than at the doleful. In the middle of final preparations for filming *A Hole in the Head* our family had a fine cry. Frank, Jr., phoned us from his Army station (Fort Monmouth, New Jersey) to tell us he had fallen in love with Priscilla Anne Pearson of Elberon, New Jersey, and would like to marry her right away, on a date agreeable to all—Junior knowing that events in our family lives were geared not to fate but to film. Well, it was "Stop the world! Our first-born's getting married!"

Checking around, all agreed that Saturday, October 4, was a suitable enough day for the world to stop. So, on that sunny suspended day in 1958, Lu and I and Lulu and Tom watched wet-eyed as our number one son took upon himself a very pretty wife, Priscilla, in St. Catherine's Catholic Church —and that night there was dancing in our hearts and in the tree-shaded streets of Elberon, New Jersey.

As has been noted before, the filming of each film creates its own unique adventures and anecdotes, some more newsworthy than the film itself. I recall two main news items about *A Hole in the Head*. Item one, of course, was Frank Sinatra—one of the spiciest bits of condiment to flavor our post-war days. There are some who say Sinatra is without a peer as a singer of popular American songs. They will get arguments from adherents of Perry Como, Bing Crosby, Eddie Cantor, and Al Jolson.

But few will accuse you of being rash if you say that Sinatra is without a peer in turning on night-club audiences. However, I will make a rasher statement: Frank would be as proficient in drama as he is in song—had he committed himself to his abundant gifts. Pity. Had Sinatra dedicated himself to the profession of acting as much as he has to his singing, he would have made a devastating combination of Bogart, Tracy, and Casanova.

Sinatra is a great singer ("a saloon singer" he calls himself), and he knows it. The excitement of moving and reaching the hearts of live audiences with his lyrical virtuosity makes his blood run hot. He has total command of his performances; selects his own songs, songwriters, orchestras, audiences. Sinatra is also a great actor, and he knows that, too.

But in films he is not Sinatra doing Sinatra's thing with song. He cannot reach and bewitch live, ever-changing "saloon" audiences. He performs for a never-changing audience of busy, dispassionate cameramen, sound men, script girls, make-up people, dead-pan electricians who have "seen it all before," and other actors who don't bewitch easily—if at all.

Nor is Sinatra in total command of the shooting of a film. There are budgets and schedules to confine, and directors to heed. But Sinatra "heeds" very badly. Directors become his bête noires. If directors keep him busy he maintains an uneasy truce; for having started something, Sinatra's next goal is to finish it—but fast. He bores easily; can't sit still or be alone; must be where the action is—preferably with his fellow "saloon" performers, the lovelies, or the less orthodox socially.

Should he not be used for a day or two—especially on location—Frank grouses, accuses directors of fooling around with inconsequentials. Regrettably, he is half-right. There is a good deal of "fooling around" inherent in directing. Sinatra gives ultimatums: "Finish with me in three days or I'm blowing" or, "Another *week* on this location? Look, fella. If you want to futz around, or want to be the 'big' man—do it on your own time—not mine. I'm giving you till *tomorrow night* to shoot my scenes." And directors *do* finish with him when he demands—admitting Sinatra is half-right.

It was during our second night of shooting at the West Flagler Kennel Club dog track, in Miami, that I discovered a quirk in Sinatra that might account for his sour attitude toward directors. It was a hard-nosed brutish scene: Flat-broke Sinatra is making a last ditch grandstand play to promote super-promoter Keenan Wynn (pals in their younger days) and one of Wynn's half-dozen "Miss America" secretaries (Joi Lansing) into financing Sinatra in a "Disneyland" deal. Filthy-rich Keenan Wynn (a Mike Todd with savagery) figures Frank out rightly as a phony—"Creeps that try to take me,

Hole in the Head.
Director-baiter Sinatra wonders
if his new director-partner is for
real.

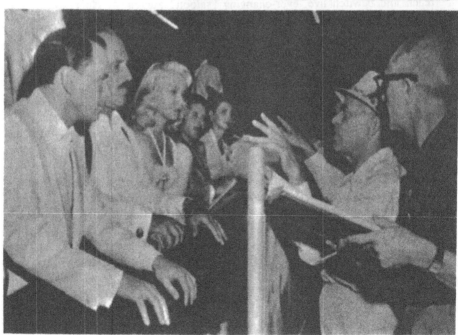

Sinatra becomes interested when he hears me tell Keenan Wynn and Joi
Lansing, "No rehearsals from now on. Frank leaves his best scenes in rehearsals.
Ad-lib, don't wait for cues, cut into each other's lines. If you flub, keep going!
Don't stop for anything till I yell 'Cut!' "

"But, Mr. Capra! I've got to have rehearsals to match the action!" cries the distraught script girl. "Honey, the vaults are full of bad pictures that match the action perfectly—"

Having no theatrical film to worry about (my last one was six years ago), Lu and I have fun with our dearest friends —Dottie and William "Wild Bill" Wellman . . .

they always get sweaty hands"—and brushes him off with, "Here's fifty, pal. See you around." Panicky, but still grandstanding, Sinatra throws the money in his face. One bodyguard grabs his arms, the other paralyzes Sinatra with a mean right hook in the solar plexus; fighting for air, Frankie boy grabs his stomach, stumbles to the nearest men's room.

The scene took place in the dog track's V.I.P. clubhouse boxes; Sinatra, Wynn, Lansing, in the front box, Miami's racing set filled other boxes. First rehearsal: Sinatra great, others need straightening out. Second rehearsal: Sinatra cools off, others improve. First photographic take: Sinatra cold, others fine.

I took Frank aside. He was in a black mood. "Something bothering you, Frank?" "Hell, yes. All those rehearsals, repeating the same jokes to the same jerks. It'd bother *anybody*." Well, well! Another Stanwyck? Could be. He's a performer first, actor second. He never repeats a song to the same audience. "Take ten, Frank. I'll call you."

I went to Keenan Wynn, an all-league pro. "Keenan, I want to try something without rehearsing it with Frank. Change your cues, mix up your lines. Joi! Interrupt Frank during his speeches, but keep the scene going, no matter what Frank does. I want it to be all new for him. Art, change the extras around in the back boxes, we don't want to see the same faces—"

Roll 'em! Action! Sinatra has the first line. Keenan jumps him with, "What'd you say?" Surprised, Sinatra says, "I ain't said nothing, yet." "Well, say it. What's on your mind?" It was a brand-new game. Sinatra lights up. They play a wonderful scene, full of natural ad libs. Well, I'll be damned. Another Stanwyck. And another king-size headache, because Edward G. Robinson, a star of major magnitude, wants to rehearse all day! And the more he rehearses the better he plays the scene. Eddie may not like it if I don't rehearse him with Sinatra.

He didn't like it at all. In fact, kind, good-natured Eddie Robinson blew his top before a set full of people when we got back to the Goldwyn Studios. In a voice choking with anger and tears he shouted, "I won't stand for this degradation any longer. I was a star for twenty years at Warners and nobody, *nobody* refused to rehearse with me. You're toadying to Sinatra. You're afraid of him. *That's* why he won't rehearse with me. But that's all. I'm finished. No more. No more. I'm out of this picture. Out. Out. I'm calling my agent—" His choking voice trailed off in sobs as he stomped toward his dressing room, leaving behind him not a closed mouth or a moving finger among crews and other actors.

"Art! Call lunch. Back at one." It was 11 A.M. "Yes, Mr. Capra. Lunchee! Back at one o'clock. Look at 'em go, look at 'em go—"

I sat in my director's chair while the cast filed past me, bursting with "news" to spread throughout Goldwyn's studio: Freckle-faced, eleven-year-old Eddie Hodges (playing Sinatra's son) gave me a wrinkled-nose smile and the "okay" sign with his fingers (I fell in love with him in Meredith Willson's *Music Man*); sloe-eyed Carolyn Jones, playing Sinatra's latest flame—a pre-hippy, kooky nymph who wanted her flame lit, lit, lit, every hour (her calling card might read: "Have muu-muu, surfboard, and bongo—let the wind blow!") —ruffled my hair as she passed by; Eleanor Parker, "the lady" of our cast marched out, nose high. Last to leave was Thelma Ritter, that best of all character actresses. She leaned down, put her arms round my neck and whispered in my ear: "Told you Robinson was going to stink. And I'm gonna stink, Sinatra's gonna stink, you're gonna stink, and THE PICTURE's gonna stink! Wait and see."

Unusual as it may sound, this bit of "encouragement" had become a ritual with Thelma Ritter. Remember, the stars had risen over Hollywood. Their one last hurdle to complete take-over was the film director. So it was open season on directors; the bigger the name the bigger the game. Morning after morning, while I sat in my chair completely absorbed in plotting the day's work, cold hands clamped suddenly over my eyes, beads and baubles tattooed my bald pate, tired perfume constricted my nose, and Thelma Ritter's harsh whisper poured her litany of "stinks" into my ears. I never batted an eye. That deviled her. But I had a film to make—my first in seven years—and not all the Ritters and Robinsons in the world were going to keep me from making it MY WAY!

I entered my stage dressing room-office. The phone rang. Sinatra. "What's the matter, Cheech? True Eddie Robinson's taking a powder?"

"No. Just butterflies; hasn't worked in some time. I'll handle this, Frank. You stay out of it—"

When there's tension and revolt in the air a director must keep his cool, must keep ahead of his cast, must keep them off-balance with discombobulating left jabs. Above all, he must keep them guessing.

Within twenty minutes, my long-time friend Phil Kellogg, of the William Morris Agency, burst in, very upset. "Frank, you of all people. Robinson called me. Wants off the picture. What happened?"

"Simple, Phil. Sinatra plays his best scenes *without* rehearsing, and Robinson plays his best scenes after an *hour* of rehearsing. If I rehearse them together they'll wreck each other. So I rehearse Robinson with someone else playing Sinatra's lines. Robinson says 'No!' Sinatra *must* rehearse with him. I say *I'll* tell Sinatra what to do, not Robinson. So Eddie ups and runs and says he'll quit. If he does, he's a damn fool. He's great in the picture. But if he does quit, if he doesn't report on the set at one o'clock ready for work, you tell him I'll sue him seven ways from Sunday for every dime it'll cost to replace him—"

Phil Kellogg wasn't with Robinson over ten minutes before he phoned. Would I please come to Eddie's dressing room. I opened the door. Eddie is sobbing like a child. He runs to me, embraces me roughly, and plants warm wet kisses all over my face. The heart and maleness of this sentimental man were something to experience. "How could I do this to you, Frank. My old, dear friend. Me! Who's been in the theater since before I could blow my own nose—How could I *do* this to you?—"

The cast and crew couldn't have been more surprised when they assembled on the set for the one o'clock call. There was Robinson on the set, clowning and laughing and joking like a happy fiddler on the roof. "Bill!" I shouted to our cameraman William Daniels. "Our first set-up is a big head close-up of the best damned actor in the world—Mr. Edward G. Robinson!" The applause was spontaneous and loud. Sinatra walked on the set—and gaped. Robinson was taking bows! Not only that—he rushed to Sinatra with a happy grin, embraced *him* roughly, and pinched *his* cheeks till they hurt. "You squirt! With all those dames. I used to be all rooster and bones, too, when I was young—"

It was a happy picture from then on, so happy that I think neither Sinatra nor Robinson—nor Thelma Ritter for that matter—ever gave warmer or better performances, though Thelma continued needling me with her routine of "stinks" each morning.

There is a show business footnote to Thelma Ritter's "get-your-goat" humor. We previewed *A Hole in the Head* for Arthur Krim and Bobby Benjamin of United Artists, at a Loew's "Something" theater in the Bronx. Lu and I took Charlie O'Curran and his wife, Patti Page, to the preview. The night was so cold and snowy that Patti, worried about getting an audience for the preview, called the captains of her Patti Page Fan Clubs and urged them to be at the theater. Our preview was an enormous success. Why shouldn't it be—with Patti Page's claque to howl it up?

We stood in the lobby, Patti greeting and thanking her fans, when beads rattled, a woman's arms encircled my neck, a tear-stained face clamped on to mine, and Thelma Ritter's voice poured happy wet noises into my ear, "Oh, Frank . . . It's so wonderful . . . so beautiful . . . I'm so proud to be a part of it . . . so proud . . . so proud . . ."

The other major news item about *A Hole in the Head* was the answer to this personal question: Could I evoke heart and humor out of a "sex and violence" entry, a story with no hero, no Mr. Deeds or Mr. Smith; a story about hard, unpleasant characters? Bitter "realism" was the trend. Could I leap a seven-year hiatus, dive into the pool of cynicism, and come up with laughs? Or, was my courage too worn and my legs too stiff to run with the times?

The advent of the sex-violence trend in films was practically forced on us by economics. Ever since American films first spread their flickering throughout the world, our "villains" had become a problem of ever-increasing magnitude. The power of films is always surprising, even to us who make them.

If we made pictures in which the villain was an African, a South American, a Frenchman, or any other nationality, those countries objected violently. They began to ban *all* pictures made by an offending American film company. Economic censorship was born.

To keep from losing foreign markets we resorted to using only American villains. But this brought on *domestic* difficulties. If our villain was a doctor, the medics objected; if a lawyer, the legal profession yelled "Foul!" as did labor unions, bankers, politicians, ministers, if one of their own was portrayed in a bad light. Pressure group censorship was born.

To keep from offending *anybody* our American villains had to be rich, white, jobless, stateless, useless playboys—cardboard myths without menace or meaning. No wonder world critics dismissed American films as "sham," "inane," "meaningless." Only Disney had it licked. His villains were animals, and animals don't go to the movies, or else Disney would have been picketed by the "Wolf's Protective League."

Well, you can't tell film stories *without* villains. So filmmakers rediscovered the ancient, *general* enemies of *all* humanity: Insanity, Poverty, Disease, War. Being hated and feared by everybody, they made ideal villains. The villain began changing from a person to an idea, a state of mind, or a condition.

The "mental health" stories spawned their corollary villains of amnesia, obsession, nymphomania, homocide, genocide, homosexuality, Freudianism, pre-natalism, can't-help-it-ism, and all the other real or invented "isms" of the ash-can or "downbeat" school.

When the lid was opened on this Pandora's box of "psychic" villains the eggs fell into the fan. With the brakes of personal responsibility removed, all sins were now somebody *else's* fault. Sex, murder, violence, rape, and robbery were not really immoral. The poor offenders were just "sick." And the screens began to crawl with this new "art." Delinquent youth came into their glory.

In Italy, screaming women with dirty necks and bosoms too big for their blouses became the rage. They didn't really *want* to be prostitutes. But they just had to have that precious chewing gum from the Americanos because of their ten little brothers and a sick, fat uncle.

The French, with Gallic logic, stuck to good old sex. They couldn't make the A-bomb, so they invented the B-bomb and called it Bardot.

In Japan, rowdy youths killed and stole and raped and blamed it all on "atom" fever.

In England, the homosexuals minced across the screen and waved their hankies at the audience. So few real actors could get work, Peter Sellers had to play all the parts.

In India, they copied Hollywood but added ten songs and dances.

In Russia, too little fertilizer and too much Stalin caused the suffering.

The Swedes, being neutral, couldn't blame *anybody*. So they just threw away the plot and dared you to understand their films. The critics couldn't understand them either so they called them "art."

The "anything goes" period was immortalized forever on film when Richard Widmark (in *Kiss of Death*) pushed a wheelchair with an invalid old woman in it down a flight of stairs—and laughed!

But, as has been noted elsewhere, out of this welter of sex and violence and "blame somebody else" films there emerged a harder type of motion picture that offered something new and fascinating in villainy—the *non-hero*. And this type of film was successful and all the rage in the forties and fifties, for example: *The Snake Pit . . . The Treasure of the Sierra Madre . . . Lost Weekend . . . All the King's Men . . . A Streetcar Named Desire . . . On the Waterfront . . . 12 Angry Men . . . The Defiant Ones . . . Room at the Top . . . Elmer Gantry . . .*

No laughs in that bunch. Evidently the post-war years were no time for comedies. In fact, in the Best-Picture Awards department (excluding Mankiewicz's *All about Eve* and Mike Todd's *Around the World in 80 Days*—not really outright comedies), there was a seventeen-year comedy dry spell (1944–60) between McCarey's *Going My Way* and Wilder's *The Apartment* —two great motion pictures that dramatized and epitomized the seventeen-year growth of cynicism in our national attitudes and in our Hollywood films. And yet the daring villainy of the non-hero of the fifties was but a pale prelude to the savagery of the *anti-hero* of the sixties.

But it was still 1958 for me. *A Hole in the Head* was filled with what we used to call unpleasant characters. The leading man was a grandstanding, dame-chasing wastrel; rearing a ten-year-old son in an atmosphere both sinful and phony. Could I fit such non-heroes into my own style of warm human comedy? If I couldn't, I might as well hang up my kind of laughs.

But after viewing *A Hole in the Head*, most of the important critics said, "Yes! Capra *can* handle the non-hero genre."

The *Hollywood Reporter* summed up press reactions with this sentence:

> The creator of a succession of the finest comedy-dramas in the history of show business . . . is back (after 8 years) with all his past techniques in full blossom and with a wonderfully new ability to capture the flavor of our times . . . [with] a comedy that registers its success not in chuckles, but in roars . . .

And *The New York Times* flipped its masthead. Here's Bosley Crowther's peroration to a most generous notice:

> . . . But the prize goes to Mr. Sinatra, who makes the hero of this vibrant color film a soft-hearted, hardboiled, white-souled black sheep whom we will cherish, along with Mr. Deeds and Mr. Smith, as one of the great guys that Mr. Capra has escorted to the American screen.

Audiences also approved of my non-hero comedy—everybody with a piece of *A Hole in the Head* made a handsome profit.

But most important, *I* realized that my style of comedy could be fitted to the hard-knock school. Technically, I handled color and the new wide film with ease. Production-wise, I brought in *Hole* one week under schedule (thanks to Bill Daniels, one of the fastest and best of Hollywood's top cameramen), and at the incredibly low cost of $1,800,000. But I knew I had something else going for me besides technical savvy, and that was a *creative* savvy uniquely mine. I could add heart and humor to the non-hero genus.

What ten thousand kinds of a fool ever persuaded me to quit films in the first place? I was only sixty-one years old. Yes, sir. One more chance at a non-hero film and I would again take my rightful place in Hollywood's room at the top. My big chance materialized before I could say, "Good night, Mrs. Calabash, wherever you are!"

I have mentioned elsewhere that directors are in some ways closer to their stars than to their families. The reverse is just as true: Actors know more about directors than fireplugs know about dogs. Out of my one-picture association with Sinatra, a mutual admiration society sprang up between us. In interview after interview I disappointed the press by extolling both Sinatra's talent and his cooperation. Whatever tales of woe other directors had to relate about Sinatra's intransigence did not apply to my experience—as witness the fact that we finished *Hole* under schedule and under budget.

My rapport with Frank was something special, and mostly unspoken. We liked, respected, and admired each other and never said anything about it. I couldn't help knowing, of course, that he did not live with the mother of his three children, or noticing that he was wildly in love with his offspring, and that at times he appeared more than just fond of their mother.

Once I praised his acting ability, told him that when he was ready to grow up, kick the hoopla habit, and take acting seriously, there was a picture I wanted to make about a dynamic, colorful personality who changed history —St. Paul: the savage persecutor of early Christians, who turned right around and became Christ's first and greatest missionary and His thirteenth Apostle. Until now I had thought only one actor had the range and the power to play the part—Jimmy Cagney. But now there was another; another with the power to attract, sway, cajole, convince. And that was Francesco Sinatra, bad boy of the saloon singers. He could play Saul who became Paul—when he was ready to kiss off rat packs, beauty queens, and hipsters.

The item made the columns; it triggered an avalanche of indignant letters from shocked readers. I still say Sinatra is top-drawer casting for Paul. For underneath "all that jazz," there is heartbreak in Sinatra's pleasure-go-round; heartbreak that could find release in total commitment to a spiritual ideal.

After retiring in 1952, then spending six quiet years making educational films in the eye of Hollywood's hurricane, *A Hole in the Head* developed. The winds blew in, tom toms beat out—and I found myself back in the present tense of make-believe's sound and fury. That's Hollywood.

On February 7, 1959, at the Directors Guild annual dinner, my fellow directors honored me with their highest tribute: the D. W. Griffith Award for outstanding contribution to the film director's art. Only four others had received this esteemed laurel—C. B. De Mille, John Ford, Henry King, and King Vidor.

A few days later, Frank Sinatra invited Lu and me (he called her Lucy) to be his guests at the Sands Hotel, Las Vegas, where he was giving solo performances. Important conference, he said. We took along Jim and Marion Warner, and were ushered to a V.I.P. table which turned out to be a table leg surmounted by a table top smaller than a pizza pie. For wherever the Leader performed there was breathing room only. And there he stood and sang! The champ. Magnetic. Sensual. The greatest saloon singer of all time, playing on the emotions of his beloved saloon audience with the artistry of Toscanini conducting Beethoven's Ninth.

It was during late supper in one of the lounge booths that Sinatra stunned me with his sudden question, "How would you like to produce and direct a film with me, Dean Martin, and Bing Crosby?"

"Geez, Frank!" I stuttered. "Throw in Garbo and I'll consider it."

"Ain't that the greatest? Sammy Cahn came up with it. The life of Jimmy Durante and his two pals, Lou Clayton and Eddie Jackson. The ups and downs of the greatest team of laff-getters to ever hit show business. You like?"

"Does Jimmy Durante like?"

"Wild about it. And so is Dino, and so is the Bingle. But we need you, Cheech, to pull it all together. Even-steven four-way split—you, me, Dean, and Bing—on everything. I'll take last billing. We'll kill 'em, Cheech! With that combo we'll murder the people—"

For Abe Lastfogel and the William Morris Agency, putting together a Sinatra-Crosby-Martin-Capra package was like trying to stuff four jacks-in-the-box into a cigarette case. Hold one down, the other three would spring out. The preliminaries alone were staggering. Four corporations were involved. Four wrangling over-officious sets of agents, lawyers, and tax experts split fees and infinitives. To appease and coordinate them, a disinterested *fifth* firm of legal minds—O'Melveny and Myers—was hired. In Hollywood there was no business but star business now.

Months passed while lawyers haggled, and the three stars busily made millions in recordings, radio, television, and other films. But I, merely the producer and director, twiddled my thumbs and took solace in John Milton's comforting line "They also serve who stand and wait."

But I belong to the lucky. Nice things happen to us even while we "stand and wait."

On May 26, I was again elected president of the Screen Directors Guild, mainly to supervise merging our Guild and the Radio and Television Guild of America into one national organization of radio, television, and film directors and their staffs.

On June 4, our daughter Lulu graduated from Pomona College with a B.A. in philosophy and literature, and made immediate plans to enter Harvard University for a Master's degree in education.

On June 12, at exactly 7 P.M., I was in Burbank attending an emergency meeting of NBC's labor negotiators and Guild officers (George Sidney and Joe Youngerman) in John West's NBC offices. The hassle: our Guild claimed jurisdiction over TV tape machines. We had made strike noises. John West suggested we go look at a tape machine. He led our angry group of eight down studio streets, and into a stage. He hushed us to be quiet—a live TV

show was being broadcast. We followed him in single file, threading lights
and ducking mike booms—when a hand clutched my arm and pulled me in
front of hot blinding lights. I heard a voice, a familiar TV voice: "Welcome
Frank Capra to *This Is Your Life.*"

It was Ralph Edwards and his famous show. NBC executives and Guild
officers had tricked me into an emergency labor meeting, then delivered me
to Ralph Edwards on the exact second.

On July 16, Frank Capra 3rd was born in Escondido's Palomar Hospital.
Californians being that way about their Golden State, Sergeant Frank, Jr.,
had sent Priscilla from New Jersey to Fallbrook so that little Frank could be
born as a fifth-generation native Californian. Dr. Edwin Powell spanked out
our first grandchild's first cry, then he and his wife, Ruth, and Lu and I
celebrated by lapping up our fair share of Escondido's quota of the bubbly.
Priscilla came home to see proud twenty-five-year-old Frank Aye, Aye, off
to Fort Monmouth, while prouder sixty-three-year-old Grandpa Frank Aye,
and proudest eighteen-year-old Uncle Tom drove Frankie Aye, Aye, Aye,
home from the hospital—with Uncle Tom lost in wonderment at the newborn
miracle in his arms.

On August 8, Lu and I put the Durante story on the shelf and went "flying
down to Rio." Brazilian President Kubitschek had invited me—through
Harry Stone, my old Indian Film Festival side-kick (now head of the Eric
Johnston office in Brazil), and also through our Ambassador, John Moors
Cabot—to address the Rio and São Paolo branches of the Society of Theater
Arts. I'll go to the dark side of the moon if anyone buys me a round-trip
ticket.

There was good news waiting for us when we returned to Hollywood. My
old friend and ex-partner, Sam Briskin (temporarily head of Columbia
Studios since Cohn's death), had offered the best deal for the Durante story.
I phoned Sinatra's office. Would Mr. Sinatra arrange a meeting of the
principals? He did. Crosby, Martin, Sinatra, and I met for lunch at Sinatra's
Puccini Restaurant on South Beverly Drive. I gave them the highlights of
Columbia's offer.

1. Columbia will put up $5 million to make film, without approval of
   script, and *without interest.*
2. Columbia agrees that Crosby, Sinatra, Martin, and Capra shall each
   draw $250,000 in salary from the venture.
3. Durante to receive $250,000 for life story, clearances from his partners
   or heirs, all music rights to Durante's songs, and film rights to Gene
   Fowler's book *Schnozzola.*
4. Film to be made at Columbia Studios as a co-venture between five
   corporations: Columbia's, Sinatra's, Crosby's, Martin's, and Capra's.
5. Each of the five corporations to own one-fifth of the film.
6. Columbia will distribute film—domestic fee: 25 percent; foreign: 35
   percent.

There was much jubilation and pumping of hands. Greatest deal ever offered. "Take it!" all said. Only Crosby was a bit rueful—like a fox. He felt hemmed in by the "Mafia" he quipped. "Hey, Capra. We're old pals, remember? You gotta take care of me. Between these two highbinders here I feel like an inside-out sandwich—a thin piece of Irish bread between two big slices of Sicilian salami." Frank and Dean gave it back to him. They know the old Groaner. Lets Bob Hope beat his brains out while he relaxes and gets all the boffos. A couple of toasts. All agree verbally. I'm instructed to move into Columbia Studios to prepare the production. The Durante story was on. Hallelujah!

On the day I moved into Columbia Studios (October 2, 1959), the *Hollywood Reporter* announced: "Columbia closes deal for *Durante Story* 3 star package deal . . ." And *Variety* called it "one of the most spectacular deals ever entered into by an independent group."

I began preparing the screenplay with two pretty good handicaps. One, there were no writers available; the Writers Guild had called a strike. And, two, strike or no strike, I could only hire people with my own money. My wealthy star partners would not advance a dime to the project until their convention of lawyers had arrived at a consensus. And so Capra, the out-of-action partner, not only "served" while "standing and waiting"; he also paid all the venture's bills.

On November 11, 1959, I sent my partners a seventy-five-page treatment, interspersed with key dialogue scenes. Anyone who had been in film production for over two weeks would have immediately seen that that treatment contained the ingredients for one of the great pictures of all time. But my partners were stars! Big business! Presidents of many corporations! They had flunkies to read for them. Silence. No comment on my treatment nor on my numerous memos.

On the fifteenth day of January, 1960—eleven months after Sinatra had called me to Las Vegas and said: "Cheech, we need *you* to pull it all together"—the mob of lawyers, agents, and tax experts that had conceived so diligently in Sinatra's office for months, now labored mightily and brought forth an agreement that was as binding as the kiss of a whore.

EXAMPLE: "No capital shall be required from any joint venturer except by unanimous approval of all parties . . ." Any partner could veto paying any bill.

EXAMPLE: Regarding what each corporation shall furnish, each star's company promises not to necessarily furnish Sinatra, Crosby, or Martin, but "to furnish the services of a male co-star of a caliber pre-eminent in the industry . . ." If said male star not agreeable to others, "this joint venture shall terminate at the option of any party . . ."

When my temperature cooled to 103, I wrote the following letter to Abe Lastfogel:

Dear Abe:

I have read the draft of the co-venture agreement for the production of the Durante story.

It is so full of ifs, ands, and buts; so filled with reservations, and so permeated with ways in which the picture can *not* be made, that I seriously doubt the picture will be made at all.

Since I have already spent about a year's time on this project without any income—besides having advanced about twenty thousand dollars of my company's money—I have to make a decision as to whether I stay with the venture, or withdraw . . .

The agreement calls for *four* producers. It's tough enough for *one* producer to prepare and complete this picture, but with four I can only see confusion compounded . . .

Therefore, Frank Capra and Frank Capra Productions are withdrawing from the co-venture forthwith. Whatever material has been written by Capra . . . will remain the property of Frank Capra Productions . . . Will you please notify the other members . . . of my decision. . . .

In Sinatra's letter (January 26) to Bing, Dean, and Frank, he admits he had four producers in mind at all times:

> . . . While Frank Capra was to be the individual producer and director, I always thought of this project as one in which all four of us would make the basic decisions. . . .

A great, great film was killed by stars. The first leak of its death was a phony. The *Hollywood Reporter* headlined (February 9): "Durante picture latest casualty in writer strike."

Louella Parsons got closer to the truth (February 13):

> It was director Frank Capra's decision to bow out of *The Jimmy Durante Story*, but he isn't talking.

Army Archer (Daily *Variety*, March 8) hit it on the nose:

> The low-down on Frank Capra's bow out is he couldn't take four producers on one film . . .

Jimmy Durante was heart-broken about the blow-up, but never a harsh word out of him. "I guess dey can't find nobody who looks like me or sounds like me," joked the possessor of the prominent proboscis to Rick Du Brow, New York *Telegraph* reporter.

> We had another problem, too—dose tree guys are too busy . . . dey got too many irons in da fire.
> Da director, Frank Capra, finally quit after waitin' for dem . . . He couldn't waste his life on da pitcher . . . I got no complaints, I can still smoke a good cigar . . . Da best ting I got, though, is my health. God gave me dat. And I'm still able to work and help a few people.

The world was in a confused turmoil—wars, H-bombs, confrontations, fear, hate, hate. And Hollywood was feeding the confusion with a steady diet of sex, violence, and lewdness. What wisdom needed, to catch up with our runaway technology, was time. And time might be bought not with violence, but with compassion—that divine unguent that lubricates and soothes our abrasive human hates. Compassion might just possibly slow down the ticking till we could defuse the world with reason.

And we had had an outside chance of buying a little precious extra time by filming the life of Schnozzola, the great compassionate clown. A chance that got lost among stars and their satellites. Pity. Pity.

Now what would I do? Certainly the world didn't need *more* films about sex, violence, and lewdness. Judging by contemporary Hollywood films, the United States was made up of sexpots, homosexuals, lesbians, Marquis de Sades, junkies, too! too! beautiful people, country-club liberals, draft-card burners, and theatrical and religious figures bleeding make-believe blood for Cause and Camera. "Shock films," they called them; "skin flicks" that dealt not with the humorous, honest, robust, Rabelaisian earthiness that *nurtures* life, but with the cologned, pretentious, effete, adulterated crud that *pollutes* life.

But what about the moral "self-policing Production Code" of the Motion Picture Producers Association? Oh, its administrators shrugged, grew longer sideburns, and "amended" the Code into sterility by slow castration. And what about the Catholic Church's "Legion of Decency," the powerful watchdog of film morals? It, too, "fell in with the times" and gradually deteriorated into a toothless, meaningless group that piously fly-specked films for any unholy depredations against such "absolute truths" as: priests wearing wrong vestments, a too flagrant flaunting of divorce "laws," and violations against the sacred rite of eating fish on Fridays. Flout the spirit of morality all you want; but respect the letter—if you want the Legion to pass your film as "okay for families." As it did for *Bonnie and Clyde*.

Forgotten among the hue-and-criers were the hard-working stiffs that came home too tired to shout or demonstrate in streets—steel workers, bus drivers, salesmen, telephone operators, secretaries, dressmakers—the old reliables who paid their bills and taxes that supported rich and poor alike, and prayed they'd have enough left over to keep their kids in college, despite their knowing that some were pot-smoking, parasitic parent-haters.

Who would make films about, and for, these uncomplaining, unsqueaky wheels that greased the squeaky? Not me. My "one man, one film" Hollywood had ceased to exist. Actors had sliced it up into capital gains. And yet—mankind needed dramatizations of the truth that man is essentially good, a living atom of divinity; that compassion for others, friend or foe, is the noblest of all virtues. Films must be made to say these things, to counteract the violence and the meanness, to buy time to demobilize the hatreds.

Someone should keep reminding Mr. Average Man that he was born free, divine, strong; uncrushable by fate, society, or hell itself; and that he is a child of God, equal heir to all the bounties of God; and that goodness is riches, kindness is power, and freedom is glory. Above all, every man is born with an inner capacity to take him as far as his imagination can dream or envision—providing he is *free* to dream and envision.

A sculptor may say: "There's a man imprisoned in this block of stone who cries to be free. I can loose that man by chiselling away the constraining dross." Well, as a filmmaker I could say—and should continue saying—"There's a divine nobility imprisoned in each man's primitive nature. I can loose that nobility by stripping away the animalistic dross."

But was I the only filmmaker that could, or would, produce films that said these things? Was that my mission? Other directors were apparently taking the violent route—violent films for violent times. Sentiment was old-fashioned. Hardness was "in." Okay. I'll be the maverick. A nonconformist. I'll make sentimental films until my audience cries, "No more!" But on one condition. I will not take orders from, or kowtow to, any fat-headed star—male, female, or guess what.

In an interview in *The New York Times* (April 28, 1960), I outlined my next three film projects:

1. Gore Vidal's hit play, *Best Man*, a modern version of Mr. Smith's idealism emerging from the no-holds-barred shenanigans at a Republican National Convention. Vidal would write the script. The film—starring Spencer Tracy, I hoped—would be produced a year hence, after I had finished—

2. *Pocketful of Miracles*, a modern version of *Lady for a Day*. I had had such good luck putting my style of heart and humor into Arnold Schulman's *A Hole in the Head*, a story of contemporary non-heroes, that I wanted to experiment with retelling Damon Runyon's fairy tale with rock-hard, non-hero gangsters. Possible casting for Apple Annie— Shirley Booth or Helen Hayes. Harry Tugend was writing new script. And—

3. Rebecca West's *The Meaning of Treason*, the fascinating political and psychological in-depth study of "Lord Haw-Haw," the Irish defector who broadcast anti-English propaganda to the British for the Nazis in World War II. A story of a traitor's redemption—from the most-hated man in England, to the best-loved prisoner, to tears at his hanging.

CHAPTER 23

Pocketful of Troubles

UNITED ARTISTS agreed to finance and distribute *Pocketful of Miracles*, if—Frank Capra Productions could sign up one incandescent superstar, or two workaday stars that could twinkle but not dazzle. So FCP bought the remake rights to *Lady for a Day* from Columbia Pictures for $225,000 (thirty years earlier we paid Damon Runyon fifteen hundred for his original story, "Madame La Gimp"), and moved into Paramount Studios on a rental basis, and searched Hollywood's heaven for a super-nova or two prosaic novas to scintillate in the starring roles.

The two biggest parts were, of course, Dave the Dude, tough, cocky, but superstitious midtown bootlegger who is feuding with the mob for control of the Manhattan territory, and Apple Annie, the ruthless ruler of the Times Square panhandlers, who gets in a jam by living a lie to her illegitimate daughter. There was another role that a third star might play: "Queenie" Martin, a cynical "over the hill" moll and night-club owner of the Texas Guinan ("Hello, sucker!") type.

I had a superb script, the end result of many talents: Bob Riskin's original version of thirty years earlier, Harry Tugend's modern version of one year ago, and the final version by Hal Kantor, aided and very much abetted by Jimmy Cannon, New York sports writer for Hearst, and superb slinger of Broadway's argot.

"What do you want me to do, Frank?" "Jimmy, take Kantor's script and rewrite every line of it in your own lingo." He did. I kept what lines I wanted. They got many an audience boffo for which Cannon was not credited. (Tugend and Kantor were the writers of record, and the Writers Guild allowed only two screen credits per screenplay.)

With such a script I anticipated no sweat signing stars. Ideal super-novas for Dave the Dude role: Frank Sinatra or Dean Martin. "Yes, yes, yes!" said United Artists. "Either one most acceptable." I sent a script to Frank. It bounced back with the speed of Don Budge's backhand. "Mr. Sinatra passes," said the secretary. I sent a script to Dean. It came back faster than Pancho Gonzales' first serve. "Mr. Martin passes," said the secretary. Two rolls, two snake eyes. We're even. I had thrown them a double six on the Durante story.

I had my sights on another ballsy young actor who threw out seismic hints of erupting into a luminary, Steve McQueen. But McQueen didn't wiggle UA's needle—yet. Unacceptable. There *would* be some sweat.

Joe Sistrom and I were having spaghetti and meat balls for lunch at the Naples Restaurant on Gower Street. Glenn Ford stopped at our table on his way out. "Glenn!" I greeted. "What're you doing out of make-up?" Glenn was in more pictures than the President's bodyguards.

"My astrologer says I'm to play the part of Dave the Dude for Mr. Frank Capra's *Pocketful of Miracles.*"

"Tell your astrologer I'll take an azimuth bearing on United Artists and let him know in an hour."

Long-distance phones buzzed at UA. The verdict: Ford unacceptable as a superstar. Acceptable if teamed with a strong female nova. Progress, at least. I called Glenn Ford's agent. One guess. Right. My agent, too—the William Morris office, Abe Lastfogel, president. Ford's terms: Make *Pocketful* as a co-venture film between Frank Capra Productions and Glenn Ford's Newton Productions. "Forget it, Abe. I want no hams co-producing my pictures."

"Frank, it's a new ball game," argued Lastfogel. "No way you can make a picture today except with a star as your partner—"

"Ridiculous, Abe. Who else can play Dave the Dude?"

"No star, Frank. Not on straight salary. Stars all want a piece of the action, the biggest piece. Take Glenn, will you? He's the most cooperative actor in Hollywood. Besides, I'll be the arbitrator for the co-venture. I can handle Ford. He's not like Sinatra—"

"You guarantee that Ford is *half* as cooperative as Sinatra and one-tenth the draw, and you've got a deal—"

It was really my first and last professional compromise. But it was fateful— the first link in a concatenation of further compromises that led to—Anyway, it was all quite incredible even in the land of make-believe.

For example—Abe Lastfogel was the agent representing all *four clients* in the Capra-Ford deal: producer-director Frank Capra (a hired man), Frank Capra Productions (a hiring corporation), actor-star Glenn Ford (a hired man), Ford's Newton Productions (a hiring corporation). Mr. Lastfogel's William Morris Agency (and all other talent agencies that put together package deals) negotiated for both employers and employees and collected 10 percent of their respective salaries and profits. Cozy. You wouldn't think there was any *additional* way in which an agency would have it made. But there was.

On paper, I was the producer-director for the co-venture. That was on paper. Legally, all partners in a co-venture have an equal vote regardless of whether individual partners own one percent or 99 percent of the venture. That meant that, technically and lawfully, Glenn Ford had a voice equal to mine in all film production decisions. What happened if we disagreed? The co-venturers had to give the tie-breaking vote to a disinterested third party. And who was the agreed-upon "disinterested" third party in our deal? Correct. Abe Lastfogel. With his power to vote either with Ford or with Capra, Lastfogel was, in fact, the *executive-producer* of the film.

At any rate, while I attended a four-day National Strategy Seminar with top U.S. Defense officials at the U.S. Army War College, at Carlisle Barracks, Pennsylvania, Lastfogel worked out the package deal for FRANTON, as the co-venture was so unimaginatively called. United Artists would get 20 percent of the profits for financing, and the Capra and Ford companies would split 80 percent. But Ford would receive a cash salary of $350,000 for ten weeks of his time—$35,000 a week! I would receive, for my sixty-five-week stint as producer-director-writer-editor, about $1,500 per week.

But United Artists would not sign the deal until I came up with a strong *female* co-star of nova magnitude. How many stars could play a drunken hag like Apple Annie? Shirley Booth? She played a wonderful slob in *Come Back, Little Sheba.*

Shirley wanted to see the old film, *Lady for a Day.* She saw it alone in a Columbia projection room; came out red-eyed; announced she could never, never top May Robson—and ran off.

There was Helen Hayes. What an interesting Apple Annie she would make. I sent her a script. Back came a telegram:

> DEAR FRANK THAT IS ONE WHALE OF A SCRIPT I
> LAUGHED AND I CRIED I SHALL BE MOST GRATEFUL
> AND HAPPY TO BE A PART OF IT ALL FONDLY
> HELEN HAYES

What a joy it would be to work with Helen Hayes. Glenn Ford, UA, and Abe Lastfogel approved her for Apple Annie. United Artists would sign the deal—as soon as Glenn Ford signed up on behalf of *his* company. But Glenn Ford suddenly developed writer's cramp. He wanted more coaxing— and more fringe benefits. His demands: The co-venture must hire his own personal make-up man, wardrobe man, secretary, chauffeur, publicity man, still man. All clothes he wore in the film must be tailor-made, and must become Ford's personal property at no cost to him. He must also have first choice on any special furniture or props bought for the film. "Frank," said Abe Lastfogel, "make the boy happy. Give him these picayune things." I made the boy happy. He promised to sign the UA deal in a day or two.

I sent Lucy Kroll (Helen Hayes's agent) a telegram asking her to please tell Helen how delighted I was, and would she please send me Helen's salary terms. Good. Now to cast the brassy "Texas Guinan" role. There was only one woman I wanted—Shirley Jones. As the prostitute in *Elmer Gantry*, Shirley nearly stole the show from Burt Lancaster. She, too, was a client of William Morris. "Frank, Miss Jones wants you to know she'll be delighted to play Queenie Martin," phoned Lennie Hirshan of the William Morris office. "Her price is seventy-five thousand for eight weeks." "Fine, Lennie. I'll clear it with Ford and call you back—"

I phoned Hirshan that Glenn Ford had approved; it was a commitment with Shirley Jones, and please give it to Louella or to Hedda for a lead story. Then I left Paramount Studios for a weekend at our Red Mountain ranch. Glenn Ford, Helen Hayes, Shirley Jones. Not bad. I whistled and sang all the way home.

"Darling," said Lu as I entered the living room, "call Abe Lastfogel right away at the Beverly-Wilshire Hotel."

"Abe, I just got here. Can't it wait?" "Gotta see you tonight, Frank. We're in a bind, but I can't talk on the phone. I'll be waiting around the pool—"

The pool area of Hernando Courtright's Beverly-Wilshire hacienda was dark. Curly-headed Abe Lastfogel sat alone at a patio table under a fringed umbrella. He motioned. I sat down. To laymen Lastfogel was only five foot four, but he rode tall in the saddle in show biz. He had put together and headed the USO in wartime. I knew by the way he whistled softly and drummed with his fingers that his computer brain was spinning its wheels.

"What's up, Abe?"

"Glenn Ford," he said and blew out some air. "Glenn doesn't want Shirley Jones to play Queenie Martin. He wants the part for his young friend, Hope Lange."

I laughed. "Abe, Glenn's ribbing you. Hope's a baby. *Twenty years* from now she'll be too young to play a Texas Guinan dame."

"He laid it on the line, Frank. If I don't vote with him on Hope Lange, he won't sign the United Artists contract."

"But did you tell Glenn that he committed himself to *Shirley Jones*? That we owe her seventy-five thousand whether she plays the part or *not*?"

"He says that's William Morris's headache, not his. He gave me till midnight. It's Hope Lange or he's out."

"Well, I'll be a sonofabitch." I jumped up to keep from blowing up. "Abe, look at me! Are you going to let some punk actor run your business? Fuck Glenn Ford! Let's replace *him*."

"With whom?" he asked with a tired sigh.

"With anybody. There must be a thousand actors in Holl——"

"Name one. That UA will lend money on. The fun's gone out of picture-making, Frank. Let's face it. If I vote with you against using Hope Lange, Ford pulls out. And UA cancels the picture unless you replace Glenn with another star. Which you're not going to do this year or next. And if you do, you'll just start all over again with a *new* co-venture. And the *new* star will tell you how to cast your film. Fun, huh?"

"Meantime, your Frank Capra company is stuck with a quarter of a million in story costs, and maybe another hundred G's for Helen Hayes if she's committed. Now, Frank. You tell me. As the third party, who do I vote for—you or Glenn? Every damn decision is a four-foot putt these days."

I have stated before that one of the prime assets a creative filmmaker *must* have is courage. Ten years earlier my choice would have been prompt and loud: To hell with Ford, Lastfogel, and money! But now I was sixty-four years old. My own statement—shouted from housetops—came back to haunt me: "It's a young man's game. Every film director over fifty should be put out to pasture."

What choice would I make as I walked alone around the block, while Lastfogel waited pool-side for my answer? Principle or money? I opted for money. And Frank Capra became a paper tiger. For Lady Luck smiles only on the valiant. And the voices of the "little people"—sprites, pixies, gremlins, genies—cheer not for the faint of heart, nor do fairy wings whir for the timid.

For forty years my films had all been shaped in the forge of enthusiasm, and filmed in an environment of gaiety. Actors were free to imagine, create, run as fast as they could with their parts. Fear was a stranger on our sets. We were young; we dared; we laughed. We had courage.

But *Pocketful of Miracles* was shaped in the fires of discord and filmed in an atmosphere of pain, strain, and loathing. Hate and fear smirked in the wings.

Glenn Ford, a garden-variety star, had accomplished what neither Mack Sennett, Harry Cohn, L. B. Mayer, nor Jack Warner had ever once been able to do: Compel me to shoot a film not my way, but *his*. Ford had challenged me, forced me to compromise, and that grinning, boyish Apollo galled me down to my last Sicilian chromosome. But he must not know it.

In a Machiavellian move to be a producer-director in fact as well as in name, I spread it around—Glenn Ford's brilliant notion to replace Shirley Jones with Hope Lange was a stroke of genius! I postponed the starting date for three months to give me time to rewrite the script and to dig and reach for magical formulas that might transmute the wisecracking Texas Guinan role into one more suitable to the callow innocence of Hope Lange.

I then sent Helen Hayes's agent this telegram:

> PICTURE POSTPONED UNTIL GLENN FORD AVAILABLE . . . AROUND MARCH FIRST. IF THAT DATE SUITABLE FOR HELEN PLEASE QUOTE ME HER PRICE FOR TEN WEEKS PLUS TWO . . .
>
> FRANK CAPRA

Back came a telegram from Lucy Kroll:

> . . . HELEN STATE DEPARTMENT TOUR . . . OPENS MARCH U.S. AND THEN 30 WEEK TOUR EUROPE AND LATIN AMERICA . . . HELEN AND I HEARTBROKEN OVER CONFLICT OF DATES . . .
>
> LUCY KROLL

And another from Helen:

DARLING FRANK WHAT A HEARTBREAK TO MISS THAT PLUM
OF A PART AND THAT WONDERFUL SCRIPT . . . LOVE
HELEN HAYES

I could have strangled Glenn Ford. Because he wanted Hope Lange, I lost Helen Hayes. Now who could play Apple Annie?

Joe Sistrom mused out loud in a casting session, "I wonder what Bette Davis is doing—" Of course. Perfect. She'd give Apple Annie the hardness we wanted. I discussed it with Glenn Ford. He lit up. "Bette! Dear old Bette! My old flame. She gave me my start as her leading man in *Stolen Life*, at Warners—"

I sent a script to Bette Davis through her MCA agent, then flew to New York to see her personally. She hit out first:

"Frank, you know Hollywood hates me, and I hate Hollywood . . . And it's a damn cinch that after five years, I'm not going back there to play a sentimental old hag . . . a bitchy part, yes . . . I like playing a bitch . . . but a sixty-year-old Cinderella? . . . Blech-h-h-h! . . . Besides your first choice was Helen Hayes . . . I wouldn't be talking to you except that my daughter read the script and said, 'Mother! You'd make the greatest Apple Annie in the world'—"

Bette Davis, a much bigger star than Glenn Ford, signed up for a salary. Away from Hollywood for years, she hadn't yet heard that stars incorporate themselves and demand "a piece of the action—the biggest piece."

Bette Davis was undoubtedly the best of all possible casting for Apple Annie, but Hope Lange? Well, she still stuck in my craw. Outwardly, I was a calm producer-director; inwardly, a vat of seething sour wine. Some bung had to blow. It blew. On New Year's Eve. Paper hats askew, we were caroling the birth of 1961 in the La Quinta Hotel dining room, when suddenly—a huge phantom bird sank three talons of its angry claw deep into my head and face, and tried to lift me. No warnings, nor preliminary signs. Just wham! A massive, killing pain over my right eye.

Leaving Lu, Jim and Marion, Frank and Priscilla to frolic it up, I clutched my head, stumbled out to the broad lawns, and skulked along oleander hedges to the deserted tennis courts. And there, in the darkness, I moaned, panted, ballooned my cheeks, blew out short bursts of air, licked hot lips, wiped tears that poured out of my right eye, and clawed at my head, trying to uproot the fiendish talons from their iron grip.

One racking hour later, the talons let go. The paroxysm eased as suddenly as it had convulsed. Euphoria set in. Lu and Frank, Jr., found me chuckling to myself. "It's gone, darling! A whopping headache. But it's gone—"

What was all that pain about? In bed, in the dark, just before we leave the conscious world, we are alone, very alone. Is falling asleep a rehearsal for death, and waking up a personal resurrection? Are dreams out-of-focus visions of life hereafter? I don't know. But I do know that just before sleep I

shed the armor of pretense and lie naked, unsure, frightened. I add up the
day's score—it's against me. I replay the day's events in slow motion—I
missed most of my assignments. Many of us reach for a pill or a prayer to
help us through the night. But ever since I was a child prayer had been a
problem. To me, most prayers were selfish. "O Lord, help *me* get a job . . .
Help *my* children . . . Save *my* soul—and to hell with all the others!"
("Three coins in a fountain . . . make it *mine*, make it *mine!*") Gimme,
gimme, God. So I made up a childish prayer that included everybody:
"Lord, help us all to be good and kind, and give us peace in our house and
in all other houses." From constant repetition the words had become as
meaningless and ritualistic as *om, mani, padne, hum* on prayer wheels.

But the night the monstrous bird sank ghostly talons into my head, the
words welled up from deep within me; real; a soul cry. And when prayer is
for real it hangs out the door latch to your innards, and conscience pulls the
latch, enters, and lets you have it. "What was that pain all about? It's the
Judas pain. You welched; compromised; sold out."

Two more attacks that night left me groveling on the floor. In the morning
I called our doctor friend Stanley Imerman. Three different neurologists examined me; tumping, thumping; X rays of the head; encephalograms of the
brain waves. All normal. The agonizing attacks continued nightly—two,
three, four. There is no known cure for "cluster" headaches, said the experts,
and strongly advised calling off *Pocketful*. One neurologist suggested a possible palliative. "Horton's treatment" was rough. It consisted of a small injection of sodium phosphate, the dose doubling every day for some ten days. I
would try anything.

Imerman's nurse, Marcella, gave me the injections. About the fifth day I
walked around in a daze. My blood pressure plummeted to 85 or 90 after
each day's injection. But—my headaches lessened in length and in number.
Two weeks after the final injection they were gone—glory be! Now to finish
preparing *Pocketful of Miracles*. Principal photography was due to start in
five weeks.

The first indication that Lady Luck had deserted me—after a forty-year
honeymoon—occurred after the third day of shooting: That night the headaches returned. One each night, then two, three, four. I climbed walls. One
hour of excruciating agony, then some fitful sleep, only to wake up screaming
with pain. Lu and I had moved into an apartment at the Beverly-Comstock
Hotel. Almost nightly Dr. Imerman would come in response to her anxious
calls. He suggested "Horton's treatment" again. No! I couldn't be a zombie
and direct a film.

No one on the set, not even Art Black, my assistant, or Frank Capra, Jr.,
my second assistant, knew of the nightly ordeal. But my son did notice that
instead of whistling in the morning, I came in with a face that looked like
something a cartoonist had etched in over-ripe liver, and that in between
camera set-ups I'd collapse on my dressing room couch. In between set-ups
I would also break down and beseech the Almighty with a "gimme" prayer:

"Lord, I can take the damn headaches at night and still shoot this film. But please, don't let me get them in the daytime . . . not in the daytime, please . . ."

During the third week of shooting a bigger can of worms was opened. Glenn Ford gave a columnist an interview, to wit: He felt so grateful to Bette Davis for having started *him* on *his* path to success, that *he* had demanded Miss Davis be rescued from obscurity, and be given the role of Apple Annie in *his* starring film.

Well. I don't know what Bette Davis did the day she started Glenn on his career, but I sure know what she did when she read Glenn's interview. She flashed, and sparked, and crackled like an angry live wire thrashing in the wind . . . god*dam*dest insult . . . that sonofabitch Ford . . . helping *me* make a comeback . . . that shitheel . . . wouldn't let him help me out of a SEWER . . . thought *you* wanted me in this crappy picture, not Ford . . . knew I shouldn't've come to Hollywood . . . I hate it . . . hate Apple Annie . . . hate the picture . . . hate you most, Capra, for bringing me out here . . .

'Tis the law of the trolls and the leprechauns. When a favorite of theirs defects to the timid, 'tis written bad cess be allotted him not singly, but in bunches, big as bananas. The cameras were rolling. I sat in my chair. Dave the Dude had just informed the reluctant Judge that he must "marry" Apple Annie. "Apple Annie!" he cries. "Preposterous! . . . A frowsy hag with the breath of a dragon!"—and Wham! The three talons strike and plunge into my head.

I rose, shouted "Cut it!" —clamped my jaws and headed for my dressing room. Art Black and Frank, Jr., followed me. "Shut the door, Art—" I flopped on the couch and tossed in agony. "Headache again, Daddy?" "Yes, Frank. Don't tell a soul, hear? . . ." If news leaked out, confusion would rock the filming, and UA and the banks would force a replacement director on me.

Operation "Horton's treatment" was the most hush-hush shenanigan since the A-bomb's Manhattan Project. Every noon hour, I would slip into a curtained limousine, be driven around the Paramount lot to the alley back of the First Aid Department, where a sworn-to-secrecy nurse would sneak me in, inject me with my daily-doubled dose of sodium phosphate and sneak me back to the car. My blood pressure: 90; my energy: that of a mouse spun dry in a washing machine.

How could the filming of *Pocketful*, torn with discord and loathings, directed by a walking zombie, stumble through to completion—within its budget and schedule? By occupational pride that transcends hazards. Amateurs play for fun in fair weather. Professionals play to win in the teeth of torments. Despite Bette Davis's hatred for Ford, for her part, and for me; despite Glenn Ford's tying a knot in my guts every time he bounced into a scene like a musical comedy funny-man; despite my unfocused state between sleeping and waking—at times I seemed to see the world from the inside of a beer bottle—I kept plugging away at my film chores . . . "Set the camera up here, Bronner . . . Dolly back with Mr. Horton . . . Eddie, turn at the door and give him one of your curled-lip sneers . . . Bette, pull up your

Pocketful of Miracles, a co-venture between Frank Capra and Glenn Ford, starts filming with sleepless nights and fearful days.

The brutal "cluster" headaches hit again; three to four each night. I silently pray they will not hit during the daytime. They do.

Toward end of film I begin to look as scrofulous as Apple Annie.

skirts and do a jig with Glenn . . . Hope, fight back till he tears everything off but your fig leaf . . . Mickey, flip every card *in* the hat when you snore, miss only when you're awake . . . Peter Falk—"

Peter Falk was my joy, my anchor to reality. Introducing that remarkable talent to the techniques of comedy made me forget pains, tired blood, and maniacal hankerings to murder Glenn Ford. Thank you, Peter Falk.

The chips were down. At 9 P.M., August 18, 1961, the gum-chewing projectionist in the booth of Oakland's Paramount Theater pressed a switch. The big wheel spun, the little ball rolled. The title: Frank Capra's *Pocketful of Miracles* flashed on the screen. A packed preview audience applauded politely. Round and round the little ball goes, and where it stops . . . ?

In the last orchestra row, Joe Sistrom, associate producer, and Frank Capra, Jr., second assistant director, sucked in deep breaths and crossed their fingers. Next to them my wife, Lu, and our daughter, Lulu (on vacation from Harvard University), prayed silently, eyes closed. From the first row balcony, film editor Frank Keller covertly lowered a microphone that would bug the "jury"—and pressed the "record" switch on my infallible spy—the tape recorder.

Five hundred miles south, on the waterfront of San Diego's Mission Bay, in the plush bar of the Islandia Hotel, chain-smoking Frank Capra was downing his fourth Vodka Gibson. The drink did little to warm icy feet, or to dry clammy hands. Jerkily, he glanced at his wristwatch. "Credit titles about over now"—this to Lu's brother, Jim Warner, and his wife, Marion. "Big red apple on the screen now. Camera pulls back, it's Apple Annie selling apples in the rain . . ."

There was much more than profits or Frank Capra's reputation riding on that Oakland preview. The fate of a whole genre of previously successful films was at stake—the sentimental "entertainment" picture. *Pocketful of Miracles* offered that preview audience a clean-cut choice. It was shamefully sentimental; Capra-corn at its best, or worst. The "jury's" verdict would influence all Hollywood.

Filmmakers were mulling; soul-searching. Millions of non-voting American youths had been killed or maimed in the three major wars of the last forty years. The period between wars was shortening, and their elders were playing patty-cake with another wacky war in Southeast Asia. Enough nuclear weapons to blow up the world had been stockpiled. What in hell was going on in the land of the brave and the home of the free? There's got to be some changes made, Mr. President, Mr. Congressman, and Mr. Supreme Court Justice.

The winds of change blew through the dream factories of make-believe, tore at its crinoline tatters. Older filmmakers urged agonizing reappraisals, but within the democratic framework. Younger radicals said, "Hell, no! The framework's been rotted by termites. Tear it down and start over." But the hedonists, the homosexuals, the hemophilic bleeding hearts, the God-haters, the quick-buck artists who substituted shock for talent, all cried: "Shake 'em!

Rattle 'em! God is dead. Long live Pleasure! Nudity? Yea! Wife-swapping? Yea! Liberate the world from prudery. Emancipate our films from morality!" To which films like *Pocketful of Miracles* answered: "No! We must never emancipate our films from morality. Morality gained us our *freedoms*. Abandon morals and we turn back the clock!"

Could *Pocketful* help stay the trend toward the lewd, the brutal, and the cup of bitterness? The little ball bounced among the numbers. And where it stopped . . . ?

My watch said eleven twenty. The preview was over. They'd be filling out cards in the lobby now. "In five minutes," I said. "Joe Sistrom will call me in five minutes . . ."

Time ticked on; planets moved in their appointed orbits; traffic lights winked red, winked green . . . 11:45 P.M. . . . midnight . . . 1:30 A.M. . . . No calls. We sat in silence. Tears glistened in Marion's eyes. Failure . . . absolute failure . . . bitter, bitter failure . . . all that pain . . . all that work, by so many great people . . . defeat . . . despair . . . black . . . black . . . sinking . . .

A hand shook me. A voice came into focus. Jim Warner's voice. "Frank! Frank! The bartender's calling you."

I stumbled slowly to the phone, delaying the coup de grace. "Hello?" I heard a jumble of noises, a party or something. A voice on the phone . . .

"Yeah. Hello? Frank? . . . Joe Sistrom . . . JOE SISTROM . . . Well, fella, you can start counting your money . . . Pipe down, for Pete's sake. I can't hear Frank . . . Frank? You hear me? . . . I said you could start counting your money!"

"What's the gag, Joe?"

"GAG, for Pete's sake? Damndest preview I ever saw . . . They howled, they applauded . . . and the cards! Highest rating in . . . Here's Lu, Frank—"

"Darling?" She was crying. "I'm *so* happy for you, dear. It's the greatest preview of *all* your pictures . . . Frank Keller? Yes, he's here—"

"El Chief-o? Don't ask me any hard ones, boss, I've had a few . . . Do I *agree* with 'em? Mr. Capra, it's a gasser! Wait'll you hear the tapes . . . they laugh over half the lines—"

Just to make sure that the trolls and leprechauns who had abandoned us through the filming of *Pocketful*, hadn't perpetrated a huge joke at the Oakland preview, we immediately previewed the film again without change at the De Anza Theater in Riverside. This time, Joe Sistrom called me *before* the showing ended. "Incredible, Frank! It's bigger than Oakland!—"

The tapes proved him right. It *was* bigger than Oakland. We sneak-previewed it a third time, at the Broadway Theater in Santa Ana. And for the third time the audience roared their way through the showing and applauded loud and long when it ended.

I played the tapes of the previews over and over. There was no way I could challenge or disbelieve the logic of their electronic verdict: *Pocketful of Miracles* was a hit of enormous magnitude!

On Sunday night, September 24, president Arthur Krim held an after-dinner strategy meeting in his private bungalow at the Beverly Hills Hotel. Present: all the United Artists bigwigs of both coasts, Abe Lastfogel, my agent, and Eddie Small, the dean and venerated sage of Hollywood's independent producers. I was there, too, of course, but not really. I was still leapfrogging clouds from last night's showing of *Pocketful* in Long Beach. Yes, for the first time since that *Lost Horizon* disaster in Santa Barbara twenty-four years ago, I had dared the emotional meat grinder of another preview.

It was difficult to persuade myself that it was not all a dream as the happiest group of salesmen I ever saw began making book on *Pocketful's* grosses . . . "A minimum of twelve million" . . . "The way that audience went for it? *Twenty* million" . . . "I'll kiss anybody in Macy's window if it's under twenty-five . . ."

"Whoa, whoa! You guys," said Eddie Small laughing. "Remember, people who see previews bought tickets to see some *other* picture."

Abe Lastfogel asked president Arthur Krim if his United Artists salespeople had any plans for selling *Pocketful.* "Plans?" broke in Max Youngstein. "Hell, yes. *Big* plans, revolutionary plans. First, with its Yuletide theme, *Pocketful's* a natural to open on Christmas week. Should knock the goyim right on their Jingle Bells. Right?"

Then all the UA men combined to enthusiastically spring their revolutionary plan: Open *Pocketful not* in the normal, but trite, stale, unimaginative way of playing in one first-run theater in New York, and one in Los Angeles. No! Some seven other big films, including four of their own besides *Pocketful* —Kramer's *Judgment at Nuremberg*, Wilder's *One, Two, Three*, Wise's *West Side Story*, and Wyler's *Children's Hour*—were opening the old hackneyed way on Christmas week. Why? Because they had Christmas themes? Of course not. They were beating the Academy's December 31 deadline for award nominations. *And*—those seven big films had booked every first-run house that was worth a damn in New York and Los Angeles for Christmas week openings.

But—we *gotta* make *Pocketful* eligible for Academy nominations. It's a cinch to cop at least two awards, and the grosses will skyrocket. But what about a first-run theater? None left. Do we open it in the sticks in some Chick Sales? Not on your sweet life. "We have a sensational plan! Open *Pocketful not* in one or two cities, but in two *hundred* cities. And not in just *one* theater, but simultaneously in *all* the important neighborhood houses and drive-ins in those two hundred cities. Blanket the nation with a *Pocketful of Miracles* during Christmas week! How about that for a grabber?"

We all agreed it was a grabber. We drank toasts to its success—six hundred prints of *Pocketful* would play day and date in six hundred theaters come Christmas week. The pixies and the nixies cackled gleefully.

I ran *Pocketful* for the Hollywood press corps at a public preview in the Chinese Theater, Sunday night, October 15, 1961. The press reactions were indicative of the hopes and fears, the intellectual schisms, and the emotional tides of the confused early sixties—that twilight period between the setting of the good old days and the advent of the tough new years.

Mike Connolly in the *Hollywood Reporter*:
. . . shows us the way out of our dreary Tennessee Williams-ish rut . . . *Pocketful* pulls us back into the clean, fresh, upper air . . . Let's stay there.

Variety:
Once upon a time, Frank Capra's *Pocketful* . . . would have been an odds-on shoo-in for a happy ending at the ticket windows. But today the tracks are faster . . . yesterday's favorite is today's long-shot . . .

Lorraine Gauguin's "Hollywood Callboard" (syndicated):
. . . The whole audience, in a mass reaction, started to cheer and sections of the audience rose to their feet in a tribute that was deafening . . .

Ivan Spear, *Box Office*:
. . . signals the reversal of a trend . . .

Dick Williams, Los Angeles *Times*:
Is sweet corn as digestible to today's blasé audiences, especially the teen-agers, as it was a quarter of a century ago? . . .

Then I put on a private showing of *Pocketful* for Hollywood's "400" at the Directors Guild Theater. Ginger Rogers' reaction to the film: "Frank, it's so wonderful! What are you trying to do—bring back movies?" George Seaton: "It's a film that should make you proud." Sam Goldwyn: "I'll never be able to put on paper how much Frances and I loved it." John Lee Mahin: ". . . a triumph of the deliriously delightful over the dull and dogmatic downbeat." Jimmy Cannon, who wrote many of the funny lines, wired: "FRANK. I LAUGHED MY HEAD OFF . . . A UNIQUE COMEDY IN THIS TIME . . ."

There were some, of course, who didn't like the film, especially the self-proclaimed avant-gardists that make it an article of their bushido never to laugh. After all, being an avant-gardist is not funny, you know. But I was happy that one of my pet "new wave" guys, John Cassavetes, a Capra fan since a kid, was most enthusiastic: ". . . gives viewers a feeling of hope . . ." he said.

Could it be that my kind of sentiment and humor was still wanted—and needed?

Perhaps I wasn't too old yet. People get old, not ideals. Fed-up youth had begun its taunting of elders: "You hypocritical old poops, we're up to here with your bungling. Your two solutions for everything—'more money, more war'—are bankrupt answers. Get out of those chairs! We're foreclosing on the world!" Fed-up black people were beginning to cry out: "We were born in this Promised Land. We live for it, work for it, die for it. We demand our share of its milk and honey NOW!"

Change was in the air. Perhaps violent change. Perhaps now more than ever the world needed films that dramatized compassion, and said to confused, anxious, angry hearts: "Whoa! Violence produces backward changes. Don't be panicked into hate. Don't be afraid to love. You have a mission to evolve upward through brotherhood, mercy, tolerance."

Avidly I devoured what the big-city critics had to say about *Pocketful of Miracles.*

In New York:

A. H. Weiler, *The New York Times*:
. . . Repetition and a world faced with grimmer problems seem to have been excessively tough competition for this plot . . .

Wanda Hale, New York *Daily News*:
. . . rowdy humor and pardonable sentiment . . . crackling dialogue and competent acting . . .

Newsweek:
. . . [He] has taken a second-story approach to the house of sentiment and robbed it blind . . . It is happy news, that after 40 years in movies, Capra's way is as sure as ever . . .

Paul V. Beckley, New York *Herald Tribune*:
. . . an organ peal of rambunctious humor, the best of the past wrapped up in the best of the present . . .

In Chicago:

Doris Arden, *Sun-Times*:
Four stars! . . . warm, sentimental, funny film . . .

Ann Marsters, *American*:
. . . And you can take all the "avant-garde" dramas of twisted sex and sin—so-called realism—and throw them back in the ash heap . . .

Nina Hibbin, *Daily Worker*:
. . . reveals the ultimate emptiness of Capra's line of thought . . . [He] emerges, not as a humanist, but only as a peddler of sunbeams . . .

But regardless of critical reactions, I knew I was not a product of film critics, film studios, or even film talents. I was adopted by the world's average guy because I could communicate in the universal language of the heart. I was the hoi polloi's boy, of them and one of them. A soul brother. I knew them. They knew me. They had crowned me king of the filmmakers. And I would remain king of the film road until the common people of the world rejected me. Then, and only then, would Frank Capra be washed up. A dream? Perhaps. But real as rain to me.

The man on the street had yet to pass judgment on *Pocketful of Miracles.*
Expectations were that he would laud it and applaud it to the skies. The
Star led the Wise Men where? To a palace? No, to a stable. The vision: a
star. The reality: a stable. Life is a mixture of star and stable; glory and
grime.

On December 19, 1961, *Pocketful of Miracles* opened in six hundred
theaters throughout the country. "It opened soft," was UA's answer to my
phoned query. Next day I called again. All executives were "in conference."
Not one United Artists executive ever again called me or returned a call.

The picture opened and closed in all the principal cities before one could
say " 'Twas the night before Christmas." A wag might have added, "And all
through the house, not a ticket buyer was stirring, not even a souse . . ."

In a few weeks the film was playing the cheap "nabe" houses and the all-
night "dirties"—then finis. Gone. Out of circulation. *Pocketful* was the flop of
the year! My shocked mind withdrew into a vacuum of white silence.

Why? How could a film that was so immensely enjoyed and cheered at all
five successive previews, whose preview cards averaged the unheard of high
rating of 91.5 percent, suddenly fail for lack of customers? Why should "my
people" reject a film that had excited wise Hedda Hopper into predicting "it
will make a mint," and stampeded the movie theaters' own trade journal,
Film Bulletin, into printing such hosannas as, "EXHIBITORS! Roll out the red
carpet and order some extra tickets, because three-time Oscar winner Frank
Capra is going to be your Santa Claus this Christmas"?

Only two industry executives had predicted the disaster. My ex-partner
Sam Briskin, vice president and elder statesman at Columbia, and Leo Jaffe,
Columbia Studios' new chief, backed me up against the bar after my private
showing of *Pocketful* at the Directors Guild Theater and double-teamed me.
"Frank, don't be a schnook!" pleaded Sam. "Don't let those United Artists
mamzers open this great picture cold all over the country—" "Open it in one
classy little house in New York," chimed in Jaffe, "and in another classy little
house in L.A. here. That's ALL! And let the film run for six months or a
year. It's that kind of a picture. It cries for a build up—"

In my four decades as a filmmaker—from *Fultah Fisher's Boarding
House* to *Hole in the Head*—I had made a score of Army information films,
four one-hour TV science shows, and thirty-eight theatrical motion pictures.
Not one had been rejected by audiences. Only two of them—*Miracle Woman*
and *The Bitter Tea of General Yen*—had lost money. Mostly because they
were banned in the British Empire, one for irreverence, the other for miscegenation. But *all* had been acceptable to the John and Jane Does. For
forty years the people and I had had a "thing" going between us. That was
my secret, my strength, my belief, my dream. I could do no wrong as long as
I knew the people were with me.

Why the surprising failure with *Pocketful?* Sam Briskin might attribute it to
the colossal stupidity of United Artists in marketing the film. United Artists
might half-agree. I did *not* agree. The film played in theaters, hundreds of

theaters. My people didn't come. Had my "thing" with the average guy still been in effect, he would have trekked to Mecca to see *Pocketful*.

No, the cause of failure was not inept marketing, not inadequate advertising, not any commercial blunder. To me the real cause was deeply personal, deeply moral. No one with the enormous power to speak to hundreds of millions of his fellow men for two hours, and in the dark, should speak with a forked tongue. What he says must come straight from his heart, not his wallet.

Pocketful of Miracles was not the film I set out to make; it was the picture I chose to make for fear of losing a few bucks. And by that choice I sold out the artistic integrity that had been my trademark for forty years. As a consequence, and by some direct perception independent of any reasoning process, those who listened in the dark sensed what my lucky elves, trolls, and leprechauns had sensed when Glenn Ford made me lick his boots—I had lost that precious quality that endows dreams with purport and purpose. I had lost my courage. Fear had tainted the aura of the hoi polloi's hero. His "thing" with people lost its magic, and the people said, "Capra—we've had it from you."

To others that belong, or aspire to belong, to that privileged group of "one man, one film" makers, I dare to say: "Don't compromise. For only the valiant can create. Only the daring should make films. Only the morally courageous are worthy of speaking to their fellow men for two hours in the dark. And only the artistically incorrupt will earn and keep the people's trust."

Had I really lost my moxie—which had carried me further than all other talents combined? Yes, I had. My chronic film fever had cooled. I was sixty-four. In Hollywood there is no tradition. As with the man who sells umbrellas there are no yesterdays—it's rain or shine today. Filmmakers are tested and challenged daily. If they flinch, if they don't figuratively spit in the eyes of their challengers, the pack moves in to elbow them off the magic carpet.

When *Pocketful* came up empty there was dancing in the streets among the disciples of lewdness and violence. Sentiment was dead, they cried. And so was Capra, its aging missionary. *Viva* hard-core brutality: *Arriba* barnyard sex! *Arriba* SHOCK! Topless-shock! Bottomless-shock! Mass intercourse, mass rape, mass murder, kill for thrill—shock! shock! To hell with the good in man. Dredge up his evil—shock! shock!

Did I spit in anyone's eyes? Nope. I avoided them and went into hiding at our Fallbrook ranch. Everything about me was set for retirement—that is, everything but my ego. That hurt like a stone in my shoe. All over the world I was known as a home-run hitter. I couldn't bow out of films with a weak pop fly. One more home run, just one more—and I'd walk out of Hollywood with honor, maybe even with a twenty-one-gun salute. One more film. And make it *my* way, with no Glenn Fords around to change my mind.

Besides, I had a commitment. When that faceless little man rescued me from the river Styx a quarter of a century earlier, hadn't I vowed that down to my dying day, down to my last feeble talent, I would be totally committed to the service of man, to the making of films about we the people?

I recalled a paragraph in Bill Boehnel's review of *Meet John Doe* in the New York *World-Telegram*. It articulated my commitment:

For if the ideal of democracy is to remain alive, to weather today's storms, as it has weathered others, it must be stated and re-stated in a manner which will capture and stimulate the imagination of those who, in the long run, will decide if it is to perish or survive. And what better way than to make the John and Jane Does themselves the heroes and the heroines?

And yet—filmmaking is not a profession in which one can mellow gracefully. It is a hot-eyed, hot-juiced, high-staked game of unrecallable hunches and gut decisions no computer can make for you. The patina of wisdom that forms on us naturally after long exposure to life is, paradoxically, a handicap. In Hollywood one moves fast, thinks fast, and fades fast—those who think logically fading the fastest. Thus the vexing question about another film: had I lost the power to make quick decisions? My experience with Gore Vidal was not reassuring.

Playwright–author Gore Vidal is a caustic intellectual, a possessor of an eloquent bitchiness that I found entertaining. One would never expect him to also be a dedicated evangelist with a life-long mission. But he was. It was during the incredible previews of *Pocketful* that Vidal checked into my Paramount office with a first draft screenplay of his Broadway hit *The Best Man*, a funny but biting probe of how the tortuous politics of smoke-filled rooms make or break Presidential candidates at our national conventions.

I called Vidal's attention to the queer coincidence that all the main characters in his script were confirmed atheists. "No coincidence," he said. "I'd like to convert the whole damn world to atheism. It's my vocation."

Well, it sure as hell was not *my* vocation. Here we go again, I thought to myself. Glenn Ford used my last film to make himself a big man with a young chick. Now this gay blade wants to use my next film as a brochure for his anti-religious vanities. So I bowed out of *The Best Man*. Of course, I could have thrown Vidal out on his ear and hired another scriptwriter. But the point is, I didn't. I backed off from another confrontation. Backing off is not the way to make films, I thought to myself at my ranch hideout where, four months after *Pocketful*'s unmiraculous box-office performance, I still remained incommunicado. Which I did quite easily, thank you, without building fences or hanging up "no trespassing" signs.

I had always wanted to know what it felt like to "remain incommunicado." It has a certain ring to it, a romantic resonance that conjured up royalty, class, fame. Like the Aga Khan, Garbo, Erle Stanley Gardner, the "beautiful people." Well, being incommunicado is my idea of nothing. No visitors, no friends, no phone calls. As far as Hollywood was concerned, I had ceased to exist—perhaps never had existed. *Cleopatra* was breaking Mark Antony and

Twentieth Century-Fox; Henry Hathaway was trying to stop runaway covered wagons, runaway Iron Horses, and runaway actors in *How the West Was Won*; Ralph Nelson was making *Lilies of the Field*, a heartwarming show with Poitier and a gaggle of nuns that I wished I were making; Tony Richardson was mixing up an old English cocktail spiked with pratfalls and sex and calling it *Tom Jones*. But I remained incommunicado, if you please, in a hole of my own making. And what fun is there in hiding when no one's looking for you?

But two wonderful things happened that yanked me out of my portable hole. On May 5, 1962, our daughter Lulu and William G. Bruch were married in the San Diego chambers of Judge James C. Toothaker.

To top the wedding in schmaltz, Mayor Sam Yorty and the councilmen of Los Angeles declared May 12, 1962, as "Frank Capra Day," in honor of a newskid who got his first nosebleeds in their fair city's alleys. And the Los Angeles Chamber of Commerce combined with the Directors Guild to throw a party in honor of the "day."

Army Archer, of *Variety*, caught the spirit of the evening in his column:

> The State Dept. would have given the A-OK sign to the goings-on in Hollywood Saturday night when Frank Capra was toasted, roasted, scrolled, plaqued, etc., by the City Fathers and L.A.'s Chamber of Commerce for his 40 years of service to industry, city, country, fellow man, etc. . . . Capra is in the ready stage to blast off again for Uncle Sam —this time to rep us at the Red Czech film parley. And there are requests for him from Germany, South America, etc. . . . General Jimmy Stewart, who co-emceed the Capra caper: "Marlon Brando's making a fortune beating up women while I'm waiting for the next Frank Capra picture." . . . George Sidney, Directors Guild prexy: "This is the first time in the history of Hollywood, that the city of Los Angeles has officially recognized a creative talent." . . . John Ford added: "This is our greatest night in 51 years of motion picture making," and reminded the black-tie'd group of Capra's ability to direct—even while standing on his head. Frank then obliged by doing a neat headstand on the Guild stage! . . . After Jack Ford recalled that Frank had received the Order of British Empire (OBE) on the recommendation of Winston Churchill, Jack Ford chided the industry for permitting Capra to talk of retiring. (Capra told us he doesn't know what pictures to attempt in these strange times) . . . "Make those human comedy-dramas," said Ford, "the kind only you can make—the kind of films America is proud to show here, behind the iron curtain, the bamboo curtain—and behind the lace curtain." . . .

Driving home, Lu said: "Darling, now that Hollywood's given you its 'well done' watch, don't you think you ought to take the hint and retire?"

"What retire?" I shot back. "I not only think it, I *know* I can still make pictures better than anybody in this town." She groaned. Then, with a rare loss of patience: "I just knew that 'Frank Capra Day' stuff would ring some old fire bells."

Marty Rackin, a swinging, full-of-beans writer, had moved into a job that had a faster turnover than *Time*'s junior writers. He became production head of Paramount. "Frank," he said to me in his new office, "I know how badly you want to film that Luke book, *Dear and Glorious Physician.* I'm with you, pappy. It'll be bigger than *Ben Hur.* All you've got to do is first go to Spain and make a circus picture with John Wayne for Sam Bronston. Paramount's putting up the Duke and half the dough. Catch on? The circus picture goes over—I'll guarantee you I can talk Paramount and Bronston into letting you make the Luke thing in Spain—"

Lu and I, Joe Sistrom, and Frank Capra, Jr., and his wife Priscilla, all flew to Madrid to make a circus picture with John Wayne for Samuel Bronston and Paramount. At the time, Samuel Bronston was looked up to as one of the more incredible characters in an incredible business—an elegant and gracious old world combination of the financial wizardry of Ponzi, the flamboyant salesmanship of Barnum, and the largesse of Diamond Jim Brady. But all these qualities were secondary to a plaintive childlike compulsion—he wanted everybody to love him.

I looked forward to making a film with John Wayne. For years he had needled me about using Cooper, Gable, and Stewart, but never Wayne. But I had kept him in mind, because I was sure that in that big hunk of solid man there was the depth and the humanity of another Mr. Deeds, a Mr. Smith, or a John Doe. What I didn't realize was that when you took on Duke Wayne you took on a small empire. And part of that empire was a personal writer by the name of James Edward Grant.

Jimmy Grant was something new to me—a writer who attached himself to a male star and functioned as that star's confidant, adviser, bosom playpal, baby sitter, flatterer, string-puller, and personal Iago to incite mistrust between his meal ticket and film directors, especially name directors. On first meeting, Jimmy Grant struck me as one of Jonathan Swift's "hail, fellow, well met" chaps as he regaled us with hair-raising adventures he had had with Errol Flynn, the first star to whom Grant had been a guiding satellite.

But then Grant bragged about how he had convinced the Duke that he had gotten too big to be directed by "decrepit old bastards like John Ford," and all that Grant and Wayne needed was a young TV director they could handle. Or better still, Wayne should direct himself (as he did so disastrously in *The Alamo*).

I dismissed Grant as a big-mouth and ordered him to get busy writing a script for the original circus story Bronston had bought from one of his vice-presidents.

"You're outta your mind, Capra," said Grant. "No use writing anything till Wayne gets here. Duke makes his own pictures, now. So relax, fella. When he gets here, he and I will knock you out a screenplay in a week. All you gotta have in a John Wayne picture is a hoity-toity dame with big tits that Duke can throw over his knee and spank, and a collection of jerks he can smash in the face every five minutes. In between you fill in with gags, flags, and chases. That's all you need. His fans eat it up—"

After six months Sistrom and I had a beautiful script worked out, while Grant played golf and laughed at our efforts. "Wayne won't like it," he warned. But Wayne wasn't showing up in Spain. Rumors were that he was cruising the Caribbean in his yacht—a holdout for better terms on his new Paramount deal.

Three months later Duke Wayne showed up at Lisbon on his yacht. Jimmy Grant rushed to him with my script. Word came back to Bronston: Wayne no likee script. Wants new one written or he won't come to Madrid. Bronston had to choose between Capra and Wayne. I made it easy for him.

Henry Hathaway, a director pal of Wayne's, had just walked off a picture in England because *his* star, Kim Novak, had insisted on telling Henry how *he* should shoot a modern version of Maugham's *Of Human Bondage*. I told Bronston that Hank Hathaway was one of our best "get it done" directors who took no guff from any actor. "Sam, I beg you to ask Hathaway to replace me—"

As prescribed in the Directors Guild by-laws, a director that is asked to replace a fellow director cannot accept the assignment until he discusses it with the replaced director.

"Frank," asked Henry Hathaway as he walked into my room at the Castellana Hilton, "why in hell are you walking out on the Duke?"

"Hank, I'm not walking, I'm *running*. So do me a favor and take over. Oh, I got a tip for you. All you need in a John Wayne picture is a big dame with big tits that Wayne can wrestle with, and every five minutes big Duke must smash some jerk in the puss, got it? And in between you fill in with gags, flags, and chases. Rotsa ruck, Hank—"

After nine months of scriptwriting, casting (David Niven, Claudia Cardinale, Lilli Palmer), and auditioning circus acts, I fled Madrid with the same relief one flees Siberia. Again I avoided confrontation with one who challenged my "one man, one film" status. Sure it had piled up on John Wayne's heels. But whose heels are entirely free from taint? I could have kicked Jimmy Grant out of the country—just as Hathaway did after he took over. I could have cowed the big Duke into giving his best performance. I could have made a rousing hit out of *Circus*, and gone on to make *Dear and Glorious Physician*. But I didn't. Wayne, Paramount, and Bronston did their stuff. I didn't do mine.

And the big black bird again sank its phantom claw into my head and tore and let go, tore and let go, in a nightmarish ritual of agony and relief, agony and relief, so torturing that only an intense concentration on the boils of Job kept my marbles together.

"Cluster headaches," New York's learned headache specialist, Dr. Friedman, called them. "Because," he explained, "in their active stage they come in clusters, like grapes. We know very little about them, and less about how to treat them. But men over fifty-five very rarely suffer them. You must be some kind of a specimen." I was sixty-five. Well, as the stout lady they laced into the first corset said, "It figures."

Was there anything left worth living for? Oh, yes! In his last year in journalism at the University of Southern California, our younger boy Tom, managing editor of the *Daily Trojan,* met a beautiful student of Swedish ancestry, Carol Ealy. Nature took its appointed course and on Saturday, February 9, 1963, they were married in Spokane, Washington, by Rt. Rev. Msgr. John J. Coleman.

In the fall of 1963, my "clusters" (excuse the expression) went into a passive stage. I felt free to do a chore for the State Department. A year earlier, in accordance with the cultural and technical exchange agreement between the U.S. and U.S.S.R., the Society of Motion Picture and Television Engineers had hosted an exchange group of visiting Russian film engineers. In organizing a reciprocal visit the State Department called on the engineering society to choose three delegates (Dr. Deane R. White [chairman], Research Division, Du Pont; W.E. Gephart, President, General Film Laboratories; and E. M. Stifle, Eastman Kodak Eastern Division); State's representative was producer-director Frank Capra.

We arrived in Moscow October 20, 1963, and left November 11. In between we visited film and television studios, schools, factories, laboratories, and research centers in Moscow, Leningrad, and Kiev; the Kinap factory in Odessa; the Kazakh-Film studio in Alma Ata. All told, the visits covered 6,400 miles. On our return we submitted a combined technical report to State and to the S.M.P.T.E., most of which was published in the latter's technical *Journal.* My contribution was mostly on the production, distribution, and exhibition of the Soviet Union's theatrical films, with comments about their artistry, their techniques, and their educational and propaganda values.

Of enormous interest, I wrote in my report, was the freedom yeast that we sensed was fermenting with new vigor among artists and filmmakers. Stalin used to give wayward artists a simple choice: the party line or the wall. In fact, to shoot or not to shoot intransigent intellectuals was one of the rifts between Stalinists and anti-Stalinists. But Soviet writers need villains for their stories, as do writers everywhere. Even toothpaste commercials have their germs. Until shortly before our visit, Soviet writers had been limited to roughly three villains: Nazi Germany, American Imperialism, and the A-bomb.

But when Khrushchev cut Stalin's reputation to ribbons, he handed Soviet artists a windfall—a new "heavy!" And they made the most of it. Films, books, articles, and poetry lamented the people's sufferings under the unlamented Stalin. What artists may or may not have realized was that attacking Stalin was a backhanded way of attacking the whole Soviet system.

But Mr K. realized it. And he didn't buy it. So in March, 1963, he called a three-day Congress of Artists and laid it on the line to them with pleadings, exhortations, and threats that *all* artists "from the most merited and famous worker in literature and art to the young beginner" must blindly follow the Party line . . . And that Mr. K. may preach peaceful coexistence to avoid a nuclear war, but on the ideological front the war must go on. And he reminded them to "keep your weapons always in readiness for battle," for the Soviet system must prove supreme, if not by war, then by the salami method —one small slice at a time.

But war on any front is probably just as senseless to their artistic intelligentsia as it is to ours. No real artist can ever find complete satisfaction in the constant cynical use of his talents to glorify world conquest by *any* political party. He is dying to do some programs *without* the "commercials." And there you have a very interesting internal struggle—the artist against the dictator. It's as old as time. If you're a betting man, put your money on the artist.

In the spring of 1964, three years after the completion of *Pocketful of Miracles,* the Martin-Marietta Corporation, builders of the Titan rocket boosters, asked me to produce a futuristic space film the Martin people could donate as the opening exhibit in the permanent Science Building in the New York World's Fair. I leaped at the opportunity.

Reaching for the Stars was a twenty-minute film—combining real action and animation—of a future Manned Orbital Laboratory (M.O.L.) and its space "taxi" that shuttled back and forth from earth to the M.O.L. with supplies and relief crews. For the final docking in space, the screen darkened, and life-sized models of the M.O.L. and space "taxi"—complete with replicas of astronauts that "moved" inside—lighted up and completed their docking maneuvers over the heads of the viewers.

In researching space details, Howard Houseman, head of the William Morris New York office, called my attention to a book a writer client, Martin Caidin, had just written. *Marooned* dealt with an American astronaut whose re-entry retrorockets fail to fire, and the consequent dramatic rescue race between Russian and American space agencies. It read like great theater. I obtained an option and presented the project to Mike Frankovich, successor to Harry Cohn at Columbia Studios. Twenty-four years earlier I had given football star Frankovich his start in motion pictures. He had played a radio announcer in *Meet John Doe.*

Mike went for *Marooned* in a big way. I moved back into Columbia Studios in May, 1964. Walter Newman began writing what was to become a most magnificent script.

Three long frustrating years later, I backed off from *Marooned,* a beaten, discouraged man. Using his powers of script and budget approvals, Frankovich finally forced me into an impossible position: Make the film for under three million dollars or give up the project. I gave up the project. Whereupon, Frankovich took it over as his personal production, engaged John Sturges to direct it, and spent *eight* million in filming it.

When a Mike Frankovich could maneuver me out of the Columbia I had helped build into a major studio—and euchre me out of a pet film project—I had had it. In younger days I ate guys like Mike Frankovich for breakfast. And so, I retired—or, more truthfully, I was retired—from Hollywood. But *nobody* shook me off my catbird seat and stuffed my talents into his straitjacket. When I realized I had lost my power to make fast decisions—and those I made I worried about—I climbed down of my own persuasion, with my colors still flying. That little cockeyed "one man, one film" flag I had raised, in ignorance, in that Jewish gymnasium in San Francisco a half century earlier, was never lowered, never struck.

And so I relaxed, looked around me, and began to laugh again. And began to be very proud, and very grateful to many, many people. For I had lived a most wonderful life, been given an extremely rare privilege—a forty-five-year ride on the magic carpet of Film! Forty-five years of creative adventures, excitements, and an occasional accomplishment that exalted me to walk among the peaks.

I had helped create the golden era of films, the era when the Hollywood filmmakers of the thirties and forties—Cecil B. DeMille, John Ford, Henry King, Leo McCarey, George Cukor, Sidney Franklin, Victor Fleming, W. S. Van Dyke, Clarence Brown, Ernst Lubitsch, William Wellman, Mervyn LeRoy, Frank Borzage, Billy Wilder, Michael Curtiz, Alfred Hitchcock, Howard Hawks, Willie Wyler, King Vidor, and George Stevens—could take an audience by the scruff of the neck and make it shriek with laughter, weep with sorrow, or shake with terror. Giants they were, who thrilled the world with their own works, creative giants in love with their medium, fiercely proud of it, fiercely jealous of it.

Now that most of their voices are still, who is to speak for the American film—Sidney Lumet, Arthur Penn, Mike Nichols, Norman Jewison, Stanley Kubrick, Martin Ritt, Arthur Hiller? Perhaps. But not by degrading the values of love and glorifying its dementia.

Willie Wyler is still talking, but his voice is growing tired. David Lean speaks with art and authority, but he's British. Stanley Kubrick is trying his best to say something. He will—when he learns to say it simply. Norman Jewison said something simply—and beautifully—in *Heat of the Night*. Robert Wise said it most profitably in *West Side Story* and *Sound of Music*, as did George Cukor in *My Fair Lady*.

But the giants are mostly gone. The Marquis de Sade took over in the Sixties. There is one game hold-out: the last vestiges of heroics are the gaspings of tired, bloated, aged John Wayne. Almost everything else has been creep-hero stuff: glorifications of the "minus" people or apologies for the "brute" people. Gone the power of morality, of courage, of beauty, of the great love story.

What about the Seventies? There is a dawning, and a promise of future, and greater giants. Witness films such as *2001, Patton, Airport, Love Story,*

Ryan's Daughter. Since periodic cycles are normal in nature, perhaps mankind has its own cycle of expansion and compression—a sort of breathing in and out—and that at present we are in the fag end of an exhalation phase.

The American campus—which *should* be the fountainhead of ideals and vigorous new adventures in life—can seemingly come up only with draft-card burning and childish parading with childish placards. And for protest, do college students pound angry typewriters or mount forensic platforms to stand and fight for ideals as fearless individuals? No. They scream slogans as spineless mobs, or huddle in "sit-ins," blocking hallways until they are ignominiously dragged away in paddy wagons.

Hundreds of Christian sects give pious lips service to ecumenism while secretly worrying about the future of their own little empires. The oldest institution in the world, the Catholic Church, wrestles with the mod agonies of birth control, married priests, Bishops' rights, and rock music. Scientists broadly hint *they* should be the new *Herrenvolk* to regiment the human race into conformity.

Is it all chaos? No. These are pains of growth—accelerated growth caused by exploding knowledge and instant communications. All are searching— philosophers, scientists, students, whites, blacks, hippies—all are searching and probing, yearning for goals, for meanings. The apparent chaos in methods is but the trials and errors of man's evolution toward the divine.

Well, now that I had retired and smugly knew all the answers—was I a happy man? Oh, sure. There is no greater punishment for a creative spirit than to wake up each morning knowing he is unneeded, unwanted, and unnecessary. Retirement was becoming slow death, until this obit appeared:

Ben Capra. Died Thursday, June 12, 1969. Born May 3, 1885.

"Ben is not an easy man to explain," said the young priest from the pulpit of Our Lady of Assumption Church in Sacramento, as he looked toward my brother Ben's coffin covered with flowers and flanked with lighted candles. "I am dispensing with the usual Catholic eulogy for the dead, for nothing that we can do or say here can help speed Ben's trip to a better world. He has done all that for himself. He doesn't need our flowers, our candles, or our incense.

"I've been a priest for only eight years. But in those eight years I have never met a man who was as humble, as good, or as honest as Ben—or who was more loved by his neighbors.

"I have told dying human beings to 'make their peace with God.' But in my heart I never really knew what I meant by that remark—until I saw Ben die. At peace with God, himself, his neighbor. Ben taught me, a priest, just how real, how deep, and how wonderful is faith. It happened to me, as I'm sure it happened to many others who knew Ben Capra—I, a priest, am a better priest for having known Ben. . . ."

Good old Ben. His name never appeared in marquee lights, nor above film titles, nor even in local papers. But even after death he was still improving the quality of the day for his neighbors. Had I accomplished as much?

I drove alone to the Sicilian ghetto I had left fifty years ago. There it was. Mama's three-room house. It seemed smaller, much smaller. And piteously run down. Its roof sagged. Pieces of the porch bannister hung brokenly; half of the once-white picket fence lay flat in the dry weeds. The big spreading pepper tree, whose limbs we climbed and dreamed in, now drooped forlornly under the weight of its scrawny, smog-blackened leaves. And a scruffy shirt-sleeved man and a stout piano-legged woman sat on the porch. They eyed me hostilely as I sat in my car across the street.

How could they know that their run-down house had been built by courage; the courage of two middle-aged, penniless, illiterate peasants who had dared travel halfway around the world to meet the unknown fearful challenges of a strange land, a strange people, and a strange language? And who slaved like oxen and fought like tigers to feed and clothe their children. And who fed them. And clothed them. And one of them became a film director. And became famous. And retired. And now he was belly-aching because he was not needed.

I closed my eyes; thought of Mama, of Papa, of Ben, of my little sister Ann—the youngest and the first to die. I said a prayer for each of them. Out of prayer came peace—and impudence. Like Antaeus (whose strength depended upon his touching the ground), I had to return to my roots for a much-needed draught of peasant courage. Out of the refill came a book that is an impertinent try at saying to the discouraged, the doubting, or the despairing what I had been presuming to say in films: "Friend, you are a divine mingle-mangle of guts and stardust. So hang in there! If doors opened for me, they can open for anyone."

INDEX

499

Made in the USA
Las Vegas, NV
19 December 2023

83280430R00302